"I shall be more than satisfied if I have
succeeded in bringing before the mind's eye
of the reader the distinctive charm
of that far northern land."

Seton Gordon, *Amid Snowy Wastes*

Spitsbergen – Svalbard

A complete guide around the arctic archipelago

Nature and history,
Places and regions,
Useful and important information

By Rolf Stange

Imprint

Author and publisher:
Rolf Stange
Email info@spitzbergen.de
Internet www.spitzbergen.de

Sale: info@spitzbergen.de

All information in this book has been researched carefully. Nevertheless, the publisher/ author will not accept claims for damage. Each traveller is responsible for making sure that he/she has proper and complete knowledge, experience and equipment to deal with with dangers that may be met anywhere in Svalbard. The fact that a source of danger has been mentioned in this book at one geographical location does not indicate the absence of this, similar or other danger sources at other localities where this has not been mentioned. The reader is herewith reminded that he/she must make sure to get up to date information about possible legal changes concerning travelling in Svalbard. Sketch maps in this book are for geographical overview only and must not be used for orientation in the field or for navigation.

This book informs independently. The author is neither employed on a long-term basis by any tour operator, nor have advertisements or other grants been accepted in relation to this book.

Text processing and layout: Christian Bönschen, Rolf Stange

First edition: May 2008
Second edition: May 2009

Printing: Druckerei Karl Keuer, Email druckerei@drukk.de

ISBN (10) 3-937903-07-0
ISBN (13) 978-3-937903-07-1

Table of contents

Foreword 11
1. Preface 12
2. Introduction 13
3. Traveling in Svalbard: Useful, practical and important information 16
   3.1 Spitsbergen – seasons 16
   3.2 Spitsbergen – how to travel 19
      3.2.1 Expedition style cruising 19
      3.2.2 Cruise ships 21
      3.2.3 Staying in Longyearbyen 22
      3.2.4 Individual hiking 22
      3.2.5 Organised hiking tours 23
      3.2.6 Canoe/kayak 23
      3.2.7 Dog sledging 24
      3.2.8 Skiing 24
      3.2.9 Snow mobile 24
      3.2.10 Horse-riding 25
      3.2.11 Helicopter 25
      3.2.12 Climbing 25
      3.1.13 Scuba-Diving 26
      3.2.14 Nonsense 26
   3.3 Tour operatours 26
   3.4 Clothing, hygiene & the environment, photography 31
   3.5 Getting to Spitsbergen 35
   3.6 Conservation, cultural heritage, protected areas, safety 36
      3.6.1 Conservation and protected areas 37
      3.6.2 Polar bears and weapons, communication, safety in the field 42
      3.6.3 Registration of tours with the administration 45
      3.6.4 Tent and hut 46
      3.6.5 Other hazards in the field: rivers, glaciers, ice and snow, mud, rabies and other diseases, drinking water, mosquitos 48
      3.6.6 Orientation 51
      3.6.7 Cultural heritage 51
   3.7 Longyearbyen 53
      3.7.1 Services and infrastructure 53
      3.7.2 Accommodation, eating and drinking 60
      3.7.3 Shopping 64
      3.7.4 Sights in Longyearbyen 65
      3.7.5 Activities near Longyearbyen 67
      3.7.6 From coal to space research: Longyearbyen through 100 years 71

4. Natural history ... 74
4.1 Geography, glaciers, permafrost ... 74
4.2 Geology ... 78
4.3 Oceanic currents ... 98
4.4 Sea ice ... 99
4.5 Driftwood, rubbish and environmental toxins ... 101
4.6 Climate and weather ... 103
4.7 Mammals ... 105
4.7.1 Polar bear ... 105
4.7.2 Arctic fox ... 108
4.7.3 Svalbard reindeer ... 109
4.7.4-4.7.8 Seals ... 110
4.7.4 Bearded seal ... 110
4.7.5 Ringed seal ... 111
4.7.6 Harp seal ... 112
4.7.7 Walrus ... 113
4.7.8 Harbour seal ... 115
4.7.9-4.7.13 Whales ... 116
4.7.9 Mink whale ... 117
4.7.10 White whale ... 117
4.7.11 Humpback whale ... 118
4.7.12 Fin whale ... 119
4.7.13 Bowhead whale ... 120
4.7.14 Introduced species ... 121
4.8 Birds ... 122
4.8.1 Red-throated diver ... 122
4.8.2 Northern Fulmar ... 123
4.8.3 Common eider ... 124
4.8.4 King eider ... 125
4.8.5 Long-tailed duck ... 126
4.8.6 Pink-footed goose ... 127
4.8.7 Barnacle goose ... 128
4.8.8 Rock ptarmigan ... 145
4.8.9 Snow bunting ... 145
4.8.10 Purple sandpiper ... 146
4.8.11 Grey phalarope ... 147
4.8.12 Arctic tern ... 148
4.8.13 Great skua ... 149
4.8.14 Pomarine skua ... 149
4.8.15 Arctic skua ... 150
4.8.16 Long-tailed skua ... 151
4.8.17 Sabine's gull ... 151

4.8.18 Ivory gull ... 152
4.8.19 Ross' gull ... 153
4.8.20 Glaucous gull ... 153
4.8.21 Black-legged Kittiwake ... 154
4.8.22 Atlantic Puffin ... 154
4.8.23 Common guillemot ... 155
4.8.24 Brünich's guillemot ... 156
4.8.25 Little auk ... 157
4.8.26 Black guillemot ... 158
4.9 Plants ... 159
4.9.1 Polar willow ... 177
4.9.2 Dwarf birch ... 178
4.9.3 Mountain sorrel ... 178
4.9.4 Knotweed ... 178
4.9.5 Arctic mouse-ear ... 179
4.9.6 Tundra chickweed ... 179
4.9.7 Fringed sandwort ... 179
4.9.8 Nodding lychnis ... 179
4.9.9 Moss campion ... 180
4.9.10 Snow buttercup ... 180
4.9.11 Svalbard poppy ... 180
4.9.12 Scurvy grass ... 181
4.9.13 Whitlow-grasses ... 181
4.9.14 Purple saxifrage ... 181
4.9.15 Yellow mountain saxifrage ... 181
4.9.16 Alpine saxifrage ... 182
4.9.17 Hawkweed-leaved saxifrage ... 182
4.9.18 Bog saxifrage ... 182
4.9.19 Drooping saxifrage ... 182
4.9.20 Tufted saxifrage ... 183
4.9.21 Spider plant ... 183
4.9.22 Mountain avens ... 183
4.9.23 Arctic bell-heather ... 183
4.9.24 Boreal Jacob's ladder ... 184
4.9.25 Polar cress ... 184
4.9.26 Wooly lousewort ... 184
4.9.27 Arctic cottongrass ... 184
4.9.28 Arctic dandelion ... 185
4.9.29 Polar dandelion ... 185
4.9.30 Grasses, mosses, lichens & fungi ... 185

5. History 187
5.1 Vikings 188
5.2 Pomors 189
5.3 Willem Barents 191
5.4 Whaling in the 17th century 193
5.5 Early expeditions and science 195
5.6 Attempts to fly to the pole: Virgohamna and Ny Ålesund 200
5.7 Trappers 202
5.8 Whaling in the early 20th century 204
5.9 The Spitsbergen Treaty 205
5.10 Mining 207
5.11 The Second World War 209
5.12 Spitsbergen after the War 210
6. Fjords and islands, settlements and stations: The regions of Svalbard 213
6.1 Isfjord 216
6.1.1 Alkhornet, Trygghamna 217
6.1.2 Ymerbukta 219
6.1.3 Borebukta, Bohemanflya 219
6.1.4 Ekmanfjord, Coraholmen, Flintholmen 221
6.1.5 Dicksonfjord, western Dickson Land 223
6.1.6 Eastern Dickson Land (Skansbukta, Pyramiden), Billefjord 226
6.1.7 Sassenfjord, Tempelfjord 230
6.1.8 Adventfjord 233
6.1.9 Grumantbyen, Colesbukta 240
6.1.10 Grønfjord, Barentsburg 243
6.1.11 Festningen, Russekeila, Kapp Linné/Isfjord Radio 248
6.2 Forlandsund east side 253
6.2.1 Daudmannsodden, Farmhamna 253
6.2.2 St. Jonsfjord 254
6.2.3 Kaffiøyra 255
6.2.4 Engelskbukta 255
6.3 Prins Karls Forland 256
6.4 Kongsfjord 275
6.4.1 Ny Ålesund 277
6.4.2 Inner Kongsfjord 286
6.4.3 Blomstrandhalvøya 289
6.5 Krossfjord 291
6.6 The northern west coast 295
6.6.1 Dei Sju Isfjella 295
6.6.2 Hamburgbukta 295
6.6.3 Magdalenefjord 296

6.7 Northwestern Spitsbergen 299
6.7.1 Sørgattet, Bjørnfjord, Smeerenburgfjord 300
6.7.2 Danskøya 301
6.7.3 Amsterdamøya 303
6.7.4 Fair Haven, Fuglefjord, Sallyhamna 305
6.7.5 Nordvestøyane: Fugløya, Fuglesangen, Klovningen, Ytre Norskøya, Indre Norskøya 306
6.8 Raudfjord 308
6.9 The Woodfjord area 310
6.9.1 Woodfjord 310
6.9.2 Reinsdyrflya, Stasjonsøyane, Andøyane 313
6.9.3 Liefdefjord 314
6.9.4 Bockfjord 316
6.10 Moffen 318
6.11 Wijdefjord 319
6.12 Ny Friesland, Verlegenhuken 338
6.13 Sorgfjord 339
6.14 Hinlopenstretet 341
6.14.1 Murchisonfjord 344
6.14.2 Lomfjord 345
Footnote one: Drift ice and circumnavigations 346
Footnote two: Through Hinlopenstretet or around Nordaustland? 347
6.14.3 Alkefjellet 347
6.14.4 Wahlenbergfjord, Palanderbukta 348
6.14.5 The islands in Hinlopenstretet 350
6.14.6 Augustabukta, Vibebukta 353
6.15 Nordaustland 355
6.15.1 Lady Franklinfjord, Brennevinsfjord, Lågøya 360
6.15.2 Sjuøyane 362
6.15.3 Nordenskiöldbukta, Rijpfjord, Duvefjord 364
6.15.4 Karl XII Øya, Brochøya, Foynøya 365
6.15.5 Isispynten, Austfonna, Bråsvellbreen 367
6.16 Storøya, Kvitøya 385
6.17 Kong Karls Land 388
6.18 Southeastern Svalbard 391
6.18.1 Agardhbukta, Dunérbukta, Mohnbukta 394
6.18.2 Barentsøya 397
6.18.3 Edgeøya 400
6.18.4 Tusenøyane, Halvmåneøya, Ryke Yseøyane 404
6.18.5 Hopen 406

6.19 Bjørnøya 411
6.19.1 Southern Bjørnøya: The bird cliffs (Hambergfjellet-Sørhamna)... 416
6.19.2 Western Bjørnøya 433
6.19.3 Northern Bjørnøya: Bjørnøya Radio 433
6.19.4 Eastern Bjørnøya: Kvalrossbukta, Russehamna, Miseryfjellet, Tunheim 435
6.20 Sørkapp Land 437
6.21 Hornsund 440
6.21.1 Gåshamna 443
6.21.2 Hornsundtind, Samarinvågen 444
6.21.3 Brepollen 444
6.21.4 Burgerbukta, Gnålodden 446
6.21.5 Isbjørnhamna 447
6.22 Dunøyane, Isøyane, Kapp Borthen 449
6.23 Bellsund 450
6.23.1 Recherchefjord 453
6.23.2 Van Keulenfjord 455
6.23.3 Van Mijenfjord, Akseløya, northern Bellsund 457
7. Arctic environmental problems and tourism 464

AECO 467
Other books written by the same author 468
The author 469
Thank you 470
Norwegian glossary 471
Geological glossary 471
Table: Earth history of Svalbard 476
Literature 477
Index 481

"Voyages begin in books."

John Harrison, *Where The Earth Ends*

NOTE: when this book was about to be printed, the following notice was published by the Sysselmannen: commercial rental of firearms for protection against Polar bears will be restricted in the future.
It is likely that anyone who wants to rent a rifle will be required to show a license (European firearms pass or equivalent).

Foreword

Svalbard is now a common destination for those connoisseurs of travel who are anxious to see nature in all its stark beauty. This arctic archipelago is ideally suited to expedition cruising and in recent years more and more companies have taken up the challenge of attempting to meet the demand. Some have employed large, sometimes very large, ships and these only permit landings at Longyearbyen and perhaps Ny Alesund, together with, if passengers are lucky, a cruise around Magdalenefjord or one of the other fjords on the west coast. These trips may serve to whet the appetite for an extended trip and perhaps a circumnavigation of the islands, and to do this much smaller, agile and nimble vessels are required. These are vessels which are able to land passengers by Zodiac inflatables in order to enable them to gain a finer appreciation of the landscape and wildlife than can be secured simply by gazing at the land from the deck of a large cruise ship. On the other hand, some may feel stimulated to make a land based trip to Svalbard and for this, of course, considerable preparation is necessary.

But there is one requirement that is even more important than the selection of an appropriate tour company and vessel if one is to secure maximum benefit from the visit. This is to ensure that one has the services of an efficient expedition leader whose responsibility it is to guarantee the traveller's personal safety and to impart to him or her knowledge of the environment into which he or she is venturing.

It is fair to say that expedition leaders come in all shapes and sizes, and most are singular characters who seem to be very much more at home in the world of eternal snow and ice than they are in "civilisation". But they all seem to manage, in an incredibly short time, to convey their enthusiasm to visitors and they have the uncanny ability of coalescing an often disparate group of tourists, different nationalities, different interests, different ages etc into a team such that friendships made on the trip often last for years afterwards.

The author of this book is expedition leader *par excellence* whose experience in both polar areas is profound. But it is fair to say that Svalbard is the area in which his expertise places him at the very top of the profession. He has devoted a great deal of effort towards compiling the present book, which represents a distillation of his extraordinary knowledge of the archipelago. This is no mere guide book of the type that makes one wonder if the author's sole acquaintance with the territory is a quick visit coupled with much study of the internet, but is a veritable encyclopaedia of the islands and covers all aspects of their geography, geology, wildlife and history. The author has been to all the places he describes and has studied the archipelago widely in all aspects of science. As well as a detailed text there are excellent photographs and maps and the book will tell travellers all they might reasonably want to know about any particular site that they are visiting.

I have the greatest pleasure in recommending this book to all visitors to Svalbard.

Ian R. Stone, Editor *Polar Record*
Scott Polar Research Institute, University of Cambridge

Chapter 1 – Preface

"Stormy shores, sterile mountains, which by the nudity of their soil, the rage of their gales, excite a sentiment in the depth of the soul deeper and more religious than the awe that pervades the mind of the traveller in the midst of the virgin forests of America."

Xavier Marmier, in *Spitsbergen Gazette,* 20 July 1897

For centuries, Spitsbergen has been a destination for travellers for a variety of reasons. The first tourists found their way to Spitsbergen in the late 19th century and today, more and more people discover the varied landscape and the history, the fascination of ice and of a flora plagued by the harsh climate and, last but not least, the richness of the wildlife. The easy accessibility of Spitsbergen thanks to regular flights contributes to this development, as does the good tourist infrastructure. Options are plentiful, from long, physically demanding, hiking or skiing tours to ship cruises of differing durations and finally to short stays in the settlements. According to taste, you can experience the Arctic in summer or winter.

Regardless of the way of travelling that you choose, be it a private expedition or an organised tour, this book tries to answer questions within all relevant fields of interest. Many questions will arise while travelling along the cold coast or across the tundra and glaciers; others may come later, at home and some have to be answered well in advance during early stages of planning. The variety of the birdlife and other wildlife, the flora, history, political situation, geology and landscape phenomena, settlements and stations, fjords, unknown islands and famous sites: Whatever you want to know, you are very likely to find the answer here in the volume you are reading now.

This book tries to draw your attention to attractive options as well as warning against impossible or possibly even dangerous actions. You can damage the fragile environment, or the sometimes violent Arctic can hurt you; great care must be taken to avoid both eventualities. This is the responsibility of tour operators and of every individual traveller: Your own behaviour is crucial to making your stay in Spitsbergen rich with memories and to ensuring at the same time that nobody can see that you have ever been there once you have left. That is how it should be!

And now: Enjoy – reading and travelling!

Rolf Stange

Chapter 2 – Introduction

"The English at first called Spitsbergen "Greenland" in ignorant good faith; they continued to do so, to assert that it was not a Dutch discovery, and so the name stuck to the island for the best part of two centuries."

Martin Conway, *No Man's Land*

Which is correct: Spitsbergen or Svalbard? The nomenclature is by no means easy to understand. In 1194, the Vikings found a cold edge or **Svalbard**, as their language had it, whatever this edge was in reality. Without any doubt, Willem Barents found several islands of the archipelago in 1596 and called the main one **Spitsbergen**. It did not take long until the whalers followed Barents. They believed for a long time that Spitsbergen was a part of **Greenland**, although the use of this name for Spitsbergen may have been, to some degree at least, politically motivated, as the quote at the beginning of this section suggests. Observations of currents led careful observers as early as 1614 to the assumption that there was no connection between the real Greenland and Spitsbergen.

The Pomors, hunters from northern Russia, had a similar word for the islands in question: They called it **Grumant**, possibly derived from the name Greenland. The German ship's doctor Friedrich Martens, who visited Spitsbergen in 1675, invented the German spelling **Spitzbergen**, which has also been adopted by some English authors.

For centuries, those interested in the cold islands at the northern rim of the world accepted **Spitsbergen** or, mostly for the German speakers, **Spitzbergen**. In 1925, the Norwegians were granted sovereignty over Spitsbergen and, along with it, the opportunity to introduce the old viking term **Svalbard**. This was from then on the official name for the whole archipelago, including Bjørnøya (Bear Island) in the south and Kvitøya (White Island) in the northeast. They also defined that **Spitsbergen** should be used when referring to the "core-archipelago", including the main island together with Nordaustland, Edgeøya and Barentsøya, but excluding the outposts of Bjørnøya, Hopen, Kong Karls Land and Kvitøya. **Vest-Spitsbergen** was invented as a name for the main island.

It took many years until it was realised that there was no need for two different words for the archipelago, one for the whole group (Svalbard) and then for a larger part of it (Spitsbergen). Spitsbergen as a geographical term for the "core-archipelago" could be dropped without any problem and was thus available again for the main island, making the artificial name Vest-Spitsbergen unnecessary. This was decided in 1969.

Since then, the situation is officially as follows: **Spitsbergen** ("Spitzbergen" in German spelling) is the main island. **Svalbard** is the name of the whole archipelago, including the remote islands of Kvitøya, Kong Karls Land, Hopen und Bjørnøya.

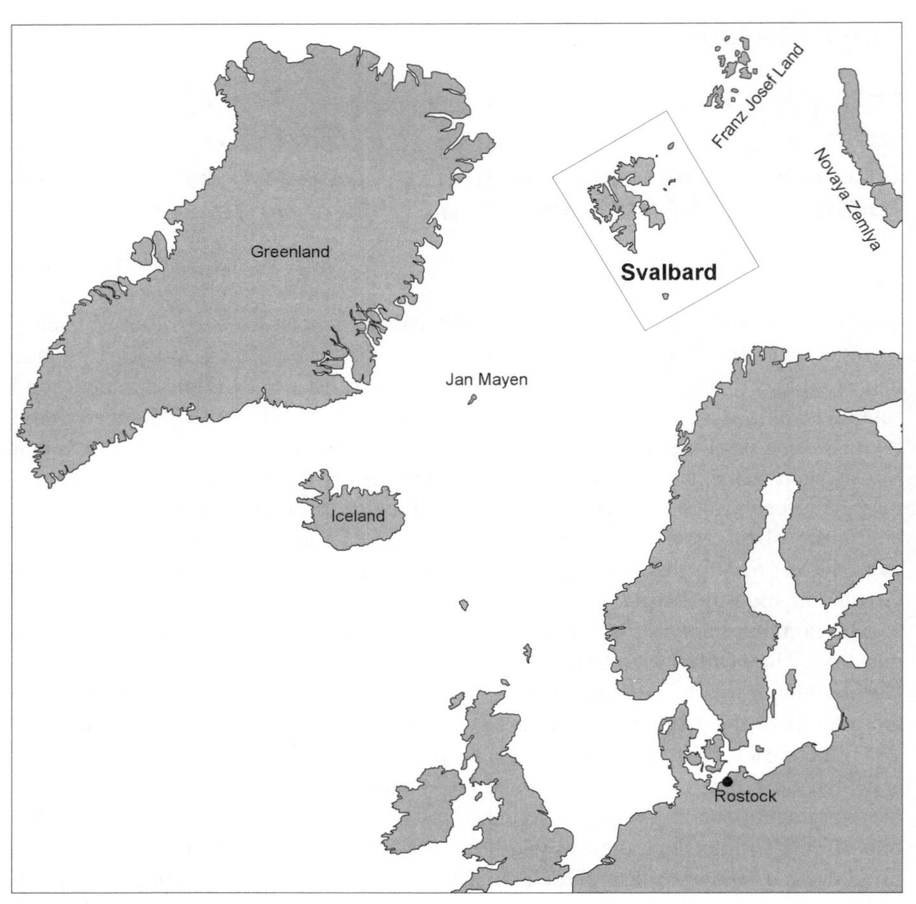

2-1 Svalbard in the north Atlantic.

In this book, I have used the names Svalbard and Spitsbergen in this sense. However, when both fit, I have mostly given preference to "Spitsbergen" rather than Svalbard because it has been used exclusively between 1596 and the early 20th century and so it historically the correct name.

Svalbard is situated between 74° and 81°N (northern latitude) and 10° and 35°E (eastern longitude). The archipelago has a land surface of 61,022 sq km, being about the size of Scotland or one and a half times larger than Switzerland (41,300 sq km) or Denmark (43,000 sq km). The surface area of the main island is 37,673 sq km, of which about 22,000 sq km is glacier-covered. The next-largest islands are Nordaustland (14,443 sq km), Edgeøya (5,030 sq km) and Barentsøya (1,330 sq km).

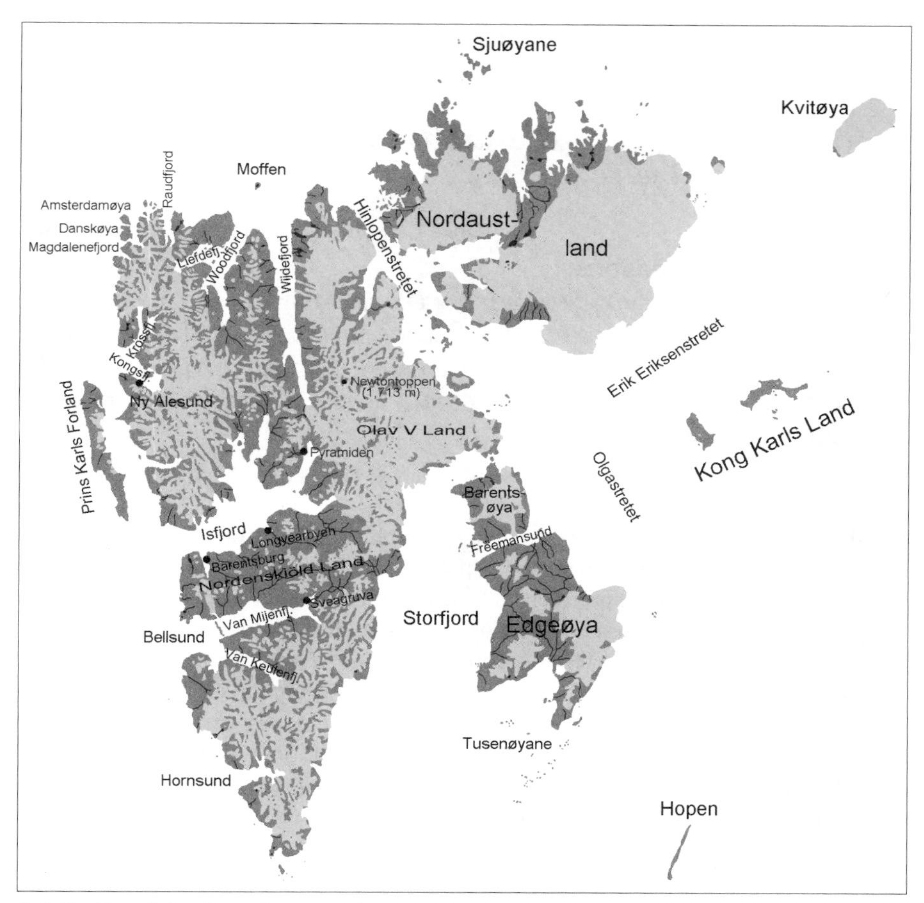

2-2 Svalbard (without Bjørnøya).

It is a distance of 2,695 km from my home in Rostock (northeastern Germany) to the port of Longyearbyen and only another 1,308 km from there to the North Pole. There is no other place where you can regularly reach a position so close to the pole with a non-icebreaking ship. Today, good accessibility is provided by the scheduled flights from Oslo and Tromsø in Norway to Longyearbyen, independent of the ice situation. This, together with the beautiful scenery, the rich animal and plant life as well as a wide choice of activities, has made Spitsbergen an increasingly popular destination for polar enthusiasts.

Chapter 3 – Travelling in Spitsbergen: Important, useful and interesting facts

"Nothing can exceed the sublime grandeur of a really fine day in these regions..."

James Lamont, *Seasons with the Sea-Horses*

3.1 Spitsbergen – Seasons

"Spring has the vigour of birth, summer is quiet and restrained, while autumn flares with the splendour of degeneracy through the gloom of approaching death. The darkness, however, presents a mystery which is pregnant with eternity."

R.A. Glen, *Under The Pole Star*

Spitsbergen is beautiful at any season of the year, but all the seasons differ in what you can do and see. There is no one season which is generally to be preferred; in the end, it depends on your personal preference. Every year is different, which means that the following description can not be any more than a guideline. Regarding temperature, weather, midnight sun etc., refer to section 4.6 *Climate and weather*.

Spring, or the **"light winter"**. This is the time from March to early May. Air temperatures will mostly remain below zero; it can be very cold, especially in March, but in contrast to the "real" winter, the daylight has returned. In March, there is regular daylight and darkness similar to central Europe, with long, beautiful sunsets and dawns. You have chances to see northern lights as long as there is some real darkness in early March. In late April, the sun is shining 24 hours a day and the risk of very cold weather is decreasing significantly.

This is the time for any sort of winter tour, be it with ski, dog sledge or snow mobile. Especially in late March and April, there is a lot of snow mobile traffic on the main routes, which can be quite annoying if you come for some quiet days on skis or with a dog sledge. Rental snow mobiles and hotel rooms may be booked up. This makes early booking important, or you can move towards the earlier or later part of the season. The winter season ends with the beginning of the melting period, usually towards mid May. You may be surprised by the small amount of snow, but don't forget that you are in a polar desert area where precipitation is generally low. Additionally, a lot of snow has been blown away or rather relocated: you may find deep snowdrifts behind obstacles, while the surroundings can be almost snow free because the last storm has blown it all away.

Between winter and summer – late spring. This in-between season lasts approximately from mid May to mid June, when there is not enough snow any more for ski- or snow mobile tours, but still too much for hiking. Depending on the ice situation, some boats may already start to offer day trips in Isfjord. The choice of activities is comparatively limited, but in exchange, this is a relatively calm season as most tourists have either gone or not yet come. Arctic birdlife starts to be busy, with the breeding season in full swing. There is still a lot of wet snow in the landscape, which makes walking difficult, but it looks beautiful. A good season for a relaxed stay in Longyearbyen.

Early summer. The summer season starts in late June. The snow will gradually disappear, allowing for hikes, although it is still too early for longer trekking because there is still wet snow, wet tundra and large amounts of meltwater in the rivers. The midnight sun is burning in the sky, which of course means that you will not see the beautiful, warm light of a sunset or sunrise. Arctic wildlife is abundant and busy, the tundra is getting more and more coloured with different flowers as the summer advances. Many bird are resting and breeding on the tundra, which means that you have to move around very carefully. The shipping season has started, and during a several-day-long cruise you are very likely to see drift ice. If you want to circumnavigate Spitsbergen by ship, then the ice will probably make this impossible in late June or early July, so you should come later in the summer. On the other hand, if there is still a lot of snow in the landscape, you may get some last "winter" impressions.

Late summer. About mid July to mid August is midsummer. The snow should mostly be gone, and the terrain is becoming increasingly dry. This is the ideal time for longer hiking tours as well as for ship-based expedition cruises into the remoter parts of the archipelago, although drift ice can make access to certain areas or a circumnavigation of Spitsbergen impossible at any time. The breeding season is advancing and, for some early breeders, already approaching the end, making some areas more accessible such as small islands, which were covered by breeding Common eiders in June and early July. By mid August, flowers are slowly disappearing again, and when the little leaves of the Polar willow change from green to yellow and reddish brown, these beautiful shades will give the tundra soft autumn colouration (not as bright as in other parts of the Arctic, where colourful species such as the Crawberry and Dwarf birch are more abundant).

Early autumn. By late August and definitely by September, the summer is over. The tundra is quite dry in autumn, which may thus still be a good time for long trekking tours, especially the first half of September. The flowers are gone, but rich tundra areas where the Polar willow is abundant will have nice yellow-brownish autumn colours. The nights are getting increasingly dark and, when the weather is good, then the low evening sun will cast the most beautiful light over the landscape. The first snowfall announcing winter will cover the mountains. Most birds will have left Spitsbergen and migrated towards warmer latitudes, leaving deserted birdcliffs and tundra areas where life was teeming just a few weeks earlier. You may be lucky to see the Aurora borealis in clear nights in the second half of September. At some stage, but unfortunately impossible to predict, autumn storms will finally terminate the short, arctic summer, leaving a thick snow cover even at sea level.

Late autumn. In October and early November, the days are getting shorter and shorter and temperatures are gradually dropping, but when the weather is fine, then the light of the low sun can be unbelievably beautiful. The choice of activities is reduced in late autumn but you can spend some calm days in Longyearbyen without having a lot of other tourists around or enjoy some cultural events such as the "dark season blues festival". This is also a good time to see the Aurora borealis, especially in the years 2010 to 2012 as there will be a maximum of sunspot activity in 2011.

Polar night. The sun does not show above the horizon from late November to mid February. It will not surprise you to read that it is mostly dark and cold, although temperatures around or even slightly above freezing and some rain may occur every now and then. If you want to see darkness, then it may not be necessary to travel to Spitsbergen to do so; a winter night somewhere in the mountains of Scandinavia will provide an experience similar enough, and for northern lights, chances in northern Norway or Sweden are actually better than in Spitsbergen, where you are almost a bit too far north for a strong and frequent Aurora borealis. It does occur in Spitsbergen but the "ring of fire", where strong northern lights are burning the sky almost every clear night is really further south, where you will also find a better infrastructure and at least some hours of weak daylight, allowing for more activities to be enjoyed.

It should be mentioned, however, that a clear night, with stars and possibly an Aurora borealis casting some bleak light over the snowy landscape, is beautiful beyond imagination.

Transition from polar night to light winter. Daylight will gradually come back in February. The twilight will be lighter and longer from day to day, with the first sunlight coming over the horizon around 20 February in the Isfjord area. This time of the year can be very cold with temperatures below -30°C, but opportunities for outdoor activities increase from now on. Additionally, it is still quiet before the flood of visitors that will come to Longyearbyen in the snow mobile season. The soft colours of the early light, ranging from dark blue to purple and soft pink and all shades in between, are incredible during periods of clear weather.

3.2 Spitsbergen – how to travel

"A long journey can best be performed when the ground is covered with snow. In this case, each traveller is provided with a pair of snow-shoes, and a sledge of eight to twelve feet in length, and one foot in breadth, on which, all the apparatus and provisions requisite for the journey, are drawn by hand. ... a strong experienced traveller can perform, on an average, about twenty miles a-day, dragging after him 100 to 150 pounds weight of articles upon his sledge."

William Scoresby, *An Account Of The Arctic Regions*

Depending on taste, time and caliber of your credit card, there is a range of different options to experience in Spitsbergen, each with specific advantages and drawbacks. Some ways of travelling are comfortable and without any risk, others include hardships and potential risks that require careful preparation and experience – within the context of an organised tour, this is mainly the responsibility of the tour operator, but he will need your cooperation regarding preparation before, and safe operation during, the tour. Notification to the Sysselmannen (governor) is required well in advance for tours into most parts of the archipelago (see section 3.6.3 *Registration of tours with the administration*). The tour operator will do this for organised voyages.

All possible ways to travel one can imagine and a few things beyond are offered by tour operators (see section 3.3 *Tour operators* and 3.7 *Longyearbyen*). Some ways of travelling can be organised individually, although this is mostly not significantly cheaper than booking a tour.

3.2.1 Expedition-style cruises

These are ship-based voyages, where comfort on board is less important than an intense experience of scenery, wildlife and history, in relatively small groups compared to a classical cruise ship. This makes expedition-style cruises an ideal way to experience Spitsbergen for many, and this way of travelling is enjoying increasing popularity. If your main interest is the nature and history of Spitsbergen (or other polar regions) and you do not mind sharing this with 30-100 like-minded travellers, you have some fitness and a spirit of adventure but you do not want to carry a heavy rucksack and sleep in a tent for days, then you should consider an expedition cruise.

- Groups are relatively small (30-100, depending on the ship) and you travel on ships with a relatively simple hotel standard, at least compared to large cruise ships. In other words, if a high standard of cabin comfort, multi-course cuisine and on-board entertainment are very important to you (more important than the nature experience), then a cruise on a larger vessel may be a better choice for you. On the other hand, an expedition ship is definitely much more comfortable than a tent, and many who are used to individual travelling are surprised by the standard.

- Do not expect a lazy holiday. Two landings each day are not unusual (duration mostly from two to three hours), and between excursions, there is always something to see from the ship. You may wish to walk for several hours across pathless terrain, so good health and physical condition are necessary. If you enjoy walking along the beach or through the forest for five kilometres or more at home, then you will enjoy the landings; but if you prefer to take the car to get your rolls from the baker's that is just around the corner, then you should keep a good distance from an expedition ship. You should also consider that the medical equipment on board an expedition-style cruise ship is rather basic and the next hospital is usually very far away. In case of emergency, it will certainly take several hours, possibly days, until a patient can receive advanced medical treatment. This means that a generally good health is imperative.
- The atmosphere on board is informal. Elegant clothes are usually not required but you will need rubber boots and warm, waterproof clothes for excursions. On most smaller ships, passengers are welcome on the bridge.
- Expedition style cruises are not safaris for any particular wildlife species, especially not "polar bear safaris", although marketing brochures sometimes deliver this impression. If you have a very strong interest in seeing polar bears, then you may want to consider a voyage to Churchill in Canada, where close-up views of polar bears are virtually guaranteed at certain seasons. There is no such guarantee in Spitsbergen. If your brochure says otherwise, then it is wrong. Also, if you have a very strong wish to see a particular bird species, then you may be lucky or you may not. Chances for most popular wildlife species such as polar bears, walrus and birds such as Little auks, Grey phalaropes and rare gulls are definitely there, but nothing is ever guaranteed. Especially for birds, make sure you chose the right season – see sections on the individual species, but late June until mid July is generally good for birds. You need a lot of luck for spectacular close-up views and photography of polar bears and walruses. Don't forget to bring binoculars.
- During landings, groups are always accompanied by guides armed with heavy-caliber rifles to protect them from potentially dangerous polar bears. These large animals have to be expected anywhere and at any time in Spitsbergen outside the inhabitated settlements; the importance of this fact cannot be overstressed. Individual excursions are not possible. Safety of humans and animals takes precedence over tourist interests. If you are not willing to accept being with a group at all times while on shore and having to curb your urge for individual exploration, then you should not join an expedition-style cruise.
- The language spoken on board is often English, but check carefully prior to booking. Some ships have special departures for French, German or other language groups, and if you happen to be with a group that you cannot understand, then this may make the situation quite frustrating for you and others, unless you are able to learn

a new language within a week or so!

- For an intense nature experience, choose a small ship and as long a duration as possible for the ship-based voyage. Some agencies offer special departures for dedicated special interest groups such as photographers or birdwatchers.
- The itinerary that you receive before departure is usually only a guideline describing what could happen, rather than a timetable that will be followed in detail. The expedition leader, who is finally responsible for the itinerary, should have good local experience and will design a voyage that pays attention to the actual ice and weather situation, to relevant observations made earlier during the season and to the interests of the group. This procedure has proven to be very effective and often results in voyages that exceed expectations. Please do not make everybody's life difficult by requesting the ship to follow the itinerary exactly as outlined in your brochure.

3.2.2 Cruise ships

Cruise ships have been visiting Spitsbergen regularly since the late 19th century and represent a classical way of travelling in this region; today, more and more cruise ships ranging in size from several hundred to more than a thousand passengers visit Spitsbergen each summer. Most of these cruises depart from or end in central Europe, with Spitsbergen being only a part of their itinerary. The nature experience is accordingly rather limited, as landings take place mainly in the settlements, usually Longyearbyen and/or Ny Ålesund. Beyond those, there is a very limited number of locations where medium-sized cruise ships can put several hundred passengers ashore. The most important is Gravneset in Magdalenefjord (see section 6.6.3 *Magdalenefjord*), although the future of this is somewhat uncertain due to a recent ban by the Norwegian authorities on navigation in National Parks for all ships that use heavy fuel (crude oil). This means most large cruise ships. It is currently under discussion whether certain sailing routes will be kept open to enable access to sites such as Magdalenefjord and Kongsfjord that have traditionally been used by large cruise ships. A decision is due in spring 2009.

The nature experience on a large cruise ship is not very intense compared to other ways of travelling in Spitsbergen, but such a voyage offers an impression of Spitsbergen as one of several destinations, combined with a level of comfort, availability of medical facilities and so on that is superior to any other way of travelling. A large ship also offers elderly and disabled persons the opportunity to visit the Arctic safely.

From an environmental perspective, there are several factors favouring these big ships, so long as they do not have accidents, particularly anything resulting in oil spills. For environmental reasons, landings of several hundred passengers are mostly restricted to settlements and to a few selected locations, leaving remote wilderness areas unvisited by large groups. The ship's passage to and from Europe also avoids carbon dioxide emissions into the upper atmosphere caused by flights to bring in cruise tourists.

3.2.3 Staying in Longyearbyen

You can settle down on the camping site or in one of the hotels in Longyearbyen for some days and explore Longyearbyen and the surroundings individually, or join guided tours that you can book with specialised agencies in Longyearbyen at the tourist information, or in hotels. The scenery around Longyearbyen is not the greatest, compared to other parts of Spitsbergen, but the variety of flora and wildlife that you can see is quite surprising – certainly no polar bears or walruses, but you may well see reindeer, Arctic fox and a range of different birds at close range inside the settlement. If you are a dedicated birdwatcher, then two days in and around Longyearbyen may well pay off – especially if you hire a guide with a rifle and good relevant, local knowledge (see section 3.7 *Longyearbyen*).

Remember that you need a rifle as soon as you leave the last inhabited houses behind you.

3.2.4 Individual hiking

The choice between day trips around Longyearbyen and several-week-long hiking tours with expedition character is almost infinite. You need to prepare carefully and bring physical fitness and some experience with hiking in pathless terrain, as well as the ability to handle a heavy-caliber rifle in case you meet a polar bear. The weight of your rucksack will quickly exceed 20 kg if you spend several days in the field. Hiking enables you to enjoy a very intense experience of arctic landscape in the silence that it deserves, as well as the exciting feeling of being exposed to the elements, especially when you sleep in a tent. Only a few things in life feel better than the first pizza after 12 days on dry food!

Trekking in the remote parts of the archipelago is virtually impossible, as there is no transportation. If you want to hike on Nordaustland or Edgeøya, then you have to organise your own logistics, which usually means that you have to charter a boat or bring your own. But things are easier in the large and varied Isfjord: Small ships taking tourists for day trips can drop hikers off and pick them up again at a date that you have agreed in advance. Such day trips may visit Barentsburg or Kapp Linné, Trygghamna, Ymerbukta, Billefjord with Skansbukta, Pyramiden and Nordenskiöldbreen or Tempelfjord. Transportation to and from the wilderness is not guaranteed, as departures may be fully booked or can be cancelled for many reasons, but there are several trips to most of these destinations per week. Organise transportation back to Longyearbyen carefully and well in advance! If you count on being picked up somewhere in the wildnerness a day before your flight leaves from Longyearbyen then you may miss your flight, as bad weather can make a pick-up impossible at any time.

You will not find detailed route descriptions in this book. The reason is neither laziness nor a lack of relevant experience of the author – I love writing and have covered many hundreds of kilometres hiking in Spitsbergen – but if you are experienced enough, then a short time spent looking at topographic maps will provide you with endless inspiration for interesting tours. If you are unable to come up with some good ideas after looking at all those colourful lines on the map sheet, then you should book an organised tour.

However, a few interesting, but demanding options need at least to be briefly indicated: You can hike from Longyearbyen to the east coast of Spitsbergen. Tireless legs and feet can carry you from Kapp Linné or Barentsburg to Fridtjovbreen in Bellsund. Dickson Land can be reached quite easily with day-trip boats from Longyearbyen, and Skansbukta or Pyramiden are excellent starting points for demanding, but very rewarding tours in different directions.

It is important to pay attention to the duty to notify the Sysselmannen (governor) of your plans well in advance, for most parts of Svalbard (see section 3.6.3 *Registration of tours with the administration*).

3.2.5 Organised hiking tours

As with individually arranged hiking tours, an organised tour will provide an in-depth, silent experience of the Arctic that some will find rather deterring, while others may consider it as close to nature and thus exciting and attractive, enjoying sleeping in tents without shower, heating and so on. You have to adjust your own rhythm and pace to that of the group. On the other hand, there are several obvious advantages: Less effort in organising your trip, solid tour planning, the group experience (which is usually nice), and pre-arranged depots which mean lighter rucksacks.

According to taste and fitness, there are different options from day tours to long, demanding tours. Collect detailed information about the tour and judge for yourself carefully. If you are not able to keep pace, then your participation may turn into a problem for the group and a strain for yourself. Once the tour has started, there may be no way back, so such a tour may not be a good opportunity to test your abilities; this is something you should do at home.

3.2.6 Canoe/kayak

Due to the lack of calm rivers and lakes, the open canoe is of no use in Spitsbergen. Strong expedition sea-kayaks, however, can be used in the fjords with good results during short excursions and long expedition-like tours. Individual organisation requires great effort, starting with the logistics of getting your equipment up to Spitsbergen and back home. It is possible to rent kayaks and relevant equipment, including survival suits, in Longyearbyen.

Specialised tour operators offer guided kayaking tours, mostly in the Isfjord or Kongsfjord areas. This way of getting around is certainly attractive and yields a different perspective to a hiking tour, but it is also exhausting and associated with specific risks. Potential dangers such as rapid weather changes, or the coastline, may make it impossible to land in many places because of steep rock cliffs and calving glaciers.

3.2.7 Dog sledging

This is a traditional way of travelling in the Arctic that can hardly be surpassed in terms of beautiful, intense and romantic nature experience. A few days of dog sledging, from hut to hut or sleeping in tents, will give you a more unfiltered arctic experience than anything else.

In Spitsbergen, snow mobile traffic is still a nuisance for quiet travellers, despite motorised traffic being more and more strictly controlled, but there are scooter-free areas, which may even be enlarged in the future. Especially from March to May, short day trips are popular and do not involve too much strain, as you will be back in your hotel after a few hours. Specialised operators also arrange several-day-long tours for the adventurous. Long dog sledging expeditions are certainly less comfortable than cruises on board a large ship, but if you are willing and able to accept sleeping in a tent in temperatures far below freezing and all the little and not-so-little difficulties that will come along with it, then you will be richly rewarded. Regarding these everyday challenges of winter-life with tents: If you are afraid of it, then stay away from it or at least try elsewhere first, but if you are curious about it, then with careful preparation and some help and advice of your guides you will manage and even enjoy it.

Another aspect is the fact that dog sledges are a very environmentally sound means of transportation. They also create local jobs in places where these are most desperately needed, for example in remote places in Greenland.

3.2.8 Skiing

There are no facilities for downhill skiing in Spitsbergen. Cross-country skiing may be compared to dog sledging, as a silent, slow and intense way to discover the wintry beauty the Arctic has to offer. It is, of course, much easier to organise a private skiing adventure without a guide than a dog sledging expedition. On the other hand, several-day-long skiing trips with all the equipment that is needed are for the sportive only; physical exertion is extremely hard especially if there is deep, soft snow. Shorter, perhaps guided, tours of a few hours duration in the vicinity of Longyearbyen are an option for a wider public, but obviously still require a higher level of sporting ability than snow-mobile tours. If you are not afraid of hard work in the snow and sleeping in tents with temperatures far below freezing, then a long cross country skiing expedition is an experience that you will never forget. Amongst the destinations that local operators offer is Newtontoppen, Spitsbergen's highest mountain, the summit of which can be reached without technical climbing.

3.2.9 Snow mobile

If you want to race through the Arctic at great speed, then a snow mobile tour is what you need. The nature experience is limited due to speed and noise. Because of exhaust fumes and noise, which disturb both wildlife and quiet travellers with skis or dog sledges, snow mobile driving is not exactly an environmentally friendly way to experience the Arctic. Officially, driving is only allowed on snow covered or frozen ground, but in areas with frequent winter traffic, you will find snow mobile tracks in the summer in the vulnerable vegetation – quite annoying, if you have walked for several days to experience "untouched" nature.

You can rent snow mobiles in Longyearbyen or join organised tours, both day trips and longer trips with an overnight or two, in Barentsburg, Kapp Linnè or Sveagruva. There are serious restrictions in force now as to where you may drive, especially for individual tourists, for guided groups and, to some degree, for locals. Legislation is changing, so get in touch with the tourist information in Longyearbyen or the Sysselmannen if you plan any private tour. Also, you will need a car driving license. For an individual tour, the driving license must have been obtained no later than 2001, otherwise a special snow mobile driving license is required. If you drive any faster than 80 km/h (30 km/h in Longyearbyen, 20 km/h in Barentsburg), without helmet or with more than zero percent alcohol in your blood, you risk not only your's and other people's lives, but also serious fines.

3.2.10 Horse-riding

You may believe it or not, but riding is indeed possible on Spitsbergen. Actually, that does not mean week-long expeditions on horseback across the tundra, but a few hours along the coast of Isfjord west of Longyearbyen, near the camp site and towards Bjørndalen, offered by a local horse enthusiast and tour operator.

3.2.11 Helicopter

Tourist use of helicopters is not allowed anymore, least of all landing in the field. Permission may be given for film teams and professional photographers, if one of the few helicopters is available, but these are heavily used by the administration and scientists. Because of the high fuel consumption and wildlife disturbance, helicopters are possibly the least environmentally sound way to travel.

3.2.12 Climbing

Large areas of Spitsbergen are unattractive terrain for climbers, as bedrock consists of soft, frost-shattered sediments. There are, however, some good climbing areas, where steep rockwalls consist of hard granites or gneisses. These can be found in the northwestern corner of Spitsbergen and in the northeast, in Ny Friesland, around Newtontoppen, which is the highest mountain in Svalbard. Despite altitudes of not much more than 1,000 metres, the strongly glaciated mountain ranges in the northwest generally have more alpine landforms with pointed mountain peaks and sharp ridges, which offer exciting climbing opportunities. So does the Newtontoppen area. Newtontoppen itself can be "conquered" on ski without technical climbing. Spectacular and technically more demanding is Hornsundtind in south Spitsbergen, the third-highest mountain of the archipelago, 1,431 metres high.

According to climbers, ice-climbing and technically challenging ski tours in steep terrain are supposed to be better than rock climbing, but the greatest difficulty still is getting to these remote areas, which are far away from Longyearbyen.

3.2.13. Diving

The high Arctic is not exactly a classical diving destination, but experienced dry-suit divers can experience the magic of the underwater world in Spitsbergen (as well as in Antarctica). An expedition cruise ship usually serves as a base for a week or ten days with almost daily dives. You will usually share the trip with a group of non-divers, and the divers are then of course welcome to join the land-based excursions of the "normal people" to see the dry part of the world as well. The dives are under controlled conditions and not technically challenging, but are nevertheless not for beginners, as experience with dry suit diving is necessary. The heavy parts of the equipment are provided on board. Ask specialised operators for more information (see section 3.3 *Tour operators*).

3.2.14 Nonsense

Bicycling: This is not possible in Spitsbergen, as there are no suitable roads outside the settlements. Bicycling on non-frozen tundra is not an option for environmental reasons and thus forbidden. Inside Longyearbyen, a bicycle is very useful, though.
Camper van: Not seriously an option without roads beyond the settlement areas. And how do you get your camper van to Spitsbergen?
Bus: Not an option for getting around on Spitsbergen for the very same reason as with camper van: There are simply no roads outside the settlements. Sightseeing-tours in Longyearbyen and, to a limited degree, also in Barentsburg, are possible and often done for passengers of larger cruise ships.

3.3 Tour operators

"Organising an expedition of this kind is a great experience, for one is trying to do something which ought to cost £ 12,000 for a third of that figure."

A.R. Glen, *Under The Pole Star*

There is a growing number of smaller and some larger companies, which offer all sorts of tours. The following list does neither claim completeness nor does it involve any judgement of the quality, but is for your orientation only. Most operators offer different day trips in and around Longyearbyen, some organise longer trips. The short descriptions below are as of 2008. You will find up-to-date contact details and programmes on the internet. Check the website of the tourist information in Longyearbyen (www.svalbard.net) for links.

Tour operators that actually organise their own trips should not be confused with agents that are selling such voyages without being present in Spitsbergen themselves. Such agencies are not included here, neither are shipping companies mentioned that operate large cruise vessels which may visit Spitsbergen occasionally.

In Longyearbyen

- **Arctic Adventures:** Small operator based in Adventdalen, about 12 km east of Longyearbyen. Emphasis is on anything that involves dogs, also kayaking etc, daytrips and longer expeditions.
  P.O. Box 480, 9171 Longyearbyen, Norway.
  Phone +47 7902 16 24, mobile phone +47 478 05 990, fax +47 7902 17 45, email info@arctic-adventures.no, internet www.arctic-adventures.no.
- **Basecamp Spitsbergen**: Shorter and longer trips, amongst others skiing, dog sledging, snow mobiles. "Trapper-hotel" in Longyearbyen, "the boat in the ice" (the sailing vessel *Noorderlicht* frozen in fast ice in Tempelfjord during the spring), Kapp Linné/Isfjord Radio.
  P.O. Box 316, 9171 Longyearbyen, Norway. Phone +47 7902 46 00, fax +47 7902 46 01, email svalbard@basecampexplorer.com, internet www.basecampexplorer.com/svalbard/no.
- **Jonathan Adventure Sailing**: Sailing with the 15 meter sailing boat *Jonathan III* (maximum 6 passengers) and *Jonathan IV* (maximum 10 passengers). Longer expeditions in Isfjord, north Spitsbergen and remote parts of Svalbard, logistical support.
  P.O. Box 243, 9171 Longyearbyen, Norway. Mobile phone +47 97 12 99 53, email info@jonathanadventuresailing.com, internet www.jonathanadventuresailing.com.
- **Polar Charter**: Day trips in summer with MS *Polargirl* in Isfjord, mostly Barentsburg and Pyramiden. P.O. Boks 330, 9254 Tromsø, Norway. Mobile phone +47 77 65 57 97, email pcharter@online.no, internet www.polarcharter.no.
- **Poli Arctici**: The Italian in Longyearbyen. Logistics also for film teams and scientists, shorter tours and longer expeditions, equipment rental (no weapons, but clothing, bicycles etc.). 9171 Longyearbyen, Norway. Phone +47 7902 17 05, fax +47 7902 17 34, mobile phone +47 91 38 34 67, email stefano@poliarctici.com, internet www.poliarctici.com.
- **Spitsbergen Experience**: Specialist for dog sledging, from daytrips to longer expeditions, P.O. Box 524, 9171 Longyearbyen, Norway. Phone/Fax +47 7902 12 39, mobile phone +47 91 70 37 25 or +47 95 96 10 51, email priita@spitsbergenexperience.com, internet www.spitsbergenexperience.com.
- **Spitsbergen Tours**: Company owned and led by Andreas Umbreit from Germany, who is present in Longyearbyen during the spring and summer season. Ski- and snow shoe tours during the spring, varied summer programme

from settlement visits to easy walking and demanding hiking tours, special arrangements on request. P.O. Box 6, 9171 Longyearbyen, Norway. Phone +47 7902-14 44 or -10 46, Fax +47 7902 10 67, email info@terrapolaris.com or terrapolaris@gmx.net, internet www.longyearbyen-camping.com, www.terrapolaris.com.

- **Spitsbergen Travel**: The largest tour company in Longyearbyen, active in all seasons, anything from easy day trips to long expeditions by all legal means: walking and hiking, skiing, snow mobiles, dog sledges, kayaks, small boats, expedition ships, smaller cruise ships. Including *Polar Star* and *Nordstjernen,* and MV *Expeditions* announced to start in 2009. The first local tour operator that has announced it has become a "Climate saver", which means that it will implement measures to cut CO_2 emissions. P.O. Box 548, 9171 Longyearbyen, Norway. Phone +47 7902 61 00, fax +47 7902 61 01, email info@spitsbergentravel.no, internet www.spitsbergentravel.no.
- **Stig Henningsen Transport og Guiding**: Logistics, transportation, snow mobile tours and invididual cruises on a small motor boat. P.O. Box 353, 9171 Longyearbyen, Norway. Phone +47 7902 13 11, mobile phone +47 91 85 37 56, Fax +47 7902 18 82, email mail@htg.svalbard.no, internet www.htg.svalbard.no.
- **Svalbard Explorer**: Specialised in visits to "Gruve 7", a working coal mine in Adventdalen just east of Longyearbyen. The future of these excursions is uncertain because the mining company has announced to stop tourist visits to the mines. P.O. Box 412, 9171 Longyearbyen, Norway. Mobile phone +47 90 76 29 33, fax +47 7902 39 77, email info@svalbardexplorer.no, internet www.svalbardexplorer.no.
- **Svalbard Hestesenter**: Your partner for horse riding in the high Arctic and more: logistics, excursions, equipment rental including rifles and trip wire to safeguard camps against polar bears. Rifle courses. P.O. Box 182, 9171 Longyearbyen, Norway. Mobile phone +47 91 77 65 95, email post@arcticriding.no, internet www.arcticriding.no.
- **Svalbard Huskies:** Based in Adventdalen, about 7 km east of Longyearbyen. Day trips with dogs, summer and winter. P.O. Box 543, 9171 Longyearbyen, Norway. Phone/fax +47 7902 57 80, mobile phone +47 98 40 40 89, email info@svalbardhuskies.com, internet www.svalbardhuskies.com.
- **Svalbard Reiser**: Mostly snow mobile tours, but offers also equipment rental, logistics etc.. P.O. Box 433, 9171 Longyearbyen, Norway. Phone +47 7902 56 50, mobile phone +47 99 52 47 30, fax +47 7902 56 51, email info@svalbardreiser.com, internet www.svalbardreiser.com.
- **Svalbard Snøscooterutleie AS**: Snow scooter tours and rental service for cars, snow mobiles and equipment. P.O. Box 538, 9171 Longyearbyen, Norway. Phone +47 7902 46 61, fax +47 7902 17 71 email post@scooterutleie.net, internet www.scooterutleie.svalbard.no.

- **Svalbard Villmarkssenter:** Based in Adventdalen, about 10 km east of Longyearbyen. Specialist for dog sledging, mostly day trips, also during the summer. The first local tour operator certified with "Ecotourism Norway", with a strong interest to develop environmentally friendly tourism in Spitsbergen. Villmarkssenter owns two houses in historical style in Adventdalen, one of them being a replica of the hut that was used by Willem Barents' expedition during their famous wintering in Novaya Zemlya (1596-97), which can be rented for courses, conferences etc. including catering.
  P.O. Box 396, 9171 Longyearbyen, Norway.
  Phone +47 7902 17 00, mobile phone +47 90 79 00 76, fax +47 7902 19 86, email info@svalbardvillmarkssenter.no, internet www.svalbardvillmarkssenter.no.
- **Svalbard Wildlife Expeditions AS**: Winter and summer, different day trips with snow mobile and boat, mine visits, basecamps in the Isfjord area, hiking on Prins Karls Forland, skiing expedition across Spitsbergen. P.O. Box 164, 9171 Longyearbyen, Norway. Phone +47 7902 22 22, fax +47 7902 22 23, email info@wildlife.no, internet www.wildlife.no.
- **Svalbard Nature**: French tour operator, specialising in kayaking. P.O. Box 594, 9171 Longyearbyen, Norway. Internet www.80-n.com.
- **Svalbard4You:** Small local operator, run by Jon Sandmo, long-time medical doctor in Longyearbyen. Day tours and several-day long tours, both snow mobile (winter) and hiking (summer).
  P.O. Box 144, 9171 Longyearbyen, Norway. Phone +47 7902 20 40, fax +47 7902 2270, mobile phone +47 901 86 536. Email post@svalbard4you.no or jsandmo@online.no, internet www.svalbard4you.no.

And finally some companies, that are not based in Longyearbyen, but are regularly active in and around Spitsbergen. The number of companies operating expedition cruise ships has been growing in recent years, visit www.aeco.no/members for more information on other operators

- **Aurora Expeditions**: Operates the expedition cruise vessel *Polar Pioneer* with a capacity of 56 passengers. The *Polar Pioneer* can be seen around the north Atlantic during the northern summer, including Spitsbergen and East Greenland. 182 Cumberland Street, The Rocks, NSW 2000, Australia.
  Phone +61 2 9252 1033, fax +61 2 9252 1373, email auroraex@auroraexpeditions.com.au, internet www.auroraexpeditions.com.au.
- **Gap Adventures**: Canadian tour operator, present in Spitsbergen with MS *Expedition* (maximum 120 passengers). 19 Charlotte Street, Toronto, Ontario M5V 2H5, Canada. Phone in North America: +1 800 708 7761, elsewhere +1 416 26 00 999. Internet www.gapadventures.com.

- **Grand Nord Grand Large**: French specialist for polar tourism, operates nordic ski and pulka expeditions and, during the summer, hiking and sea kayak trips in Isfjord and Kongsfjord. GNGL, 15 rue du Cardinal Lemoine - 75005 Paris, France. Phone +33 140 46 05 14, fax: +331 43 26 73 20, email infos@gngl.com, internet www.gngl.com.
- **Lindblad Expeditions**: with roots going back to Lars Erik Lindblad who "invented" expedition cruising, operates among others the *National Geographic Explorer* (max 148 passengers) and the *National Geographic Endeavour*. Lindblad Expeditions, 96 Morton Street, 9th Floor, New York 10014, USA. Email explore@expeditions.com, internet www.expeditions.com.
- **Oceanwide Expeditions**: Dutch company specialised in expedition style cruises, operating ice-strengthened motor vessels with passenger capacity of about 54 (*Professor Molchanov* and *Professor Multanovskiy*) and the larger *Antarctic Dream* (84 passengers), which are in Spitsbergen from mid June to late August. Starting in the 2009 season, Oceanwide will also operate the larger *Plancius* (112 passengers). Much smaller, but also a member of the Oceanwide family, is the sailing vessel *Noorderlicht,* which is a regular and beautiful sight in Spitsbergen's fjords. Oceanwide Expeditions also offers voyages with scuba diving options. Oceanwide Expeditions, Bellamypark 9, 4381 CG Vlissingen, The Netherlands. Phone +31 118 410 410, fax +31 118 410 417, email info@oceanwide-expeditions.com, internet www.oceanwide-expeditions.com.
- **Origo Expeditions:** This Swedish company offers voyages on the vessel *Stockholm*, one of the smallest ships (max 12 passengers) doing commercial tours to the remote parts of Svalbard on a regular basis. Origo Expedition AB, Kyrkåsliden 3, 433 31 Partille, Schweden. Phone +46 314 41 143, fax: +46 313 36 4329, email info@origoexpedition.se, internet www.origoexpedition.se.
- **Polar Quest:** Operates the *Origo* (up to 24 passengers), *Stockholm* (12 passengers) and the *Quest* (53 passengers) in Spitsbergen waters and offers trips to other, mostly polar, destinations. PolarQuest Ltd, Stora Nygatan 29, P.O Box 180, 401 23 Göteborg, Sweden. Phone +46 31 333 17 30, fax +46 31 333 17 31, email info@polar-quest.com, internet www.polar-quest.com.
- **Quark Expeditions:** One of the larger companies in the business, Quark operates icebreakers and ice-strengthened vessels, mostly of Russian origin, in most polar waters of the world. *Akademik Sergey Vavilov* and *Akademik Ioffe* are scheduled to sail in Spitsbergen for Quark Expeditions in 2009, usually with optional sea kayak excursions. 47 Water Street, Norwalk, CT, USA, 06854. Phone +1 (203) 852 5580, fax +1 (203) 857 0427. Email enquiry@quarkexpeditions.com, internet www.quarkexpeditions.com.

- **Waterproof Expeditions:** The specialist for diving in polar waters, including Spitsbergen. Singel 292, 4381 VM Vlissingen, The Netherlands. Phone +31 118 435 885, fax: +31 842 272 044, email: info@waterproof-expeditions.com, internet www.waterproof-expeditions.com.
- **69 Nord:** Small French company based in Tromsø, offering sailing voyages with the aluminium sloop *Southern Star* in Spitsbergen and Norway. Some trips with skiing or paragliding option. Postboks 499, 9255 Tromsø, Norway. Mobile phone +47 993 625 70 (English, Français), office in France +33 05 56 58 50 42, email : info@69nord.com or olivier@69nord.com, internet www.69nord.com.

3.4 Clothing, hygiene & the environment, photography

"... one night Brownie, to Richard's amazement, began to wash his clothes. Richard considered the matter, and decided that the whole thing was bad. His reasons were conclusive. First of all, it was a nuisance ; then, it was no good washing clothes if one did not wash oneself, which he had no intention of doing ; finally, if something fits, why ask it to shrink?"

A.R. Glen, *Under The Pole Star*

If you book a trip to Spitsbergen, you should receive from your agency detailed information about clothes and equipment that you need. Pay close attention to this information – good preparation on the participant's side, especially good clothing and equipment, is a key factor in making your trip enjoyable. Once you have left Longyearbyen, you will normally not be able to get hold of anything anymore, and even in Longyearbyen, things may not be available in the size you need.

Of course, clothing depends totally on the season and the way of travelling that you plan. It is not possible to give detailed advice for all situations. Winter tours especially require excellent and functional clothing without any compromise. Such clothing may be provided by your tour operator in the case of an organised trip. For summer trips, you will usually bring your own equipment, although your tour operator may help you with rental equipment on request.

What you read below is my personal recommendation which I have tried and tested extensively in different conditions. It works as well for a day trip near Longyearbyen as it does for a challenging, week-long tour in the field; the main differences will be some extra sets of certain items and, of course, different footwear.

Clothing is always very personal. Some may be happy in comparatively thin clothes, while others under the same conditions may feel freezing despite many layers. In the end, you have to decide what works for you. Decide carefully! This is not the time to save money.

During a summer trip at or near sea level, you will not encounter temperatures below freezing. Normal temperatures from late June to mid August will be slightly above freezing, between +1 and +7°C. Your temperature perception also depends largely on the presence or absence of wind and sun.

In the case of an expedition-style cruise, be prepared for long cruising in small boats under wet and windy conditions, as well as for some mountain walking. You may experience both within one excursion. The layer principle will enable you to adjust flexibly. If your clothing consists of many thin layers instead of one thick one, then you can always quickly add or remove a layer. All you need is a small rucksack to keep something in reserve. A spare pair of gloves may come in handy if your main ones are getting wet, and the same can be said about an extra pair of warm socks.

The outermost layer should always be wind- and waterproof. This applies even in sunny weather, as weather changes can be very sudden and water splashes may make you wet during a speedy boat ride even under calm conditions. A breathing membrane is excellent, but for shorter walks, cheaper rain clothes will also do.

You must always have gloves, a hat and a scarf, in your rucksack at least, to be prepared for unpleasant weather changes. There is an old saying which goes something like "if you have cold feet, then put on a hat". There is something in this. Thin finger gloves will enable you to handle binoculars and camera without exposing your fingers completely. I find that the sort of gloves which combine finger and mitten are very useful; the fingers of the gloves are cut off, and if it is really cold, then you can use a little bag that is attached to the gloves to cover your fingers.

Leave your jeans at home or at least on board. They are neither wind- nor waterproof, and they take a long time to get dry.

Footwear is always a matter of passionate debate, and there are as many opinions as travellers. For expedition-style cruises, rubber boots are generally recommended and most professional expedition leaders and guides will hardly use anything else. The crux of the matter is to avoid cheap boots that you may use at home in your garden. Rather get solid hiking rubber boots with a strong, profiled sole, that give protection up to your knees. Most people find out that they can walk in such boots much better than expected. They are useful not only for the first step ashore during landings with small boats, but also on the tundra which is often wet and has small rivers that you may have to cross. Choose boots slightly larger than you normally would. Your feet swell slightly after some intense hiking, and you need space for an extra pair of thick socks.

For good rubber boots, try outdoor equipment stores or shops selling fishing and hunting gear.

For longer summer hiking and trekking tours, you will need strong hiking boots, and for long tours in areas with a lot of coarse scree, which is quite common in Spitsbergen, plastic mountain boots can be a good choice. These are strong boots resembling those used for downhill skiing, with a robust outer layer of plastic and separate inner shoe, which is also useful during the evening. The outer part may be used alone for crossing rivers, or together with Neoprene® socks (as used for windsurfing), to protect your feet from stones and ice-cold water. Others prefer to carry an extra pair of rubber boots for this purpose (an improvised, lightweight construction to make them higher is useful, such as rain trousers glued on to them) or simply use their hiking boots, claiming rightly that after some days in the field in Spitsbergen you will have wet feet anyway, so you may as well save the effort …

There are a number of options, none of them being ideal. But do not try to cross rivers in bare feet! Stones are moving rapidly at the bottom and can quickly hurt your feet. The temperature of the water is impossible to stand for more than a few moments. To make it even worse, arctic rivers tend to have many channels, which you may have to cross one after the other, so your toes would fall off sooner rather than later.

One person may hate wet feet but not mind carrying a heavier rucksack, while the next one does not care about moist feet, but wants to reduce weight. In the end, both will enjoy the very same tour with different equipment.

Change of subject, from cold feet to preventing the upper end of your body from becoming burnt. The sun can be surprisingly strong in high latitudes, even through clouds and fog, and large surfaces of ice, snow and water amplify radiation that is burning your skin. Use strong **sun cream** and **sun glasses**.

For summer tours, I recommend the following (adjust and add items according to your individual needs):

- A layer of long, warm underwear.
- A warm pullover.
- Robust dungarees of wind- and waterproof, breathing membrane. The dungarees will also protect your belly from wind.
- Scarf, cap and gloves are always at hand, as well as sunglasses and sun cream.
- Shoes:
    - For ship-based voyages, choose robust, knee-high rubber boots with strong profiled sole, available from shops selling hunting, fishing or outdoor equipment.
    - For hiking tours, according to need: hiking boots or plastic mountain boots, possibly completed with rubber boots or even Neoprene® socks.

Personal hygiene and environment: Because of the low temperature, chemical processes need much more time in the Arctic than they do anywhere warm. Thus it goes without saying that only biologically degradable soap, toothpaste, shampoo etc. should be brought to Spitsbergen. We can certainly survive some days with less chemical products and possibly take the experience back home that the use of less and at the same time environmentally less harmful substances for washing and cosmetics is possible anywhere on Earth.

Do not leave toilet paper or other unappetizing evidence of human presence visible in the landscape. Digging anything into the ground is not a solution, as frost action will bring everything back to the surface after a while. Burn whatever can be burnt, leave faeces where it will not annoy anybody (certainly not in or near any river or lake) and take everything else back to Longyearbyen.

Photography: This is not an introduction to photography, but some advice may be useful. Always protect your camera and binoculars (unless waterproof, of course) from rain and splash water, especially during boat transfers. A waterproof camera bag comes in handy. This may seem too obvious to be mentioned here, but practical experience tells a different story. Do not expect any photographic equipment to be available outside Longyearbyen, including film rolls and memory cards. Even if the brochure says it should be available on board – it can be sold out. Do not expect that you can download memory cards on board a ship; the more independent you are, the better. Bring at least an empty CD or DVD, in case somebody is able to help you with his private computer. Sufficient film material, memory, batteries, chargers will decrease any risk.

Plugs from the UK do not fit into wall sockets in Longyearbyen or on board many cruise ships, so bring an adapter to be sure you can use your equipment.

If you plan to go hiking or any other tour that involves being away from civilisation for days or even weeks, then you should test carefully to see if your camera and batteries can stand the temperatures that you expect. Arctic weather conditions are a serious challenge for all electronic equipment in the summer and even more so in the winter.

A small camera with a viewfinder will yield nice snapshots for your photo album, but hardly allows spectacular wildlife photography. For any serious wildlife photography you will need a telephoto lense. Having a selection is certainly useful: If light, a tripod and enough time to put it up, are available, then 400 mm is a good focal length and you may even want to add a tele converter. If time is limited or a tripod is not an option for weight reasons, then focal distances beyond 300 mm are usually too unwieldy and you can do without anyway: It is always better to enlarge a sharp image than have a full-frame one that is blurred. For this reason, you should bring film with ASA values of at least 200 or even 400. In June and July there is usually plenty of light, but in August you will notice that already the light is getting scarce in the evening, as your light meter will suggest rather unpleasant shutter speed values.

If weight does not matter, then a small backup camera is a good idea in case your main equipment suddenly conks out. It goes without saying that this usually happens at the most inconvenient moments, such as the very first day of a long voyage.

If you have to carry all your luggage, then you should definitely not underestimate the weight of camera gear with several lenses. During hiking tours, you will mostly photograph scenery and flowers rather than wildlife, and for this purpose, a small, but good camera with viewfinder and in-built zoom lens will do for most people. Digital or analogue does not matter, as long as you bring sufficient batteries.

Now, finally some hints:

For flower photography, it is well worth lying down flat on the ground, not only because it gives everybody nearby a good laugh, but also because a good background will definitely increase the aesthetic value of the result.

For photos of large areas with ice and snow, underexpose a little bit, especially against the light. Don't overdo it; 1/3 or 1/2 step should be sufficient, depending on your camera and film material. You did not come to the high Arctic to save a few bucks on film! In good situations, take several pictures with different f-stop values.

But don't forget: The key factor for a great photo is the rare opportunity of being there when it happens … good luck!

3.5 Getting to Spitsbergen

"From Tromsö in the extreme north of Norway, it took us six days' steaming to reach Spitsbergen, the only halt during that time being a few hours' stay at Bear Island."

Seton Gordon, *Amid Snowy Wastes*

Citizens of signatory states of the Spitsbergen treaty (including most EU countries, Switzerland, the United States of America) do not need a passport to visit Svalbard, including the Russian settlements. Passing through Norway, however, requires a passport, as Svalbard is not part of the area of the Schengen treaty, so you are entering Schengen territory from outside when you travel from Longyearbyen back to Norway.

Every visitor has to pay an environmental fee, currently 150 NOK, which is added to the flight ticket or, if you come to Spitsbergen by ship, paid by the shipping company. Either way, you are unlikely to realise that have have actually paid the fee.

There is no regular passenger ship traffic between Norway and Spitsbergen, which means that visitors and locals mostly have to rely on the scheduled flights from Oslo and Tromsø to Longyearbyen. The airport, which is located about five kilometres west of Longyearbyen, opened in 1976 and was not made for the quantities of passengers passing through today. Consequently, a larger terminal building was built during 2007. It has Cafeteria and a post box.

During the tourist seasons (March to early May and late June to late August), many flights are fully booked, which makes excess luggage expensive and hand lugggage is strictly restricted to one piece per passenger. The usual security rules apply. When leaving Spitsbergen, customs procedures are complicated, as Svalbard is not part of Norway from the customs authorities' perspective: If you fly from Longyearbyen to Oslo and have an overnight there, then you will usually have to take your main luggage out in Tromsø, go through customs clearance and deliver it again, even if it was checked through to Oslo in Longyearbyen. The procedure is certainly confusing. To avoid difficulties, ask the airport staff or flight attendants for details. A similar procedure is applied upon entering Norway: even if you go straight to a connecting flight to Longyearbyen or elsewhere in Norway and your luggage is checked through, you have to take your luggage in Oslo, go through customs and hand it over again. Your luggage will stay in Oslo if you forget to do this.

There are good reasons to arrive at least one day in advance, before an organised tour starts. You will, for example, have time for individual or guided activities before or after a ship cruise. Secondly, you reduce the risk of boarding a ship while your luggage is still sitting somewhere at another airport further south. Spontaneous shopping for a complete new set of equipment is expensive and annoying.

You could also decide to spend a day in Oslo or Tromsø. Many flight passengers from outside of Norway have to spend a night in Oslo anyway. You will quickly find comprehensive tourist information about Oslo or Tromsø on the internet or in any guidebook, and there is no need to copy it all again here. Nevertheless, it should not remain unmentioned that a visit to the *Fram*, the legendary polar ship used by the likes of Fridtjof Nansen, Roald Amundsen and Otto Sverdrup, is a great way to round off an arctic trip when you have time in Oslo. You can see the *Fram* on the museum peninsula Bygdøy. From Oslo's international airport at Gardermoen, there is regular transportation by train and bus to Oslo centre. The bus needs some more time (about 40 minutes instead of 20), but it is cheaper.

If your journey up to Spitsbergen is part of an organised tour, then you will often be picked up at the airport in Longyearbyen. If not, it is nevertheless all very easy. After each arrival and before every departure, there is a flight bus between Longyearbyen and the airport. The flight bus stops at all hotels and guest houses. The only exception is the camping site, which is just a few hundred metres walking from the airport, across the car park down towards the Isfjord. You have to pay cash for the airport bus (50 NOK from summer 2008). A taxi from Longyearbyen to the airport costs about 100 NOK (payable in cash or by credit card), but as you may have to wait a while for a taxi before departures and after landings, the airport bus is not only cheaper, but most likely as quick as a taxi.

3.6 Conservation, cultural heritage, protected areas, safety

"Here we can live, we can also die, just as it pleases us; nobody will stop us."

C. Ritter, *A Woman in the Polar Night*

This quote is from the 1930s and things have definitely changed since then. Everyone who is travelling in Svalbard has laden a veritable burden of responsibility upon his or her shoulders, both for their own safety and for the protection of the vulnerable natural and historical environment in the far north. There are a number of rules, some of which are common sense, while others come in the shape of Norwegian legislation in Oslo or the rules of the Sysselmannen in Longyearbyen.

The following list draws your attention to some important aspects, but cannot claim completeness. If you plan to travel in Svalbard, then you have to make sure that you know the relevant regulations – this is especially true for individually organised voyages. In the case of organised tours, the tour operator is responsible, but needs your active cooperation to make sure neither common sense rules nor relevant laws are violated. If you choose to ignore these, then you risk very unpleasant consequences such as heavy fines or, in extreme cases, imprisonment for environmental damage and/or safety risks.

Trips to most parts of Svalbard need approval of the Sysselmannen (www.sysselmannen.no) in advance. Amongst the requirements that have to be met are insurance cover for expensive search- and- rescue operations, and certain equipment (see section 3.6.3 *Registration of tours with the administration*).

3.6.1 Conservation and protected areas

The official motto is that it is impossible to be an invisible visitor, but it is appreciated that you try. Do not take anything away with you but photos, memories and souvenirs that you have bought legally, and do not leave anything behind but unavoidable footprints.

It goes without saying that **rubbish** must not be left behind, neither ashore nor at sea. This includes cigarette butts, which do not belong in the water or on the tundra. One reason is that seabirds such as fulmars may try to eat them with potentially fatal consequences and beyond this, there is the respect for the still relatively untouched beauty of the Arctic, which requires that we do not use the place as an ashtray. Regarding rubbish, burying it does not help because frost action or animals will most likely bring it back to the surface. The only acceptable option is disposal in Longyearbyen.

It is not allowed to leave any traces. This includes building cairns. If you collect stones to secure your tent from strong wind, then make sure you don't leave artificial stone rings behind when you move on. Such rings are now becoming a common, but quite annoying sight in the Isfjord area. Most of us come to the Arctic to experience "untouched" nature; and any signs of camp sites are not exactly helpful in this respect. It is a different story with ancient tent rings in areas with a native population such as Greenland.

It is strictly forbidden and totally unacceptable, to cut your name, the name of your boat or anything else into wood, the wall of a hut or paint or spray it on rocks.

Any **disturbance of wildlife** is generally forbidden. Keep your distance from breeding birds, especially ones that are breeding on flat tundra such as geese, ducks and Arctic terns. If the adults leave the **nest**, then the egg or chick will soon freeze to death or fall victim to larger birds (e.g. Glaucous gulls) or the Arctic fox. Do not try to photograph nesting birds or abandoned nests, unless the nest has obviously been abandoned a long while ago. Special care needs to be taken during the late spring and early summer, when geese arrive after their spring migration and gather in large concentrations in certain areas (including Adventdalen, Sassendalen, Colesdalen, Reindalen, the west coast between Isfjord and Bellsund and north of Isfjord (Daudmannsøyra), and in southern Dickson Land), before they spread out to their breeding areas. Pink-footed geese are most easily disturbed, with a flight distance of well over a kilometre and a high risk of predation on eggs and chicks when the adults have left the nest.

If you are **being attacked by Arctic terns**, then you are most likely too close to their nesting area. The birds attack the highest point, so you may simply hold your hand with glove, a walking stick, tripod, piece of driftwood or your guide above your head. Do not try to hit the birds! If you do hold anything up, then just hold it, don't wave it.

Following animals with snow mobiles, boats or any other means is forbidden. There is a wide distinction between careful, respectful approach and inconsiderate or even ruthless pursuit; the boundary between them can be transitional and does sometimes require some experience. But at the latest, when an animal (Polar bear, walrus, …) changes its behaviour, or when it moves away from you at some speed, then the distance is too small, your approach has been too fast etc. Every animal may react in a different way. It may choose to come close to you out of curiosity, and this is the ideal situation, provided it is safe. A reindeer approaching you does not imply any danger, and neither does a Bearded or Ringed seal or an Arctic fox (unless you touch it, as it may have rabies). It is a different story, obviously, with Polar bears and walruses: from both, you must keep your distance for your own safety. In the vicinity of a bear, you are safe in a manouvreable boat, but when walruses are around, then solid ground under your feet is better than a vulnerable small boat. **It is generally forbidden to feed animals**. Regarding Polar bears, there are also vital safety reasons for not feeding them, because they will then expect to get food from humans and may react with aggression if disappointed next time. Under no circumstances must Polar bears be fed from ships, although this was common practice in the past.

You can collect loose **fossils** outside protected areas as of 2008, but it is not allowed to damage larger rocks to retrieve fossils. Larger and scientifically important fossils, including remains of dinosaurs, are likely to be legally protected in the future.

Exporting **driftwood** is prohibited unless you have special permission. From 2008, it is still allowed to collect some young (!) driftwood for a small **fire** at a safe distance from cultural heritage sites (minimum 100 metres). Make sure you do not burn any wood that has been worked, for example beams and boards, parts of wrecks or pieces of wood with old nails. Neither must old driftwood which you find away from and above the present-day shoreline, or pieces of wood that carry vegetation including mosses and lichens, be burnt. Keep your fire small and **make sure there are no visible traces of the fire place once you have left**. Despite all these restrictions, making a fire is still a nice thing to do and is possible, but it is annoying to see that old remains of the cultural or natural heritage have been damaged carelessly.

It is possible to collect single **reindeer antlers** that the animals shed every year, but you must not remove antlers from dead animals. **Plants** are generally protected and must not be collected. Avoid damage as much as possible. Especially moss beds can be very vulnerable to footsteps. Damaging plants is generally forbidden, except from unavoidable footsteps while walking in a normal, respectful way. Try to step on stones rather than on vegetation. Dry vegetation is normally less vulnerable than on wet areas, especially wet mosses.

Most parts of Svalbard are protected. There are several different kinds of protected area, each one having its specific set of rules which can go as far as a complete ban on any kind of traffic even in the surrounding sea. As from 2007, this applies to the bird sanctuaries and selected parts of the nature reserves such as Moffen and Kong Karls Land. There may be more "no go" areas in the future, especially in eastern parts of Svalbard; you will get updated information from the Sysselmannen or the tourist information office in Longyearbyen.

Amongst other things, it is prohibited to collect stones and fossils in all protected areas.

Protected areas

A large and still increasing proportion of the Svalbard archipelago has come under protection since 1973, when the national parks Northwest Spitsbergen, Prins Karls Forland and South Spitsbergen, together with the nature reserves Northeast Svalbard and Southeast Svalbard, were established. Further areas followed in 2002 and 2005, leading to 65 % of the total land area of Svalbard now being protected (see map further down in this section). The degree of protection varies, depending on the protection status. Violation of relevant laws can lead to fines or imprisonment of up to one year or, in exceptional cases, up to three years.

Boundaries of protected areas, including those with a total ban on all traffic, are not marked in the field. You have to know them.

Observe special regulations for motorized traffic in the air or on the ground (such as snow mobiles). Contact the Sysselmannen if such traffic is part of your plans.

National parks

The following is prohibited:

- All technical intervention, i.e. no forms of industrial intervention are allowed, including erection of buildings, establishment of mines and wells to search for or extract fossil fuels. This applies also to the sea floor.
- Any disturbance of the sea floor. Shrimp fishery is allowed at depths below 100 metres.
- Dumping of refuse.
- Hunting and disturbance of mammals and birds and their lairs or nests.
- The introduction of alien plant or animal species.
- Removal or damage of plants and fossils.
- Use of cross-country vehicles and landing with aircraft.

These regulations do not apply to police and rescue services. The Sysselmannen can give dispensation from regulations, for example for scientific studies.

Additionally, a ban on certain ship fuel types is currently (2008) under consideration. This may have consequences for cruise ship traffic for example in Madgalenefjord.

Nature reserves

The same regulations as for National Parks are in force, but the Sysselmannen can introduce traffic bans in addition. The near future is likely to see significant restrictions on tourist traffic in the large nature reserves in eastern Svalbard. Landings from tourist ships may be limited to selected locations in order to preserve large reference areas for science, and several historical sites may receive special protection. This recent development is quite controversial and currently under discussion, a decision being likely during spring 2009.

The following regulations have recently been put in force for ship traffic in the large nature reserves in eastern Svalbard:

- Ships must not carry or use any fuels other than "quality DMA referring to ISO 8217 fuel standard". In practice, this means that crude oil is banned.
- The maximum number of passengers is limited to 200.

Bird sanctuaries

The same regulations as for Nature Reserves are in force. Additionally, there is a general ban on all traffic in the period 15 May to 15 August. All traffic including boats have to keep a minimum distance of 300 metres to the nearest coast, including small rocks, inside the bird sanctuary. The purpose is to protect important breeding sites of birds such as Common eider and geese. Currently, there are 15 bird sanctuaries, most of them small islands.

There is a total ban on all traffic in the following areas (as from December 2008):

- 15 **bird sanctuaries** (see above)
- It is not allowed to approch **Moffen** during the period 15 May to 15 September any closer than 300 metres.
- You must not appproach **Kong Karls Land** any closer than 500 metres at any time of the year.
- The huge bird cliffs at the **southern end of Bjørnøya** enjoy special protection. You must not approach them from land during the period 01 April to 31 August. All vessels longer than 40 feet (12.2 metres) must keep a minimum distance of one nautical mile (1.852 kilometres or 1.15 statute miles).
- In the **northern part of Bjørnøya**, you may not enter the area around the lakes Kalven, Laksvatnet and Lomvatnet, situated southeast of the weather station or northwest of Tunheim, between 15 June and 31 August.
- It is generally prohibited to enter **Virgohamna** on Danskøya. The Sysselmannen, however, can give permission to visit Virgohamna also for touristic purpose.
- The fenced-off areas on Gravneset in **Magdalenefjord** must not be entered.

It is likely that access restrictions will be introduced in 2009 at the following historical sites: Ebeltofthamna (Krossfjord), Ytre Norskøya and Likneset (northwestern Spitsbergen), Haudegen Station (Rijpfjord, Nordaustland), Andréeneset (Kvitøya), Habenichtbukta (southwestern Edgeøya), Zieglerøya/Delitschøya/small surrounding islands (near Andréetangen, southeastern Edgeøya), Halvmåneøya (possibly except the trapping station Bjørneborg), Tiholmane and Schareholmane (Tusenøyane), Lægerneset (Recherchefjord), Midterhukhamna (Bellsund/Van Keulenfjord).

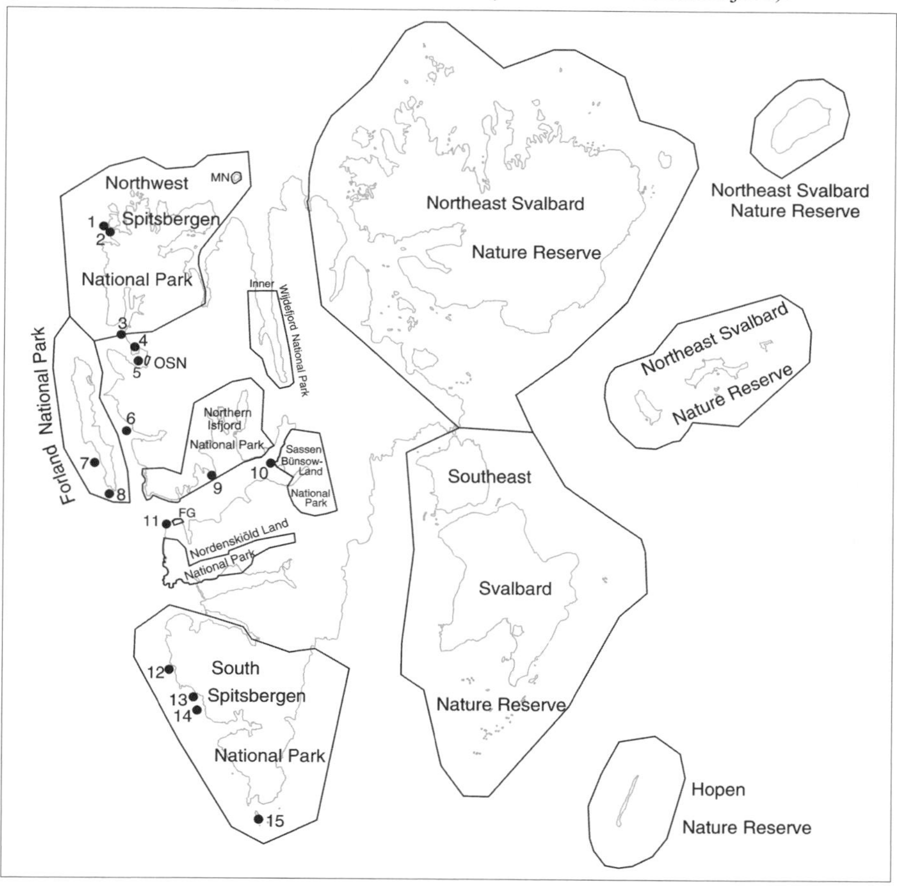

3.6.1 Protected areas (for Bjørnøya, see page 411).
FG = Festningen geotope. MN = Moffen nature reserve.
OSN = Ossian Sarsfjellet nature reserve. Black dots: Bird sanctuaries.
1 = Skorpa, 2 = Moseøya, 3 = Kapp Guissez, 4 = Blomstrandhamna,
5 = Kongsfjord, 6 Hermansenøya, 7 = Forlandsøyane, 8 = Plankeholmane,
9 = Bohemanflya, 10 = Gåsøyane, 11 = Kapp Linné, 12 = Olsholmen,
13 = Isøyane, 14 = Dunøyane, 15 = Sørkappøya.

Biotopes and geotopes

Areas of particular importance to the flora or fauna or that contain important or distinctive geological formations may be given protected status as biotopes or geotopes. In such areas, activities that may affect or disturb the flora or fauna or damage geological formations contrary to the purpose of the protection measure shall be avoided. The only protected area of this category so far is the Festningen geotope.

3.6.2 Polar bears and weapons, communication, safety in the field

There are more Polar bears than humans in Svalbard and seeing the king of the Arctic in his own environment is certainly amongst the most beautiful and impressive arctic experiences to be had. If you want to see a Polar bear, then you need patience and luck. The choice of the right voyage will also increase your chances: Although nobody can give you a serious guarantee, chances are certainly better on a long cruise in the remote parts of the archipelago than during a short stay in Longyearbyen, where you will probably have to make do with one of the stuffed bears, for example in the museum. There, at least, it is possible without any danger even close to.

With real Polar bears however, there is always a serious risk involved. During several decades and into the 1990s, there have been a number of accidents, some of them resulting in human fatalities. Every year, several Polar bears are shot in Svalbard in self defence, mostly by scientists or locals, including trappers.

It should obviously be in everyone's interest to do everything possible to reduce the risk of having to shoot a bear and in any case, they are protected by law. Shooting a bear is illegal and must immediately be reported to the Sysselmannen. Detailed investigations will follow every case, and so will serious punishment unless the Polar bear has been shot in self defence in a situation which occured through no fault of one's own. In a case where the shooting could have been avoided, not only the shooter may face punishment, but also the person who has caused the situation due to irresponsible behaviour, for example by leaving the group.

It is under all circumstances strictly forbidden to lure or to feed Polar bears or to follow fleeing bears.

As participant of a guided tour, your responsible behaviour is the key to avoiding incidents. This is for your own safety, for the safety of the group including the armed guides and, of course, the well-being of the bear. Follow strictly the guidelines given by your guides! The main points are briefly outlined here:

Outside of the inhabited settlements, **you have to expect a Polar bear anywhere and at any time**, no matter how unlikely you consider it to be. The coastline is a common place for Polar bears to wander about, but you can also meet them far inland, even at high altitudes and on glaciers. In flat terrain, there is always a rock or a little depression where a bear may be sleeping, not being visible even from a short distance. Blind areas such moraines, uninhabitated settlements and canyons are especially dangerous.

The only places where you are generally safe are the permanently inhabited settlements Barentsburg, Longyearbyen, Ny Ålesund and Sveagruva. If a Polar bear comes close to these places, then he will usually be seen and scared away. In Longyearbyen, the road between the settlement and airport / camping site is considered safe at least in the summer. West of the camping site, you are in the wildnerness, despite a number of weekend huts that are standing between the camping site and Bjørndalen. These huts are not regularly occupied and Polar bears show up in this area almost every year. In the summer of 2007, a bear was even seen on the road near the harbour! This was certainly a rare event.

Outside the inhabitated settlements, you must have an appropriate firearm at any time and, of course, relevant experience. This applies also for walks in the direct neighbourhood of Longyearbyen, including Adventdalen, Bjørndalen and Platåberget. In Longyearbyen, you can rent **rifles** (for contact details of suppliers, see end of this section). You do not need a special license, but of course you have to be able to handle the weapon. The minimum calibre for a rifle is .308 winchester, 30.06 is commonly used. Short weapons such as revolvers are not recommended and must not be used by guides who carry responsibility for the safety of a group. In Longyearbyen, some locals use heavy-caliber revolvers when out on tour, especially those who do not spend a lot of time in the field, for example during snow mobile tours or field police out on shorter inspections.

Beyond rifles, it makes sense to carry signal guns. **Signal pistols** are more effective than the smaller signal pens. To scare a Polar bear away, you should use ammunition that explodes at a distance of approximately 50 metres with a loud bang, rather than ordinary signal ammunition. As drift ice and glacier fronts often make similar sounds, it may fail to make a big impression on the Polar bear; sometimes it works well, sometimes it simply does not have any effect at all. Make sure you are used to the handling of such ammunition: If you get the distances wrong and the bullet explodes behind the bear, then it may run in the wrong direction, that is towards you …

Inside the settlements, you may carry weapons only for transportation to the field or shooting range. This applies to Barentsburg, Longyearbyen, Ny Ålesund and Sveagruva. If technically possible, weapons must be visibly unloaded. With rifles, the bolt must be removed. Carrying weapons inside public buildings is not allowed. Some places, for example the Svalbardbutikken (the large supermarket) and some hotels, have rifle safes.

For safety measures for camps, see section 3.6.4 *Tent and hut*.

There are more items that you should carry in the field for safety. These include various **means of communication**. Modern-day technology has come to Spitsbergen and **mobile phones** work in the near neighbourhood of Barentsburg, Longyearbyen and Sveagruva (not Ny Ålesund). Whether your phone works or not, depends on your device and your contract. In case of emergency, you can try to establish mobile phone connection anywhere in the Isfjord area. To increase the chances of success, try to get to a place where you can see Longyearbyen or Barentsburg, or climb up a mountain slope to reach some altitude. You may be lucky, but do not rely on your mobile phone when it comes to safety unless you really know where it works – and even then, the battery may fail. By the way – do yourself and everybody around you a favour and turn your mobile phone off when you are in the wilderness.

During longer tours in remoter areas, you should have a **PLB** (Personal Locator Distress Beacon). These small boxes contain modern technology, but are designed to be robust, waterproof and easy to use. If activated, they emit a signal that will be picked up by satellites and transmitted to the nearest search-and-rescue system. The received signal includes the information that you are in distress and your position. The kind of emergency remains unknown to the outside world until they have found you. This means that a large-scale search-and-rescue expedition will be launched. In practice, this usually means that the large and expensive helicopter will take off and try to find you; if suitable, boat or snow mobile expeditions are also possible. The perpetrator of a search-and-rescue expedition has to be prepared to carry the huge costs; individual tourists should check with their insurance in advance if this is covered.

The position of the sender cannot be determined with great accuracy, which means that under unfavourable conditions it may take quite some time to find you, involving increased costs.

The PLB technology has certainly saved lives and will continue doing so but if you carry one, than it should not lead you to make decisions that you would not have made without a PLB. If you start your PLB because you are running out of chocolate supplies, because you risk missing your flight, your shoes don't fit or you simply don't like the tour, then the reaction of the rescuers will be expensive and unpleasant.

It is compulsory to carry a PLB in areas where tours are subject to permission by the Sysselmannen, even if you have got a satellite phone. You can rent a PLB in Longyearbyen (see end of this section of contact details of suppliers).

Compared to PLBs, **satellite phones** have the clear advantage that you can not only transmit an emergency signal, but you can also communicate with the outside world. You can pass on a GPS position and describe your location or you can notify a harmless delay and thus prevent an expensive search-and-rescue expedition from being launched. In case of a less serious emergency, you can inform the authorities about the nature of the case and thus reduce the efforts significantly, saving costs and resources. As with PLBs, satellite phones should not lead you towards risky decisions thinking "if it does not work, I can still call the helicopter". The disadvantage is that satellite phones are rather expensive, but they are definitely cheaper than an unnecessary search-and-rescue expedition. You can rent satellite phones in Longyearbyen (see below for contact details of suppliers). A satellite phone does not release you from the liability to carry a PLB for tours that need permission from the Sysselmannen.

For suppliers for rental safety equipment in Longyearbyen, check with the following addresses or see section 3.3 *Tour operators*. Book well in advance for vital parts of your equipment.

Arctica AS: The outdoor- and mountaineering department in Svalbardbutikken, the large supermarket in Longyearbyen centre. Svalbardbutikken, phone +47 7092 25 40, email arcticas@online.no, internet www.arctica-as.no.

Ingeniør Paulsen (or short: **IGP**): The shop is near the coastline at the road towards Adventdalen, below the large, brown building that houses the university UNIS, the tourist information and the museum. Phone +47 7902 32 00, fax +47 79 02 18 10, email igp@spitsbergentravel.no, internet www.spitsbergentravel.no/igp.

Sportscenteret: Outdoor outfitter in the Lompensenter, amongst others weapon rental. Phone +47 7902 15 35. Email sports.centeret@longyearbyen.net, internet www.sportscenteret.no.

Price examples (Norwegian kroner per day): Rifle 100 NOK, PLB 150 NOK, satellite phone 300 NOK, signal pistol starting at 50 NOK. Prices per day get better when you rent for a longer period. Ask the suppliers for their updated conditions. You need relevant knowledge and experience. Insurance cover in case of accidents, search-and-rescue expeditions or loss of rental equipment is important.

3.6.3 Registration of tours with the administration

It is normal to make sure somebody knows about your whereabouts before you leave and to agree a time at which this person will alarm the Sysselmannen in Longyearbyen if you have not returned. The more accurate the information, the better; spontaneous deviations from your original plan may be expensive, if not fatal. You can also register with the Sysselmannen before and report about your return after the tour, this is compulsory for tours in large parts of the archipelago of Svalbard. The only area, where you may go on tour without registering with the Sysselmannen, is the so-called administration area 10. If you plan to travel anywhere in Svalbard outside administration area 10, then you have to notify the Sysselmannen about your plans prior to your arrival. This also applies at sea within the 12 mile zone around the coasts of Svalbard including Bjørnøya.

Together with details of your planned itinerary, the Sysselmannen will require contact details of a contact person at home and the names of participants, duration, destination, means of transportation, equipment, especially safety-relevant parts such as weapons and means of communication. You must carry suitable firearms and a PLB (personal locator beacon, see previous section).

The Sysselmannen will then determine the sum that has to be covered by your insurance in case of search-and-rescue operations. It is highly advisable to contact the Sysselmannen well in advance to inquire about these details and especially to make sure that your insurance coverage is sufficient, that it covers the potential risks that you will face during your tour and that you carry insurance evidence that you can present to the administration in Longyearbyen. If you only find out in Longyearbyen that you need (or want) an insurance then the choice is not great, but you can check with Ingeniør Paulsen for insurance cover (see end of previous section).

As an alternative to an insurance policy, the Sysselmannen will accept a bank guarantee; that is, a bank account containing the required amount, which the Sysselmannen can access easily during search-and-rescue operations.

3.6.3 Administration area 10 (hatched).

In the field, you have to carry with you documentation of your notification that you receive from the Sysselmannen. Expect inspection by field police at any time.

After the tour, the first thing that you have to do – at the latest after you have finished your first hot shower and good meal – is to let the Sysselmannen know that you are back to make sure that the helicopter does not search Spitsbergen's valleys for you while you are sitting in your bath tub at home.

3.6.4 Tent and hut

In the settlement areas, you may put up a tent only on the designated camping sites. These exist in Longyearbyen and Ny Ålesund. In the surroundings of huts and cultural heritage sites, there is a "no camping" policy in force, the required minimum distance being 100 metres (It is currently under discussion whether camping should be permitted within 100 metres of historical sites when the ground is frozen or snow-covered. A final decision has not yet been made). Remember that cultural heritage sites are sometimes very inconspicuous in the field, especially if there is snow; the ban on camping takes no account of snow cover and violation may result in heavy fines. Other than that, you may camp anywhere; if possible, you have to do so on vegetation-free ground. You must move your tent after one week at the latest to avoid damage to the vegetation. If you intend to camp at one site for more than one week, then you have to apply for permission from the Sysselmannen even within administration area 10 (see section 3.6.3 *Registration of tours with the administration*).

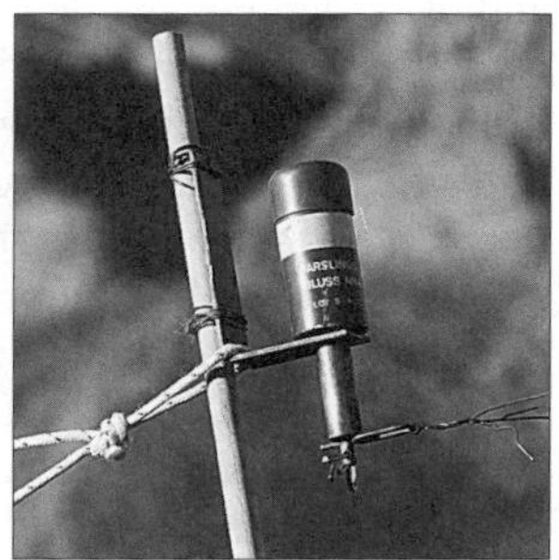

3.6.4 Mine for Polar bear alarm fence

Because of the potential of Polar bear visitors during the night, you have to put up a special alarm fence around your camp (does not apply to the camping site in Longyearbyen). This fence consists of a trip wire, fastened to strong posts at a distance of approximately ten metres from the nearest tent. The wire is connected to small alarm mines which explode with loud noise if anything walks through the wire. This will most likely be wind, reindeer or your friend who needs to go to the toilet, but you never know ... ideally, the bang is supposed to scare the bear away and to wake you up. If you have got enough resources, then it is a good idea to use two wires on the same posts: A lower one at knee-height, and a second one about one metre above the ground. Beyond question, such an alarm fence makes sense, but it cannot give hundred percent safety. Mines may fail to explode, and Polar bears have been seen crawling under the wire and into camps. If you are hiking inland, then you will have to carry not only the alarm mines and wire, but also posts, that have to be secured with cords to make sure that they stand firmly. For mines and related equipment, ask Ingeniør Paulsen in Longyearbyen (see end of previous section). Rental alarm fences should be available for about 350 NOK per week, but supply may be short if you have not ordered well in advance.

If you have the opportunity to take a sledge dog with you, then you not only have a loyal and funny friend, but also an alarm system that is more reliable than a construction of wire and mines, the assembling of which is amongst the less pleasant everyday duties of camping in Polar bear territory. A strong dog can carry its own food for several days in bags resembling saddle bags. Next to the trip wire or a dog, a person on bear watch is another recognized method to secure a camp against bears. It is strongly recommended to use at least one of these measures. Some of the local tour operators in Longyearbyen who have dogs offer to rent them out.

It is also strongly recommended that food and rubbish are placed outside the camp, avoiding attracting a bear to the camp, although practicability and benefit are disputed and will at least vary according to the situation. If you have failed to use an acknowledged warning system (fence, dog, watch) or you have food or rubbish stored inside the camp, then this will influence the official judgement if you have to shoot a bear.

You should not establish a camp directly on the shoreline, as Polar bears often walk along beaches. There is no infrastructure whatsoever outside the settlements. There are no **huts** that you can rent as a tourist, with a few exceptions near Longyearbyen (see section 3.7.2 *Accommodation, eating and drinking*). Additionally, in 2007, the Sysselmannen has granted permission to several local tour operators to establish huts in Nordenskiöld Land (central Spitsbergen) and Billefjord for commercial use within a strict framework of rules that excludes use for invididual tourists. Using huts without explicit permission is illegal – every hut in Spitsbergen is owned by somebody. Without approval of the owner, you may use a hut only in cases of real emergency. Bad weather does not justify a break-in. Nowadays, most huts are locked. If you have to break into a hut, notify the Sysselmannen as soon as possible and be prepared to pay costs for repair and to replace anything that you have used.

There are **no marked paths**. The best topographic **maps** that are available come at a scale of 1:100,000 and are accordingly not very detailed. Often, it is not clear from the map if you can pass a certain area or not. This is something that you have to live with in Spitsbergen unlike other areas in the world and, if you travel individually, then you have to find your own route in the field.

3.6.5 Other hazards in the field: rivers, glaciers, ice and snow, mud, rabies and other diseases, drinking water, mosquitos

Walking on glaciers and crossing rivers and similar obstacles requires adequate equipment and experience. In particular, the difficulties and risks involved in the **crossing of large rivers** are often underestimated, especially the rivers in the large, ice-free valleys in Nordenskiöld Land and in the neighbourhood of Longyearbyen during the melting season. This applies, amongst others, to the rivers Adventelva, Sassenelva and Reindalselva in the valleys of the same names. Water levels can vary greatly within a short time span. During and shortly after the snow melt in June is statistically the period with the highest water levels, but even in late summer, until mid September, water discharge can be huge especially on warm days. In the late autumn and early winter, freezing will terminate summer melting of snow and ice, resulting in river levels falling to almost nothing. Some experience will enable you to find spots where crossing is comparatively easy; if you are faced with a river too deep and torrential to cross, it may help to wait a couple of hours. Even though daily temperature cycles are not very pronounced, there are slight differences that may cause significant changes in water run-off, especially on sunny days. Run-off follows the sun with a delay of several hours; the lowest water levels will be in the early morning. Every tributary stream that you pass while walking up a valley will also make the crossing easier.

Many **glaciers** in Svalbard have only few crevasses and are accordingly easy to traverse in the late summer when large parts of the glacier's surface are free of snow, making crevasses visible. Large meltwater channels are more likely to cause difficulties than crevasses and can sometimes force long detours. Walking on glaciers can be great fun in Spitsbergen and it can actually be much easier to walk on a glacier than covering a similar distance on the ice-free tundra with all its rivers, little canyons and wet spots.
Nevertheless, you must never forget that **specific risks are always inherent in walking on glaciers** (crevasses, meltwater channels with rapid torrents, sub-surface caves that may collapse, etc.). It goes without saying that you have to bring and use appropriate safety equipment, knowledge and experience; it should, however, be mentioned that often a relatively "relaxed" approach is taken when dealing with "easy" glaciers (rather flat, no snow hiding any crevasses) in Spitsbergen, compared to the Alps or other glaciated mountain areas.

Icebergs breaking off from **glacier fronts**, an every-day event in Spitsbergen, often cause large waves. These are especially dangerous when they break in shallow waters and at the shore. Get away from the shoreline: If you are ashore, walk upslopes; if you are in a boat, make sure you quickly get into deeper water. Never camp directly on the shoreline close to large calving glaciers! If too close, then calvings can be dangerous even to larger ships, as a cruise ship painfully had to experience in Spitsbergen in the summer season in 2007, when several people got hurt during a major calving that flooded the front deck with water mixed with pieces of glacier ice.

When travelling in a small boat or kayak, do not forget that **drifting icebergs** can collapse or turn over very suddenly, causing an effect similar to a calving glacier front. Keep your distance!

But there is also some good news: As meltwater production is zero during most parts of the year, **meltwater caves** become dry during the winter. Equipped with helmet, torches, crampons etc., you can explore glacier caves, which is an absolutely fascinating experience! This is possible, for example, on Longyearbreen, one of the glaciers near Longyearbyen. Guided tours are available.

Snow avalanches are hazards during the winter season, especially after heavy snowfall near steep slopes. There has been an increasing number of accidents with such avalanches in recent years, also near Longyearbyen.

The whole topic of **ice** is highly complex in relation to safety and can only be touched on briefly here. During the spring, frozen fjords can be excellent and frequently used traffic ways, but there is always some inherent danger. There are places, where fjord ice is always thin or absent because of currents underneath. Heavy storms may destroy fjord ice at any time; something that you have to consider for your return trip in the case of long winter expeditions. In Van Mijenfjord, the ice will be broken during the spring by icebreakers – quite inconvenient if you happen to be on the wrong side of the fjord and just want to go back … the dates are published in the local press (Svalbardposten) and you can also contact the Sysselmannen.

During the late spring and early summer, the so-called **ice-foot** is a very dangerous place to walk on. The ice-foot consists of a small rim of fjord ice that is attached to land, being not much more than one or two metres wide and seemingly providing very convenient paths to get around difficult terrain. However, more than one careless wanderer has taken a bath in icecold water when the seemingly strong, but actually fragile, ice structure collapsed under his boots, skiis or sledge. During ship-based voyages in the early shipping season, the ice-foot or high snow walls can make landings difficult or even impossible.

The **tundra can be very wet** during the summer melting season. This makes walking difficult, but does not pose any particular danger, but there are spots with unpleasant, deep and possibly even dangerous mudholes. You have to expect these especially within young moraines, but also in terrain influenced by solifluction. This is water-saturated, soft sediment on a gently sloping surface, that is slowly flowing downslope, a few centimetres during each melting season, under the influence of gravity. Even for the experienced eye, it can be difficult to see dangerous spots in solifluction areas. It may be useful to know that, in Svalbard, they often occur in areas with poorly solidified, fine-grained Mesozoic (Triassic, Jurassic, Cretaceous) sediments. This makes areas such as Wilhelmøya, Barentsøya and Edgeyøa favourites for walkers to disappear in the mud up to their knees or even deeper. Everybody who has been several times to Dolerittneset ("Kapp Lee") at northwesten Edgeøya will know what I mean …

Polar foxes can have **rabies** or **tapeworm** *(Echinococcus multilocularis)*. Never touch a fox, be it alive or dead; or fox faeces. Avoid drinking from still waters in the tundra; preferably take water from little streams. It may be a good idea to boil drinking water, especially in the vicinity of settlements. This is definitely recommended in and near Grumantbyen, an abandoned settlement in Isfjord west of Longyearbyen, where an introduced mouse species (*Microtus rossiaemeridionalis*) is abundant. So far, the occurance of this mouse population is restricted to the near neighbourhood of Grumantbyen. These mice can be temporary hosts to the tapeworm of the Polar fox in its larval stage that is mostly spread by faeces and can be dangerous also to humans: without proper treatment, an infection can end fatally. An infection will show only after a long time, making treatment difficult and expensive and complete curing impossible. There is some evidence suggesting that only long-term exposure leads to infections, as people concerned are mostly owners of dogs and cats.

But finally, there is at least some good news: Mosquitos, usually the inevitable and ever-present plague of the arctic summer, are mostly scarce in Spitsbergen. Only warm, calm summer days will bring those little tormentors in any numbers, and only rarely in amounts that makes them a real pain. This is most likely to happen in inner parts of Isfjord such as Billefjord, Dickson Land and Ekmanfjord. If you have ever really been plagued by mosquitos in Spitsbergen, then you may find some comfort in the fact that you have experienced something quite rare – a fact that will most likely change as the climate is getting warmer, unfortunately.
After having read this chapter, do you still dare to come?

3.6.6 Orientation

The most precise topographic maps are published by the Norwegian Polar Institute at a scale of 1:100,000; for most parts of Svalbard, you won't find any better. They are available in Longyearbyen and at home from specialised geographic book traders, or they may be ordered directly from the Norwegian Polar Institute (www.npolar.no). The scale makes it impossible to see all details of the terrain on these maps and, additionally, arctic landscapes can alter quickly, especially the exact position of glaciers, glacial lakes and rivers.

Provided visibility is good, then orientation is usually quite easy with some basic experience in reading maps, as there are never any trees or houses in the way and you will usually have a good overview of the terrain. Relevant experience with maps and compass is absolutely necessary; a small GPS-receiver is useful, but does not help without a detailed map or waypoints.

Nautical charts are often very incomplete and not very precise, especially in the remoter parts of Svalbard where you find surprisingly large white, uncharted areas on the charts. Currently, Norwegian authorities are considering closing badly charted areas for navigation.

Magnetic deviation is surprisingly small, about four degrees to the east around Longyearbyen. It varies across the archipelago and can be stronger locally, depending on the occurence of magnetic rocks such as basalt-like bedrock (Diabas, Dolerite). If you anticipate orientation with the compass, then check the magnetic deviation in time before the visibility gets poor.

3.6.7 Cultural heritage

There is a whole set of special rules. Generally, everything that is man-made and older than 1946 is automatically protected, be it even a piece of broken glass or a rusty nail. Younger artefacts may also be protected.

A lot has been stolen or damaged under careless boots in recent decades; please take your part of the responsibility to protect all that is still there. In the vicinity of cultural heritage sites, you may not camp, put up a tent or make a fire within the required minimum distance of 100 metres from the nearest part of the site. This applies also if the cultural heritage is covered by snow, thus being invisible. Remember that often such sites of cultural heritage are not very evident; in some cases it may even be difficult for the experienced eye to see them (It is currently under discussion whether camping should be permitted within 100 metres of historical sites when the ground is frozen or snow-covered. A final decision has not yet been made).

If you are **collecting rubbish** in the wildnerness – something that is generally very welcome – then special care is needed in areas with cultural heritage sites. Do not collect anything that you cannot positively identify as rubbish, especially plastics. Actually, in some cases it can be difficult to decide or even be a matter of debate if a certain item is rubbish or a protected part of the local history. If in doubt, assume it is protected even if the item in question looks like rubbish to you. In the end, it is up to the Norwegian authorities to decide on this.

Virgohamna (illustration 6.7.2 page 323) on Danskøya is something like a high-arctic Cape Canaveral: It was from there that pioneer explorers Salomon August Andrée and Walter Wellman started their attempts to fly to the North Pole in the late 19th and early 20th century. Both have left behind a bit of a mess. What looks like a rubbish dump to the inexperienced eye, is actually one of a few key sites for experts in polar exploration. Virgohamna has been closed to visitors to protect the site. Tourists can, however, apply for a permission to enter the site under strict conditions.

It is likely that access restrictions will be introduced in 2009 at the following historical sites: Ebeltofthamna (Krossfjord), Ytre Norskøya and Likneset (northwestern Spitsbergen), Haudegen Station (Rijpfjord, Nordaustland), Andréeneset (Kvitøya), Habenichtbukta (southwestern Edgeøya), Zieglerøya/Delitschøya/small surrounding islands (near Andréetangen, southeastern Edgeøya), Halvmåneøya (possibly except the trapping station Bjørneborg), Tiholmane and Schareholmane (Tusenøyane), Lægerneset (Recherchefjord), Midterhukhamna (Bellsund/Van Keulenfjord). Thus, make sure you have got complete and up-to-date information, especially if you travel individually.

Violation of laws relating to the protection of the cultural heritage may lead to serious fines or even imprisonment for up to a year.

Strict laws to protect historical sites are, unfortunately, important as many sites have already suffered heavily from carelessness – both intentional and unintentional but, in the end, do make a difference from the conservation point of view. Do not forget that the purpose of strict laws is to protect historical sites in the interest of future visitors, both tourists and scientists.

Much has been stolen or damaged under careless boots. It has become a habit in recent times to blame tourism for this, so it may be appropriate to mention here that vandalism and theft were much more common in the early and mid 20th century, before public awareness for the problem started to grow. Carelessness and collecting illegal souvenirs are as much a habit amongst scientists and locals as amongst (organized) tourists where responsible guides usually put a lot of effort into preventing such damage. On the other hand, there are cases where guides obviously need more training and experience.

3.7 Longyearbyen

"Skal du gjøre bare en ting i Longyearbyen, reis til Gruve 7, sitt der en halv time uten å si et ord, og du er et nytt menneske."

"If there is only one thing you will do in Longyearbyen, then make it a trip to mine seven, sit down for half an hour without saying a word, and you will be a new human being."

Arne Holm, *Gruvebyen gjennom 100 år*

Longyearbyen is commonly called the capital of Spitsbergen. Spitsbergen / Svalbard, however, is not a country and it does not have a capital. The administration and most public services in Spitsbergen are in Longyearbyen.

For most tourists, Longyearbyen will be the first place they see in Spitsbergen, and for many, it will be the base for all activities. This is reason enough to give some priority to the description of Longyearbyen and its tourist infrastructure; the surrounding landscape and nature is the subject of section 6.1 *Adventfjord*. Longyearbyen or Longyear City, as it was originally called, was founded in 1906 by the US-American entrepeneur John Munro Longyear. Today, there are about 1,700 people living in the still-growing settlement.

It is a common custom to take off your shoes before entering flats and some public buildings such as the museum, church, hotels and the Sysselmannen's office. You can keep your shoes on in shops and most restaurants.

3.7.1 Services and infrastructure

Airport – Air tickets – Bank / post office – Bicycle rental service – Car rental service – Cinema – Communication – Emergency phone numbers – Fire brigade – Hospital / medical services – Library – Lompensenter – Newspaper – Pharmacy – Port – Post office – Sewing – Sports complex – Sysselmannen (governor) / police – Taxi – Toilets – Tourist information – University UNIS

Airport: The airport, official name **Svalbard Lufthavn**, is situated about five kilometres west of Longyearbyen, just above the camping site, and was opened in 1975. In 2007, a new terminal was built, as the old one became too small for the increasing air traffic. There are almost daily flights from and to Tromsø and Oslo, and local flights to Ny Ålesund and Sveagruva. Telephone +47 7902 38 00.

Car rental:

Arctic Autorent AS: Office in the airport, opening hours at flight arrivals and departures. Mobile phone +47 917 02 258, fax +47 7902 70 51.
Email info@autorent.as, internet www.autorent.as.

Longyearbyen Bilutleie AS: Office in Sjøområdet, which is the part of Longyearbyen near the fjord. Telefone +47 7902 11 88, mobile phone +47 906 84 113, fax +47 7902 10 82. Email post@bilutleie.no.
Svalbard Auto AS. Telefone +47 7902 49 30, fax +47 7902 49 31, email auto.svalbard@lnsn.no.
Svalbard Reiser AS: Telefone +47 7902 56 50, email johansl@online.no.

Cinema: Once or twice a week in the "Huset" in upper Longyearbyen, usually on Sunday evenings. The selection of films is usually not too exciting.

Communication: In Longyearbyen, Barentsburg and Sveagruva (not Ny Ålesund), there is mobile phone coverage that includes the near surroundings of the settlements and even larger parts of Isfjord. If you spend a longer period, you may consider buying a pre-paid Norwegian SIM card at Telenor (the Norwegian telecommunication company) or in the electronics department of the Svalbardbutikken.

There are public card telephones in the bank / post office building, in the Lompensenter, in the guesthouse in Nybyen and in the harbour master's office in the port (Bykaia). You can buy telephone cards in the Svalbardbutikken (in the main building, this time) and in the harbour master's office. Furthermore, there are public card telephones in the hotel in Barentsburg, in Ny Ålesund and in Sveagruva.

For internet, try the public library. There are two computers that can be used for free, as well as wireless internet access if you bring your own computer. Several hotels offer internet services to their guests, including wireless access in some cases.

Emergency telephone numbers: Sysselmannen (including **Police**) +47 7902 12 22 or mobile phone +47 41 40 31 65. **Fire brigade** +47 911 09 700. General emergency numbers 110 (fire brigade), 112 (police) and 113 (ambulance).

Hospital / Medical services: The hospital, located between the centre and the Radisson Hotel, is the address of choice in case of any medical problems, including teeth. For an appointment, call +47 7902 42 00, or +47 7902 42 30 for the dentist, in an emergency 113.

Library: The public library is situated on the first floor of the Lompensenter and welcomes everybody provided you take your shoes off. Next to a selection of literature, both general and local interest but mainly in Norwegian, there are two computers with internet access. Sign on in the list at the counter to make a reservation for one of the computers.

Lompensenter: Large building in the centre of Longyearbyen with different services including a range of shops and Cafés (Busen, Fruene), public library etc.

Newspaper: The *Svalbardposten* comes weekly and informs in Norwegian about local and regional news, leaving out international news. In 2004, 3,380 copies were circulated, and out of 2,600 subscribers, about 2,200 were living somewhere south of Spitsbergen. You can also subscribe to a digital version on the internet (www.svalbardposten.no).

Some international newspapers are available in the Svalbardbutikken supermarket.

It is likely that you have brought some newspapers from home for your journey up. If you want to do your guides a favour, then do not throw them away, but bring them along – you will make them happy if they are written in a language that the guide can read.

Pharmacy: In the Lompensenter. The hospital will also be able to help.

Port: There is a port with three quays in Longyearbyen. Most passenger vessels go alongside at "Bykaia", about 15 minutes walking distance from the centre of Longyearbyen (taxi: about 65 NOK). Bykaia is situated directly next to the road between the airport and Longyearbyen and you cannot miss it. Next to it, there is the harbour building with harbour master's office, shipping agent and a small souvenir shop. With a little bit of luck, one of the offices may even be occupied during opening hours. You can buy telephone cards, and there is a washing machine, toilet etc. Fuel, water, electricity, disposal of water and rubbish are available for yachts and larger vessels. During the summer season, the small port can be quite heavily frequented, and priority is usually given to larger vessels (they pay more) even if reservations have been made in advance. This means that smaller ships sometimes have to take passengers on board with small boats.

The port of Longyearbyen is secured with a fence against terrorist attacks, and the security personnel are usually strict. This means for you as a passenger, that you should not arrive prior to boarding time, as you will normally not be able to get to the vessel. Walk around for a little while or have a coffee in Longyearben until it is time for boarding.

Telephone (during the summer season, starting 01 June, officially 24 hours a day) +47 91 12 23 00, VHF (dito) channel 12 and 16, fax: +47 79 02 13 15, email bykaia@ssd.no, internet www.portlongyear.no. Port security: telephone +47 48 19 27 45.

Post office: See bank / post office.

Sewing: If your clothes are falling apart, then **Randi's Systue** may be the place to try (together with Atelier Aino in "the house with the green door" behind Skinnboden, near the restaurant Kroa). Randi prefers to sew fine dresses and traditional costumes, but will also help you with outdoor clothes, as much as possible. Do her a favour and wash your clothes before you bring them. Telephone +47 7902 11 00.

Sports complex: Officially called **Svalbardhalle**, it is near the school and has, amongst other things, an indoor pool and a climbing wall. Telephone +47 7902 23 05, fax +47 7902 35 30.

Sysselmannen (Governor) / Police: The Sysselmannen is the highest representative of the Norwegian government on Svalbard. Amongst many other duties, he (or she) has police authority and is responsible for search-and-rescue operations. Sysselmannen på Svalbard, P.O. Box 633, 9171 Longyearbyen, Norway. Office hours: Monday to Friday 0830-1530, telephone (during office hours) +47 7902 43 00, 24 hours +47 7902 12 22 or mobile phone +47 41 40 31 65, general emergency telephone number 112, fax +47 7902 11 66, email Firmapost@sysselmannen.no, internet www.sysselmannen.no.

Taxi: There are two taxi companies in Longyearbyen.
Svalbard Maxi Taxi AS: Operates a minibus for up to 15 persons, offers taxi services and guided minibus sightseeing tours in Longyearbyen. Telephone +47 7902 13 05, fax +47 7902 35 96.
Longyearbyen Taxi: Telephone +47 7902 13 75.
Toilets: The most important part. In Longyearbyen centre, there are public toilets in the Lompensenter.

Tourist information: Is located together with the museum in the eastern part of Svalbardporten, the large, dark-brown building that also houses the university UNIS. Both when you plan your individual tour and when you are in Longyearbyen, the tourist information offers a lot of useful information including the complete programme of tours and day trips that you can book, accommodation, contact details of service companies, an overview of up-to-date office hours of all services of interest in Longyearbyen, brochures, maps and pretty much anything else you may think of. Office hours: 01 May to 30 September every day 1000-1700, 01 October to 30 April 1200-1700, special office hours on public holidays. Telephone +47 7902 55 50, fax +47 7902 55 51, email info@svalbard.net, internet www.svalbard.net.

University UNIS: There will not be too many settlements of the size of Longyearbyen that have got a university. Strictly speaking, UNIS ("The University Centre in Svalbard") is not a university on its own, but a common outpost of the Norwegian universities in Bergen, Oslo, Tromsø and Trondheim. Approximately 350 students, about half of them from Norway, the others from many different countries around the globe, study biology, geology, geophysics or technology, all of this, of course, with a focus on the arctic perspective. Together with the scientific centre "Forskningsparken", the tourist information and the museum, UNIS is located in the large, brown building between the centre and Adventfjord. Telephone +47 7902 33 00, fax +47 7902 33 01, email studadm@unis.no, internet www.unis.no.

There is a shuttle bus service between the airport and Longyearbyen (all hotels) before and after each flight (50 NOK, cash only). The availability of taxis can be limited near flight times, which makes the bus not only the cheaper, but also often the faster solution. Hand luggage is restricted to one piece, and the usual security rules apply (see also section 3.5 *Getting to Spitsbergen*).

Air tickets: SAS Ground Services, the service address of the airline SAS, Monday to Friday 0900-1600, Sunday 1200-1600, telephone +47 7902 45 00, internet www.sasbraathens.no.

Otherwise, **Spitsbergen Travel AS** and **Svalbard Wildlife Service AS** may help you with ticketing issues in Longyearbyen, for contact details see section 3.3 *Tour operatours*.

Bank / Post office: Both are directly next to each other in the same building in the centre of Longyearbyen. In the bank, you can exchange money; there is also a cash dispenser. 100 Norwegian Kroner (NOK) equals roughly 12.4 Euro or 9.3 British Pound (January 2008).
Bank: telefone +47 7902 29 10, fax +47 7902 29 11. Post office: telefone +47 7902 16 04. Opening hours: Bank Mo-Fr 1000-1530, post office Mo-Fr 0930-1700, Sa 1000-1500.

In Spitsbergen, you will find post boxes at the post office (surprise, surprise), at the airport, at the hotel in Barentsburg, in Sveagruva and at the shop in Ny Ålesund. All post from Spitsbergen, including that from Barentsburg, will be sent via Longyearbyen and Norway. Allow at least a week for delivery from or to Longyearbyen, and parcels before Easter and Christmas will need more time. Barentsburg, Longyearbyen, Ny Ålesund and Sveagruva have still got their own postal franks.

Bicycle rental service: A bicycle is very convenient in Longyearbyen with its rather long roads, especially if you stay in Nybyen or at the camping site. Rental bicycles are available at Basecamp Spitsbergen (see section 3.7.2 *Accommodation, eating and drinking*), Spitsbergen guesthouse (dito), Ingeniør Paulsen (see section 3.6.2 *Polar bears and weapons, communication, safety in the field*), Poli Arctici (see section 3.3 *Tour operatours*) and on the camping site (see 3.7.2 *Accommodation, eating and drinking*).

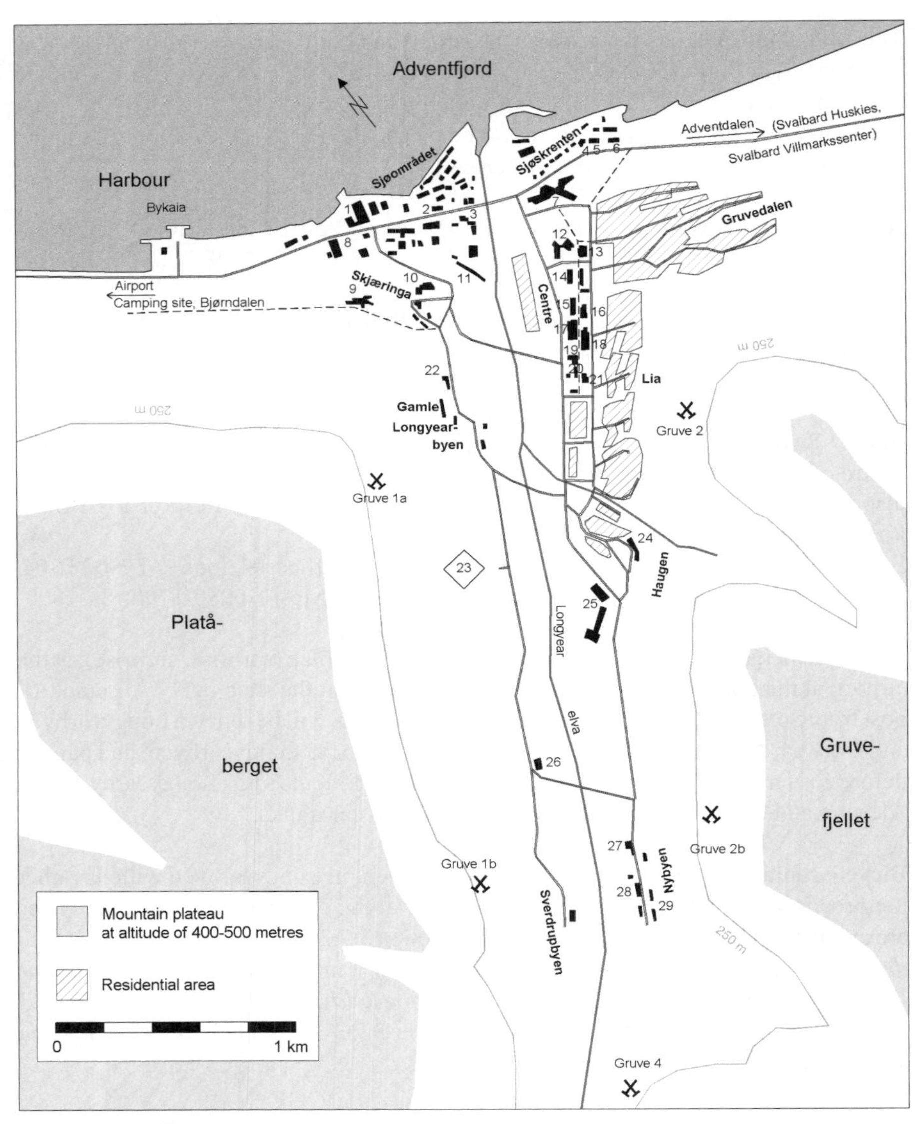

3.7 Longyearbyen.

Sjøområdet ("Sea-area", near Adventfjord)
1 = Store Norske Spitsbergen Kullkompanie
2 = Svalbard Reiser
3 = Longyearbyen Bilutleie
Sjøskrenten ("Sea-shore", near Adventfjord)
4 = Henningsen Transport & Guiding
5 = Ingenieur Paulsen
6 = Svalbard Snøscooterutleie
7 = UNIS, Tourist information, Museum
8 = Power station
Skjæringa ("The Notch", referring to a notch that was blasted into the slope for the cable railway)
9 = "Taubanesentralen", the old cable railway station.
10 = Sysselmannen
11 = Mary-Ann's Polarrigg
Centre
12 = Radisson SAS Hotel
13 = Spitsbergen Travel
14 = Krankenhaus
15 = Næringsbygget
16 = Bank/Post
17 = Lompensenter (Kafe Busen, Kafe Fruene, library, public toilets, shops)
18 = Svalbardbutikken
19 = Svalbard Arctic Sport
20 = Shops and Randis Systue (sewing)
21 = Basecamp Spitsbergen/Kroa
Gamle Longyearbyen ("Old Longyearbyen")
22 = Church
23 = Cemetary
Haugen ("The Hill")
24 = Spitsbergen Hotel ("Funken")
Not part of any specific quarter
25 = School/sports complex
26 = Huset/Kino
Nybyen ("New Town")
27 = Galleri Svalbard
28 = Spitsbergen Gjestehus (Guesthouse)
29 = Gjestehus (Guesthouse) "102"

3.7.2 Accommodation, eating and drinking

Accommodation: There is a full range of places in Longyearbyen where you can sleep, for different tastes and credit card calibers. Prices, telephone numbers and the like given here are for 2009 or 2008. They have been researched carefully, but may have changed. Check with the individual supplier for up-to-date prices.

The cheapest option is the **camping site**, which is the northernmost equipped camping site on this planet (the one in Ny Ålesund is just a piece of tundra without any facilities, and the one at the North Cape in Norway is, by comparison, almost in the tropics). It is open from late June to early September and additionally during special events such as the Spitsbergen Marathons (check in advance) and, on request, outside the season for groups. It is located between the airport and the coast, but noise is not too much of a problem, as the number of landings and departures is quite limited. Thoughtless tourists putting up their tent with a lot of noise in the middle of the night, when the midnight sun is shining, are more likely to disturb your sleep than flights. The view across Isfjord is beautiful, and a service building is available; it is open at least 0800-1000 and 2000-2200, often 24 hours a day unless somebody gives the staff a reason to lock it, with a self-service kitchen and showers: the friendly staff, usually Michelle from the Netherlands, can offer five hot minutes under the shower for 10 NOK – in the shape of a token for the hot water automat, unless you prefer cold water. It is about five kilometres walking along the road to Longyearbyen, but you can rent bicycles on the camping site. The only bus service is the airport bus after landings and before departures, which does not stop at the camping site, but the airport is near, as already mentioned. A night is 90 NOK, and it is possible to rent a place in a tent, isolation mattress or sleeping bag. If you need tent space or rental equipment, advise in advance especially if you arrive in the middle of the night; otherwise, it is not necessary to make a reservation for individual travellers.

During the season, you may be surprised by the number of people who stay at the camping site, and the service building can be crowded at times. But on the other hand, you will always meet people to exchange information and stories. As an additional service, the staff will often organise and offer **day trips** in the surroundings of Longyearbyen. Longyearbyen Camping, P.O. Box 6, 9171 Longyearbyen, Norway. Telephone +47 7902 14 44, mobile phone +47 977 44 696,
Email info@longyearbyen-camping.com, internet www.longyearbyen-camping.com.

It is highly recommended that you book in advance if you want to stay in any **hotel or guesthouse in Longyearbyen**, especially during the summer season and even more so during weekends around Easter. Outside the tourist season, especially during the dark time, accommodation is cheaper.

Several companies offer to rent **flats**:

Svalbard lodge: Flats for 4 or 6 persons in central Longyearbyen, equipped with all

that may be needed for daily life. Prices from 1,900 to 3,950 NOK. Svalbard Snøscooterutleie, P.O. Box 538, 9171 Longyearbyen, Norway. Phone +47 7902 46 64, faks +47 7902 46 71, email utleie@scooterutleie.net, internett: www.scooterutleie.net.
Stefano Poli has several flats and appartments for rental. Prices between 650 NOK (1 person) and 1,500 NOK (4 persons). Poli Arctici A/S, P.O. Box 89, 9171 Longyearbyen, Norway. Phone Tel +47 957 35 742, mobile phone +47 91 383 467. Email stefano@poliarctici.com, internett: www.poliarctici.com.

There is no real budget accommodation, but several **guesthouses** offer comparatively affordable beds. What you get is a relatively simple, but tidy room with breakfast and self-service kitchen.

Spitsbergen Guesthouse is located in Nybyen, the upper part of Longyearbyen, towards the glacier. From Nybyen, it is about 20 minutes walking to the centre. Single, double, triple rooms and small apartments are available between 315 and 1,595 NOK. Spitsbergen Guesthouse, P.O. Box 500, 9171 Longyearbyen, Norway, telephone +47 7902 63 00, fax +47 7902 63 01, email spitsbergen.guesthouse@spitsbergentravel.no, internet www.spitsbergentravel.com.

Guesthouse "**102**" is also in Nybyen, about 20 minutes walking from the centre. The "102" offers double and larger rooms ranging from 390 to 950 NOK. Gjestehuset 102, P.O. Box 164, 9171 Longyearbyen, Norway. Telephone +47 7902 57 16, fax +47 79 02 56 81, email 102@wildlife.no, internet www.wildlife.no.

Mary-Ann's Polarrigg is situated between the centre and the Sysselmannen's office building, 5 minutes walking from the centre, and has triple, double rooms and "luxusriggen". Prices between 495 and 2,500 NOK depending on room and season. Regarding quality of rooms and services, it is somewhere between the guesthouses and the more expensive hotels; for example, it is closer to the centre, you can get a warm meal in the evening and it has got an interesting design. Mary-Ann's Polarrigg, P.O. Box 17, 9171 Longyearbyen, Norway. Telephone +47 7902 37 02, mobile phone +47 958 04 108, fax +47 79 02 10 97, email post@polarriggen.com,
internet: www.polarriggen.com.

If you like to be more comfortable, then try one of the following **hotels**.

Basecamp Spitsbergen AS has a hotel in central Longyearbyen, the interior of which has been designed to create a rustic trapper's hut atmosphere even in every single room. Single, double, triple rooms and suites. Prices vary from 990 to 3,120 NOK. Basecamp Spitsbergen AS, P.O. Box 316, 9171 Longyearbyen, Norway. Telephone +47 7902 46 00, Fax +47 7902 46 01, email svalbard@basecampexplorer.com, internet www.basecampexplorer.com/svalbard/no.

You will find high-end comfort near central Longyearbyen in the **Radisson SAS Polar Hotel**. The building was originally used during the Olympic winter games 1994 in Lillehammer and was then relocated to Longyearbyen. Prices from 1,390 to 4,190 NOK. During the dark season, flats with self service kitchen are available for prices between 800 and 1,200 NOK including breakfast. Radisson SAS Polar Hotel Spitsbergen, P.O. Box 554, 9171 Longyearbyen, Norway. Telephone +47 7902 34 50, Fax +47 7902 34 51, email sales.longyearbyen@radissonsas.com, internet www.spitsbergentravel.com.

Spitsbergen Hotel, commonly called Funken, about 10 minutes walking from the centre. Single and double rooms with higher standards, prices between 750 and 3,650 NOK. Spitsbergen Hotel, P.O. Box 500, 9171 Longyearbyen, Norway. Telephone +47 7902 62 00, fax +47 7902 62 01, email hotel@spitsbergentravel.no, internet www.spitsbergentravel.com.

Wherever you sleep, from the camping site to the expensive hotels, you can order taxis and book day trips at the reception. The **airport bus** stops at all guesthouses and hotels in Longyearbyen.

Even if located not in Longyearbyen itself, all accommodation places that you can book in Spitsbergen are mentioned here.

Kapp Linné, situated at the entrance to Isford, houses a small but fine hotel in the buildings of the former coastal radio station Isfjord Radio. It opens from March to October and on request also during the dark season. Currently, single rooms are available for 2,220 NOK or 2,800 NOK, depending on the season, and double for 1,600 or 1,900 NOK; transportation from and to Longyearbyen is extra. Most guests come with a guided snow mobile or boat trip, but you can stay individually. Especially during the early summer, Kapp Linné offers a great opportunity to spend some calm days in an area that does not have large glaciers nearby, but is nevertheless beautiful and rich in things to see, including some fine birdlife. For excursions, you have to bring a rifle. The operating company is currently planning some re-building, but promises to preserve the station-like character of the place. Kapp Linné, 9172 Isfjord på Svalbard, Norway. Basecamp Spitsbergen, P.O. Box 316, 9171 Longyearbyen, Norway. Telephone +47 7902 46 00, fax +47 7902 46 01, email svalbard@basecampexplorer.com, internet www.basecampexplorer.com/svalbard/no.

The **boat in the ice** may be the most unusual accommodation that you can book in Spitsbergen. During the winter, the sailing ship *Noorderlicht* is frozen into the ice in one of the fjords, usually Tempelfjord. You can reach it from Longyearbyen by snow mobile or dog sledge. *Noorderlicht* then serves as a destination for day trips and offers the opportunity to spend a night. There are ten double cabins for 2,960 NOK with full board, and if you just happen to be around, you can have lunch for 270 NOK. Basecamp Spitsbergen, P.O. Box 316, 9171 Longyearbyen, Norway. Telephone +47 7902 46 00, fax +47 7902 46 01, email svalbard@basecampexplorer.com, internet www.basecampexplorer.com/svalbard/no.

For accommodation in Barentsburg and Ny Ålesund, see the relevant sections in Chapter 6 *Fjords and islands, settlements and stations*.

Eating and drinking in Longyearbyen

Nowadays, Longyearbyen has a good choice of restaurants. It is recommended to reserve a table for most places. You can pay with Norwegian currency and credit cards, but foreign currencies are not generally accepted in cafés and restaurants. Clothing is usually casual; you may dress more formally in the restaurants for dinner, but you don't have to. Trekking clothes that you have just had on for two weeks in the field will not be appropriate clothing for any place on Earth with a solid roof where other people are around.

Snacks, small or liquid meals:

The **Karlsberger Pub**, located together with Café Busen in the Lompensenter, is a bar with a wide selection of different drinks.

Barents Pub & Spiseri is a bar in the Radisson SAS Polar Hotel, that besides drinks also serves small meals. Every day 1600 to 0200.

Kafé Busen is a classical place for a lunch in Longyearbyen. In recent years, it has changed its menue from "ordinary" and fast-food style food to an emphasis on salads and organic food.

Café La Recherche is part of the Galleri Svalbard and offers an opportunity to have a coffee or light snack in Nybyen, the upper part of Longyearbyen. Opening hours depend on the gallery.

Basecamp Hotel also operates a bar, which is called **Cognachemsen**.

A nice and quite popular place for a piece of cake and coffee is the café **Fruene Kaffe & Vinbar AS**, located very centrally in the Lompensenter.

Funken Bar in the Spitsbergen Hotel (commonly known as "Funken") opens not only for drinks in the evening, but is also a cosy place to relax with coffee and waffles during the afternoon. Open every day 1100 to 0200.

Svalbar, the most recent establishment of its sort in Longyearbyen, between Svalbardbutikken and Basecamp Hotel/Kroa.

Restaurants:

Brasseri Nansen in the Radisson SAS Polar Hotel (see section on accommodation for contact details). Hotel restaurant with nice fjord view. More recently, the Brasseri Nansen has been enlarged with an upmarket section on the second floor for more exclusive occasions.

Funktionærmessen Restaurant, part of the Spitsbergen Hotel (see section on accommodation for contact details).

The **Huset** in upper Longyearbyen, about 20 minutes walking from the centre, is a restaurant with a long tradition and, during the evening, a bar. The disco is open during Friday and Saturday evenings and not a place for teetotallers. You can get a coffee and a snack starting at 1600 (1400 on Saturdays). The restaurant opens every day at 1900, including the famous wine cellar. Telephone +47 7902 25 00, Fax +47 7902 25 01, email post@huset.com, internet www.huset.com.

You will find the **Kroa** (officially: Steakers Svalbard AS) in the same building as the Basecamp Hotel near the centre of Longyearbyen. Like the hotel, it has a very rustic trapper atmosphere with a lot of wood, skins and old photos on the walls from the wild days of the trappers. Kroa, P.O. Box 150, 9171 Longyearbyen, Norway. Telephone +47 7902 13 00, fax +47 7902 35 86, email post@kroa-svalbard.no.

Restaurant Vinterhagen belongs to **Mary-Ann's Polarrigg** (see section on accommodation for contact details). Bar and restaurant in nice atmosphere.

3.7.3 Shopping

Nowadays, you will find pretty much everything that you need for everyday use in Longyearbyen and quite a lot of things beyond this. There is a shop offering electronic equipment including a small selection of (digital) camera gear, several shops with outdoor equipment, a number of souvenir shops and so on.

Spitsbergen is a low-tax area because of the regulations of the Spitsbergen treaty. This makes a lot of items cheaper than they are in Norway, especially things that you don't really need, such as alcohol and tobacco. Other items are more expensive because of shipping costs, including everything that is fresh. You can save money with the TaxFree-regulation, as Svalbard is not part of Norway, customs-wise. A lot of shops issue relevant documents.

Opening hours differ and vary depending on the season, but may typically be Monday to Friday 1000-1800 and Saturday 1000-1500. Most shops close on Sundays.

Books and maps: The museum is the best place to buy books on natural history and other regional interest, as well as maps. For the complete catalogue of topographic, geological and other maps of Svalbard and Jan Mayen, contact the Norwegian Polar Institute (www.npolar.no, no public sales in Longyearbyen).

Souvenirs: There is a wide range of souvenir shops offering different products, such as **Gullgruva**, the local "gold mine" located in the Lompensenter, where you can get the products of a local goldsmith next to the "usual" selection of T-shirts and postcards. **Rabi's Bua**, close to the Lompensenter, specialises in knitwear and clothing. If you really want to buy parts of animals, then try **Skinnboden**, where you can also buy Polar bear skins imported from Canada or Greenland – in Svalbard, they are strictly protected.

Supermarked: The largest shop is the **Svalbardbutikken** in the centre of Longyearbyen. Next to food stuffs, you will find outdoor equipment, stationary, souvenirs, books, maps and a small selection of international newspapers (at least during the tourist season), as well as an electronics department. This is your place not only for video and audio stuff, but also if you need to replace your broken digital camera or if you want to buy a Norwegian SIM card for your mobile telephone. The food department of the Svalbardbutikken is also open on Sundays.

Trekking and outdoor equipment: Svalbard Arctica AS (in the Svalbardbutikken), **Ingeniør Paulsen** (IGP) near Adventfjord below UNIS towards Adventdalen and **Skandinavisk Høyfjellutstyr** in the centre have already been mentioned in section 3.6.2 *Polar bears and weapons, communication, safety in the field* (see there for contact details). Additionally, there are two shops in the Lompensenter that offer equipment (**Sport 1 Svalbard**, telephone +47 9702 32 50 and **Sportcenteret**, telephone +47 7902 15 35) and a newer one not far from the Lompensenter, on the other side of the road that parallels the river.

3.7.4 Sights in Longyearbyen

Atelier Aino: Little exhibition with Spitsbergen-inspired art in the centre of Longyearbyen, in "the house with the green door" behind Skinnboden near the restaurant Kroa. Atelier Aino, P.O. Box 372, 9171 Longyearbyen, Norway. Telephone +47 7902 10 02, mobile phone +47 481 20 227, email ag@ainogrib.com.

Cemetery: The old cemetery is near the church under the slopes of the Platåberg. The first burial took place in 1917, the last one in 1950. Urn burials are still possible, but deceased inhabitants of Longyearbyen will usually be buried in their home community in Norway. Some graves have been opened in 1999 by Canadian scientists who had hoped to find the virus that caused the 1919 Spanish influenza in the graves in the permafrost, but with little success.

Galleri Svalbard is the gallery with the longest tradition in Longyearbyen and is located in Nybyen. Permanent sales exhibition and café, closed on Tuesdays, otherwise open 1300-1700 during the season. Galleri Svalbard, P.O. Box 350, 9171 Longyearbyen, Norway. Telephone +47 7902 23 40, fax +47 7902 15 57, email galleri.svalbard@lokalstyre.no, internet www.gallerisvalbard.no.

Goldsmith: Dutch goldsmith Marina van Dijk has settled in Longyearbyen to be inspired by arctic nature. You can see and buy her art in the souvenir shop Gullgruva in the Lompensenter. Gullsmed M. van Dijk, P.O. Box 72, 9171 Longyearbyen, Norway. Telephone +47 7902 11 96.

Historical Longyearbyen: Longyearbyen has a very interesting local history and traces from the mining period and the Second World War are visible in many places. Those with historical interest will find a little stroll worthwhile; the Svalbardmuseum has announced the establishing of a historical footpath with information signs as a plan for the future. To see some of the most interesting places, you could start with Skjæringa, that is the oldest part of Longyearbyen under the Platåberget, near the Sysselmannen's office building. The oldest buildings fell victim to a large-scale German attack in 1943, but you will find traces in the shape of burnt beams, parts of the former foundation, for example near the church. Above the church, you will also see the oldest mine, Gruve 1a, the so-called "Amerikanergruve" ("American's mine"), operating from 1906, temporarily closed in 1920 after a major explosion on 3 January, during which 26 miners lost their lives. The "Amerikanergruve" was finally closed in 1958. It is amazing to see the steepness of the slopes on which the miners established their installations.

Not far from the "Amerikanergruve", you will see a strange building standing on poles, resembling a giant spider. This is the old cable railway station. The first cable railway was built in 1907 to transport coal from the mines to the coal quay. More and more cable railways were added, coming together in the cable railway station in Skjæringa, until they were replaced by lorries in 1987. You can continue your historical walk to the church and the cemetery.

There are several **monuments** in Longyearbyen, including an eight metre high obelisk in Skjæringa, for the victims of the Second World War, and a monument near Huset for Einar Sverdrup, managing director of the coal company, who died in 1942 under German fire in Grønfjord near Barentsburg.

If you start your historical walk from the camping site, then half-way to Longyearbyen you will pass the old coal shipping crane, which is quite obvious. Near the coal crane, there is an old cannon from the Second World War that was stationed with the Norwegian garrison on Kapp Heer near Barentsburg.

The **church** is very obviously located on the western side of Longyear valley and opens every day during the summer 1000-2200. Services will be held in Norwegian on Sundays and on most public holidays; they are usually followed by coffee and tea in the church building. Everybody is welcome, but it is appreciated that you do not film or photograph during church survices. The original church was built on the same place in 1921 and destroyed during the German attack of 1943.

Cultural events: These take place mostly in the calm period. There is a blues festival in Longyearbyen in late October, followed by the "Kunstpause" ("art pause") in November with art and music and later, in January, by a jazz festival. The return of the sun to Longyearbyen is celebrated during one whole week in early March ("Solfestuke"). If running a **Marathon** is on your wish-list, then you can do so on skis in late April / early May or on foot in early June, and when your breath has normalised again in late June, then you can join the traditional Norwegian Saint Jons celebrations with a large bonfire on the beach.

Museum:

The **Svalbardmuseum** moved in 2006 and is now situated in Svalbardporten, the large, brown complex between Longyearbyen centre and Adventfjord. There is a modern exhibition about all possible aspects of Svalbard, from geology to history and wildlife. English translation of the explanations is somewhat limited, but that should certainly not keep you from visiting the very interesting exhibition. And when you are there, then stock up with books on Spitsbergen or maps, as this is the place that has the best selection on offer. You are welcome in the museum if you take your shoes off and then pay 75 NOK (reduced price 30 NOK) for your ticket, opening hours May to September every day 1000-1700, other seasons 1200-1700. Outside regular opening hours, groups can arrange visits for 350 NOK additional (!) to the individual admission fee. Svalbard Museum, P.O. Box 521, 9171 Longyearbyen, Norway. Telephone +47 7902 64 92 or +47 7902 64 90, fax +47 79 02 64 91. Email kontor@svalbardmuseum.no, internet www.svalbardmuseum.no.

The Spitsbergen Airship Museum: A new museum has been opened in Longyearbyen in 2008, featuring a permanent exhibition based on the three airships that were used during attempts to fly from Spitsbergen to the North Pole: the *America* (Wellman 1906, 1907, 1909), the *Norge* (Amundsen and Nobile in 1926) and the *Italia* (Nobile, 1928), including the rescue expeditions that went out after the crash of the *Italia* north of Nordaustland. It is located in the old cowshed near the church, where the Svalbardmuseum was located until it moved a few years ago. The Airship Museum, Postbox 644, 9171 Longyearbyen, Norway. Phone +47 79021705 or +47 95735742 or +47 91383467, fax +47 79021734, email ingunn@spitsbergenairshipmuseum.com, internet www.spitsbergenairshipmuseum.com.

The **Svalbard Global Seed Vault** (SGSV) or "Doomsday Vault", as it has been called by the press, brought Spitsbergen considerable international attention when it was officially opened in February 2008. It is supposed to receive 4.5 million samples of food crop seed, each sample with several thousand seeds. These will come from more than 100 countries over the next few years, following the first delivery of seeds on 26 February 2008 from Syria, Germany and the Philippines. The SGSV is thus to become the most comprehensive and by far the safest collection of its kind in the world. It is located above the airport in the slopes of Platåberget, the large entrance with its reflecting surfaces being readily visible. The site was chosen because it is believed it will survive even in the case of a global catastrophe such as nuclear war or extreme climate change leading to complete melting of the ice caps in Greenland and Antarctica. Even in the worst-case-scenario of global warming, the natural permafrost deep in the mountain is expected to last for at least 200 years: three highly secured rooms, cooled down by the permafrost aided by only minimal use of artificial cooling systems to minus 18°C, are situated at at the end of a 125 metre long tunnel. Security systems include four strong doors and motion detectors. Norway has financed the construction work. The purpose is to preserve the diversity of food crops despite the current loss of species. Samples from the SGSV will only be released again if all other seed sources have been destroyed or exhausted. The SGSV is not open to the public. Internet: www.seedvault.no.

3.7.5 Activities near Longyearbyen

The surroundings of Longyearbyen offer a wealth of opportunities for interesting day trips. It has to be mentioned that you need a suitable weapon as soon as you set a foot beyond the last inhabited house. Polar bears have been seen in the valleys and on mountains close to Longyearben at any season of the year.

If you want to explore the surroundings of Longyearbyen individually, then a look at the map will provide you with plenty of inspiration. If not, then you should consider a guided tour. This is why I do not include detailed route descriptions here: If you are not able to find your own way, then you should not walk around on your own in the arctic wildnerness. But this is not a problem, as there is a wide choice of interesting day trips to choose from. Options vary with the seasons, but there is always something to do and to explore, depending on your interest and abilities. For most tours, you have to be energetic to some extent.

Local tour operators are quite creative, expanding their programmes gradually, so it is clear that this overview cannot claim completeness. The local tourist information has up-to-date information on day trips with all tour operators. You can book in the tourist information, in your hotel or guesthouse (also camping site) and, of course, directly with the individual tour operator. During the tourist season, there are usually several options every day, depending on booking situation and weather, of course.

If you come to Longyearbyen to join a several-day ship-based tour and arrive a day before your ship's departure, or if you have a day after disembarkation, then it may be a good idea to check for day trips before you come to Spitsbergen. Hanging around in Longyearbyen without doing anything is a waste of time, considering the choice of options that you have, even if you have got only half a day.

Day trips in winter

Options are quite limited during the polar night, and the main tourist season lasts from early March to early May. Especially around Easter, you have to expect large numbers of visitors, making early booking of accommodation, excursions and rental equipment highly advisable.

Ice cave: Meltwater channels of glaciers become dry outside the melting season and are then accessible with proper equipment. You can walk up, use skies, snow mobile or dog sledge to get to the entrance of a meltwater cave in the Longyearbreen (Longyear glacier). You do not need to bring skills or equipment related to glaciers, but the narrow and dark caves are definitely not for the claustrophobic. Walking around inside a glacier is definitely an unforgettable experience!

Dog sledge: There are different offers for trips, lasting from a few hours to a whole day. As soon as there is enough snow, you can use this beautiful way of getting around in the Arctic to explore Adventdalen or some glaciers near Longyearbyen. Depending on the tour operator and your taste and ability, you can relax and sit on the sledge or drive your own dog team within a guided group of several sledges.

If you are interested, specialised tour operators can arrange longer tours, including week-long expeditions, into remote areas. It does not get any better if you are out for an intense experience of the Arctic, but don't forget that these expedition-like trips are physically quite demanding.

Snow mobile tours are the focus of winter tourism in Spitsbergen. These vehicles enable you to cover large distances, so you can reach, for example, the glaciers in Tempelfjord, the abandoned Russian mining settlement of Pyramiden, the active settlement of Barentsburg, Kapp Linné or the east coast of Spitsbergen within a day. Sitting a whole day on a snow mobile requires some staying power and the warmest clothes that you have (warm overalls and special equipment will normally be provided by the tour operator). Being at least 16 years old is one of the legal requirements (refers to the driver, not to the snow mobile), another one is a car driving license (obtained no later than 2001 for individual tourists) or a special snow mobile driving license. Do not drive a snow mobile without a helmet or with the slightest amount of alcohol in your blood.

Friends of motor sport can do several-day trips. The "Nordenskiöld round" around Nordenskiöld Land is quite popular and will take you from Longyearbyen to the east coast and from there via Sveagruva to the west coast and possibly Kapp Linné; finally from there or Barentsburg back to Longyearbyen. Duration usually three days, staying overnight in the hotels in Sveagruva and Kapp Linné or Barentsburg.

If you wish for a quiet, intense experience of arctic nature in the winter, then you may find a large group of snow mobiles rather annoying.

Ski tours: There are different options for shorter ski tours around Longyearbyen, partly in snow mobile-free areas. Ski tours are generally a great and affordable way to experience the beauty and silence of the arctic winter (unless a group of snow mobiles is racing past you at great speed). There are guided tours that do not require alpine ski experience, but it should not be your first time on skis and you should bring some sporting ability and attitude.

There is also the option to do longer, demanding tours for those with the desire for adventure and the physical ability to cover some snowy ground with luggage for several days. It is especially attractive to have a sledge dog with you. They may help to transport your luggage and keep an ear and nose open for Polar bears while you are sleeping.

Day trips in summer

EISCAT Station: Visiting the EISCAT satellite ground station near mine seven with a nice view into Adventdalen includes an introduction to space science in the Arctic.

Fossil collecting: You can find fossils in many places in Spitsbergen, and outside the protected areas you may even collect them and take them home with you (please observe possible future changes in relevant legislation). Around Longyearbyen, you can find beautiful leaf imprints from the lower Tertiary or – a bit further away – Mesozoic shells and ammonites. Guided walks or boat trips will take you to the right spots, which will be more rewarding if you come early during the season, before large numbers of fossil hunters have turned every stone around. Frost action makes sure there will be something to be found again next summer.

Dog sledge: This is on offer as long as there is some snow left on mountain plateaus and high glaciers during the early summer. These are short excursions, but they offer a good impression of this beautiful way of getting around and, of course, the landscape.

During the summer, sledge dog teams have been seen pulling a VW beetle that has been rebuilt and turned into a demotorized cabrio vehicle along the road into Adventdalen … Why not? I can not think of an environmentally more friendly way to drive a car.

Kayak: Short guided excursions that will take you across Adventfjord to the remains of the old mining settlement of Hiorthamn are possible for every energetic person during good weather, even without specific experience. You can also do several-day long tours, mostly in the Isfjord, but also in the Kongsfjord and Krossfjord.

Horse riding: Experienced horsemen as well as Greenhorns of all age groups can join half-day excursions on the backs of Iceland ponies along the south coast of Isfjord, west of Longyearbyen.

Sightseeing tours: You can do guided city tours in Longyearbyen by car or bus. The taxi companies provide this spontaneously if seats are available. Book in advance if you require any specific language.

Boat excursions: Boat trips of about eight hours duration provide a nice opportunity to appreciate the landscape variety of the Isfjord. There are several boats with a capacity of about 40 passengers offering tours during the day and, sometimes, in the evening. A warm meal is included. Barentsburg and Pyramiden are classical destinations, usually combined with a visit to the glaciers Nordenskiöldbreen, opposite Pyramiden, or to one of the glaciers on the north side of Isfjord such as Esmarkbreen in Ymerbukta. Another interesting and beautiful fjord is Tempelfjord with the impressive mountain of the same name on its northern side. Tours to Barentsburg and Pyramiden include guided walks of about one and a half hours duration.

Longer trips to Prins Karls Forland or Ny Ålesund are occasionally offered, or tours up to three days long along the west coast to Smeerenburg and Moffen. Longer tours on slightly larger vessels include circumnavigation of Spitsbergen or Svalbard with a duration of one week or more (see section 3.2.1 *Expedition-style cruising*).

Several operators also offer zodiac tours from Longyearbyen ranging from shorter visits to the other side of Adventfjord, to several day long tours in Isfjord.

Hiking: There is a range of different options for hikers to choose from, mostly mountain tours on the high plateaux surrounding Longyearbyen and also up to some higher peaks. Other routes may take you into one of the valleys near Longyearbyen. The highest mountain top near Longyearbyen is the Nordenskiöldfjellet with a height of 1,050 metres. Some excursions include crossing one or several glaciers, may be steeper and include walking over boulders, thus requiring good balance in uneven terrain. There are also easy walks.

Some tour operators arrange walks with sledge dogs in the summer.

Day trips around the year

Mine excursion: The historical roots not only of Longyearbyen, but also of most other settlements in Spitsbergen, are beyond doubt the coal mines. Most mines near Longyearbyen have been shut down; only mine seven in Adventdalen is still operating on a small scale to supply the local coal power plant. Guided excursions to several of the mines near Longyearbyen, including the still active mine seven, could be booked and provided a fascinating opportunity to get some impressions of coal mining and to see a mountain from inside - unless you are claustrophobic. The temperature in the mines is constant and a little below freezing. The future of the mine excursions is unfortunately rather uncertain, as the mining company has announced it intends to close the mines to visitors.

There is a limited choice of activities which are possible in any season. It will not come as a surprise that activities during late autumn and the dark period are of a more leisurely and less sporting character. This does not mean that they do not deliver a nice and atmospheric experience.

There are several options to have a **meal in the wildnerness** somewhere near Longyearbyen. Depending on the season and weather, this ranges from a barbecue on the beach or in a tent, to a meal in a rustic hut. You will hear stories of the days of old, from tropical islands … no, wrong … about Polar bears and trappers, and some tours include slide presentations.

"Trapper station": There is a replica of a trapper station near the dogyard in the entrance to Adventdalen, that serves as destination for leisurely, but atmospheric excursions. This will certainly include meeting sledge dogs, possibly with puppies, a meal and Spitsbergen-stories.

3.7.6 From coal to space research: Longyearbyen through 100 years

The early history of Longyearbyen started in 1901, when the American entrepeneur **John Munro Longyear** realised the potential of the area for coal mining during a visit to Spitsbergen on board a cruise liner, together with his family. In 1903, he came back for further investigations, bought the area south of Advenfjord from a Norwegian company in 1904 and started in 1905 with the first preparations for coal mining. 1906 was the year when coal mining actually started, at the place that was called Longyear City from that time onwards. Traces from those early days of mining can be seen above Skjæringa (the part of Longyearbyen above the power plant) in the shape of mine 1a, the so-called "Amerikanergruve" ("American's mine"). After various difficulties, Longyear sold the property to the Norwegian mining company "Store Norske Spitsbergen Kullkompani" ("Great Norwegian Spitsbergen coal company" or short SNSK) in 1916. Longyear City became the residence of the Norwegian administration (Sysselmannen) as soon as the Spitsbergen treaty came into force in 1925; since 1926 the place is called Longyearbyen, which is just the Norwegian translation of Longyear City.

The **population** of Longyearben has been growing slowly since those early years. About 230 people, including 37 women and children, wintered in 1919-20. During the winter of 1934-35, there were already 550 people in Longyearbyen. This number remained more or less stable well into the 1980s. Nowadays Longyearbyen has got about 1,700 inhabitants, although available statistics are surprisingly inaccurate. Fluctuation is much larger than with any settlement of comparable size in Norway. According to official statistics most Norwegians gave "desire for adventure" and "nature experience" as their reason to move to Longyearbyen, followed by "good job offer" (men) and "partner got a job in Longyearbyen" (women). Next to the nature experience, taxes that are low in comparison with Norway are certainly amongst the reasons that keep many Norwegians in Longyearbyen for some years.

Most important sectors on the job market in the Norwegian settlements in Spitsbergen (including Ny Ålesund and Sveagruva) are mining (233 employees), building and construction (194), transportation and storage (177), administration (147), schools, health and social system (133), tourism (120) and retail trade (107). These numbers are for 2003 and do not include temporary jobs. Especially within tourism, there is significant seasonal employment.

During the **Second World War** Longyearbyen was evacuated in 1941. The only inhabitants of Longyearbyen during those dark years were the soldiers of a small Norwegian garrison. Together with all other settlements in Spitsbergen with the exception of Pyramiden, Longyearbyen was destroyed during the large German attack of 1943.

The **first landing of a civilian plane** took place in February 1958 on flat tundra in Adventdalen, to evacuate an emergency patient to Norway. After that a 1,800 metre long piece of tundra was flattened to create a primitive runway that was used by a passenger plane for the first time in 1959. The following years saw one landing per year on average. Against diplomatic resistance from the Soviet Union, who feared that it could be used for military purposes, today's airport was built and opened in 1975. From then on, isolation of Longyearbyen for most parts of the year was history and there were no more obstacles for the politically motivated development of the settlement towards a "normal" Norwegian community.

The history of Longyearbyen during the 20th century is reflected in its **urban development** that took place in a counterclockwise movement around the river in the valley Longyeardalen. It all started in 1906 in Skjæringa above today's coal power plant, followed in 1937 by Sverdrupbyen in the inner part of the valley. Sverdrupbyen is now deserted and mostly destroyed. The first parts of Longyearbyen on the eastern side of the valley were built in 1946 and called Nybyen ("new town") and Haugen ("the hill"). Recent development of Longyearbyen is taking place mainly in the centre, in Sjøområdet near the ford and in the entrance area of Adventdalen.

In the late 1980s, tourism started to play an ever-increasing role in the economic landscape of Longyearbyen. Just the number of no less than six guesthouses and hotels, plus other accommodation for visitors, says a lot about the importance of tourism, including visiting scientists and business traffic.

The **only mine still operating** near Longyearbyen is mine seven in Adventdalen. In 2004, 62,000 tons of coal were mined, most of which was used to supply the local coal power plant. Another important factor that leaves its stamp on this rather small community, is **science**. The first scientific installation was the northern lights observatory that was opened in Adventdalen in 1978; in 2007, it was moved up to a mountain plateau near mine seven and the EISCAT station where it is now operating at an altitude of 520 metres. The year 1978 also saw the opening of the MAB-station (MAB = man and biosphere, a Unesco research project) at the end of the road into

Adventdalen. In 1993, UNIS followed and in 1996 EISCAT (European Incoherent Scatter), a large installation near mine seven for research on northern lights. A whole forest of mighty antennas to control satellites in polar orbits and receive their signals is located on the Platåberg near Bjørndalen since 1997. In 2004, a glass fibre cable was laid from Longyearbyen to Norway to accommodate the large data volumes that are constantly received from satellites. Recent years have seen a significant increase of the scientific infrastructure in and around Longyearbyen. It is considered desirable to become independent of coal mining, which can obviously not be continued forever, but currently a large number of jobs in Longyearbyen still depend directly or indirectly on mining.

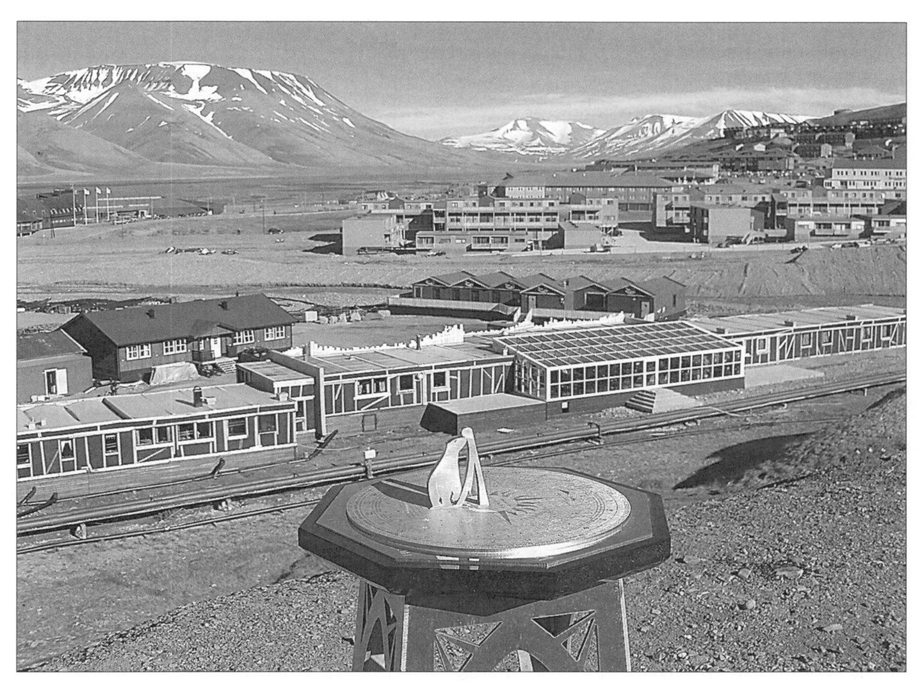

Longyearbyen seen from Skjæringa. Sundial and Mary-Ann's Polarriggen in the foreground, Adventdalen in the background.

Chapter 4 – Natural history

"One of the most interesting appearances to be found in Spitzbergen, is the Iceberg. This term, written Ysberg by the Dutch, signifies ice-mountain. I speak not here of the islands of ice which are borne to southern climates on the bosom of the ocean, but of those prodigious lodgments of ice which occur in the valleys adjoining the coast of Spitzbergen and other Polar countries, from which the floating icebergs seem to be derived. Where a chain of hills lies parallel to the line of the coast, and within a few miles distance of the sea-beach, having lateral ridges jutting towards the sea, at intervals of a league or two, we have a most favourable situation for the formation of icebergs."

William Scoresby, *An Account Of The Arctic Regions*

The landscape itself makes for a great part of the fascination of Spitsbergen. Regarding both the landscape and the geology, you will find further details of individual areas in the respective sections of chapter six.

The book "Rocks and Ice. Landscapes of the North", written by the same author (see www.spitzbergen.de) is dedicated to the landscapes of Spitsbergen and northern East Greenland, including the geology, glaciation and permafrost phenomena in a detailed but nevertheless understandable way.

4.1 Geography, glaciers, permafrost

"Along the edge of the ice runs a narrow stretch of moraine, red sands and gravels, cut into fantastic shapes. Its steep cones and turreted battlements resemble nothing so much as an uninhabited Nigerian village, transported by the imagination to within 600 miles of the North Pole."

R.A. Glen, *Under The Pole Star*

Svalbard has an impressive variety of landscapes. The geological mosaic and climatic differences interfere in a way that makes it possible to experience very different landscape types within relatively short distances – from steep, glaciated mountain peaks and ridges to wide, plateau-shaped mountains and finally to open, coastal tundra plains.

About 36,500 sq km or 60 % of the land surface of Svalbard is covered by **glaciers**. In Spitsbergen it is generally true to say that the higher and more mountainous the landscape, the more heavily it will be glaciated. Accordingly, almost all valleys near the west coast are filled with a network of glaciers. Many of these have impressive calving fronts such as you can see, for example, in Hornsund, Kongsfjord, Krossfjord, Magdalenefjord, Smeerenburgfjord and Liefdefjord. As there is no expanse of inland ice in these glaciers' catchment areas that would compare to Greenland or even Antarctica in size, icebergs in Spitsbergen do not reach the gigantic volumes of their counterparts in those areas.

You will find some **ice caps** in northeastern Svalbard; For instance, the whole eastern and southern part of Nordaustland is covered by the ice caps Austfonna and Vegafonna which cover a total area of about 8,450 sq km; comparable to that of the large glacier, Vatnajøkull, in southeast Iceland. The south and east coast of Nordaustland consists almost entirely of a glacier front that is about 190 km long – the longest in the northern hemisphere! You will find large **ice-free land** areas mostly in central parts of Spitsbergen, the average altitude of which is generally lower compared to the mountains near the west coast. Nordenskiöld Land, the neighbourhood of Longyearbyen, has most of the large ice free valleys of the archipelago. The low-lying plateau-shaped hills and coastal plains of Kong Karls Land in the far east of Svalbard are almost completely free of ice, and so are the outposts Hopen and Bjørnøya.

Most glaciers in Svalbard have been retreating since the late 19th century. Large moraine ridges, far away from and above today's glacier rims, together with a comparison of the visible landscape with historical maps, charts and photographs, do not leave any doubt regarding this tendency. If you approach a glacier front with a boat or ship, then in most cases you will be well inside the glacier – at least according to the chart, which usually gives the position in the 1960s or 70s.

During the ice age, the whole area of Svalbard has repeatedly been covered by a huge ice cap; at its maximum, there was an inland ice sheet that stretched from the northern part of the Svalbard archipelago across Scandinavia to northern Poland and Germany, covering large parts of Great Britain at the same time. The disappearance of such a large ice mass has left obvious traces in the landscape such as **raised beach ridges**. The heavy weight of the ice-age glaciers pressed the crust of the Earth down several hundred metres over large areas. When most of the ice disappeared, the land surface rose accordingly, initially at a rate of more than a centimetre per year, and later increasingly slowly. At the same time, global sea level was rising because of the discharge of huge volumes of meltwater into the world's oceans. As land uplift was, in some regions including Svalbard, faster than global sea level rise, the result was a coastline that was retreating from the sea. Low ridges of sand and gravel, piled up along the coastline during heavy storms, seemingly migrated landwards to form fossil raised beach ridges. In Svalbard, wide, very gently sloping surfaces with fascinating geometrical patterns of many old beach ridges documenting the positions of coastlines of the past, are quite a common sight.

Along these beach ridges, everything that was washed ashore hundreds and thousands of years ago remained where it lay. You may find whalebones and decaying driftwood, literally as old as the hills, at a large distance from today's shoreline.

The oldest and highest raised beaches are more than 10,000 years old and are situated more than 100 metres above present-day sea level. You will find raised beaches in most more or less flat, unglaciated parts of Svalbard. You will get the best views of these from a slightly higher vantage point. The view that you may have from a hill of a series of well-developed and preserved raised beaches is very beautiful and fascinating.

All unglaciated land areas of Svalbard are affected by **permafrost**. This means that only the uppermost layer of the soil, the so-called active layer, will thaw during the short summer months. Below the active layer, which varies in thickness from half a metre to 1.5 metres, the ground remains frozen throughout the year.

In other words, permafrost describes a certain temperature regime of the ground and does not necessarily imply any visible landscape features, but when other factors are present, conspicuous and strange phenomena may be the result: ice wedges, pingos and rock glaciers require permafrost for their active existence, whereas stone rings and solifluction often have especially favourable conditions in permafrost areas, but they do also exist in non-permafrost territory (for further details of these phenomena, see "Rocks and Ice" by this author).

You will find **ice wedges** in many flat tundra areas. What you can see is a pattern of large cracks in the ground, ideally forming hexagons resembling honeycombs in shape, but being eight to 20 metres wide. At depth below the active layer, the cracks are permanently filled with ice due to the permafrost.

A **pingo** may be described as a frozen spring in the widest sense. Under the permanently frozen part of the ground, at depths of possibly several hundred metres, there can be groundwater flow. If groundwater penetrates through a weak zone in the permafrost, then it may rise to near the surface, where it will freeze to form a huge ice lens. This ice lens may form a hill, covered by a thin layer of sediment, up to 20-30 metres high and more than 100 metres in diameter at the base. This is the pingo in a stricter sense, the visible part of the system. You will find most pingos in Spitsbergen in the ice (that is glacier ice) free valleys of Nordenskiöld Land such as Adventdalen and Reindalen. As sub-permafrost, pressurized groundwater is a precondition for pingo formation, you will not find pingos near the edge of permafrost areas (or if you do, then they are mostly of a different kind like the one described here). Accordingly, you will rarely find any pingos close to the coast in Spitsbergen, which makes it difficult to see this phenomenon unless you walk a long way inland (although there are a few exceptions to this rule).

Rock glaciers are another, little known, but nevertheless quite common permafrost phenomenon of some size. They consist of large bodies of coarse scree, roughly resembling a tongue in shape, several hundred metres in length with a more or less sharp edge near the lower end. Rock glaciers move downslope at a rate of a few centimetres each year. They come into existence when meltwater penetrates scree, then freezes due to the permafrost regime and finally fills the interstices completely with ice. The internal friction of the scree decreases as a result, making the whole thing unstable, so that it starts to move slowly downslope, under the influence of gravity. You can see from Longyearben two nice examples, one on the far side of the Adventfjord on the slope of Hjorthfjellet, the other one actually within the settlement: After the War, Sverdrupbyen (between Huset and the glacier Longyearbreen), which is now largely destroyed, was built on a rock glacier. They were probably not aware of this fact when they built it.

Stone rings are quite common in Svalbard although, as already mentioned, their existence does not require permafrost,. Their development depends on intense, frequent repetition of freezing, thawing and re-freezing of water-saturated ground that consists of sand and gravel. During freezing, water expands by nine percent in volume, which causes strong pressure in the soil. The interplay of a number of complicated processes results in separation of coarse and fine particles of the soil. The final result is a ring with a diameter of one to three metres. The outer part consists of the coarse parts: stones and gravel, whereas the fine particles: sand, silt and clay, will form a sharply defined core.

Due to the varied geology and climatic differences, stone rings come in endless shapes and variations. Additionally, they can be deformed by gravity on sloping surfaces, resulting in shapes resembling half-moons or garlands or, even strips following the gradient. A convenient term for all these phenomena is **frost patterned ground**, which also includes ice wedges.

Soft, water-saturated sediment may slowly move downhill on a sloping surface. This phenomenon, called **solifluction**, can affect large surfaces in permafrost areas where water cannot seep down into the soil due to the eternal frost, thus allowing only the uppermost layers to thaw and soften. This makes solifluction an efficient factor in landscape development in the Arctic, despite of rates of movement of only a few centimetres per year, depending on the geology and water supply. Solifluction is especially efficient below snow patches and in areas with soft, fine-grained sediment. Solifluction areas can be very muddy and thus rather unpleasant terrain for hikers.

Pingo in Vendomdalen, Nordenskiöld Land.

4.2 Geology

"Yet there was a time when fetid tropical forests steamed where now the white deserts of ice have their domain. The span of man is nothing ; the life of an ice-age a fraction ; a geological period a moment ; and eternity is beyond time or space."

R.A. Glen, *Under The Pole Star*

Anybody interested in geology should have a copy of the "Bedrock map of Svalbard and Jan Mayen, 1:750,000", published by the Norwegian Polar Institute; very useful if, for example, you travel large parts of the archipelago during a cruise. If you spend more time in a smaller area, then you may want to have the relevant map sheets at a scale 1:100,000 in your rucksack.

Spitsbergen has been called a geologist's Eldorado. This description is well justified: Large areas are free of vegetation, making bedrock readily visible, unlike "civilised" latitudes that are mostly covered by soil and vegetation, buildings and asphalt. Rocks of almost all sorts and dating from most chapters of earth history are present. Within the large groups of sediments and metamorphic rocks in particular, you will find all kinds of rocks you can possibly imagine and, most likely, even more … Only rocks originating from surface volcanic eruptions (lava) are scarce, due to an obvious lack of active volcanoes. But they are not so far away, in Iceland and on Jan Mayen.
For some good close-up views of Spitsbergen's solid rock geology, you have to go to the right places. The lower slopes of mountains are mostly covered by scree, the upper ones steep and inaccessible, and valley floors tend to be covered with gravel and solifluction lobes. There are, however, many good outcrops, for example in little river valleys that are deeply incised (like small canyons), or at little coastal cliffs, that are sometimes accessible during low tide and in good weather. If you come for the geology, then the late summer is your season, as many interesting spots are occupied by breeding birds during the early summer and thus not accessible.

You can find beautiful fossils from different periods. Collectors must, however, pay attention to relevant laws before they start picking them up, as collecting of any rocks including fossils is forbidden within protected areas that comprise most parts of Svalbard. Outside the protected areas, collecting is still allowed.

You will find a short summary of the **earth history and geology of Svalbard** in the following pages. For the geology of individual areas, refer to the relevant sections in chapter six. Some technical terms are explained in the geological glossary in the appendix, where you will also find a summary of Svalbard's earth history in the form of a table.

Spitsbergen is the northwestern corner of the continent of Eurasia. There is at present a shallow shelf sea between Spitsbergen and Norway, only a few hundred metres deep. This contrasts with oceans that are several thousand metres deep, further west and north. Half-way between Spitsbergen and the North Cape of Norway, the bottom of the sea rises above sea level, forming the island of Bjørnøya.

As on all continents, Spitsbergen has a geological foundation, the so-called **basement**. This is an old, heterogenous body of rocks that has been influenced by tectonic activity a long time ago, but has been more or less stable since then. Due to this activity, that happened during several stages, old rock masses were exposed to heat and pressure and thus partly molten and then cooled down to form crystalline rocks such as granites, or metamorphic rocks like schist and gneiss.

In Spitsbergen, such events took place on several occasions during earth history. The last tectonic event that significantly influenced the basement happened about 400 to 500 million years ago (mostly Silurian). An ancient ocean, the Iapetus, was closed during this episode and a mountain chain was formed along the seam. Remains of those mountains, the Caledonides, once a proud chain with high peaks, can still be found in the shape of metamorphic rocks, granites and deformed sediments in Svalbard, East Greenland, Norway and Scotland.

In many places, those Caledonian basement rocks were later covered by sediments, some of which have later been removed by erosion, exposing the ancient basement at the surface once more. In Svalbard, the basement is also called **Hecla Hoek**, after a mountain near the Sorgfjord in northeastern Spitsbergen. This term, however, is nowadays mostly regarded as old-fashioned and geologists tend to use the general term **basement**, which has also got the advantage that it is a general term that can be used anywhere on Earth.

The Hecla Hoek or basement is exposed in Bjørnøya, along the whole of the west coast and parts of the north coast of Spitsbergen, in the northern Hinlopen Strait and along the northern coast of Nordaustland and Kvitøya. The highest mountains of Spitsbergen, Newtontoppen (1,713 metres) and Perriertoppen (1,712 metres) can be found in Ny Friesland (northeastern Spitsbergen) in an area that consists entirely of basement rocks, rising up from an elevated plateau.

Fossils are rare in Hecla Hoek rocks, as is normal for strongly metamorphic and magmatic rocks. There are, however, fossils in some places, but these are mostly not very handsome and not easily seen. You may find nice stromatolites in upper-Proterozoic carbonate rocks (600-700 million years old) around the northern Hinlopen Strait.

The formation of the basement was followed by the deposition of various sediments over a period of several hundred million years. The oldest comprise a series of coarse conglomerates, sandstones and fine-grained siltstones that formed as a weathering and erosion product of the Caledonian mountains. These rocks, which often have a beautiful reddish colour due to the high content of Hematite, are collectively called **Old Red** (illustration 6.9.1 page 328) and date back to the Devonian (408-360 million years ago) and the lowermost Carboniferous. You can see those beautiful rocks within a narrow, north-south trending strip in the central Hornsund area, east of the Kongsfjord and on the eastern side of Raudfjord. The main Old Red area, however, is located in Andrée Land and in northern Dickson Land, an area that collectively forms the so-called Andrée Land Graben. Fossils are rare in these rocks, although geologists have found, amongst others, perfectly preserved fish fossils – the first fish to have lived on the earth.

During and after the deposition of the Old Red, Svalbard, as part of the larger tectonic plate that comprised Europe and North America (including Greenland), continued its slow but steady journey northwards at a pace of some millimetres each year. In the heat of equatorial latitudes, large watermasses evaporated in shallow lagoons, leaving so-called evaporites behind; minerals like gypsum. Large amounts of organic matter were deposited in neighbouring swamps and later turned into coal. Occasionally, sand was washed in by rivers to form layers of sandstone, and large masses of calcarous organisms such as brachiopods, corals and bryozoa died to be turned into fossil-rich layers of limestone. Today, we can see these varied sedimentary layers from the upper Palaeozoic (**Carboniferous** and lower **Permian**) in central Spitsbergen in the Billefjord-Tempelfjord area. Carboniferous coal was mined at Pyramiden until the settlement was abandoned in 1998. Fossil-rich layers of very hard limestones from the lower Permian, the so-called **Kapp Starostin formation**, can be found in many places over large parts of the archipelago, often forming prominent landscape features such as cliffs, capes or islands.

This era was followed by the **Mesozoic**, a relatively calm period in the region in question, at least tectonically. Still being part of a large continental plate, Spitsbergen continued its slow drift northwards, mostly without large movements within the crust of the plate. Slow subsidence led to ingression of shallow shelf seas, causing deposition of associated sediments over large areas. Some of these sediments were later eroded again, when the land rose above sea level during subsequent periods of uplift. The remaining, rather uniform, mostly dark and fine-grained depositional rocks can be seen over large areas in eastern Svalbard: in central and southeastern parts of Spitsbergen and the neighbouring, large islands of Barentsøya and Edgeøya, Wilhelmøya, Kong Karls Land, Hopen and in the far south on Bjørnøya. Many of the inhabitants of those shallow, sub-tropical Mesozoic seas have left characteristic traces such as ammonites and shells in the rocks. There are also fossils of larger animals including dinosaurs. Quite spectacular discoveries of dinosaur skeletons have been made in 2006 and 2007 in Isfjord (Kapp Thordsen area and near Diabasodden).

The Atlantic ocean did not exist at all during this long chapter of earth history. The opening, however, was soon to come and was heralded by **volcanic activity**, which did not take place at the surface, but at shallow depths below surface, where liquid rocks of basaltic composition forced their way between layers of older sediments. This

3.1-1: Mid-April in Van Mijenfjord, view towards Midterhuken (Bellsund).

3.1-2: Late snow melt. Mid-June, Trygghamna (Isfjord).

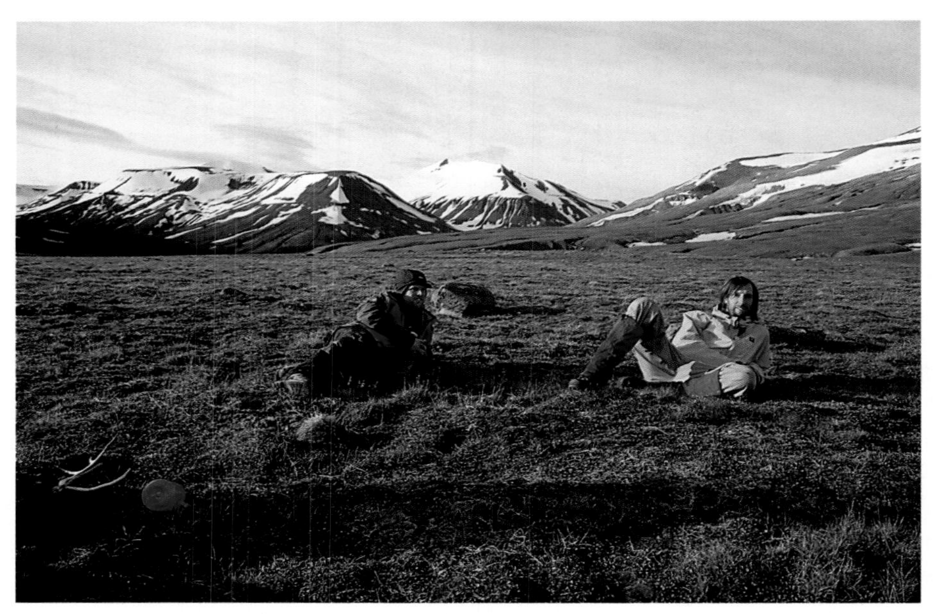

3.1-3: Enjoying arctic high summer. Mid July, Lundstrømdalen (Nordenskiöld Land, central Spitsbergen).

3.1-4: Low autumn sun. Early September, Sassendalen.

3.1-5: Late polar night. Mid-February, Longyearbyen.

3.2-1: Expedition cruise ship.

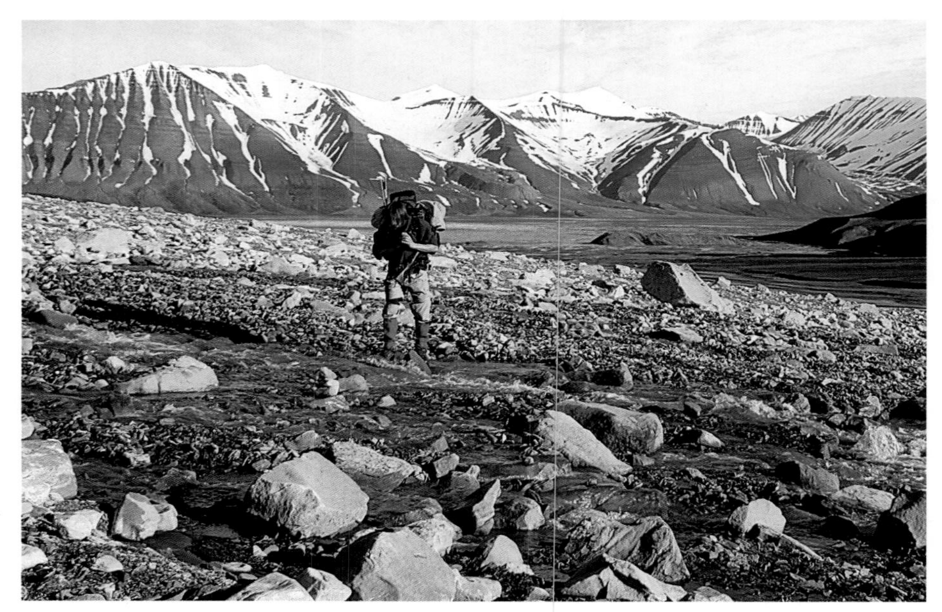

3.2-2: Several-day summer hiking in Lundstrømdalen (Nordenskiöld Land, central Spitsbergen).

3.2-3: Glacier hike. Hørbyebreen, Dickson Land.

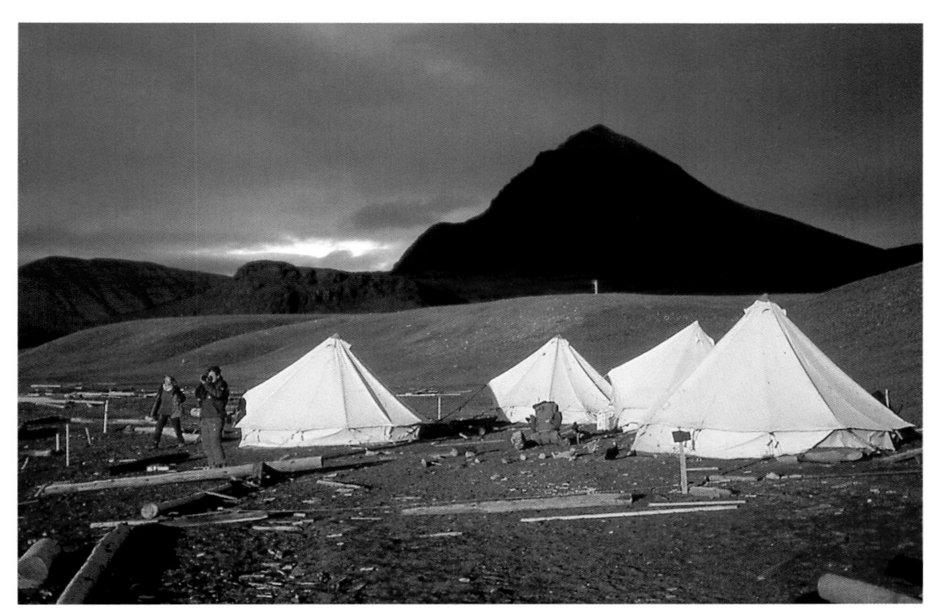

3.2-4: Camp near Diabasodden, Sassenfjord.

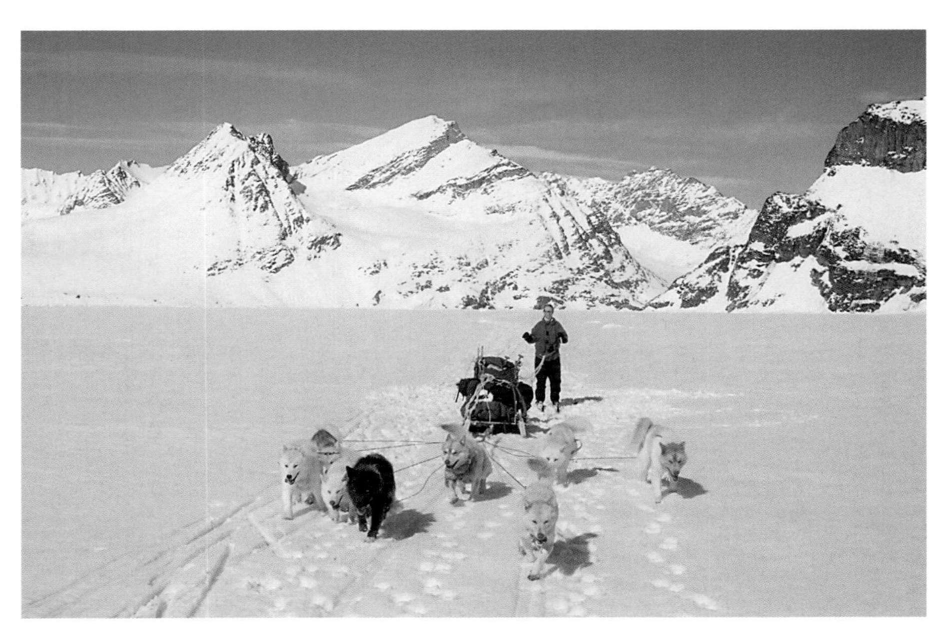

3.2-5: Dog sledging (East Greenland).

3.2-6: Cross-country skiing tour, Van Mijenfjord.

3.2-7: Camp. Lyckholmdalen, Dickson Land.

3.6-1: River crossing. Adventelva, inner Adventdalen.

3.6-2: Cultural heritage sites are often unobtrusive.
Pomor site, Kingodden, Prins Karls Forland.

3.7-1: Longyearbyen seen from Platåberget, with Adventdalen in the background.

3.7-2: This modern building houses UNIS, the tourist information and the museum.

3.7-3: Central Longyearbyen with Svalbardbutikken (supermarket, left), miners' monument and Lompensenteret (shopping centre, right).

4.1-1: Glaciers in central Spitsbergen. Mittag-Lefflerbreen (centre, flowing from right to left) seen from Tarantellen.

4.1-2: Calving glacier. Fjortende Julibukta, Krossfjord.

4.1-3: Terminal moraine. Lomfjord.

4.1-4: *Medial moraine. Hannabreen, Liefdefjord.*

4.1-5: *Raised beaches. Martensøya (Sjuøyane).*

4.1-6: Ice wedges with small streams at Alkhornet.

4.1-7: Pingo at Brentskardet (Nordenskiöld Land, central Spitsbergen).

4.1-8: Stone circles. Mushamna, Woodfjord.

4.2-1: Gneiss, a typical rock of the basement. Andréeneset, Kvitøya.

4.2-2: *Devonian Old Red. Bockfjord.*

4.2-3: *Triassic sediment layers. Diskobukta, Edgeøya.*

4.2-4: Folded layers of Permian sediments at Selmaneset (southernmost point of Värmlandryggen, Trygghamna), Isfjord.

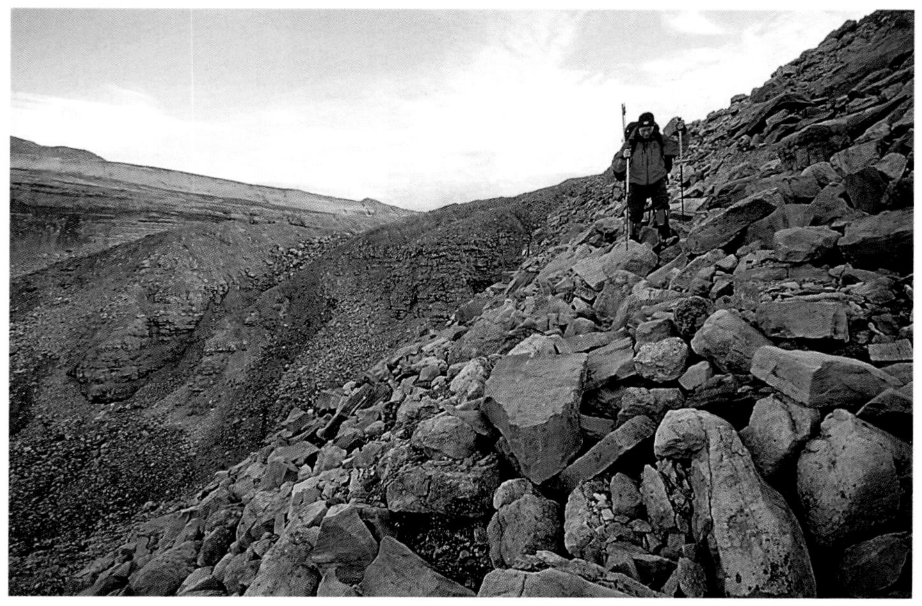

4.2-5: Scree slope in Skansdalen.

4.4-1: Drift ice.

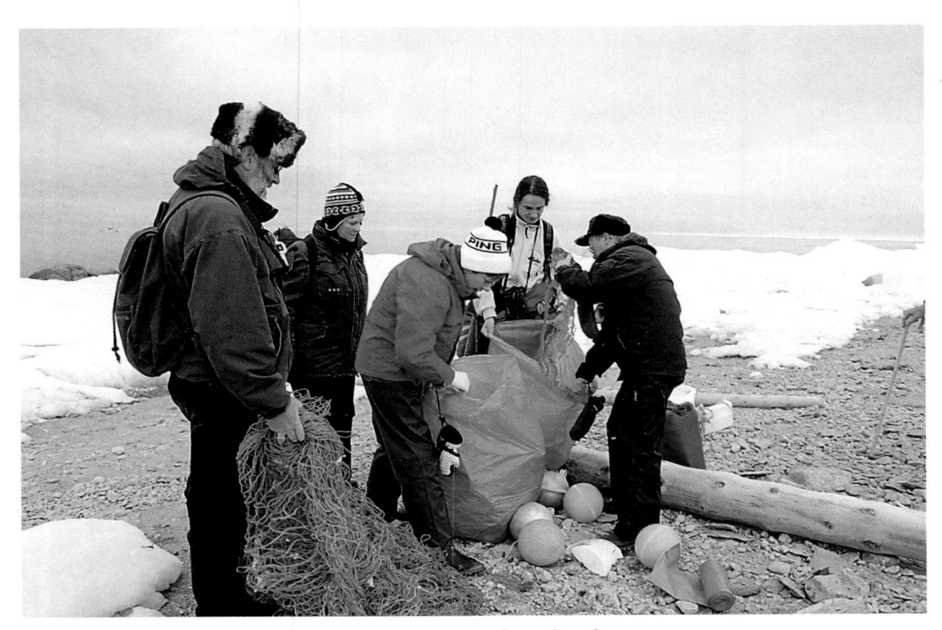

4.5-1: "Clean up Svalbard". Birdvågen, Nordaustland.

happened during a long period in the upper Jurassic and Cretaceous eras, between 150 and 100 million years ago. They cooled down to form hard **intrusions**, which, depending on their exact composition, can most commonly be called **Dolerite** (diabase). Today, these intrusions have come to see the light of day thanks to erosion of the surrounding, mostly softer sediments. Due to their hardness, they often stand out in the landscape as cliffs, capes or small islands. You can find these intrusive rocks spread out over large areas of central and eastern Svalbard, in Isfjord (e.g. Diabasodden), in Hinlopen Strait (Alkefjellet and many islands), in the Storfjord area (e.g. Kapp Dufferin or Dolerittneset/"Kapp Lee") and south of Edgeøya (Tusenøyane).

The next and very important chapter in the geological development of the area is the **opening of the north Atlantic** with all its consequences. Announced by the volcanic activity mentioned above, the opening took place in several steps starting approximately 100 million years ago in the lower Cretaceous. The direct and obvious consequence was the separation of Spitsbergen and northeast Greenland, which had been direct neighbours for a long time. Land masses around the evolving ocean were uplifted to form high coastal mountain areas: This is the reason for the spectacular coastal landscapes on both sides of the Atlantic, in East Greenland, Norway and at the west coast of Spitsbergen. Older rocks involved in these movements experienced strong deformation.

As can be expected, these mountains suffered weathering and erosion from the moment they were uplifted above sea level. The result was the deposition of thick piles of sedimentary layers (shallow marine and coastal conglomerates, sandstones, siltstones including several coal seams) during the **lower Tertiary**, about 50 million years ago. In Spitsbergen, this coal has been mined in Barentsburg, Grumantbyen, Longyearbyen, Ny Ålesund and Sveagruva. Traces of a rich plant life have been preserved in the shape of beautiful leaf imprints.

4.2 Bockfjord with the volcanic ruin Sverrefjellet in the centre.

The deposition of the Tertiary sediment layers almost completed the development of Spitsbergen's "hard rock geology". Subsequent times saw some small, but real **volcanic eruptions** in northwestern Spitsbergen, leaving the remains of a volcano in the Bockfjord area and some small warm springs (illustration 6.9.4 page 330). The Quaternary ice age then removed large rock volumes through strong glacial erosion and saw the deposition of sediments by glaciers, rivers and along the ever-shifting coastline, thus creating the landscape that we can see today.

4.3 Oceanic currents

"From the fact of the sea near Spitzbergen being usually six or seven degrees warmer at the depth of 100 to 200 fathoms, than it is at the surface, it seems not improbable that the water below is a still farther extension of the Gulf Stream, which, on meeting with water near the ice lighter than itself, sinks below the surface, and becomes a counter under-current. ... In some situations near Spitzbergen, the warm water not only occupies the lower and mid regions of the sea, but also appears at the surface."

William Scoresby, *An Account Of The Arctic Regions*

Next to the geology, it is especially the climate that leaves its unmistakable mark on Spitsbergen's ecology, and the climate is in turn strongly influenced by the position of the archipelago in the boundary zone between two very different oceanic currents.

The **Gulf stream** with its warm water masses, that drifts northwards along the coast of Norway, is of decisive importance. One branch flows around the northern tip of Norway to the east, whereas another one follows the edge of the continental shelf northwards, towards Spitsbergen. Called the **West-Spitsbergen current**, this relatively (!) warm current then follows the west coast and even the north coast of Spitsbergen, before it fades out northeast of Svalbard under the influence of cold water masses from the arctic ocean. The influence of the West-Spitsbergen current reaches as far as Sjuøyane, the northernmost islands of the Svalbard archipelago, or even beyond, which becomes clear from the distribution of drift ice in the area (see next section).

With **water temperatures** of up to 8°C during the arctic summer, the West-Spitsbergen current does not actually create good playgrounds for swimmers, but this is better than the area of the cold **East-Spitsbergen current** with temperatures as low as –1,7°C to +2°C. These cold waters originate near the north coast of Siberia and drift across the North Pole towards the Atlantic, splitting up into several branches. One part drifts southwards on the east side of Svalbard, thus being responsible for the significantly heavier ice conditions and slightly colder climate of that part of the archipelago as compared to the west coast. Another branch follows the east coast of Greenland with cold water and huge masses of heavy drift ice.

The mixing zone of cold and temperate watermasses at the surface of the sea and corresponding airmasses in the lower atmosphere is an area with frequent **fog**, especially during the spring and summer.

Locally, the **tides** can create strong currents despite a relatively small tidal movement of between one metre and one and a half metres from low to high water. The narrow straits of Heleysund and Ormholet between Spitsbergen and Barentsøya are notorious for tidal currents of up to ten knots (18 kilometres per hour).

4.4 Sea ice

"If the masses of ice which usually prevent the advance of navigators beyond the 82nd degree of north latitude, be extended in a continued series to the Pole (of which, unless there be land in the way, I have no doubt), - the expectation of reaching the Pole by sea, must be altogether chimerical."

William Scoresby, *An Account Of The Arctic Regions*

The ice conditions around the coasts of Svalbard are somewhat surprising and not at all what you may expect in those latitudes, around 80°N. Nowhere else you can get so close to the North Pole with a non-icebreaking vessel at any time of the year. The northernmost branch of the Gulf stream keeps the west coast largely open, and the big fjords in the central west coast area rarely freeze completely during the winter. The large Isfjord usually stays open nowadays, whereas it was frozen during most winters in the early 20th century. Its inner branches are, however, usually covered by fjord ice that developes quite late in the winter after a long period of cooling down, but may persist well into June. The ice conditions in other fjords in the same area, like Kongsfjord and Krossfjord, are similar. Van Mijenfjord is a bit of an exception, as its entrance is almost completely blocked by the long, narrow island of Akseløya, which supports ice formation and delays break up. It may, however, be destroyed early in the spring by icebreaker traffic to Sveagruva.

The cold East Spitsbergen current transports large masses of drift ice from the arctic Ocean, that can block the northern and especially the eastern coasts of the archipelago well into the summer. The exact position of the ice edge varies greatly from year to year and even from day to day during any given season. Whereas dense drift ice can make access to the north coast of Spitsbergen, east of Amsterdamøya, impossible as late as July during one summer, in the next summer even the Sjuøyane can be free of ice as early as late June. The "normal" situation, if such exists at all, is somewhere in the middle of these two quite extreme situations. In general it can be said that there is much more drift ice in the east than in the west within the Svalbard archipelago. It is quite normal to reach the little island of Moffen at 80°N from the west coast early in the season (June), while Barentsøya and Edgeøya are still surrounded by ice for several weeks despite of their more southerly position.

One branch of the cold East Spitsbergen current brings drift ice around the southern tip of Spitsbergen to the southern west coast, which means that drift ice at the southern and central west coast usually comes from the south and not from the north. Hornsund, which is the southernmost fjord of Spitsbergen, is blocked by ice for a much longer time during the early summer than the fjords further north. Occasionally, however, single fields of drift ice make it into Isfjord even in mid summer. This is rare, but has in the past caused difficulties to larger cruise ships without ice strengthening. Obviously, the ice conditions are of great importance for shipping in Svalbard waters. Ideally, during a cruise you want to see drift ice, but not too much of it if you want to reach certain destinations. If you want to be more or less sure that you are able to circumnavigate Spitsbergen, then you should not come before late July (no serious guarantee, even then!), but some years you may miss the ice completely (see also footnote one *Drift ice and circumnavigations* and footnote two *Through Hinlopen Strait or around Nordaustland* in section 6.14 *Hinlopen Strait*). In the end, it depends on your wishes, but the ice conditions are and remain unpredictable even at the time of booking which may be several months before your voyage. On the other hand: Spitsbergen is really the high Arctic, and not a zoo or a theme park, and this is all part of the adventure,

Not only the position, but also the appearance of the ice edge varies greatly. If the wind is blowing from the ice towards open water, then more and more ice floes will drift into the open area. The result is a very gradual boundary from first, very open patches of drift ice to a densely packed ice cover, that is dense enough to be called pack ice. If the wind is blowing from the open water towards the ice, then it will push the ice floes densely together and thus create a very abrupt boundary between open water and dense ice.

Sailing into the drift ice can be part of an itinerary during a cruise in Spitsbergen on an ice-strengthened ship. Next to the fascinating experience of the ice itself, there is the potential for exciting wildlife encounters, that makes this well worthwile: Several seal species (Bearded seal, Harp seal, Ringed seal), Walrus, Polar bears, even whales (Minke whales, for example) and rare birds (Pomarine skua, Ivory gull, the rare Sabine's gull, theoretically even a Ross' gull – but don't expect it!) are amongst the inhabitants of this icy world, that may show up. What you need is good weather, as many sharp eyes on deck as possible, binoculars and, most importantly, luck. And while you are there, don't forget to spare some thoughts for the explorers of the heroic age, who spent weeks, months or, in some cases, years in this environment. In Svalbard, this includes the expeditions of Phipps, Parry, Nordenskiöld, Nansen and Andrée (see chapter 5 *History*).

In these modern days, you can check the **actual position of the ice edge on the internet**. The Norwegian meteorological institute in Tromsø publishes ice charts for different areas in the North Atlantic (http://retro.met.no/kyst_og_hav/iskart.html) including Spitsbergen. The lack of accuracy of even these up-to-date ice charts can be surprising. The ice is described in terms of the percentage of the water surface, given as a fraction, that is covered by ice. The highest category is "very close drift ice" with an ice cover of 9/10-10/10 (90-100 %), followed by "close drift ice" with 7/10-9/10, "open drift ice" with 4/10-7/10 and finally "very open drift ice", 1/10-4/10. Additionally, there is the category "fast ice", which is ice still attached to the coast and accordingly does not drift. Even if an area is generally accessible, quite small remnants of fast ice can make landings impossible. On the other hand, solid ice in the fjords makes winter travelling by dog sledge, skis or snow mobile much easier.

In practice, the actual ice cover is usually overestimated: If you can hardly see open water anymore from the deck of a ship, then the ice cover is unlikely to be beyond 7/10.

4.5 Driftwood, rubbish and environmental toxins

"The shores are a treasure-board of romance. Across the Polar Ocean a current flows from the Siberian coasts, bringing with it driftwood, which is carried high up the beaches by the winter ice. With the logs and timber there are relics of every kind. Fishing floats, many hundred years old, from Murmansk; remnants of long-wrecked ships; a battered sea-chest; perhaps the mortal remains of a long-dead seaman."

R.A. Glen, *Under The Pole Star*

You will find amazing amounts of driftwood on many beaches in Svalbard, that comes with the currents either from Siberia or from the Carribean Sea where the Gulf stream originates. The vast majority, however, comes from the Siberian far east. Most logs reach Spitsbergen without roots. These logs obviously do not come from trees that fell naturally into the river, but they have been cut down by foresters and then floated down the large Siberian rivers. A large percentage gets lost during this voyage and then drifts, together with the ice, across the North Pole area, finally ending up either on the sea bottom or on the beaches of East Greenland, Jan Mayen, Svalbard or Franz Josef Land. The driftwood could not reach these islands without the ice which prevents it from sinking.

Because of this origin mostly from Siberian forestry, it is apparent that there was less driftwood on Spitsbergen's beaches for example when whalers frequented those shores in past centuries. You might even call it industrial rubbish, even though it does not cause any damage and is actually quite decorative; it has been used as a "local" resource for heating and occasionally as building material.

While the northeastern current brings most of the driftwood, there is a different sort of rubbish coming with the Gulf stream from the south, unfortunately in large volumes. This rubbish comes from all countries that are neighbouring the North Atlantic on either side and consists mostly of plastics from the fishing industry such as nets, boxes and buoyancy devices made of plastic, cork or metal.

The large volumes of plastic rubbish, that you can see even on the most remote beaches of Svalbard, is thus not of local origin, but comes from so-called "civilised" countries. It is in these countries that the the abuse of the world's oceans as the planet's rubbish dump, has to be fought; locally, you can only cure the symptoms, which nevertheless makes sense and is being done with significant success. This is important, not only because plastic rubbish is not what you want to see in the "untouched and pristine" arctic wilderness, but especially because it is dangerous for wildlife that may get entangled in old ropes and fishing nets and then die a slow and painful death. This concerns not only marine life such as fish, dolphins, seals, walruses and seabirds, but also reindeer.

The Norwegian administration has started the project "**Clean up Svalbard**" to reduce the amount of rubbish that is already there. This project encourages tourists officially to collect rubbish anywhere they find it – or almost anywhere, as there are some designated reference areas that are cleaned by the authorities exclusively for comparison (Poolepynten on Prins Karls Forland and Vesle Raudfjord on the north coast of Spitsbergen). Burning of plastic rubbish on site is explicitly not desired. The Sysselmannen provides strong rubbish bags of different sizes, which can then be disposed of in Longyearbyen. The collected volume should be registered; ask the Sysselmannen for information, bags and forms. Also the inhabitants of Longyearbyen contribute to this project with logistic support by the administration. Hundreds of tons of rubbish have disappeared in recent years from Svalbard's beaches, and everybody who is travelling the area over a longer period of time can witness a significant improvement.

Do not collect garbage in the mentioned reference zones and near cultural heritage sites unless you are really sure what you are doing. Remember that many cultural heritage sites have a very inconspicuous appearance, others look like rubbish dumps, but all are protected by law. As a general rule, collect plastics, but leave wood, glass and metal. Net balls are not dangerous to wildlife and thus of secondary importance.

At the same time, the Norwegian administration is working to reduce rubbish disposal from fishing fleets at sea, but this is obviously difficult to enforce.

Next to the visible rubbish, currents in the sea and atmosphere also bring invisible, but unfortunately even more dangerous waste to the Arctic: **Environmental toxins**. Concentrations of heavy metals, for example mercury, and chemicals such as PCBs (Polychlorinated Biphenyls; banned, but long-lived), DDE (resulting from the breakdown of DDT) and POPs (Persistant Organic Pollutants; volatile, but long-lived, toxic organic compounds) have reached alarming levels especially in the Atlantic sector of the Arctic. The Gulf stream and longitudinal air currents provide effective conveyor belts for dangerous waste water and gas from industry, traffic, energy production, agriculture and individual households, which accumulate in the tissues of animals at increasing levels; the higher they are in the food chain, the higher the level. This endangers top predators such as Polar bears and Glaucous gulls in particular, to mention only two examples.

If the concentrations of these toxins (and those that quickly replace the forbidden ones) are not reduced very soon, then the north Atlantic Polar bear population, together with other species, will be faced with serious consequences, including infertility, in the near future. This development is obviously a catastrophe, not only for the wildlife, but also for native hunters who still live on what nature supplies. This is not an issue in Spitsbergen which has never had a native population, but it is a serious problem in Greenland and Nunavut (arctic Canada) where people still hunt to supply their own food needs. Due to the consumption of meat and animal fats, the pollution levels of which would certainly cause a food scandal in the EU or US, these people are exposed to slow poisoning (see also chapter seven *Arctic environmental problems and tourism*). Sources of these toxins include seemingly harmless industrial processes as the production of nonstick frying pans and flame retardants containing bromine.

In recent years, marine sediments near the settlements in Isfjord have been shown to have a high concentration of PCBs. This includes Longyearbyen to a lesser degree, but concentrations reach higher levels in the vicinity of Pyramiden and Barentsburg. These pollution sources are, however, not significant on a larger scale and the Norwegian administration plans to remove the sources.

4.6 Climate and weather

"In den zwey ersten Spitsbergens Sommer-Monaten ist das Zahnklappern sehr gemein/ die Begierde deß Essens ist auch grösser als in andern Ländern."

"During the first two summer months in Spitsbergen, teeth chattering is very common / also the desire for food is larger than in other countries."

Friedrich Martens,
Spitzbergische oder Groenlandische Reisebeschreibung

Corresponding to the high latitude, the climate is high arctic. The summers, however, are cooler and the winters less severe than is the case in comparable latitudes in Greenland, Canada and Russia. Svalbard is an archipelago of relatively small islands, and the mild influence of the West Spitsbergen current is evident. This makes the climate maritime high arctic. The mildest area is the central west coast (Bellsund, Isfjord, Kongsfjord). The influence of the West Spitsbergen current is, however, largely restricted to the west coast and parts of the north coast, whereas the east is under influence of the cold East Spitsbergen current and accordingly high arctic with a smaller maritime component. The effect of these currents on the ice situation is significant (see chapter 4.4 *Sea ice*).

The mean temperature in Isfjord is –7,5°C. July is the warmest month (5 to 6°C on average) and temperatures below freezing are very rare at sea level at this time between late June and mid August; temperatures below 2°C are as rare as ones above 10°C. Nevertheless, a very pleasant feeling of summer heat (well, relatively) may be experienced locally on calm and sunny days, though even these are rare events. You are certainly more likely to experience such pleasant days in protected branches of the inner Isfjord than at the outer west coast, and T-shirt-weather in northwestern Spitsbergen is about as common as snowfall in Dubai.

Warm spells with moist, unpleasant thaw do occur even in mid-winter, although with decreasing frequency in February and March, when the mercury will stay around a frosty –14°C on average. There may be week-long periods during which it does not get any warmer than –20°C.

Precipitation has a strong local variation, but is generally low, about 200-300 mm per year (for comparison: 838 mm per year in England). March and August/September are months with maximum precipitation. This does not mean that you will experience Spitsbergen as a very dry place: Even light precipitation will make you feel wet and cold, although the actual volume of water is rather small.

Fog is unfortunately not an unknown phenomenon in the maritime Arctic, especially during the summer. Often there is a thin layer of fog with clear spots on the leeward side of mountains or near large glaciers. Mountaineers may be lucky and leave the fog layer below while ascending a mountain – or find out that it has got a seamless transition into a cloud cover.

There is no precise weather forecast for Spitsbergen, as the local variation is very pronounced and changes can come rapidly at any time. It can be different in every fjord and behind every cape, and there is no weather forecast for the individual areas within the archipelago. You can check the weather forecast for Longyearbyen on the internet (http://met.no/svalbard/longyearbyen.html?fylkesvis) and the actual weather situation on the UNIS website (www.unis.no).

The **midnight sun** shines for approximately four months, in Longyearbyen from 19th April to 23rd August. In June and July, the sun is high above the horizon 24 hours a day, which also implies that there are no warm colours during the night. Beautiful sunset-colours come back to these latitudes in mid August, and the sun will remain below the horizon throughout the period 26th October to 16th February. The official **polar night**, during which the sun will always stay at least four degrees below the horizon, lasts from 14th November to 29th January.

4.7 Mammals

"These things must seem wonderful to all who may hear of them, both what is told about the fishes and that about the monsters which are said to exist in those waters."

King's Mirror, Chapter XVII.
Unknown author, Norway, 13th century.

Mammalian fauna is represented by few species. The only truly terrestrial mammal is the reindeer that occurs on most islands of the archipelago. The Arctic fox is not a true terrestrial mammal, as it will often follow Polar bears on the drift ice during the winter. There are no rodents, with the exception of some introduced species in the settlements.

Marine mammals are more varied; the Polar bear belongs to this group. Walruses, a characteristic animal of the high Arctic just as is the Polar bear, were almost exctinct in the waters around Spitsbergen in the 1950s, but are now recovering thanks to strict protection. Other seal species are common, for example Bearded and Ringed seals in the fjords or in drift ice.

Several mammals, such as Muskoxen and Arctic hare, have been introduced during the early 20th century, but have died out again.

In this book, it is not possible to describe all species that you may encounter in Spitsbergen. I have chosen those that you are likely to see and, additionally, some others that are important as rarities. Refer to specialised literature for descriptions of other species.

In the description of distribution, "circumpolar" means that you can find the species in question anywhere around the North Pole; in the north American, Russian and European Arctic.

4.7.1 Polar bear (*Ursus maritimus*)

Eisbär (D) – Isbjørn (DK) – Ours blanc (F) – Orso bianco (I) – Isbjørn (N) – Ijsbeer (NL) – Isbjörn (S)

Description: Illustration page 129. The Polar bear is currently the largest bear species on Earth. Males may reach weights of 300-700 kg (length from nose to tail 1.80-2.60 metres) and females 150-350 kg. Weight varies greatly according to season and food availability. In 1995, a male bear was shot on Hopen that weighed 800-850 kg. The colour ranges from dirty yellow to creamy yellow to almost white, but never snow-white. If a Polar bear has spent longer periods on land, the fur will become dark yellow and during periods of starvation, when it neglects beauty culture, it will appear dirty and unsightly. Telling the sexes apart is anything but trivial, especially from a distance, and requires good observation opportunities and experience. Males grow larger, but how do you tell a sub-adult male apart from a large female? Males have a very strong neck and a broad skull base, females tend to have a (relatively!) slim neck and a longer skull. Pay attention to the bridge of the nose: It is shorter and often heavily scarred with males, but in comparison longish with females.

Distribution / Migrations: Polar bears have a circumpolar distribution in the Arctic, with several regional populations, but there is interchange between all areas. The Svalbard – Franz Josef Land area is considered one population, but exchange with Polar bears further east in the Russian Arctic does certainly take place. A helicopter census in 2004 (213 flight hours) yielded a result of approximately 3,000 animals in the Barents Sea area, with an estimated 25,000 on a global scale.

You have to expect Polar bears anywhere and at any time in Svalbard outside the permanently inhabited settlements (see section 3.6.2 *Polar bears and weapons, communication, safety in the field*). The probability of meeting a bear increases towards the north and east.

As the latin name *Ursus maritimus* already suggests, Polar bears are marine mammals. They are great swimmers and can cover distances of many tens of kilometres without any problems; swimming distances of more than 100 kilometres have been observed. Whether these bears will be able to get back to land or ice is another question. Recent observations suggest that there is increased mortality due to drowning because of unintentional long-range swimming induced by decreasing sea ice cover in Alaska. It is reasonable to expect a similar situation for Svalbard and this cause of death will increase in the future due to climate change with the obvious decrease in the sea ice cover around the islands.

The true habitat of Polar bears is dense drift ice. It is there and on the ice of frozen fjords and bays where they spend most of their life and find their most important prey: Bearded seals and Ringed seals, of which they need about one per week, or maybe more in the case of smaller Ringed seals. If necessary, well-fed Polar bears with a thick layer of fat may survive up to eight months without food!

In theory, a male bear never has to go back to land after he is born. Some animals however stay on land, more or less intentionally, during the summer and wait for the ice to return. Some of them have adapted quite well and spend the early summer on small islands, plundering birds' nests, or near glacier fronts trying to catch seals that are lying on small pieces of ice. Female bears seem to have stronger regional bonds, whereas many males show a very well-developed migratory behaviour and cover large distances, potentially roaming the whole Arctic.

Polar bears are loners and do not usually tolerate the presence of other Polar bears unless there is an overabundance of food, for example a beached whale. Females stay out of the way of males outside the mating season, as strong males may kill their offspring if they are hungry or as a precursor to mating. Even fully-grown females are not safe from aggression from their hungry, male counterparts.

Biology: Peak mating season is in April and early May. Females and males stay together for a couple of days for repeated mating and then go their ways. Strong males (ten years and older) may mate with several females, and females do not disdain mating with different partners. The further development of the fertilized egg is delayed until September, and in late December, two (rarely one, very rarely three) rat-sized, naked cubs will be born in a snow cave. Important denning areas are in eastern parts of Svalbard, on Edgeøya and Barentsøya, Hopen, Kong Karls Land and Nordaustland. The highest density of dens is on Kongsøya in Kong Karls Land with up to twelve dens per square kilometre! The young family will leave the den in late March or early April, when the female has not had any food for about four months, but has nursed the cubs during the same period. Good hunting results are critical and only experienced mothers will be able to raise both cubs to reach an age of one year. The young bears become independent at an age of two and a half years. Mortality is high again during the first year of independence, until they have got sufficient hunting experience. Once they have survived this stage, they have a reasonable chance to become 15 to 25 years old.

Polar bears do not like to run, but can reach more than 30 km/h over short distances.

Miscellaneous: In Svalbard, Polar bears were hunted until 1973 when Norway followed other arctic nations in the protection of this species. Since then, they have been globally protected, with the exception of limited hunting by natives in Greenland, Canada, Alaska and Russia. Unfortunately, illegal hunting is still part of a Polar bear's real life: 200 to 300 bears fall victim to poachers each year in the Russian Arctic. This is, however, a regional problem without any implications for the global population which is threatened more by climate change and its dramatic consequences for the extent of the arctic drift ice, and by poisoning with environmental toxins (heavy metals, PCBs etc.), that are transported by oceanic and atmospheric currents from industrial countries to the Arctic. Consequences include impairment of the immune system and decrease in fertility and, possibly, increased mortality of cubs.

In Svalbard, Polar bears are strictly protected and may be shot only in case of direct danger to human life or health. Before you shoot a bear, you must do all that is possible to avoid a direct conflict: Don't go there in the first place if a Polar bear is too close, and if one shows up, try to scare it away. Shouting, shooting flares or metallic noise may help. Keep groups together, don't get between the rifle(s) and the bear (in tents, lie down to get out of the way), try to occupy an elevated position. If all this does not help, then you have to shoot to kill: A wounded bear is a worst case scenario. Aim for the breast / shoulder area, where you are most likely to hit either vital organs or bones, which will kill or immobilize the attacking animal. The head is too small. Then, shoot several times until you are 200 % sure that the bear is dead, before you go closer. The killing of a Polar bear must be reported to the Sysselmannen as quickly as possible and will always be followed by detailed police investigations.

4.7.2 Arctic fox (*Alopex lagopus*)

Eisfuchs (D) – Polarræv (DK) – Renard arctique (F) – Volpe artica (I) – Fjellrev (N) – Poolvoos (NL) – Fjällräv (S)

Description: Illustration page 129. Adult Arctic foxes are about 60 cm long and 2.5-5 kg in weight. They have a very dense, thick, usually completely white winter fur, that is brown during the summer; moulting is from May to early July and September to December. Additionally, there is a small proportion that remains dark brown throughout the year. These types belong to the same species, but it is the dark morph, the so-called "blue fox", which is very rare in Spitsbergen.

Distribution / Migrations: Arctic foxes have a circumpolar distribution. They roam over large areas, preventing sub-populations from being isolated. In Svalbard, foxes appear on all the islands and in all habitats from the drift ice at sea to mountains, although they prefer the tundra in the vicinity of bird cliffs during the summer. In favourable areas with good food availability an Arctic fox may manage with a territory of less than 10 sq km, otherwise 10-20 sq km.

Biology: Arctic foxes eat pretty much everything they can get hold of, typically eggs and chicks during the summer. They have to make do without rodents in Svalbard, as these do not occur in this region. Food availability during the summer is generally good, but the winter is a meagre season, during which Ptarmigans, carrion, hidden stocks and, near settlements, rubbish are important items on the menu. Some Arctic foxes follow Polar bears out onto the drift ice and feed on the left-overs of their meals. Starvation during the winter seems to be the main cause of death.

During the mating season, Arctic foxes have a territory, the size of which depends on food availability: The more food that is available, the smaller the territory. Mating is in March, and the female will give birth in a den, often under large rocks, in late May or early June. Five or six cubs, even more in good years, are born to enjoy the rich, early arctic summer, but many will die during the first winter. Those who survive have a good chance to reach an age of three or four or, in exceptional cases, even ten years or more.

Miscellaneous: The population is sound and stable in Svalbard despite centuries of intense hunting. Outside the protected areas, locals are still allowed to hunt during a certain period in the winter, but only very few people are actually doing this. Arctic foxes have traditionally been caught during the winter with wooden traps that kill the fox with a heavy weight of stones without damaging the precious fur which provided a very important income for trappers.

Nevertheless, Arctic foxes are often quite inquisitive and with a bit of luck you may observe them from a close distance. Remember, however, that they can have rabies or tapeworms in Svalbard. Both can be very dangerous for humans, so don't touch unnaturally friendly or dead foxes or fox excrement.

4.7.3 Svalbard reindeer (*Rangifer tarandus platyrhynchus*)

Spitzbergen-Rentier (D) – Svalbardrensdyr (DK) – Renne du Spitzberg (F) – Renna (I) – Svalbardrein (N) – Rendier (NL) – Svalbardsren (S)

Description: Illustration page 130. The Svalbard reindeer is the only reindeer species in Svalbard. It is a unique, relatively small subspecies. Both sexes have antlers, but those of the males are bigger. Male reindeer grow their antlers from April to July, shed the bast in August and September and finally the antlers in late autumn, after the breeding season. Females get their antlers in June and carry them until spring next year.
Females: Weight 53 kg in spring, 70 kg in autumn. Length 1.50 metres.
Males: Weight 65 kg in spring, 90 kg in autumn. Length 1.60 metres.

In contrast to Scandinavia where semi-wild reindeer stay together in large herds, you will see either single animals or small groups in Svalbard. Herds of more than 20 animals are exceptional. Svalbard reindeer are not domesticated and do not belong to anybody.

Distribution / Migration: Reindeer occur everywhere in the Arctic, but the subspecies "Svalbard reindeer" is endemic to Svalbard. They were driven near to extinction in the early 20th century due to extensive hunting, but have recovered well and can now be found in most parts of the archipelago, although man has helped on some occasions by moving small stocks within Spitsbergen to suitable areas. There are even some reindeer chewing on the very meagre vegetation in the polar deserts on Nordaustland, but they do not occur on the remotest islands of Storøya, Kvitøya, Hopen and Bjørnøya. Highest population densities occur in areas with rich tundra vegetation, mainly Nordenskiöld Land and the large islands of Edgeøya and Barentsøya. Within these areas, they do not show a very pronounced seasonal migration pattern, as winter and summer feeding grounds are within the same regions. Reindeer walk across fjord ice and glaciers to move around.

Biology: Svalbard reindeer will eat almost anything that has roots and leaves, with a few exceptions such as Arctic bell-heather (*Cassiope tetragona*). During the summer, they spend most of the time feeding to accumulate a thick layer of fat, which is their main energy source for the winter when food availability is low. Reindeer spend the winter in places where the snow has been blown away by the wind, to have access to some vegetation, often at some altitude. Late winter and spring are the most difficult time of the year, when the tundra is still hidden under snow and their fat reserves are used up. Especially when periods of thaw are followed by frost and everything is covered with an impenetrable layer of hard ice, reindeer are faced with difficult times. Starvation during such periods and when the teeth are worn down after about ten years are the main causes of death. Few reindeer die during the rich summer season.

Mating is in October. During this time, strong bulls will defend a harem of up to ten cows. During the following early summer, around June, a single calf will be born. The proportion of females that give birth varies strongly from ten percent in difficult years up to 90 percent in good times. There are accordingly very pronounced fluctuations of the population size.

Miscellaneous: The size of the total population is estimated to be around 10,000 animals, thereof about 4,000 in Nordenskiöld Land, but varies from year to year. Reindeer have been protected in Svalbard since 1925, but limited hunting has been introduced for locals in 1983 in designated areas in Nordenskiöld Land. The hunting season is in September and it is assumed that hunting does not affect the population. In 2006, 296 permits were issued, but only 178 reindeer were shot.

Despite hunting, reindeer can be very curious and sometimes approach groups of tourists to a distance of within ten metres. They spend most of the day walking slowly over the tundra, feeding permanently, and do not pay any attention to humans to begin with. Then, they are typically undecided between running away and coming closer. Snow mobiles can pose serious strain on reindeer during the most difficult season, when they need to save energy. Pay attention to this and give reindeer the right of way. During the summer, you will often find reindeer hair on the tundra. Wishful thinking suggests that this is Polar bear fur, but the distinction is easy: Reindeer fur is much coarser, but breaks easily, whereas the finer Polar bear hairs are much thinner and stronger.

4.7.4-4.7.7. Seals

The most common seal species in the coastal waters of Spitsbergen is the Bearded seal, followed by the Ringed seal. There is a Harbour seal colony on the west coast, and Walrus occur in the northern and eastern parts of the archipelago. Harp seals are quite common at the ice edge.

In contrast to the large concentrations of seals that you may know from other parts of the world, you will usually "only" see single animals in the high Arctic, with the exception of Walrus colonies and during the breeding season, when some species occur in large numbers within certain areas, but never densely crowded. The simple reason for this is that any concentration of seals ashore would attract the attention of Polar bears in no time at all.

4.7.4 Bearded seal (*Erignathus barbatus*)

Bartrobbe (D) – Remmesæl (DK) – Phoque barbus (F) – Foca barbata (I) – Storkobbe (N) – Baardrob (NL) – Storsäl (S)

Description: Illustration page 130. Bearded seals are up to 2.5 metres long and 300 kg in weight; in exceptional cases even up to 400 kg. They are the second biggest seal species in the Arctic; only Walrus grow bigger. The female is slightly bigger than the male, but the difference is virtually impossible to see. Their proportions help to identify Bearded seals: If you see a large, fat, almost box-shaped "sausage", with a small head at the end, then it is likely to be a Bearded seal. They owe their name to their strongly developed moustache. Normally, you will see single animals lying on ice floes, or occasionally two, but never large numbers together and hardly ever on shore; just swimming or basking on ice floes.

Distribution / Migration: Bearded seals occur in most regions around the North Pole. They prefer shallow coastal waters with drift ice, often fjords with calving glaciers. They spend the whole year in Svalbard waters.

Biology: Moulting takes place over most of the year. They eat pretty much anything that lives near, on and in the sea bottom, such as mussels, crabs, squid and fish. The whiskers are organs with a very sensitive sense of touch, thus helping to find prey at depths of up to 200 metres. Many Bearded seals end their lives as a Polar bear's meal, but Orcas, Greenland sharks and Walrus with slightly abnormal taste can also be dangerous predators.

Females give birth on ice floes in early May, and the single pup is able to swim after only a few hours. To begin with, they live on approximately eight litres of milk each day with a fat content of about 50 percent. After about three weeks, they can dive and find their own food. Bearded seals have a life expectancy of 20-25 years.

Miscellaneous: With some luck and a boat you can often approach Bearded seals quite closely. They are hunted outside the protected areas and outside the breeding season. As in Greenland, seal meat is mostly used to feed dogs. Hunting is limited in popularity, as you cannot refuel snow mobiles with seal meat.

4.7.5 Ringed seal (*Phoca hispida*)

Ringelrobbe (D) – Ringsæl (DK) – Phoque annelé (F) – Foca dagli anelli (I) – Ringsel (N) – Ringelrob (NL) – Vikare (S)

Description: Illustration page 131. Ringed seals reach about 1.1-1.6 metres in length, weighing 50-100 kg with a weight minimum in May to June and a maximum in autumn. In other words, they are much smaller than Bearded seals. It is virtually impossible to tell the sexes apart. The belly is silver-grey, the sides and the back much darker with a varied pattern of rings, to which this species owes its name.

Distribution / Migration: The Ringed seal occurs everywhere in the Arctic including the northernmost areas. It is the only arctic seal species that is able to keep a breathing hole open even in thick ice with the claws of its foreflippers. Ringed seals occur in Svalbard waters throughout the year, but mostly near the ice edge north of the archipelago. This seal spends its whole life in or at least near drift ice or fjord ice. As long as the fjords are still frozen, they stay in quite large numbers on the fjord ice. After moulting, which happens in June and July, they retreat to open waters near the ice edge. Observations of Ringed seals, especially good photo opportunities, are quite rare, in contrast to Bearded seals.

Biology: Ringed seals can dive several hundred metres deep and spend up to 45 minutes under water, to catch small fish and crustaceans. They give birth in April or May in snow caves on fjord ice. In years with little snow, the seal pup hardly has a chance to survive the first days. The pup is white, about 60 cm long and weighs 4.5 kg. It spends

six weeks with its mother, half of this time in the water, and will reach a weight of 20 kg during this nursing period. The female will mate again when the pup is about to become independent, but it takes another four months until pregnancy actually proceeds with the development of the fertilized egg.
Miscellaneous: The Ringed seal is the most abundant arctic seal species; the global population is estimated at several million individuals. They are the preferred meal of Polar bears, but Greenland sharks and occasionally Walrus may also take a Ringed seal. New-born pups may fall victim to Arctic foxes or Glaucous gulls, if snow is lacking to hide in. Man has hunted Ringed seals in their thousands and is still doing so everywhere in the Arctic; in Svalbard it is possible for the locals to hunt Ringed seals outside the protected areas and the breeding season. Catches are actually low, whereas this is a main target species for hunters in Greenland. The meat is mainly used as dog food, but also for human consumption. If a Ringed seal escapes from all these dangers, it may well become several decades old.

4.7.6 Harp seal (*Phoca groenlandica*)

Sattelrobbe (D) – Grønlandssel (DK) – Phoque du Groenland (F) – Foca dala sella or Foca della Groenlandia (I) – Grønlandssel (N) – Zadelrob (NL) – Grönlandssäl (S)

Description: Illustration page 131. Harp seals are relatively small seals, measuring 1.70 to 1.80 metres and weighing 120 to 140 kg. The fur pattern of the adults is mainly silverish grey, but has a large, dark spot across the back that looks vaguely similar to a saddle, hence the name. This pattern is more strongly pronounced with males than femailes. The head is also partly black.

Harp seals are easily identified by their behaviour: in Spitsbergen waters, they are mostly seen in larger groups near the ice edge or within drift ice, often swimming in a very lively and playful way. Sightings in fjords are rare.
Distribution/ migration: Harp seals can be found in the Arctic from Newfoundland to West and East Greenland and into the Barents sea, mostly in the vicinity of drift ice.
Biology: Harp seals dive down to 200 metres and feed on a variety of fish and crustaceans. Mating occurs in January and February, but the fertilized egg is implanted after a delay of about 4 months in May or June. The pup, approximately 85 cm large, is born next January or February. It suckles for only about 12 days, but gains about 2 kg weight per day during this period. It will then spend another 2 weeks on the ice, until its fur, originally white, has changed to a pattern with dark spots. The fur develops the characteristic „saddle“ pattern of the adults only after 7 (males) or 12 years (females). Polar bears, Greenland sharks and Orcas are the Harp seal's worst enemy; if they manage to escape those, then they may live for up to 35 years.
Miscellaneous: The global Harp seal population, once numbering many millions, has been reduced dramatically throughout centuries of industrial hunting, but is still estimated around 7 million. Several 100,000 are still taken each year, most of them in Canada.

4.7.7 Walrus (*Odobenus rosmarus*)

Walross (D) – Hvalros (DK) – Morse (F) – Tricheco dell'Atlantico (I) – Hvalross (N) – Walrus (NL) – Valross (S)

Description: Illustration page 131 and 335. The Walrus is the largest seal species in the Arctic and the second-largest one on a global scale; only male Elephant seals outgrow Walrus. The tusks, that can be up to one metre long, make them unmistakable; tusks of Walrus cows are slightly smaller than those of bulls. Bulls can be up to 3.5 metres long and 1,500 kg in weight, while cows reach 2.5 metres and a weight of 900 kg. A newly born Walrus baby is 1.3 metres long and weighs sweet 60-85 kg. The Pacific Walrus (*O. r. divergens*) is slightly bigger than its Atlantic relative. Both are considered subspecies of the same species.

The colour is brown, but variable: Once they have spent some hours ashore, the skin tends to have a pinkish shade, especially in warm weather, as an increased blood circulation in the thick skin prevents overheating. When they come out of the water or if it is cold, they decrease blood circulation to preserve heat; then they will appear almost dark-grey.

Telling the sexes apart is difficult. Adult males are significantly larger than females. Males have got more scars and characteristic calluses around the neck, whereas the cows have smoother skin.

The significance of the tusks is not clear. It is known that they are not needed to obtain food. They are certainly useful for defence against Polar bears, although this is rarely needed, and for climbing up on ice floes. The most important purpose is certainly as a status symbol and weapon for fighting during the mating season. The tusks may break off, which certainly affects the breeding status of males, but it does not influence life expectancy.

Walrus are very social. Single animals are the exception. They stay in groups, often with more than 20 individuals. Herds of more than 100 animals are not the rule in Svalbard, but such large or even larger groups do occur.

Distribution / migration: Walrus occur in several areas around the Arctic. There are several, more or less isolated populations in northeastern Canada and West Greenland as well as northeastern Siberia and the Bering Strait. The Atlantic Walrus is spread from Northeast Greenland to Svalbard, Franz Josef Land and Novaya Zemlya. Svalbard and Franz Josef Land are a key region for this population, although the majority stays in the east, in the Russian Arctic. There is an interesting sexual segregation: The bulls tend to stay in Spitsbergen, while the cows together with their calves obviously prefer the northeasternmost parts of Svalbard and Franz Josef Land. In recent years, sightings of females and calves have increased also in Spitsbergen. This very positive tendency is due to the general return of Walrus to their original range pre-dating the arrival of Europeans in Spitsbergen, who introduced hunting that almost led to regional extinction of Walrus in Spitsbergen in the 1950s. Even today, most Walrus in Svalbard are found in the northeastern parts of the archipelago, which was not visited by early whalers. One well-known colony is at the southern tip of Moffen.

Walrus spend the whole year in the same region, but move away from the coast and towards open water during the winter. They need polynyas: areas that remain ice-free during the whole winter due to currents. Polynyas occur on the northern sides of both Svalbard and Franz Josef Land. As soon as the coast becomes ice-free, walruses return to their traditional haul-out sites. They tend to use the same sites year after year: beaches near shallow, productive waters with muddy bottom, where they find good feeding grounds. After a successful feeding trip, they may rest for several days ashore – up to eleven days of siesta have been observed (who has observed this for eleven days?), and in historical reports there is talk about Walrus sleeping on the beach for about seven weeks!

During the little ice age, there were very rare sightings of Walrus in the River Thames, and in the early 20th century, a Walrus even got lost in the southern Baltic sea.

Biology: The preferred diet consists almost exclusively of the mussel Bluntgaper (*Mya arenaria*), which lives in the mud at the sea bottom and filters plancton. Walrus can sense the mussels with their whiskers and use their nose, and possibly a strong jet of water that they produce to uncover the mussel. Then they will suck the meat out of the shells. The stomachs of Walruses have been found to contain up to 70 kg of mussel meat, but not a single shell! Productive and shallow waters are obviously an important part of their habitat.

There are single individuals that have a different taste and predate on seals. These Walrus have got a particularly high level of contamination with environmental toxins (heavy metals, PBCs etc.).

Mating is between December and February and copulation takes place in the water near the ice edge. Bulls have heavy fights for females, during which serious injuries occur. A single calf is born 15 months later, in May of the following year. The female will separate from the herd to give birth on an ice floe. The calf spends about two years with its mother.

Miscellaneous: The size of the Walrus population in Svalbard and Franz Josef Land is estimated to be around 2,000 animals, but is increasing. The strong skin, that was used amongst other things for machine belts during the early days of industrialisation, and also the ivory were highly sought-after goods. Since the 17th century, there has been heavy hunting pressure on Walrus in Spitsbergen. On countless occasions, several hundred animals were killed within hours. Before those cruel days, Walrus must have been very abundant anywhere in Svalbard, even including Bjørnøya.

Hunting was finally banned completely in 1952, and this total protection is still in force in Svalbard. The population is increasing, but still nowhere near its original size. Recent threats include disturbance at the haul-out sites, contamination with environmental toxins, climate change and oil spills.

Polar bears occasionally try to kill a Walrus, although they have respect for the strong tusks. Orcas may be dangerous for Walrus in the water. Other than that, there is no predator that Walrus would have to fear. Little is known about the life expectancy, but it will surely be beyond 30 years, possibly 40.

Walrus are easily disturbed ashore. Anybody who approaches Walrus that are hauled out on the beach, has to exercise the greatest care: Slow approach, no noise, no sudden movements, no smell being blown towards the Walrus and, especially, a respectful distance are key factors to avoid disturbance. 30 metres should definitely be the minimum distance for any approach, and in many cases you will have to stay further away, depending on the animals and the situation. Let them know you are there at an early stage; this is definitely better than them finding out about your presence when you are already close. The worst case scenario is a whole herd leaving a resting place in panic, all rushing into the water. For reasonable photos, you need a telephoto lens, but 300 mm should normally do.

Next to the view, it is the sound that can be quite impressive; just imagine up to 70 kg of raw mussel meat being digested in every stomach! Considering this, it is not surprising that also the smell can leave you with unforgettable impressions.

4.7.8 Harbour seal (*Phoca vitulina*)

Seehund (D) – Spættet sæl (DK) – Phoque commún (F) – Foca comune (I) – Steinkobbe (N) – Gewone zeehond (NL) – Knubbsäl (S)

Description: Illustration page 132. With a length of about 1.5 metres and a weight of a good 100 kg, Harbour seals are slightly larger than Ringed seals. The colouration of their fur varies from almost black to dark grey and brown, with patterns that can be similar to those of Ringed seals. Already at birth, their size approaches one metre and the fur also resembles that of adults. Main features to distinguish Harbour seals from Ringed seals are the location and situation of the observation: You will find Harbour seals, if at all, only on the west coast of Spitsbergen and you will rarely see one only, as they tend to stay in groups. Also, if you see any seals lying on rocks, then they should be Harbour seals, as other seals in Spitsbergen rarely show this behaviour. In contrast to other seals, Harbour seals usually do not rest on ice floes unless the shore is not accessible.

Distribution / Migration: Generally, Harbour seals are amongst the seal species with the widest range, but they are more at home in temperate and sub-arctic areas. In central Europe, they are well-known from the North Sea coast. The world's northernmost occurrence is the one and only colony at Spitsbergen, which is on the northeast coast of Prins Karls Forland. They spend the whole year in the area, but can swim quite far. Thus, you may also see them in Isfjord, Kongsfjord or at the northwestern corner of Spitsbergen. The Spitsbergen population is possibly a relict dating back to a period with milder climate several thousand years ago.

Biology: In Spitsbergen, Harbour seal pups are born in early to mid June. The offspring sees the light of day for the first time in shallow water and is immediately able to swim. The young seal will live for three to four weeks on its mother's milk, until it has increased its body weight from ten or twelve to 25-30 kg and then starts to find its own food. As soon as the young become independent, the mating season begins, but pregnancy is delayed by a good two months, until September or October. Harbour seals moult in late August to early September and will then build up a thick fat layer for the winter, feeding on almost anything they find in the water that is small enough for them to eat, such as fish, jellyfish and crustaceans. Females and males tend to go their separate ways outside the mating and moulting seasons.

Their main enemies are Orcas, Greenland sharks and, exceptionally, those Walrus who have abnormal diet requirements. Polar bears rarely take Harbour seals, as their distribution ranges overlap only marginally.

The life expectancy of Harbour seals in Svalbard is, for reasons not yet known, significantly shorter compared to their relatives further south; the oldest one found was 22 years old (normally up to 35 years).

Miscellaneous: The size of the local population is estimated to be around 1,000 animals. Chances to see them lying on rocks are better during low water, since they tend to search for food during high tide.

Hunting, losses as bycatch in fishing nets and pollution including oil spills have put pressure on Harbour seal populations in many areas. While the Spitsbergen population is assumed to have a normal size, it is on the Norwegian red list and thus totally protected.

4.7.9-4.7.13 Whales

"Auch Wale wurden mir versprochen, und ich fand es beeindruckend, daß das Reisebüro das Leben im Meer dermaßen gut unter Kontrolle hatte."

"They promised me also whales, and I was impressed that the travel agency had life in the sea so well under control."

Anne B. Ragde, *Mord in Spitzbergen*

To begin with, it needs to be noted that, after several centuries of intense whaling, Spitsbergen is not prime whalewatching territory. But whales do sometimes show up. Several weeks can go by without any sightings at all, and then they are suddenly around in considerable numbers. If you travel on a ship, then spend as much time looking out for whales as you possibly can. Many sightings are too brief to be announced on the ship's intercom.

4.7.9 Minke whale (*Balaenoptera acutorostrata*)

Zwergwal (D) – Vågehval (DK) – Petit rorqual (F) – Balenottera minore (I) – Vågehval (N) – Dwergvinvis (NL) – Vikval (S)

Description: Illustration page 132. The Minke whale or "Minkie" is the smallest baleen whale, but is still a very impressive animal, considering its size of about ten metres. It resembles other baleen whales in shape and colouration: slim and streamlined, dark-grey to black back with a pale belly. Next to the relatively small size, the dorsal fin is important for identification: It is large in relation to the body, at least in comparison to other whales. In shape, it resembles a sickle and is placed to the front of the last third of the body length. The blow is small and does not have any specific shape; the fluke (tail fin) remains invisible when it dives. It does not spend much time at the surface, unless feeding there.

Distribution / migration: Minke whales occur in all of the world's oceans, predominantly in high latitudes. The population in the north Atlantic is thought to be about 100,000 animals, but estimates vary between official studies in countries that allow whaling (Iceland, Norway) and other scientists from many countries.

Minke whales are not very abundant in Spitsbergen, but show up regularly in fjords, coastal and offshore waters and near the ice edge. Sightings of single animals are most common, but small herds occur occasionally. During winter, they retreat to latitudes somewhere between Portugal and the Carribean.

Biology: In the North Atlantic, Minke whales feed on a range of small fish species as well as plankton (in Antarctica, you would call it krill) which they filter with their baleen plates. They also take larger fish species, but only to a very subordinate degree; competition with commercial fishing is thus not significant. Mating is generally between October and March, depending on the region and population. After a pregnancy of ten months, a 2.5 metres long calf is born in the wintering area.

Miscellaneous: Minke whales show up only for moments, dive again and then show up again at a different place and are thus difficult to observe and to photograph. Spectacular observations such as curious individuals approaching boats and displays of acrobatic behaviour are rare, but do happen.

Minke whales have been hunted for many centuries in the North Atlantic. Norway still allows its small whaling fleet an annual quota of several hundred animals, although this is highly contentious even in Norway.

4.7.10 White whale (Beluga) (*Delphinapterus leucas*)

Weißwal (D) – Hvidhval (DK) – Beélouga/ Baleine blanche (F) – Beluga (I) – Hvitfisk/ Hvithval (N) – Beluga (NL) – Vitval (S)

Description: Illustration page 133. The White whale, often called Beluga, is a medium-sized toothed whale. Bulls can reach four and a half metres in length and 1,500 kg weight; cows are slightly smaller. They cannot be confused with any other

whale because of their creamy-white colour, although they are grey during their first years. White whales tend to stay in groups of 20 or more animals.
Distribution / migration: Many different areas around the North Pole have a White whale population. They can be found in coastal waters anywhere in Svalbard, often in fjords near glacier fronts. The size of the regional population is not known, but they are among the more common whales in Svalbard. Bulls and cows seem to stay in separate herds, but individuals may be flexible with regards to their bonds to a specific group. Their biology, including migration patterns, is still largely unknown, but they seem to spend the winter in areas with drift ice.
Biology: White whales are slow swimmers, but dive down to depths of 1,000 metres and have something like echo location to find food and for orientation. They feed on a range of species: fish, squid and, in other regions, salmon. Mating is in spring (April-May); the cows give birth between May and August of the following year. They may reach 40 years in age, being predated on by Polar bears and Orcas.
Miscellaneous: White whales have been hunted in Svalbard for centuries into the 1960s by Pomors and then by Norwegians. Now they are protected in Svalbard waters, but still hunted in Canada and Greenland. The regional population seems to be increasing slowly.

4.7.11 Humpback whale (*Megaptera novaeangliae*)

Buckelwal (D) – Pukkelhval (DK) – Baleine à bosse (F) – Megattera (I) – Knølhval (N) – Bultrug (NL) – Knölval (S)

Description: Illustration page 133. Humpback whales are between 12 and 13 metres long (maximum 18) and weigh up to 30 tons, which makes them significantly smaller than Fin or Blue whales, but larger than Minke whales. Female Humpback whales are slightly larger than males. They belong to the group of baleen whales and have 270 to 400 baleen plates on each side of their mouth to filter plankton. The pectoral fins are proportionally the longest of any whale, they can be as long as one third of the total length of the whale. The tail fin has wavy rear edges and a distinctive black and white marking that is unique for each individual animal. Head and lower jaw are covered with knobs called tubercles. The dorsal fin is stubby and, relative to the body size, smaller than that of a Minke whale.

Identification of Humpback whales is often made easy by their behaviour: they are by far the most acrobatic and playful of all whales, often showing the large tail fluke elegantly just before diving, although it is a myth that this means that they do not show up again once you have seen the tail fluke. Occasionally, they breach spectacularly, showing up to a good two thirds of their entire body length.
Distribution / migration: Humpback whales are at home in all of the world's oceans. They spend the summer in polar waters and the winter in tropical latitudes. It is believed that there are southern populations that migrate to Antarctica and northern ones which spend the arctic summer in the north Atlantic or Pacific, respectively. Individual animals occur as well as groups of a few animals; larger pods are uncommon, although occasionally seen.

Biology: Humpback whales feed on krill and small schooling fish during the summer in polar waters, whereas they live largely off their fat reserves in the winter in tropical areas. This is the time for mating, and competition for females is high. Cows give birth to one calf that is one third of its mother in length after 11.5 months. For six months, the calf will live on the fat-rich milk of the mother, until it gradually gets used to securing its own prey. The life span is believed to be 50 to 60 years, but recent research indicates that it may actually be much longer.
Miscellaneous: The species was severely brought down by whaling until it was protected in 1966. Humpback whales are definitely not an every day sight in Spitsbergen's coastal waters, but they are seen every now and then, mostly individual animals near the west coast. Their sometimes playful and curious behaviour makes them a photographer's favourite amongst all whales.

4.7.12 Fin whale (*Balaenoptera physalus*)

Finnwal (D) – Finhval (DK) – Rorqual commun (F) – Balenottera comune (I) – Finnhval (N) – Gewone vinvis (NL) – Sillval (S)

Description: Illustration page 133. Fin whales are the second largest whale species after the Blue whale. Females reach 24 metres body length and up to 75 tons weight; males reach a size of 22 metres. The body is long and slim, with a dark-grey upper side and a pale underside. The sickle-shaped dorsal fin is far back at three quarters of the body length. The asymmetric colouration of the head is an important diagnostic feature: The left side is dark-grey, the lower part of the right side is white. Also the baleen is dark on the left and pale on the right side. Fin whales have a strong blow, up to six metres high. Distinguishing them from other whales can be tricky.
Distribution / migration: Fin whales occur in all of the world's oceans. They spend the winter in temperate waters where mating and birthing take place, but prefer the rich feeding grounds of high latitudes during the summer. The north Atlantic population winters in the open sea, possibly in the latitudes between Spain and the Gulf of Mexico or even in the Mediterranean. During the summer, they can be seen in Spitsbergen, especially off the west coast in the area where the continental shelf drops down to the deep sea basin, but they are most common in East Greenland.
Biology: Fin whales tend to stay in smaller groups, but both single animals and larger herds occur, if food availability is good. Cows and bulls go separate ways. They are fast swimmers and can reach up to eight knots (14 kilometres per hour) while travelling and up to 14 knots (27 km/h) during sprints. Fin whales rarely dive longer than 15 minutes or deeper than 200 metres on their search for plankton, which is their exclusive diet.
Miscellaneous: This large whale species has been hunted extensively since the invention of the explosive harpoon in the late 19th century. The global population may be around 75,000 animals, of which about 25,000-30,000 are in the North Atlantic. They are globally protected, with the exception of limited hunting in West Greenland,

and numbers are increasing, although there is some loss as bycatch in fishing nets. Overfishing of food resources and environmental toxins are current dangers. The latest threat for these and other whales is the LFAS system (Low Frequency Active Sonar) of the US Navy, which creates incredible sound pressures of up to 215 decibels, meaning that the noise at a distance of as much as 480 kilometres is still 140 decibels, equivalent to a rifle shot.

The life expectancy of these majestic animals is close to a century.

4.7.13 Bowhead whale (*Balaena mysticetus*)

Grönlandwal (D) – Grønlandshval (DK) – Baleine boreale (F) – Balena della Groenlandia (I) – Grønlandshval (N) – Groenlandse Walvisch (NL) – Grönlandsval (S)

Description: The Bowhead whale, sometimes also called Greenland whale, is a large, dark animal up to 20 metres long and 100 tons in weight. The mighty mouth alone can occupy a good third of the body length. The baleen plates that hang down from the upper jaw, can be three or even four metres long, the longest of any whale species on Earth. Bowhead whales are slow swimmers, with a strong, V-shaped blow. The most important diagnostic feature is the absence of a dorsal fin.

Distribution / migration: The Bowhead whale is a high-arctic whale species that tends to stay near drift ice. They have been extremely abundant well into the 17th century, but have been driven close to extinction by whalers during subsequent decades. In recent years, single Bowhead whales have been seen again in Svalbard waters. During the summer of 2006, one animal was even seen near Longyearbyen – the first sighting of this species on the west coast of Spitsbergen for a very long time and thus quite a sensation! In 2007, five Bowhead whales were seen south of Kvitøya.

4.7.13 Bowhead whales. Drawing by Friedrich Martens (1675).

Nevertheless the Bowhead whale must unfortunately be considered practically extinct in the area, and nobody is able to say if the population will ever recover. There are still a few hundred animals in the Russian and north American Arctic. Recent data suggest a slight recovery of the West Greenland population.
Biology: Little is known about this extremely rare species. Like other baleen whales, Bowhead whales swim slowly through surface waters of the oceans, filtering immense volumes of seawater for plankton. A cow may give birth to a 3.5 metre long calf every second year.
Miscellaneous: The fine oil that was boiled out of the blubber (=fat) layer was a precious product, as was the baleen. This made the Bowhead whale the preferred target species of a very intense, international whaling period in the north Atlantic during the 17th and 18th centuries. In Spitsbergen, the species was protected in 1911, but internationally, this happened as late as 1939 – far too late, obviously.

Today, it is hard to imagine the abundance of whales that must have crowded the fjords of Spitsbergen in the past. Old chronicles and logs can give only a slight idea.

4.7.14 Introduced species

Several species have been introduced intentionally in the early 20th century, to have game for hunting available near the settlements, where reindeer where already overhunted. In 1929, 17 young **Muskoxen** from Greenland were released in Hiorthamn opposite Longyearbyen. To begin with, they seem to have liked their new home and multiplied well. But in the end, it turned out not to be their environment, as the last one was seen in 1985 not too far from Longyearbyen. 30 **Arctic hares**, that were moved in 1930 from Greenland to Spitsbergen without being asked, finally joined the fate of the Muskoxen; the last ones were seen in the 1970s.

Several species have been introduced unintentionally, most likely together with hay for livestock that was held in the settlements, Norwegian and Russian, in the past. One **mouse** species (*Microtus rossiaemeridionalis*) is obviously feeling well in the surroundings of Grumantbyen and has recently been seen in other places near the coast between Longyearbyen and Barentsburg; rarely also inland, away from the coast, but so far it has not moved further away (see section 3.6.5 *Other hazards in the field* for health risks related to mice in Spitsbergen).

4.8 Birds

"We went ashore (at Vogelhook = Fuglehuken) for about two hours, investigating the wonderful bird rookeries, first discovered by Barents in 1596. The vegetation was luxuriant with rich mosses, scurvy grass, and many arctic plants. Birds were countless - Bruennich's guillemots, razorbills, puffins, little auks, dovekies, kittiwake gulls, burgomaster gulls, skuas, fulmar petrels, pink-footed geese, purple sandpipers, and snow-buntings."

William S. Bruce,
The exploration of Prince Charles Foreland, 1906-1907

Out of approximately 30 bird species that come to Svalbard as regular breeders, the 26 most important are described here. "Important" means that either they are so common that most visitors are likely to see them, or they are prominent because of their rareness. This "method" and the resulting choices are definitely subjective.

In total, 163 species have been seen in Svalbard as of 1998, mostly as vagrants, who happened to be "blown" to the Arctic but do not belong there. Some of the **30 or so regular breeders** occur only on Bjørnøya, such as the Great Northern diver and the Common guillemot.

The descriptions refer to the breeding plumage, which is what you will see in Spitsbergen. If you are, for example, from the UK, then you will certainly know some of the species in their winter plumage.

4.8.1 Red-throated diver (*Gavia stellata*)

Sterntaucher (D) – Rødstrubet lom (DK) – Plongeon catmarin (F) – Strolaga minore (I) – Smålom (N) – Roodkeelduiker (NL) – Smålom (S)

Description: Illustration page 134. Sea diver, that reminds one of a large duck both in flight and on the water. There are four species of sea divers worldwide. The Red-throated diver is the smallest, being 53-69 cm long and weighing 1.500-1.700 g, and is the only sea diver breeding in Spitsbergen, apart from the Great Northern diver of which a few single pairs are breeding on Bjørnøya in the far south. Their long, pointed, slightly down-bent beak is characteristic, together with the brownish-red throat and the grey head. Male and female birds look the same. In flight the long slim neck is slightly bent downwards, which gives these divers a very specific silhouette. Typical observations are either in flight or near small freshwater lakes in the tundra or sitting on the water where they will quickly retreat if anything is coming close. Red-throated divers float deep in the water and have a very elegant outline, that is always bent a

little forward. When walking, which the bird will only do if necessary, it looks rather clumsy as the legs are far back under the body. Red-throated divers call frequently when in flight; their monotonous calls carry a long way.
Distribution/Migrations: The Red throated diver has a circumpolar distribution in the Arctic and sub-Arctic down into the boreal zone. In Svalbard, they are most common on the west coast of Spitsbergen, in the southeast (Tusenøyane) and on Bjørnøya. They come to their breeding grounds in May or June and spend a long summer in the North, well into September or even October. Then, they move south, into coastal waters anywhere from Norway to the Mediterranean.
Biology: Pairs usually breed on their own; only occasionally will you see several pairs of Red-throated divers close to each other. Usually they build their nests on flat tundra on the shores of small lakes; occasionally also on little islands within such waters. Being good divers, as the name suggests, they find their food in the sea: They live mostly on small fish, but will additionally take plant pieces and invertebrates (mostly insects) on shore. In late June or early July, as soon as the lake near the nest is free of ice, the female will lay one to three eggs (normally two). Both parents take part in the 26-28 days of incubating, and in feeding the chick(s) until they become independent after six to seven weeks.
Miscellaneous: The regional population size is unknown, but it will not be large. Red-throated divers are beautiful, elegant birds, and the sight of a Red-throated diver next to a romantic little lake in the tundra is a great experience. They are, however, very shy and will leave the nest quickly as soon as they see somebody, even at a distance of 100 or 200 metres; eggs and chicks will then cool down or fall victim to an Arctic fox, Great skua or Glaucous gull. Thus great care is needed. Keep a good distance away and be aware of your silhouette when you walk over the hills, suddenly appearing in a Red-throated diver's view.

For good photos, you will need a very good telephoto lens, a tripod and you should be on your own and have a lot of time – or you have to be very quick when they are flying over you.

4.8.2 Northern fulmar (*Fulmarus glacialis*)

Eissturmvogel (D) – Mallemuk (DK) – Pétrel fulmar (F) – Procellaria cenerina (I) – Havhest (N) – Noordse stormvogel (NL) – Stormfågel (S)

Description: Illustration page 134. Length 45-53 cm, 650-1,000 g in weight. The streamlined body is dark grey without any significant contrast, unlike gulls. There are different colour variations (morphs) of the fulmar; the dark-grey one is common in Spitsbergen, and the lighter one is common further south, for example in Iceland. In flight they are easily recognised by their stiff wings and their very elegant, perfectly controlled long glides, often just above the crests of waves; a behaviour not shown by gulls. The small tube on top of the beak makes them unmistakable from short range.

Distribution/Migrations: Northern fulmars have a wide range from Newfoundland and northern France, up to Spitsbergen where they breed almost everywhere on steep cliffs; they are not breeding on the remote, high arctic islands in the far northeast. Outside the breeding season, they are truly pelagic, which means that they will stay on the high seas at all times and not come to land. They spend most of the year around Spitsbergen except for the darkest months, when they move a little bit south towards the open Atlantic. The main breeding areas in Svalbard are on the west coast of Spitsbergen and Bjørnøya.
Biology: Northern fulmars breed in loose colonies on steep cliffs. They live off squid, small fish and plankton and find their prey close to the surface on the open sea and in drift ice, covering huge distances on their search for food.

Belonging to the tubenoses, they are closely related to the Albatrosses of the southern hemisphere and, just like these, they have a slow reproduction rate but a high life expectancy. They can reach ages of more than 60 years. In late May, they lay a single egg into a very simple nest or even directly on rocks. Both parents sit for about 50 days. Adults and chick can defend the nest effectively by spitting very smelly and sticky oil, and they can aim quite well.
Miscellaneous: Northern fulmars are not related to gulls but belong to the tubenoses, most of which live in the southern hemisphere. The size of the population in Svalbard is not known, but they are among the most commonly seen birds in the area. They are always around ships, often in large numbers. The view of a fulmar that glides elegantly over breaking waves, is an impressive and beautiful image of the adaptation of wildlife to a harsh environment.

4.8.3 Common eider (*Somateria mollissima*)

Eiderente (D) – Ederfugl (DK) – Eider à duvet (F) – Edrodone comune (I) – Ærfugl (N) – Eidereend (NL) – Ejder (S)

Description: Illustration page 135. The Common eider is a large diving duck (58 cm long, 1.2-2.8 kg in weight) and can hardly be confused with any other species in Spitsbergen. King eiders are the possible exception, as there may be a pair of King eiders amongst a flock of Common eiders. The females are indeed very similar, so distinguishing female King and Common eiders is rather for the experienced birdwatcher. This is, on the other hand, a marginal problem, as King eiders are quite rare in Svalbard. Within Common eiders, males and females are easily distinguished: The male catches the eye with a contrast-rich plumage, the details of which change with age, whereas the female has a brown camouflage plumage. Distinctive is the shallow forehead, which contrasts with the bulging forehead of the King eider.
Distribution/Migrations: Common eider ducks are widely distributed in the Arctic and sub-Arctic. They spend the winter largely in the breeding areas; only the northernmost populations move further south. Common eiders from Svalbard winter in northern Norway and Iceland. In Svalbard, they breed everywhere in the

archipelago in dense colonies on small islands that are inaccessible for Arctic foxes, once the ice is broken up.

Biology: Male and female stay together from autumn onwards and then in many cases for several years, but they do not pair for life. The breeding season starts as soon as the nesting sites are free of snow (late May – mid June). The female builds the nest, a shallow hole in the tundra upholstered with bits of plants and down, and then lays four to six eggs, occasionally even more. Sometimes two females share a nest. The well-camouflaged female sits for 24 to 26 days, living on her fat reserves during this period. The male will stay near the nest to begin with, but then joins other males in larger groups for moulting. As soon as the chicks have hatched, they follow their mother to the water and stay there, near the coast, until late summer or autumn.

A typical system for raising the offspring is the formation of a "Kindergarten" where a few females take care of a large group of young birds.

Miscellaneous: The Svalbard population is estimated at somewhere between 13,500 and 27,500 breeding pairs, not including non-breeding individuals and young birds. In the early 20th century, trappers collected down from the nests, which is still being done in so-called "Eider-farms" in Iceland and, to a very limited degree, in Spitsbergen. Provided it is done carefully, it does not do any harm to the adults or the eggs. Nowadays, Common eiders are protected, and most of their important breeding islands have been declared bird sanctuaries where all traffic is generally banned during the breeding season. Many eggs and chicks fall victim to Glaucous gulls and Arctic foxes. Polar bears that are "stranded" on islands with Common eider colonies will live on scrambled eggs for several weeks, reducing breeding success to zero.

As with other birds, human visitors have to be careful during the breeding season to avoid disturbances, which can be difficult due to the good camouflage of the females; this reduces predation of eggs and chicks.

4.8.4 King eider (*Somateria spectabilis*)

Prachteiderente (D) – Kongeederfugl (DK) – Eider à tête grise (F) – Re degli Edredoni (I) – Praktærfugl (N) – Koningseider (NL) – Praktejder (S)

Description: Illustration page 135. With a length of 55 cm and a weight of 1.5-1.8 kg, the King eider is slightly smaller than the Common eider. The difference between the females of both species is confined to some small details. Distinguishing the males is much easier: The male King eider has a grey head, a bulging forehead and a read beak which is a real eye-catcher. Another difference is the black back (Common eider: white back), which can be seen even from a distance.

Distribution/Migrations: King eiders have a circumpolar distribution and are largely confined to arctic latitudes, even more so than the Common eider. In Svalbard, the King eider is generally rare, but most common on the central west coast and at Reinsdyrflya. So far as is known, they spend the winter on the coast of northern Norway.

Biology: The preferred habitat is flat tundra with small freshwater ponds. King eiders live on a range of invertebrates and crustaceans which they find on the bottom near the shoreline. They do not breed in colonies, but form small groups after the breeding period. They come back to the breeding areas slightly later than the Common eiders and lay four to six eggs, which are incubated by the female for 22 to 24 days. The male leaves the nest shortly after egg laying. The female leaves together with the chicks before these can fly, to join other females on the water.
Miscellaneous: The male King eider is a beautifully coloured bird that is high on the wish list of many birdwatchers who come to Spitsbergen. It needs a bit of luck to see them. Check carefully any large flocks of Common eiders, as a King eider or two may occasionally mix in with them. King eiders are usually quite shy in Spitsbergen and accordingly difficult to photograph.

4.8.5 Long-tailed duck (*Clangula hyemalis*)

Eisente (D) – Havlit (DK) – Harelde de Miquelon (F) – Moretta codona (I) – Havelle (N) – Ijseend (NL) – Alfågel (S)

Description: Illustration page 135. Relatively large duck with marked sexual dimorphism: Due to their long tail, which alone is a good 12 cm long, males reach 55 cm in length, females only 40 cm. The weight is for both 650-900 g. Both have a contrast-rich plumage. Most conspicuous are the white ring around the neck of the female and the white side of the head of the male.

Long-tailed ducks have a complicated moulting pattern: They moult three times per year; before breeding, in late summer and in late autumn. In Spitsbergen, they have their breeding plumage.
Distribution/Migrations: Long-tailed ducks occur in the sub- and high-Arctic around the pole and live both in mountain areas and in flat tundra; in Spitsbergen mainly in lowlands with small lakes near the west coast. Northern European Long-tailed ducks leave Spitsbergen in October or even November to spend the winter in northern Norway or the northern Baltic sea.
Biology: Long-tailed ducks have a mixed diet of some plants, but mainly mussels, larvae and little crustaceans. They nest on dry patches of tundra near small ponds. Males tend to return to the same nest each year and like to keep some distance from their nearest neighbour. As soon as the snow-melt allows, normally in late June, the females lay five to nine eggs and sit for about four weeks, while the males gather at the coast in groups for moulting. The female stays with her chicks near a lake or on the coast, until they can fly after five to six weeks.
Miscellaneous: Long-tailed ducks are skilled flyers and can reach 100 km/h.

4.8.6 Pink-footed goose (*Anser brachyrhynchus*)

Kurzschnabelgans (D) – Kortnæbbet gås (DK) – Oie à bec court (F) – Oca delle zampe rosse (I) – Kortnebbgås (N) – Kleine rietgans (NL) – Kortnæbbet gås (S)

Description: Illustration page 136. The Pink-footed goose is a medium-sized goose (length 60-75 cm, weight 2.2-3.5 kg) with a relatively short neck, largely black beak and pink legs. Resembling the Bean goose (*Anser fabalis*) or the Greylag goose (*Anser anser*) to some degree, its plumage appears to be less rich in contrast compared to that of the Barnacle goose.

Distribution/Migrations: Pink-footed geese are high arctic birds that breed in Iceland, East Greenland and Svalbard, where they feel at home on the whole archipelago, particularly the western parts. They spend the winter near the coasts of the North Sea and use the island Andøya in northern Norway as an important resting place during their migration. When they arrive in Svalbard in mid-May, it is some days before they continue to the actual breeding areas. Adventdalen is an important resting site for the first days after the spring migration, and other areas with high densities of Pink-footed geese include Sassendalen, Colesdalen, Reindalen, the west coast between Isfjord and Bellsund and north of Isfjord (Daudmannsøyra) and southern Dickson Land.

Biology: Leaves and buds are on the menu of Pink-footed geese. They arrive in the breeding areas in mid or late May and breed individually or in small colonies on the tundra near cliffs. In early June, the female will lay two to five, exceptionally even seven eggs and sit for almost four weeks. The male does not directly take part, but will guard the nest and defend it if necessary. The young birds leave the nest quickly and will have learnt to fly at an age of two months. Moulting of the adults takes place in July. During moulting, they cannot fly and will form larger flocks for safety, until they fly back south in September. The family will stay together until the next spring migration.

Miscellaneous: The Pink-footed goose is the most numerous goose in Svalbard, but is hunted both there and in the wintering areas and is thus quite shy; they may leave the nest when disturbed even from a distance of more than a kilometre! Exposed eggs or chicks are likely to be taken by predators such as Glaucous gulls or Arctic foxes; Pink-footed geese are at higher risk than other geese in Svalbard due to their low threshold against disturbance. Be as careful as possible in sensitive areas (see above) at relevant times or try to avoid these areas altogether. Keep your distance from nests and moulting birds. Resist the desire to approach to take photos.

The population has increased significantly from about 20,000 in the 1970s to 60,000 in 2007 and this trend will probably continue, especially if temperatures keep rising due to climatic changes. Pink-footed geese could then occur in higher numbers in areas along the west coast of Spitsbergen and the tundra areas of southwestern Edgeøya.

4.8.7 Barnacle goose (*Branta leucopsis*)

Weißwangengans (D) – Bramgås (DK) – Bernache nonnette (F) – Oca a faccia bianca (I) – Hvitkinngås (N) – Brandgans (NL) – Vitkindad gås (S)

Description: Illustration page 136. Barnacle geese are medium-sized geese (58-70 cm long, 1.5-2 kg in weight) with contrasty plumage: black neck and partially white head. They are easily distinguished from the other two commonly breeding geese in Spitsbergen.

Distribution/Migrations: Barnacle geese breed in three different areas: Northeast Greenland, Svalbard and northwestern Russia down to the Baltic sea. Birds from Svalbard spend the winter in northern England and southern Scotland, using Bjørnøya as a resting place on the way down south and the west coast of Norway during the spring migration. Barnacle geese from Greenland winter in Iceland and western Scotland, and those from Russia on the German and Dutch North Sea coast. They spend a couple of days after the spring migration mainly around Vårsolbukta and the Hornsund area, before they move on to their breeding areas.

The most important breeding areas in Svalbard are the west coast of Spitsbergen and Tusenøyane.

Biology: Rock terraces on top of cliffs and small islands in lakes or near the coast are their preferred breeding habitat, where they are largely undisturbed by foxes. They lay four or five eggs on which the female will sit for 24-25 days. The male will stay around and defend the nest against foxes or other predators. As soon as the chicks have hatched, the goose family will leave the nest and spend the following weeks on rich tundra near a lake or the coast, so that they can retreat to the water in case of any danger. This time is also the moulting period of the adult birds, so the whole family is unable to fly for some weeks until the young geese are ready for take-off at an age of 40-45 days. After moulting, Barnacle geese will gather in large numbers in areas with rich vegetation, where they will build up energy for the long flight to the wintering grounds. The family will stay together until the next spring. Barnacle geese are vegetarians and feed on plants and mosses.

Miscellaneous: Barnacle geese that walk through the settlement of Ny Ålesund without hesitation, are much less nervous about human presence than Pink-footed geese which have been hunted for a long time in Spitsbergen. Barnacle geese were driven near to extinction in Svalbard, but have recovered well, and limited hunting may be re-opened in the future. The overall population is stable or even growing slowly, with an estimated 25,000-30,000 birds in the year 2000. The strong concentration of large numbers during certain times of their migration makes Barnacle geese vulnerable to disturbances.

4.8.8 Rock ptarmigan (*Lagopus muta hyperborea*)

Alpenschneehuhn (D) – Fjeldrype (DK) – Lagopède des Alpes (F) – Pernice bianca (I) – Svalbardrype (N) – Sneeuw hoen (NL) – Fjällripa (S)

Description: Illustration page 137. Ptarmigan are 35-40 cm long and 490-1.200 g in weight. During the winter they are white, but have a brownish camouflage-plumage in summer. Males moult later than females. The well-camouflaged birds are difficult to see, but unmistakable once you have spotted them. Normally, you will hear them before you see them.
Distribution/Migrations: Ptarmigan can be found in high latitudes and mountain areas around the North Pole. The subspecies *L. m. hyperboreus* is confined to Svalbard and Franz Josef Land. In Svalbard, they breed on all islands and they are the only birds that do not leave the breeding areas during the winter. As many as 25 subspecies are described worldwide, although differences are minimal.
Biology: Ptarmigans are vegetarians. The male occupies the breeding territory as early as mid March. This is often a steep, rocky slope, where some vegetation is still available. Mating takes place in May and egg laying (nine to eleven eggs) in early or mid May, depending on the timing of the snow melt. The female sits for three weeks.
Miscellaneous: The size of the population in Svalbard is not known, but ptarmigan are quite abundant. In suitable terrain, there may be three to five males with one or two hens each per square kilometre. In Spitsbergen, ptarmigan are hunted by locals in autumn and early winter.

The scientific name used to be *Lagopus mutus*, but it has recently been changed into *Lagopus muta*, because *lagopus* is derived from an ancient Greek word of feminine gender, which indicates "hare foot".

4.8.9 Snow bunting (*Plectrophenax nivalis*)

Schneeammer (D) – Snespurv (DK) – Bruant des neiges (F) – Zigolo della neve (I) – Snøspurv (N) – Sneeuwgors (NL) – Snösparv (S)

Description: Illustration page 137. Snow buntings (length 16-17 cm, weight 25-40 g) are smaller than Blackbirds and have a contrast-rich plumage with white belly, pale head and brownish-spotted wings and backs. The male has a completely white head, is largely black and white and thus more contrast-rich than the female. Snow buntings are not only the most colourful birds of their small size in Spitsbergen, but also the only singing bird in the high Arctic.
Distribution/Migrations: The Snow bunting has a circumpolar distribution in the Arctic and spends the winter in temperate latitudes. In Svalbard, it can be seen everywhere from late March or April to late August or even September. These birds migrate to the White Sea area in northern Russia or to the steppe north of the Caspian Sea or Kazakhstan.

Biology: Snow buntings feed on seeds and, to a lesser extent, insects. They are not too particular with regards to their breeding habitat, as long as the nearest neighbour is not too close. Nests may be anywhere, in lush tundra areas, near large seabird colonies or on thinly vegetated mountain slopes near the coast or far inland. The small, well isolated nest is usually well hidden. Upon arrival, they may build a small cave in the snow for temporary protection from severe weather. Shortly after arrival in the breeding areas, the male will establish a territory and attract a female with its beautiful voice. The female will lay four to seven eggs in late May or early June and sit for 12 to 14 days. The male does not take part in this, but assists while the chick needs food for 12 to 14 days after hatching.
Miscellaneous: The exact size of the breeding population in Svalbard is not known, but it will be variable around several thousand breeding pairs. There is no evidence for a long-term increase or decrease of the regional population. Snow buntings are a common sight. Their melodic voice is a welcome sound in the tundra, announcing the end of the winter.

4.8.10 Purple sandpiper (*Calidris maritima*)

Meerstrandläufer (D) – Sortgrå ryle (DK) – Bécasseau violet (F) – Piovanello violetto (I) – Fjæreplytt (N) – Paarse Strandloper (NL) – Skärsnäppa (S)

Description: Illustration page 138. The Purple sandpiper is a small, sturdy wader (21 cmlong, weight 60-100 g) with a 3 cm long, slightly down-bent beak. The sexes look alike. During summer, the plumage is brownish with a pale belly. Amongst the small birds that occur on the coast, often on the beach, and in the tundra of Spitsbergen, the Purple sandpiper is the most common one and it is not unusual to see several together.
Distribution/Migrations: Purple sandpipers occur from northeastern Canada to northwestern Russia. In Svalbard, they breed on flat, dry tundra. In early May, they come to the breeding areas and stay to late August or September. They spend the winter in Scandinavia.
Biology: Purple sandpipers live on crustaceans and insects and accordingly spend a lot of time on the shoreline and in the tidal zone, searching for food. They can also be seen further inland and at some altitude. Breeding pairs build a nest of plant material on the tundra. Both parents take their share of incubating, altogether about four weeks, but the male spends most time on the eggs and with the offspring, leaving the nest soon after hatching.
Miscellaneous: If you approach too close to the nest, the Purple sandpiper pretends to be injured and runs away, catching your eye with a raised wing, trying to lead the potential predator away from the nest. If you see this, you must move away quickly to make sure that eggs and chicks are not exposed any longer than necessary. You can follow the bird until it flies back, as it will lead you away from the nest. But when looking for food on the beach, Purple sandpipers are not shy and are quite easy to observe.

4.8.11 Grey phalarope (*Phalaropus fulicarius*)

Thorshühnchen (D) – Thorshane (DK) – Phalarope à bec large (F) – Falaropo beccolargo (I) – Polarsvømmesnipe (N) – Rosse Franjepoot (NL) – Brednäbbad simsnäppa (S)

Description: Illustration page 138. The breeding plumage of the Grey phalarope is rusty red, apart from the more camouflaged upper sides of the wings and head and a white spot around the eyes. It is a small bird (length 20 cm, weight 40-75 g). There are some unusual differences between the sexes: The female is not only slightly larger, but also has the more contrast-rich plumage, unlike the normal situation with most birds. This has to do with its unusual breeding behaviour (see below).

Distribution/Migrations: The Grey phalarope occurs in the high Arctic everywhere around the North Pole. In Svalbard, it breeds everywhere near the coast, but is most abundant on the west coast and western north coast of Spitsbergen, in Tusenøyane and on Bjørnøya. In winter, Grey phalaropes like it warm and migrate as far as the Tropics. Those coming from Svalbard, probably winter near the coast of West Africa. They come back to the breeding areas in early or mid June and stay until late July or early August. The females leave first, and the males stay until breeding is completed.

Biology: Grey phalaropes breed in solitary pairs or loose colonies on flat, moist tundra with rich vegetation, often near small ponds. Often, they return to the same nest for several years. They find their food, mostly insects and small crustaceans, in the tundra in small ponds, or on the coast. Sometimes they are seen sitting on shallow water, rotating quickly to whirl up prey.

Compared to many other birds, Grey phalaropes have swopped roles for breeding. Laying the four eggs in mid June is still the female's business, but then the male takes over for incubating (18-20 days) and taking care of the offspring (16-18 days). This enables the female to breed again with a different male. Once the second set of eggs is laid, the female will move south.

Miscellaneous: The wintering plumage is grey (hence the name) and rather unsightly, hence the common desire of many birdwatchers, who have seen this bird in Europe during the winter, to see it in the Arctic in summer plumage. The breeding behaviour also makes this bird quite interesting. With some luck and in the right place, you may see several individuals together on the beach where they can actually be quite approachable, if you are careful.

4.8.12 Arctic tern (*Sterna paradisaea*)

Küstenseeschwalbe (D) – Havterne (DK) – Sterne arctique (F) – Rondine di mare coda lunga (I) – Rødnebbterne (N) – Noordse stern (NL) – Silvertärna (S)

Description: Illustration page 138. The Arctic tern is the only tern that breeds in Spitsbergen, and it is thus unmistakable. Female and male look the same to human eyes. Being 35 cm long and weighing 100-125 g, the Arctic tern is a relatively small bird.

Distribution/Migrations: The Arctic tern has a circumpolar distribution in the sub- and high Arctic. It is the northernmost breeding tern species and the bird with the longest annual migration: The breeding sites in the north and the wintering sites as far south as coastal Antarctica are up to 15,000 kilometres apart! Arctic terns return to their breeding sites in late May or early June and stay there until late August or early September.

They breed in the vicinity of settlements, such as near the camping site and near the shore of Adventfjord in Longyearbyen or inside Ny Ålesund. If you come to Spitsbergen in the summer, you should know what you have to expect near Arctic tern colonies (see below; Miscellaneous).

Biology: Arctic terns breed in more or less dense colonies on flat tundra, mostly near the shore and on the beach or on small islands. They are often seen diving down onto the water surface to catch small fish, crustaceans or insects.

They will start breeding as soon as the nesting areas are free of snow, but may lose a whole season if the snow melt comes very late. The nest is in a little depression directly on the ground. Here, the female lays two eggs (occasionally one or three), which both parents sit on for about three weeks. The chick will leave the nest after three days, stay another three weeks with its parents and then become independent.

As with other sea birds, Arctic terns have a low reproduction rate, but a high life expectancy. One individual was seen 21 years after ringing and had obviously changed much less in appearance than the biologist who had ringed it.

Miscellaneous: Arctic terns defend their colonies fiercely against any intruders: predating birds, Arctic foxes, Polar bears and humans are all dive-bombed without hesitation and occasionally scratched by the sharp beaks. This can annoy Polar bears to such a degree that they decide to retreat. If you come under attack from Arctic terns, leave the area quickly. Do not try to photograph the nest (same as with any other bird). The birds will attack the highest part of you with a lot of noise. The easy solution is to hold up your tripod, walking stick, shooting iron, or partner calmly over your head – but never hit these small and vulnerable birds; don't even wave whatever you hold up. As Arctic terns defend their colonies so effectively, other birds such as Common eider like to breed amongst them. If annoyed too much by persistent aggressors such as foxes or bears, the terns may try to find another place in the next season.

The total population numbers around 10,000 breeding pairs (feels rather like 10,000,000,000 near aggressive colonies); the population trend is unknown.

4.8.13 Great skua (*Stercorarius skua*)

Skua (D) – Storkjove (DK) – Grande labbe (F) – Stercorario maggiore (I) – Storjo (N) – Grote jager (NL) – Storlabb (S)

Description: Illustration page 139. The Great skua is the largest skua (50-58 cm, 1.2-1.8 kg in weight) and has a rather uniform, brown camouflage plumage. The only white patches are on the underside of the wings and thus visible only in flight. With its broad wings and the strong beak, which has a slightly curved point, it resembles a bird of prey.

Distribution/Migrations: The Great skua has a primarily sub-arctic distribution and breeds in the eastern north Atlantic in Iceland, the Færøe Islands, Shetland Islands and Norway. The first breeding pair in Svalbard was recorded in 1970 on Bjørnøya and in 1976 on Spitsbergen but since then, the species has occupied most parts of the archipelago with the exception of the high-arctic northeast. Great skuas spend the winter on open ocean, not too far south of the breeding areas.

Biology: Great skuas like fish, especially if others have caught it. As with other skuas, they chase other seabirds until they drop their prey. They also take eggs and chicks from other birds when the opportunity arises.

Great skuas lay two eggs into a shallow nest on flat tundra. Both parents sit for a good four weeks. The family will then stay near the nest for another six to seven weeks, until the chicks can fly.

Miscellaneous: Great skuas are strong birds and defend their nest and offspring aggressively. Leave quickly if you happen to become the target of a divebombing skua.

Genetically, they are very similar to the Arctic skua. Great skuas are primarily Southern Ocean birds, where five out of six species breed (South Polar skua, Brown skua etc.).

4.8.14 Pomarine skua (*Stercorarius pomarinus*)

Spatelraubmöwe (D) – Mellemkjove (DK) – Labbe pomarin (F) – Stercorario mezzano (I) – Polarjo (N) – Middelste jager (NL) – Bredstjärtad labb (S)

Description: Illustration page 139. Medium-sized (44-51 cm long, 550-900 g in weight) skua with long tail, that looks like a spoon from the side. The sexes look alike. The plumage has a pronounced dark-light contrast, although there is a rare, completely dark morph. Pomarine skuas can be confused with the far more common Arctic skuas.

Distribution/Migrations: Pomarine skuas breed in the high Arctic of North America and Siberia. They spend most of their time at sea. For breeding, they come to flat tundra areas near the coast, often near lakes or rivers. Svalbard is not amongst the main breeding areas, but nevertheless, Pomarine skuas are regularly seen around the archipelago. During the winter they like it warm and move to tropical latitudes off west Africa.

Biology: Small rodents are the preferred prey of the Pomarine skua, which is also the explanation why they do not breed in Svalbard. There they prefer to steal food from other birds and take eggs and chicks.
Miscellaneous: Despite not being a breeding bird in Svalbard, the Pomarine skua is regularly seen and for many dedicated birdwatchers, sightings are highlights of a Spitsbergen voyage. Chances are best near the ice edge.

4.8.15 Arctic skua (*Stercorarius parasiticus*)

Schmarotzerraubmöwe (D) – Almindelig kjove (DK) – Labbe parasite (F) – Labbo (I) – Tyvjo (N) – Kleine jager (NL) – Kustlabb (S)

Description: Illustration page 139. The Arctic skua is a compact, medium-sized skua (length including tail feathers 46 cm, weight 350-600 g). It has a contrast-rich plumage with dark cap, white neck and belly and dark back and upper wings. The Arctic skua is often confused with the Pomarine skua and Long-tailed skua, although the latter two are much less common in Spitsbergen. The size and the shape of the tail are diagnostic. The Long-tailed skua is slightly smaller and more elegant in shape; the Arctic skua has a shorter tail than both Long-tailed and Pomarine skuas.

As well as the "normal", contrasty plumage, there is a dark morph with completely dark feathers. The dark morph is rare in Svalbard.
Distribution/Migrations: The Arctic skua breeds everywhere in the Arctic and sub-Arctic. In Svalbard, it breeds in tundra areas anywhere in the archipelago, but is most common on the west and north coasts of Spitsbergen. During the winter the open sea is their preferred habitat, usually off west and southwest Africa.
Biology: Single pairs of the Arctic skua breed on rather flat tundra, often on a very shallow rise in the ground for a good overview. Arctic skuas come to the breeding areas in early June, often returning to the same nest. After egg-laying in early July, both parents incubate the eggs (one or two) for 26 days. Soon after hatching, the young bird(s) leave the nest together with the parents. The family stays together until the chick can fly after about five weeks. As the Latin name suggests, Arctic skuas do not like to look for food themselves, but prefer to chase other birds such as Kittiwakes or Brünich's Guillemots in flight until they drop their prey. Occasionally, they may also steal eggs or chicks from other birds. In areas where rodents occur, these are another welcome food source for the Arctic skua.
Miscellaneous: The Arctic skua is by far the most abundant skua in Svalbard, with an estimated local population of about 1,000 breeding pairs, and it is a common sight on flat tundra. Because of its good camouflage, it can be difficult to see. If you approach close to a nest, one of the adults will pretend to be hurt to lure you away. If you see this, then move away quickly either where you came from, or you can also follow the bird as it will lead you away from the nest. If you approach even closer, then the bird will attack. If this happens, move quickly away from the nest. Do not stop to take any photographs.

4.8.16 Long-tailed skua (*Stercorarius longicaudus*)

Falkenraubmöwe (D) – Lille kjove (DK) – Labbe à longue queue (F) – Labbo coda-lunga (I) – Fjelljo (N) – Kleinste jager (NL) – Fjällabb (S)

Description: Illustration page 140. Judged by its length of about 53 cm, the Long-tailed skua is larger than the Arctic skua, but in fact it is smaller, as this measurement includes the tail feathers which alone are 15 cm long. It weighs 220-350 g and has a smaller and more elegant appearance. With a dark cap, yellowish-white chest and neck but otherwise brown plumage, it resembles the Arctic skua. The long tail and the elegant flight resembling that of a swallow, are diagnostic for the Long-tailed skua.
Distribution/Migrations: The Long-tailed skua has a circumpolar distribution in the Arctic, including some scattered breeding pairs in northern Norway. As its main prey, rodents, are lacking in Svalbard, it is very rare in this area. There is at least one breeding pair on the northern side of Kongsfjord, possibly another one in the northern Isfjord area and it is occasionally seen in the drift ice, possibly on the way from or to its breeding grounds in Greenland or the Russian Arctic. Long-tailed skuas spend the winter in the south Atlantic.
Biology: Rodents are the main prey of the Long-tailed skua. It is accordingly quite common in East Greenland, but rare in Spitsbergen, where it has to make do with insects, carrion and marine crustaceans.

Solitary pairs breed on flat, dry tundra. Both parents incubate the two eggs (rarely one) for 23 days. The chicks stay a few days only on the nest and then stay for another three weeks with their parents until they are able to fly.
Miscellaneous: Breeding Long-tailed skuas may be curious and come quite close to visitors. Of course you must still keep a good distance from the nest.

4.8.17 Sabine's gull (*Larus sabini*)

Schwalbenmöwe (D) – Sabinemåge (DK) – Mouette de Sabine (F) – Gabbiano a coda forcuta (I) – Sabinemåke (N) – Vorkstaartmeeuw (NL) – Tärnmås (S)

Description: Illustration page 140. Being 33 cm long and weighing only 150-210 g, the Sabine's gull is a rather small gull. It is the only gull in Svalbard with a black head and is thus easy to identify – if you happen to see this very rare bird at all. The sexes look alike. The flight of a Sabine's gull is very elegant and resembles a swallow's; the wing tips are black.
Distribution/Migrations: The Sabine's gull breeds in the sub-Arctic and high Arctic from north America, Greenland and Svalbard to the Russian Arctic. With a few breeding pairs in northern parts only (Moffen, Lågøya and a very few other sites in the north and northeast of Nordaustland), it is one of Svalbard's rarest breeding birds. Sabine's gulls spend the winter off southwest Africa and southwestern South America.
Biology: Important food sources include small fishes and marine invertebrates, occasionally also eggs and chicks from other birds. The Sabine's gull nests on flat,

dry tundra in the vicinity of small ponds. Chicks hatch after 23 to 26 days from the two or three eggs. They leave the nest after only a few hours, to follow their parents to the coast or to a pond where they wait until they are able to fly. Young birds probably spend their first summer in the wintering areas.
Miscellaneous: There are probably fewer than ten breeding pairs in Svalbard and sightings are accordingly very rare. Similarly globally, with about 10,000 breeding pairs, this species is not very abundant. Trained eyes with good binoculars or telescopes may be lucky to spot it near Moffen or north of Nordaustland, especially if there is drift ice around. Sabine's gulls like to breed in colonies of aggressive Arctic terns that chase any aggressor away.

The species owes its name to Sir Edward Sabine, who discovered the bird in 1818 in Greenland.

4.8.18 Ivory gull (*Pagophila eburnea*)

Elfenbeinmöwe (D) – Ismåge (DK) – Goéland sénateur (F) – Gabbiano eburneo (I) – Ismåke (N) – Ivoormeeuw (NL) – Ismås (S)

Description: Illustration page 140. The Ivory gull is a medium-sized gull (length 44 cm, weight 400-500 g) with completely white plumage, yellow beak and black eyes and legs.
Distribution/Migrations: Ivory gulls breed in certain areas in the high Arctic. In Svalbard, they breed in the high-arctic northeastern and eastern parts of the archipelago (Sjuøyane – Nordaustland – Kong Karls Land). Colonies are small, changing their location after a while and usually situated on steep cliffs, usually far inland on Nunatakker (plural of Nunatak, a mountain surrounded by glaciers). There are exceptions, as some Ivory gulls breed on flat tundra or smaller mountains near the coast.

Ivory gulls spend their lives mostly in waters with a lot of drift ice. They like to follow ships for a while and are thus regularly seen from ships in areas with drift ice, as well as in the vicinity of settlements, as they find food near rubbish dumps and sewage water outlets. Ivory gulls spend the winter probably near the ice edge.
Biology: Ivory gulls build a simple nest of plant material and lay one or two eggs in late June or early July. Both parents take part in incubation which lasts for about 25 days. The offspring will leave the nest after another seven weeks. They live on a wide selection of food, from small fishes and near-surface zooplancton to leftovers from Polar bear's meals and seal placenta. Glaucous gulls can be dangerous to eggs and chicks. Polar bears and Arctic foxes will plunder nests on flat ground.
Miscellaneous: The global population was estimated at 14,000 breeding pairs, most of them in the Russian Arctic, but a census in 2006 showed that recent numbers are much smaller, around one third of the original estimate. The reasons for this development are unknown, although the decreasing pack ice cover and environmental toxins are believed to be important factors. Ivory gulls from the Russian arctic were found to have high levels of PCB and DDE in their tissue.

4.8.19 Ross' gull (*Rhodostethia rosea*)

Rosenmöwe (D) – Rosenmåge (DK) – Mouette de Ross (F) – Gabbiano polare di Ross (I) – Rosenmåke (N) – Ross' meeuw (NL) – Rosenmås (S)

Description: Illustration page 141. Small (32 cm long, 200-250 g in weight), very elegant gull, resembling a swallow in flight. Light-grey upper side, otherwise whitewith black stripe around the neck and a shade of pink on the chest; black beak and red legs.
Distribution/Migrations: The most important breeding areas are in northeastern Siberia, east of the Taymyr peninsula. After breeding, they leave this area to spend the later summer at sea near the ice edge. In Spitsbergen, there was only one unconfirmed sighting of a breeding pair of the Ross' gull near Kapp Linné in 1955.
Biology: Ross' gulls feed on small crustaceans and fish. They breed on flat, boggy tundra on small islands in lakes and lay two or three eggs in mid June. Incubation lasts three weeks.
Miscellaneous: The Ross' gull is a very beautiful, rare, high-arctic bird and thus high on the wishlist of many birdwatchers. It is extremely rare in Svalbard, but it has even happened that strong northerly winds blow it down to the UK, where it then becomes an attraction for birdwatchers, until it disappears again after a short time.

4.8.20 Glaucous gull (*Larus hyperboreus*)

Eismöwe (D) – Gråmåge (DK) – Goéland bourgmestre (F) – Gabbiano bianco (I) – Polarmåke (N) – Grote burgemeester (NL) – Vittrut (S)

Description: Illustration page 141. The Glaucous gull is by far the largest of the regular gulls of Spitsbergen (65-78 cm, 1.3-2.2 kg in weight). It is not possible to distinguish the sexes by eye. The plumage is largely white, except for the light-grey upper wings. The size, and the absence of black wingtips, makes it easy to distinguish from Kittiwakes.
Distribution/Migrations: Glaucous gulls breed in all parts of the high Arctic and spend the winter in the open sea not too far from the breeding areas, or occasionally in coastal waters. They breed everywhere in Svalbard in seabird colonies.
Biology: In Svalbard, where rodents are absent, the Glaucous gull occupies the role of bird of prey. It takes almost anything it can swallow: Fish, mussels, crustaceans, eggs, chicks and even adult Kittiwakes, Brünich's guillemots and Little auks. It likes to breed in colonies of those species, much to their disgust, but often without any other breeding Glaucous gulls in the same area, unless food availability is very good. Glaucous gulls build a nest of grass, mosses and seaweed, usually in an elevated position. Both parents will incubate the two or three eggs for four weeks. For breeding, Glaucous gulls often return to the place where they were born. Once they have found a suitable nesting site, they will keep using it for several seasons.

Miscellaneous: There are several thousand breeding pairs in Svalbard, although exact counts are lacking. It is believed currently that the population is declining slightly. Being at the top of the food chain, Glaucous gulls accumulate high concentrations of environmental toxins in their fat tissue and liver.

4.8.21 Black-legged kittiwake (*Rissa tridactyla*)

Dreizehenmöwe (D) – Ride (DK) – Mouette tridactyle (F) – Gabbiano tridattilo (I) – Krykkje (N) – Drieteenmeeuw (NL) – Tretåig mås (S)

Description: Illustration page 142. Black-legged kittiwakes are medium-sized gulls with black legs, yellow beaks and grey upper wings with black tips. The sexes look alike. Length 41 cm, weight 330-350 g.
Distribution/Migrations: Kittiwakes are common everywhere in the Arctic and sub-Arctic. In Svalbard, there are dense colonies on steep rock cliffs in all parts of the archipelago, the largest being on Hopen and Bjørnøya. There are some breeding sites of a different sort on windowsills in Barentsburg and Pyramiden. The population in Svalbard is estimated at about 270,000 breeding pairs (one third of these being on Bjørnøya). They spend the winter on the open sea, not too far from the breeding areas.
Biology: Colonies are situated on steep cliffs where they can breed without being disturbed by Arctic foxes or Polar bears. Kittiwakes feed on a wide range of food, mainly crustaceans and fish, but they also follow fishing vessels. Their eggs and chicks and even adult Kittiwakes are preyed on by Arctic foxes, Glaucous gulls and the Great skua.

In contrast to other cliff breeders, Kittiwakes build a nest of plant material on narrow rock ledges. Egg-laying takes place in the first half of June. The female lays two eggs (three in the sub-Arctic), both parents sit for 27 days. Usually, one chick will hatch one or two days before the second one, and it is often only the older one that will survive.
Miscellaneous: A slight increase of the Svalbard population since the mid-1990s is, for unknown reasons (bad food availability?), being followed by a minor decrease. The population is however generally healthy and Kittiwakes are among the most commonly seen birds in Spitsbergen.

4.8.22 Atlantic puffin (*Fratercula arctica*)

Papageitaucher (D) – Lunde (DK) – Macareux moine (F) – Pulcinella di mare (I) – Lunde (N) – Papegaaiduiker (NL) – Lunnefågel (S)

Description: Illustration page 142. The Atlantic puffin is a relatively small member of the family of the alcids (length 30 cm, weight 320-550 g). Puffins in Svalbard are slightly larger than birds of the same species in the sub-Arctic (Iceland, Færøe Islands, Scotland, northern Norway). In summer it is unmistakable due to its strong, colourful beak.
Distribution/Migrations: Puffins breed mainly in the sub-Arctic, also in smaller numbers in high Arctic areas in the Atlantic (there is a similar species in the northern

Pacific). Most birds in Svalbard breed on Bjørnøya, but others are at home on the west and north coasts of Spitsbergen and as far as Sjuøyane, but in much smaller colonies compared to those in the sub-Arctic. There are a surprisingly large number of Puffins breeding on Vesle Tavleøya, the second-northernmost island of the archipelago.

The wintering areas are not exactly known but will be somewhere in the north Atlantic. Puffins return early to their breeding sites in early or mid May and stay well into August.

Biology: In the sub-Arctic, Puffins breed in large numbers in small caves on the top edge of steep cliffs. Lack of suitable soil and permafrost make this mostly impossible in Svalbard, so they have to breed on ledges of steep cliffs, as other auks, and occasionally in crevices between large boulders. Colonies are smaller and less dense than further south. Both parents incubate the single egg for six weeks. The chick stays at the nest for another five to ten weeks, until it is able to fly. The slow reproduction rate is balanced by a high life expectancy: Once a Puffin is fully grown, it has a good chance to reach an age of 30 years or even more.

Miscellaneous: Don't expect observation opportunities as good as in Iceland, the Færøer Islands, Scotland or Norway, but there is often a Puffin flying by. Recent years have seen dramatic collapses of breeding colonies for example in Lofoten (Norway) for reasons that are not yet fully understood, but overfishing is likely to be an important factor, directly or indirectly..

4.8.23 Common guillemot (*Uria aalge*)

Trottellumme (D) – (Atlantisk) Lomvie (DK) – Guillemot de Troïl (F) – Uria comune (I) – Lomvi (N) – Zeekoet (NL) – Sillgrissla (S)

Description: Illustration page 143. The Common guillemot has a white belly and is otherwise black; it is 41 cm tall and weighs 900-1,100 g. The mostly-sub-arctic Common guillemot is very similar to its high-arctic relative, the Brünich's guillemot. The different beaks enable experienced eyes to tell these two apart: the beak of the Common guillemot is longer and more pointed and it does not have the white stripe along the upper mandible, which is characteristic for the Brünich's guillemot. Also, the white belly can be used for identification: The Brünich's guillemot has a white stripe with a rather pointed end, running from the belly towards the throat; this is more rounded in the case of the Common. A small proportion of the Common guillemots have white 'spectacles'.

Distribution/Migrations: The common guillemot does not breed in Spitsbergen, apart from a few small occurrences in Bellsund and at the northern tip of Prins Karls Forland. The northernmost large colonies are on Bjørnøya where Common and Brünich's guillemots breed in mixed colonies with hundreds of thousands of breeding pairs of each species. The Common guillemot thus tends to inhabit more sub-arctic areas, but is also found everywhere at higher latitudes and is one of the most numerous seabirds of the North. Probably spending the winter in open waters largely in the region of the

breeding colonies, they are not very migrative. Common guillemots breeding in the northernmost parts of the species' range (Bjørnøya) move a few hundred kilometres south towards the Norwegian coast.
Biology: Common guillemots are seabirds, which means that they spend all of their life at sea without coming to land, except in the breeding season. Their menu is more specialised than that of the Brünich's guillemot and comprises mostly fish which they catch at depths between 20 and 30 metres, exceptionally even beyond 100 metres.

The steeper and denser the colony site, the better the breeding success of the Common guillemot. One reason for this is protection against predators such as Arctic foxes and Glaucous gulls. The breeding cycle is very similar to the Brünich's guillemot. A single, pear-shaped egg is laid in late May or early June. Both parents sit for 32 days and take part in foraging for the chick for another three weeks until, still unable to fly, the chick has to jump from the cliff into the water or, if necessary, down onto the tundra. Many young birds die during this hazardous operation or fall victim to Arctic foxes. To reduce the risk, the breeding cycle is largely synchronized within a colony: The more chicks walking over the tundra at the same time, the smaller the risk for the individual bird to end up as fox food.
Miscellaneous: In 1987, the Common guillemots' colonies on Bjørnøya collapsed by 85 %. Out of approximately 245,000 breeding pairs from the year before, only 36,000 returned to breed. The Brünich's guillemot, which breeds at the same colonies in comparable numbers, was not affected. The reason was overfishing and thus a depletion of the food resources of the Common guillemot, whereas the Brünichs were better off because of their more varied diet. Since then, the breeding population of Common guillemots on Bjørnøya is recovering, but has not yet reached its original size.

4.8.24 Brünich's guillemot (*Uria lomvia*)

Dickschnabellumme (D) – Polarlomvie (DK) – Guillemot de Brünnich (F) – Uria grossa (I) – Polarlomvi (N) – Dikbekzeekoet (NL) – Spetsbergsgrissla (S)

Description: Illustration page 143. With their black back and head and white belly, Brünich's guillemots look like flying Adelie penguins. They are 41 cm tall and weigh 700-1,200 g. The high-arctic Brünich's guillemot is very similar to its close sub-arctic relative, the Common guillemot, which makes these two difficult to distinguish. The Brünich's guillemot has a shorter, thicker beak with a white stripe from the root almost to the tip on the lower edge of the upper mandible (see also above, description of the Common guillemot).
Distribution/Migrations: Brünich's guillemots are widely spread throughout the high Arctic. They appear in smaller numbers in northern Norway, with more substantial colonies in northern Iceland, Greenland and Jan Mayen and in very large numbers in Svalbard and Franz Josef Land. The population in Svalbard is estimated at around 850,000 breeding pairs, the largest colonies being on the southeastern coast of Spitsbergen, on Hopen and on Bjørnøya, but there are small and medium-sized

colonies everywhere in the archipelago. Brünich's guillemots from Svalbard winter in the open sea around Iceland, southern Greenland and Newfoundland. The regional population is largely stable, with only small fluctuations.
Biology: Brünich's guillemots nest on steep rock cliffs on narrow ledges, out of reach of Arctic foxes and Polar bears. Upon arrival of the birds in April or May, the nesting places are still inaccessible because of ice and snow. The female will lay one pear-shaped egg in late May or early June. Both parents sit for 32 days and feed the chick for three weeks until it has to jump down from the cliff, like young Common guillemots (see above). Brünich's guillemots feed mostly on fish and crustaceans.
Miscellaneous: Brünich's guillemots breeding in Spitsbergen may end up in a cooking pot in Greenland or Newfoundland. Despite pressure from hunting in the wintering areas, they do not seem to mind human visitors too much near their breeding place, if you move carefully and quietly. Guano-proof clothing is generally recommended near birdcliffs!

4.8.25 Little auk (*Alle alle*)

Krabbentaucher (D) – Søkonge (DK) – Mergule nain (F) – Gazza marina minore (I) – Alkekonge (N) – Kleine alk (NL) – Alkekung (S)

Description: Illustration page 144. Measuring 20 cm in length and weighing between 120 and 180 g, the Little auk is the smallest of the alcids in the North Atlantic. It has a stocky appearance with its large head, short beak and a strong neck. In flight, Little auks can be distinguished from Brünich's guillemots by their smaller size and faster wingbeats.
Distribution/Migrations: The Little auk is the most numerous seabird of the high Arctic. Apparantly, it finds Iceland too warm or, more probably, diet requirements force the Little auk to stay in areas with colder water masses, which it finds in the high Arctic from Baffin Island in Canada to Severnaya Zemlya in the Russian Arctic. In Svalbard, it nests almost everywhere, but the largest colonies are around the northwestern corner of Spitsbergen and in Bellsund and Hornsund. Dense colonies require certain geomorphological characteristics such as steep scree slopes with boulders of a certain size, as Little auks breed under boulders. A minimum size of rocks is needed to create hollows of sufficient size, but if they are too large, then Arctic foxes can plunder the nest. The largest colonies comprise several tens of thousands of breeding pairs, but exact surveys have not yet been carried out.

The Little auk is amongst the first migratory birds to return to their breeding sites in the high Arctic, where they arrive as early as April or early May. They leave in mid August and spend the winter in open sea near southwest Greenland.
Biology: During the breeding season, Little auks live primarily on crustaceans. They lay one single egg in the second half of June and incubate it for another 29 days. The chick stays for four weeks in the nest, until it can fly.
Miscellaneous: Attempts to count Little auk colonies in Spitsbergen have so far

been more or less unsuccessful because of great practical difficulties, but the regional population may exceed one million breeding pairs. Because of the large numbers, Little auks play a significant role for the terrestrial ecology, as they transport energy in the form of guano from the sea to the tundra. It is estimated that each Little auk carries about 250 g of natural fertilizer to the tundra during the breeding season.

Breeding colonies are always on steep scree slopes and thus rather difficult to access. It is almost impossible to see the nest as it is usually under large rocks or in crevices. Nevertheless, you can observe them at the colony, as they like to spend some time sitting on boulders and are not very afraid of humans, provided you do not move. It is important to stay outside the actual breeding area, as any intrusion would create disturbance. Patience is needed until, sooner or later, a Glaucous gull patrols the area and the Little auks take off. This is a good moment to move closer until you have reached the outer edge of the colony. After a while, the birds will come back, but remember that you have to be very calm and motionless. Sometimes, the colonies are very active and visits are then an exciting experience, but at other times it is quite calm and then there is not a lot to see. This is also the case when a strong wind is blowing or at other, unpredictable times when the birds may be out searching for food or at home watching TV.

There are several smaller Little auk colonies on steep scree slopes around Longyearbyen (the slopes of the Platåberg towards the settlement, near Gruve (mine) one, in the little valley that leads down from the plateau to the moraine of Longyearbreen, on the slopes above Nybyen and, a bit further away, on the slopes east of the entrance of Bjørndalen. With local knowledge and a rifle (for protection), you can see them by taking a short day trip from Longyearbyen, but some walking in steep, rocky terrain is necessary. Seeing a busy Little auk colony is an experience that you will not forget. The small, numerous, lively, noisy birds are the epitome of concentrated, intense life in the Arctic. An experienced birdwatcher once called them the "soul of the Arctic".

4.8.26 Black guillemot (*Cepphus grylle*)

Gryllteiste (D) – Tejst (DK) – Guillemot à miroir (F) – Uria nera (I) – Teist (N) – Zwarte zeekoet (NL) – Tobisgrissla (S)

Description: Illustration page 144. With a length of 34 cm and a weight of 350-450 g, the Black guillemot is a medium-sized auk, somewhere between Brünich's guillemots and Little auks in size. They are completely black, apart from a characteristic white, oval spot on the upper wings, which can easily be seen when the bird is sitting on the water. Legs and the inside of the beak are red. The sexes look alike.
Distribution/Migrations: The Black guillemot has a circumpolar distribution in the high- and sub-Arctic. The Svalbard population does not migrate far, but spends the winter near the ice edge.
Biology: While searching for food, breeding Black guillemots stay closer to the coast than other auks. They find their food, which consists of small fish and crustaceans, near

the surface. Compared to Common and Brünich's guillemots, the Black guillemots are rather unsocial birds, as they breed in small, loose colonies in rock crevices, under large stones and on steep cliffs. Colonies larger than 100 breeding pairs are the exception. It is the only auk that normally lays two eggs, which both parents incubate for about four weeks. The chicks can fly after 30 to 40 days and are then immediately independent.
Miscellaneous: The population in Svalbard numbers around 20,000 breeding pairs and they are a common sight. The Black guillemot is hunted to a limited degree in Spitsbergen. When sitting on the water, it can dive quickly and will usually do so at exactly the moment when you press the trigger of your camera.

4.9 Plants

"Viewed from the sea, the greater part of Spitsbergen appears as an altogether barren and lifeless country. A place of wild beauty, it is true, but incapable of supporting the life of even the most hardy plants. Yet this first impression is an inaccurate one, and a close search reveals that on the most lifeless and rock-strewn hill-sides plant-life is generally present, with many and beautiful, though minute, flowers."

Seton Gordon, *Amid Snowy Wastes*

For most visitors, the vegetation will not be the main motivation to come to the high Arctic, and the first glimpses from the regular flight of strongly glaciated southern Spitsbergen suggest a total absence of anything that has roots, leaves and flowers. Once you are there, however, you will soon realise that things are different and most people cannot help but fall for the spell of the beautiful, small, tough flowers in such a hostile environment.

The vegetation of Spitsbergen forms a varied mosaic. If you think that "tundra" and "tundra" are the same, then you will be surprised during every excursion in different parts of the archipelago.

For an overview, the tundra of Svalbard has been organised into a "middle arctic" and a "high arctic" zone and these have been subdivided again into two vegetation zones each, totalling four **vegetation zones** as a first approach to simplify the complex distribution of species associated with certain ecological conditions. Certain species, that are especially abundant, are characteristic of these vegetation zones, but what you can actually see in any given location depends on the local habitat.

The central and northern west coast, the north coast and central parts of Spitsbergen are considered "middle arctic", at least in a regional context. The Arctic bell-heather

(*Cassiope tetragona*) and Mountain avens (*Dryas octopetala*) are characteristic of the two vegetation zones that can be found in these areas. These zones are accordingly called "*Cassiope tetragone zone*" or "*Arctic bell-heather zone*", which is in the climatically mildest parts of the archipelago, followed by the "*Dryas octopetala zone*" or "*Mountain avens zone*". In these zones, the warming influence of the Gulf stream is most prominent and the inner fjords give protection from the colder maritime air during the summer. This is where the richest vegetation and three out of four plant species can be found.

In contrast, southern Spitsbergen and the whole east of Svalbard belong to the high Arctic from a plant-ecological perspective. There, the cold waters of the East Spitsbergen current create a rather harsh, high arctic climate. The "*Polar willow zone*" (or "*Salix polaris zone*"), which can be found mostly on the western side of Edgeøya and Barentsøya, still has a rather dense vegetation cover, whereas the "*Svalbard poppy zone*" ("*Papaver dahlianum zone*") includes true polar deserts, strongly contrasting with other ecological zones due to their emptiness.

This rough distribution is influenced mainly by the climate and oceanic currents, together with local factors such as altitude, moisture, soil, nutrients, snow cover and daylight, which evidently create a very complex, varied, colourful mosaic. The very uneven thickness of the winter snow cover and the timing of the snow melt are especially decisive for plant growth. It is clear, however, that the whole archipelago of Svalbard, from Bjørnøya in the south to Sjuøyane in the north, belong to the zone of arctic **tundra**, as there are no woods and no free-standing trees. Plants do not grow taller than 20 or 30 cm. The five tree species (Polar willow, three other quite rare willow species, and Dwarf birch) creep along or even in the soil surface and do not even grow into bushes.

Plants have developed different and sometimes quite surprising strategies to survive in this extreme environment. Creeping just over the ground or even growing, at least partly, directly under the surface, gives protection from wind and cold, and so does the snow cover during the winter. Another adaptation is the asexual reproduction by means of scions, instead of creating seeds. Scions to not require insects or wind, both of which are unreliable. The same species may use both ways of reproduction, depending on conditions during a given year. Many flowering plants reproduce only every second year or at even longer intervals.

Animals have a significant influence. Vegetation is usually very rich near large seabird colonies or in the immediate vicinity of nests. Seabird colonies provide large amounts of natural fertilizers, but these create a soil with extreme conditions such as an abnormal pH-value, resulting in a vegetation cover that is lush, but poor in species. Next to Scurvy grass and Mountain sorrel, specialised mosses and grasses (e.g. *Alopecurus borealis*) thrive there. Grazing reindeer create the opposite result and keep the tundra short. The plant cover, including mosses and lichens, is markedly richer and more strongly developed in areas without reindeer.

At least 173 species of flowering plants have been found in Svalbard (mostly after Elvebakk & Prestrud (1996), see *literature*). 38 of these plant species are unknown on the mainland of Scandinavia, but many of the others can be found in Norway and Sweden, Scotland and the higher Alps. Many of the 173 species are very rare and can be found at only a few locations. At least five are introduced (other sources state 17 of the species were brought to Spitsbergen by man). Other introduced species have been eradicated or did not survive.

26 species are briefly introduced in this chapter. The selection does not follow scientific criteria, but I have tried to include mainly species that you are likely to see when you visit Spitsbergen. I have included some characteristic saxifraga species, rather than buttercups where the different species are very difficult to distinguish. If you have ever seen experienced botanists creeping over the tundra with magnifying glasses, heatedly discussing the identification of Whitlow grasses, of which twelve species (plus hybrids!) exist in Spitsbergen, then you will understand why I do not even try to get involved with this – an abstinence that I seriously recommend to everybody who comes with a general interest; any effort to tell the Whitlow grasses apart only brings frustration. Nevertheless, if you come to Spitsbergen in the summer, then you should certainly get down on your knees at least occasionally and try to identify some of the small flowers. You will quickly be able to recognize the most common species and then they will not only be beautiful colour spots in a seemingly empty environment, but additionally bring variety and familiarity to this exotic landscape.

Not all species in Spitsbergen have English names whereas some flowers have several different names. In the end it is the Latin name that counts, but even then confusing situations can occur.

Endemic means that this species occurs only in one area (region, island).

Circumpolar = Distributed in all areas around the North Pole: Alaska, arctic Canada, Greenland, Svalbard and the Russian Arctic.

4.9.1 Polar willow (*Salix polaris*)

Polarweide (D) – Polarpil (DK) – Saule polaire (F) – Salice Polare (I) – Polarvier (N) – Poolwilg (NL) – Polarvide (S)

Illustration page 161. The Polar willow is by far the most common of Spitsbergen's five tree species; there are three other willow species (Dwarf willow (*Salix herbacea*), Net-leaved willow (*Salix reticulata*), Tundra willow (*Salix arctica*) plus the Dwarf birch. The small, oval-round leaves of the Polar willow are not easily confused with any other plant, apart from the other willow species which are very rare. Only the Net-leaved willow has a wide-spread (but never dense) occurrence, especially on the west coast of Spitsbergen. It is quite similar to the Polar willow, but has a distinct net-like pattern on the leaves. The stems of the Polar willow are normally no thicker than knitting needles and creep directly over the ground, often covering large parts of the tundra and thus creating little "forests", no higher than two or three cm, so not even a mouse could get lost in there. Large individual Polar willows may be several decades old, as they grow no faster than a few millimetres per year. They occur everywhere in Svalbard, but are most abundant in tundra areas on the west and north coasts of Spitsbergen, and on Edgeøya and Barentsøya. In valleys near Longyearbyen such as Adventdalen and Bjørndalen, it covers large parts of the valley bottom. In the autumn, it brings beautiful reddish-yellow colours to the tundra, not only in Svalbard, but also in northern Russia and Canada.

4.9.2 Dwarf birch (*Betula nana*)

Zwergbirke (D) – Dværg-Birk (DK) – Bouleau nain (F) – Betulla Nana (I) – Dvergbjørk (N) – Dwergberk (NL) – Dvärgbjörk (S)

Illustration page 161. Next to the willow species, the Dwarf birch is the only other "tree" in Svalbard. It is very rare, and most tourists will not see it. Friends of the Dwarf birch should try their luck in the protected, climatically more favoured valleys of Nordenskiöld Land. There is a locality on the flat tundra northwest of Janssonhaugen in Adventdalen, between the rivers of Adventelva and Janssonelva, which you can reach within a few hours walking from the end of the road. This requires a rifle, as well as rubber boots to cross several rivers, and then patience to find the toothed leaves and the stems which can reach the diameter of a little finger. They creep directly over or partly even in the ground.

4.9.3 Mountain sorrel (*Oxyria digyna*)

Alpensäuerling (D) – Fjeldsyre (DK) – Oxyria à deux carpelles (F) – Acetosa soldanella (I) – Fjellsyre (N) – Bergzuring (NL) – Fjällsyra (S)

Illustration page 162. Mountain sorrel grows anywhere in Svalbard, and is widespread in the Arctic and in mountain areas of northern and temperate latitudes. It prefers moist locations and can be up to 20 cm high. It is a pioneering plant and grows on calcarous, often rocky ground. Its deep-green leaves have a sour taste and contain vitamin C, which made it an important part of the menu of indigenous cultures and whalers in the Arctic as an anti-scorbutic. Today, reindeer like to graze on mountain sorrel. It is especially lush and abundant near birdcliffs which provide rich nutrition.

4.9.4 Knotweed or Knotgrass (*Polygonum viviparum* or *Bistorta vivipara*)

Knöllchenknöterich (D) – Tospirende pileurt (DK) – Renouée vivipare (F) – Poligono viviparo (I) – Harerug (N) – Levendbarende Duizendknoop (NL) – Ormrot (S)

Illustration page 162. Knotweed grows up to 15 cm high and has conspicuous, long and pointed leaves. For reproduction, knotweed often uses scions that sprout on the stem. This strategy enables knotweed to occupy freshly exposed surfaces such as new moraines as a pioneering plant. It is abundant anywhere in Svalbard, as well as elsewhere in the Arctic and in northern and temperate mountain areas, and is unmistakable. Knotweed is a favourite food for reindeer and ptarmigan.

4.9.5 Arctic mouse-ear (*Cerastium arcticum*)

Arktisches Hornkraut (D) – Arktisk hønsetarm (DK) – Céraiste arctique (F) – Peverina Artica (I) – Snøarve (N) – Poolhoornbloem (NL) – Svalbardsarv (S)

Illustration page 163. Arctic mouse-ear grows in small cushions and occurs as different sub-species everywhere in Svalbard and in other places in the Arctic and sub-Arctic. It prefers calcarous and nitrogen-bearing, moist soil. Under favourable conditions, it may cover a high proportion of the surface and is then an important food resource for animals.

4.9.6 Tundra chickweed (*Stellaria crassipes*)

Schneesternmiere (D) – Stilkfladstjerne (DK) – Stellaire succulente (F) –

Snøstjerneblomst (N) – Sneeuwmuur (NL) – Polarstjärnblomma (S)

Illustration page 163. You can find the small, white flowers and slim, quite long stems of the Tundra chickweed anywhere in Svalbard; usually not in abundance, although it can occur in large numbers at favourable sites. In Svalbard, Tundra chickweed develops two different kinds of flowers: female and bisexual ones. It prefers dry, calcareous ground.

4.9.7 Fringed sandwort (*Arenaria pseudofrigida*)

Wimper-Sandkraut (D) – Kalkarve (DK) – Sabline des pays froids (F) – Kalkarve (N) – Gewimperde Zandmuur (NL) – Polarnarv (S)

Illustration page 164. Fringed sandwort is not a very common plant, but you may find it on the west or north coast of Spitsbergen, mostly on dry ground in inner fjord sections. It develops cushions that look a bit similar to those of the Moss campion, but has slightly larger, white flowers.

4.9.8 Nodding lychnis (*Silene wahlbergella*)

Nördliche Alpennelke (D) – Lygte-Pragtstjerne (DK) – Silène de Wahlbergue (F) – Silene di Wahlberg (I) – Blindurt (N) – Knikkende Silene (NL) – Fjällblära (S)

Illustration page 164. The Nodding lychnis grows five to ten cm high and examples can be found in small numbers at suitable locations in most parts of Svalbard except Bjørnøya. Beyond this, it also occurs in many other places in the Arctic.

4.9.9 Moss campion (*Silene acaulis*)

Stengelloses Leimkraut (D) – Tue-limurt (DK) – Silène acaule (F) – Silene a cuscinetto (I) – Fjellsmelle (N) – Stengelloze Silene (NL) – Fjällglim (S)

Illustrage page 165. A common plant that grows in dark-green cushions and catches the eye with small, pinkish-red flowers that can occasionally also be white. Normally, the flowers begin to blossom on the side that receives most sun radiation, which means that, at least in theory, the first flowers should point southwards. The Moss campion owes its unofficial name "Compass flower" to this fact. The compact cushion-shape provides good protection against cold and dry wind and is thus an excellent adaptation to the extreme climate. Moss campion grows mostly on rather dry soil and can be found everywhere in Svalbard and in most other regions around the North Pole. The fact that reindeer do not like it, certainly contributes to the high life expectancy of up to 100 years.

4.9.10 Snow-buttercup (*Ranunculus nivalis*)

Schnee-Hahnenfuß (D) – Sneranunkel (DK) – Renoncule des neiges (F) – Ranuncolo delle Nevi (I) – Snøsoleie (N) – Sneeuwboterbloem (NL) – Fjällsörblomma (S)

Illustration page 165. The Snow-buttercup is included here as one example of a range of buttercup species that occur in Svalbard, most of which are quite similar to each other and many are quite rare. The bright yellow flowers can be found mostly in moist places in Svalbard (except Bjørnøya), but the Snow-buttercup is most common on the west and north coasts of Spitsbergen. Beyond this, it grows in most other arctic regions. It seems to have a disappointing taste for reindeer, as they usually ignore it.

4.9.11 Svalbard poppy (*Papaver dahlianum*)

Svalbardmohn (D) – (Fjeld-)Valmue (DK) – Pavot Dahlia/P. de Svalbard (F) – Papavero delle Svalbard (I) – Svalbardvalmue (N) – Spitsbergen Papaver (NL) – Spetsbergsvallmo (S)

Illustration page 166. Svalbard poppy is often called the "national flower" of Spitsbergen, although it can also be found in northern Greenland, northern Scandinavia and the Russian Arctic. There are two variants of this species, one with white flowers and another with yellow flowers. Svalbard poppy is abundant everywhere in Svalbard with a tendency towards dry ground with some lime content. No other flowering plant has been found in Spitsbergen as high as the Svalbard poppy, which can grow at heights of more than 1,000 metres above sea level.

4.9.12 Scurvy grass (*Cochlearia officinalis* or *C. groenlandica*)

Gebräuchliches (or Echtes or Grönländisches) Löffelkraut (D) – Grønlandsk Kokleare (DK) – Cranson officinal (F) – Coclearia medicinale (I) – Skjørbuksurt (N) – Lepelblad (NL) – Vanlig skörbjuggsört (S)

Illustration page 167. Scurvy grass grows everywhere in Svalbard and in all other parts of the Arctic, but thrives mostly under seabird colonies. It has been used against scurvy in the past because of the vitamin C content of the leaves. The name of the mountain behind the old whaling station Smeerenburg on Amsterdamøya, "Salatberg", still reminds us of whalers who went there to collect vegetables as their only chance to get hold of something fresh to fight malnutrition.

4.9.13 Whitlow-grasses (*Draba spec.*)

Felsenblümchen (D) – Draba (DK) – Drave (F) – Draba (I) – Rublom (N) – Hongerbloempjes (NL) – Draba (S)

Illustration page 167. There are twelve different species of Whitlow-grasses in Svalbard, seven of which have white flowers and five with yellow ones. To make things more complicated, there are in addition four hybrids. Identification of these species, most of which are widely spread in large parts of the Arctic, is for experts only.

4.9.14 Purple saxifrage (*Saxifraga oppositifolia*)

Roter Steinbrech (D) – Purpur-Stenbræk (DK) – Saxifrage à feuilles opposées (F) – Sassifraga a foglie opposte (I) – Rødsildre (N) – Zuiltjessteenbreek (NL) – Purpurbräcka (S)

Illustration page 168. Purple saxifrage, which grows slowly in small, loose cushions or often with thin strings that creep over the ground, is abundant everywhere in Svalbard as well as elsewhere in the Arctic. It can also be found in many mountain areas in central and even southern Europe. Its many, small flowers cast a beautiful shade of purple-red on large tundra areas in July before the colour fades again relatively early in the summer (before the end of July). The Purple saxifrage is a pioneering plant with shallow roots, which enables it to be amongst the first species to occupy freshly exposed, geomorphologically active surfaces such as young moraines and rock slopes.

4.9.15 Yellow mountain saxifrage (*Saxifraga aizoides*)

Fetthennensteinbrech (D) – Solstenbræk (DK) – Saxifrage jaune (F) – Sassifraga cigliata (I) – Gulsildre (N) – Gele bergsteenbreek (NL) – Gullbräcka (S)

Illustration page 168. The cushion-shaped forms of the Yellow mountain saxifrage are generally not very abundant, but can be quite numerous especially in dry localities with calcarous bedrock on the west coast of Spitsbergen. There, its yellow flowers are a pleasure to see in August when many other flowering plants have already faded. It also occurs in other arctic and sub-arctic areas as well as in the Alps.

4.9.16 Alpine saxifrage (*Saxifraga nivalis*)

Schneesteinbrech (D) – Snestenbræk (DK) – Saxifrage des neiges (F) – Sassifraga delle Nevi (I) – Snøsildre (N) – Sneeuwsteenbreek (NL) – Fjällbräkka (S)

Illustration page 169. The high stem of the Alpine saxifrage catches the eye on suitable locations everywhere in Svalbard and elsewhere in the sub-Arctic and Arctic. It is very similar to its close relative, the Hawkweed-leaved saxifrage. The Alpine saxifrage is not very particular about habitat, but it is not very competitive and thus it often has to live, for example, in dry rock crevices because more favourable habitats are taken by other, more competitive plants.

4.9.17 Hawkweed-leaved saxifrage (*Saxifraga hieracifolia*)

Habichtskrautblättriger Steinbrech (D) – Rank stenbræk (DK) – Saxifrage à feuille d'éperviere (F) – Sassifraga nordalpina (I) – Stivsildre (N) – Havikskruidbladige Steenbreek (NL) – Styvbräcka (S)

Illustration page 169. The Hawkweed-leaved saxifrage can be up to 20 cm tall in Spitsbergen and it is thus almost as impressive as its name. It grows on wet soil, often within moss cushions and is less common than the similar Alpine saxifrage, especially in eastern parts of the Svalbard archipelago where it is quite rare. It can be found in many other arctic regions around the pole.

4.9.18 Bog saxifrage (*Saxifraga hirculus*)

Moorsteinbrech (D) – Gul stenbræk (DK) – Saxifrage oeil de bouc/Saxifrage dorée (F) – Sassifraga delle torbiere (I) – Myrsildre (N) – Bokjes Steenbreek (NL) – Myrbräcka (S)

Illustration page 170. The Bog saxifrage grows in small, loose cushions and has bright yellow leaves. It is, however, quite similar to other saxifrages and to buttercups. It occurs in the whole archipelago of Svalbard and beyond this in many other parts of the Arctic, and prefers moist ground where it can be quite numerous.

4.9.19 Drooping saxifrage (*Saxifraga cernua*)

Nickender Steinbrech (D) – Knop-Stenbræk (DK) – Saxifrage penchée/à bulbilles (F) – Sassifraga incurvata (I) – Knoppsildre (N) – Knikkende Steenbreek (NL) – Knoppbräcka (S)

Illustration page 170. Small, loose cushions of the Drooping saxifrage with their fragile stalks grow everywhere in Svalbard and other arctic areas, mostly in damp locations.

4.9.20 Tufted saxifrage (*Saxifraga cespitosa*)

Rasensteinbrech (D) – Tuestenbræk (DK) – Saxifrage en touffe/en coussinet (F) – Tuesildre (N) – Groenlandse Steenbreek (NL) – Tuvbräcka (S)

Illustration page 171. The Tufted saxifrage grows in small cushions with white flowers and is abundant not only in Svalbard, but also everywhere else in the Arctic. It can be very abundant in suitable locations. In cases of low nutrient availability or infection with fungi, the leaves, normally green, appear bright red to orange.

4.9.21 Spider plant (*Saxifraga flagellaris*)

Fadensteinbrech (or Schlangensteinbrech) (D) – Edderkop-Stenbræk (DK) – Saxifrage toile d'araignée/à flagelles (F) – Sassifraga del ragno (I) – Trådsildre (N) – Spinneplantje (NL) – Trådbräcka (S)

Illustration page 171. The Spider plant is not abundant on Svalbard, but it can be found in locations everywhere in the archipelago except Bjørnøya. Beyond this, it has a circumpolar distribution. The Spider plant has a characteristic flower which nicely demonstrates a strategy that is typical for many arctic flowering plants, as it has readily visible scions. It is one of the few species that are disdained by reindeer.

4.9.22 Mountain avens (*Dryas octopetala*)

Silberwurz (D) – Almindelig Rypelyng (DK) – Dryade à huit pétales (F) – Camedrio alpino (I) – Reinrose (N) – Achtster/zilverkruid (NL) – Fjällsippa (S)

Illustration page 172. This nice plant with its yellowish-white flowers grows on dry tundra everywhere in Svalbard except Bjørnøya, but it is especially abundant on the west and north coasts of Spitsbergen in locations with a calcarous substrate. Beyond this, it occurs almost everywhere in the Arctic. In some locations it is so abundant that the tundra seems to have a silvery gleam in the sunshine, which gives pleasure to tourists and reindeer alike, though for different reasons. Mountain avens is common also in Scandinavia and was widespread in Europe during the ice age, the last cold spells of which have been called "Younger Dryas" after the Latin name.

4.9.23 Arctic bell-heather (*Cassiope tetragona*)

Vierkantiges Heidekraut (D) – Almindelig Kantlyng (DK) – Cassiopée tétragone (F) – Campanula Artica (I) – Kantlyng (N) – Vierkante Lavendelheide/Kantheide (NL) – Kantljung (S)

Illustration page 172. Arctic bell-heather is amongst the most eye-catching and easily identified of all plants. It grows everywhere in the Svalbard archipelago except Bjørnøya and in most other parts of the Arctic. Arctic bell-heather prefers dry ground which is reliably snow-covered during the winter, but it is most abundant on the west and north coasts of Spitsbergen, where it can cover large areas. The otherwise not-too-particular reindeer disdain this tough plant, which is a significant ecological advantage. In some locations, it is so abundant that it gives the tundra a gentle, whitish gleam.

4.9.24 Boreal Jacob's ladder (*Polemonium boreale*)

Nördliche Himmelsleiter or N. Jakobsleiter (D) – Polarjakobsstige (DK) – Polémoine Boréal (F) – Polemonio Boreale (I) – Polarflokk (N) – Arctische Jacobsladder (NL) – Polarblågull (S)

Illustration page 173. Plants with blue flowers are the exception in the Arctic. The rare Boreal Jacob's ladder is one of those exceptions, but it grows only at a few locations in the inner parts of the fjords on the west coast of Spitsbergen. In some of these places, it can reach considerable size and in July has beautiful purple-blue flowers. Beyond Spitsbergen, it also occurs in northern parts of Russia, Canada and Alaska.

4.9.25 Polar cress (*Cardamine nymanii* or *C. pratensis Polemonioides*)

Polarschaumkraut (D) – Engkarse (DK) – Cardamine de Nymani (F) – Crescione Polare (I) – Polarkarse (N) – Pinksterbloem (NL) – Polarbräsma (S)

Illustration page 173. The Polar cress with its delicate pink to light-blue flowers grows generally everywhere in Svalbard, as well as in other parts of the Arctic, on moist, nutrient-rich tundra. It is, however, mostly restricted to very few, scattered individuals and is thus not easy to find. It has adapted quite well to the arctic environment, where helpful insects can be rare, by reproducing asexually: Falling leaves develop roots and grow into independent plants, whereas the flowers are mostly "decoration" only.

4.9.26 Wooly lousewort (*Pedicularis lanata* or *P. dasyantha* or *P.l.d.*)

Wolliges Läusekraut (D) – Uldhåret troldurt (DK) – Pédiculaire à anthères épaisses (F) – Ullmyrklegg (N) – Kartelblad (NL) – Ullspira (S)

Illustration page 174. The Wooly lousewort is an eyecatcher in slightly moist locations in the fjords on the west and north coasts of Spitsbergen. Beyond this, it occurs only at a few locations in the Russian Arctic. It is closely related and thus quite similar to the Hairy lousewort which is smaller and slimmer and occurs everywhere in Svalbard. All louseworts are poisonous.

4.9.27 Arctic cottongrass (*Eriophorum scheuchzeri*)

Scheuchzers Wollgras (D) – Polarkæruld (DK) – Linaigrette de Scheuchzer (F) – Pennacchi di Scheuchzer (I) – Snøull (N) – Eenjarig wollegras (NL) – Polarull (S)

Illustration page 174. Arctic cottongrass is a sedge and thus a grass; these are briefly discussed in the next section. It is a real eye-catcher, a beautiful plant that is characteristic of boggy and wet tundra areas. It occurs generally at suitable locations everywhere within Svalbard except Bjørnøya, especially on the west coast of Spitsbergen and, beyond this, in large parts of the sub- and high Arctic and mountain areas of temperate latitudes. Some of the nicest occurrences in Spitsbergen are within Longyearbyen. It is a good idea to walk carefully in areas with Arctic cottongrass, as it clearly indicates wet spots.

There is one more cottongras species in Svalbard (*Eriophorum triste* or *E. angustifolium*), which is slightly smaller.

4.9.28 Arctic dandelion (*Taraxacum arcticum*)

Arktischer Löwenzahn (D) – Arktisk mælkebøtte (DK) – Pissenlit arctique (F) – Tarassaco Artico (I) – Arktisløvetann (N) – Arctische Paardebloem (NL) – Arktisk maskros (S)

Illustration page 175. The Arctic dandelion is not amongst the plants that you will see everyday, although it generally occurs all over Svalbard (except Bjørnøya). It is the most common of three dandelion species that grow naturally in Svalbard (one only on Bjørnøya); additionally, there are introduced species in the settlements. The Arctic dandelion has widespread occurrences in locations in Northwest and East Greenland, Novaya Zemlya, the Taymyr peninsula and the Siberian far east.

4.9.29 Polar dandelion (*Taraxacum brachyceras*)

Polarlöwenzahn (D) – Bredbladet mælkebøtte (DK) – Pissenlit à dents/cornes courtes (F) – Polarløvetann (N) – Poolpaardebloem (NL) – Polarmaskros (S)

Illustration page 175. The Polar dandelion is similar to the Arctic dandelion, but unmistakable because of its yellow flowers. Being quite specialised on dry ground, it is fairly rare and occurs only at favourable sites on the west- and north coasts of Spitsbergen.

4.9.30 Grasses, mosses, lichens & fungi

Plants that are usually called **"grasses"** are common on the tundra in Spitsbergen. In total, there are 59 different species: Four rushes (*Juncaceae*), four Wood-rushes (*Luzula*), 17 sedges (*Cyperaceae*. Thereof three *Carex* species; two cottongrasses, genus *Eriophorum;* one *Kobresia*) and another 34 grasses in a stricter sense (*Poaceae*).

Out of these, less than ten are widespread and abundant (for example *Juncus biglumis, Luzula confusa, Luzula arctica, Carex rupestris, Deschampsia alpina*). Many of the others are restricted to very small occurrences in a few locations, and at least five have followed man up to Spitsbergen and grow nowadays near the settlements. Most tourists will probably notice these plants just as "grass" (and so does the author, admittedly) and will refrain from identifying single species, which can be a challenge even for trained specialists.

"Officially", there are 373 **mosses**, which grow sometimes in colourful cushions and stripes on wet tundra and in streams everywhere in Svalbard, even in the most barren parts. The colours not only depend on the species, but also on the availability of nutrients in the soil: In areas of low nutrition, a moss that is usually deep-green may show red cushions. Mosses are quite vulnerable and you should avoid stepping on them.

Lichens are front-runners in terms of species numbers in extreme environments. This applies also to Svalbard, where experts have counted 597 different species. Each lichen consists of a symbiotic combination of a fungus and an alga and is, strictly speaking, not one organism and thus not exactly a species. Lichens occupy otherwise dead surfaces such as barren rocks and endure the most extreme conditions like large temperature variations, dryness and malnutrition. Dust falling out of the clean, arctic air is often the only food source – just trying to imagine this, makes the author hungry. Lichens have developed a number of strategies to adapt to such extreme conditions. There is also strong competition for good sites such as the sunny side on suitable rocks, and lichens do not hesitate to use internationally banned methods including chemical warfare to chase away their neighbours.

Algae inhabit large areas of moist and wet tundra, forming a blueish-black film on otherwise barren surfaces. Other species, such as the Snow algae (e.g. *Chlamydomonas nivalis*), live in the snow and colour snow fields and glaciers with a reddish or greenish tint at the end of the summer when the snow melts and the algae concentrate near the surface.

"Primitive" plants such as mosses, lichens and algae are altogether the most varied and successful organisms in the tundra environment and thus deserve occasional attention, even if they do not catch the eye at first glance.

There are more than ten different species of **fungi** in Spitsbergen, all of which are also known from northern Scandinavia and Russia. They say that all of them are eatable (no guarantee from the author!), and those who know the good spots can prepare some good mushroom dishes during the autumn. The passion for collecting mushrooms is, however, unevenly distributed, at least according to a Russian brochure from the Pomor-museum in Barentsburg: "Citizens of the Russian settlements of Spitsbergen are fond of gathering mushrooms as a habitual rest time spending. The Norwegians prefer to look at (sic!) mushrooms in the shops!" ☺

Chapter 5 – History

"In the following chapters I propose to relate the story of the succession of events recorded to have happened in and on the coasts of Spitsbergen since its discovery in 1596. They will be found more numerous, more varied, and often more dramatic than the reader may be prepared to expect."

Martin Conway, *No Man's Land*

In the history of Spitsbergen, events follow each other, some overlapping in time and others separated by long time intervals. Most have one thing in common; that they are not directly connected to each other. Within the context of Spitsbergen, it is possible to look at and understand each historical episode independently. It is the wider story of European and Russian history that provides the thread that runs through the whole story. Interest in any area has usually had its roots in the economic, scientific and political developments in other parts of the world – especially in regions such as Spitsbergen that have never had an indigenous population.

The order of the sections in this chapter is a little arbitrary. A strictly chronological sequence would be confusing, since some chapters overlap in time. The history of Spitsbergen is more easily understood if it is subdivided into periods of certain activities.

This chapter cannot claim completeness in any sense, but it gives an introduction to readers with a general interest. A little bit of historical background can turn an inconspicuous relic seen on the tundra into an exciting discovery, rather than a piece of rubbish. Maps become history books once the significance of placenames and their status in Spitsbergen's history is understood.

Whichever of the many cultural heritage sites you visit in Spitsbergen you will always find yourself in the middle of the most beautiful landscapes. Wildlife will also pay an occasional visit alongside you, such as reindeer, foxes or even Walrus – like the one that I once saw sleeping on top of one of the famous blubber ovens in Smeerenburg.

There was never a **stone-age** population in Spitsbergen. Legend has it that the **Vikings** first discovered the island, but there is no evidence for this theory either. The first people who saw Spitsbergen may have been **Pomors** – hunters from the north coast of Russia – although the exact timing of their first voyages to this part of the Arctic is also disputed. There is, however, no doubt about the well-documented, "official" discovery of Spitsbergen during **Willem Barents**' third voyage in 1596. A few years later, **whalers** from different European countries started to harvest the rich Walrus and whale populations. When the Pomors disappeared in the 19th century, **Norwegian trappers** started to hunt Polar bears, Arctic foxes and other arctic animals. At the same time, **scientists** from different nations discovered the Arctic as an interesting field not only for discovery, but also for science in a stricter sense. They were followed by **record-hunters** who wanted to reach the highest latitudes and companies who wanted to exploit **mineral occurences**. This made it necessary to have an administration for the land area. In 1920, the **Spitsbergen Treaty** was signed, putting the archipelago under Norwegian administration and coming into force in 1925.

The 1920s saw important events in the history of polar exploration in Spitsbergen: The legendary expeditions of **Roald Amundsen** and **Umberto Nobile** were launched from **Ny Ålesund** and resulted in triumph and tragedy, respectively. As everywhere in the world, the **Second World War** put its dramatic stamp on the arctic. **Modern times** are influenced by a coexistence of Norwegian and Russian settlements, mining, science, tourism and modern service industry. Despite all this, there is still room for adventurers and trappers.

The name Svalbard has been used since 1194 in an Icelandic chronicle. The origin of the name is, at best, unclear and it was hardly used again until 1925, when Norway revived it. During most of the history of the archipelago, the Dutch name Spitsbergen has been in use. The official situation regarding the main placenames **"Spitsbergen"** and **"Svalbard"** is explained in Chapter 2 *introduction* and the practical advantages of having two different words for the main island (Spitsbergen) and the whole archipelago (Svalbard) are obvious, but from a historical perspective, it should be noticed that Spitsbergen is the term which has enjoyed a far more extensive usage over the centuries.

5.1 Vikings

"Opp gjennom årene har det vært spunnet mange myter omkring norrøne ferder nord i ishavet med mulige oppdagelser og ilandstigninger på Svalbard."

"Throughout the years, many myths have been spun around Viking voyages northwards towards the ice sea, including the possible discovery of, and landings on Svalbard."

Sysselmannen på Svalbard,
Kulturminneplan for Svalbard 2000-2010

Whether or not the Vikings reached Spitsbergen in 1194, as has often been claimed by Norwegian historians, is unclear. There is no solid evidence that could support or reject this theory which goes back to an Icelandic chronicle where it is mentioned that "Svalbarði", the "cold rim", was found in 1194. Considering the given translation, it becomes clear that "Svalbarði" was not even necessarily an island: It may also have been the edge of the pack ice. Otherwise, Newfoundland, Greenland and Jan Mayen are other possible candidates for the "cold rim". There is no archaeological evidence in Spitsbergen that points to Viking visits. This is in contrast to Newfoundland and Greenland, where remains of ancient Norse settlements have been found.

Even if Vikings had really seen or even landed in "Svalbarði" in the 11th or 12th century, then this event neither influenced the further course of the local or European history, nor did it contribute to geographical knowledge. Nevertheless, this hypothetical event was extensively stressed by Norwegian historians and authorities who, much later, claimed Norwegian sovereignty for the archipelago. This was underlined by the introduction of the rather artificial name "Svalbard" for the whole island group, in the years that followed the Spitsbergen Treaty.

5.2 Pomors

"There must have been a strange fascination about an arctic hunters's life for the people of the White Sea, or it would not have been possible to recruit them year after year, in spite of all the tragedies, frost-bites, and narrow escapes that they witnessed or experienced. One year eighteen men were sent forth. Twelve of them died and only six returned home after terrible experiences, yet everyone of these six was ready to go back the first time he had a chance."

Martin Conway, *No Man's Land*

The Pomors were people who lived on the coast of the White Sea in northern Russia. They were hunters and fishermen and had a long tradition of hunting voyages to the Arctic. Without any doubt, they were active for centuries in Spitsbergen, which they called "Grumant". This name may be derived from "Greenland", which was believed to form one continuous landmass in the north, including Spitsbergen.

Next to the quest for good hunting grounds, religious reasons may have been important for the long stays of the Pomors in the Arctic. It is said that the Pomors belonged to the Raskol movement that had separated from the Orthodox church in the second half of the 17th century and was thus persecuted.

The beginning of the Pomor period lies in the shadows of the past. The timing of the arrival of the first Pomors in Spitsbergen has been and still is a matter of heated discussion: Was it earlier than Willem Barents' "official" discovery of the island in 1596, or later? It was especially during the years of the Cold War that Soviet scientists tried to secure evidence for an early arrival of people from Russia in Spitsbergen. They have presented both archaeological discoveries and historical documents that seem to suggest Pomor hunting stations existed in Spitsbergen as early as the middle of the 16th century, but no really unequivocal proof has been found so far. Half a dozen hunting stations from the central and southern west coast of Spitsbergen were dated prior to

1596. The methodological problem that remains is that it is actually the age of the timber that has been dated by means of dendrochronology, rather than the timing of the establishment of these stations in Spitsbergen. All equipment and furnishing that has been dated so far, is from the 18th and 19th centuries – the historical "smoking Kalashnikov" still remains to be found.

It is, however, undisputed that the Pomors were the people with the longest history of presence and activities in Spitsbergen. After a prime period in the late 18th century, the small stations were abandoned in the first half of the 19th century. The hunting grounds were still good, as can be concluded from the increasing activities of Norwegian hunters in those years. Political and economic reasons may have been involved in moving the Pomor's attention away from Spitsbergen.

They came to hunt wildlife. For this purpose, they established hunting stations which were, at least in some cases, small settlements. Up to 20 or so persons occupied a station that included a sauna, smithy, storage and living houses and other facilities that Norwegian hunters in later periods would not even dream of. Chessboards have been found during excavations, some of them obviously home-made during long winter evenings. Typical for Pomor sites are bricks from chimneys, in contrast to the Norwegian metal ovens of later years.

The families, however, remained in Russia: Spitsbergen was a preferred hunting area for the Pomors, but was never their home.

In 1743, four Pomors became stranded somewhere in Edgeøya and three managed to survive until they were finally found and rescued in 1749.

The most famous individual Pomor was Ivan (or Ermil, depending on the source) Starostin, who spent most of the time between 1787 and 1826 in Spitsbergen. Legend has it that during the last 15 of these years, he did not even bother to sail to Russia. He lived at Russekeila between Kapp Linné and Grønfjord and was buried near Kapp Starostin after his death in 1826.

Remains of Pomor hunting stations can still be seen near the coast in much of the archipelago (illustration 3.6.2, page 87). Orthodox crosses made of wood and used for both orientation and religious purposes, were an integral part of all stations, but most have fallen victim to later visitors who collected firewood. Nowadays, only two original crosses remain that are still standing, both in the entrance to Murchisonfjord (illustration 6.14.1-2, page 336).

5.3 Willem Barents

"At noon on June 17th ... they came in sight of land which was visible for about 32 to 26 miles trending almost from west to east. "It was high land and entirely covered with snow." Undoubtedly the north coast of Spitsberen between Hakluyt's Headland and the mouth of Liefde Bay was what they saw and this was the memorable day of the island's discovery, ..."

Martin Conway, *No Man's Land*

The undisputed honour of the "official" discovery of Spitsbergen falls to the Dutch navigator **Willem Barents**, who started his third and most famous area voyage with two ships in 1596 to find a navigable seaway to China. What he found instead of such a passage, was an island where they killed a white bear after a long fight. They called the island "Beeren Eyland" (Norwegian: Bjørnøya). A few days later, they reached Spitsbergen somewhere in the northwest. Barents sailed up and down the coast for some time and called the land **Spitsbergen** ("Pointed mountains") because of the impression that the alpine terrain made on him. From Spitsbergen, Barents tried to force a passage to the East, but was finally forced to spend a winter in the north of Novaya Zemlya. Several men, including Barents himself, died from scurvy in the spring of 1597. The others made it back home after an adventurous journey. They brought with them tales of fantastic treasures in the shape of whales and other animals that were just waiting to be harvested.

There are no archaeological findings in Spitsbergen that date back to Willem Barents' expedition, but they left a number of placenames on the maps. Some of them have survived until today. They are the oldest genuine placenames in Spitsbergen: Beeren Eyland (Bjørnøya), Inwyck (Bellsund), Grooten Inwyck (Isfjord), Vogelhoek (Fuglehuken), Keerwyck (northern Forlandsund) and, last but not least, Spitsbergen itself.

In the centuries following, a number of larger geographical features have been named after Barents to immortalise the pioneer discoverer of Spitsbergen. Next to Barentsøya, Barentsfjellet near the north end of Prins Karls Forland, Barentsgattet between Fuglesangen and Klovningen and Barentsburg, nothing less than the shelf sea itself has been named after the brave Dutchman: the Barents Sea, extending from Spitsbergen southwards all the way to the North Cape of Norway.

5.4 Whaling in the 17th century

"The supply of whales appeared unlimited. One day, writes Poole, "the whales lay so thicke about the ship that some ran against our cables, some against the ship, and one against the rudder. One lay under our beake-head and slept there for a long while. At which time our carpenter had hung a stage close by the water, whereon his tooles lay. And wee durst not molest the said whale for feare he should have overthrowne the stage and drowned all his tooles. In the end he went away, and carried the ships head around, his taile being foule of the cable"."

Martin Conway, *No Man's Land*

Both the survivors of Barents' voyage in 1596-97, and other discoverers such as Henry Hudson (1607), brought knowledge of the richness of marine mammal life in the Arctic back to Europe. It was not long before whalers from various European countries sailed northwards. To begin with, they had Basque whalers on board as the Basques were the only people who had experience of hunting large whales.

First were the Englishmen of the Muscovy Company, who sent their first ships to the Arctic in 1603. The purpose of this voyage was actually to hunt Walrus rather than whales. They started their bloody business at Bjørnøya, but soon continued further northwards. The first whaling ships came from England to Spitsbergen in 1610, followed by the Dutch in 1611. Both nations soon had large fleets involved in "fishing" whales in Spitsbergen waters, as well as a number of land-based stations to process whale oil from "blubber" (fat). Whale oil was the prime product that could be sold for good prices in Europe to be used for lamp oil, soap production and lubrication. Baleen plates ("whalebone") were another, sought-after product for umbrellas and corsets.

The Bowhead whale or "Right whale", as it was commonly called during the 17th century, was the preferred target species: It was the "right" whale to hunt as it was a slow swimmer, stayed afloat at the surface even when dead and yielded huge amounts of the valuable blubber. The hunt itself was done with hand-thrown harpoons from open rowing-boats; hard and dangerous work that was done by experienced men. The crew of such a whaling boat consisted usually of six: Four oarsmen, one helmsman and one harpooneer. Once the whale was tired from many hours of hunting, it was killed with a lance and then towed to the whaling station to be flensed (cut into pieces) on the beach. Pieces of blubber of a handy size, called "bible", were boiled down into whale oil; everything else was wasted during the early years. Only later was it found out that other parts of the whale, including the bones, could also be boiled to extract oil.

Technically, it was not possible to operate the blubber ovens on the small, wooden ships. This made it necessary to have shore-based whaling stations, which gave islands in good whaling waters, such as Jan Mayen and Spitsbergen, an immense strategic significance. A good location for a whaling station had to meet a number of requirements: Good access to the open sea and coastal waters, protection against wind and waves, drinking water and a shallow beach where whales could be hauled up. Occurrences of Mountain sorrel and Scurvy grass in the vicinity were appreciated, as the positive effects of these herbs in the fight against scurvy was already known. A lookout point, such as a small mountain that could easily be climbed, was another advantage.

There was a good number of whaling stations in Spitsbergen. The most famous was and is still the Dutch "establishment" Smeerenburg ("Blubber town") on Amsterdamøya at the northwestern corner of Spitsbergen (illustration 6.7.3-2, page 324). The size of these stations has, for a long time, been described with considerable exaggeration in the literature, but archaeological excavations have made it clear that even the larger stations could never have housed more than a maximum of 200 men – mostly well below this number – during the short summer season. Large settlements with churches, brothels and other facilities are nothing but legend. The most important feature of a shore whaling station consisted of one or several blubber ovens: a foundation and walls of bricks that had been imported from Europe, a chimney and an insulation layer made of local material such as sand, gravel and whale oil. This mixture has also been referred to as semi-natural concrete. What you can still see today, about 350 years after the stations were abandoned, is mostly pieces of bricks and remains of the foundations and, in some cases, the actual foundations. Additionally, there have been houses for the men who worked on the stations. To begin with, they had to make do with tents, but later they could move into more solid housing which, from habit, they still called "tent". There were storage houses, workshops and a smithy, at least in larger stations. These operations were expensive, and it took at least 100 whales to cover the costs of a season.

The stations were usually abandoned during the winter. On several occasions, there was a plan to leave a wintering party, but only once did the Dutch dare to leave seven men behind in Smeerenburg at the end of the summer. The first attempt in 1633-34 was successful, but a second attempt the following year resulted in a catastrophe when all seven men died of scurvy. When the first ships came in the early summer of 1635, all they found was the frozen corpses in a squatting position; scurvy causes strong abdominal pain. This was the last attempt by Europeans to spend a winter in the Arctic for a long time, although there have been several unintentional winterings when crew members have got lost and found themselves stranded somewhere, not able to leave the cold coasts for a year. Often such events ended fatally, but in 1630-31, actually before the Dutch winterings in Smeerenburg, eight tough English whalers managed to survive a winter in Recherchefjord, probably near Renardbreen. This was the first successful wintering of Europeans in Spitsbergen and may be the first ever, unless perhaps the Pomors were earlier.

There are many burial areas from the days of the whalers in Spitsbergen, especially in the northwest (illustrations 6.7.3-3, page 324, and 6.7.5-2, page 326). Whaler's graves in permafrost areas are not only important sites for archaeological research on early whaling in the Arctic, but also on simple, everyday European clothing from those days, which has not been preserved or documented elsewhere. From our modern point of view, the whaler's clothes were not at all suitable for the climate and the hard working conditions. Most of the dead found in the graves died young, less than 30 years old, from scurvy or injuries. All the skeletons are male, and there is no archaeological or historical evidence for the presence of women in Spitsbergen in the 17th or 18th century.

Both Spitsbergen and Jan Mayen were developed as centres for whaling. Jan Mayen was under Dutch control but in Spitsbergen, there was competition for good hunting areas and suitable sites for land stations. There were clashes and conflicts, and the whaling ships were accompanied by warships at times. After a few years, the prime whaling nations, England and the Netherlands, agreed that the former were to colonize the coast south of Spitsbergen up to Magdalenefjord and the latter would use the northwestern corner, thus satisfying both parties without any major conflicts. The other, smaller whaling nations were more or less tolerated, when they built their stations in less favourable locations.

There was one real sea battle, when three French warships brought up about 40 French whaling ships in 1693 in Sorgfjord at the northeastern corner of Spitsbergen. After several hours of gunfire, 13 French ships were captured. This was not the only violent incident, and during that summer, some 28 ships were captured by the French, who took eleven back to France and destroyed the others on the spot.

In the late 17th century, the heyday of land-based whaling stations was already past. Stations such as Smeerenburg and all the others had seen their most active seasons in the 1630s. They were gradually abandoned in the 1650s as the once so abundant whales moved from the fjords to more pelagic waters and the whalers had to follow them out to the open sea, either taking unprocessed blubber back home or using the newly developed technique of boiling the blubber down into oil on board ship.

There were more than 250 ships in Spitsbergen waters in peak seasons in the 1630s, catching a total of 250 to 750 whales per year, with records of more than 1,000.

5.5 Early expeditions and science

"The expedition started from Tromsö (in 1861) in two vessels, the schooner "Aeolus" and the sloop "Magdalena". Nine naturalists took part in the voyage ... The result was what might have been expected: by this expedition ... a safe foundation was laid, for the first time, of the knowledge of Spitzbergen in almost every department which could be the object for the scientific exploration of that time."

A. G. Nathorst,
Swedish Explorations In Spitzbergen 1758-1908

The whalers who frequented Spitsbergen from the early 17th century were driven exclusively by economic motives. Discovery and science were of no importance to them, with a very few exceptions such as **Friedrich Martens** from Hamburg, who joined a voyage to Spitsbergen in 1671 on board the whaling ship *Jonas im Walfisch* and subsequently published the very first, quite accurate description of Spitsbergen and its plants and animals. A whaling Captain who made numerous discoveries and observations and published them in books, was the great **William Scoresby** junior from the early 19th century. But most whalers kept their discoveries for themselves as they did not want any competitor to know where they had made their catches, or they simply did not care about publishing their considerable knowledge.

It was only in the 18th century that expeditions were launched that were not commercially motivated, at least not directly. The quest for a passage to the far east, which was of great interest to merchants, was certainly an important reason to finance such voyages. However, the desire to reach high latitudes or even the North Pole, to find new islands or whaling grounds or to make other important geographical discoveries played an increasingly important role. Additionally, the British Admiralty wanted to have seamen competent in navigation in northern waters, which could best be achieved by sending out expeditions.

On a number of occasions Spitsbergen served as a base for North Pole expeditions, due to its position at a high latitude, combined with good accessibility by ship. The Russian scientist **Mikhail Lomonossov** initiated an expedition that was to winter in Recherchefjord and then sail across the North Pole to the Bering Strait. Lomonossov himself died at home before the whole project started. His successor, **Vasilij Vakovlevitsj Tsjitsjagov,** had to accept that neither in 1765 nor the following summer could he get very far in the ice with his three ships. Nor was the opportunity to do scientific work used to any extent.

The next explorers on the scene were the British who sent a whole series of expeditions in search of a northwest passage to the Pacific, but also tried the way via

Spitsbergen across the Pole. In 1773, **Constantine John Phipps** sailed northwards with his two ships, the *Carcass* and the *Racehorse*. His instructions to turn around at the North Pole instead of a voyage to the Bering Strait turned out to be quite superfluous as, despite several persistent attempts, Phipps did not make it any further than Sjuøyane and was faced with considerable difficulties when he finally tried to leave the ice. Some scientific observations were made and one of Phipps' officers was no less than Horatio Nelson, 14 years young. Legend has it that he almost perished during an unauthorized Polar bear hunt. There is, however, no historical evidence for this anecdote.

The next voyage was made in 1827 when the Englishman **William Edward Parry** sailed to Spitsbergen with a crew and eight reindeer on board his ship *Hecla*. He had boats designed to be pulled across the ice as sledges, if necessary. Like many scientists of his day, Parry expected to find open water after an initial belt of drift ice, hence the sledge boats. The *Hecla* anchored in Sorgfjord in the bay which is today called Heclahamna, and Parry started with his sledge boats towards the north, but had to leave his reindeer behind for space reasons. After an open boat journey across open water, he met with ice and started to drag the boats. Out of necessity, his men had to assume the role of the reindeer to do the pulling. They turned back at 82°40'N due to slow progress, but they had at this point reached a latitude that would only be beaten in 1895 by Fridtjof Nansen. Prior to turning back, Parry realized that the ice was actually drifting southwards, thus preventing him effectively from reaching significantly higher latitudes. They made other important discoveries confirming earlier conjectures. The ice situation would certainly not allow any navigation between Spitsbergen and the North Pole. The ice was not, as expected, smooth and flat, but on the contrary very uneven. Marching over the ice was not only hampered by its very inconvenient surface, but also by the unfavourable direction of the current. This made Spitsbergen altogether uninteresting for any further attempt to reach the North Pole until aviation became available, and there were very few attempts to reach high latitudes from Spitsbergen between Parry's expedition and the famous Balloon flight attempted by the Swede Andrée in 1897 (see section 5.6 *Attempts to fly to the pole: Virgohamna and Ny Ålesund*).

In the same year as Parry, 1827, the mayor of Burscheid in Germany, **Barto von Löwenigh**, was in Spitsbergen for a voyage that primarily served his desire for adventure. In Norway, von Löwenigh invited the Norwegian geologist **Balthazar Matthias Keilhau** at short notice to join him, turning his trip into something more than a pure pleasure trip. After the expedition, Keilhau published his geological and other observations that he made in southern Spitsbergen, on Edgeøya and Bjørnøya; hence the reputation of this voyage for having started scientific investigation of Spitsbergen. It may, by the way, also have been the very first tourist voyage to the area.

This new scientific orientation was continued on an exemplary level in 1838-40 by the French on board the ***Recherche***. They visited a number of different locations in the north Atlantic, and Spitsbergen played a subordinate rule during this famous expedition. In 1838, Recherchefjord was visited for some weeks and received its name on this occasion and, in 1839, Magdalenefjord was the scene of some detailed investigations. This expedition was distinguished by careful preparation and the participation of scientists from different countries, and it yielded results that filled more than 20 volumes.

It was, however, mainly the Swedes, who started systematic scientific work in Spitsbergen in the 19th century. The first was marine biologist **Sven Lovén** with a small expedition in 1837. Following him, figures such as **Otto Torell**, an early advocate of the ice age theory, and more especially **Adolf Erik Nordenskiöld,** stepped onto the scene. Nordenskiöld became one of the most famous personalities in polar exploration when he completed the northeast passage on board the *Vega* in 1878-79. However, it was Torell who really started a whole series of Swedish expeditions when he investigated glaciated landscapes, making self-financed voyages to Switzerland, Iceland and, in 1858 for the first time, Spitsbergen, accompanied by the young Nordenskiöld. In 1861, Torell led a larger expedition on board the vessels *Aeolus* and *Magdalena*. His scientific staff reads like a who's who of the later scientific scene in Sweden: Nordenskiöld, Jakob Chydenius and Nils Dunér were amongst those who were with Torell to solve scientific problems in the Arctic. Both ships operated for about four months, partly separated, and brought home a rich scientific harvest, especially from northern parts of the archipelago.

In 1864, Nordenskiöld took over as leader of the Swedish expeditions. One result of the Swedish expeditions so far was the first more or less accurate map of Spitsbergen, which was published in 1865. Next to his scientific interests, the mineralogist Nordenskiöld had ambitions to reach the North Pole, possibly to make his voyages more attractive to sponsors. In 1868, Nordenskiöld tried a steamship of 60 horsepowers. Despite three stubborn attempts, all that could be achieved was confirmation of Parry's conclusion that it was not possible to get anywhere near the North Pole from Spitsbergen with a ship. This made Nordenskiöld consider a sledge journey across the ice. In 1872-73, after some training in East Greenland, Nordenskiöld wintered at "Polhem" in Mosselbukta on the north coast of Spitsbergen, to be able to start early in the following year. Shipwrecked crew members from other ships put an additional burden on his provisions. To make things worse, the 40 reindeer that Nordenskiöld had brought to pull the sledges, all sensibly sought their well-being in freedom, and ran away. Soon after the start of the sledge journey, in 1873, it became clear that the Pole could not be reached. Nordenskiöld decided reasonably to change his plans in favour of some scientific work in the largely unknown interior of Nordaustland before returning home. He never returned to Spitsbergen, but colleagues such as Alfred Nathorst kept the Swedish tradition of solid scientific work alive for some years. During those expeditions, large parts of coastal Spitsbergen were mapped geologically and topographically.

The first **international polar year** of 1882-83, initiated by **Karl Weyprecht**, is generally considered to mark the beginning of coordinated scientific work in polar areas.

During this period, a number of nations cooperated to sustain a network of scientific stations at high latitudes, mostly in the Arctic. The task of establishing a station in Spitsbergen naturally fell to Sweden, and for one year, detailed data in various fields of geophysics were successfully collected at Kapp Thordsen in Isfjord. One of the members of this expedition was Salomon August Andrée, who was later to become famous for his tragic attempt to reach the Pole by balloon in 1897. In 1882-83, he was responsible for the observation of geomagnetism and electricity.

The next large, internationally coordinated scientific enterprise was the **Swedish-Russian Arc de Meridian expedition**, which is remarkable for a number of reasons. The scientific objective was to determine the shape of the Earth by means of a combination of very precise astronomic determinations of latitude and longitude, using triangulation to establish the exact distance between the points where astronomic observations were carried out. The intention was to measure the length of one degree of latitude along a meridian, which was then to be compared to equivalent data from equatorial areas. If the Earth was a perfect ball, then one degree of latitude had to be the same length, regardless of the position between equator and pole. But if the Earth was flatter at the poles, as many scientists suspected, then the distance between two parallels (latitudes) had to be slightly less near the poles. It was decided to measure along a north-south profile in Hinlopen Strait towards the south cape of Spitsbergen. Astronomic fixing was done at two observatories, a Swedish one at Crozierpynten in Sorgfjord and a Russian one in Gåshamna in Hornsund. These observatories also served as wintering stations. The triangulation that connected the observatories topographically, was done in the summers from 1898 to 1904, with 1899 to 1902 as the main working period. This logistically and scientifically demanding task, to measure the length of a meridian between two degrees of latitude, was successfully accomplished thanks to the cooperation of the two countries: The Swedes worked in the north, while the Russians measured in the south. Both the purely scientifically defined objective and the international cooperation in those years, at a time of strong nationalism in Europe, and the successful realization without any loss of human life, make the Arc de Meridian expedition one of the most interesting of those years. Scattered remains of the observatories can still be seen in Sorgfjord (illustration 6.13, page 333) and in Hornsund (illustration 6.21.1, page 423).

In the early 20th century, the **Norwegians** finally turned their attention to the exploration of Spitsbergen. Hunting and fishing in the Arctic had already been a Norwegian activity for a long time. The spectacular expeditions of Fridtjof Nansen amplified the Norwegian interest in the Arctic and this young nation, which had just become independent from Sweden in 1905, saw a new and rewarding challenge in the development of the islands between its own north coast and the North Pole. Spitsbergen also stimulated some political interest: The temporary establishment of a Norwegian postal connection from Adventfjord to Norway, the purchase of claims, and a telegraph station built in 1911 in Green Harbour (Grønfjord), were episodes manifesting the growing interest in control of Spitsbergen, within some circles in Norway.

In fact the scientific exploration of Spitsbergen, as well as all the other activities, remained international. There were a number of expeditions, more or less hunting and yachting voyages by rich adventurers, during which geographical knowledge was occasionally obtained and later published. The boundary between science and tourism was obviously gradual, but the expeditions of the Prince (later Duke) **Albert of Monaco** brought such a wealth of fresh knowledge, mostly in the shape of new charts of coastal waters, that their scientific character can hardly be denied. The Duke financed and joined expeditions to Spitsbergen in 1898, 1899, 1906 and 1907. A good number of placenames still remind us of the noble explorer, in the fjords where he carried out his scientific work; for example Krossfjord and Liefdefjord (Monacobreen!).

One of the Duke of Monaco's collaborators was the Norwegian officer **Gunnar Isachsen** who joined the expeditions in 1906 and was soon to become a major driving force in the **Norwegian exploration** of Spitsbergen. Expeditions were sent out almost on a yearly basis, and a lot of systematic work was done mainly within the fields of topography and geology. The leading character from 1908 onwards was geologist and lecturer **Adolf Hoel**. It is fair to say that Hoel's interests were not exclusively scientific; he had also a strong motivation to bring the islands, which were a no man's land, under Norwegian sovereignty. This was finally achieved in 1920. In the meantime, the scientific focus was on topographic mapping and geology, the possibility of mining activities being kept in mind. To support the expeditions, an organisation called *De Norske statsunderstøttede Spitsbergenekspeditioner* ("The Norwegian governmentally funded Spitsbergen expeditions") was founded and later renamed *Norges Svalbard- og Ishavsundersøkelser*, that finally developed into today's *Norwegian Polar Institute* (NPI).

Despite all these regular and mostly very successful scientific expeditions, there were failures and even catastrophes. One of the biggest dramas was the "Deutsche Arktische Expedition" ("German Arctic Expedition") in 1912-13, as it was officially called; now better known as the "Schröder-Stranz expedition", after its leader. A group of four men, including Schröder-Stranz, was left on the north coast of Nordaustland for a sledge journey, but they were never seen again. The expedition ship, the *Herzog Ernst*, was forced by drift ice to winter in Sorgfjord. Three more men died during attempts to walk to Longyearbyen, while others survived only with severe frost bite. Several expeditions were launched in the spring of 1913 to rescue the remaining survivors who were finally evacuated from Sorgfjord by Gunnar Isachsen.

5.6 Attempts to fly to the pole: Virgohamna and Ny Ålesund

"... *when, one day, you hear that I have got him (the balloon Örnen) out of his house all right, you may tell the world that Andrée is as contented and feels himself as safe, as if he were in his own home in Stockholm.*"

Salomon August Andrée in Virgohamna (1897), quoted in *Spitsbergen Gazette* No. 6, August 1897

As neither ship-based voyages nor sledge journeys from Spitsbergen towards the Pole had yielded any real success, this field remained relatively calm for a while.

Being an engineer, the Swede **Salomon August Andrée** believed in the developing technology of the late 19th century. An expedition with one of the new-fashioned, hydrogen-filled balloons seemed to be a promising way to reach the North Pole. In 1896, Andrée established his base camp in Virgohamna on Danskøya (illustration 6.7.2, page 323), but could not launch his balloon *Örnen* (Eagle) because of unfavourable weather conditions. His second expedition in 1897 resulted in the take-off of his airy vehicle and its subsequent disappearance. Engineer Knut Frænkel and meteorologist Nils Strindberg crewed the *Örnen,* together with Andrée. After a good two days and various technical difficulties, the ice crust that formed on the balloon had become so heavy that the three men had finally to land on the ice. They struggled across the uneven drift ice and ended up on Kvitøya (illustration 6.16.2, page 381) where they established their last camp. They were not seen or heard of again until 1930 when the camp was accidentally found by a Norwegian expedition. The photographs from the dramatic days in 1897 could still be developed after 33 years in the ice. The three brave Swedes received a state funeral in Stockholm.

Another one who believed in polar aviation was the American journalist **Walter Wellman**. After two fruitless attempts to reach the North Pole by ship from Spitsbergen and with sledges from Franz Josef Land, Wellman put all his faith in the latest technological developments and brought an airship, the *America*, to the very same place where Andrée had launched his balloon only nine years before. Wellman's first attempt in 1906 was doomed to failure from the start, as the engine of the airship was not at all capable of propelling the vessel or keeping it manouvreable. His second attempt, in 1908, ended after a few kilometres with a semi-controlled crash landing on a small glacier. The third and last attempt was started in 1909. After a short flight and some technical problems, *America* was landed on drift ice north of Spitsbergen and towed back by a Norwegian ship to Virgohamna. When Wellman heard of the news of Robert Peary and Frederick Cook, who both claimed to have reached the North Pole in the meantime, he never returned to the Arctic.

Another man, who saw himself as destined to reach the North Pole, was the famous Norwegian explorer **Roald Amundsen**. For a while, he was busy with other adventures such as conquering the South Pole and the subsequent *Maud*-expedition in the northeast passage, but Amundsen then left the *Maud* when he realized that it would not offer opportunities for anything but solid science. Instead, he became convinced that it was now possible to reach the North Pole by air, enabling him to realize his old dream. Amundsen chose Ny Ålesund as a base for his expeditions because there he could then start from a position relatively close to the pole and at the same time he could benefit from the good accessibility to ships and the presence of the miners who could help him during his preparations. For his first attempt, in 1925, Amundsen's choice fell on two Dornier-Wal flying boats, N-24 and N-25. The two craft did not return after their start from the ice of the Kongsfjord on 21st May and were believed to be lost. After an emergency landing at 87°41'N, the six men had to create a runway in the uneven ice to enable one of the two flying boats to take off. This dramatic attempt proved successful, and a single, heavily overloaded Dornier-Wal flew back to Spitsbergen, only to be forced to crash-land again near Brennevinsfjord at the northwestern coast of Nordaustland due to lack of fuel. A Norwegian sealing ship happened to be in the area and brought the adventurers safely back to Ny Ålesund.

Amundsen returned in 1926, this time with an airship called *Norge* which had been constructed by the Italian **Umberto Nobile**. While Amundsen and Nobile were preparing their expedition in Ny Ålesund, the American **Richard Byrd** arrived in Kongsfjord and took off on 9th May in his Fokker airplane *Josephine Ford*. Byrd returned a good 15 hours later and claimed to have reached the North Pole by air. Nowadays, historians have strong reservations about Byrd's claim, but at the time Amundsen, of course, was not aware of this. He started on 11th May on board the *Norge*, together with his American sponsor Lincoln Ellsworth, and with Umberto Nobile and his Italian crew. The mast that held the airship during the last moments before this start (and again in 1928) is still standing on the tundra close to Ny Ålesund (illustration 6.4.1-3, page 271). The *Norge* flew across the Pole and reached Teller in Alaska without difficulties. The most dramatic part of this expedition was the argument which later started between Amundsen and Nobile as to whether the fame should go to the young nation of Norway or to fascist Italy.

The result was another all-Italian expedition in 1928. Nobile returned to Ny Ålesund with a new airship, the *Italia*, to repeat the flight over the North Pole. After some successful flights across the Russian Arctic, the final advance towards the Pole was started. What resulted was one of the greatest dramas in the history of polar exploration, and the biggest media event of the 1920s. *Italia* flew over the Pole and was then turned around to fly back to Ny Ålesund. North of Nordaustland, the airship crash-landed on the ice. A part of the airship drifted away together with five crew members, one of whom was later found dead; the remaining nine were stranded on the ice. Two persons were seriously injured, including Nobile who had broken a leg. The following weeks saw the largest search-and-rescue expedition ever launched in the Arctic. More than 20 aircraft and 14 ships from six nations tried to rescue the Nobile expedition. Amundsen started out from Tromsø with the French flying-boat *Latham* in the seach of his old rival. *Latham* crashed somewhere near Bjørnøya together with its crew, including Amundsen; only a small part of the wreck was later found on the coast of Norway.

Finally, Nobile's radio operator managed to send an SOS, together with their position. The Swedish pilot **Ejnar Lundborg** managed to land a small plane on the ice close to the Italian camp; the famous "red tent". Lundborg evacuated Nobile, who was most severely injured amongst those who were still on the ice, but crash-landed on the ice during his second attempt to land near the red tent. Finally, the Soviet icebreaker *Krassin* reached the camp and rescued everybody remaining. In the meantime, two Italians and the Swede Malmgren, who had been second-in-command and meteorologist on board the *Italia*, had tried to walk to Spitsbergen. *Krassin* found and rescued the two Italians, but Malmgren was lost under doubtful circumstances.

More than 1,400 people were involved with these rescue expeditions during which 17 men died, including Amundsen. The fact that Nobile was the first to be evacuated, together with the mystery of Malmgren's disappearance, cast a very bad light on Nobile, amplified by the heroic sacrifice of his competitor Amundsen.

With the flight of the *Norge* in 1926, both Poles had definitely been reached on the ground or by air and it had become clear that there were no large landmasses left to be discovered in the Arctic. The flights from Ny Ålesund thus constitute the final chapter of those polar expeditions; they were out for records, sensation and the conquest of geographical extremes, rather than scientific progress: The "heroic" age was over and gave way to systematic research.

5.7. Trappers

"Heller til Svalbard på en nøtteskal enn arbeidsledig i Norge."

"Rather in a nutshell to Svalbard than jobless in Norway."

Karl J. Bengtssen, *Tretti år rundt Svalbard*

The Pomors were hunting in Spitsbergen for centuries, but their activities decreased and finally stopped altogether in the 19th century. The reasons for this are not fully understood, but they may have to do with economic problems at home, as the hunting grounds in Spitsbergen remained good enough for trappers to follow from Scandinavia, mostly from Norway. The main targets of their activities were the valuable winter fur of Polar bear and Arctic fox, that could be sold in Norway. Beyond this, they collected down from Common eider nests and occasionally hunted Belugas. Other species such as reindeer, seals, birds and birds' eggs were taken to supplement their supplies, as dogfood and as bait for fox traps.

It was not only Norwegians, but also Swedes, Finns, Germans, Baltic people and Russians, all of whom tried to make some income by wintering in Spitsbergen, but the scene and the trade were clearly dominated by Norwegians. The trapper culture (if you want to call it that) in Spitsbergen has its roots in summer voyages to the icy sea to catch seals at the ice edge, together with anything else that did not run, fly or swim away early enough. Such short hunting expeditions had already been a tradition in north Norway for a long time and always remained economically much more important than the relatively limited number of men and, later, also a handful of women, who spent years in Spitsbergen to hunt during the winter. The first Norwegian wintering in Spitsbergen took place during 1795-96, probably in Isfjord. In 1822-23, 16 men wintered in Krossfjord. By this time, the set-up was known and the business was established. A number of failed winterings then resulted in catastrophes so that activities remained low for a long time, until the heyday of overwintering and hunting began in 1892.

Depending on the region, the focus was either on Polar bears or on Arctic foxes. Foxes were caught with wooden traps that killed the animal with a heavy weight of stones without damaging the fur. Iron traps that caught foxes by the feet were hardly used in Spitsbergen. The best fox territories were in Bellsund and Isfjord, but the west coast further north and the north coast were also used. Bears were caught with armed traps: wooden boxes with bait and a short-barrelled rifle connected via a piece of trip-wire to the trigger. If a Polar bear smelled the bait, then it had to place its head in the wooden box directly in front of the barrel and would shoot itself between the eyes as soon as it pulled on the bait. This simple, but very effective system worked with single animals as well as with female bears who had offspring to look after. The trapper would sooner or later come along to check his traps, and would try to keep the little bears alive to sell them to zoos for a lot of money; a trade that mostly went through Hagenbeck in Hamburg. Polar bears were also caught with poisoned bait, a technique that was soon forbidden but remained in practice for a long time. The most important hunting areas for Polar bears were those areas that were in the ice for most of the year, especially Hornsund, the southeastern part of Edgeøya and the surrounding small islands and Hopen.

The usual strategy was to have one "hovedstasjon" (main station, illustration 6.18.4-3, page 420), a slightly bigger and more comfortable hut to live in, and a number of smaller shelters to increase the area that could be worked (illustration 6.1.1-1, page 257 or 6.1.6-5, page 262). In the early years, groups were quite large and comprised four to six men or even more. Later, there was an increasing tendency towards teams of two persons or even loners who wintered on their own. Thus, trapping developed more and more from an industry that was organised by merchants in Tromsø or Hammerfest to a lifestyle of dropouts who liked the free life in the Arctic. In the early 20th century, the idea of hunting Polar bears in Spitsbergen, which included lots of adventure and the possibility to make a lot of money, attracted so many that in some years, good hunting areas were verging on crowded. Most trappers made just enough money to cover the costs of their adventure. It should not be forgotten that many were terrified after a lonely winter and returned back home as soon as they could, but some liked it so much that they spent many years in Spitsbergen. A few became legendary figures, and names like Hilmar Nøis, Arthur Oxaas, "Polar bear king" Henry Rudi and a very few brave women such as Wanny Woldstad, who wintered several times in the Hornsund area in the 1930s, together with her children, are still well-known today and their adventures have been told in many books. These stories from the "fangstmannsperiode" influence the images that many have of life in the Arctic, especially in Norway.

Interrupted only by the Second World War, professional hunting in Spitsbergen continued on a large scale until 1973 when Polar bears became protected internationally. Today, trappers are a rather rare phenomenon in Spitsbergen. The only one who still really deserves to be called a trapper is a Norwegian who has for many years, and still is, living in one of the northern branches of Isfjord. Another has specialized in collecting Eider down, but he only comes to Spitsbergen during the relevant season. One further trapper's station on the west coast is occupied by a Norwegian couple, sometimes together with their children. Other "trappers" can apply to the Norwegian administration for a hut in Wijdefjord or Woodfjord, but these people are attracted by the outdoor life and the experience, although they are obliged to catch foxes. The Norwegian who has moved into the hut in inner Wijdefjord (Austfjordnes) may actually stay for a longer period, while the future of the hut in Woodfjord (Mushamna) is currently slightly uncertain, as the Sysselmannen has anounced it may be closed because the necessary resources to run it might not be available in future.

5.8 Whaling in the early 20th century

"Es ist ein ziemlich betrübendes Bild, das diese Geschichte des Walfanges in unserer Zeit von der Art gibt, wie der Mensch mit den Reichtümern der Natur haushält. ... Die Geschichte wiederholt sich selbst, aber die Menschen lernen herzlich wenig daraus, sei es, daß sie nicht wollen oder daß sie nicht können."

"The story of whaling in our days gives rather a sad picture of the way man treats the wealth of nature. History is repeating itself, but man does not learn from this, either because he will not or he cannot. "

Fridtjof Nansen, *Spitzbergen*

Once stations such as Smeerenburg had been abandoned in the early second half of the 17th century, whaling became more pelagic. Whales and ships moved away from the shores, towards the ice edge, and Spitsbergen's fjords remained peaceful for a long time. This changed when the Norwegian **Svend Foyn** realised the potential for whaling, during his first voyage to the area. The turning point was his invention of the explosive harpoon gun that enabled whalers to take even the largest species, including Fin and Blue whales, which had thus far swum in relative safety around the ships that killed their smaller and slower relatives. The new slaughter of the largest whales started on the coast of north Norway but, in 1890, Foyn went to Spitsbergen and caught nine Blue and three Fin whales within a short season. After a few years, it became big business, and from 1905 onwards, these whales were seriously hunted for their blubber. During this summer, about 15 ships harpooned some 800 large whales. Most whaling ships processed their prey directly at sea, but others used land-based stations in Spitsbergen, at Finneset in Grønfjord and on Bjørnøya. This new rush for oil and blood was rather shortlived. By 1906, results were already rather meagre, and by 1912, whaling ships were largely going elsewhere. Altogether about 2,000 whales were caught during those years, most of them Fin and Blue whales. Even one century later, the populations have still not recovered, and sightings of these majestic creatures, especially of Blue whales, are quite rare in Spitsbergen.

The catches of White whales (Belugas) are a different story. They had been hunted or caught with nets in the fjords for centuries, first by Pomors, later by Norwegian trappers. A hunting station which was often used to catch Belugas was near Kapp Toscana (Ingebrigtsenbukta) in Van Keulenfjord. Piles of bones still remind us of the slaughter of the past.

5.9 The Spitsbergen Treaty

"Article 1. The High Contracting Parties undertake to recognise, ... , the full and absolute sovereignty of Norway over the Archipelago of Spitsbergen, comprising, with Bear Island or Beeren-Eiland, all the islands between 10° and 35° longitude East of Greenwich and between 74° and 81° latitude North, ...

Article 3. The nationals of all the High Contracting Parties shall have equal liberty of access and entry for any reason or subject whatever to the waters, fjords and ports ...;
subject to the observance of local laws and regulations, they may carry on there without impediment all maritime, industrial, mining and commercial operations on a footing of absolute equality."

The *Spitsbergen Treaty*, signed 09 May 1920 in Paris

Spitsbergen belonged to no-one until well into the 20th century. Several nations, mostly in northern Europe, had occasionally shown some interest, but were content with keeping it neutral; as long as nobody else started any trouble, it was simply not worth the effort and possible repercussions for other political issues. Most of the marine resources such as whales and fish were in any case not related to the land sovereignty question.

The picture changed when mining became an increasingly important issue early in the 20th century. Incidents such as labour disputes between Norwegian workers and their American and British employers in the mines around Adventfjord suddenly made a working administration and legislation necessary. Several options were put on the table, including a joint administration by Norway, Sweden and Russia. The First World War drew everybody's attention to areas far away from Spitsbergen and reduced the political influence of previously interested powers such as Germany and Russia.

During the post-war negotiations in Versailles, Norway convinced the other nations that Norwegian administration and sovereignty would be the appropriate solution for Spitsbergen and its neighbouring islands. The Spitsbergen Treaty was signed in 1920 in Versailles and came into force in 1925; it is commonly referred to as "Svalbard Treaty", but the term "Svalbard" is not used in the original document. The Spitsbergen Treaty defines some restrictions to Norwegian sovereignty, including:

- Spitsbergen would be part of the kingdom of Norway and under Norwegian administration and legislation.
- Citizens of all the signatory powers would have free admission and the same legal status.
- Spitsbergen would be demilitarized. No country including Norway would be allowed to install military facilities but this should not hamper the execution of sovereignty by police and coastguard.

In practice, the definition of what is "military" and what is not has proved to be a difficult question. Sharp protests came from the Soviet Union when the airport near Longyearbyen was opened in 1975, since this could be used for military purposes. On the other hand, the size of the helicopter fleet in Barentsburg during the coldest years of the Cold War could hardly be explained as meeting the daily needs of a mining company.

In 1925, the archipelago was re-named "Svalbard", as if the islands had been Norwegian ever since the mysterious Viking voyage in 1194 to the "cold rim", whatever that was. The years from 1596 to 1925 were treated as nothing but a little historical confusion (see chapter 2 *introduction* for further details on the main placenames).

Next to Norway, Russia is the only country that makes any use of its right to economic activities such as mining. During the Cold War, the different settlements kept a watchful eye on each other but for the most part lived peacefully together at close range, with occasional official contacts and some limited cultural exchange. Nowadays, there is regular official and private contact between Norwegians and Russians, although Barentsburg follows Russia in terms of autocratic structures.

5.10 Mining

"Besides coal and oil-bearing rocks, Spitsbergen has other valuable products. An extensive layer of iron was recently discovered in a hill-face at Recherche Bay ... and at Cape Thordsen phosphatic deposits occur. There exist ... enormous quantities of gypsum of great purity, and in King's Bay the British Northern Exploration Company have marble quarries. Asbestos occurs in various districts in large quantities."

Seton Gordon, *Amid Snowy Wastes*

The fact that there was coal to be had in Spitsbergen was already known to the early whalers, but it was the systematic geological mapping carried out in the late 19th and early 20th century that fuelled hopes for natural treasures in the frozen ground of the far north. Soon, a number of companies started activities that remind one a little of the gold rush in north America, if not in terms of scope, then at least regarding the enthusiasm that some characters put into their enterprises. In many instances, business projects were started in a rush and considerable resources were used to exploit mineral occurrences, the quality and quantity of which were at best uncertain and occasionally highly doubtful. In other cases, a lack of financial backing put a stop to projects that seemed promising but failed finally because of adverse logistical or natural circumstances. A handful of mines have survived until recent years. These are the foundation of today's settlements in Spitsbergen.

For a long time, coal had been used intermittently to supply the whalers' or other ships' own needs, whenever this was convenient. It was not until 1899 that Spitsbergen coal was, for the very first time, exported with commercial intentions. It was the Norwegian sealer, **Søren Zachariassen** from Tromsø, who took a small load of coal from Bohemanflya in Isfjord, back home for sale in Norway. This is generally considered to be the beginning of commercial mining in Spitsbergen.

In the following years, a number of quickly-formed companies from different countries claimed large areas of Spitsbergen which at that time was still no man's land. In many cases, these companies simply paid some money to trappers for local inspections. Actual activity was required if the claim was to have at least some substance; to give a contract to somebody who was there anyway was the cheapest method of installing a guard. In other cases, trial mining was done and mining installations were sometimes established, with the purpose of industrial extraction of minerals, which subsequently turned out to be short-lived. The most famous example within Spitsbergen may be the old marble mine on Blomstrandhalvøya in Kongsfjord, although there is a surprising number of other similar instances. The English *Northern Exploration Company* (NEC), with **Ernest Mansfield** as its colourful leading figure, distinguished itself by numerous attempts, all of which turned out to be failures. Successful mining on an industrial scale was the exception rather than the rule, and the expense of the operations meant that the ventures changed their owners, sometimes frequently. Profitable mining was hardly ever achieved.

In the 1920s, when the Spitsbergen treaty had just been signed and Norway was about to exercise its sovereignty as completely as possible in Spitsbergen, the Norwegian government bought many mining claims from foreign companies, most of whom were happy to escape from bankruptcy; it also subsidised most domestic companies.

The first mining settlement with year-round industrial mining was **Advent City** that had been established in 1905 on the northern side of Adventfjord by an English-Norwegian company. Activities were hampered by numerous labour disputes and brought to an end as early as 1908. The American entrepeneur **John Munro Longyear** founded Longyear City in 1906 and sold it to Norway in 1916; it was renamed **Longyearbyen** in 1926. For many decades, it remained the focus of the activities of the Norwegian state-owned mining company *Store Norske Spitsbergen Kullkompani* (SNSK). The SNSK, often just called "Store Norske", is still mining coal in Longyearbyen, but only on a symbolic level to supply local needs, mainly those of the coal-powered power station. The company is still the land-owner and an important employer in Longyearbyen and is thus one of the major players in the development of the settlement.

The history of **Ny Ålesund** is roughly comparable, but after a series of accidents, mining was finally stopped in 1962. Subsequently, the settlement was turned into a modern, international research village. Nowadays, **Sveagruva** is the centre of Norwegian mining activities in Spitsbergen. For a long time, the Russian state-owned company *Trust Arktikugol* used to run several coal mining settlements in Spitsbergen, but **Grumantbyen** together with the associated harbour facilities in **Colesbukta** was closed in 1962 and all activities in **Pyramiden** were stopped in 1998. Today (early 2009), **Barentsburg** is the only active Russian settlement in Spitsbergen, although mining has currently been stopped and there are plans to open a new mine in **Colesdalen** between Barentsburg and Longyearbyen. Colesdalen is one of the valleys with the richest tundra areas in Spitsbergen. The coming years will show how serious the Russians are about their plans.

To summarize, mining was clearly the dominant economic activity in Spitsbergen throughout the 20th century, interrupted only by the war years. After some "wild" early years, the Spitsbergen Treaty made the legal situation clear and a number of less serious or non-viable companies soon left the stage. A smaller number of localities, where mining on an industrial level was established, have survived the early "gold-rush period". These form the basis of today's system of settlements in Spitsbergen.

5.11 The Second World War

„In the arctic all men have a common enemy in the climate, and it has always been an unbroken tradition there that men are friends; and so it seemed incredible to the men at Eskimoness when they found themselves, at the end of that winter, suddenly faced with human enemies, forced to hunt men instead of polar bears, and foxes, and to discover what it felt like to be hunted.“

David Howarth (1957), *The Sledge Patrol*

The occupation of Norway by Nazi-Germany in 1940 did not, to begin with, have any consequences for Spitsbergen and its mining settlements. This situation changed when Hitler attacked the Soviet Union in June 1941, when the Barents Sea suddenly became of great strategic importance as a seaway to Murmansk. In August 1941, 1,955 Russians were evacuated to Arkhangelsk and 765 Norwegians to England. Most settlements in Spitsbergen were effectively destroyed to make sure the enemy would not use them. This was quickly realized in Germany and advantage was taken of the opportunity to establish weather stations in Spitsbergen. Reliable weather data from the Arctic was important for warfare not only for the battlefields in Europe, but also for the Barents Sea itself and thus for the Murmansk convoys. Their significance for the war in eastern Europe made the convoys' safe completion or destruction, respectively, an issue of high priority on both sides. Accordingly, a lot of effort was put into establishing war weather stations and putting those of the enemy out of action. Competition between different branches of the German armed forces led to the somewhat strange fact that, for several years of the war, more than one station wintered in Spitsbergen; for example in the winter of 1941-42 "Bansö" (Adventdalen) and "Knospe" (German: bud. Signehamna, Krossfjord) were manned and operated.

In the spring of 1942, a Norwegian military operation with British participation tried to bring Spitsbergen back under Norwegian/Allied control. Two small vessels, *Isbjørn* and *Selis,* sailed to Spitsbergen, but were attacked by four German planes in Grønfjord during the night of 14th May 1942. *Isbjørn* sank and *Selis* was burning; 14 men died and a number were injured. The survivors established a garrison of about 80 Norwegian and British soldiers in the largely destroyed Barentsburg.

In the autumn of 1942, another weather station with the code name "Nussbaum" (German: walnut tree) was established at the same site as "Knospe" in Signehamna (Krossfjord). "Nussbaum" was discovered by the Norwegians in spring 1943. One German soldier died during a small exchange of shots. The German submarine that arrived to pick up the German weather team, attacked the Norwegian's boat; one Norwegian soldier drowned during this attack.

In September 1943 the German northern fleet, that had been inactive in Norway's fjords for some time, launched a large-scale attack on Spitsbergen, which came as a surprise to Norway and the allies. The large battleships *Scharnhorst* and *Tirpitz*, supported by nine other warships, bombed Barentsburg and Longyearbyen. Nine Norwegian soldiers were killed and another 41 captured during this attack. Eight German soldiers also lost their lives. The Norwegian garrison was soon re-established in the ruins of Longyearbyen.

In the meantime, the "war for the weather" continued. During the winter of 1943-44, German war weather stations were active in Liefdefjord and on Hopen, followed in 1944-45 by stations on Hopen, in Stormbukta (south Spitsbergen) and on Bjørnøya. At the same time, the most famous of all war weather stations was working in the remote Rijpfjord on the north coast of Nordaustland. Only evacuated in September 1945, this station, called "Haudegen" was the very last active German military unit of the war.

The fact that no less than four German weather stations were active in Spitsbergen during the last year of the war, not counting similar expeditions in northeast Greenland, is evidence of the attention that was paid to the "war for the weather", at least on the German side. All stations were staffed both by military personnel and scientists and secured against attacks. Fighting relating to these stations was rare, but it did happen and it cost human lives on both sides.

Few remains have survived until today. Time, the tough weather conditions, souvenir hunters and, in some cases, nearby settlements or stations have mostly destroyed the traces. In Svalbard, the remote "Haudegen" station on Nordaustland is the only one that is more or less well-preserved (illustration 6.15.3-1, page 377). On other sites, some traces tell the experienced eye what was once there.

Pyramiden was the only settlement that survived the war without any damage. All the other settlements, as well as some small huts, were destroyed mostly by German fire, but both Norwegians and Russians soon re-established their mining installations to supply their domestic needs for coal in the difficult years that followed the war.

5.12 Spitsbergen after the War

"Stikkordet var ‚normalisering', men hva var nå det?"

"The key words were "normalization", but what should this now mean?"

Thor-Bjørn Arlov, *Svalbards Historie*

This section includes a short overview of today's settlements and stations in Svalbard. For further details, see the relevant sections in chapter six.

Mining activities were quickly resumed both by Russians and Norwegians. For Norway, the need for a reliable energy source for a country that was otherwise not exactly blessed with natural resources, certainly played an important role in the meagre years after the war (nothing was known at that time about the oil occurrences of the North Sea).

It was the Swedes especially, who resumed systematic scientific research in Svalbard during the International Geophysical Year 1957-58. In Kinnvika on the western side of Nordaustland, a relatively large station with several buildings was erected to observe geophysical phenomena simultaneously with other stations in the Arctic and Antarctic.

At the same time and for the same purpose, Polish scientists established a station at Isbjørnhamna in Hornsund. Originally built for the Geophysical Year, this station was kept operational, initially as a summer station and, since 1978, as a year-round facility.

In the following years, scientific research was taken up again by a growing number of expeditions from various countries. Expeditions from the UK, especially Cambridge University, established a tradition of systematic geological research under W.B. Harland as a famous leading figure, to mention just one example. Also the re-orientation of **Ny Ålesund** as a scientific village gave a huge impetus to international polar research in Spitsbergen, which is still growing in the first years of the third millenium AD.

In the meantime, a different kind of research was established in Spitsbergen. Due to its position close to the Pole, Spitsbergen is an ideal site for antennae that receive signals from satellites in polar orbits. Due to the good infrastructure and accessibility, **Longyearbyen** soon gained importance in this new "market with the large dishes". A glass fibre cable was laid from Longyearbyen to Norway in 2004 to accommodate the huge data volumes, at the same time supplying the locals with high-speed internet access.

Together with other modern activities, this has created new markets and economies with an associated need for a labour force, putting mining into a more marginal position, at least in Longyearbyen.

The centre of modern Norwegian coal mining is **Sveagruva** in the innermost part of Van Mijenfjord. There, in recent years, mines have been developed and are so productive that, according to the state-owned mining company *Store Norske Spitsbergen Kullkompani* (SNSK), the books have balanced or actually moved into profit. In the recent past, technical difficulties including fire, water in the mines and accidents have put things back into a more normal mode and it can be assumed that public support continues to play a vital rule in this business in Spitsbergen. Sveagruva is still a mining settlement only and other activities such as tourism are not on the wishlist. The workers mostly live in Longyearbyen or even in Norway.

Next to the Norwegians, the Russians are still mining coal in Spitsbergen, though the state-owned mining company Trust Arktikugol has closed the settlement of **Pyramiden** in the innermost part of Isfjord in 1998. Nowadays, Russian activities are concentrated in **Barentsburg**, although this settlement has also obviously seen better days in the past. There are plans for a new Russian mine in Colesbukta between Barentsburg and Longyearben. Such a new mine would not exactly be part of an environmentalist's dream, but permission has already been given by the Norwegian authorities. Time will show how serious the Russian plans are.

Next to these settlements, there is a number of smaller **stations**. The coastal radio station **Isfjord Radio**, situated at Kapp Linné in the mouth of Isfjord, is run automatically since 1999 and is not staffed anymore. The glass fibre cable that was laid from Longyearbyen to Norway in 2004 can supply all needs for communication and thus makes Isfjord Radio technically unnecessary. The buildings are, however, still used occasionally to accommodate tourists in a hotel named **Kapp Linné**.

There are still permanently staffed Norwegian weather stations on **Bjørnøya** and **Hopen** as well as on Jan Mayen, which is not part of Svalbard. There is an active **Polish research station** in **Hornsund**.

All settlements and stations used to have their own postmark and codes, but these have mostly been withdrawn since 2002. Nowadays, the settlements have their own postmark, but not the outposts Isfjord Radio, Hopen and Bjørnøya anymore.

5.12 EISCAT (European Incoherent Scatter) near mine 7 in Adventdalen..

Chapter 6 – Fjords and islands, settlements and stations: The regions of Svalbard

"The rugged western coast of Spitsbergen, with glaciers descending from icefields and peaks of 1,000 m, gives way to relatively ice-free dissected tablelands in the centre, with further high ice mountains (up to 1,717 m) in the northeast. To the northeast of Spitsbergen lies Nordaustlandet ... that is almost totally buried under two ice caps. Various smaller islands complement the two main islands of the archipelago."

Dowdeswell and Hambrey, *Islands of the Arctic*

Very few people will have been to all the sites that are described in this chapter and they will be, for the most part, scientists and professional expedition leaders and guides. Hardly anyone else has the chance to get to these remote places. In recent years, expedition style cruise ships have landed passengers at more than 150 different localities throughout the whole archipelago of Svalbard, but only at ten or so during any one voyage. Your influence as a passenger on where you will make excursions during a cruise is actually very limited. This may seem disappointing but, for most people, it will not matter at all. Most passengers will wish to experience as much as possible of the wildlife, the landscape and ice, flora and some history, within the time available. For example, the barren, desert-like landscape on the north coast of Nordaustland and the surrounding islands is an interesting area to visit – if the ice conditions allow. But where exactly you land, in which bay or on which island you go ashore, does not make a big difference in the end. "Pars pro toto"; according to this motto, you can experience the geographical and biological character of a whole area at one or two exemplary sites. Every single site has, of course, got its own special features and you could spend weeks and months following the lonely coasts step by step, always exploring and always finding new things, but this is impossible for most of us and probably not something that everybody would actually enjoy (I would! – The author).

It will be clear, then, that this chapter cannot describe every possible site in detail. The most famous and – relatively – frequently visited "classics" are certainly included, so that you can prepare for a voyage or look up facts about the places you have visited. Perhaps you will visit a site that is not described here; better still, because it is always exciting to explore something new. You can still read about the area in general for some background on the landscape and geology, history, wildlife and flora of the region.

The wildlife is somewhat tricky. You may have been to Antarctica or other areas, where many beaches are full of life. These places are well known and we know what

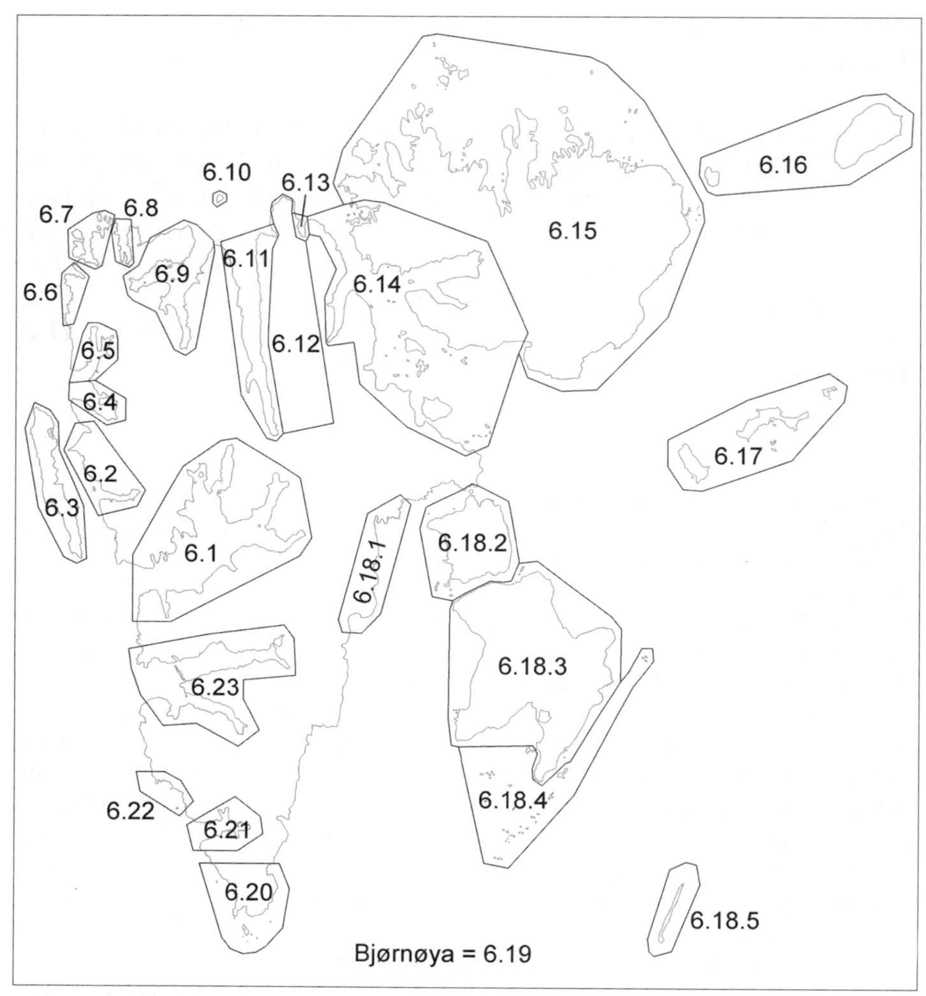

6. Geographical affiliation of the sections in chapter 6.

kind of wildlife will be there before we go ashore. In Spitsbergen, some of the wildlife is predictable too, for example the bird colonies. Arctic foxes, Polar bears and reindeer, however, roam over large areas and you need some luck to see them. You may one day see a group of reindeer at a particular spot on the tundra and, on the next day, nothing. We (leaders) know from experience that some places offer a better chance for seeing certain wildlife than others, but there are no rules and no one can predict what will actually be there on the day of your visit. What you need is patience, good binoculars and a bit of luck.

Walrus colonies are a special case. They are mostly stationary during the summer months, but it may happen that a haulout site is occupied by a large group one day and then by only one or two walrus next week – even none at all if your luck is out. Scientists and experienced expedition leaders know where to find good walrus sites, but I don't reveal their exact position in these pages simply to protect these animals from too many visitors. Experience has shown, in Antarctica for example, that private yachts can reach the most remote areas without any relevant experience of how to treat sensitive wildlife properly and this can cause environmental problems. The number of yachts visiting Spitsbergen has grown significantly in recent years.

This may be an appropriate place to remind readers of the necessity to treat the arctic environment with respect, regardless of the means of travel. Please read chapter 3.6 *Conservation, cultural heritage, protected areas, safety* carefully, with its individual sections, and do not forget the code of responsible behaviour when you are in the field; the urge to take good photographs can easily become stronger than the need to keep a proper distance from a bird's nest. On organised voyages, safety and conservation depend not only on the expedition leader, guides and other staff, but also to a great extent on you – the visitor.

To structure the information in the following pages, individual sections mostly follow the scheme "general – placenames – geology – landscape – flora and fauna – history".

Some of the most important **Placenames** are explained because they can transform a map into a history book, describe the landscape or remind one of anecdotes. Placenames have often been given thematically, within certain areas. Most placenames have been "Norwegianised" in the 20th century. The choice in this book is, of course, subjective.

The section on **Geology** is mostly rather short and requires that you have read chapter 4.2 *Geology*. For an explanation of technical terms, refer to the geological glossary at the end of this book. Some of the contents of the geology sections may be of interest mostly to (amateur) geologists who already have some basic knowledge. Further information, easily understood by everybody, can be found in "Rocks and Ice. Landscapes of the North" written by the same author (see www.spitzbergen.de).

In the section **Flora and fauna**, some characteristics of each individual area are described. It is impossible to mention every small, inaccessible bird colony, or the "usual suspects" that you may or may not meet almost anywhere. Unexpected encounters with migrating wildlife (Polar bears, reindeer, seals, whales) are possible almost everywhere and at anytime.

The numbers of the illustrations correspond with the numbers of the relevant section in the text. Additional reference to illustrations is made only where appropriate, to refer to illustrations from the general chapters (chapter 4 *Natural history* and chapter 5 *History*), which may also document individual locations.

6.1 Isfjord

"Beautiful indeed, and highly characteristic, is the scene of entering (Isfjord) with the fine mountains on either hand, the great glaciers, coming down from the north, and the strange table-hills stretching away to the south."

Martin Conway, *The First Crossing of Spitsbergen*

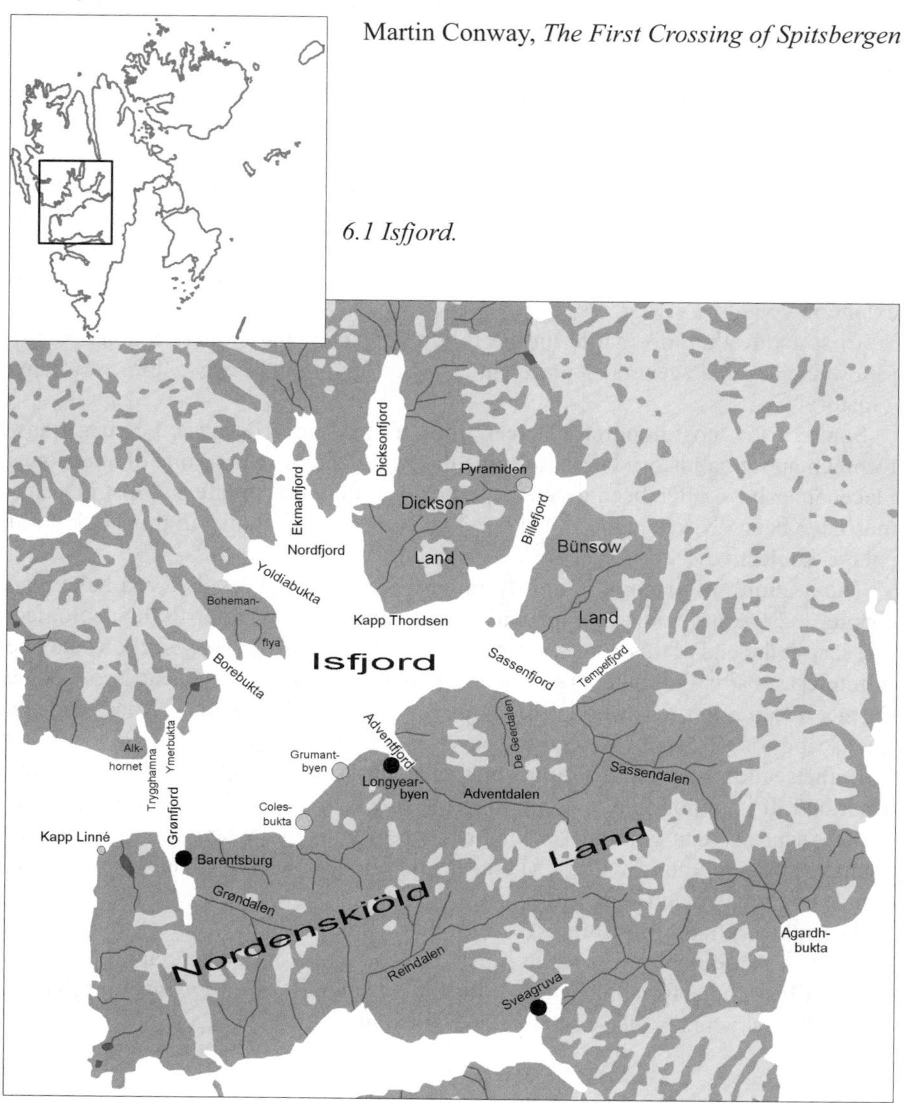

6.1 Isfjord.

Isfjord cuts 107 kilometres deep into Spitsbergen. On the basis of its surface area and the number of branches, it is certainly the largest fjord in the whole archipelago, although Wijdefjord, which runs from the north coast into central Spitsbergen, is one kilometre longer, according to official statistics.

Almost the whole spectrum of landscapes, geology, biology and history of Spitsbergen is represented in the Isfjord area. No other fjord offers such a variety of scenery. Several of today's active settlements are in Isfjord and accordingly there is a wide choice of tourist activities, mostly in and around Longyearbyen.

The following sections are organized in such a way that they follow the shores of Isfjord from the northern side of the entrance in a clockwise direction.

6.1.1 Alkhornet, Trygghamna

General: The mountain Alkhornet is situated at the entrance to the small fjord Trygghamna on the northern side of the mouth of Isfjord. Trygghamna might be called "Spitsbergen in a nutshell", because the area has most of those features that attract visitors to the Arctic: beautiful mountain and glacier scenery; wide, rich tundra; reindeer and Arctic foxes; a bird cliff, and historical relics from different periods. Trygghamna is part of the Northern Isfjord National Park.

Placenames: Alkhornet: Refers to the shape of the mountain, which resembles a horn, and its inhabitants, the alkets. **Kjerulfbreen**: Theodor K. (1825-88), Norwegian geologist. **Trygghamna:** "Safe harbour"; the deep and well- protected bay was frequently used as a natural harbour since the 17th century. The Dutch whalers called it "Behouden haven", which means the same as Safe harbour.**Vermlandryggen**: after a province in Sweden.

Geology: Metamorphic basement on the western side of Trygghamna, including slate, phyllite and quartzite, all strongly deformed and in places cut by conspicuous, light-coloured veins. The eastern side of Trygghamna, in contrast to this, has younger sedimentary layers. The hardness of some of these layers, together with their sloping attitude (they are dipping towards the east), strongly influence the geomorphology. These sediments, some of which are rich in fossils, date back to the upper Palaeozoic (Permian) and, towards the neighbouring Ymerbukta, the Mesozoic (Triassic), and became tilted during Cretaceous and lower Tertiary times. The upper Palaeozoic layers are exposed with beautiful folds at Selmaneset, the southern tip of the mountain ridge east of Trygghamna.

Landscape: The landscape is beautiful and varied. Trygghamna is surrounded on all sides by steep, striking mountains and has several smaller glaciers (Protektorbreen, Harrietbreen, Kjerulfbreen). The inland area north of Trygghamna is mountainous and strongly glaciated. West of Trygghamna, there is a wide, open, coastal tundra plain. Directly under the mountain Alkhornet, there is an extremely well developed field of ice wedges.

Flora and fauna: Alkhornet, as the name already suggests, is home to a large seabird colony with several thousand breeding pairs of Kittiwakes and Brünich's guillemots.

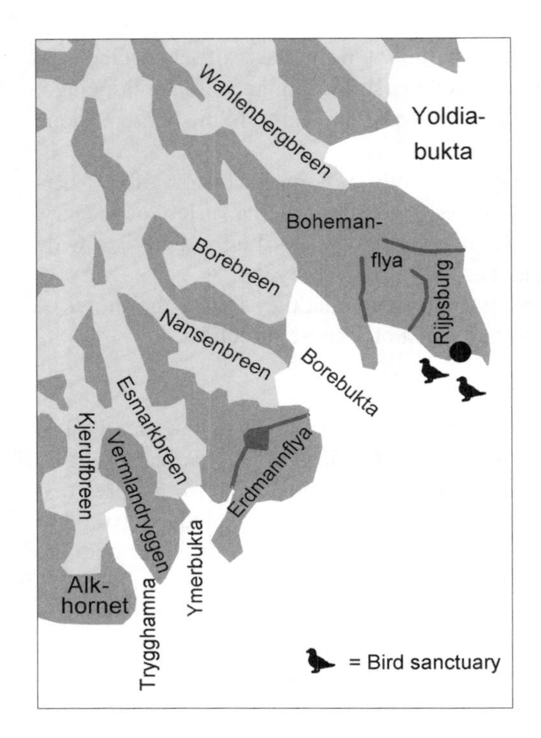

Alkhornet - Ymerbukta - Bohemanflya

Due to the mild west coast climate and fertilization from the bird cliff, the tundra below Alkhornet has very rich vegetation which provides feeding for reindeer. Arctic foxes have several dens in the area, taking advantage of the birdcliff as a source of eggs and young birds that occasionally fall out of the nests. Geese also breed on many cliffs near the coast, so visitors have to move around with great care in the early summer. Polar bears are not an everyday sight in Isfjord, but whoever thinks that they will never show up in the area could be in for a creamy-yellow shock. In some summers, bears seem to hang around in this area.

History: The central west coast is the part of Spitsbergen that has the longest recorded history of the whole archipelago and Trygghamna has been used throughout this time. There are relics of most chapters of Spitsbergen's history on the western side of the bay. The oldest ones are remains of blubber ovens and graves from whalers, probably English, dating back to the 17th century, though the blubber ovens are not amongst the best preserved examples in Spitsbergen. In the 18th century, Pomors used the area as a hunting ground and established a smaller and a larger station, also on the west side, not far from the old whaling station (on the plain north of the modern hut). The larger consisted of five houses and was one of the largest Pomor-sites in Spitsbergen.

Near the entrance to the fjord, there are remains of a trapper's huts just under the Alkhornet; now a ruin, it dates back to 1905. During WWII, there was a lookout of

Norwegian soldiers on the point at the entrance to Trygghamna. The modern hut, close to the beach with the Pomor and whaler sites, belongs to the Sysselmannen and was built in the 1980s when the relationship betweeen Norwegians and Russians was not always easy. It is no coincidence that, from this hut, you can see Barentsburg, including its helicopter base, across Isfjord.

6.1.2 Ymerbukta

General: The glacier Esmarkbreen in Ymerbukta, usually together with Barentsburg, is frequently visited during day trips from Longyearbyen using small excursion boats. Ymerbukta belongs to the Northern Isfjord National Park. For map, see section 6.1.1 *Alkhornet* (page 237).

Placenames: Erdmannflya: probably after Axel Joachim E. (1814-69), Swedish mineralogist. **Esmarkbreen**: Jens E. (1763-1839), Norwegian mineralogist. **Vermlandryggen:** after a region in Sweden. **Ymerbukta**: after a Swedish scientific journal. Ymer was a giant in Norse mythology.

Geology: The ridge Vermlandryggen, on the western side of the Ymerbukta, consists of steeply dipping sedimentary layers that are increasingly older to the west, spanning the time from the Permian to the lower Cretaceous (with several hiati; that is, missing strata). The mountains in the inland area further north consist of sediments of the same ages, but these have been strongly deformed by Cretaceous-Tertiary tectonic action to form a complex mosaic. Erdmannflya, the plain east of Ymerbukta, is built up of sediments dating back to the lower Cretaceous and lower Tertiary; the youngest solid bedrock in the area. Areas near the glacier are covered with large, recently deposited moraines.

Landscape: The calving front of the crevassed Esmarkbreen, surrounded by picturesque mountains, is the impressive highlight of the scenery in Ymerbukta. Another characteristic feature is the wide, rather flat plain of Erdmannflya on the eastern side of the bay. Large, fresh moraines near the shore show how much larger the glacier must have been in recent centuries.

Flora and fauna: There are no faunal highlights of tourist interest specific to this area, but interesting encounters with seals or even White wales and Polar bears are always possible near a glacier front.

History: There are remains of a Pomor station in the outer moraine area on the eastern side of Ymerbukta.

6.1.3 Borebukta, Bohemanflya

General: Borebukta has two large, beautiful glaciers, but is relatively rarely visited because of shallows in the entrance area and because Ymerbukta is more conveniently located for boats visting Barentsburg from Longyearbyen. Wide areas of very shallow water make landings difficult but there is a lot to see, not only in terms of history, but also the scenery, the tundra and the birdlife. The area is part of the Northern Isfjord National Park. Furthermore, some small islands on the southern side of the

Bohemanflya have been declared bird sanctuaries where all traffic is banned from 15 May to 15 August (this includes 300 metres of the surrounding waters). For map, see section 6.1.1 *Alkhornet* (page 218).
Placenames: Bohemanflya: Carl Henrik B. (1796-1868), Swedish scientist. **Borebreen, -bukta:** Boreas, god of the cold, northerly winds in ancient Grecian mythology. **Fridtjofbreen:** F. Nansen (1861-1930), Norwegian polar explorer.
Geology: The mountains around Borebukta consist mainly of strongly deformed Triassic sedimentary rocks; the bay itself is fringed with large moraine ridges dating into the little ice age. The large, coastal plain Bohemanflya consists of tectonically deformed Mesozoic sediments (Triassic to lower Cretaceous). The lower Cretaceous that can be found in the southern parts contains some coal seams which are well exposed near the coast in the vicinity of the huts at Rijpsburg (see below, *history* section). Large parts of Bohemanflya are covered with young superficial deposits, mostly raised beaches.
Landscape: Borebukta is dominated by the glaciers Borebreen and Nansenbreen, although both have retreated considerably in recent times. Wide-open, more or less flat, tundra that continues out from the shore, with extensive shallows. The surf has created small coastal cliffs on large parts of the shore.
Flora and fauna: Tundra vegetation covers large areas. Elevated parts are dry and easy to walk on; some of the lower areas are wet and accordingly difficult to walk on, and the vegetation of these wetlands, mostly mosses, is easily damaged. There is not so much wildlife in this area. Winterers have actually called Bohemanneset (the point at the southern end of Bohemanflya) "Kapp ingenting" (Norw., "Cape nothing") because of the lack of game. There are bird colonies, mostly Common eider, on the small islets off the south coast of Bohemanflya; they are bird sanctuaries and thus not accessible. With some luck, you can see Grey phalaropes and even King eiders on small lakes or on the shore.
History: It is the history that is of most interest at Bohemanflya, strictly speaking the area west of Bohemanneset. Outcrops of coal seams have been known for a long time and it was here that the Norwegian **Søren Zachariassen** extracted the first small load of coal for the purpose of export and sale. This is commonly considered to be the beginning of commercial mining in Spitsbergen. Zachariassen took about 90 tons on board and sold most of it in Tromsø. In the following year, he built a house for 16 people but did not do any more mining. It was in this hut that **Hjalmar Johansen** and **Theodor Lerner** wintered in 1907-08. Johansen had wintered with Fridtjof Nansen in Franz Josef Land in 1895-96, and "fog prince" Theodor Lerner was a German journalist and self-declared polar explorer. They made a sledge journey to north Spitsbergen with the very ambitous intention of discovery and geographical surveying of the northeasternmost parts of the archipelago (Kvitøya), but they finished their journey on the northwest corner of Spitsbergen where they were picked up by a boat.

In 1920 the mine was sold by the Norwegians to the Dutch mining company *NeSpiCo* (Nederlandse Spitsbergen Company). More houses were built and in 1920-21 a trial mine was constructed which was then called "Rijpsburg". In 1922, NeSpiCo removed most buildings and concentrated activities on the second mine of the company in Grønfjord, which they called Barentsburg. Only the Norwegian building and another house, now a ruin, were left behind. Both Rijpsburg/Bohemanneset and Barentsburg were sold to Russia in 1932.

The Norwegian hut, that dates back to 1900, is still in good condition. There are other remains all over the place in the vicinity, including a well, several pits, signs of annexation and the grave of the Norwegian trapper Arne Olsen, who died in April 1926 after a lonesome winter. He has the dubious honour of being the last person to die from scurvy in Spitsbergen.

6.1.4 Ekmanfjord, Coraholmen, Flintholmen

General: Beautiful scenery and interesting geology are the main features of Ekmanfjord which is part of the Northern Isfjord National Park.

Placenames: Coraholmen: *Productus cora*, fossil Brachiopod that is often found in Carboniferous and Permian sediments in Spitsbergen. **Ekmanfjord:** Johan Oscar E. (1812-1907), Swedish businessman and Patron of Swedish polar expeditions. **Flintholmen**: After the rock, flint.

Geology: There is a lot to see. In contrast to areas further west, the sedimentary layers are still mostly horizontal, as tectonic movements that took place just before and during the opening of the north Atlantic were less pronounced because of the larger distance from the west coast. The oldest rocks belong to the Devonian Old Red

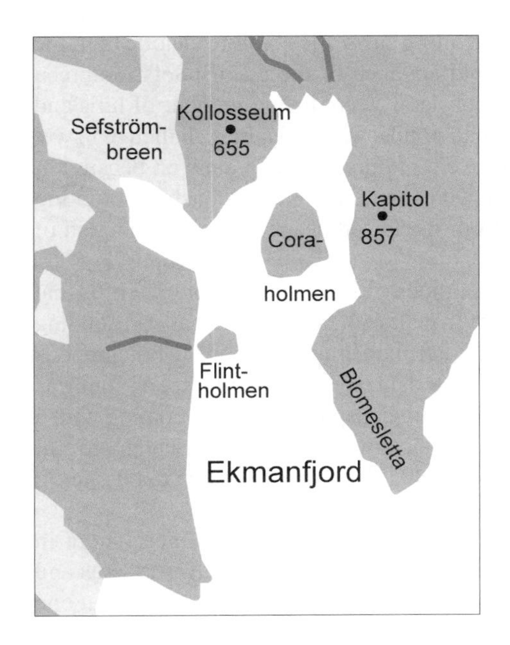

formations, which are a real eyecatcher because of their reddish colour. They can be seen in the lower slopes of the mountains north and east of Coraholmen. The colours of the Devonian sandstones and conglomerates, caused by hematite and iron oxides, are responsible for the reddish colouration of meltwater and moraines.

The upper Palaeozoic is represented by layers from the upper Carboniferous and lower Permian, consisting of various sandstones, carbonate rocks and evaporites, the latter being mostly white. These sediments build up most of the mountain slopes around Ekmanfjord above the Old Red. The extensive, very hard, fossil-rich Permian layers form prominent cliffs on the upper slopes. In some cases, as on the mountain Kapitol, the mountain tops are "crowned" by hard layers of basaltic intrusions which have now been exposed due to erosion.

The youngest solid bedrock in the area dates back to the lower Mesozoic (Triassic and lower Jurassic) and can be found on the western side of the entrance to Ekmanfjord (Bertilryggen).

The Quaternary geology ("ice age dirt") is also quite spectacular, especially on the small islands of Coraholmen and Flintholmen (see below).

Landscape: The Old Red gives a reddish-brown colouration which contrasts with the younger sediments. The slopes of the mountains Kollosseum (519 metres) and Kapitol (857 metres), that consist of characteristic horizontal layers of Carboniferous and Permian sediments, are dissected by erosion to form regular, vertical protrusions which remind one of a castle or a gothic cathedral.

The islands of Flintholmen and Coraholmen are little gems in terms of scenery and Quaternary geology. They have flat plains with old, tundra-covered raised beaches on their southern and eastern sides. On the remaining sides, they feature chaotic moraine landscapes that were created during a rapid advance of the glacier Sefströmbreen in the late 19th century. These moraines consist of a confusing number of hills and steep cones separated by mudholes and small ponds, which can be a challenge in wet conditions; they leave the visitor with the overall impression of a lunar or, because of the reddish colour, a Martian rubbish dump. The material that was pushed up during the advance of the glacier was derived from the raised beaches consisting again of former Old Red sediments.

Sometimes there are brachiopods that are much older than the (moraine) hills that contain them (which date back to the late 19th century), but are as old as surrounding bedrock, which makes them Carboniferous or Permian in age (there are no brachiopods in the terrestrial Old Red sediments). More abundant, are shells which are as young as a few 1,000 years. These are often covered with a conspicuous, white coating with a very uneven surface. This coating consists of calcarous algal colonies which are still living in fjords surrounded by calcarous bedrock. It is frequently taken to be a fossil coral, but this is not the case.

Flora and fauna: On Coraholmen and Flintholmen, you will find nice tundra in the flat parts outside the moraine areas, with breeding birds such as Arctic terns and geese (keep a good distance!). In some places, there are little hummocks, about one

foot high. These consist of tundra vegetation which keeps growing on a core of peat. The lowermost peat layers can be several thousand years old. Calm and sunny days may produce a regional faunal rarity in the shape of a mosquito plague. This can be quite annoying, although it does not compare with the level of torture that one has to endure, for example, in parts of Scandinavia.
History: There are remains of Pomor hunting stations and huts of Norwegian trappers on the eastern side of the Ekmanfjord.

6.1.5 Dicksonfjord, western Dickson Land

General: The area features beautiful, characteristic landscapes, and good hiking opportunities. It is part of the Northern Isfjord National Park.
Placenames: Dickson Land, -fjord: Oscar D. (1823-97), patron of Swedish polar exploration. **Fiskefjellet:** "Fish mountain", after Devonian fossils. **Hugindalen:** Hugin and Munin, Odin's ravens in Norse mythology. **Kapp Smith:** Lars Olson S. (1836-1913), Swedish businessman, patron of Swedish polar expeditions. **Kinamurfjellet:** "Chinese wall mountains", describring the shape. **Lykta:** "lantern", after the shape of the top. **Nathorstdalen**: Alfred Gabriel N. (1850-1921), Swedish geologist and polar explorer. **Sauriedalen**: after Triassic saurier fossils. **Triungen**: Tri = three, referring to the three mountain tops.
Geology: The slopes around northern Dicksonfjord consist of **Old Red** with its characteristic, reddish-brown colours. Most mountains, including Triungen and Lykta, have prominent, pyramid-shaped tops consisting of layers of hard, Carboniferous limestone. The Devonian Old Red and overlying **Carboniferous** limestones are separated by an angular unconformity: some layers are missing. They may have been removed before the deposition of the next sediments or they may never have been deposited. Additionally, the Devonian layers were tectonically folded and tilted before the Carboniferous limestones (which are still mostly horizontal in this area) were deposited. This characteristic structure gives evidence of tectonic activity during the uppermost Devonian. This late phase in the sequence of events linked to the Caledonian orogeny is regionally called **Svalbardian phase**.

A bit further south (Lyckholmdalen – Skansdalen), the Old Red disappears below sea level and the Carboniferous appears in the lower slopes, now topped by hard **Permian** sediments. Some of the upper Carboniferous layers include evaporites such as anhydrite.

Even further south, in southern Dickson Land, the Carboniferous and Permian layers disappear below sea level due to the general southward dipping attitude of the strata. Still visible above sea level are younger shales and sandstones from the **Triassic**, that have in places been intruded by basaltic sills and dykes. A lot of interesting fossils have been found in the Triassic sediments in southern Dickson Land, including skeletons of marine dinosaurs (Plesiosaurs) in 2006.
Landscape: Dickson Land, together with Andrée Land further north, is the area with the least glaciation in the whole Svalbard archipelago, as the higher mountain areas to

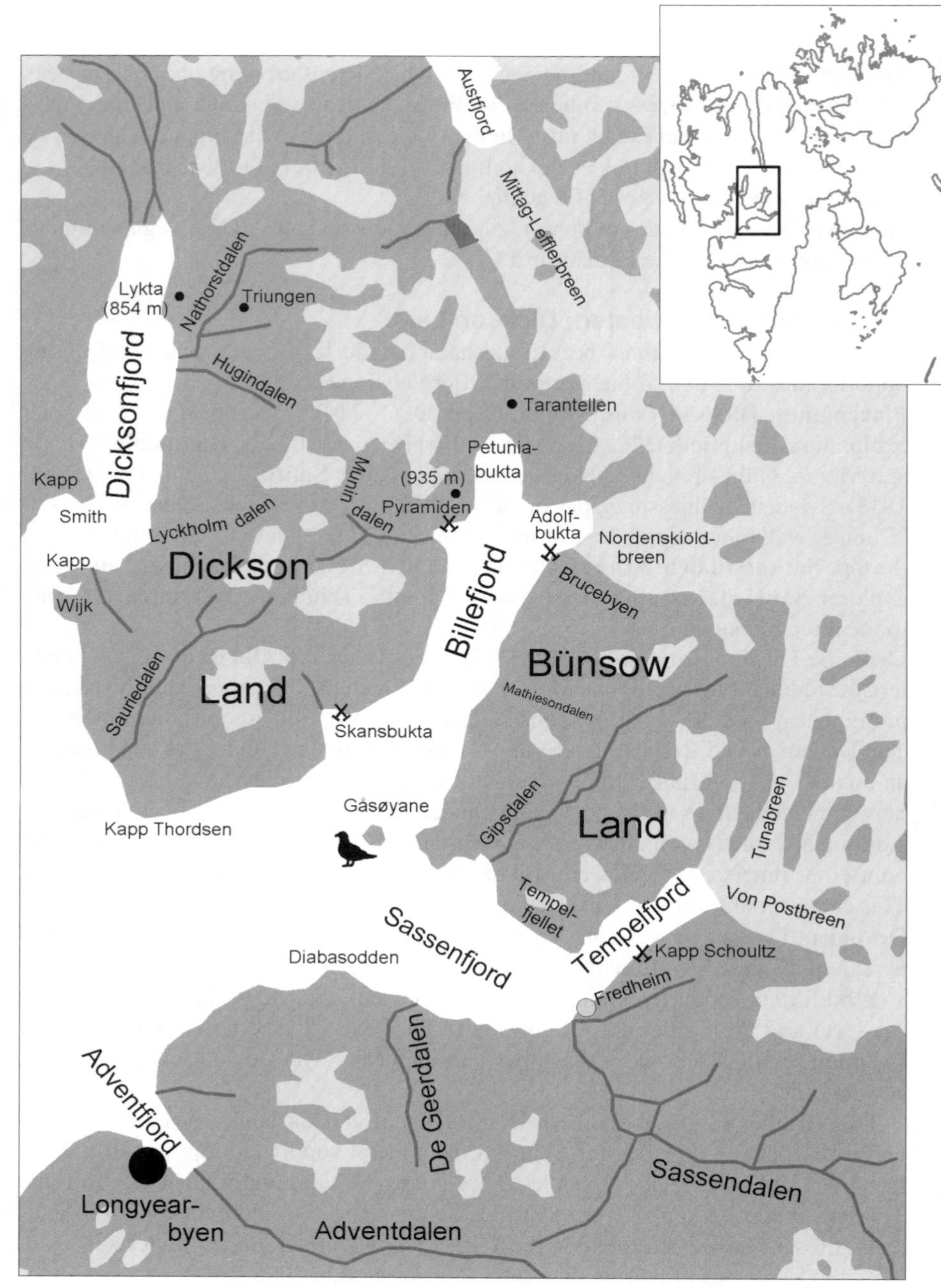

Dicksonfjord – Dickson Land – Billefjord – Sassenfjord – Tempelfjord.

the west and high plateaux further east catch most of the precipitation. This, together with the attractive scenery and the relatively good accessibility of Pyramiden by boat from Longyearbyen, makes Dickson Land a good area for demanding, several-day-long trekking tours.

Every geological unit has its own landscape characteristics. The Triassic in the south gives rise to rather soft landscapes with wide valleys, and mountains with extensive summit plateaux of modest altitude. The higher of these plateaux are partly covered by small ice caps, whereas there is rich tundra on the plains and valley bottoms near sea level. The hard Permian and Carboniferous sediments create spectacular valleys and canyons, with slopes that are dissected by erosion to form regular, vertical protrusions. These valleys include Skansdalen and Lyckholmdalen.

Further north, you get into the realm of the Old Red (Hugindalen, Nathorstdalen). The valleys are wider, with large valley bottoms filled by braided rivers characterised by multiple channels. The slopes are more rounded, but often topped by steep walls of Carboniferous sediments that make access to the mountain tops difficult or even impossible. Next to these wall-like mountain tops, the reddish colour of the rocks is the most striking landscape feature in this area, caused by the Devonian Old Red. Mountains that combine these characteristic, pyramid- or wall-shaped tops with red middle and lower slopes include Fiskefjellet/Lykta, Kinamurfjellet and Triungen as well as Pyramiden further to the east.

Flora and fauna: The protected and climatically relatively favoured branches of the inner reaches of Isfjord have quite rich vegetation. Arctic bell-heather and Mountain avens are abundant plants characteristic of this "middle Arctic" tundra type, and in places small hummocks are a sign of relatively high biomass productivity; a rare feature of Spitsbergen's tundras. There is not a lot of wildlife in Dickson Land. On warm, calm, summer days, mosquitos can occasionally be a plague, but not as bad as in Scandinavia or Greenland, for example.

History: At **Kapp Smith,** on the western side of Dicksonfjord, there are remains of a Pomor hunting station. In 1936, the first systematic aerial surveys of large parts of Svalbard were made by Norwegians who built several huts, including a radio house and darkroom, for this purpose at Kapp Smith. These huts have later been recycled by Norwegian trappers, but the pioneers of aerial surveying in the Arctic did not forget to leave a little memorial to themselves, which is still there.

There are several Norwegian trapper huts on the eastern side of Dicksonfjord, amongst others the station at Kapp Wijk that has a long history. It was established in the 1930s by **Arthur Oxaas**, one of Spitsbergen's legends of those years. Built as a simple hut when Oxaas wintered on his own, it was later turned into a more comfortable and spacious house when he lived there together with his wife. After WWII, they realized that life in the Arctic was not for them anymore, and Arthur continued his career in Tromsø, selling sausages in the street and achieving fame as a storyteller of his own adventures.

Historically the most interesting site is, without any doubt, near **Kapp Thordsen** in southernmost Dickson Land. The famous Swedish geologist and polar explorer **Adolf Erik Nordenskiöld** found coprolite (fossilized dinosaur droppings) in the Triassic sediments and had a large house ("Svenskehuset") built in 1872, from which to investigate the occurrence for its economic potential as a phosphate-bearing deposit which was a sought-after raw material for the production of fertilizers. As it turned out, the occurrence could not be exploited economically.

1872 was a heavy ice year in Spitsbergen and several sealing ships had to be abandoned on the north coast of Spitsbergen. 17 Norwegians travelled in open boats from the north coast to Isfjord and moved into this house that had so conveniently been recently built at Kapp Thordsen and was still well equipped with supplies and all sorts of useful things. However, all of them died during the spring of 1873; scurvy is generally assumed to have been the cause of death, although lead poisoning has also been suggested. Two were already buried by January, some hundred metres to the east of the house, and the others found their final resting place in one shared grave near the house; the wooden cross can still be seen. There is some uncertainty concerning the number of skeletons in the grave; one or two are believed to be missing. The "Svenskehuset" has since then also been known as "Spøkelseshuset" (ghost house), but the midnight sun takes away most of the terror of the "witching hour". Traditionally, scurvy has been assumed to have been the cause of death for those unlucky sailors, but small samples taken in 2008 showed toxic concentrations of lead, which points towards lead poisoning from badly sealed tins – a fate similar to that of the tragedy of the Franklin expedition that was lost in arctic Canada in the years following 1845.

The 1872-73 tragedy did not keep some brave Swedish scientists from using Nordenskiöld's house at Kapp Thordsen in 1882-83, which was the first International Polar Year. The original plan was to spend the year in Mosselbukta on the north coast, but this was not possible due to heavy ice conditions. Amongst the members was a young engineer named Salomon August Andrée, who was to achieve fame in a tragic way in 1897 during his ill-fated attempt to reach the North Pole by balloon from northwestern Spitsbergen. It is said that Andrée did not enjoy his first year in Spitsbergen either, but the Swedish expedition to Kapp Thordsen in 1882-83 worked very successfully and produced valuable scientific results.

Miscellaneous: There is still a working trapper station at Kapp Wijk in Dicksonfjord. You should consider the station area as private property and respect the owner's privacy, unless he has invited you in.

6.1.6 Eastern Dickson Land (Skansbukta, Pyramiden), Billefjord

General: This area is relatively easily accessible thanks to more or less regular day trips by boat during the summer from Longyearbyen to Pyramiden. There are excellent opportunities for demanding, several-day trekking trips in Dickson Land and north of Billefjord. Billefjord and its surroundings have some fantastic scenery and very interesting geology to offer. Bünsow Land, between Billefjord and Tempelfjord, is part

of the Sassen – Bünsow Land – National Park. In the entrance of the Billefjord, there are some small islets called Gåsøyane, which have protection status as bird sanctuaries (all traffic banned within 300 metres around the islands from 15 May to 15 August).
Placenames: Adolfbukta: see Nordenskiöldbreen. **Billefjord**: Cornelius Claeszoon B. (arond 1675), Dutch whaler. **Brucebyen**: William Spiers B. (1867-1921), Scottish polar explorer. **Dickson Land**: Oscar D. (1823-97), patron of Swedish polar expeditions. **Hørbyebreen**: Jens Carl H. (1815-1906), Norwegian scientist. **Mimerdalen**: Swedish expedition ship used in 1872. **Munindalen**: Munin and Hugin, Odin's ravens according to Norse mythology. **Nordenskiöldbreen**: Nils Adolf Erik N. (1832-1901), Swedish mineralogist and polar explorer. **Petuniabukta**: After the Scottish expedition ship *Petunia*, used in Spitsbergen in 1919. **Pyramiden:** describes the shape of the mountain top. **Skansbukta**: named after the neighbouring mountain Skansen, from the Norwegian word for a sloping surface, which describes the shape of the wide plateau that tops the mountain.
Geology: For the geology of the western side of Billefjord (Dickson Land), see also previous section 6.1.5 *Dicksonfjord, western Dickson Land.* Some fine geology can be seen on the northern side of Skansbukta where upper Carboniferous evaporites occur. These are layers that include anhydrite, a mineral that is chemically identical with gypsum (calcium sulfate) but with a lower water content in its crystal structure. Anhydrite has been mined without commercial success at several locations, including Skansbukta. There are some excellent outcrops of these layers at the outer point on the northern side of Skansbukta, called Kapp Fleur de Lys (accessible by boat; be aware of rockfalls).

The geological history and structure of Billefjord is largely determined by the complex **Billefjorden fault zone (BFZ)** that has been active at different periods spanning altogether many hundreds of millions of years, moving blocks horizontally alongside each other for several hundred kilometres. Both Billefjord, and Wijdefjord further north, follow this structural lineament. The rocks on either side of these fjords are accordingly different from each other. They are older than the last extensive movements along the BFZ, which date probably into the upper Devonian and Carboniferous. During the Permian, the developments on either side of the fault zone gradually converge and the differences between rock types are lost. The fault finally becomes almost totally lost in the Mesozoic rocks south of Sassenfjord. The various branches of the BFZ have created a conspicuous, complex mosaic of basement rocks (mostly gneisses) and cover sediments (mostly Carboniferous) in the area to the north of Billefjord, in the area around the glacier Hørbyebreen and the lake Ålandvatnet.

The Carboniferous and Permian sediments to the north and east of Billefjord comprise, amongst others, some coal seams and evaporites, the latter consisting of multicoloured gypsum / anhydrite. This colourful series of sediments catches the eye in a very pleasant way around Adolfbukta (near the glacier Nordenskiöldbreen) and to the west of Hoglandvatnet (Trikolorfjellet); the large valley of Gipsdalen owes its name to the gypsum layers. **Fossils** from different periods can be found at many sites. Near the river bed in the middle parts of Munindalen, fossilised tree trunks (*Lepidodendron*, "Scale tree") and impressions of tree trunks in surrounding sediments are prominent because of their age. They are as old as Devonian, which was the time when larger plants just started to colonise dry land. The fossil trees from Munindalen are amongst the oldest of their kind on Earth. In other places, including the slopes of Pyramiden just behind the settlement, similar fossils can be found that are a bit younger; these trees grew in the Carboniferous era, when vegetation was already much more developed than during the Devonian. In the upper Carboniferous and Permian eras, marine life including brachiopods, sponges and corals have left a well-preserved fossil record in some layers.

The youngest deposits are Quaternary, in which there are some unusual phenomena. The good solubility of the evaporite bedrock has produced dolines and, by means of precipitation of dissolved minerals from groundwater, locally well-cemented young fluvial conglomerates and moraines (north of Hørbyebreen, Mathiesondalen, Gipsdalen). This means that young sand and gravel that would normally still be loose, deposited by rivers, is already solidified due to natural cementation during the geologically recent past. There are some nice dolines near the river in the lower reaches of Mathiesondalen; also, in a low cliff just south of the river where it enters the delta area, a good cross-section through delta sediments a few thousand years old can be seen.

There are some fantastic raised beaches especially around Brucebyen and in Gipsdalen. Large moraines near the glacier Nordenskiöldbreen give evidence of pronounced glacial retreat during recent centuries.

Landscape: Generally beautiful, varied and characteristic. The geology makes an important contribution due to rocks with differing colours, hardness and structure. Also, the degree of glaciation varies strongly around Billefjord. Dickson Land and Bünsow Land have only small glacier and some local ice caps, but Olav V Land, directly east of Billefjord and Bünsow Land, is almost completely covered with large glaciers and ice caps that send the large glacier Nordenskiöldbreen down to Adolfbukta on the east side of Billefjord. Nordenskiöldbreen, in combination with a walk through Pyramiden, is a popular destination for boat trips from Longyearbyen during the summer.

There are impressive, characteristically steep cliffs in hard Carboniferous and Permian layers. On the western side of Billefjord, they can be seen on the northern side of Skansbukta. On the eastern side, they dominate all mountain slopes south of Adolfbukta and into Tempelfjord. All these slopes are dissected by erosion into regular protrusions that resemble towers reminiscent of castles or churches. Waterfalls, a landscape feature not common in Spitsbergen, are frequently seen in central parts of Dickson Land, the largest being Sjursethfossen that falls down into a natural amphitheatre. Well-trained feet can carry you from Pyramiden to Sjursethfossen and back within a day.

Another peculiar geomorphological feature, prominent around the northern part of Billefjord (Petuniabukta), are steep walls of hard carbonate rocks on the tops of the mountains. In some cases, they form smaller, pyramid-shaped mountain tops, for example at the "type locality" for this mountain type, Pyramiden (935 metres high). In other cases, north and east of Petuniabukta, these layers are exposed over larger areas and resemble walls. In places they have been bent by tectonic movements to form elegant curves and occasionally, erosion has by chance created fantastic shapes. The most spectacular example may be Tarantellen, a mountain top that looks like a giant stone spider. Situated a good 750 metres above sea level, it is an exciting destination for well-trained hikers who do not mind steep slopes covered with coarse scree. A view over several fjords, mountain ranges and large glaciers is the reward for the long ascent from Petuniabukta.

Flora and fauna: There are nice tundra areas with quite rich vegetation around Billefjord. The protected position in the innermost part of Isfjord, together with the geology, have created a relatively favourable local environment which is classified as "middle Arctic", with abundant Mountain avens and Arctic bell-heather as characteristic species. Yellow mountain saxifrage, a species that is otherwise not too common, is widespread in Petuniabukta and shows its nice yellow flowers in August. The Northern Jacob's ladder is a botanical highlight in July, at the bottom of the slopes on the north side of Skansbukta. There are small seabird colonies on steep cliffs everywhere around Billefjord, for example in Skansbukta, where mostly Brünich's guillemonts and Kittiwakes breed together with the occasional Puffin. Often, one of these colourful birds can be seen flying by.

Pyramiden: In 1910, the Swede Bertil Högbom took the coal field of Pyramiden in possession. Mining started in 1911, but success was limited and, in 1926, the property was sold to Russia. In 1931, it was taken over by the Russian state-owned company Trust Arktikugol, together with all other Russian interests in Spitsbergen. Pyramiden was evacuated in 1941, but was the only settlement that had been active up until 1941 and was not destroyed during the following years, so mining was able to start again quickly in 1946. By 1989, there were 715 men, 228 women and 71 children living in Pyramiden; Gorbachov's Glasnost lead to the opening of a hotel for tourists in that year.

Pyramiden was abandoned in 1998. Frost action and the river have done a lot of damage to the buildings during subsequent years and Trust Arktikugol has been slow in meeting its obligation to clear the place up. Theoretically, the idea is to remove everything that is environmentally sensitive together with all valuable equipment, but to preserve some of the buildings; some have already been pulled down. The future of the place is uncertain. There have been rumours of Russian plans to re-open the hotel, but nothing has happened so far, and the condition of the building makes this unlikely. In the meantime, doors and windows have been locked to prevent theft and vandalism, which have occurred in the past and done great damage to buildings and their interiors. Until only a few years ago, much was still there, for example the library and film library; it was as if the inhabitants received only very short notice of the evacuation of the place.

A very small number of Russians are still in Pyramiden to continue with clearing up and to collect "harbour fees" from visitors. Pyramiden is usually visited in the summer by boat from Longyearbyen. This includes a walk through the settlement of about one hour's duration. If you visit Pyramiden individually, remember that buildings may collapse and Polar bears may be having a nap around any corner, so you need to carry a rifle. It is certainly fascinating to experience the combination of a ghost town with Soviet-style architecture surrounded by arctic landscape. The scenery is nicer than near Barentsburg and the buildings and many other interesting details provide good photo opportunities, together with mount Pyramiden or Nordenskiöldbreen in the background.

History: The Carboniferous coal seams attracted mining companies throughout the 20th century. The *Scottish Spitsbergen Syndicate* (SSS), founded in 1909 by the famous Scottish polar explorer **William Spiers Bruce**, investigated coal-bearing beds on the eastern side of Billefjord. The SSS built several huts in the area. **Brucebyen** south of Adolfbukta comprised several huts that were mainly used in 1919-20. Four huts and a small railway line are still there, together with various remains from the trial mining days, although the stage of real mining was never reached. A larger, single hut now called **Skottehytte,** was built at the entrance of Ebbadalen in a fine scenic setting. All the huts are now locked and may not be used without permission. Coal seams in Gipsdalen were investigated with plans for extraction in the 1980s, but mining did not take place. A rusty tractor and tracks still remind visitors of these relatively recent activities and of the environmental damage that any mining would inevitably imply.

The coal seams were not the only occurrences of potential economic interest. Evaporite layers from the upper Carboniferous and lower Permian have also attracted mining enthusiasts. Remains of attempts by the *Dalen Portland Cement Works* to extract gypsum in 1918 in Skansbukta on the northern side of Skansbukta, still catch the eye. Most of those remains may actually be slightly younger and date from the 1930s when another mining attempt was made, but real mining never started as the occurrence consists mostly of anhydrite instead of gypsum. Anhydrite is chemically very similar, but without commercial value. Today, there are a mine entrance, a short, but nicely twisted railway line, and a shipwreck to be seen. The old boat may have been intended to transport gypsum from the shore to another, larger ship.

Most of these remains, especially the wooden parts of the railway line, have suffered significantly in recent years, as Skansbukta is a popular excursion site and many visitors walk not only between, but also over the remnants. Please observe the legal and moral obligations to protect the site; nothing is to be gained by stepping on wood and moving things around.

6.1.7 Sassenfjord, Tempelfjord

General: It is actually one single fjord, the innermost part of which is called Tempelfjord and the outer part Sassenfjord. The fjord has beautiful scenery, dominated by the glaciers at the head and by the mighty mountain Tempelfjellet. It is a popular destination for day trips from Longyearbyen, by boat during the summer and, in the winter, by snow mobile. There are places where the winter fjord ice is generally unsafe due to currents underneath, and attempts to extend the snow mobile season as much as possible, despite thinning ice cover, has led to dangerous situations in the past. There are a number of sites of historical and biological interest in the Sassenfjord area, most of which belong to the Sassen – Bünsow Land – National Park. A small group of islands at the corner, between Billefjord and Sassenfjord, called Gåsøyane, has been declared a bird sanctuary and is accordingly protected (no traffic closer than 300 metres to the islands in the period 15 May to 15 August). For map, see section 6.1.5 *Dicksonfjord, western Dickson Land* (page 224).

Placenames: De Geerdalen: Gerard Jacob D. G. (1858-1943), Swedish geologist and polar explorer. **Diabasodden:** after Diabas, a basaltic rock. **Gipsdalen**: after the mineral gypsum. **Gåsøyane**: "Geese islands". **Tempelfjellet**: after the appearance of the slopes, which resemble a temple or a gothic cathedral. **Sassenfjord**: origin unknown, possibly after an old Dutch word that indicates anchoring positions. **Tunabreen:** After Ultuna, a Swedish college, where von Post worked for a long time. **Von Postbreen**: Hampus Adolf v. P. (1822-1911), Swedish scientist, pioneer of the ice age theory.

Geology: 1) Structure. The Billefjorden Fault Zone (BFZ, see section 6.1.6 *Eastern Dickson Land (Skansbukta, Pyramiden), Billefjord*) is clearly visible in the southeastern slope of the mountain Gipshuken, at the corner between Billefjord and Tempelfjord. South of Tempelfjord, it continues in the slope of Marmierfjellet, west of Sassendalen. Here it is much less prominent, but Permian sediments have been uplifted east of the BFZ to a degree that brings them above sea level, whereas rocks of this age remain completely below sea level to the west of the BFZ. The Permian-Triassic boundary is, however, not well exposed.

At the same time, the strata generally dip gently southwards. This means that the further south you are, the younger the rocks seen at a given altitude.

2) Solid bedrock. The fault structure already described leads to the following pattern. Carboniferous and Permian layers form the prominent slopes on the north side of Tempelfjord/Sassenfjord. On the southern side, the BFZ that runs through Marmierfjellet, separates two geologically different areas. East of the BFZ, around lower Sassendalen, Permian limestones crop out in the lower slopes and are topped by darker Triassic shales and sandstones. East of Sassendalen, even Carboniferous layers including evaporites come to the light of day above sea level. In contrast, west of the BFZ, all Palaeozoic rocks (Carboniferous, Permian) are below sea level and the mountains consist exclusively of Triassic sediments overlain in upper slope sections by Jurassic sediments. The highest mountain tops south of the outer part of Tempelfjord include lower Cretaceous sandstones. These Mesozoic sediments are comparatively uniform and dark. Some of the layers contain abundant fossils such as bivalves, ammonites and belemnites. South of Diabasodden, spectacular finds of dinosaur skeletons in Jurassic sediments were made in 2006. The attention of international scientists has been caught by, amongst other things, fossil remains of no less than 21 Plesiosaurs and six Ichthyosaurs; all marine reptiles. Skeleton remains of a pliosaur from the mountain Knorringfjellet near Diabasodden suggest that this marine predator was no less than 15 metres long – the longest of its kind found so far.

The Mesozoic rocks have, in places, been cut by basaltic intrusions which now form the small islands of Gåsøyane, the point to the east of these islands (Gipshukodden), Diabasodden and several dykes in the area De Geerdalen – Botneheia. Hyperittfossen is a nice waterfall in the lower De Geerdalen that cascades down over an outcrop of a hard basaltic intrusion.

3) Quaternary. Gipsdalen may be the most interesting place in the area from a Quaternary geologist's point of view. It has a beautifully developed series of raised beaches, some karst phenomena (dolines and solidified young sediments) and rock glaciers on the lower slopes of Tempelfjellet. There are more well-developed raised beaches a bit further east, at Bjonahamna.

Landscape: Tempelfjellet is the eye-catching centre of the scenery. It owes its name to its slopes that erosion has shaped into regularly protruding towers. Softer Mesozoic sediments are responsible for the darker, more rounded slopes on the southern side of Tempelfjord, occasionally interrupted by steep cliffs where harder basaltic intrusions occur. The hardness of these intrusions is also responsible for landscape features such as the islands Gåsøyane, the cliffs at Diabasodden which are used as a breeding site by seabirds including Puffins, and the waterfall Hyperittfossen in De Geerdalen. There are several wide, ice-free valleys with rich tundra areas (De Geerdalen, Sassendalen).

The inland area east of Sassenfjord is mostly covered by glaciers and ice caps. At the head of the fjord, the calving front of Von Postbreen is another scenic highlight and is frequently visited during the snow scooter season.

Flora and fauna: The richest vegetation is to be found in lowlands and valley bottoms on the southern side of the fjord, especially around Diabasodden and in the lower reaches of De Geerdalen and Sassendalen. Reindeer and Arctic fox are common. There are seabird colonies on many of the steep cliffs, the best known being at Diabasodden where some Puffins breed next to Brünich's guillemots.

History: The remains of an old tractor are rusting away near a hut on the beach in **Gipsdalen**. The tractor was used to transport equipment from the shore deeper into the valley, along a track that is still readily visible, for the purpose of investigation of coal occurrences. This took place for the first time in 1921 when the SSS (see section 6.1.6) operated in the area, but the coal in Gipsdalen attracted attention into the 1980s, although activities never went beyond the stage of research.

On the southern side of the fjord, remains of mine installations up on the slopes above **Kapp Schoultz** are a reminder of attempts to mine anhydrite that was mistaken for gypsum.

In 1910, the German explorer **Wilhelm Filchner** ascended Von Postbreen to the ice-covered inland between Sassenfjord and the east coast of Spitsbergen to prepare for his forthcoming Antarctic expedition (he went down south with essentially the same plane that was later adopted by Ernest Shackleton for his famous *Endurance* expedition which was to cross Antarctica, but Filchner was forced to turn back before the actual crossing started).

The whole fjord has been an important hunting area both for Pomors and for Norwegian trappers. The most famous of the latter is, without any doubt, **Hilmar Nøis**, who spent no less than 38 years in Spitsbergen during the first half of the 20th century, wintering pretty much everywhere in Isfjord and on the north coast of Spitsbergen. He decided, finally, to build a hut that he called **Fredheim** on the coast in Sassendalen. His wife Helfried made sure Fredheim was turned into a cosy home, and lived there together with Hilmar for a good number of years. Fredheim is one of the very few trapper huts in Spitsbergen that have two floors. When Helfried and Hilmar Nøis finally left Spitsbergen to retire in Norway, they left it "to the people in Spitsbergen". It is now owned by the Sysselmannen and mostly closed to the public.

Miscellaneous: In winter, the sailing boat *Noorderlicht* lies frozen in the ice in Tempelfjord, to provide visitors with food and accommodation (see section 3.7.2 *Accommodation, eating and drinking*)

6.1.8 Adventfjord

Longyearben is situated on the southern side of Adventfjord. The settlement with its services, history and other aspects of tourism is described in chapter 3.7 *Longyearbyen*.

General: Adventfjord is a small side branch on the southern side of Isfjord, seven kilometres long and three to four kilometres wide. The area does not have the most beautiful scenery in Isfjord, or Spitsbergen as a whole, but it has various opportunities for day trips; anyone with some interest in birdwatching, natural history or the local history can enjoy several rewarding days there.

You should be prepared for a surprise encounter with a Polar bear at anytime and anywhere, once you leave behind the permanently inhabited area. The settlement itself is of course safe, and it is also generally considered safe to walk in the summer without a weapon on the road between the airport/camping site and Longyearbyen. This is exactly where a Polar bear was wandering about in the summer of 2007, but this was a very rare event. As soon as you walk into one of the neighbouring valleys (Adventdalen with its side valleys or Bjørndalen) or one of the nearby mountains (Platåberget, Sarkofagen, Nordenskiöldfjellet), you need a suitable weapon. In the spring of 1995, two female Norwegian students walked up to Platåfjellet without a rifle, and one of them was killed by a bear. The site is marked by a simple memorial ("Ninavarden").

The only place near Longyearbyen where you are allowed to put up a tent is the Camping site (no problem in Bjørndalen, Adventdalen etc.).

Its central position in northern Nordenskiöld Land makes Longyearbyen a good starting place for longer, quite demanding hiking tours. It is possible to hike to Barentsburg, to Fridtjovbreen in Bellsund or to the east coast of Spitsbergen (requires notification to the Sysselmannen in advance), to mention just a few options. Wherever

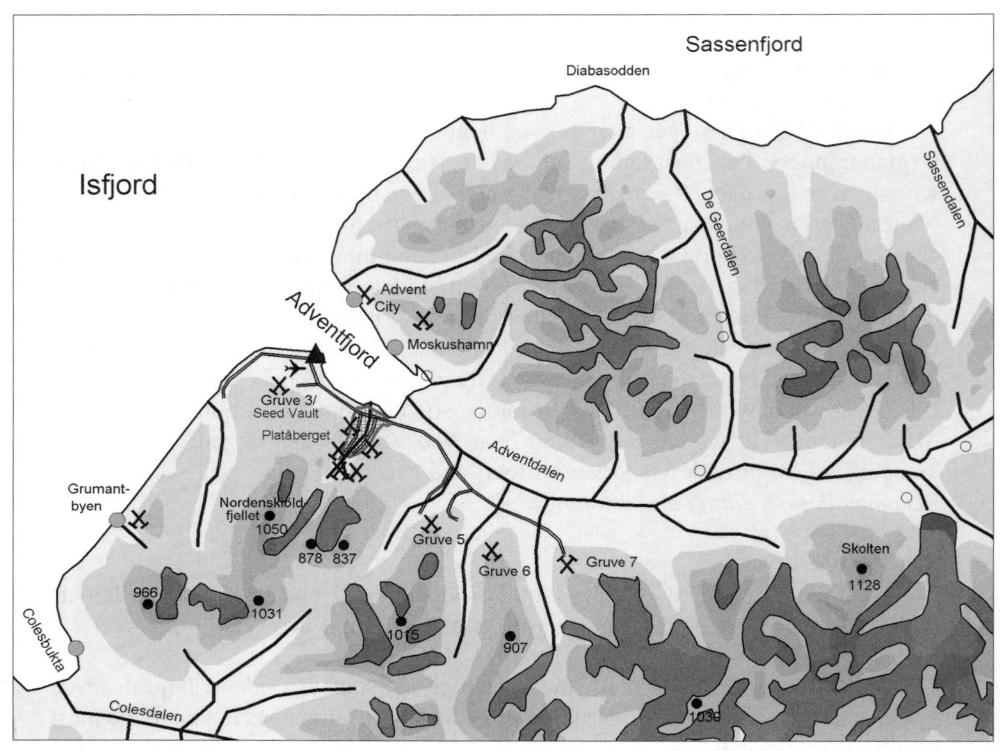

 *Mine (abandoned)*

Mine

Circle (grey): Settlement (abandoned).

Triangle: Camping site.

Shaded area: Longyearbyen.

Circle (empty): Pingo.

you choose to go, you will be faced with trackless wilderness with all that is needed to make your trip exciting: torrential rivers with ice-cold meltwater, glaciers and large, muddy moraines, soggy tundra, steeply incised canyons … If you are able to negotiate all this safely and you don't mind carrying the heavy weight of your equipment and several day's supplies, then you can spend as much time as you like in the countryside surrounding Longyearbyen.

Placenames: Adventfjord, -dalen: probably after the English whaling ship *Adventure*, that visited Isfjord in 1656. **Bjørndalen**: "Bear valley". **Hiorthamn:** Fredrik H. from Norway (1851-1923), founder of the mining company that established a mine on the northern side of Adventfjord. **Hotellneset**: location of Spitsbergen's first hotel in 1896-97 and now the area of the camping place and airport. **Larsbreen**: L. Johan Hierta (1801-72), Swedish author, politician and patron of Polar research in the 19th century. **Longyearbyen**: Norwegian translation of the original name "Longyear city". After the American John Munro L. (1850-1922), founder of the mining settlement. **Moskushamn**: indicates the place where Muskoxen from East Greenland were released in the early 20th century. Officially, the name is not in use anymore and has been replaced by the original name "Hiorthamn". **Nordenskiöldfjellet**: Adolf Erik N. (1832-1901), Swedish mineralogist and polar explorer. **Sarkofagen**: describes the shape of the mountain which resembles a coffin.

Geology (short version): Around Longyearbyen, you find near-horizontal layers of sandstones and similar sediments that were deposited about 60 to 40 million years ago as sand and mud in rivers that were surrounded by swamps and woodlands. These were repeatedly buried by mud during periods of flooding. The buried organic matter of the swamps and woodlands is the origin of the coal layers that have been mined around Longyearbyen. During other periods within the same era, the water level rose even further and the whole area was covered by shallow sea. Fine-grained, dark shales were deposited under these conditions.

The coal seams are not the only traces of by-gone forests. In some sediment layers, you may find beautiful imprints of, for example, leaves that resemble hazelnut leaves. The best places to find them are the moraines of the glaciers near Longyearbyen.

Geology (more detailed): The area consists of near-horizontal sediments from the lower Cretaceous and lower Tertiary, which are separated by a hiatus, which means that strata are missing. The upper Cretaceous is not represented anywhere in Svalbard, it may have been eroded prior to the deposition of the following layers or maybe it was never deposited. The hiatus is not clearly seen.

The strata are gently dipping southwards, which means that the further south you are, the younger the sediments at a given altitude. You will find lower Cretaceous rocks in the upper slopes on the northern side of Adventfjord where only the highest parts of the mountains consist of lower Tertiary sediments. The boundary between lower Cretaceous and lower Tertiary around Longyearbyen is, in contrast, only about 200 metres above sea level.

Layers of quartzitic sandstone make a contrast due to their hardness relative to softer, more fine-grained siltstone and shale. The sandstones form obvious cliffs in the slopes, which have been dissected by erosion to form regular towers. The eye-catching cliffs in the slopes around Longyearbyen belong to the lower Tertiary, and the same strata can be seen further upslope on the northern side of Adventfjord. The Cretaceous-Tertiary boundary (abbreviated as CT boundary) is situated under these cliffs, about 500 metres above sea level north of the Adventfjord and 200-250 metres high around

Longyearbyen. Trained geologists, especially palaeontologists, get goosepimples when they see the CT boundary, as it marks one of the largest extinction events in Earth history: the time when the dinosaurs, together with many other species, died out. As many as 90 % of all marine species may have died out in those years, although it was not a single catastrophic event, but a process that happened over millions of years due to a combination of unfavourable environmental factors, including global climate change (sounds familiar?). In practice, this means that the fossil contents of the layers below and above the CT boundary are dramatically different. Do not expect too much if you simply look up at the slopes from central Longyearbyen: there is nothing to be seen from a distance. The CT boundary is, unfortunately, not very spectacular in Spitsbergen, as it is mostly covered by scree and, secondly, the upper Cretaceous is missing, which makes the sedimentary sequence incomplete and thus also the record of the dramatic evolutionary and environmental development at that time.

Both Cretaceous and Tertiary consist of fluvial, coastal and shallow-marine sandstones, siltstones and shales. The sandstones were deposited in deltaic environments, similar to today's Mississippi delta.

The fine-grained, dark shales, in contrast, indicate the marine influence: they were deposited in times of rising sea levels (which could also be caused locally by land subsidence), when shallow seas were covering the land area. The increasing distance to the coast meant that only fine-grained sediment was transported far enough to reach the area. More coarse-grained sediments, such as coastal sandstones and fluvial conglomerates, where deposited elsewhere at the same time: as a result, the rock composition changes depending on whether you go up and down at one site or follow the same layer horizontally over a larger distance. There have been several transgression/regression cycles (relative rise and fall of sea level). This means that sandstones (with coal seams) are overlain by finer-grained siltstones and shale which indicate the marine influence and, later, by another younger standstone series. This becomes very obvious during a hike up to Nordenskiöldfjellet, a mountain near Longyearbyen that is 1,050 metres high. The alternating sequence of darker shales (transgressive phase) and sandstones (coastal deposits, regressive phase) is especially obvious in the upper part of Nordenskiöldfjellet, above Platåfjellet. The uppermost beds are amongst the youngest solid rocks in Spitsbergen, belonging to the so-called Aspelintoppen formation and have been dated as Eocene, possibly lower Olicogene (divisions of the lower Tertiary), which makes them about 40 million years old.

Some of the lower Tertiary sandstones have nice fossils, including beautiful imprints of leaves that resemble hazelnut leaves. You have a good chance of finding fossils in the moraines of the glaciers near Longyearbyen.

There are coal seams both in the Cretaceous and in the Tertiary. Coal has been mined on both sides of Adventfjord (see section on history); the seams mined in and around Longyearbyen are Tertiary.

How to experience the local geology? A walk along the road between Longyearbyen and the airport, focussing on the area near the harbour, is a good start for some insight into the geology of the area. The outcrops of lower Cretaceous shallow-marine sandstones are excellent and mostly easily accessible. What you see is shallow marine siltstones, in places with some infilled tidal channels, and some smaller folding and faulting near the harbour. An energetic day trip to the top of Nordenskiöldfjellet will make you familiar with the lower Tertiary, although the outcrops are not always excellent, especially within the older layers that are mostly scree-covered or inaccessible on steep slopes. For the geology, the highlight is the part that leads you from the plateau at an altitude of 450-500 metres up over one of the ridges on either side of the glacier to the top of Nordenskiöldfjellet. There is no technical climbing, but the ridge is a little airy and made up of brittle and unstable rocks, so it may not be for everybody; do not go up in bad weather. For nice coastal outcrops of the lower Tertiary, you can make an excursion to the coast of Isfjord just west of Bjørndalen, at the foot of Fuglefjellet. There is a road to Bjørndalen, then you have to cross the river. You need calm weather and low tide to access the cliff from Isfjord; be aware of the risk of rockfalls. Finally, a visit to one of the coal mines, offered by local tour operators, is recommended for some insight into mining practices.

Landscape: The main feature of Adventfjord is the relatively dense settlement including many huts and infrastructure outside Longyearbyen. Other areas of Spitsbergen certainly have more attractive scenery but the site was chosen because of its coal mining opportunities and not for tourist reasons. However, this does not mean that there are no natural attractions. The landscape is mainly characterised by wide plateaux at an elevation of 400 to 500 metres, which are typical of large areas of central Spitsbergen. These elevated plateaux are like rocky deserts with frost-patterned ground and little vegetation. There were, at one time, substantially more rock layers lying on today's surface, but most of them have been removed by erosion over a very long period of time. Some remnants have survived and are still visible as the mountains that are towering above the plateau. The most prominent of these around Longyearbyen are Nordenskiöldfjellet (1,050 metres) and Trollsteinen (837 metres).

The plateau was, originally, a complete plain at sea level before it was brought to its present altitude by tectonic uplift. Since then, it has been dissected by erosion. Rivers and subsequent ice-age glaciers have created valleys with rather steep slopes, where harder layers form prominent cliffs. Hard tertiary sandstones are responsible for the eye-catching regular towers around Longyearbyen; these rocks have formed a cliff that has been cut into regular towers by erosion. The lower slopes are covered with vast amounts of scree. The appearance of the landscape is, on the whole, not very rich in colour contrasts, due to the dark, grey-brown colour of the rocks.

The area around Longyearbyen is amongst the least glaciated in Spitsbergen with less than 18 % being covered by ice in contrast to 60 %, the average for the whole archipelago. There are three glaciers near Longyearbyen, one of them in the upper part of Longyeardalen. All three glaciers have large moraines.

Raised beaches and ice wedge polygons are common signs of (sub)recent landscape development on flat areas near sea level, for example between the airport and

Bjørndalen. Typical arctic rivers with many channels, so-called braided rivers, are flowing in all these valleys during the summer months, the largest being in Bjørndalen and Adventdalen. There is a nice view into Adventdalen from an altitude of 400 metres from the road near mine seven in Adventalen, which you can enjoy without any physical effort simply by taking a taxi.

If you follow the river in Adventdalen a good eight kilometres into the valley, crossing some smaller tributary rivers and carrying the mandatory rifle, then you will find a nice example of a pingo on the northern side of Janssonhaugen. To reach the pingo, you have to cross the river, Adventelva, which is a challenge and not entirely without danger especially at times of higher water levels, but at Janssonhaugen, it is certainly easier than further down the valley. Keep an eye open for the very rare Dwarf birch when you approach Janssonhaugen from the west. There are some smaller pingos in Adventdalen closer to Longyearbyen, but they are on the "wrong" side of the river which is almost impossible to cross here during the summer. In spring, when fjord and river are frozen, it is a nice ski excursion to the pingo in Moskuslaguna, which will then appear as a small, ice-covered mound.

There are two nice examples of rock glaciers in the Adventfjord area: one opposite Longyearbyen on the northern side of Adventfjord, situated in a natural amphitheatre in the slopes of Hiortfjellet. The other is actually in the settlement area: Sverdrupbyen in upper Longyeardalen near the glacier, now deserted and mostly destroyed, was actually built on a rock glacier. It is doubtful that those who built the houses were aware of this.

Flora and fauna: Biologically, the area has quite a lot to offer, in spite of rather extensive land use. There are tundra areas with rich vegetation, mostly Polar willow, on large areas of Longyearbyen and in the nearby valleys and flat areas near the coast. In Adventdalen, you may be lucky to find the Dwarf birch which is very rare in Spitsbergen. Try the tundra west of Janssonhaugen, if you are interested in seeing the Dwarf birch, between the rivers Adventelva and Janssonelva – good luck! For the less sporting tundra enthusiast, all you have to do is walk around in Longyearbyen for some good first impressions of arctic vegetation, including some very nice fields of Arctic cottongrass. Additionally, there is a little "botanical garden" in the form of some strips with flowers near the car park at the Sysselmannen's office, where a number of Spitsbergen's typical plant species can be seen.

Bird enthusiasts can see a surprisingly large number of interesting birds in and around Longyearbyen. There are several small colonies of Little auk breeding in the steep scree slopes, for example above Nybyen, on the slopes of Platåberget near mine one (above the Sysselmannen's building in Longyeardalen) and above Huset, in the little valley that leads up from the moraine of Longyearbreen to the plateau on Platåfjellet; also in Bjørndalen. For Arctic terns, Kittiwakes, possibly even Grey phalaropes and other species, have a look around the Camping site and the nearby lagoon (keep a distance from breeding birds).

You may be lucky to see King eiders on small ponds in Adventdalen, which you can see from the road by car (taxí), and the Ivory gull is often seen near the dog-yard on the road that leads into Adventdalen. Some Common eiders have decided to establish their breeding colony near the dogyard at the road into Adventdalen, just east of Longyearbyen. Wildlife enthusiasts wanted to put up a warning sign to prevent traffic accidents with the ducks, but this turned out to be impossible due to beaurocratic reasons.

Reindeer and Arctic foxes are no rarities in the settlement or at the Camping site. It is certainly fair to say that everyone with some interest in Arctic wildlife can spend several rewarding days in and near Longyearbyen and its surroundings.

History: For the history of Longyearbyen, refer to chapter 3.7 *Longyearbyen*. Mining is obviously the activity that has characterised the recent past in Adventfjord, but the history of the area goes further back, although nothing is known about Pomor or early whaling sites. Being a convenient and well-known natural harbour, Adventfjord was developed early on as a centre for tourism. A hotel was opened at the entrance to the bay as early as 1896, to accommodate tourists who came to Spitsbergen with the postal steamer. It proved to be unsuccessful and was closed by 1897; today the name of the place, "Hotellneset", is all that is left of this early tourism.

The interior of the country was largely unknown until the Englishman, **Martin Conway,** together with several companions, ventured to make the first known crossing of Spitsbergen during the summer of 1896. The timing implies that one of his fellows named Garwood was able to take advantage of the presence of the above-mentioned hotel – in Conway's absence, but at his expense. It is said that the main reason for Garwood's attempt to climb Hornsundtind in south Spitsbergen was to avoid being around when Conway, upon his return, was presented with the hotel bill. In the meantime, Conway had spent weeks following the major valleys from Adventfjord (or Advent bay, as it was called then), surveying the area topographically and geologically, until he reached Agardhdalen which drains to the east coast of Spitsbergen. It is characteristic of the lack of geographical knowledge in those days that Conway expected to be travelling mainly on inland ice and so brought horses and sledges which proved rather useless in the snowy and wet tundra. This was in spite of the fact that Conway had prepared thoroughly for his voyage by reading everything he could get hold of; unfortunately, he was not able to read the Scandinavian literature.

In subsequent years, systematic scientific research of this early period was also carried out near Longyearbyen: in 1911-12, a German expedition ran a **meteorological station** on the top of **Nordenskiöldfjellet**. The station was re-opened by Swedish scientists for another season during the International Polar Year 1932-33.

There are the remains of two mining facilities from the early 20th century on the north side of Adventfjord. There is not a lot left to be seen in **Advent City**, but **Hiorthamn** is worth a visit if you are interested in the mining history. Starting in 1903, Cretaceous coal was mined in Advent City, near the fjord entrance, in a mine that was 80 metres above sea level. The scale of mining activities was investigative rather than industrial and after various difficulties, including quarrels between the work force and their superiors, mining was stopped in 1908. Most buildings were moved some kilometres along the fjord, when mining started in Hiorthamn in 1917. Hiorthamn was soon renamed Moskushamn, but the original name has been re-introduced again in more recent years. The mine entrance was 580 metres above sea level, reaching for the lower Tertiary coal seams. Mining at Hiorthamn also was faced with a range of difficulties and it was stopped temporarily in 1922 and finally in 1940. Hiorthamn did not suffer any significant damage during the war, whereas most other settlements (except Pyramiden) were destroyed in 1941. You can reach Hiorthamn in the summer by boat or kayak and in the winter by foot, ski or sledge, provided the fjord ice is strong and safe.

The German air force operated the weather station "Bansö" in Adventdalen, between Endalen and Todalen, in 1941-42.

A German reconnaissance plane was shot down by a Norwegian position in Hiorthamn on 23rd July 1942; the wreck is probably still lying at the bottom of Adventfjord, near Hiorthamn. A small Norwegian garrison was stationed in Hiorthamn during the war, and remained there until 1947. Other relicts from the war period in and near Adventfjord include burnt wooden beams in Longyearbyen, for example in the vicinity of the Sysselmannen's office. A German weather reconnoissance plane was destroyed on the ground on the old airstrip in Adventdalen, near the old northern light observatory. The plane, a Junkers 88, had not been able to take off again due to the soft ground and was soon attacked by British aircraft; the wreck can still be seen on the small slope near the river Adventelva, not far from the old observatory building that has the plexi-glass hemispheres on the roof. There is also a cannon on the point near the old coal crane between the harbour and the Camping place, which was originally stationed with the Norwegian garrison at Heerodden near Barentsburg. After the war, most activities in the area concentrated on Longyearbyen (see chapter 3.7 *Longyearbyen*).

6.1.9 Grumantbyen, Colesbukta

General: Grumantbyen and Longyearbyen may be considered the settlements representing the eastern and western hemispheres respectively, that were closest to one another during the Cold War years without being separated by a wall or anything of that sort. Day trips by boat to Barentsburg pass Grumantbyen and Colesbukta. If you want to have a closer look at Grumantbyen, then the route across the 400 metres high plateau of Fuglefjellet is an option provided you bring surefootedness and a rifle. You can get to the entrance of Bjørndalen by bicycle or car (taxi); from there, follow the valley until you find a route up to the plateau. Another route that has been done, follows the coast of Isfjord along the foot of the near-vertical cliffs of Fuglefjellet, but this is possible only at low tide and with calm weather; the route is hazardous because of sudden weather changes and rockfalls.

There are also good options for hiking further away from the coast. Many valleys have routes across passes, some easier and some steeper, that enable crossing from one valley to the next. Although the terrain often makes walking strenuous, the im-

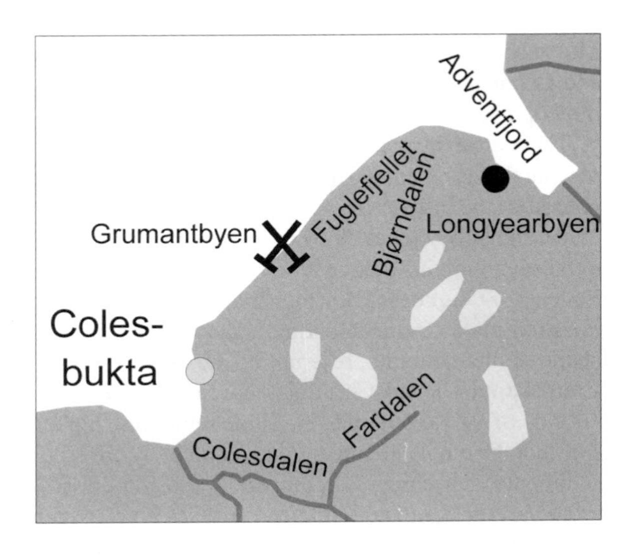

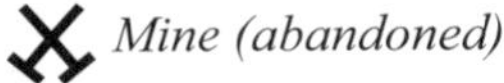

Grey circle: Settlement (abandoned)

pressions that you can get in these valleys will certainly make the effort worthwhile, as some of the richest tundra areas of Spitsbergen are to be found in this area; reindeer are, accordingly, abundant. At the same time, the decaying ghost settlements of Grumantbyen and Colesbukta have their own charm of a different, slightly morbid sort perhaps; don't forget that the houses were built in times when asbestos was still commonly used and that they may collapse. Around Grumantbyen, there is an introduced species of mouse that can transmit parasites which are dangerous to humans (see section 3.6.5 *Other hazards in the field*). It is officially recommended that water from the Grumantbyen area should be boiled before consumption.

The area has the advantage that hikers can start directly from Longyearbyen or at the end of the road to Bjørndalen, avoiding costly boat transfers to other hiking areas in Isfjord. If you are out in the winter, beware of snow avalanches on steeper slopes. Also, you must not forget the risk of a potential Polar bear encounter. The risk of a bear being around is definitely smaller than in Hinlopen Strait, but there may always be the odd bear having a siesta in a room or behind any building in the deserted settlements.

Placenames: **Bjørndalen:** "Bear valley". **Colesbukta**: "Coal bay", originally "Coal harbour". **Fardalen**: "Valley of passage", common inland snow mobile route out of Longyearbyen. **Fuglefjellet**: "Bird mountain". **Grumantbyen**: Grumant, old Pomor name for Spitsbergen, possibly related to "Greenland". **Lindströmfjellet**: Gustaf L. (1829-1901), Swedish palaeontologist.

Geology: Fuglefjellet consists of near-horizontal lower Cretaceous and lower Tertiary sediments, all fluvial or shallow marine sandstones, siltstones and shale. The Cretaceous outcrops are close to sea level near Bjørndalen. Access is possible in calm weather and at low tide but be aware of potential rockfalls. The rest of Fuglefjellet is Tertiary.

The only obvious sign of tectonic disturbance is an oblique fault between Bjørndalen and Grumantbyen, the so-called Grumantbyen-fault, that caused difficulties for the miners in Grumantbyen.

There are a few mountains around Colesdalen, towering higher than the ubiquitous plateau that is extensive between 400 and 500 metres altitude. Higher mountains that consist of the last surviving remnants of the youngest solid rocks in Spitsbergen, include Lindströmfjellet (966 metres) and Vesuv (739 metres). The sediments preserved in these mountains belong to the so-called Aspelintoppen formation and are dated as Eocene(?)-Oligocene(?), which makes them approximately 40 million years old. The question marks indicate dating uncertainties. The name Vesuv refers to the conical shape of the mountain, resembling a classical volcano, but sedimentary in origin.

Landscape: The most striking landscape feature is the wide, rocky high plateau at an altitude of 400 to 500 metres. Some remaining higher mountains bear witness to the fact that the whole area was once completely covered with another thick sequence of sediments, subsequently removed by erosion down to the level of the plateau. This erosion actually created a plateau near sea level, which has since then been uplifted to its present elevation. The latest step in the geomorphological history was the incision of the valleys, first by rivers and later by glaciers, as soon as uplift enabled this process to start. The valley shapes seen today, with their typical glacially-created U-shaped cross section, flat bottom and steep slopes, are thus rather young. As a result, the high plateau often ends at a sharp edge, where steep cliffs fall down to the valley or fjord.

The valley of Colesdalen is very wide and has a flat valley bottom with a thick vegetation layer, large wet areas and many river channels. Smaller tributary valleys leading down to Colesdalen and other valleys are often incised to form small but steep-sided canyons. These features do not make walking easy, but fit and experienced hikers should be able to negotiate them. One key factor is, as always, careful planning and proper route selection.

Flora and fauna: One of the tundra areas with the richest vegetation in the whole archipelago is in Colesdalen, where reindeer are abundant. There are quite large seabird colonies on the steep cliffs around Grumantbyen, with Kittiwakes and Brünich's guillemots as main breeding species. Intense fertilisation has allowed for an unusually large accumulation of biomass, in the shape of peat layers, on the steep slopes. Only a few plant species, including Scurvy grass and Mountain sorrel, are able to grow on this very acidic "soil", but these grow large and abundant, making the bright green colour that is visible from a distance. The peat layers have been addressed as "hanging bogs", but when they become too heavy, they collapse into the fjord under their own weight; a process that limits the thickness of the peat to 1 or 1.5 metres. Arctic foxes are common near birdcliffs.

Whereas most introduced mammalian animals have died out in Spitsbergen, mice still thrive in the vicinity of Grumantbyen, including the hanging peat. So far, they seem not to be having any significant influence on the local ecosystem.

History: The coal field of Grumant was claimed in 1912 by the Russian geologist, **V.A.**

Rusanov, who disappeared later in the same year, with his ship, in the northeast passage. Some items that are connected to Rusanov are on display in a hut at Rusanovodden, east of the old settlement in Colesbukta. Mining started in 1913 and was continued, with some interruptions, until 1961. The inhospitable landscape with steep cliffs and very limited accessible space makes it hard to believe that Grumantbyen was once the largest settlement in Spitsbergen. Together with Colesbukta, there were more than 1,000 people living and working in the coal field in the early 1950s; in 1951, for example, the double settlement had 1,106 inhabitants in total. The lack of any natural harbour at Grumantbyen made it necessary to establish shipping facilities a bit further west in Colesbukta. A small railway line provided the local transport. The settlements were abandoned in 1962, soon after the end of mining activities. Many buildings are still there, though in deteriorating condition, and all sorts of rubbish is lying around. A hammer and sickle on the beach at Grumantbyen, welded together from metal pipes, ensures that there is no doubt about the political background of the whole installation.
Miscellaneous: The Russian mining company Trust Arktikugol is developing plans to open a new coal mine in Colesdalen, the best days of Barentsburg being over. This prospect has not received much sympathy from environmentalists, but the Norwegian government has given approval to the plans.

6.1.10 Grønfjord, Barentsburg

General: This area is dominated by the active Russian mining settlement of Barentsburg which is a popular destination for day trips from Longyearbyen, with snow mobiles in the winter or, in the summer, by boat. A visit to Barentsburg may not offer a great experience of nature or scenery, but is an essential part of a visit to Spitsbergen if you wish to understand what has been, and still is going on there in terms of history, politics

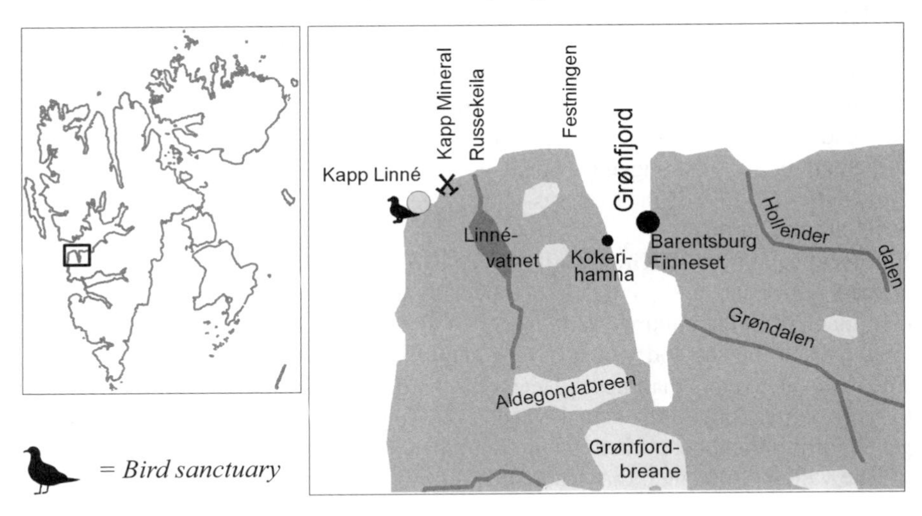

and mining. Russia has been the only country, apart from Norway, to have made substantial use of the terms and conditions of the Spitsbergen treaty. The consequence of this was not only the special situation during the Cold War, when the short distance between the settlements involved a relationship where everybody kept a watchful eye on his neighbour and yet maintained some friendly contacts. It cannot be denied that Russia is still a key player in the future development of Spitsbergen and the Arctic in general; recent political moves, including the spectacular setting of a Russian flagg on the sea bed under the North Pole in 2007, have made it very clear that the last word has not yet been spoken in arctic politics, although attention is currently focussed on the off-shore shelf areas rather than on any particular land or island. As far as Spitsbergen is concerned, one possible prospect is that a new Russian mine will be opened or other land activity started, including research, to maintain a presence. Environmental factors are likely to suffer in such an event.

Apart from all this, Barentsburg has almost daily boat connection to Longyearbyen during the summer and is thus a convenient starting point for several-day hiking tours to the inner Grønfjord which has more attractive scenery than the near neighbourhood of Barentsburg itself. Longer tours can take you further south towards Bellsund, to the Isfjord coast west of Grønfjord including Festningen and Kapp Linnè, or to the outer west coast with its large tundra plains.

There are both Russian and Norwegian mobile phone grids in Barentsburg.

Placenames: Barentsburg: Willem B. (ca. 1550-1597), official discoverer of Spitsbergen in 1596. **Finneset**: "Good point", referring to the good natural harbour. **Grønfjord**: originally "Green harbour" during the 17th century, for whatever reasons. There is not a lot of green in Grønfjord. **Kokerihamna**: anchoring place for floating whale oil factories ("kokeri") in the early 20th century.

Geology: The geology around Grønfjord is dominated by lower Tertiary sandstones, siltstones and shales, with several intercalated coal seams. The horizontal attitude of the layers on the eastern side has created a relatively uniform, unattractive geomorphology. On the west side of Grønfjord, the layers have been tilted to a steep or vertical position, which makes the landscape on this side more varied and interesting, especially at the head of the fjord in the area around Aldegondabreen and Kongressvatnet, and at the entrance at Festningen (see next section 6.1.11 *Festningen, Russekeila, Kapp Linné/Isfjord Radio*). In the Kongressvatnet area, the age of the sediments goes further back into the Permian.

Landscape: The name "Grønfjord" (Green harbour) is misleading, as the landscape appears rather dark and contrastless, especially around Barentsburg. There are some nice glaciers in the southwestern corner of Grønfjord, Grønfjordbreane, which no longer reach the sea and which have a gently sloping surface with few crevasses. The meltwater rivers that these glaciers discharge into the fjord are not always easy to cross, depending on the actual water level. Together with Aldegondabreen, these glaciers form the most attractive feature in the Grønfjord landscape.

The valley Grøndalen, that leads inland from Grønfjord towards the east, is one of Spitsbergen's major ice-free valleys with large tundra areas, a number of Pingos and several nice, smaller tributary valleys.

Small, steeply incised valleys make hiking difficult in the Grønfjord area. In the winter, they can be a hazard to careless snow mobile drivers without good local knowledge.

Flora and fauna: Grøndalen with its wide tundra areas and a good reindeer population may be the most interesting part of the area, from a biological viewpoint. There are also tundra areas on the western side of the fjord.

History: Being a good natural harbour, Grønfjord has been used constantly since the 17th century. **Kokerineset** on the western side is believed to be a site where both Pomors and early whalers had their stations; archaeological research will hopefully show what has actually been there, but any remains are buried by sediment and vegetation.

Søren Zachariassen from Tromsø must have been quite an inventive character when it came to business. The fame of having started commercial coal mining in Spitsbergen (1899 at Bohemanflya) belongs to him. In 1901, he returned to Spitsbergen with a new idea. He built a hut at Kokerineset to fish for Arctic char which occurs in nearby rivers and lakes. The idea was to can them locally and to sell them in Tromsø. At the end of the season, Zachariassen wrecked his boat and was only just rescued, together with his canned fish. Today nothing remains to be seen of Zachariassen's hut; it may have fallen victim to traffic and other activities associated with the Russian water supply station, Vannposten.

Only a few years after Zachariassen, larger marine species were targeted when a modern Norwegian whaling station was built at **Finneset** in 1905, but this was closed again in 1912 after a few busy years. During that period Norwegian whalers harpooned an estimated 2,000 large whales, mostly Fin and Blue whales, near Spitsbergen; the populations have not yet recovered. In 1911, when the whaling station was still in existence, Norway established a wireless telegraph station at the same site at Finneset, the first of its kind in Spitsbergen. The telegraph station was moved to Longyearbyen in 1930. Today, there are only a few remains that tell us of the busy years at Finneset; these include some foundations, a wooden platform (or "plan") to process whales, and the concrete fuel storage.

Coal mining has obviously been the dominant activity in this area during the 20th century. The first mining at the site of today's **Barentsburg** was started in 1912 by a Norwegian company. The Finn Knut Emil Glad was hired by the company to guard the site during the winter from 1912 to 1913. Glad came, together with his wife Anna Josefine and they built a hut and stayed for the winter. On 09th May 1913, Anna Josefine gave birth to **Spitsbergen's first baby**, a boy who was called Charles Emil Polar Glad, and all seems to have gone well afterwards. In 1920, the Dutch *NeSpiCo* (Nederlandsche Spitsbergen Compagnie) purchased the coal field and founded Barentsburg which, in 1932, changed its owner once more and became the property of the Russian state-owned Trust Arktikugol.

In August 1941, Barentsburg was evacuated and largely destroyed, the coal deposits were set on fire and all personnel, 1,955 Russians and Ukranians including those from Grumantbyen and Colesbukta, were taken to Arkhangelsk. The exiled Norwegian government wanted to re-establish Norwegian control over Spitsbergen and sent the two ships, *Isbjørn* and *Selis,* for this purpose. German aircraft attacked them in Grønfjord on 14 May 1942. *Isbørn* was sunk and *Selis* was burning when the attack came to an end, by which time, 14 men had died and a number were injured. The survivors established a garrison of about 80 Norwegian and British soldiers in Barentsburg. After the war, in 1946, mining was re-started as soon as possible. Between 2000 and 2004, approximately 300,000 tons of coal were exported each year, but production varies and is said to have gone down in recent years. There have been difficulties with accidents and a burning coal deposit in 2006, but the biggest disaster to have struck the Russian communities in Spitsbergen was certainly the crash of an airoplane in 1996 during its descent to the airport in Longyearbyen. Almost 130 miners, crew and others lost their lives instantly when the plane collided with a slope of Operafjellet, not far to the northeast of Longyearbyen.

Barentsburg: Barentsburg is currently the focus of all Russian activities in Spitsbergen. Nevertheless, visitors are left with the impression that daily life in the settlement must be a challenge for the inhabitants. Dilapidation is almost ubiquitous. Coal mining in Barentsburg was stopped in early 2008 after a fire in the mine that cost the lives of two miners. Mining is not expected to start again before November 2009 at the earliest. The number of inhabitants has been reduced to around 400 people, by far a smaller population than was present in the late 1990s. The greenhouse and the cowshed, once with cows and pigs, are now closed, only the pigs are still there, but are facing an uncertain future, so they should be considered an endangered species in Spitsbergen. Shortage of various supplies, bureaucracy and corruption do not improve the situation. This contrasts with official plans to install, amongst other things, a "shopping centre", a modern, environmentally friendly power station and a new mine in Colesbukta. We will wait and see what happens. Currently, the energy demand is supplied from a coal power station. Water comes through a pipe from Kokerineset on the opposite side of the fjord. The small crew of the pumping station, "Vannposten", tries to ensure that Barentsburg's water supply does not fail inspite of equipment that is increasingly falling apart. Hard to believe, but true, is the story of a man from Vannposten, who was attacked by a Polar bear and saved his life by poking his thumbs into the bear's eyes. The man survived with injuries. When you are in the area, keep your eyes open for a Polar bear with dark sunglasses.

In 2008, a large number of old electrical items containing toxic PCBs have been removed from Barentsburg and transported to Longyearbyen for proper disposal, in a joint effort by Norwegian and Russian authorities. The Sysselmannen praised good cooperation with the Russians on this environmentally important issue.

Little has been done in Barentsburg to encourage tourism which, accordingly, has hardly developed beyond day trips from Longyearbyen which include a visit of one or two hours to the settlement. There could well be potential to do more, as a number of interesting sites are within reach of day trips from Barentsburg. The biggest obstacle for those visitors to Barentsburg who come by boat, is to have to negotiate the long staircase that leads up to the centre, although a new one has been built in 2008. If you want to avoid the staircase, then you can follow the road from the harbour to the left or you can hike from Longyearbyen to Barentsburg, this takes a few days and is possible along the coast or through inland valleys. The reward for accomplishing this comes in shape of the luxurious Pomor hotel in Barentsburg, that offers accommodation for 550 to 650 NOK (double room, additional bed 150 NOK, from 2007). Phone/fax 0047 7902 1814. There are no shops, and no foodstuffs, equipment or fuel are available for tourists.

With the coal field being Russian property, but at the same time part of Spitsbergen and governed by the Spitsbergen treaty, you do not need to go through any immigration procedures to visit Barentsburg. Norwegian laws apply, and visitors use Norwegian currency. The Pomor museum was definitely worth the entrance fee of 40 NOK (as of 2007), and was opened on request, but it was closed in 2008. There are plans to re-open it in the old cafeteria at the upper end of the staircase from the harbour (it is announced that it will be moved temporarily into the culture house). There are permanent exhibitions on various fields of interest, one highlight of which is definitely the Polar bear heart preserved in alcohol (Vodka?)! Other places of interest include the hotel, which also houses a branch office of the Norwegian mail service, a Norwegian public card telephone and a bar with a selection of drinks, most of them not suitable for young customers. When groups visit, the souvenir shop in the large culture house is opened. It is worth a visit and you can stock up on Russian souvenirs such as Matruschkas (a doll that contains successively smaller dolls), different handicrafts, some fossils and a nice Russian photo book of Spitsbergen. There is another, smaller souvenir shop in the hotel. So far, everything has to be paid in cash (NOK, Euro, US-$), but rumour has it that it may be possible to use credit cards in the future.

The most important places of tourist interest – harbour, culture house with souvenir shop, museum, hotel with post office and bar – are in the centre of Barentsburg, only a few minutes walk from one another. Signposts have been put up to eliminate any remaining risk of people becoming lost.

This description may possibly not increase the attraction of a visit to Barentsburg. But, on the other hand, your experience of Spitsbergen is not complete without a visit to one of the Russian settlements, and the combination of two different worlds, both exotic in their own way to most visitors – the Arctic and a slowly declining Russian mining settlement – has an atmosphere that can be described as unique. Impressions will be plentiful, and photographers can certainly find opportunities. The most popular photographic subjects are possibly the Kittiwakes that breed on the sills of windows.

As of early 2009, it is not possible to buy anything you might need while out on tour (food, fuel, equipment).

There are some common-sense rules to observe in Barentsburg, as in any such place:

- Barentsburg is an active mining settlement; the work and life of the inhabitants have priority.
- Do not enter any buildings unless they are marked as public (souvenir shop, museum, hotel with post and bar) or you are expressly invited in.
- Respect the privacy of the locals, especially when you are taking pictures. Ask before you photograph or film any persons. Other than that, there are no general restrictions for photography in Barentsburg.

6.1.11 Festningen, Russekeila, Kapp Linné/Isfjord Radio

General: The area comprises a length of about ten kilometres of the Isfjord coast between Grønfjord and the outer coast. This section of the coast is exposed to the open ocean without protection. The use of the former radio station at Kapp Linné to accommodate tourists (see further down in this section) makes the area accessible; well-trained, equipped and experienced hikers can also walk from Barentsburg. Small boats and kayaks have to be careful in places, which are shallow even at some distance from the coast: north and east of Festningen and north of Kapp Starostin are the main danger zones.

If you are out to see large animals, calving glaciers and other attractions of the dramatic sort, then this rather open, coastal landscape may not be what you are looking for, but for everyone who is interested in attractions of the less eye-catching kind, including many interesting landscape features, history and geology, the area has a lot to offer. Most of it is protected: the geologically and geomorphologically very interesting coast and inland between Festningen and Russekeila has been declared a geotope. Kapp Linné itself, together with the nearby lakes, especially Fyrsjøen, is a bird sanctuary, where traffic is banned in the period 15 May to 15 August. The boundary is directly south of the station area. For map, see section 6.1.10 *Grønfjord, Barentsburg* (S. 266).

Placenames: Festningen: "Fortress", after the appearance of the small island. **Kapp Linné**: Carl von L. (1707-78), Swedish botanist. **Kapp Mineral**: refers to mineral occurrences. **Kapp Starostin**: Ivan S., see *history* further down this section. **Russekeila**: "Russian bay". The site was used by Pomor hunters, who had a large station there.

Geology: The coastal section between Festningen and Russekeila is one of the most important geological localities in Spitsbergen and has been the subject of detailed investigations at several times in the 20th century. The main reason has to do with the near-vertical attitude of the layers: every step along the coast literally covers millions of years of Earth's history, and a walk of a few kilometres follows a sedimentary succession from the lower Tertiary (Grønfjord entrance) to the Carboniferous and finally the basement ("Hecla Hoek", furthest west), covering most of the geological history of Spitsbergen. The site has been named "Festningen section", after the small island that marks its eastern end. The following description starts with the oldest part in the west and covers gradually younger rocks towards Grønfjord in the east.

The station Isfjord Radio, at Kapp Linné, has been built on solid basement rocks: strongly deformed phyllites with quartz veins. The oldest prominent sedimentary group in Spitsbergen, the Devonian Old Red, is unfortunately missing in this area. This makes the Carboniferous coarse quartzitic conglomerates and sandstones north of Linnèfjellet the oldest component of the sedimentary cover that extends from the upper Palaeozoic into the lower Tertiary. The boundary between basement and Carboniferous is easily seen on the northern ridge of Linnéfjellet: the lower part of the sharp ridge itself consists of Carboniferous sediments with a clearly visible, steeply dipping layering, whereas the rest of the mountain is built up of metamorphic rocks (phyllites) that belong to the basement. The Carboniferous sediments do not include evaporites or coal in this area.
The hard and fossil-rich carbonates of the Permian Kapp Starostin formation appear at their type locality with steeply dipping strata that have created a rugged ridge. East of Kapp Starostin you are walking on Mesozoic layers that are mostly fine-grained, dark siltstones and shales with relatively little variation. The most eye-catching Mesozoic strata are the youngest, on the eastern point of the section, where vertical hard quartzitic sandstones display well their ability to withstand erosion. On land, they stand out as a wall that continues out to sea as the very narrow, wall-shaped island Festningen, with extensive shallows on its northern and eastern side. This sandstone is called Festningen sandstone – this is the type locality – and dates into the lower Cretaceous. It attracted attention in the late 1960s when foot imprints of Iguanodons were found on some rock surfaces at Festningen. Iguanodons were large vegetarian dinosours with three strong toes and a shoe size around 200. Unfortunately, the relevant parts of the cliff have collapsed and do not exist anymore, but new ones were discovered in late 1990 just south of Festningen on some low cliffs at the coast of Grønfjord. If you follow the coast a bit further to the south, then you will soon reach the lower Tertiary where you can read the youngest layers of the geological textbook that nature has so nicely provided at the Festningen section – if you can read it. Unfortunately, some pages of this book are creased or even missing (especially upper Permian, upper Cretaceous, upper Tertiary): several faults, most of them hardly visible for the untrained eye, cut through the layers.

The Festningen section is certainly a major geological highlight, but not the only one in the area. The Quaternary geology is also certainly worth having a good look at. Raised beach ridges cover large areas of the tundra plain. You can get an insight into these young, un-solidified sediments in the valley of Linnéelva, where some of the steeper slopes provide good outcrops. Another special feature are the dolines in the plain between Linnéelva and Kapp Starostin.

For geological excursions, come late in the summer when the breeding season has finished. Birds are obviously interested in geology as they tend to nest at sites with the best outcrops, including Festningen. Late August is perfect (not before 16 August), as you are then allowed to walk around within the bird sanctuary of Kapp Linné.

Landscape: Most of the coast between Kapp Linné and Festningen consists of low cliffs. Bays with beaches that allow small-boat landings are Randvika east of Kapp Linné and the little bay west of Festningen, although none of them is protected in rough weather. There is a several-kilometre-wide tundra plain between this coastline and the mountains surrounding Linnévatnet. Some areas are quite wet and there are many lakes near the outer coast. Walking is easy on rocky ridges and raised beaches in this area except past the outlets that drain the lakes; these are mostly quite deep. There are some very well developed stone rings (frost patterned ground) in wetlands southeast of Kapp Linné, between Randvika and the little lake Tunsjøen. There are generally a lot of interesting and beautiful landscape details to be seen: next to the frost patterned ground, there are nice raised beaches, old pieces of driftwood in the tundra, some old whalebones and so on.

The tundra within the triangle Russekeila – Kapp Starostin – Linnevatnet is mostly dry and easy to walk on. Don't miss the dolines in this area. The river Linnéelva is quite deep near the coast and near the lake, if you want to cross it, then try somewhere halfway.

The landscape around Linnévatnet, one of the largest lakes in Spitsbergen, is very rocky and barren. Solifluction soil (muddy ground) makes walking difficult in places but a hike in this area will give you the impression of being back in the ice age. There are some perfectly developed stone stripes (frost patterned ground influenced by solifluction) on slopes near Linnévatnet.

Kapp Starostin is the next cape further east and continues southwards into a jagged ridge and finally into a mountainous backbone which can be followed all the way down to Bellsund. The hardness of the steeply standing layers of the Kapp Starostin formation is reflected in this landscape pattern. To the north of Kapp Starostin, extensive rock shoals will give every careless kayaker or boat pilot a taste of the submarine version of the same geomorpholoy, which eventually finds its continuation on the northern side of Isfjord (Vermlandryggen).

The landscape east of Kapp Starostin is again determined by the geology, but with the opposite result: the relatively soft Mesozoic sediments provide rather flat tundra without any eye-catching rock formations, but the vegetation takes advantage of the easily weathered fine-grained rocks and appears significantly richer, greener and wetter in this area. The far, eastern end of the coast is dominated by the islet of Festningen, which again is a striking example of how the geology influences the landscape.

Flora and fauna: The geology is not only reflected in the landscape, but also in the vegetation. Depending largely on the bedrock, it is either dense and green (between Kapp Starostin and Festningen) or relatively barren. The patterns of the old raised beaches are another important influence, especially south and southeast of Kapp Linné: the exposed ridges are mostly barren, whereas small wetlands or ponds often fill the depressions. The wetlands have thick moss beds that are easily damaged by footsteps.

Kapp Linné itself has protection status as a bird sanctuary because of large numbers of breeding Common eiders in the area. When the station was staffed, the eiders were breeding between the houses and even on doorsteps, but as the houses are now only temporarily occuppied, Arctic foxes have the area under control again and have greatly reduced the numbers of eider nests. Kapp Linné is nevertheless a very good place for keen birdwatchers in the early summer. Common eiders are still around, together with Long-tailed ducks or even King eider, Grey phalaropes and other tundra birds. Reindeer and Arctic foxes are common.

Freshwater fish are rare in Spitsbergen but Linnévatnet has a good part of the regional population of Arctic char. They used to be caught at the mouth of the Linnéelva and in the lake. Fishing with a fishing rod is still possible but licenses are required, which can be obtained from the Sysselmannen.

History: When you walk along the coast between Kapp Linné and Festningen to absorb Earth history, then there is also a good deal of human history to be seen along the way. The remains are mostly rather subtle and inconspicuous, but they tell their stories from times past; sometimes quite dramatic times. All remains are protected by law.

The most obvious site is the old coastal radio station **Isfjord Radio**, that was built in 1933 at **Kapp Linné** and later provided telecommunications between the Norwegian settlements and Norway. Isfjord Radio shared the same fate as most other settlements during WWII and was destroyed, but put back into use in 1946. It was staffed all-year-round until 1999, when the technology was re-designed to run automatically and require only occasional attention. In 2004, a fibreglass cable was laid between Longyearbyen and Norway to accommodate the large volumes of data obtained from satellite receivers. The cable made Isfjord Radio technically obsolete. Since the late 1990s, the station buildings have been used as a hotel during the tourist seasons. Kapp Linné is open during the snow mobile season and, on request, during the summer (see section 3.7.2 *Accommodation, eating and drinking*). It is one of my favourite places in Spitsbergen and I can recommend it to anybody who wants to spend some calm days in an environment that is certainly more inspiring than Longyearbyen, although it can be crowded during the winter, especially during the weekends around Easter.

The next historical site is located about three kilometres east of Kapp Linné at **Kapp Mineral**, where the Norwegian engineer Arthur Levin scratched some tons of lead ore out of basement phyllites in 1923 and 1924. In 1925, the English *Northern Exploration Company* continued work on the site and dug a vertical mine shaft about 25 feet deep. The tunnel entrance and some other leftovers are still visible.

If you follow the coast eastwards from Kapp Mineral, then you will find the remains of a wooden open boat on the beach. This may not seem worth any attention, but is a reminder of a drama from the war years that cost the lives of 49 humans. The story started in October 1942 in Philadelphia when the English cargo ship ***Chumleigh*** left with 5,000 tons of military equipment on board, bound for Murmansk. A German attack was almost certain, and a northerly course was chosen from Iceland in an attempt to escape the threat. Prolonged bad visibility made it impossible to get any bearings, and eventually the *Chumleigh* ran into reefs off the southern tip of Spitsbergen. As soon as the crew had got into the three lifeboats, five German aircraft appeared and bombed the *Chumleigh*, which was still sitting on the rocks, but soon sank. Two of the three boats disappeared during a desperate attempt to reach an inhabited area, and only one boat with 23 survivors managed to reach the coast near Kapp Linné or possibly Russekeila, where they found a little hut. What followed was a time of incredible hardship due to fierce cold and lack of the most essential equipment and provisions. Eventually, nine survivors were found and rescued by a Norwegian ski patrol from the garrison in Barentsburg. It is uncertain if the boat on the beach is really the lifeboat of the *Chumleigh* but it is the right sort of boat in the right area, and the remaining uncertainty should not keep you from devoting some thought to the incredible hardships those people had to endure.

The next history stop is **Russekeila** at the mouth of Linnéelva; an obvious site with several huts. The largest belongs to the Russians in Barentsburg and houses a little glass showcase with some Pomor items that archaeologists have found at this site during excavations. As is often the case in the Arctic, the most interesting things are the ones that are most easily overlooked: whereas the standing huts are all relatively recent, remains of Pomor stations can be found on both sides of the river, with wooden foundations and broken bricks as the most obvious parts. Everything has been subject to thorough archaeological investigation, which has resulted in the conclusion that the site was almost a small settlement with main dwelling house and an additional hut for accommodation, workshop, smithy, warehouse and sauna. Up to 20 men lived at Russekeila during the most active period which was the second half of the 18th century. The most famous inhabitant from that period is the patriarch Ivan Starostin who lived at Russekeila between 1787 and 1826 (or 1828, according to source). He did not even bother to return home during the last 15 years and he died in his adopted country and was buried at Kapp Starostin, not far from Russekeila.

Russekeila is one of the best known and most important cultural heritage sites from the Pomor period in Spitsbergen. The site is subject to the usual protection laws and certainly deserves respectful behaviour from all visitors. This means, first of all, not to walk inside the old foundations.

Continuing further along the coast from Russekeila towards the east, a small wall of local rocks indicates the site of a lookout post used by the Norwegian garrison in Barentsburg during WWII. Furthest back on the time scale is a site near Festningen where 17th century whalers, probably English, used to boil whale blubber into oil, but there is hardly anything to be seen.

6.2 Forlandsund east side

"It was at one o'clock in the morning of the 6th of August, 1856, that, after having been eleven days at sea, we came to an anchor in the silent haven of English Bay, Spitzbergen.
And now, how shall I give you an idea of the wonderful panorama in the midst of which we found ourselves?"

Frederick Temple Hamilton-Temple Blackwood,
Marquis of Dufferin and Ava,
Letters from high latitudes

The west coast of Spitsbergen between Isfjord and Kongsfjord, well hidden and more or less protected by the long island of Prins Karls Forland, has varied scenery with wide plains, open bays, fjords and glaciers. The area is rarely visited despite its position between Longyearbyen and Ny Ålesund. The main reason is that there are shallows south of Engelskbukta in the northern part of Forlandssund, the strait that separates Spitsbergen from Prins Karls Forland. Only the smallest boats can sail across these shallows and most ships have to stay on the outside of Prins Karls Forland, to the regret of all those who suffer in rough seas, knowing at the same time that the strait is not only protected from the swell of the open ocean, but has some varied and, in places, rather spectacular scenery. The Forlandsund area is out of reach for most individual tourists unless you spend a lot of money on logistics or you bring your own boat.

6.2.1 Daudmannsodden, Farmhamna

General: Wide coastal plain with many offshore rocks and reefs; a landscape that may appear bleak and featureless when seen from a distance, but is in fact beautiful and varied, with many beautiful details and a rich wildlife. For map, see section 6.3 *Prins Karls Forland* (page 274).

Placenames: Daudmannsodden: „Dead-man-point", name given by Norwegian hunters to commemorate a deceased comrade. **Farmhamna:** After the Norwegian Navy vessel S/S *Farm*, used in 1909-1910 to support scientific expeditions.

Geology: Strongly deformed sediments and metamorphic rocks, mainly schists, quartzite and carbonates, all belonging to the basement.

Landscape: Wide coastal plain with some rocky hills near the west coast and many small lakes. The largest river is Vetternbreen, which is difficult to cross during the melting season. Parts of the plain that are located at some distance from the coast can be very wet and difficult to walk. Lots of driftwood and old whalebones cover many of the beaches.

Flora and fauna: Reindeer are roaming the tundra in large numbers, and polar foxes have their dens in many of the rocky hills. Birds such as geese, ducks and others find

good feeding grounds on the tundra. Especially during the early summer, when geese are abundant in this area, you have to move around with great care.
History: On the hill nearest Daudmannsodden (the southern point of the coastal plain), there is a double grave from the whaling period in the 17th or possibly 18th century. Trappers have often used the area because of its strong fox and reindeer populations; old fox traps can still be seen at many places near the coast, and the ruin of an old hut is still visible in a small bay just 1 or 2 kilometres south of Steinpynten.
Miscellaneous: The trapper station at Farmhamna is still in use. The huts and surroundings should be respected as private.

An evening not to be forgotten at Daudmannsodden.

6.2.2 St. Jonsfjord

General: Relatively small fjord (20 kilometres long) with several glaciers and mountains that display beautiful colours in good light conditions. Nice scenery, not of the obtrusive sort, but the mountains, glaciers and colours are beautiful. The innermost part, near the glaciers, is white on the chart and depth information is missing, which hinders navigation. The island Hermannsenøya near the fjord entrance is a bird sanctuary (all traffic banned within 300 metres from the shore in the period 15 May to 15 August). For map, see section 6.3 *Prins Karls Forland* (page 274).
Placenames: St. Jonsfjord: after the evangelist.
Geology: Strongly deformed sediments and metamorphic rocks, all basement. The tectonic history makes itself visible in the faults and folds that create nice patterns and a colourful mosaic of the various rocks.

Landscape: St. Jonsfjord is surrounded by mountains that reach heights of 700 to 800 metres. There are no large, flat tundra areas inside the fjord, so easy walking is relatively limited, although the slopes near the fjord are not vertical. Surefooted, energetic hikers will have good opportunities to walk, with good views of the scenery. Any longer hiking or skiing expeditions further inland will certainly produce unforgettable scenic impressions of the glacier- and mountain-landscape.
History: St. Jonsfjord has not been used a lot. In 1919, the English *Northern Exploration Company* (NEC) investigated copper ores on the south side and built a hut called **Copper Camp** for this purpose, but the occurrence was not economic. The area was occasionally visited by Norwegian trappers during the early 20th century; a hut on the north side is evidence of those activities.

6.2.3 Kaffiøyra

General: Kaffiøyra is rarely visited by tourists. The Polish Nikolaus-Kopernikus University has, during the summers since 1975, run the Torun Polar Station, south of Aavatsmarkbreen, to provide research opportunities for international scientists. The local glaciers are the main targets of scientific interest; results confirm the general retreat of recent decades. The nearby island Hermannsenøya is a bird sanctuary (all traffic banned within 300 metres from the shore in the period 15 May to 15 August). For map, see section 6.3 *Prins Karls Forland* (page 274).
Placenames: Kaffiøyra got its name when Norwegian scientists prepared some coffee on the shore in 1909 (the procedures for giving names to geographical features have obviously become more bureaucratic since then).
Geology: Upper Proterozoic basement, mostly strongly deformed sediments and metamorphic rocks, widely covered with Quaternary sediments near the coast (raised beaches, moraines, fluvial deposits).
Landscape: Coastal plain with strongly glaciated hinterland.

6.2.4 Engelskbukta

General: The bay Engelskbukta is north of the shallows in Forlandsund. Access from the north is easy for medium-sized ships. It can be reached in a day's hiking from Ny Ålesund and is thus often visited by scientists for research and during their spare time. For map, see section 6.3 *Prins Karls Forland* (page 274).
Placenames: Comfortlessbreen: after "Comfortless Cove", name used by English whalers in the 17th century. **Engelskbukta:** "English bay".
Geology: Complex mosaic of basement rocks (slate, phyllites, weakly crystallised limestones ("marble") and Carboniferous sediments.
Landscape: The mountain slopes on both sides are gentle enough to allow short, easy tundra walks and mountain hikes. The glacier Comfortlessbreen, at the head of Engelsbukta, has retreated dramatically in recent decades and left a large moraine complex behind. In good visibility, there are nice views from Engelskbukta across the Forlandsund to Prins Karls Forland with its wild glacier scenery.

History: The name already suggests that Engelskbukta was used by English whalers during the 17th century. Remains of a blubber oven and a grave can still be seen on the northern side of the bay.

6.3 Prins Karls Forland

"Down towards either horn run two ranges of schistose rocks about 1,500 feet high, their sides almost precipitous, and the topmost ridge as sharp as a knife, and jagged as a saw; the intervening space is entirely filled up by an enormous glacier ..."

Frederick Temple Hamilton-Temple Blackwood,
Marquis of Dufferin and Ava,
Letters from high latitudes

General: Prins Karls Forland is a conspicuously narrow but elongated island off the west coast of Spitsbergen, between Isfjord and Kongsfjord. The island is 86 kilometres long but only five to eleven kilometres wide and has a surface area of 640 sq km. It has varied and dramatic scenery, important and unusual wildlife features and interesting historic sites. The surrounding waters are very shallow in places, especially near the northern point (Fuglehuken) and east of Murraypynten, where the shallows stretch all the way across Forlandsund and make passage impossible for all but the smallest ships. In other places, the waters are too deep to anchor even close to the coast. The west coast of Prins Karls Forland is completely exposed to the surf of the open ocean, but even landings on the more protected eastern side need fair weather – when the wind is blowing through the Forlandsund, then it is better to seek shelter in one of the bays on the west coast of Spitsbergen. The central west coast of Spitsbergen including Prins Karls Forland and Kongsfjord are influenced by the relatively warm waters of the West-Spitsbergen current ("gulf stream"), which keeps the area largely free of ice for most of the year. There is normally local ice formation in Forlandsund during the spring.

Prins Karls Forland is a National Park on its own. There are two bird sanctuaries on the outer coast, where all traffic is banned during the period 15 May to 15 August: Plankeholmane near the south point and Forlandsøyane a bit further north.

Placenames: Aberdeenflya: "Aberdeen plain", name given by the Scottish polar explorer William Spiers Bruce (1867-1921). **Fuglehuken:** "Bird point", referring to bird colonies. Name given by Willem Barents in 1596. **Monacofjellet:** see section on history. **Prins Karls Forland:** after Charles I. (1600-1649), Prince of Wales, later King of England.

Geology: Prins Karls Forland and Forlandsund are geologically a complex mosaic that determines the main landscape features. Most of the island consists of metamorphic basement rocks (schist, phyllite, carbonates etc), that form an uplifted crustal block ("horst"). The long and narrow shape of this block is a reasonable explanation for the

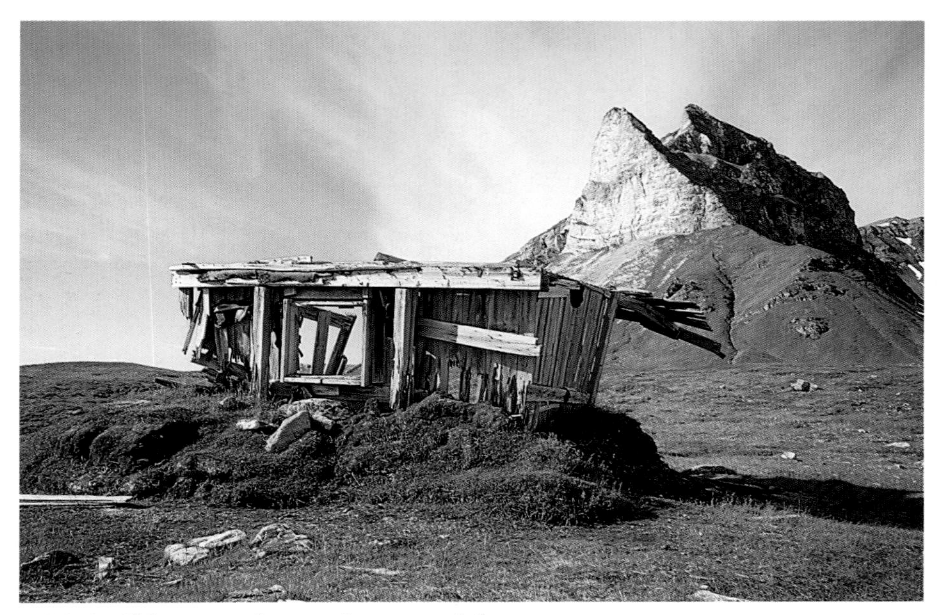

6.1.1-1: Alkhornet with ruin of a trapper's hut.

6.1.1-2: Trygghamna.

6.1.2: Ymerbukta with Esmarkbreen.

6.1.3: Rijpsburg, an old mining settlement on Bohemanflya.

6.1.4: Flintholmen in Ekmanfjord.

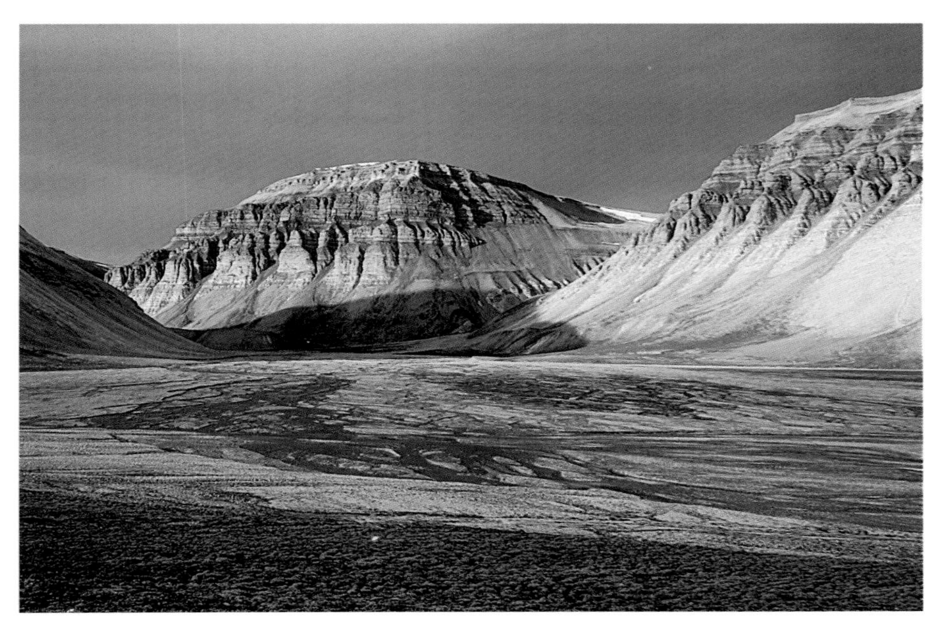

6.1.5-1: Lyckholmdalen in western Dickson Land.

6.1.5-2: Svenskehuset near Kapp Thordsen, Dickson Land.

6.1.6-1: The former Russian mining settlement of Pyramiden under the mountain of the same name. Billefjord.

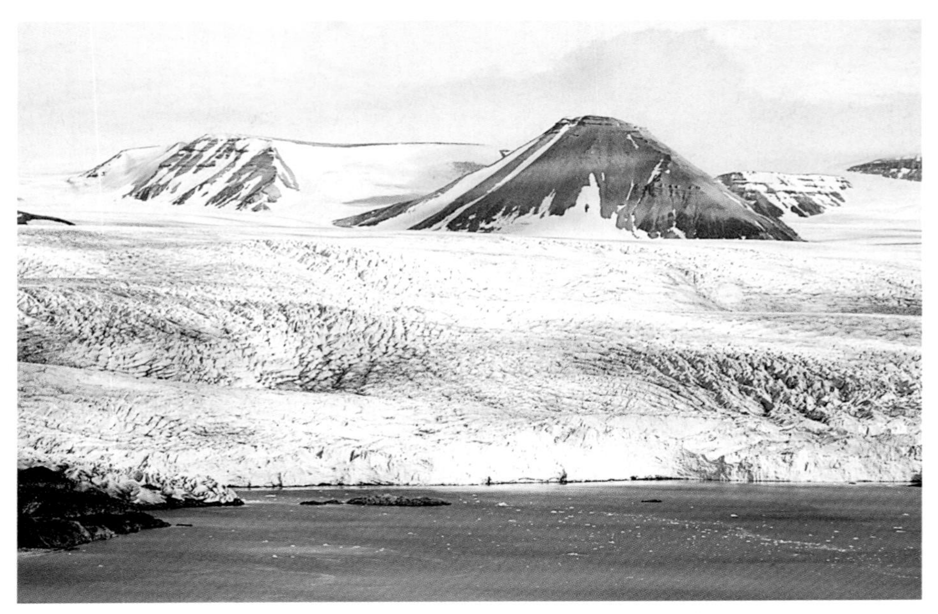

6.1.6-2: Nordenskiöldbreen seen from Wordiekammen.Billefjord.

6.1.6-3: Brucebyen.

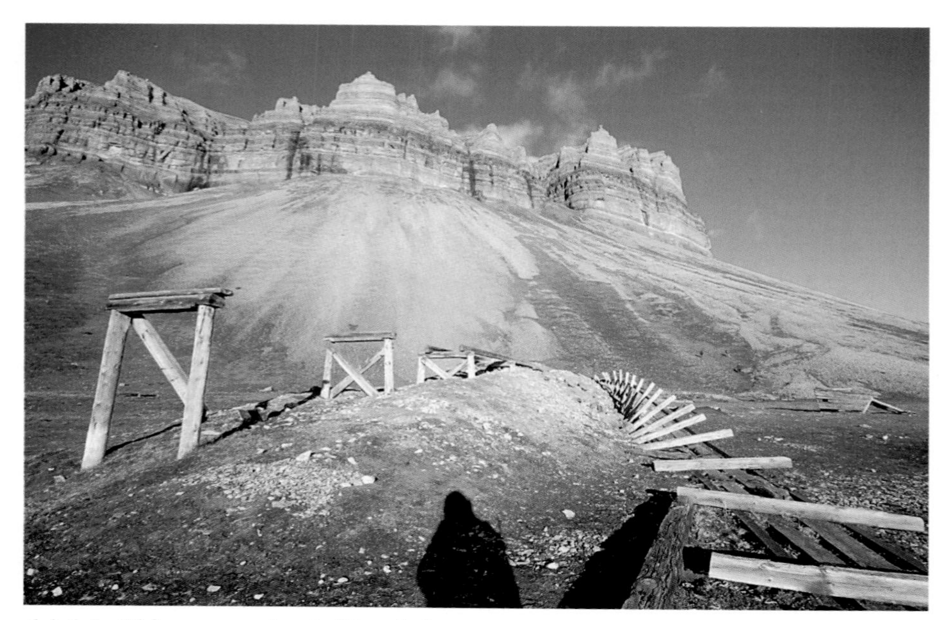
6.1.6-4: Old gypsum mine in Skansbukta.

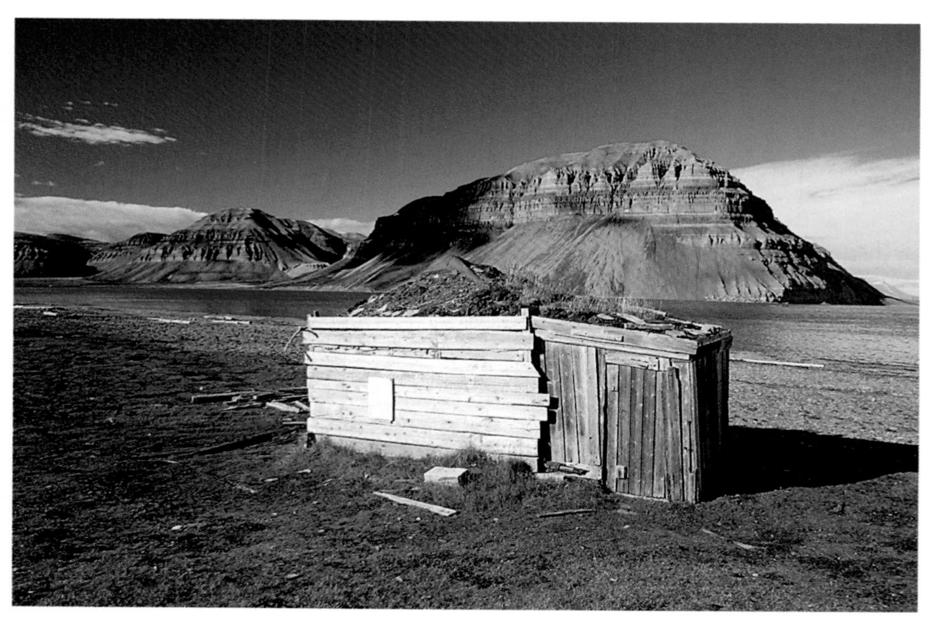
6.1.6-5: Old trapper's hut in Skansbukta.

6.1.7-1: Sassendalen seen from the mountain Trehøgden, Nordenskiöld Land.

6.1.7-2: Inland south of Sassenfjord (De Geerdalen), Nordenskiöld Land.

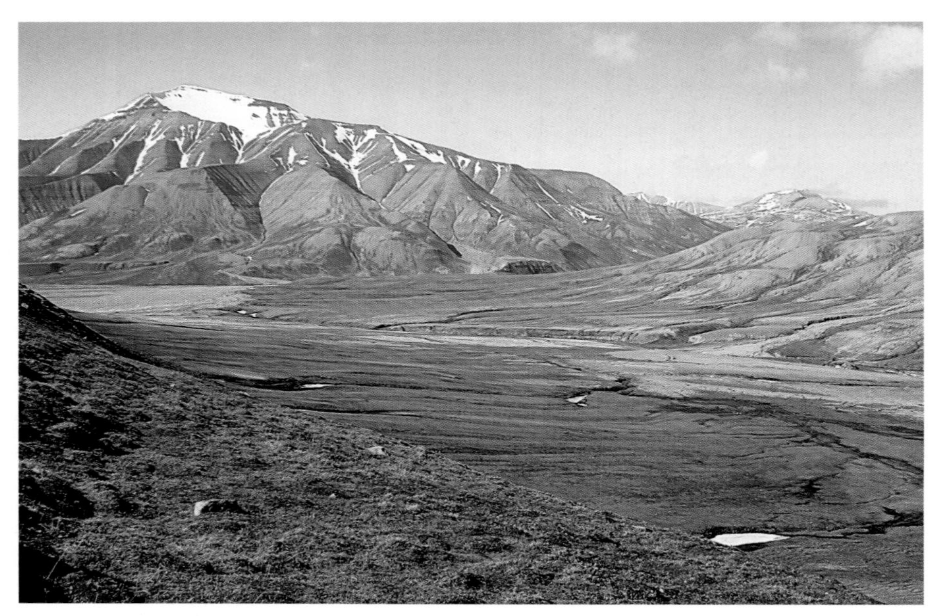

6.1.8-1: Adventdalen with Helvetiafjellet, seen from Janssonhaugen.

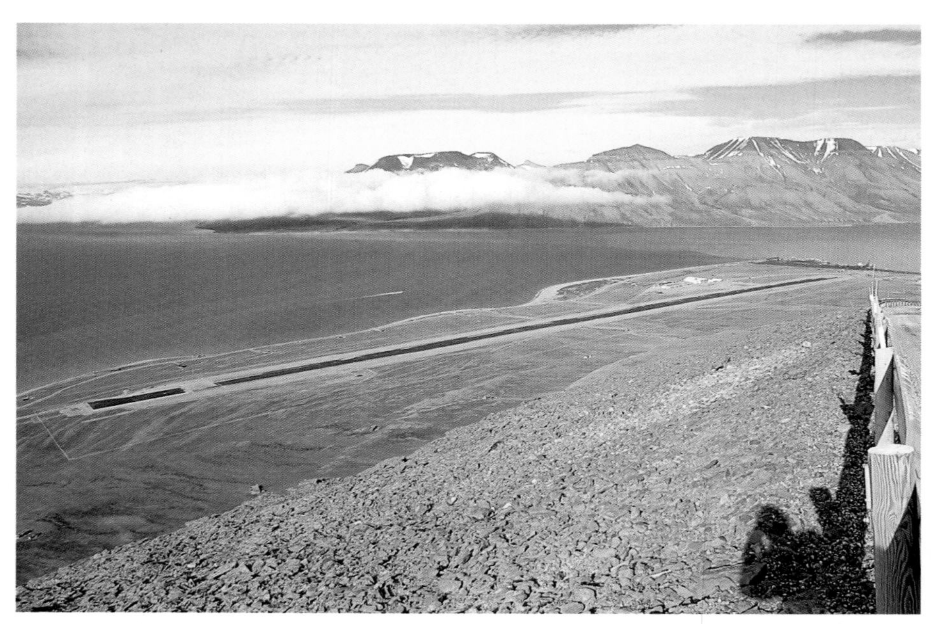

6.1.8-2: Adventfjord with airport and camping site (behind the right-hand end of the runway). Photo: Michelle van Dijk.

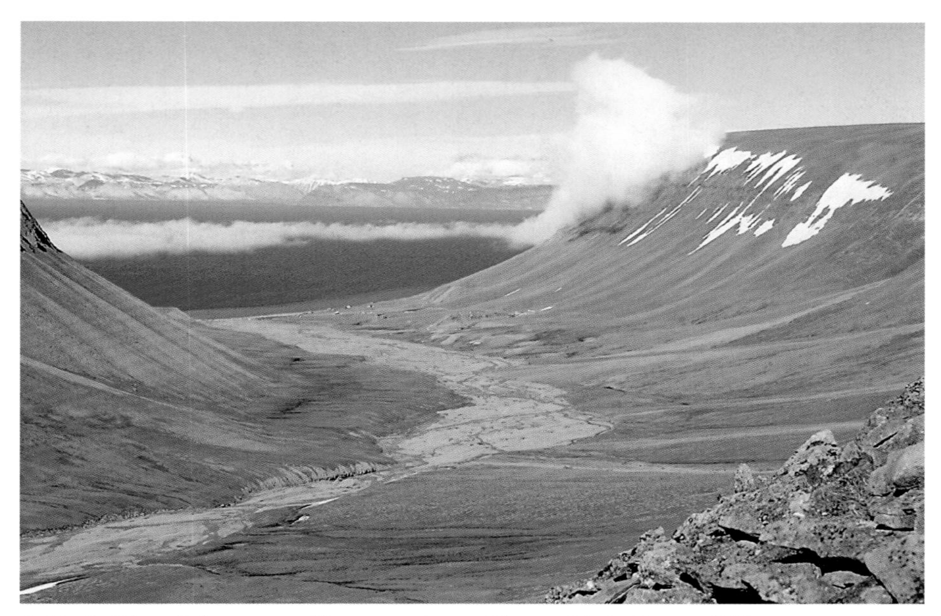

6.1.8-3: Bjørndalen west of Longyearbyen. Photo: Michelle van Dijk.

6.1.9: Grumantbyen.

6.1.10-1: Barentsburg.

6.1.10-2: Lenin in Barentsburg.

6.1.11-1: Festningen.

6.1.11-2: Kapp Linné/Isfjord Radio.

6.2.1: St. Jonsfjord.

6.2.3: Engelskbukta.

6.3-1: Glacier landscape on the east side of Prins Karls Forland.

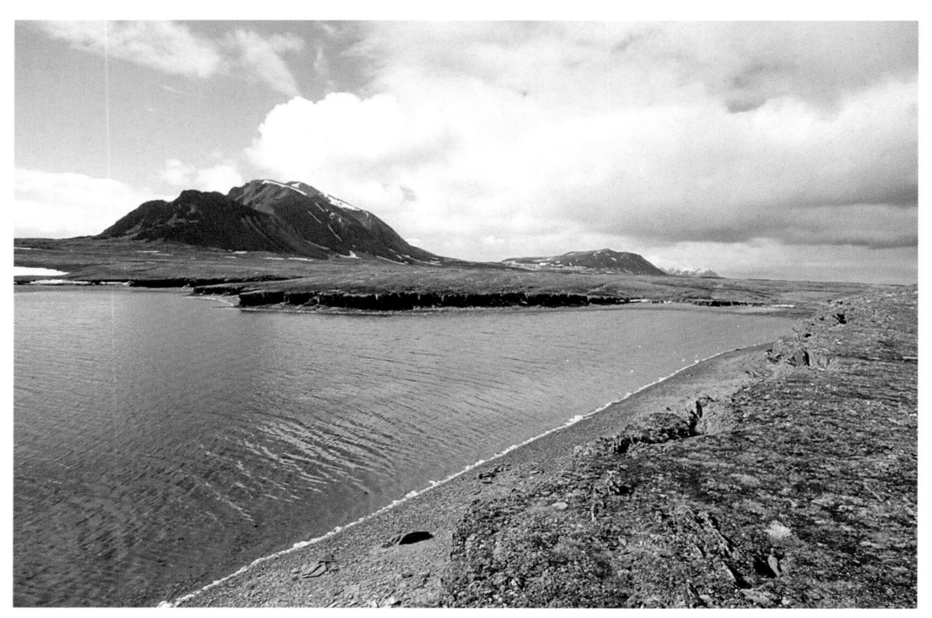

6.3-2: Coastal landscape at Kingodden, southeastern Prins Karls Forland.

6.4.1-1: Old steam railway engine in Ny Ålesund.

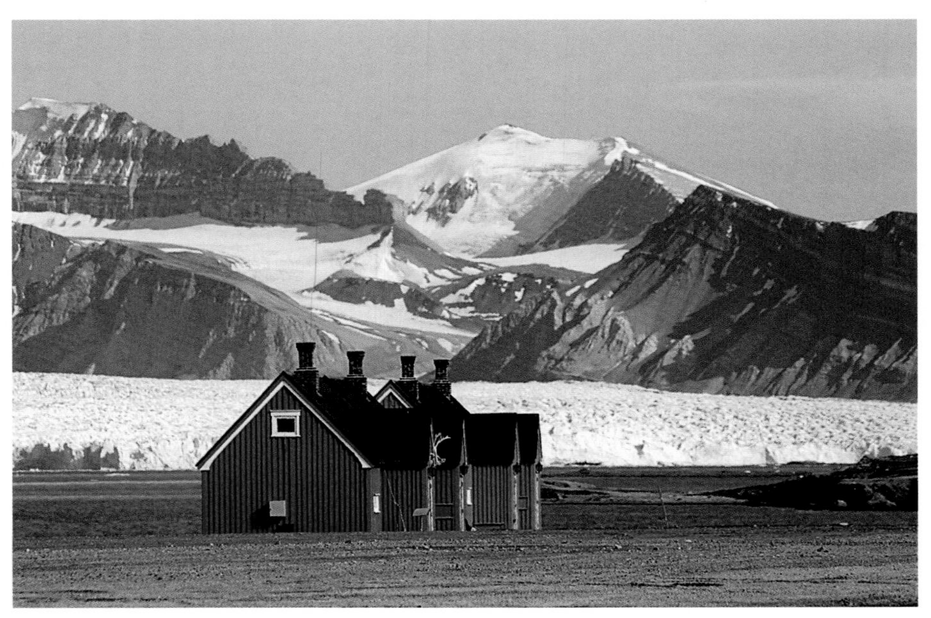

6.4.1-2: Houses in Ny Ålesund with Kongsvegen in the background.

6.4.1-3: The historical airship mast near Ny Ålesund.

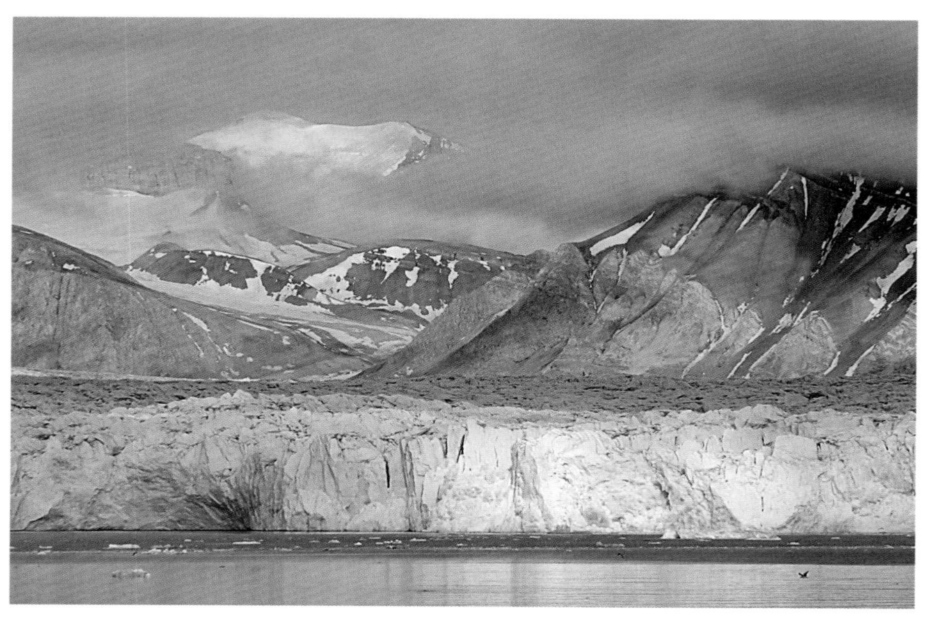

6.4.2-1: Kongsvegen in inner Kongsfjord.

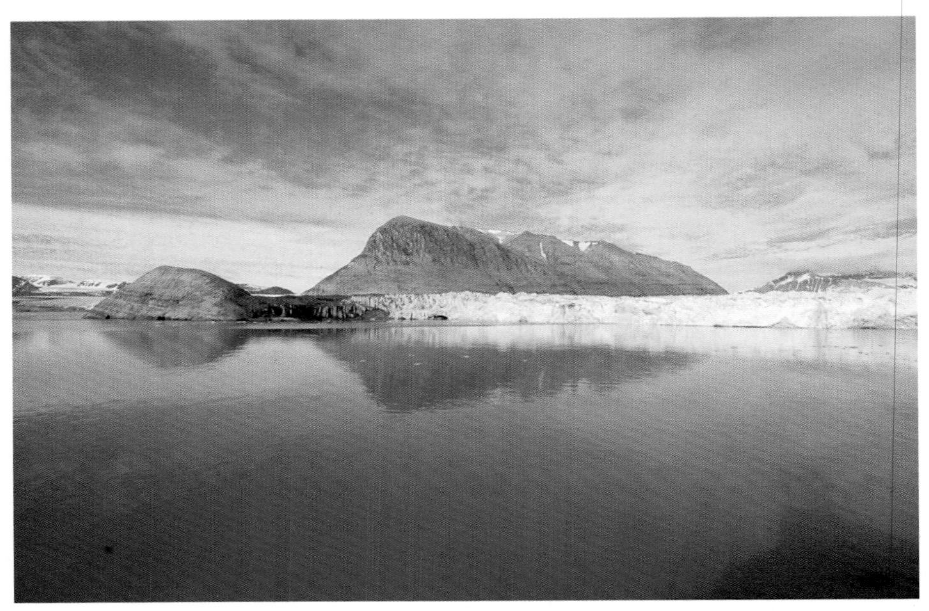

6.4.2-2: Meltwater at Kongsvegen, Kongsfjord. The reddish colour is due to suspended sediment derived from eroded Old Red.

6.4.2-3: Conwaybreen in inner Kongsfjord.

shape of the island. The height of the mountain tops, up to a good 1,000 metres, is directly related to the strong uplift of the "horst". The opposite structure to a "horst" is a "graben", where a piece of crust has subsided. The surface depression is then usually occupied by rivers, lakes or the sea, depending on its elevation, and subsequently filled with sediments. Forlandsund follows almost exactly a graben that was active during the lower Tertiary. Steeply dipping conglomerates that belong to the filling of the Forlandsund-graben, are exposed at the northeastern coast of Prins Karls Forland.
Landscape: Prins Karls Forland has an interesting landscape division. A saddle-shaped mountain in the south is separated from the mountain ranges further north by lowlands so that from a distance, Prins Karls Forland appears as if it were two separate islands. There are coastal plains in many parts of the coast and no bays that offer protection for anything but the smallest boats. In the southern half, smaller landscape features including streams, lagoons and low, elongated hills follow the north-south trend that is determined by the geology. This structure has also created some nice bays that run parallel to the main direction of the coast. The geometrical patterns are quite obvious on the topographic map.

The middle and northern parts of Prins Karls Forland have wild alpine mountain and glacier scenery, culminating in the Grampianfjella with several peaks above 1,000 metres. The highest mountain is Monacofjellet at 1,081 metres. The Grampianfjella are strongly glaciated on their eastern slopes, with hanging glaciers that are reminiscent of the Antarctic Peninsula.

Most of the flat coastal forelands are very rocky and barren with nice frost-patterned ground and patterns of raised beach ridges in many places. There are a larger number of perfectly developed rock glaciers on many slopes, especially those near the northern end of Prins Karls Forland.
Flora and fauna: Vegetation is mostly scarce and only tundra areas near bird cliffs are greener and quite covered by rich vegetation. Large numbers of breeding seabirds occupy the steep cliffs, especially at Fuglehuken near the northern tip. The most abundant species are Brünich's guillemots and Kittiwakes; rarer ones include Puffins and even some Common guillemots.

Forlandsund is home to the world's northernmost Harbour seal colony, probably a relict colony from times some thousand years ago when the waters around Spitsbergen were slightly warmer than today. Sometimes there are Harbour seals resting on rocks on the northeast coast of Prins Karls Forland. The Harbour seals are quite shy. Keep a good distance and approach carefully.

Another faunal highlight is Walrus that occupy several haul-out sites in the Forlandsund area; the only ones on the west coast of Spitsbergen. Great care is needed when you move around in areas with resting Walrus (see section 4.7.6 *Walrus*).
History: Prins Karls Forland was one of the very first parts of Spitsbergen seen in June 1596 by Willem Barents and some placenames in the area go back to the chart he drew; for example "Vogel Hoek", later Norwegianised and turned into "Fuglehuken". Whalers, Pomors and trappers have all used Prins Karls Forland and its surrounding

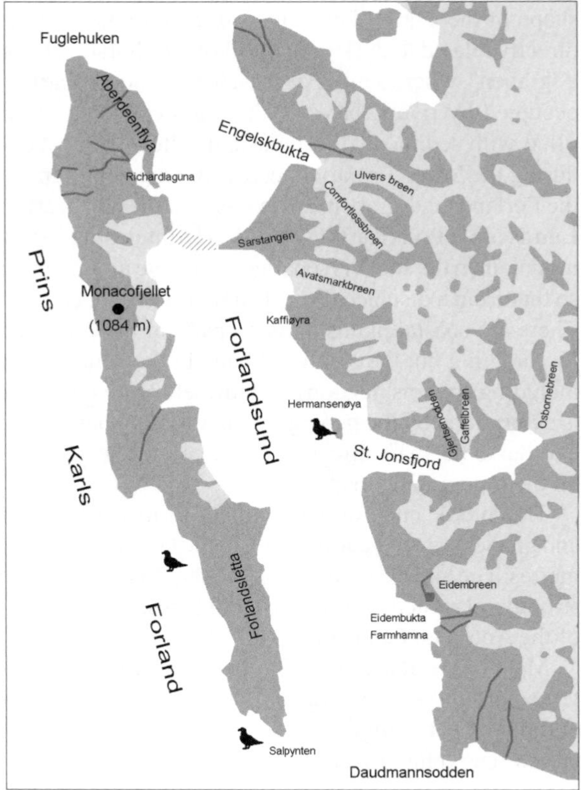

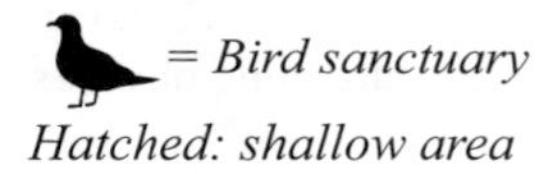

waters. The northernmost part is richest in cultural remains, including a little whalers' graveyard and the ruin of a trapper's hut southeast of Fuglehuken. On the other hand, Prins Karls Forland has never been amongst the really busy hunting areas, which may in part be due to the lack of natural harbours, but winterings of Norwegian trappers took place during 16 seasons in the early 20th century. The small hut, now not much more than a ruin, that is shortly southeast of Fuglehuken was built in 1929.

The Scottish polar explorer **William Spiers Bruce** explored and mapped the island in 1906, 1907 and 1909, hoping for coal or mineral occurrences. The ruin of a hut near Dawespynten, on the southern east coast of Prins Karls Forland, was built during these expeditions. He was supported by the Duke of Monaco who, in those years, was leading expeditions to Spitsbergen. Bruce took the opportunity to thank his supporter when he named the highest mountain of Prins Karls Forland as Monacofjellet.

6.4 Kongsfjord

"Some of the mountains of Spitzbergen are well proportioned four-sided pyramids, ... in a style of grandeur exceeding the famed pyramids of the East, or even the more wonderful Tower of Babel, the presumptive design of which, was checked by the miraculous confusion of tongues. An instance of such a regular and magnificent work of Nature, is seen near the head of King's Bay, consisting of three piles of rocks, of a regular form, known by the name of the Three Crowns."

William Scoresby, *An Account Of The Arctic Regions*

Kongsfjord or, originally, King's Bay, cuts into the west coast of Spitsbergen at latitude 79°N. It reaches about 24 kilometres inland and is about four to ten kilometres wide. Kongsfjord has been one of the most frequently visited and used parts of Spitsbergen since the days of the early whalers. The reasons for this lie in the good ice conditions in this part of the coast, under influence of the West-Spitsbergen current ("gulf stream"), in the presence of natural harbours and in coal occurrences on the southern side of the Kongsfjord which were exploited at Ny Ålesund during the 20th century. This former coal mining settlement was subsequently turned into a scientific village that is becoming more and more international. Next to researchers, tourists are attracted by the beautiful scenery of Kongsfjord, most of them coming on cruise ships of varying sizes.

Several parts of Kongsfjord have been given special protection: The bird sanctuary "Kongsfjord" comprises the lake Solvatnet in Ny Ålesund and the small islands in the fjord (Prins Heinrichøya – Dietrichøya – Mietheøya directly east of Ny Ålesund and the little archipelago Lovénøyane in the inner Kongsfjord). All traffic in these areas is banned from 15 May to 15 August, this includes the waters at a distance of up to 300 metres around the islands. Additionally, Ossian Sarsfjellet, east of Lovénøyane, has been declared a nature reserve where, to protect the vegetation, camping is forbidden.

Placenames for the sections 6.4-6.4.2: Brøggerhalvøya: Waldemar B. (1851-1940), Norwegian geologist. **Colletthøgda:** Robert C. (1842-1912), Norwegian zoologist. **Conwaybreen:** William C. (1856-1937), English mountaineer and explorer, expeditions to Spitsbergen in 1896 and 1897. **Dronningfjella:** "Queen's mountain". **Garwood-toppen:** Edmund Johnston G. (born 1864), English geologist, came to Spitsbergen together with Martin Conway. **Kongsfjord:** "King's Bay". **Kongsvegen:** "King's way". **Kronebreen:** "Crown glacier". **Kongsbreen:** "King's glacier". **Kvadehuken:** originally Quade hoek = "bad corner", an area that provided navigation hazards to early whalers. **Lovénøyane:** Sven Ludvig L. (1809-95), Swedish zoologist, came to Spitsbergen in 1837. **Ny Ålesund:** "New Ålesund", after the Norwegian town

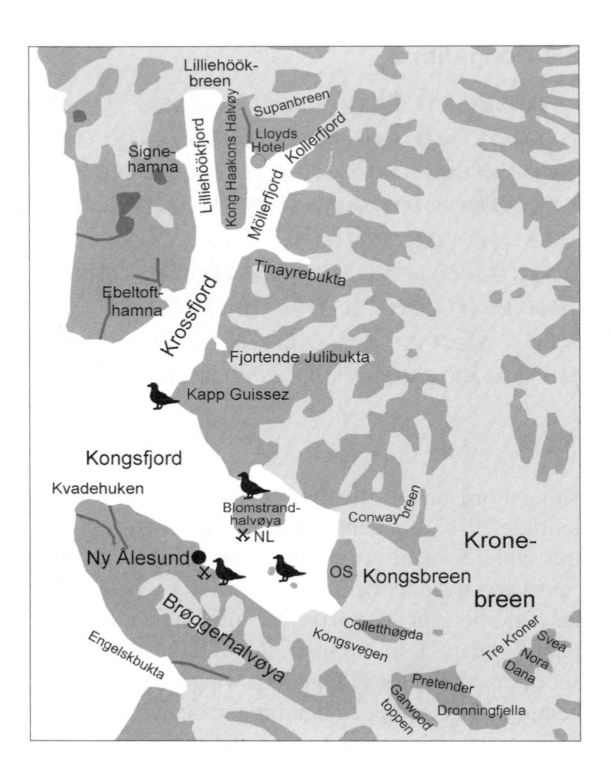

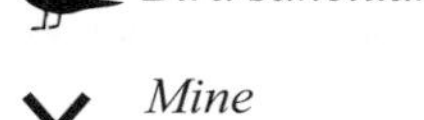

Bird sanctuary

Mine (abandoned)

NL = Ny London
OS = Ossian Sarsfjellet

Ålesund, where the company that founded the mine was based. **Ossian Sarsfjellet:** Georg O. S. (1837-1927), Norwegian zoologist, came to Spitsbergen in 1878. **Tre Kroner:** "Three crowns". The individual mountains are called **Dana, Nora** and **Svea,** the Norse names for Denmark, Norway and Sweden.

The following placenames in Kongsfjord were given during the German expedition of count Zeppelin in 1910 (see section on *history*): **Dietrichholmen:** Max Konrad Johannes D. (1870-1916), Captain of the expedition's ship *Mainz*. **Mainzodden:** after the ship used by the expedition. **Mietheholmen:** Adolf M. (1862-1927), chemist, expedition member. **Prins Heinrichøya:** Prince Heinrich of Prussia (1862-1929), patron and expedition member. **Zeppelinfjellet:** Ferdinand Graf (count) Z. (1838-1917), expedition leader.

Geology: Kongsfjord is a complicated geologial puzzle due to intense tectonic movements at several stages in Earth history, the latest and most important being related to the opening of the North Atlantic in the upper Cretaceous. Decisive for the existence of the fjord is a large fault, a crack along which different crustal blocks have moved. Rivers and, during the ice age, glaciers have been able to erode large rock volumes along this line of weakness, thus creating the fjord. The presence of the fault is also the reason for the striking fact that there are rocks of totally different types, ages and origins to be found on each side of the fjord. Refer to the following sections for further information.

History: Kongsfjord was already known to 17th century whalers and it is a bit surprising that there are no visible remains left from those early years. Pomors and trappers also used Kongsfjord and its adjacent bays extensively. One of the earliest scientific accounts of the Arctic was made by the famous English whaling Captain **William Scoresby junior**, including some descriptions of the area and the story of the ascent of a mountain near Kapp Mitra in 1818; a name given by Scoresby.

A German expedition led by **Hugo Hergesell** and **Ferdinand Graf (count) Zeppelin** spent the summer of 1910 in Kongsfjord, doing research mainly on meteorology and topography, to investigate the options for further research and exploration based on the use of airships.

Norway ran a geophysical station at **Kvadehuken** from 1920 to 1924, to collect data on meteorology, Earth magnetism and electricity and the northern lights. Today, there are only some foundations left.

In the late 1950s, Norwegian individuals took the initiative to build an "airport" at Kvadehuken. The idea was to enable aviation across the North Pole to America which, at that time, required a stoppover somewhere in the middle. In 1959, the Norwegian government decided that it was not interested in this project, because Russia feared that the airfield might be used for miltary purposes and thus violate the regulations of the Spitsbergen Treaty. There are still the remains of a track and "terminal building" to be seen at Kvadehuken; a simple wooden building proudly called "Roald Amundsens Institut". See the following sections for further information about the history of Kongsfjord.

Miscellaneous: The summer weather on the west coast of Spitsbergen can be windy, grey and wet, and it needs some luck to see the scenery of Kongsfjord in all its splendor from the beach up to the mountain tops.

6.4.1 Ny Ålesund

General: Of all the settlements in Spitsbergen that are still used, Ny Ålesund is without any doubt the one with the most attractive scenery. The mountains and glaciers of inner Kongsfjord are only a few kilometres to the east. The town is one of the most important sites in the history of the exploration of the North Pole, with Virgohamna being the only other place in Spitsbergen of comparable significance. Coal mining, originally the reason for the settlement's existence, is history. Since 1964, the place has been developed as an international research village, with scientific stations from a large and still growing number of nations, coordinated by the Norwegian Polar Institute. All stations run long-term measurement programmes of various data and, additionally, supply logistic support for shorter research projects. This structure implies pronounced seasonal variations in Ny Ålesund's population. About 130 scientists and other staff "crowd" the village during the hectic summer months, reducing to less than 30 people who work there all-year-round. There is no permanent population of families or children. The nearest hospital is in Longyearbyen. There are scheduled flights between Longyearbyen and Ny Ålesund twice a week with additional fixed-wing aircraft and helicopter traffic during the busy season.

All land and infrastructure is owned by *Kings Bay AS*, the state-owned successor to the former mining company *Kings Bay Kullkompani AS*. This was originally founded in the Norwegian coastal town of Ålesund, which readily explains the name Ny Ålesund. Kings Bay AS is the only supplier of general infrastructure, including the airfield, roads (almost ten kilometres, without a single gram of asphalt), the port, waste disposal, water supply (from a lake) and electricity (diesel generators).

As well as nice views and some impressions of the life and work of scientists in the Arctic, a relaxed stroll through Ny Ålesund can yield a good introduction to Spitsbergen's wildlife (see section on *flora and fauna* further down). The village also claims to be the northernmost settlement on Earth, but this depends on your definition of a settlement. There are permanently staffed military and weather stations further north in Canada (Alert, Ellesmere Island, 82°30'N) and Greenland (Station Nord, 81°40'N). Alert even had a larger population in the 1990s, but of military staff only. Ny Ålesund itself is at 78°55'N and thus nine kilometres south of the 79th parallel and 1,231 kilometres south of the North Pole. In anticipation of a further northwards drift of Spitsbergen, together with the continental plate of Eurasia, at a rate of a few millimetres each year, the far-sighted staff in Ny Ålesund have already made sure that all souvenirs say "79°N" to ensure they can still be used in some millions of years time. In Ny Ålesund, thinking and planning generally are future-orientated. The settlement is proud to be a "Green village", which means, among other things, that nothing is dumped in the local environment. There is a very sophisticated programme to reduce and recycle waste, and the local motto is "reduce – reuse – recycle". There are several bird sanctuaries close to the settlement where entrance is forbidden (see map on page 302).

Orientation in Ny Ålesund is so easy that there is no chance of getting lost. There is just one "main road" that leads you from the port into the village (a distance of about 200 metres) and then makes a loop through the settlement, a walking distance of no more than 15 to 20 minutes on level ground. There are several signposts along the way to explain the various buildings in Norwegian, English and German. If you follow the road from the port, you will pass the following places of interest in this order (loop to be followed in a clockwise direction).

One of the most famous photographic subjects in Spitsbergen is the old **railway engine** near the harbour. It operated from 1917 to 1958 to transport coal from the mines. Behind it is the lake **Solvatnet** with some interesting **birdlife**, including Barnacle geese, possibly Red-throated divers, Long-tailed ducks, Common eider, King eider and smaller waders. Rare vagrants of different sorts may also be seen occasionally in Ny Ålesund. The lake is part of the Kongsfjord bird sanctuary and must not be approached and, in Ny Ålesund, everybody is asked to stay on the road (see below). Good binoculars and photographic equipment are certainly useful.

As you follow the road, you pass the first buildings on the left hand side, including the british Harland House, before coming to the shop. Keep your eyes open – a **fox family** lives under the houses and young foxes are often running around and playing between the houses in the early summer. On the right hand side you find the **visitor centre** with a small permanent exhibition and information about Spitsbergen in general and Ny Ålesund in particular. In the same building, but accessible through the door from the road, are the **museum** (no staff but a box for a small entrance fee) and **public toilets**.

Kongsfjordbutikken, located just across the road from the museum, is the only shop in Ny Ålesund and open on request. It closes as soon as the last person has left the building. If you are with a small group, make sure you get your shopping done in time. The shop has a large selection of souvenirs: books, maps, T-shirts, postcards with stamps and so on. There are also some articles of daily use such as toothpaste, chocolate and beer. Norwegian currency, Euro, Sterling, US-$ and major credit cards are accepted. You will find the one and only **post box** in Ny Ålesund at the entrance to Kongsfjordbutikken.

The **old post office**, another minute walking down the road from the shop and clearly visible thanks to a sign and its mint-green colour, is not in use anymore. The door is actually normally open and you are welcome to walk in, where you will find several souvenir cachets which you can use to stamp your diary or anything you want. It is not an official stamp.

From the old post office, it is a stone's throw to the **Amundsen monument**, the "town square" of Ny Ålesund. Buildings around the "square" include the **Amundsen-Villa**, owing its name to the Norwegian explorer who used to stay in this house during his expeditions from Ny Ålesund, the Norwegian **Sverdrup-Station** and the **"Blaues Haus"** ("Blue house" or, formerly, Koldewey Station, now part of the shared French-German research station and used for accommodation).

Follow the road around Amundsen's monument to get to the **dogyard**; a further five minutes walking. There are still a few sledge dogs kept for leisure purposes. Sometimes there is some dogfood hanging on a wooden rack in the form of some seal meat which occasionally attracts Ivory gulls; keep your eyes open for a pure-white gull.

At the dogyard, the road splits into several branches. Some lead away from the settlement, towards the old mine field, Zeppelinfjellet or the airfield. Do not walk beyond this point without a rifle; you are in Polar bear territory and these potentially dangerous animals are seen in Kongsfjord every year. In the past, they have even come into the settlement, but that happens only very rarely.

The proper road to follow is the one leading to the right (coming from the Amundsen monument), towards the old coal grading plant. There are some small ponds and wet areas near the road and it is certainly worth having a good look around: Barnacle geese, Ivory gulls, reindeer and Long-tailed ducks are only a few of the species often seen in this area from which you also have a fine view of the mountains and glaciers in the inner fjord with the town in the foreground.

Go past the old coal grading plant and the modern power station to get back to the harbour area. There is a story to tell about the **coal grading plant**; a large, grey concrete block: After the mine accident in 1962 which caused 21 casualties, the number of victims was painted in large letters on the side of the building facing the fjord, to remind official visitors of the duties to ensure safety in the coal field that they had neglected. The director found this a little bit too embarassing and requested his workers to paint over the figures, which they did – in shape of a large coffin. This is still visible when you look from the fjord.

The site that has the most important historical significance is actually located a few hundred metres to the east of Ny Ålesund: the famous **airship mast**, that was used in 1926 and 1928 during the *Norge* and *Italia* expeditions, respectively (see section 5.6 *Attempts to fly to the pole: Virgohamna and Ny Ålesund*). Start a walk to the mast from the Amundsen monument and follow the road to the east (to the left, as you come from the harbour). As soon as you have left the last houses behind you, there is a small track that leads towards the very obvious mast. Remember that walking over the tundra is not allowed in and near Ny Ålesund and, once again, it is Polar bear territory and a rifle is mandatory. Smaller ships usually offer guided walks; without such an excursion, you will have to make do with a look from the village. The old cemetery, used for deceased miners, is on the tundra not far from the mast. If you follow the track further towards the fjord, you will soon reach the Camping site, the only place near Ny Ålesund where camping is allowed. It is not much more than a designated place on the tundra and does not really deserve the name "Camping site" but, nevertheless, a little fee is due to be paid to Kings Bay AS for this luxury. For slightly more comfortable **accommodation** in Ny Ålesund, refer to the **North Pole Hotel** in the heart of the settlement, run by Kings Bay (Kings Bay AS, 9173 Ny Ålesund, Norway. Phone + 47 7902 72 00, Fax + 47 7902 72 01, internet www.kingsbay.no, email booking@kingsbay.no).

Recent years have seen bigger and bigger cruise ships visiting Ny Ålesund and passenger capacities of 1,000 are no longer exceptional. It is no surprise that the local population of about 150 persons is watching this development with mixed feelings, and the future may see access restrictions to Ny Ålesund or even to Kongsfjord. Some **binding rules** have been imposed by Kings Bay to control the current visitor traffic. They are mostly common sense:

- "Reduce – reuse – recycle": control the waste volume. Do not drop litter. Avoid leaving rubbish; dispose of it properly, or take it back home. This includes cigarette butts.
- Keep a respectful distance from all technical and scientific installations, even if they do not seem to be in use.
- Stay on the roads to avoid damage to vegetation etc.
- Do not disturb any wildlife, especially breeding birds. There are nests even near the roads in the settlement, mostly of the aggressive Arctic tern. Keep your distance and never try to hit attacking birds; just walk away.

- Do not feed animals. This is valid throughout Spitsbergen, but is especially important in Ny Ålesund because of the Arctic foxes that have decided to live in the settlement.
- Respect historical sites and protected areas.

It is mandatory that visitors are familarised with these rules before they enter Ny Ålesund.

History: The English whaler Jonas Poole found bits of coal on the shore of Kongsfjord as early as 1610. It was, however, not until 1916 that Kings Bay Kull Kompani AS (KBKC), from Ålesund in Norway, started to prepare the coal field for mining. The railway was built in 1917 (in operation until 1958) and, in 1918, about 300 workers were employed to extract coal (150 during the winter). The whole business turned out to be unprofitable, mining was stopped for the time being in 1929 and the Norwegian state bought all the shares. It was mainly geological conditions that made mining difficult and dangerous: the coal seams are 210 to 340 metres below sea level and restricted to a relatively small area below Zeppelinfjellet. Several faults cut through the layers, and the high methane content led to repeated accidents, many involving casualties.

In the meantime Ny Ålesund had achieved worldwide fame thanks to the dramatic attempts to fly to the North Pole in the 1920s (see section 5.6 *Attempts to fly to the pole: Virgohamna and Ny Ålesund*).

During the years from 1935 to 1939, KBKC tried to make some money by offering harbour services to fishing vessels and opening the North Pole Hotel for tourists, but without any real success. Ny Ålesund was evacuated on 29th August 1941 and important mining facilities were destroyed and coal deposits set on fire. After WWII, mining started again in 1945, because Norway wanted to secure important coal supplies for urgent domestic needs. The village was on it's way to being developed as a "normal" mining settlement, with 158 men, 53 women and 38 children living there in 1959-60. There were then several setbacks when the prices on the world market dropped in the late 1950s, and the small community was shaken by a series of accidents, for example on 19 March 1953 (19 casualties) and on 05 November 1962 (21 victims). The loss of about 10 % of its population came hard to a small, isolated community at the beginning of the polar night in days when air travel was not available. The last accident marked the end of mining in Ny Ålesund and led to a government crisis in Norway because the government, as KBCK's only shareholder, had put a lot of taxpayer's money into the dangerous mines in Kongsfjord. It was not long before a new use was found for the old mining settlement. Good accessibility in a position relatively close to the North Pole, together with the infrastructure already there, were the main reasons for establishing antennae to receive data from satellites in polar orbits. In 1964, it was decided to build a Norwegian satellite-based telemetric station (closed in 1974). Additionally, French and English scientists discovered the research opportunities and established temporary bases in 1964-65, followed in 1966 by a Norwegian northern light observatory. Ny Ålesund's future as a research base really

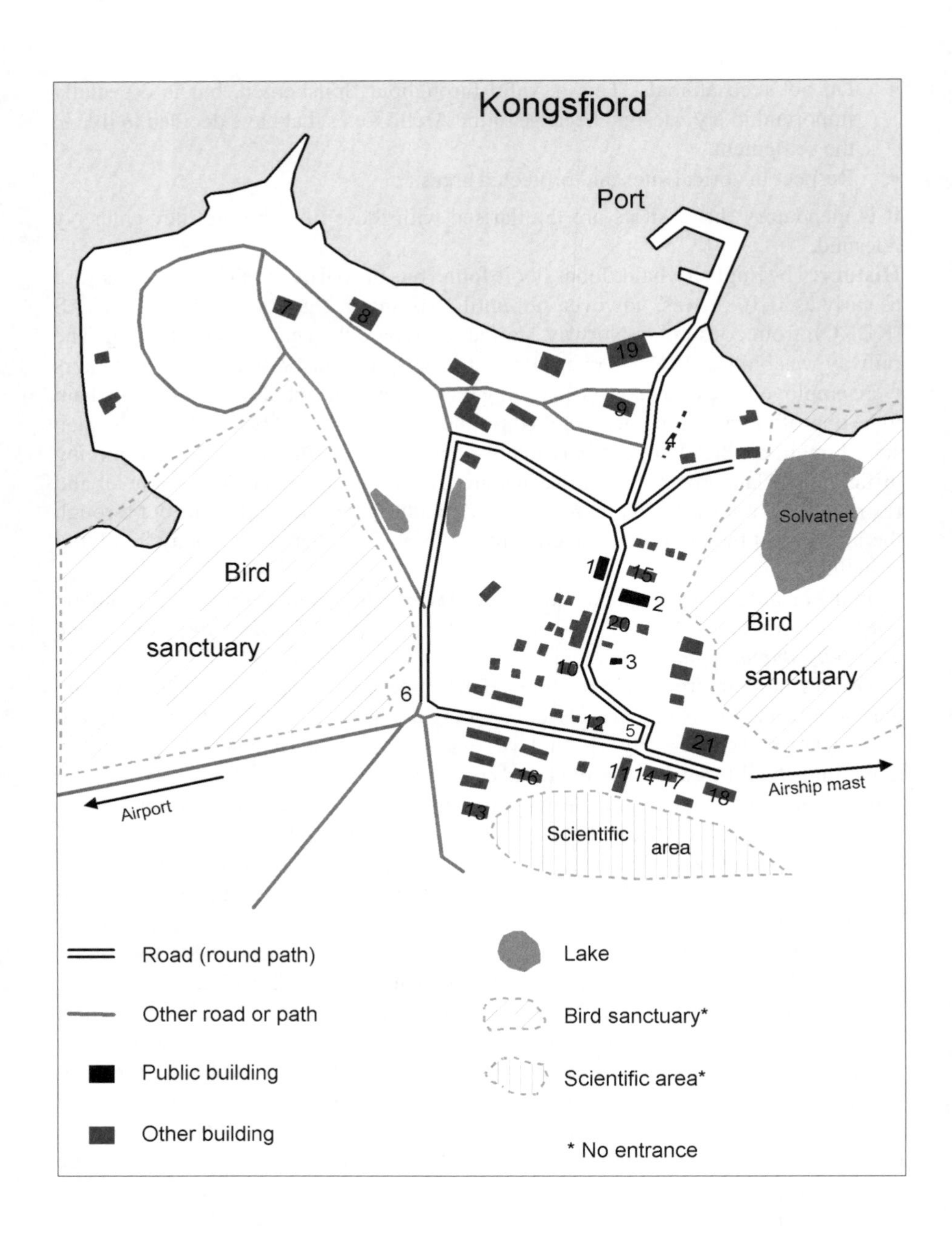
Kongsfjord
Port
Bird
sanctuary
Bird
sanctuary
Solvatnet
Scientific
area
Airport
Airship mast
1
2
3
4
5
6
7
8
9
10
11
12
13
14
15
16
17
18
19
20
21
Road (round path)
Other road or path
Public building
Other building
Lake
Bird sanctuary*
Scientific area*
* No entrance

Map of Ny Ålesund

Tourist interest
1. Visitor centre/museum/public toilets
2. Kongsfjordbutikken (shop)
3. Old post office
4. Old railway engine
5. Amundsen memorial
6. Dogyard
7. Old coal grading plant
8. Old power station
Other
9. Harbour master building
10. Hotel

Stations
11. Sverdrup Station, Norwegian
12. Blaues Haus (previously "Koldewey-Station"), German-French
13. NDSC-Station, German-French
14. Rabot Station, German-French
15. Harland Station, British
16. Dirigibile Italia, Italian
17. DASAN-Station, South-Korean
18. Yellow-River-Station, Chinese
19. Marine laboratory, Norwegian/international
20. Himadri Station, India
21. Administration, canteen

Scientific installations outside the map (not comprehensive): Japanese station and Norwegian geodetic station (both at the airfield), atmospheric station on top of Zeppelinfjellet.

started in 1968 when the Norwegian Polar Institute began to carry out permanent scientific work programmes. This paved the way for all further development in Ny Ålesund up to the present day.

Stations and research:

- The Norwegian Polar Institute (NPI) has been present year-round since 1968 and in 1999, moved into the modern building "Sverdrup Station" near the Amundsen monument. Research programmes cover most fields, including seismology (earthquakes), earth magnetism, northern lights, glaciology (glaciers), ecology, environmental monitoring (environmental toxins) and climate change. Since 1989, the NPI has run the atmospheric station on top of Zeppelinfjellet at 470 metres altitude, to monitor the chemistry of the atmosphere, including carbon dioxide. There is a cableway up to the station, but not for the public. The NPI is, since 1994, coordinating all scientific activities in Ny Ålesund, through a comittee that was established for this purpose (**NySMAC**, Ny Ålesund Science Managers Committee). The latest installation is the marine laboratory near the harbour.
- **Geodetic Station**: Large antennae near the airfield are operated by the Norwegian mapping authority (Statens Kartverk) to obtain high-precision reference data as a background for topographic measurements. Comparison of shifting positions of similar stations all over the globe allows direct measurements of tectonic plate movements.
- **SvalRak**: Facility to launch scientific rockets for research on the upper atmosphere.
- **Koldewey Station**: German research station, originally established in 1991 by the Alfred Wegener Institute (AWI) in the "Blue House", followed in 1994 by a scientific laser for research on the upper atmosphere, including depletion of the arctic ozone layer. The laser is in a special building not far from the dogyard, easily recognised by the large hemisphere on the roof (**NDSC**-Station, Global Network for Detection of Stratospheric Change).
- **Rabot Station**: Established in 1999 by the French Institute Polaire Française Paul Emile Victor (**IPEV**), now run jointly with the German facilities.
- Since 2003, French and German research facilities in Ny Ålesund have been run jointly under the acronym **AWIPEV** which combines the abbreviated names of both research institutes. Scientific work is focussed on changes in the upper atmosphere (NDSC-Station).
- The **Japanese National Institute for Polar Research (NIPR)** is working mainly on atmospheric and glacier research at a station at the airport.
- In 1991, the English **Natural Environment Research Council (NERC)** moved into their first station building and in 1992, extended this with the aquisition of **Harland House**. Scientific work includes research on the regional ecosystem in the light of climatic change.

- In 1995, Dutch scientists from the **University of Groningen** moved into one of the yellow-brown "London houses" to do biological work, with Barnacle geese being one of their favourite subjects. Much to the disgust of the biologists, a fox family has discovered the basement of the London houses as a comfortable den and has since then reduced the main research object considerably.
- The Italian **Consiglio Nazionale delle Ricerche (CNR)** followed in 1997 with a station called **Dirigibile Italia**.
- South Korea started in 2002 with the **DASAN-Station** (marine biology, glaciology, atmospheric physics).
- The **Chinese Arctic and Antarctic Administration (CAAA)** were the last ones to follow, moving into a building called **Yellow-River-Station**, as neighbours of South Korea.
- In summer 2008, India opened its **Himadri Station** to work mainly on climate change.
- The next major scientific installation will be the 30 metres high **Amundsen Nobile climate change tower**, planned by Italy to be operating in 2009.

Further nations have already expressed their interest in having stations in Ny Ålesund. Many of these stations run websites on the internet; check the author's website for links (www.spitzbergen.de).

Placenames: see section 6.4 *Kongsfjord*.

Geology: Brøggerhalvøya, the pensinsula between Kongsfjord and Engelskbukta further south, is made up of a complex mosaic of different blocks. The main structure is defined by Permocarboniferous carbonates and fine-grained clastic sediments in the west and basement schists in the east. The lower Tertiary sediments that include the coal seams are restricted to several smaller tectonic blocks in the plain southeast of Ny Ålesund.

The whole Kongsfjord area has been strongly influenced by tectonic events and several faults cut through Brøggerhalvøya. Some of the layers are dipping steeply, others seem undisturbed at first glance, as in Scheteligfjellet west of Ny Ålesund, but if you look closely, you see that the strata are not exactly parallel, but at slight angles to one another: a fault cuts almost horizontally through the mountain, along which one block has been pushed on top of the other. The result is that you find the same layers twice as you follow the slope from the bottom to the top – not a normal situation and an impressive example of how forcefully the movements in the crust work over time.

Landscape: It has been said of Kongsfjord, as of many others, that it is the most beautiful of Spitsbergen's many fjords; rather similar to the waterfalls on Iceland where every single one is the most beautiful, if only the sun shines. There is a coastal plain on the southern side of Kongsfjord, about two kilometres wide at Ny Ålesund and widening further west, opening into the wide plain of Kvadehuksletta. Behind Ny Ålesund, there is a mountain range reaching heights of up to 785 metres and several small glaciers, including Brøggerbreane (two glaciers) and Lovénbreane (three glaciers east of Ny Ålesund).

Flora and fauna: The whole coastal plain in the Ny Ålesund area is covered by tundra. The local reindeer population has, in the past, collapsed completely, but 15 reindeer were moved from Isfjord to Brøggerhalvøya in 1978 and have since then multiplied well. There are several medium-sized and larger seabird colonies on steep cliffs on Brøggerhalvøya, including Brünich's guillemots, Kittiwakes and Fulmars as the main breeding species.

Ny Ålesund offers a good introduction to Arctic wildlife. Often there are Barnacle geese in the settlement and, much to their disgust, a fox family has found a home under some houses not far from the shop. Common eider, King eider, Long-tailed eider, Grey pharalope and Purple sandpiper are amongst those species that are more or less commonly seen at the ponds in and around Ny Ålesund; good binoculars, or a telescope with tripod, are certainly useful to observe these birds. A main attraction for birdwatchers is the Ivory gull, often seen near the dogyard.

Miscellaneous: Visitors to Ny Ålesund have to pay a fee of about 65 NOK per person, plus anchoring or mooring fee, to Kings Bay AS. This is usually inclusive for cruise ship passengers.

Ny Ålesund harbour master, Kings Bay AS, 9173 Ny-Ålesund, Norway. Telefone +47 7902 72 40 or +47 7902 72 81, Fax +47 7902 72 46 or +47 7902 72 01. Email harbour-master@kingsbay.no or driftsleder@kingsbay.no, internet www.kingsbay.no.

6.4.2 Inner Kongsfjord

General: It is often said that Kongsfjord is the most beautiful fjord in Spitsbergen, which is evidently a matter of taste and weather, but there is little doubt that the innermost part is the most beautiful within Kongsfjord. Most of the scenery can be seen from Ny Ålesund. The small islands Lóvenøyane have been given protection as a bird sanctuary (no traffic any nearer than 300 metres from the shore during 15 May to 15 August), and Ossian Sarsfjellet is a nature reserve where, to protect the diverse flora, camping is forbidden. For map, see section 6.4 *Kongsfjord* (page 276).

Placenames: see section 6.4 *Kongsfjord*.

Geology: Varied; the mountains in the glaciated inland area east of Kongsfjord consist of a colourful geological mosaic. It is quite complicated if you go into too much detail, but the main building blocks are relatively easily recognisable from Kongsfjord. You will see the following rocks (from young to old).

- Sediments, mainly carbonates, from the Carboniferous and Permian. These rocks have a colour that ranges between brown and yellow, and a clearly visible layering.
- Old Red: Devonian sandstones and conglomerates with an eye-catching reddish colour.
- Basement: low to medium grade metamorphic sediments (quartzite, various schists, recrystallised marble), which are mostly grey or darkbrown with inconspicuous layering.

The complex geological history, including intense tectonic activity during the opening of the North Atlantic (upper Cretaceous), has created faults along which blocks containing these rocks have been moved around. As a result, what you see now does not have any obvious relationship with the original structure. There are some nice faults and folds exposed in the mountain slopes.

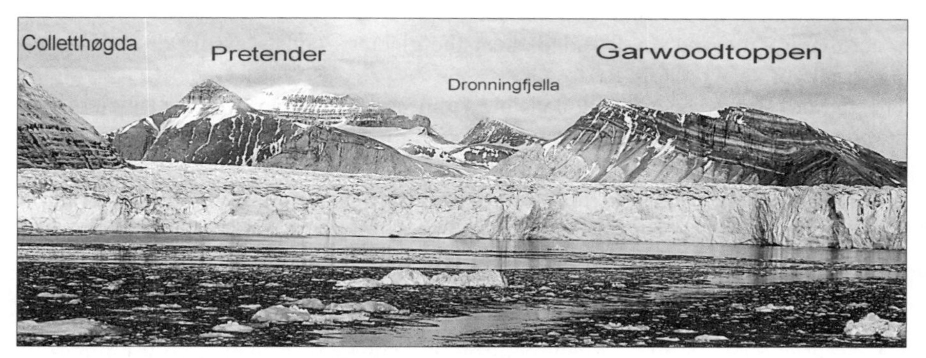

The mountains east of Kongsfjord.

From the perspective of a ship that is close to the glaciers in Kongsfjord, you will see the following from south to north (counterclockwise):

- The mountains south of inner Kongsfjord (**Brøggerhalvøya**) consisting of middle and upper Proterozoic metamorphic sediments (basement).
- **Garwoodtoppen**, the mountain that separates the glaciers Kongsvegen and Kronebreen, which is composed of Permocarboniferous sediments, nicely folded and cut by a clearly visible fault in the upper right corner.
- The mighty **Dronningfjella** towers behind Garwoodtoppen. The only part that you can see from Kongsfjord is the top with its layers of Permocarboniferous sediments.
- **Pretender**, Garwoodtoppen's immediate neighbour to the northeast, has two peaks, each with different geology. The one furthest away, in the background and thus not very prominent, is made up of Permocarboniferous layers that rest on Devonian Old Red which can just be seen. More striking is the nearer, pyramid-shaped peak of Pretender, for well-travelled Spitsbergen enthusiasts reminiscent of some mountains in Dickson Land (Lykta, Triungen, Pyramiden etc.). The trained eye will quickly realise that both peaks share a very similar geological structure. All three regionally important rock groups can be seen in the western (nearer) part of the Pretender massif: yellow-brownish Permocarboniferous in the lower right and forming the pyramid on top, below which there is a strip of Old Red. The bottom part consists of dark-brown basement rocks.
- **Colletthøgda**, the massive mountain block that separates Kronebreen and Kongsbreen at sea level, has a less complex structure than Pretender: the visible part consists throughout of Permocarboniferous sediments (the underlying Old Red is not visible from the fjord).

- **Ossian Sarsfjellet**, that forms a wide barrier between the glaciers and the fjord, consists of dark basement rocks (phyllite and mica schists, with some slightly metamorphosed marble beds). The geology of the mountains further north is similar to that of Ossian Sarsfjellet.
- **Lovénøyane**, the small islands near the glaciers, consist partly of marble and partly of very red Old Red.

The famous Tre Kroner are not visible from a position close to the glaciers, but dominate the scenery when seen from a distance, for example from Blomstrandhalvøya or Ny Ålesund. These spectacular mountains with their markedly pyramid-shaped peaks, have a geological structure similar to that of their similar-looking "relatives" in Dickson Land: hard Permocarboniferous sediment layers have created a steep peak, resting on colourful, but softer Old Red. The beautiful trio is named from south to north in alphabetical order: Dana, Nora and Svea, symbolising the ancient kingdoms of Scandinavia.

Landscape: The geology largely controls the appearance of this very impressive mountain scenery. The glaciers are another clear landscape feature and an obvious highlight. There are four major glaciers with calving icefronts in the inner Kongsfjord: furthest south, Kongsvegen and Kronebreen that share the same calving front (the future is likely to see some changes here); Kongsbreen between Colletthøgda and Ossian Sarsfjellet; finally Conwaybreen in the north. All these glaciers have retreated a lot during the 20th century; the ice volume loss has accelerated in recent years. Large amounts of meltwater drain under the glaciers into the fjord, for example south of Colletthøgda at the northern end of Kronebreen. Fine suspended particles derived from eroded Old Red are responsible for the striking red colour of the meltwater. With some luck, you may even see icebergs breaking off from the glaciers and falling into the water with a thunderous crash.

Flora and fauna: Most land surfaces have been glaciated in the recent past and are thus covered with large rocky moraines. The only flat areas with significant vegetation cover are on Lovénøyane where Barnacle geese and Common eider breed in large numbers. Ossian Sarsfjellet also has a dense and varied plant life. Biologists from Ny Ålesund are doing annual surveys and have discovered that the local population of geese is declining.

History: The geology and glaciology in Kongsfjord has been studied repeatedly by various expeditions during the 20th century. Ernest Mansfield's *Northern Exploration Company* built a hut on Storholmen, the westernmost and largest of Lovénøyane, during investigative work from 1910 and 1920 on marble occurrences on nearby Blomstrandhalvøya (see section 6.4.3 *Blomstrandhalvøya*). This hut was used in 1913 by a small expedition under Kurt Wegener, brother of the famous Alfred Wegener, as a base for a brave attempt to rescue surviving members of the ill-fated Schröder-Stranz expedition (see section 5.5 *Early expeditions and science*).

Miscellaneous: Good luck with the weather!

6.4.3 Blomstrandhalvøya

General: The name Blomstrandhalvøya (called "Marble Island" in the early 20th century) is misleading. Firstly, the name "Blomstrand" is not derived from a flower-covered beach, but is in memory of a Swedish 19th century chemist and, secondly, the "halvøya" is not a peninsula anymore but is actually an island, as the glacier that once connected it to the main island has retreated in recent years. Being situated only a few kilometres across the fjord from Ny Ålesund, Blomstrandhalvøya is a popular destination both for scientists and for tourists: there is good wildlife and vegetation as well as an interesting bit of history on the southern, most frequently visited, side, and relaxed strolls and some mountain hiking are possible, all with the splendid scenery of the glaciers and mountains of the inner fjord.

All traffic is banned within 300 metres from the shore during the period 15 May to 15 August in the little bird sanctuary Blomstrandhamna on the north side of Blomstrandhalvøya, comprising the small islands of Breøyane. For map, see section 6.4 *Kongsfjord* (page 276).

Geology: Almost exclusively basement marble, believed to be middle Proterozoic in age, which makes these rocks about one billion years old. These old limestones were metamorphosed probably during the Caledonian phase, a good 400 million years ago. This process, that changed the sedimentary structure of the rocks into a more crystalline one, was not very strong. The degree of metamorphism is rather low and the grey limestone does not show nice, large crystals. A later tectonic phase caused ubiquitous cracking of the rock. These cracks are quite obvious, and it does not take a trained geologist to tell that careful investigation will be necessary before any resources are expended on quarrying activities in the marble.

Some small "rock pockets" in the upper slopes, distinct due to their colour, contain Devonian Old Red that has been mixed tectonically with the marble.

The large boulders that are lying around on Blomstrandhalvøya deserve attention. These are erratic boulders that have been transported by glaciers during the ice age. Blomstrandhalvøya appeared probably about 10,000 years ago from under the last Pleistocene ice cover. The rock type often looks very much like fossilised wood, but is actually phyllite, a low grade metamorphic schist. There are also boulders of coarse breccia that originated in the Old Red. All of these rocks came with the glacier ice from the inland area east of Kongsfjord.

Landscape: The landscape of Blomstrandhalvøya consists mostly of rounded rocky hills and has obviously been glacier-covered during the ice age. There are some tundra areas near the coast and between the hills, some of which show nice frost-patterned ground.

Flora and fauna: Large parts of Blomstrandhalvøya are barren rock surfaces, but there is tundra with an interesting variety of plant species in some places. Purple saxifrage gives the tundra a reddish shade during the early summer, whereas the yellow flowers of the Yellow mountain saxifrage are abundant in August. Other common flowers include Arctic bell-heather and Mountain avens, both typical for the relatively mild west coast areas under the influence of the West-Spitsbergen current, and for calcarous soil. There are also interesting faunal highlights. Reindeer and Arctic foxes are not uncommon and birds such as Long-tailed ducks and Red-throated divers breed on some small ponds. The latter are very shy, so care is needed when you are in the area. For reasonable photography of these birds, you will need a telephoto lens with a long focal length, a tripod and most of all, time and luck. The good news is that the main attraction for birdwatchers is often much easier to see and to photograph: There is a nest of Long-tailed skuas not far from the old huts of Ny London. This is the only confirmed breeding site of this species in Svalbard (a second one in the northern Isfjord area is likely, though). Sometimes, these birds are curious and come close to visitors.

History: The classical landing site on Blomstrandhalvøya is the little bay Peirsonhamna on the southern side. Close to the beach you will find two old huts, several foundations and other remains of the past, including some metres of railway line with some old steam boilers and drills that were used for geological investigations. These facilities were built in the years between 1910 and 1913 when the *Northern Exploration Company* (NEC), a company initiated by the enthusiastic Englishman **Ernest Mansfield,** invested heavily in geological investigations and some trial mining in the hope of finding large quantities of high-quality marble. However, Mansfield was fired in 1913 when the NEC had to realise that although there was indeed a lot of marble, it was of low quality because of the many cracks. The aesthetic quality of this marble was in any case, not comparable to existing sources, although the opposite had been claimed. Up to 70 men worked there during the summers to build the little mining settlement "London". Some last attempts to establish a marble quarry were made in 1919-20. During the years of the First World War, some equipment was stolen and moved to Ny Ålesund, including several of the houses.

The mining period on Blomstrandhalvøya was one of the largest projects in the "gold rush years" of mining in Spitsbergen and the remains represent the largest enterprise of one of the most important companies in those years, the NEC. In other words, the remains form one of the most important sites of cultural heritage in Spitsbergen. They are protected by law and nothing must be changed or removed. Nevertheless, the remains have suffered from increasing visitor traffic in the past. As a visitor to the site, please take your share of responsibility to ensure that you to not step on anything, including seemingly robust wooden boards and especially the little platform around the steam boilers on the railway line. Both huts are nowadays taken care of and used by people from Ny Ålesund for scientific and recreational purposes.

6.5 Krossfjord

"Poole named it Cross Road, because "upon the side of a hill, a mile to the westwards of the Road, I set up a Crosse, with a writing upon it, signifying the Day of my arrivall first in this land, by whom I was set out, and the time of my being heere." Several days were spent in this neighbourhood, and excellent sport was enjoyed."

Martin Conway, *No Man's Land*

General: Krossfjord, about 30 kilometres long and five kilometres wide, has several branches and shares its entrance with Kongsfjord. It has various biological and historical highlights, splendid scenery, is well protected and has a number of interesting excursion sites. The whole Krossfjord area lies within the Northwest Spitsbergen National Park. Additionally, there is a bird sanctuary at Kapp Guissez (no traffic allowed within 300 metres from the shore and on land from 15 May to 15 August). The southern side of Ebeltofthamna is on the list of sites that may be closed to visitors in the future. For map, see section 6.4 *Kongsfjord* (page 276).

Placenames: Kong Haakons Halvøy: Håkon VII (1872-1957), king of Norway from 1905. **Kollerfjord:** Alfred K. (born 1878), member of many expeditions to Spitsbergen since 1906. **Krossfjord:** "Cross bay". The English whaler Jonas Poole erected a wooden cross at the entrance in 1610. **Möllerfjord:** Didrik M. (1830-96), Swedish astronomer. **Lilliehöökfjord:** probably after Gustaf Bertil L. (1836-99), member of Torell's 1861 expedition to Spitsbergen. **For further placenames,** see section on history.

Geology: The geology of Krossfjord and its side branches is mostly dominated by middle Proterozoic (more than one billion years old) metamorphic rocks, mostly schist, mica schist, phyllite and some subordinate quartzite. There is low-grade marble in some places, similar to that found on Blomstrandhalvøya, but not close to the coast. There is a different basement province characterised by harder gneiss and granites east of Möllerfjord, where mountains are generally higher and with sharper peaks and ridges compared to those around Krossfjord with its comparatively soft schists. Several large thrust faults cut the slopes east of Krossfjord and Möllerfjord and can be seen in the slopes surrounding side bays (Fjortende Julibukta, Tinayrebukta), affording evidence of pronounced "crustal shortening" during periods of tectonic activity. These may date back to the Caledonian phase or, believed to be more likely, to the lower Cretaceous when activity related to the early stages of the opening of the North Atlantic involved some compressive movements.

Landscape: Mostly steep and mountainous, the only large flat area being the outer coast west of Krossfjord, which is also where the only lakes in the area are situated. In most other places, the land rises steeply from the fjord. Most mountains are between

500 and 800 metres high and the highest peaks near the fjord are Kronprins Olavs Fjell at Kollerfjord (1,006 metres) and Fallièresfjella on the north side of Tinayrebukta (1,025 metres). The long, narrow and steep Kong Haakons Halvøya that divides the northern half of Krossfjord into Lilliehöökfjord and Möllerfjord is one of the most dominant topographic features. The highest part, a peak called Septeret, is 710 metres high. The inland northeast of Möllerfjord has very alpine scenery with strong glaciation and many peaks higher than 1,000 metres.

Several medium-sized and one large glacier drain parts of the ice caps of northwest Spitsbergen into Krossfjord. Most of them have attractive calving ice fronts, including (counterclockwise) Fjortende Julibreen in the bay of the same name, D'Arodesbreen (no calving front), Tinayrebreen, Mayerbreen and Kollerbreen, all in bays that have the same name as the respective glacier. The largest one is Lilliehöökbreen with its seven kilometre wide, semi-circular glacier front. The massive ice loss of this particular glacier system has been shown by the Dukes of Monaco. Albert I. of Monaco photographed the glacier in 1906, and his great-grandson Duke Albert II did the same in 2006, allowing for an interesting comparison. An estimated 40 % of the total ice volume of the glacier has been lost within a century, with an accelerating tendency in recent years. When you are near the ice cliff on a ship, then you should actually be inside the glacier – at least according to the sea chart, which usually indicates the position of the glacier from the 1960s or 70s. As is often the case, the innermost part of the fjord which has most recently been glaciated, is uncharted. Other glaciers in the area have also retreated significantly, as indicated by the large fresh moraines that have almost always been left behind.

Despite all this dramatic development, Lilliehöökbreen is certainly the scenic highlight in inner Krossfjord. There are about ten larger and an even greater number of smaller tributary glaciers feeding into this glacial system, connected via a low glaciated pass to Raudfjordbreen which flows northwards into Raudfjord on the north coast. The distance between the glacier fronts of Lilliehöökbreen and Raudfjordbreen is a good 30 kilometres.

There is a phenomenon hidden in the moraine of Supanbreen north of Möllerfjord, that is rare in northwest Spitsbergen: a pingo.

Flora and fauna: Vegetated areas are limited due to the mountainous character of the landscape, but in many of the places that do have vegetation, it seems as if nature wanted to compensate for this with an abundance of flowers that is exceptional by regional standards. Several favourable factors are involved: the relatively mild climate of the central west coast fjords; the easily weathering schists that form the subsoil, local fertilisation from bird colonies, and only few grazing reindeer. Mosses, lichens and flowering plants occur, with a large range of species, and they grow to impressive sizes. You could almost talk about "hanging gardens" under some bird cliffs. One of those places is on the northern side of Fjortende Julibukta. Species include Drooping saxifrage, Alpine- and Hawkweed-leaved saxifrage, Moss campion and many others. It is natural that such places deserve to be treated with the utmost respect.

Character plants for a "middle Arctic" tundra type such as Arctic bell-heather and Mountain avens thrive on more or less flat tundra areas. In places like Ebeltofthamna and Signehamna, it is the mosses and lichens that are especially rich and give the tundra a patchy pattern of green, brown and all shades in between. It is quite obvious that the area has not seen many reindeer for quite a while.

Large bird cliffs are the main faunal feature in Krossfjord. There are a number of seabird colonies on steep cliffs, most of them high up in the mountain slopes, for example on Kong Haakons Halvøya where large numbers of Brünich's guillemots and other species breed (Kittiwakes, Fulmars, Glaucous gulls, a few Puffins, ...). In Fjortende Julibukta, there is a smaller bird colony on a low cliff at sea level on the northern side, that has, besides the "usual" species, one or two breeding pairs of Razorbills and several Puffins as a speciality. Chances are good to see a Puffin, at least in flight, if you are in the area. Geese breed on top of the cliffs, so keep a respectful distance to avoid disturbance.

History: The history of Krossfjord is almost as colourful as its vegetation. The fjord was certainly known to whalers and Pomors, although traces from those early years are very scarce. **Duke Albert I. of Monaco**, who had a strong interest in oceanography, charted the fjord during his summer expeditions in 1906 and 1907, completed by investigations carried out by other expedition members. Worth mentioning is the Norwegian **Gunnar Isachsen** who was responsible for topographic surveys. The Duke did not miss the opportunity to put a good number of **placenames** down on the map, including **Grimalditoppen** (802 metres) near Kapp Guissez, named after the family of the Dukes of Monaco; **Fjortende Julibukta** ("Fourteenth of July Bay") to pay homage to the French National Day, and **Tinayrebukta** to commemorate the expedition's artist, Jean Paul Louis Tinayre. **Signehamna** is named after Isachsen's wife.

The almost ubiquitous NEC (*Northern Exploration Company*) had a hut on the southern side of **Tinayrebukta**, which was built in 1911 by "Polar bear king" Henry Rudi and named "Camp Zoe" after the daughter of NEC's founder Ernest Mansfield. It is still occasionally used by scientists from Ny Ålesund.

If I tell you that there is a building called **Lloyds Hotel** in the innermost Möllerfjord, at the point between Möllerhamna and Kollerfjord, then you should not expect an establishment that could provide accommodation or any other sort of service. It is a simple but slightly unusual-looking hut, painted in bright orange and decorated with three stars; star-providing standards were obviously lower in Spitsbergen during the early 20th century than they are today. Numerous plates remind one of cruise ship visits, most of them German, and it is still a popular landing site thanks to the beautiful scenery.

There are remains in **Signehamna** that remind visitors of the darkest chapter of 20th century history. The German marine weather station "Knospe" was hidden behind a hill during its operational period from 1941 to 1942. The station worked successfully without any complications and a second one, named "Nussbaum", was run during the following winter in the same place. The existence of "Nussbaum", however, was uncovered by the Allies and the station found by a Norwegian boat in the spring of 1943. A German died during a small exchange of shots on shore. Soon thereafter, the German submarine that was supposed to pick up the crew of the station, found the Norwegian boat in Signehamna. The submarine attacked and the Norwegian boat was quickly sunk. One Norwegian soldier drowned. Remains of the weather station, mostly foundations and rusting pieces of equipment, can still be seen at the original site in Signehamna, although a lot has been destroyed by careless feet, or else stolen, particularly all items that showed the Swastika.

Ebeltofthamna could almost be called an Arctic open-air museum with remains from many chapters of Spitsbergen's varied history, although all remains are very inconspicuous or scarcely visible anymore at the surface. Whalers, most likely from England, had a land station with blubber ovens and a little graveyard in Ebeltofthamna which was the very first centre of English whaling in Spitsbergen, according to Conway. The Pomors also used the area for hunting and built a hut, and one of the very first winterings by Norwegian trappers in Spitsbergen in the early 1820s, may have been based in this bay. Ebeltofthamna continued to be used by trappers in the early 20th century. Some of them took advantage of the NEC's claim on the territory by receiving a small salary for "guarding services". The last trapper liked the place so much that he spent no less than five winters there, all on his own. Ebeltofthamna was also the site of one of the earliest scientific stations in Spitsbergen, when "Das Deutsche Observatorium" ("The German observatory") was collecting meteorological data from 1912 to 1914 for Graf Zeppelin. The aim was to investigate the suitability of the area for airship expeditions. In the end, the First World War made it impossible to follow up such plans. There is some uncertainty over the further history of the German observatory building; it was probably moved to Ny Ålesund. The rumour that it was destroyed by a British warship is probably German propaganda from the years of World War One. Today, there is not much more than the foundations remaining to be seen.

6.6 The northern west coast

"The whole of the western coast is mountainous and picturesque ; and though it is shone upon by a four months' sun every year, its snowy covering is never wholly dissolved nor are its icy monuments of the dominion of frost ever removed."

William Scoresby, *An Account Of The Arctic Regions*

6.6.1 Dei Sju Isfjella

General: "Dei Sju Isfjella" is the coastal stretch between Krossfjord and Hamburgbukta; strictly speaking, this old name is used to address the seven glaciers that calve into the sea. Passenger ships pass this coast regularly, although this happens usually at some distance and during the night, on the passage from Kongsfjord/Krossfjord to destinations further north. In good weather, the coastal panorama with its glaciers and mountains is quite impressive, but there are no suitable landing sites due to the lack of natural harbours along this coast which is totally exposed to the open ocean. The area is part of the Northwest Spitsbergen National Park. For map, see section 6.6.1 *Hamburgbukta* (page 296).

Placenames: The glaciers are named according to their order from south to north: **Fyrstebreen:** "First glacier", **Andrebreen** "Second glacier" and so on. **Dei Sju Isfjella:** "The seven icebergs", referring to the seven glaciers. The name, originally "Sieben Eisberge", was probably given by Friedrich Martens who published the first accurate account on Spitsbergen in 1675.

Geology: Basement phyllites and schists in the southern part. Further north, these metamorphic rocks are replaced by harder granites and gneisses (see also section 6.6.3 *Magdalenefjord*). There, the mountains reach higher altitudes of about 900 metres.

Landscape: It is hard to imagine a more inhospitable coast. The mountains drop steeply down to the sea, and flat coastal areas, if any, are restricted to narrow strips of land, mostly rocky moraines. The calving glacier fronts, once famous amongst whalers for their sheer size, are now diminishing and steadily being replaced by growing areas of moraine.

History: The adjacent open sea has been an important whaling area for centuries. In early 1922, the two Norwegians **Torgeir Møkleby** and **Harald Simonsen** had to endure an Odyssey of several weeks drifting up and down this coast in a small boat that was caught in the ice (see *history* in section 6.7.2 *Danskøya*).

6.6.2 Hamburgbukta

General: Hamburgbukta is a very small bay about three kilometres south of Magdalenefjord and hardly visible from the open sea. The entrance is narrow and only two metres deep, but the bay offers a reasonably protected natural harbour for small ships. It is the only one between Krossfjord and Magdalenefjord and so was

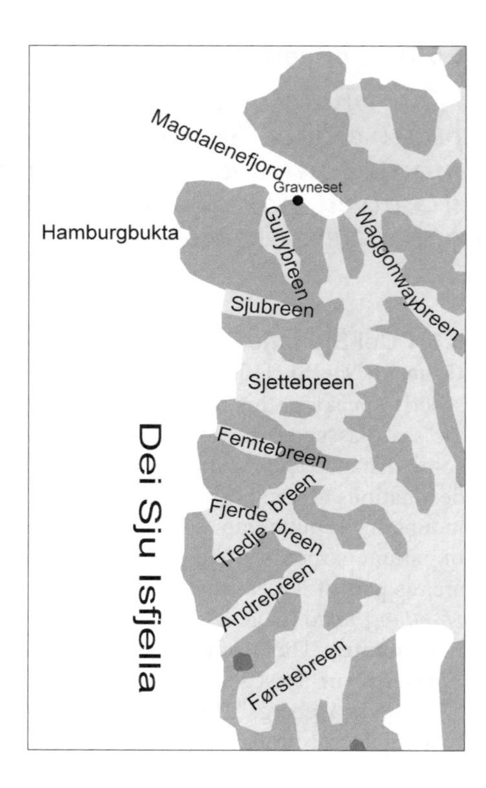

often used by early whalers. Hamburgbukta is part of the Northwest Spitsbergen National Park.

Geology: Granite-gneiss-complex, with an age of around one billion years (pointing to a possible "Grenville event").

Landscape: Barren and rocky, with small level areas at the coast. The inland is very mountainous and heavily glaciated. Two smaller glaciers flow down to Hamburgbukta, but no longer reach the water.

Flora and fauna: There are Little auk colonies in some steep scree slopes around Hamburgbukta.

History: Hamburgbukta was used by whalers from Hamburg for some years during the 1640s. Some graves are still visible south of the entrance. Norwegian trappers built a hut not far from those graves in the early 20th century, but it was only occasionally used during travelling.

6.6.3 Magdalenefjord

General: Magdalenefjord cuts about ten kilometres straight into the coast. It is two to three kilometres wide and is usually accessible year-round. It does not freeze regularly during the winter because of the influence of the West-Spitsbergen current

("Gulf stream"). The small bay, Trinityhamna, sheltered by the peninsula Gravneset (officially Gravnesodden), provides a convenient natural harbour that was frequently used by whalers during the 17th century. Except for some rock shoals, the bathymetry of the fjord allows larger ships to enter and anchor in this scenic environment, which makes Magdalenefjord a popular destination even for large cruise ships. As a result, Gravneset is the place in Spitsbergen (apart from the settlements) that receives the largest visitor numbers outside the settlements: 17,277 persons were registered ashore at Gravneset in official statistics in 2001. Most of those come on board ships with several hundred, or even more than one thousand, passengers and which usually do not make more than one landing outside the settlements. To prevent further damage to the cultural heritage sites, which have already suffered significantly from careless boots and from theft, several small areas were fenced off in 1996; a measure so far unique in Spitsbergen. Two members of the Sysselmannen's field police are usually stationed in a small hut on Gravneset during the season, to keep a watchful eye on visitors. The future is at the moment a bit uncertain due to a ban on the use of heavy oil inside the National Park, which includes Magdalenefjord, but the passage into this fjord may be excluded from the ban.

An Austrian mountaineer was killed inside a camp by a Polar bear in 1977. The risk of surprise Polar bear visitors should not be underestimated in Magdalenefjord.

Placenames: Alkekongen: "The Little auk". **Gravneset:** "Grave-peninsula". **Gullybreen, -bukta:** refers to the steep, narrow glacial valley. **Magdalenefjord:** after the biblical Mary Magdalene. **Trinityhamna:** originally "Trinity harbour". **Waggonwaybreen:** refers to the medial moraines of the glacier, that look like a paved road from a distance.

Geology: Magdalenefjord is surrounded by mountains made up of migmatites and gneisses. The age is not easily determined, but reflects the complex geological history of the region. Most structures and rocks were created during a tectonic event about one billion years ago ("Grenville event"), but the much younger Caledonian orogeny has also left its traces about 400 million years ago. The most recent major event, the opening of the north Atlantic, led to pronounced uplift of the area and thus eventually to the forming of the spectacular scenery by glacial erosion.

Landscape: The spectacular scenery is the main attraction in Magdalenefjord and it fills thousands of cruise-ship passengers with enthusiasm every summer – as long as the weather does not thwart their plans. The mountains on the north side of the fjord are 600 to 900 metres high, while those on the south side are slightly lower. The largest glaciers are Gullybreen, that debouches into a side bay on the southern side of Magdalenefjord, and Waggonwaybreen, the main glacier at the head of the fjord.

Flora and fauna: Large numbers of Little auks are breeding in the scree that covers most lower and middle slopes, especially on the mountain Alkekongen on the northern side, but the colonies are not easy to reach. There is hardly any tundra due to the lack of suitable terrain, but there are colourful vegetation patches near the bird colonies where those species thrive that are adapted to the well-fertilised environment: mosses, Mountain sorrel and Scurvy grass.

Old photographs show that Gravneset was once completely covered with vegetation, but this has largely been destroyed by great numbers of visitors. The damage is fortunately restricted to a relatively small area.
History: It is likely that **Willem Barents** visited Magdalenefjord in 1596 and held a ceremony to take the land in possession for The Netherlands. In 1614, the Englishman **Robert Fotherby** erected a cross on Gravneset and followed Barents' example by performing a similar ceremony to take the land in possession, this time for James I. of England.

As with many other parts of northwestern Spitsbergen, Magdalenefjord is known for its cultural heritage from the 17th century whalers. English whalers called the natural harbour on the inside of Gravneset, "Trinity harbour", and ran a shore station there until about 1623. Remains of blubber ovens and a graveyard are amongst the remains that are still visible at the surface. The grave site has about 130 graves and is thus one of the three largest of its kind in Spitsbergen. It was in use far longer than the other on-shore facilities, and the last whalers to die were probably buried as late as the late 18th century when whaling had already been pelagic for a long time and land was only visited for fresh water, repairs and burials. Not only accidents, but especially diseases such as scurvy took their toll, and whalers mostly made the effort to give their dead comrades a dignified burial somewhere on shore. The graves used to have wooden crosses, but these have fallen victim to the weather or to a trapper's need for heating material.

Repeated freezing and thawing of the ground brings large objects back to the surface. This process does not stop at coffins, and as a result most graves are in a condition that would be called scandalous elsewhere. Coffin boards are lying around on the ground and parts of skeletons have been scattered or removed both by Polar bears and by human visitors. We should all do our best to make sure that the condition of Spitsbergen's many historical sites does not deteriorate any faster than is unavoidable due to the harsh natural conditions.

Both **Pomors** and **Norwegian trappers** followed the whalers to Magdalenefjord to exploit the biological resources. Many expeditions have visited Magdalenefjord, including the French **Recherche**-expedition in 1838 and **Graf Zeppelin** on board the *Mainz* in 1910.
Miscellaneous: The alpine inland area east of Magdalenefjord, especially the granite massifs of Losvikfjella (1,095 metres) east of Waggonwaybreen and Hornemanntoppen (1,097 metres) have been visited several times by mountaineering expeditions during the 20th century and are still good climbing areas, but difficult to reach.

6.7 Northwestern Spitsbergen

"Thus in 1614 the Dutch for the first time appropriated the site afterwards occupied by their great whaling station, Smeerenburg; for the shore in the north harbour most suitable for the operations of flensing and boiling down blubber was the flat spit that runs south-eastwards from the hilly centre of Amsterdam Island."

Martin Conway, *No Man's Land*

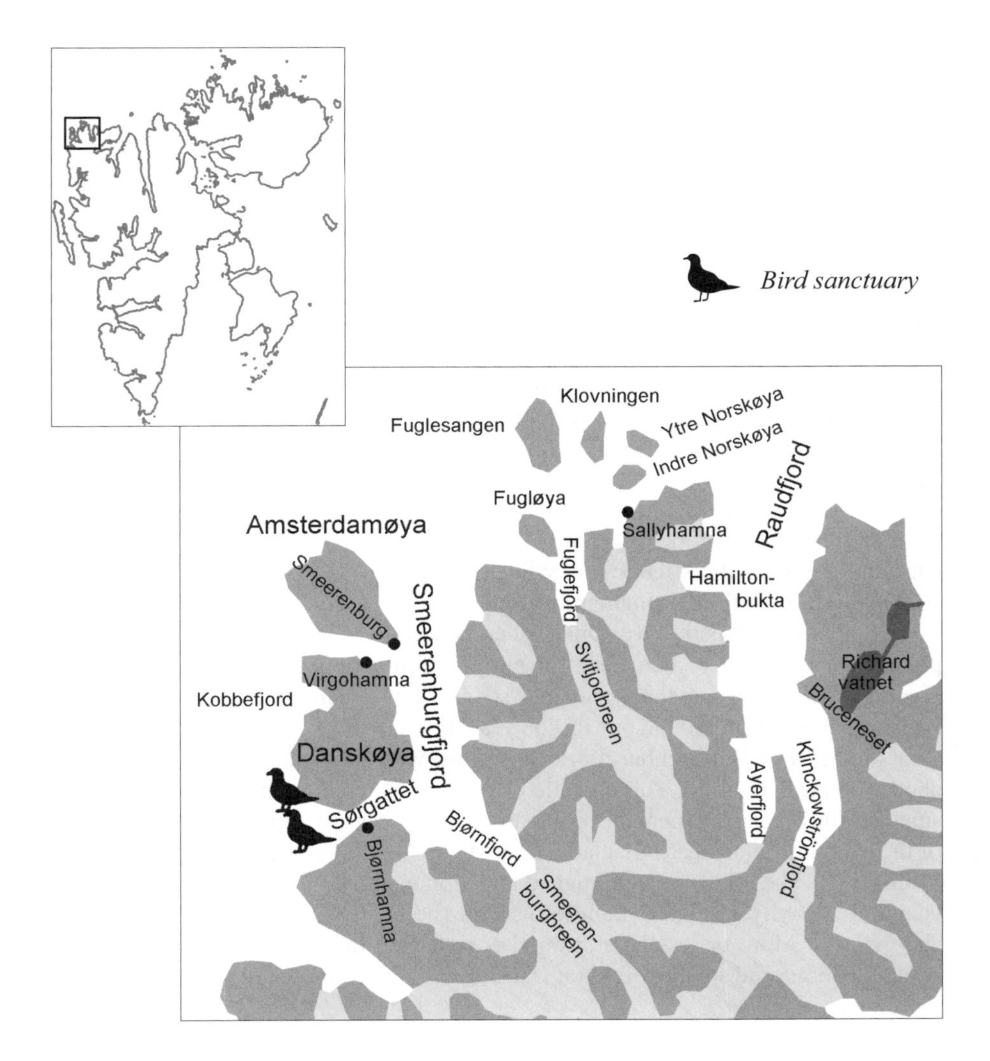

The northwestern corner of Spitsbergen is dissected by several fjords and sounds into a number of islands and peninsulas, which make for a varied landscape and a number of interesting places to explore: there is exciting scenery with rugged mountains and large glaciers around almost every corner. The area was the most important whaling ground in Spitsbergen in the 17th century and there are many remains dating back to those years. More recent expeditions have used the area as a springboard to the North Pole. The combination of the spectacular scenery and the historical sites has made northwestern Spitsbergen a frequently visited area. The best-known sites are Smeerenburg and Virgohamna, but these are not the only interest. Having the weather gods on your side is certainly important as always: the area tends to be windy, cold and often wet, and you need luck for good views of all the scenery from the shore to the mountain tops.

The whole area is inside the Northwest Spitsbergen National Park; additionally, there are several bird sanctuaries on the small rocky islets Skorpa and Moseøya southwest of Danskøya, where all traffic is banned within 300 metres from the shore from 15 May to 15 August. Access restrictions to the cultural heritage sites at Ytre Norskøya and Likneset must be expected in the future, probably in 2009.

6.7.1 Sørgattet, Bjørnfjord, Smeerenburgfjord

General: The narrow strait, Sørgattet, separates Spitsbergen from Danskøya and connects the open sea to Smeerenburgfjord, which makes this bay strictly speaking a sound and not a fjord. The narrow and short passage through Sørgattet is difficult to navigate because of several shallows and tidal currents. Larger ships tend to avoid this strait and sail into Smeerenburgfjord from the north. The two little islands of Skorpa and Moseøya in the western entrance of Sørgattet are bird sanctuaries (no traffic within 300 metres from the shore 15 May to 15 August). The whole area is part of the Northwest Spitsbergen National Park. There are plans to close Likneset to visitors in the future.
Placenames: Aurivilliusfjellet: Karl Wilhelm Samuel A. (1854-99), Swedish zoologist. **Bjørnfjord:** "Bear fjord". **Hornemanntoppen:** Hans Henrik H. (born 1878), member of the Spitsbergen expedition of Duke Albert I. of Monaco in 1906. **Likneset:** "Corpse point", site of a whalers' cemetery. **Sørgattet:** "Southern passage".
Geology: Migmatites, granites and gneisses of the basement, mostly pre-Caledonian with ages that cluster around one billion years ("Grenville event"). There is an inland area southeast of Smeerenburgfjord/Bjørnfjord with younger granite (Caledonian, about 400 million years). This so-called Hornemanntoppen-granite is often found as small erratics and gravel near the coasts around Smeerenburgfjord and gives evidence of the extent of Pleistocene glaciation that at one time filled today's fjords with ice.
Landscape: The relief is steep, rugged and alpine, and all inland areas on the main island are heavily glaciated. Landforms near the coast have been rounded by ice-age glaciers. More or less level ground is restricted to the southeastern corner of Amsterdamøya and smaller areas on Danskøya, but even these are mostly rocky and not for easy walking.

The innermost part of Smeerenburgfjord is called Bjørnfjord and it has a very nice medium-sized glacier, Smeerenburgbreen, at its head. This glacier is no exception to the general retreat of glaciers in recent decades, and the innermost part of the fjord is accordingly blank on sea charts, making navigation difficult. There are a number of smaller glaciers with small calving fronts on the eastern side of Smeerenburgfjord.

The area of the Hornemanntoppen-massif with its associated granite provides some excellent climbing areas with sharp ridges and steep peaks – a mountaineer's paradise, but remote and difficult to reach. The highest mountains are Hornemanntoppen (1,097 metres) and Aurivilliusfjellet (1,150 metres).

Flora and fauna: The vegetation is quite sparse and mostly restricted to smaller, steep spots below bird colonies, which are obvious even from a distance due to their intense green colour. It is astonishing to see that some reindeer can survive in this inhospitable landscape. The most important faunal features are the bird colonies, especially Little auks which are breeding in large numbers in some scree slopes.

History: The largest whalers' grave site in Spitsbergen is at Likneset on the east side of Smeerenburgfjord. Norwegian trappers used the area in the early 20th century, and there is still a nice hut at Bjørnhamna on the south side of Sørgattet, that is now used by the Sysselmann (field police and other official use). The first ascent of Hornemanntoppen was made by Austrian mountaineers in 1931.

6.7.2 Danskøya

General: Danskøya is a small (41 sq km) rocky island that is known as something like an arctic "Cape Canaveral" amongst Polar historians. History is obviously the main attraction on Danskøya and there is not a lot to be seen or done beyond it. You need to know the stories of Andrée and Wellman to appreciate the significance of the site (see section 5.6 *Attempts to fly to the pole: Virgohamna and Ny Ålesund*); if you don't know them, then Virgohamna will appear to you as a rubbish dump but the site is a holy grail for everybody who is interested in the discovery of the North Pole.

Danskøya is part of the Northwest Spitsbergen National Park and there are two small bird sanctuaries southwest of the island, Skorpa and Moseøya (no traffic within 300 metres from the shore 15 May to 15 August). Since 2000, access to Virgohamna is strictly regulated. Virgohamna is a bay on the north side of Danskøya and the main historical site on the island, and visits are possible only with a written permit from the Sysselmannen. Permission is given also for tourist purposes, but regulation is strict: No more than 15 persons per guide and there is a detailed map on the permit form that makes it clear where you are actually allowed to walk. This is a bit tricky and you need either good local knowledge or you have to keep a watchful eye on your guide in order to respect the regulations, which are necessary to preserve the site. The Sysselmannen has two field police officers stationed in a hut not far away, and violation of laws can be more expensive than a trip to Spitsbergen. Landings in Virgohamna should not be made when the historical site is covered with snow. For map, see section 6.7 *Northwestern Spitsbergen* (page 299).

Placenames: Danskøya: "Danish Island", refers to a Danish whaling station in the 17th century in Kobbefjord. **Kobbefjord:** "Seal fjord". **Virgohamna:** after *S/S Virgo*, the ship used by Andrée's expedition in 1896.
Geology: Gneisses and fine-grained granite, all basement rocks with ages around one billion years ("Grenville event").
Landscape: Danskøya is unglaciated and very rocky. The rounded hills make it quite obvious that the island was completely covered by glaciers during the ice age.
Flora and fauna: There is not a lot of vegetation on Danskøya; mainly mosses, lichens and some flowering plants, including Svalbard poppy and saxifrage species. Seabirds nest on higher cliffs but you should not expect any particular wildlife, although encounters with migrating mammals such as Polar bears are always possible.
History: Danskøya would hardly ever be visited if it was not for the dramatic history. The oldest part is probably the Danish whaling station from the 17th century in **Kobbefjord**, although this small and very rocky bay on the west side of Danskøya is certainly not amongst the common tourist sites. Most activities were concentrated in **Virgohamna** on the north side of Danskøya, just opposite Amsterdamøya. The oldest remains are again related to early **whaling**: there are three small mounds near the beach, which were foundations of blubber ovens used between 1636 and approximately 1650. Virgohamna was called Houker Bay in those years and frequented by Dutch whalers. There are also some graves on the eastern side of the bay, not far from the ovens.

The next famous visitor was a rich Englishman, **Lord Arnold Pike**, who wanted to spend a winter in the Arctic, mainly to hunt Polar bears. His plan was to winter somewhere in eastern Spitsbergen, but this was not possible due to the ice situation, so finally Lord Pike ended up on Danskøya where his experienced Norwegian attendants built a spacious hut to spend the winter in comfort of which Pike's nearest "neighbours" could not even dream. Unfortunately, the house was pulled down in 1925 and moved to Barentsburg, and its current whereabouts remain unknown. The foundations, at least, can still clearly be seen and are a witness to Lord Pike who can be remembered as the first tourist to spend a full year in Spitsbergen.

Virgohamna received its modern name and became worldfamous in 1896 and 1897, when the Swedish engineer **Salomon August Andrée** ventured to balloon to the North Pole with a hydrogen-filled balloon (see section 5.6 *Attempts to fly to the pole: Virgohamna and Ny Ålesund*). Andrée established his base on the east side of Virgohamna and the most obvious original artefact may be the hydrogen-filter that is still lying next to the site of Pike's house. Later, the Swedish navy erected a monument to Andrée and his companions, at the site of the balloon house on the eastern side of the bay.

It did not take any more than nine years after Andrée's disappearance before the next adventurer showed up in Virgohamna with plans to fly to the Pole. The American journalist **Walter Wellman** had already tried to sledge there from northern Svalbard and Franz Josef Land, and was now determined to try something more comfortable and promising. All of his three attempts to start with his airships from Virgohamna, in the years 1906, 1907 and 1909, failed and, looking back, the whole project certainly has a comic side to it. Wellman achieved at least something where many other "polar heroes" failed: he returned alive.

There is, finally, another adventure connected to Danskøya, much less well known, but highly dramatic and centered on **Kobbefjord** where the Norwegians **Torgeir Møkleby** and **Harald Simonsen** spent some desperate weeks in the spring of 1922. They had left the Norwegian geophysical station at Kvadehuken (Kongsfjord entrance) earlier in the same year with a small boat in an attempt to find a missing friend. After being caught in the ice and drifting up and down the coast between Kongsfjord and Magdalenefjord for 18 very cold days, they managed to get ashore in Kobbefjord where they finally starved to death.

There is a small skerry in the entrance to Kobbefjord called **Postholmen**, that is a reminder of a tradition: any ship that was sailing north to the seal hunting areas, could leave mail on a nearby spit of land, and any ship that passed by on the way south would take it back to Norway. This is one of the few bright moments in the history of Danskøya, which is otherwise pretty grim since the early whalers started their bloody business hundreds of years ago.

6.7.3 Amsterdamøya

General: Amsterdamøya is directly north of Danskøya. Being even smaller (19 sq km) and separated from its southern neighbour by only a narrow strait, its general landscape appearance is similarly rocky and barren. Smeerenburg, at the southeastern tip of Amsterdamøya, is the most famous site of 17th century whaling in Spitsbergen and a popular landing site. Landings at Smeerenburg should not be made if the site is covered with snow, unless you know the place really well enough to be sure that you do not step on any historical remains. Amsterdamøya is part of the Northwest Spitsbergen National Park. For map, see section 6.7 *Northwestern Spitsbergen* (page 299).

Placenames: Amsterdamøya: "Amsterdam island", refers to Dutch whalers. **Hakluythovden, -odden:** Originally Hakluyt headland. Richard H. (1533-1616), British geographer, published accounts of arctic voyages. **Hollendarberget:** "Hollander mountain", also referring to Dutch whalers. **Salatberget:** "Salad mountain", refers to occurrences of Scurvy grass that the early whalers collected to cure scurvy. **Smeerenburg:** "Blubber town".

Geology: Gneisses and fine-grained granites, mostly pre-Caledonian with ages around one billion years ("Grenville event"). Smeerenburgsletta, the plain in the southeast, is covered by a Pleistocene moraine.

Landscape: Most of Amsterdamøya is occupied by the flat-topped, 480 metres high Hollendarberget, and the only more or less flat area at sea level is Smeerenburgsletta, a gently undulating plain of less than one square kilometre, with several small lagoons. This plain is covered with remnants of a Pleistocene moraine and thus quite muddy in places; elsewhere it is covered with rocks. There are some large erratic boulders and well-developed stone rings (frost patterned ground). The weathering of the crystalline rocks of the old moraine has provided enough quartz sand to create a real sandy beach at Smeerenburg, almost white and a rarity in Spitsbergen. Amsterdamøya is unglaciated apart from one small glacier on the northern slope of Hollendarberget.

Flora and fauna: The area around Smeerenburg is quite barren, apart from mosses and lichens. The densest vegetation on Amsterdamøya is on the slopes of Hollenderberget under bird colonies, where Scurvy grass and Mountain sorrel thrive in abundance. The whalers in the 17th century did not know anything about the vitamin C content of the leaves of these flowers, but they knew that they helped to fight the ever-present demon of scurvy, so they collected it and called the southeastern slopes of Hollendarberget Salatberget.

Sometimes reindeer or Arctic fox are seen searching the plain for food, and the lagoons near Smeerenburg can be very interesting for birdwatchers (Arctic terns, Snow buntings, geese, Arctic skua, possibly Ruddy turnstone and others). Seals are occasionally seen near the beach, sometimes even Harbour seals from Prins Karls Forland that may have a rest on the stones near the beach. It can also happen that one or two Walrus sleep somewhere on the beach, not too far from the old blubber ovens; the nearest Walrus colony is on Moffen. Polar bears have been seen walking across the historical remains; obviously they can not read and do not know that the site is protected.

History: As with Danskøya, it is mainly the history that makes Amsterdamøya a popular landing site. Smeerenburg was one of the largest and is certainly now the best known whaling station from the 17th century in Spitsbergen. Seven Dutch companies from different towns in the Netherlands had their facilities in Smeerenburg, including two houses and at least one (double) oven each to render down oil from blubber (fat layer of whales); there was also a Danish company for a while. The most obvious remains are foundations of the blubber ovens with parts of the walls that were built around the ovens for insulation. The black material that was used for this purpose was local sand and gravel mixed with whale-oil. The easternmost ovens, belonging to the chamber (company) of Amsterdam, have unfortunately fallen victim to changes in the shoreline; a development that is likely to continue in the future. The next one, furthest east on the present beach, also belonged to Amsterdam, followed westwards by Middelburg, Vlissingen, Veere, the Danes, Enkhuizen, Delft and Hoorn.

The heyday saw about 200 men working in Smeerenburg during the short summer season, living and working in 16 or 17 houses that stood behind the ovens. There was probably also a "fortress" – a small battery to defend the site. The busiest years in Smeerenburg were the early 1620s, and the settlement was gradually abandoned during the following decades, finally starting to fall apart in the 1660s.

Smeerenburg was also the site of the first intentional wintering of Europeans in Spitsbergen, when a guard of seven men wintered successfully in 1633-34. A second team was left behind for the following winter, but this time the seven men were not able to fight scurvy and were all found dead the next season. They were buried on the plain

not far from the old settlement. Altogether, archaeologists have found 101 graves in several small grave fields in this area (see also section 5.4 *Whaling in the 17th century*).
Miscellaneous: Often the weather provides conditions that make it easy to imagine the hard life of the whalers. Most tourists, after a few hours on shore, are happy to get back on board a warm ship, have a hot drink and get all the Gore-Tex® dry again. If you start to feel cold on shore, then spare some thought for the whalers who had to survive a whole summer in clothes that we would certainly find unsuitable even for a short landing.

6.7.4 Fair Haven, Fuglefjord, Sallyhamna

General: The fjords on the northwestern corner of Spitsbergen, for example Fuglefjord, are of great scenic beauty due to their picturesque mountains and glaciers. Additionally, there are several historical sites to make the area more interesting, as you may expect in this part of Spitsbergen. Today, Fair Haven is the strait between Fugleøya and Spitsbergen in the south and Fuglesangen and Klovningen in the north. In the 17th century, the name was used for a slightly larger area and it is one of very few old placenames in Spitsbergen that have not been "Norwegianised". Despite several rock shoals, the straits generally provided what the old name suggests: sheltered waterways and some convenient natural harbours. See next section (6.7.5 *Nordvestøyane*) for the off-lying islands. The area is part of the Northwest Spitsbergen National Park. For map, see section 6.7 *Northwestern Spitsbergen* (page 299).
Placenames: Fair Haven: Name given by whalers in the early 17th century, referring to convenient navigation conditions. **Fuglefjord:** "Bird fjord", after Little auk colonies. **Sabineodden:** Sir Edward S., see section 6.7.5 *Nordvestøyane*. **Sallyhamna:** see *history* further down in this section. **Svidtjodtbreen:** after a region in eastern central Sweden.
Geology: Upper Proterozoic (600-1,000 million years, "Grenville event") granites and migmatites.
Landscape: Very rocky and barren. Hardly any level ground; most slopes fall steeply into the sea. The few narrow, more or less level coastal strips are covered with rocks and boulders. The smaller islands are ice-free, whereas the interior of Spitsbergen is strongly glaciated. Svidtjodtbreen is a larger glacier with a nice calving front at the head of Fuglefjord; it is one of only a few glaciers that have not retreated to any significant degree in recent decades.

The ice-age glaciation left obvious traces everywhere near the coast in form of rounded landforms and polished rock surfaces, especially when looking at the numerous shoals, rocks and skerries in Fair Haven and in Fuglegattet east of Fugleøya. The steep and inaccessible terrain makes hiking largely impossible, unless you are a real mountain goat or you are equipped for glacier hiking. Landing sites are few, the most convenient being the little bay at Sallyhamna which has a small beach and a small area of rocky, but more or less level ground.
Flora and fauna: The only places with significant vegetation are slopes under bird cliffs. The main biological attraction of the area are Little auk colonies, to which

Fuglefjord and Fugleøya owe their names. Even though the actual breeding sites are on inaccessible, steep and rocky slopes, the view and noise of large swarms of Little auks flying by is quite impressive.
History: Sallyhamna on the east side of Fair Haven is a little bay protected by a small peninsula; it is one of very few places where the terrain permits limited activity. Sallyhamna was used by 17th century whalers who have left the remains of several blubber ovens and graves, one of the latter inside the foundations of an oven.

The hut was built in 1937 by the Norwegian trapper **Waldemar Kræmer** who wintered there several times, occasionally together with his wife **Sally** after whom Waldemar named the place. The hut is actually standing on top of an old blubber oven with a whaler's grave inside.

Sabineodden is a small point about one kilometre north of Sallyhamna and is the northern end of a small bay called Birgerbukta. Sabineodden is another historical site with remains from different eras: there are remains of a Pomor station, probably from the 18th century, next to a more obvious ruin of a trapper hut that was built in 1920. **Arthur Oxaas**, a well-known trapper from Tromsø, who later settled down together with his wife at Kapp Wijk in Dicksonfjord, obviously liked Sabineodden; he wintered there no less than seven times, including three years on his own.

6.7.5 Nordvestøyane: Fugløya, Fuglesangen, Klovningen, Ytre Norskøya, Indre Norskøya

General: Geographically, the islands and straits near the northwestern corner of Spitsbergen are slightly confusing to the regional novice. Some of the sounds are not navigable due to shallows, and the steep terrain does not provide a large number of landing sites. On the other hand, there are several highlights and the scenery is generally superb. Main landing sites are on Ytre Norskøya and Fuglesangen, but the terrain is rocky and walking is not easy. The whole area is part of the Northwest Spitsbergen National Park. For map, see section 6.7 *Northwestern Spitsbergen* (page 299). There are plans to close the historical site at Ytre Norskøya to visitors in the future.
Placenames: Fugløya: "Bird island". **Fuglesangen:** "Bird song", referring to Little auk colonies on this island. **Klovningen:** "Gap island", describing the shape. **Sabineodden:** see *history* in this section. **Utkiken:** see *history* in this section. **Ytre/Indre Norskøya:** "Outer/inner Norwegian island".
Geology: Granite and migmatite from the upper Proterozoic (600-1,000 million years, "Grenville event"). There is some marble at the south end of Klovningen, which contrasts in colour with the overlying darker granite.
Landscape: Generally steep and rocky; most slopes are covered with coarse scree and fall directly into the sea, thus making the terrain very difficult for walking. There are no glaciers on the islands. The only significant more or less flat land is on the south side of Ytre Norskøya. Klovningen is easily recognised due to its shape, with a steeply incised gap that almost cuts off the northern end. Barents noticed in 1596 that Klovningen is a good navigation mark.

Flora and fauna: The land is very barren and vegetation correspondingly scarce, apart from thick moss beds near bird colonies. The south side of Ytre Norskøya is the only place which deserves to be called tundra.

Names such as Fugleøya and Fuglesangen indicate the main biological attraction of the area: many thousand Little auks which together are responsible for a remarkable level of noise at their colony, the exact size of which is not yet known but may be in the order of several tens of thousands of breeding pairs. In contrast to all other birds in Spitsbergen, Little auks have their nests under large boulders on steep scree slopes, and most colonies are accordingly inaccessible. Fuglesangen has a Little auk colony that is relatively accessible, although the landing itself is on a steep beach with large rounded boulders and not exactly easy. What you need is calm weather, not only because it is not possible to land otherwise, but also for the Little auks to display nicely (see section 4.8.24 *Little auks*). If a visit to breeding Little auks is high on your wishlist, then do not come too late in the summer; you may even consider an extra day in Longyearbyen to pay a visit to one of the smaller colonies there.
There are also some Puffins breeding on these islands, and if you watch out for a while, then you should see one of these colourful birds flying by.

History: The area is amongst the first places that were visited during Barents' expedition in 1596; it is likely that he anchored in Fair Haven. Most of the islands have hardly ever been stepped on due to the inhospitable terrain but, in the early 17th century, whalers used every convenient beach. Dutch whalers had a station on the south side of **Ytre Norskøya**, where remains of several blubber ovens (four

View from "Zeeussche Uytkyk", Ytre Norskøya.
James Lamont, Yachting in the Arctic Seas

single and four double) still remind us of their former presence. Dutch activities started in 1617 and must have lasted for quite some time, as there is a grave site, with about 165 graves, on a rocky ridge nearby – the second-largest whaler's graveyard in Spitsbergen. Archaeological excavations have contributed to our present knowledge of inadequate clothing and of what caused the deaths. Next to injuries, scurvy took a large toll. All skeletons found in Spitsbergen were male.

The 150 metre high hill on Ytre Norskøya was used as a lookout point by whalers, who called the mountain **Zeeussche Uytkyk**, after Zeeland their home province in the Netherlands. The ascent is steep and rocky, but energetic, surefooted hikers can enjoy the view and try to see the North Pole.

In 1823, an expedition was sent out from England with Captain **Charles Clavering** and the astronomer **Edward Sabine** to make pendulum observations at different localities in high latitudes. The purpose was to determine the local value of gravity and then make deductions about the shape of the Earth; the question was whether or not the Earth was slightly flatter at the poles. Sabine built a small observatory on **Indre Norskøya**, made his observations and then the expedition moved on to East Greenland. He was certainly successful at leaving his name on the map: places named after him include Sabineodden on Spitsbergen's coast south of Indre Norskøya, Sabineøya on the north coast of Nordaustland and Sabine Ø in East Greenland. Last but not least, there is the beautiful Sabine's gull *Larus sabini*, that he found and described first.

6.8 Raudfjord

"Towards eleven o'clock we approached the mouth of the magnificently grand Arctic inlet known as Red Bay. At its end a great glacier wall, estimated at close on 200 feet sheer from a distance of several miles, met the waters of the sea."

Seton Gordon, *Amid Snowy Wastes*

General: Raudfjord is the first fjord eastward as you follow Spitsbergen's north coast from the western corner. It is a good 20 kilometres long and five kilometres wide and has a number of side bays on the west side, all having calving glaciers and shallow waters in common. Innermost Raudfjord has two branches, Ayerfjord with Chauveaubreen and Klinckowströmfjord with Raudfjordbreen. The whole area is part of the Northwest Spitsbergen National Park. For map, see section 6.7 *Northwestern Spitsbergen* (page 299).

Placenames: Ayerfjord: Name used since the early 17th century, origin unknown. **Bruceneset:** William Spiers B. (1867-1921), Scottish polar explorer. **Buchananhalvøya:** John Young B., member of the 1899 Spitsbergen expedition of Duke Albert I. of Monaco. **Chauveaubreen:** Henri Jean Charles Albert C., member of Duke Albert I.'s Spitsbergen expedition. **Hamiltonbukta:** Count Hugo Vilhelm H. from Sweden, Captain of a ship used by the Swedish section of the Arc-de-meridian expedition in 1899.

Klinckowströmfjord: Baron Axel K. (1867-1936), Swedish zoologist and polar explorer, late 19th/early 20th century. **Raudfjord:** originally "Red bay", referring to red Old Red sediments on the east side. The red colour is not very prominent and the name would more appropriately have been given to Bockfjord or inner Woodfjord, but it has been used in different variations ("Red-cliff sound") since the early 17th century.
Richardvatnet: Jules R., discovered the lake during Duke Albert I.'s expedition.
Geology: Most rocks around Raudfjord are crystalline and part of the basement: migmatites on the west side, mostly pre-Caledonian with ages near one billion years ("Grenville event"), partly with signs of Caledonian reactivation. On the east side of the fjord mostly middle-Proterozoic phyllite.

Raudfjord follows a tectonic graben, that is a subsided slice of Earth's crust bounded by steep faults on either side. The graben consists of Devonian Old Red sediments, mostly sandstones and conglomerates, normally with a distinct brownish-red colour due to a high hematite content. Old Red sandstone occupies a larger part of the eastern shore of Raudfjord, Buchananhalvøya in the inner fjord, and a small area around Konglomeratodden on the west side. This distribution suggests that the whole sea bed of Raudfjord consists of Old Red which is softer than the surrounding basement rocks and was thus eroded more easily. This would account for the existence of the fjord. The red colouration of the Old Red is restricted to certain layers and is not particularly prominent in Raudfjord.
Landscape: Nice ☺. The west side of the fjord, that consists of hard, strongly uplifted basement rocks, is mostly glaciated: ten glaciers have calving fronts on the shore, including the larger ones at the head of the fjord, Chauveaubreen and Raudfjordbreen. Raudfjordbreen is the largest; its calving front is three kilometres wide and it is connected at its head to Lilliehöökbreen which flows south. The glaciers in Raudfjord are no exception to the general trend of glacial retreat which has increased in recent years. Freshly exposed surfaces, nicely polished and showing glacial striae ("scratches"), are witnesses to this dramatic development. The hard rocks on the west side often show near-vertical cliffs that have been created by ice-age glaciers.

The rocks on the east side are softer and have fewer high areas. This, together with less precipitation, most of which is caught by the mountains further west and east, produces a lower degree of glaciation. The glaciers are fewer and smaller, and not a single one has a calving front on the east side – a striking contrast to the western shore of the same fjord. This, however, means that the east side has much better hiking opportunities, especially in the Solanderfjellet area where energetic hikers can enjoy splendid views over Raudfjord or over a valley that connects the fjord with the sea further east and is filled by several lakes, including Richardvatnet. The terrain is rocky and requires surefootedness.
Flora and fauna: Vegetation is mostly scarce, although there are some rich spots that resemble hanging gardens on some slopes, for example near Bruceneset and under birdcliffs – of which there are several. The largest is in Hamiltonbukta; Brünich's guillemots are the most abundant breeding species.

History: Being the westernmost fjord on the north coast of Spitsbergen, the influence of the West-Spitsbergen current is still noticeable in Raudfjord which therefore has a long history of human activity. It was already known to whalers in the early 17th century, who left some graves at Bruceneset. Norwegian trappers later discovered Raudfjord as good territory offering opportunities to hunt both Arctic fox and Polar bear. On the north side of Hamiltonbukta, the wind blows through the ruins of a hut that was built in 1927, and there is another hut at Bruceneset, which is still in good condition.
Miscellaneous: The area around Raudfjord seems to be something of a weather divide. It is not too unusual for the sun to be shining in Raudfjord and further east while, at the same time, a strong wind is blowing low clouds through Smeerenburgfjord. But as always, hope for the best; be prepared for the worst …

6.9 The Woodfjord area

"Across the fjord the conical mountains to the south displayed the most wonderful tints. One hill was of a dark red colour, so that, although the sky was actually clouded, it seemed as though here a flood of sunlight lingered. Near by was a second hill which, at a distance, seemed of pale green. ... On the surface of the fjord there floated an iceberg, a fitting foreground to the inscrutable and snow-flecked mountains."

Seton Gordon, *Amid Snowy Wastes*

The second fjord along the north coast of Spitsbergen is the large Woodfjord with its side branches. Many visitors to the area will have fond memories of Liefdefjord.

The average ice conditions were ideal for earlier "users": the West-Spitsbergen current usually kept Woodfjord open in the summer and, during the later winter and spring in most years, the fjord ice made it easy to get around.

6.9.1 Woodfjord

General: Trending approximately north-south, Woodfjord cuts about 65 kilometres into the north coast. It has two side branches on the west side, Liefdefjord and Bockfjord, and two minor bays, Mushamna and Jakobsenbukta, on the east side. The western part of Woodfjord is inside the Northwest Spitsbergen National Park.
Placenames: Andrée Land: Salomon August A. (see section 6.7.2 *Danskøya*). **Gråhuken:** "Grey hook", descriptive name referring to the colour of the rocks. **Jakobsenbukta:** Kristian J., Captain of a ship used in 1906 and 1907 by the Duke of Monaco. **Mushamna:** "Mouse bay", origin unknown. **Woodfjord:** earlier "Wood bay", referring to the large amounts of driftwood that cover some beaches in Woodfjord.

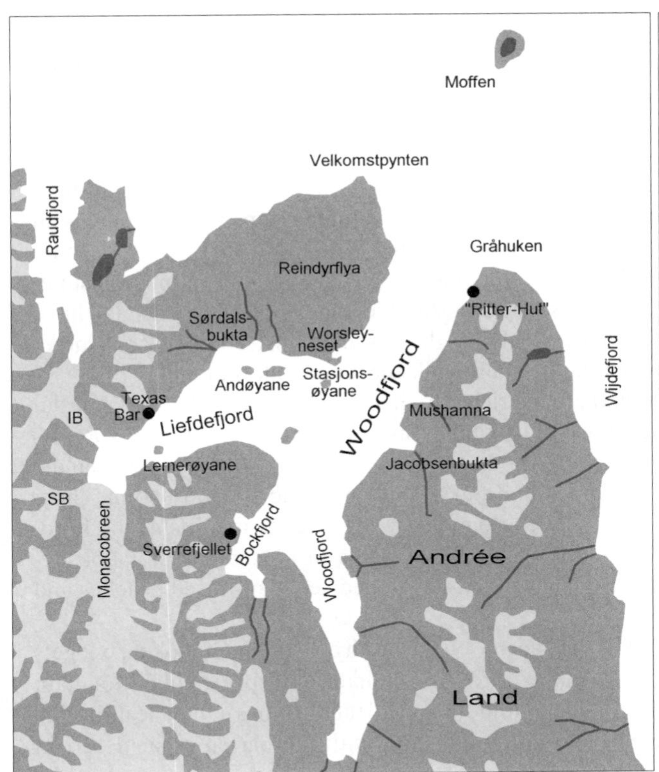

IB = Idabreen,
SB = Seligerbreen

Geology: The entire Woodfjord area consists of Old Red sandstone, although you will quickly realise that not everything that is called "Old Red" is actually red (it is at least old). The red layers are prominent in the southern part of Woodfjord, south of Liefdefjord. The rocks further north are rather grey (Mushamna, Gråhuken). Fragments of fossil fish have been found, particularly in the more fine-grained layers.

The fact that Devonian sediments were deposited with an astonishing total thickness of around ten kilometres and that they have largely suvived until today is due to areas of tectonic subsidence; so-called graben systems. The largest graben in Spitsbergen is the Andrée-Land graben, that comprises Andrée Land between Woodfjord and Wijdefjord, and parts of Dickson Land further south. Woodfjord and parts of Bockfjord and Liefdefjord also belong to this graben.

The graben filling, the Old Red, has been folded and faulted in the uppermost Devonian ("Svalbardian phase"). The layers are accordingly "crisscross", cut by faults and bent by folds, that produce nice geometric patterns in some mountain slopes.

Some volcanic activity occurred in Andrée Land in the Miocene (upper Tertiary, about 15 million years ago), and the valleys which then existed (before the glaciation) were partly filled with lava flows. Remains of these lava flows still exist, now forming the tops of some mountains in Andrée Land: the former valley fillings have been transformed into mountain peaks by glacier erosion. These Miocene volcanic rocks are the youngest Tertiary solid rocks in Spitsbergen. There was also some Quaternary volcanism, see section 6.9.4 *Bockfjord.*

Landscape: Old Red sediments are prone to frost shattering, and there are accordingly no vertical slopes in Andrée Land and no pointed mountain tops that compare with basement areas further west. The mountains around Woodfjord are characterised by more rounded slopes covered with vast amounts of scree. Precipitation is mostly caught by the higher mountains further west and east; Andrée Land is thus fairly dry and has a low degree of glaciation without any calving glaciers at all. Instead, there are a larger number of ice-free valleys that invite short walks or longer hikes inland.

Larger areas of level ground are restricted to the fjord entrance. The wide coastal plain of Reinsdyrflya is the largest of its kind in Spitsbergen (see section 6.9.2 *Reinsdyrflya, Stasjonsøyane, Andøyane*). Another wide coastal plain stretches between the northernmost mountains of Andrée Land and Gråhuken, the northermost point. There are smaller areas of more or less level ground near sea level further inside the fjord, providing opportunities for tundra walks, for example in Mushamna or Jakobsenbukta. Most of these tundra areas have well-developed series of raised beaches and frost-patterned ground.

Flora and fauna: Vegetation is very scarce on the north coast near Gråhuken, but gets richer the further south you are in the fjord. An abundance of species like Mountain avens and Arctic bell-heather indicate "middle-arctic" tundra types under the influence of the mild West-Spitsbergen current, contrasting with the barren polar desert in northeastern Svalbard, geographically not too far away.

The lack of steep slopes makes Woodfjord unsuitable for cliff-breeding seabirds, but birds such as Common eiders and the aggressive Arctic terns are abundant. Minke whales seem to be more or less regular visitors to the entrance of the fjord, and White whales have been seen more than once.

History: Woodfjord was a traditional hunting area for Norwegian trappers, and there is a trapper hut that is still in use. Nothing is left of older huts, some of which were destroyed by German forces during WWII. It is a bit surprising that no traces are left from more distant periods by Pomors or whalers, apart from some whalers' graves at Mullerneset (see section 6.9.2 *Reinsdyrflya, Stasjonsøyane, Andøyane*). Pomors must certainly have known Woodfjord, but remains of their houses have not survived.

In 1934-35, Hermann and **Christiane Ritter** from Germany wintered, together with Karl Nikolaisen from Norway, southwest of Gråhuken. This wintering resulted in a book called "Eine Frau erlebt die Polarnacht", a classic in German Spitsbergen-literature that can be recommended to anyone. It is also available in English translation under the title "A Woman in the Polar Night". The famous Norwegian trapper Hilmar Nøis sometimes hunted in this area and on one occasion was accompanied by an Englishman Paul Adams who subsequently wrote the book "Arctic Island Hunter" about his experiences.

Several of Nøis' huts still existed in 1959. Two are still standing, one near Worsleyneset (the southeastern corner of Reinsdyrflya), another one is Texas Bar in Liefdefjord.

6.9.2 Reinsdyrflya, Stasjonsøyane, Andøyane

General: Reinsdyrflya is a gently undulating coastal plain in the entrance area to Woodfjord and Liefdefjord with a surface area of approximately 250 square kilometres. The small islands Stasjonsøyane and Andøyane are part of this plain, at least geologically and biologically, even though they are separated by a belt of water from the main part of Reinsdyrflya and thus belong to Liefdefjord on the map. The bays and straits between the islands and the south side of Reinsdyrflya often hold onto fjord ice until well into July. The area is part of the Northwest Spitsbergen National Park.
Placenames: Andøyane: "Duck islands". **Reinsdyrflya:** "Reindeer plain". **Stasjonsøyane:** "Station island", after a photogrammetrical station in 1907. **Sørdalsbukta:** "South valley bay". **Velkomstpynten:** see *history* further down in this section.
Geology: Devonian Old Red, mostly of the red sort (Wood Bay group, lower Devonian, about 390 million years old). The solid rock is covered with recent sands and gravels of raised beach deposits that give evidence of post-glacial isostatic land uplift. No rocks have been preserved that are younger than the Old Red, but older than the upper Quaternary – a gap of 390 million years, and an impressive example of intense erosion that has taken place in recent chapters of earth history, removing anything that might possibly have been there.
Landscape: You will not find steep slopes on Reinsdyrflya: the highest elevation on this gently undulating plain is near the northeastern corner and no higher than 95 metres above sea level. The plain continues southwards into Liefdefjord, but several small former valleys are now below sea level, thus separating the small island groups Andøyane and Stasjonsøyane.

Such coastal plains, called **Strandflate**, are common geomorphological features in Spitsbergen, and a number of theories have been suggested to explain their origin. No single theory has been accepted as the one and only true explanation, and the impressive plains seem to have a long and complex history. Constant wave action that cuts into rocky shores, combined with shifting sea levels (partly caused by repeated glacio-isostatic land subsidence and uplift), seem to be important factors in many cases. This cannot explain all instances, however, as there are some "strand flats" in relatively protected situations; for example those in Isfjord and Forlandsund. Ice-age glaciers may have contributed, and in some cases the plains may be very old, dating back to times when no glaciers existed in the area, when warmer climates gave rise to different landscape-forming processes. Small coastal cliffs, often found at the shoreline of the strand flats, are evidence of the recent effects of waves. There are also large coastal plains, partly submerged, on parts of the Norwegian mainland coast.

Next to the conspicuous plain, it is the pleasing contrast between colourful tundra and strongly reddish rocks that makes visits to Reinsdyrflya and the associated small islands delightful, at least in fine weather.

Flora and fauna: Names such as Reinsdyrflya and Andøyane are a clue to the inhabitants of the area. Reinsdyrflya has a large reindeer population that is free to walk anywhere in the fjord system, once the fjord ice is solid in the winter and spring. The wind usually ensures that vegetation on higher ridges remains snow-free and thus accessible to reindeer. Large areas are covered by "middle-arctic" tundra, with abundant Mountain avens and Arctic bell-heather; rarer species include the Spider plant.

A rich bird life can be seen in the early summer near the coast of Reinsdyrflya and on Andøyane and Stasjonsøyane. Common eiders and Arctic terns breed on the islands, out of reach of Arctic foxes. Always look closely at supposed Common eiders, as one of them may easily turn out to be a King eider. Grey pharalopes are not uncommon near the beach or on lagoons.

History: Whalers used to keep a look-out from Velkomstvarden, a cairn on a 95 metre high hill near Velkomstpynten near the northeast corner of Reinsdyrflya. The designation "Velkomstpynten", originally "Welcome point", may indicate that occasional landings were a welcome change from the daily hard work for whalers, or else that a walk up the hill provided Captains with welcome information about ice conditions or the presence of whales. The name "Velkomstpynten" was attached to several points on various old charts until it stuck in its present position, but all of them may have served a similar purpose.

In more recent years, during the early 20th century, Reinsdyrflya was used by Norwegian trappers. There is still a hut standing west of Worsleyneset, the southeast corner of the plain. It was built in 1924 by the famous Norwegian hunter Hilmar Nøis.

Some scattered remains can still be seen near the coast in **Sørdalsbukta**, where the German weather station "Kreuzritter" ("Knight of the cross") operated during the winter 1943-44. A cross on a hill marks the grave of the station leader who died during an accident with explosives, shortly before the party was picked up.

6.9.3 Liefdefjord

General: Liefdefjord is often on tourist itineraries because of the great scenery and options for various excursions. Being 13 kilometres wide at the entrance from Woodfjord, the sides become more and more mountainous the deeper you sail into the 30 kilometres long bay. There are various excursion options, from relaxed tundra walks to mountain hikes and then there is the mighty Monacobreen at the head of the fjord. The islands Andøyane near Reinsdyrflya also have plenty of smaller attractions to offer (see section 6.9.2 *Reinsdyrflya, Stasjonsøyane, Andøyane*). Sheltered parts of Liefdefjord are normally still covered by fjord ice in the early summer. Liefdefjord is inside the Northwest Spitsbergen National Park. For map, see section 6.9.1. *Woodfjord* (page 311).

Placenames: Idabreen: After the wife of the German surveyor Paul Seliger, who constructed a map of the area in 1907. **Lernerøyane:** Theodor L. (1866-1931), German journalist, Spitsbergen-traveller, self-declared polar explorer; leader of an expedition in 1907 that made topographical surveys in Woodfjord. **Liefdefjord:** Dutch name from the 17th century, "Love bay". Origin unknown, possibly after a ship. **Monacobreen:** After Duke Albert I. of Monaco, who led the expeditions that mapped the glacier in 1906/07. **Seligerbreen:** see Idabreen. **Stortingspresidenten:** "President of the Storting". Storting is the Norwegian parliament and granted funds to the Duke of Monaco's expeditions.

Geology: The mountains around Liefdefjord display a rather complex geological mosaic, but it is not too difficult to get some ideas that help to explain the main landscape characteristics. The rocks can roughly be divided into two main groups, basement and Old Red. Most layers within the Old Red in Liefdefjord have a nice reddish colour, and they tend to form softer, more rounded slopes because they weather rather easily.

This contrasts with the crystalline basement, mostly migmatites and marble in this region, that makes itself visible in the landscape by giving rise to many higher, pointed peaks and sharp ridges. There are two north-south trending strips of Old Red running through Liefdefjord, separated by a basement block. The eastern Old Red section is part of the Andrée Land graben (see section 6.9.1 *Woodfjord*), including the mouth of Liefdefjord with Reinsdyrflya and the islands in outer Liefdefjord (Andøyane, Stasjonsøyane, Måkeøyane) and the conspicuously round Roosfjella on the southern side. The western and much narrower Old Red strip runs through the innermost fjord, under and to the east of Monacobreen. It is much less prominent and surrounded by impressive alpine mountain tops that highlight the crystalline basement.

Landscape: The geology has a significant influence on the general appearance of the scenery, as outlined in the previous paragraph. Next to the hardrock geology, Monacobreen is the natural focus of Liefdefjord's scenery. Currently it shares one calving front with Seligerbreen, altogether about five kilometres wide. Recent glacial retreat is dramatic and the shared glacier front will probably be lost sooner or later, when it has retreated behind the first ridge of the mountain Stortingspresidenten that separates the two glaciers. The waters near the eastern section of the glacier front are quite shallow, and a new islet, or rock, has appeared from under the retreating glacier in recent years; not an uncommon event in the Arctic these days. The attempt by a person claiming to be the one who "discovered" the island, to propose a name for it, was rejected by the Norwegian topographic authority.

There is a small group of islands not far from Monacobreen called Lernerøyane, which were still glacier covered only a few thousand years ago. The landscape-shaping influence of the glacier ice is evident on every square metre, and it is interesting to compare the most recently exposed areas near today's glacier front to Lernerøyane and finally to the islands in the outer Liefdefjord which have been ice-free for a long time, perhaps more than 10,000 years.

Flora and fauna: The same goes for the vegetation: it is interesting to compare areas in the inner Liefdefjord to places closer to its entrance into Woodfjord. The closer to Monacobreen you are, the scarcer the vegetation. The timing of deglaciation is one important factor, but others like bedrock, local climate and topography are just as important in creating the complex vegetation pattern.

There are some small colonies of seabirds on steep cliffs on the west side of Liefdefjord, all in crystalline basement areas (even the birds have their geological favourites). A spectacle can often be seen near the calving front of the Monacobreen, where subglacial meltwater rivers wells up from the bottom, bringing plankton to the surface. This attracts thousands of Kittiwakes and Arctic terns, and you can see large concentrations of these birds hectically trying to secure some food. Other beneficiaries of this arctic Cockaigne, such as seals, are often around. If you add to all this the possibility that a Polar bear might be sitting on a piece of ice somewhere not far away, White whales could show up, and the glacier could drop a large piece of ice at any moment into the middle of this spectacle, then you will probably think that this is all too good to be true. It has happened, so keep your eyes open and your fingers crossed.

Keen birdwatchers should keep a close eye on the bird concentrations near the glacier front, as the rare Sabine's gull is occasionally seen, together with the Kittiwakes and terns; it takes well-trained eyes and good binoculars to see them, should they be around … good luck!

You should also have a careful look at the fjord ice if you come to Liefdefjord (or any other fjord) early in the season. It may seem empty at first glance, but the closer you look, the more seals you are likely to spot, and it is not too unusual to see more than a hundred Bearded and Ringed seals on a few kilometres of fjord ice.

History: On the west side of the fjord, there is a hut with the promising name "Texas Bar", which was built by the famous Norwegian hunter Hilmar Nøis in 1927. Do not expect any beverages, but the scenery and walking opportunities are nice. The hut now belongs to the Sysselmannen and is occasionally used by scientists.

The German weather station "Kreuzritter" that operated in 1943-44 on the south side of Reinsdyrflya has been mentioned previously (see section 6.9.2 *Reinsdyrflya*).

The whole Liefdefjord area was investigated in detail by scientists of various disciplines in 1990-92 during a German-led expedition to understand high-arctic ecosystems. One expedition member died during a sudden low-angle avalanche of meltwater mixed with snow and stones on the east side of Liefdefjord; a cross stands near the place where he died.

6.9.4 Bockfjord

General: Bockfjord is a smaller branch of Woodfjord. It is about eight kilometres long, but has nice and varied scenery and some geological highlights. Bockfjord is part of the Northwest Spitsbergen National Park. For map, see section 6.9.1. *Woodfjord* (page 311).

Placenames: Bockfjord: Franz-Karl von B. (born in 1876), surveyed Woodfjord topographically during an expedition organised by the German journalist Theodor Lerner in 1907. **Jotunkildene:** "Jotun springs", jotuns are giants in Norse mythology.

Trollkildene: "Troll springs". **Sverrefjellet:** S. Sigurdsson (1151-1202), Norwegian king.

Geology: Mostly Old Red with its specific colour and landscape-shaping characteristics. Basement rocks, mainly marble, on the west side of inner Bockfjord. One of Spitsbergen's special geological features can be found in Bockfjord: Sverrefjellet (506 metres high) is the ruin of a volcano that erupted a few hundred thousand years ago under glacier ice. There are more volcanic features further inland in the Bockfjord area, but these are the only Quaternary volcanoes in Spitsbergen. The lavas of Sverrefjellet have brought some interesting presents for geologists to the surface: rock samples from deeper parts of the Earth's crust, or so-called xenoliths. These are pieces broken off the inside of the volcano and brought to the surface in the lavas. They show the dark-green colour that is typical of minerals from deeper in the earth's crust.

Sverrefjellet was covered by ice-age glaciers several times in its geologically rather short history and has thus lost the characteristic volcanic shape; the mountain seen now is just a volcanic ruin (see photo on page 105).

This relatively recent volcanic activity makes itself felt in the form of several "warm" springs north of Sverrefjellet, close to the shore of Bockfjord. Sinter terraces have been deposited from the mineral-rich waters that cool rapidly at the surface. There is another area with similar springs in the valley south of Bockfjord, about seven to eight kilometres inland. These sinter terraces are unique in Spitsbergen. They are vulnerable and must not be stepped on. The springs themselves are quite small, not much more than holes with water within the terraces.

Landscape: The contrasting rock formations of the Old Red and the basement with their respective characteristics (basement: sharp ridges and peaks, Old Red: rounded slopes, warm colours) together create a very pleasant panorama, completed by several glaciers (all terminating on shore) and the dark, pyramid-shaped volcanic ruin Sverrefjellet. The terrain is mostly quite rocky.

Flora and fauna: Only small tundra areas due to the topography, but these are interesting for trained botanists, as the warm springs have attracted several plant species that do not exist anywhere else in Spitsbergen; these are mostly inconspicuous grasses, but nevertheless unique in the region.

Miscellaneous: NASA has used Sverrefjellet since 2003 for geological investigations and equipment testing related to the preparation of future Mars missions; the Sverrefjellet area is suitable because of similarities in geology and terrain. These summer field camps will continue for some time in the future.

9.10 Moffen

"At two in the afternoon we had little wind, and were in sight of Moffen Island, which is very low and flat. ... Sent the master on shore, who found the island to be nearly of a round form, about two miles in diameter, with a lake or large pond of water in the middle, all frozen over, except thirty or forty yards round the edge of it, which was water, with loose pieces of broken ice, and so shallow that they walked through it, and went over upon the firm solid ice. The ground between the sea and the pond is from half a cable's length to a quarter of a mile broad, and the whole island covered with gravel and small stones, without the least verdure or vegetation of any kind. ... They saw three bears, and a number of wild ducks, geese, and other sea fowls, with birds nesting all over the island. There was an inscription over the grave of a Dutchman, who was buried there in July 1771."

Constantine John Phipps, *Voyage towards the North Pole*

General: Moffen is an unusual little island, only four or five square kilometres in area and situated 25 kilometres north of Gråhuken. Moffen is home to the best-known and most frequently visited Walrus colony in Svalbard and enjoys special protection: it has been declared a Nature Reserve, and from 15 May to 15 September all traffic is banned not only on the island, but also within 300 metres of the shore line. Aircraft have to keep a minimum distance of 500 metres. Most ships have to keep a distance larger than 300 metres because of the shallow waters around the island.

Moffen is situated a fraction north of the 80th parallel, crossing which, appears to be a fundamental part of any voyage to northern Spitsbergen. The remaining distance to the North Pole from 80°N is ten degrees of latitude, each degree having 60 minutes of latitude. Ten degrees of latitude thus equal 600 minutes = 600 nautical miles = 600 x 1.852 km = 1,111 kilometres or 690 statute miles – this is the distance from 80°N to the North Pole. The Walrus experience at Moffen is usually not too exciting because of the requirement to keep a distance. For map, see section 6.9.1. *Woodfjord* (page 311).

Placenames: see *history* further down in this section.

Geology: Moffen is entirely made up of a series of beaches that have been thrown up on the shallow sea bottom by currents and storms from different directions.

Landscape: Moffen is completely flat and has the shape of a doughnut with a large brackish lagoon in the middle. The lagoon was used as a convenient natural harbour by whalers in the 17th and 18th centuries.

Flora and fauna: As far as can be seen from a distance, there is no vegetation beyond some mosses on the island, but Moffen has some faunal highlights. Arctic terns are breeding in large numbers, together with one or two pairs of Sabine's gulls that are extremely rare in Spitsbergen. Foxes are usually around, even though it is an island.

The obvious attraction are the Walrus that find ideal feeding grounds on the shallow sea bottom around Moffen. Walrus must have been far more abundant, both on Moffen and in Spitsbergen in general, before the advent of Europeans who have driven the regional population close to extinction through several centuries of intense hunting. Moffen was the first place on the north coast of Spitsbergen to be re-colonised and is thus an important stepping stone in re-establishing the walrus population.

History: The 17th century whalers knew Moffen well, and they not only slaughtered thousands of Walrus, but also buried their own deceased comrades on the island. Some parts of Moffen are still covered with Walrus bones. According to one theory, the term "Moffen" was used by Dutch whalers referring to Germans who worked on the ships; it was certainly not a polite expression. However, the name is more likely to describe the shape of the island.

6.11 Wijdefjord

"Here we were not to be disappointed. The scenery of Wijde bay is superb."

Martin Conway, *The First Crossing of Spitsbergen*

General: Wijdefjord stretches 108 kilometres southwards into Spitsbergen and is thus the longest fjord of the archipelago. It is more than 20 kilometres wide at the entrance and looks like a strait when seen from the north; it follows a dead straight line and has only one branch, the small Vestfjord. The main fjord south of Vestfjord is inventively called Austfjord. The neighbouring land areas are Andrée Land and Dickson Land to the west and Ny Friesland in the east.

Wijdeford is mostly blank on sea charts and not often visited by ships. Energetic hikers who can negotiate glaciers can reach Austfjord from Billefjord. The southern part of Wijdefjord was declared a National Park in 2003. For map, see section 6.14 *Hinlopenstretet* (page 342).

Placenames: Austfjord: "East fjord". **Krosspynten:** "Cross point", refers to the grave of a Norwegian trapper who died and was buried there in 1912. **Mittag-Lefflerbreen:** Magnus Gustav M.-L. (1846-1927), Swedish mathematician and one of the organisers of the Arc-de-Meridian expedition. **Mosselbukta:** Name used since the 17th century, exact origin unknown, possibly after a ship. **Vestfjord:** "West fjord". **Wijdefjord:** "Wide fjord".

Geology: The remarkable shape of the fjord – more than 100 kilometres in a straight line – is determined by a large tectonic structure, the Billefjorden fault zone (BFZ, see section 4.2 *Geology* and 6.1.7 *Eastern Dickson Land, Billefjord*). This fault is the eastern boundary of the Andrée Land graben, on the west side of Wijdefjord, that is filled with Devonian Old Red. Basement rocks make up almost all of the Ny Friesland side of Wijdefjord. These basement rocks include sediments of various metamorphic grades (quartzite, slate, schist, phyllite) and crystalline rocks such as migmatites, granites and marble. The only younger rocks on the Wijdefjord side of Ny Friesland are some small areas of Carboniferous carbonates.

The youngest rocks in Wijdefjord are doleritic ("basaltic") intrusions at Krosspynten that date to the upper Jurassic.

Landscape: The most striking landscape element is the dead straight Wijdefjord itself, that reaches almost as far as Isfjord, cutting Spitsbergen into two halves. The land bridge separating Wijdefjord from Isfjord is only 30 kilometres across.

The basement block that now makes up Ny Friesland, has experienced strong uplift and now forms an elevated plateau that catches most precipitation from the east. It is thus much more strongly glaciated than Andrée Land. As a result, there are four smaller glaciers calving into Wijdefjord on its eastern side, but no glacier anywhere near the shore west of the fjord. The head of Wijdefjord (Austfjord) is dominated by the calving front of Mittag-Lefflerbreen, which is approximately five kilometres wide.

The slopes on either side of Wijdefjord do not fall straight down to sea level, and in most places there is a small strip of more or less level ground between the shore and the mountains.

The lakes in northwestern Ny Friesland, south of Mosselbukta, are quite rare landscape elements in Spitsbergen.

Flora and fauna: There is an interesting geographical distribution of vegetation zones from the mouth to the head of Wijdefjord. The north coast of Spitsbergen including the tundra to either side of the entrance of Wijdefjord is very barren, but the further south you get within the fjord, the more vegetation you will find. The reason for this is the improving local climate: an increasing degree of continentality, as the distance from the outer coast increases, implies slightly warmer summer temperatures. As a result, almost all the general vegetation zones of Spitsbergen can be found in Wijdefjord, from polar desert in the north (Verlegenhuken) via "middle-arctic" tundra of the "Mountain avens type" followed by the "Arctic bell-heather type", until the "inner fjord zone" is reached in Austfjord with dense tundra vegetation that resembles heathland – well, almost, but the vegetation cover is nearly 100 % in suitable terrain, and the species diversity is rich. This interesting botanical cross section makes Wijdefjord unique in Spitsbergen and was an important reason for declaring the inner part of the fjord a National Park in 2003.

The fauna is inconspicuous by comparison. There are bird cliffs on steeper slopes, mostly within the hard-rock basement areas of Ny Friesland that have been carved out by recent erosion. The lakes south of Mosselbukta have a large proportion of Spitsbergen's population of Arctic char.

6.9.1: Warm colours displayed by the Old Red in inner Woodfjord.

6.9.2: Stasjonsøyane in Liefdefjord.

6.9.3-1: Liefdefjord and Woodfjord (in the background), seen from Wulffberget near "Texas Bar".

6.9.3-2: Inner Liefdefjord seen from Lernerøyane.

History: Pomors appreciated Wijdefjord as a good hunting area, not least due to the rich Arctic char population of the lakes. The three best preserved Pomor huts in Svalbard are in Wijdefjord; at least the only ones which still have standing walls. Two huts, one in Rekvika southwest of Verlegenuken almost exactly at 80°N and the other at Dirksodden near Lakssjøen, have been repaired and are thus not completely original, though in comparatively good condition. The third hut at Elvetangen is not in good shape, but it is the most authentic, apart from the hut of a Norwegian trapper that was built directly next to it in 1910 or 1911.
Another hut built in Wijdefjord in the early 20th century by a Norwegian trapper has since been moved to the Polarmuseum in Tromsø, where it is now on permanent display.

A historically important site is **Polhem** in **Mosselbukta**. It dates to 1872 when the famous Swedish polar explorer Adolf Erik **Nordenskiöld** arrived with his expedition. A house was built to occupy for the winter and called "Polhem", the plan being to use reindeer to sledge to the North Pole during the following spring. The reindeer all took to their heels in the autumn, and Nordenskiöld finally cancelled his North Pole trip in favour of a scientifically more productive sledge journey to the totally unknown interior of Nordaustland.

Interior, provisions and finally parts of the building material of Polhem were gradually plundered by trappers, until the house came to play an important rule during another expedition, the fame of which is entirely based on its complete and tragic failure. Several men of the German **Schröder-Stranz expedition,** who were forced to winter in Sorgfjord, tried to walk along Wijdefjord to Longyearbyen, using Polhem and several huts in Wijdefjord as stepping stones. Three men froze to death in Wijdefjord during chaotic attempts either to reach Longyearbyen or to retreat to the expedition ship in Sorgfjord. Remains of two of them were found some years later on the east side of Wijdefjord; the third man was never seen again. Since then, Polhem has collapsed and unfortunately there is not much left.

6.12 Ny Friesland, Verlegenhuken

"A series of easy snow-slopes seemed to lead from the glacier to near the top, and it suddenly struck us that it would be a really amusing feat to sledge the dogs right up to the summit. Moreover, why should not the dogs enjoy the view as well as we ourselves? We steadily climbed, hauling and shoving, but always making headway, until at last we gained the summit, the dogs having won the `honour` of being the first team to climb Spitsbergens highest mountain."

R.A. Glen, *Under The Pole Star*

General: See sections 6.11 *Wijdefjord*, 6.13 *Sorgfjord* and 6.14.2 *Lomfjord* for the coastal parts of Ny Friesland. The inland is very remote and thus only rarely visited by tourists. Mountaineers occasionally accept the long journey there in exchange for the exciting rock- and ice climbing possibilities on the crystalline massifs of southern Ny Friesland. Ice climbing and extreme skiing options are said to be better than the rock climbing, according to some who have been there.

The ice cap Åsgårdfonna that covers the wide high plateau of Ny Friesland is not too varied and is technically easy terrain, but distances, temperature and wind, together with the ubiquitous danger of hidden crevasses, must not be underestimated. Private and even commercial skiing expeditions venture regularly on ascents to the summit of **Newtontoppen**, the highest mountain on Svalbard. The 1,713 metre high summit can be reached from one side without technical climbing, and both skiis and snow mobiles are regularly used for ascents. When you stand on top of Newtontoppen, you have the whole of Svalbard around and under you and some truly excellent views.

The one and only fact that distinguishes **Verlegenhuken** from other parts of the coast is that this low, rocky headland is the northernmost tip of Spitsbergen (but not of Svalbard). It is a nice section of coast, but there isn't anything special to see other than a wooden navigation beacon, raised beaches on nearby coastal plains, and a lot of driftwood and plastic rubbish on the beaches. The eastern part of Ny Friesland is part of the Nordaust Svalbard Naturreservat. For map, see section 6.14 *Hinlopenstretet* (page 342).

Placenames: Newtontoppen: Sir Isaac N. (1642-1727), English mathematician and physicist. **Ny Friesland:** After Friesland, a Dutch province and home to many whalers who visited Spitsbergen in the 17th century. **Verlegenhuken:** "Mislaid corner" that was often misplaced on old charts. Possibly also referring to awkward situations caused to the whalers by the pack ice that is often "attached" to Verlegenhuken. **Åsgårdfonna:** Åsgård, home of the gods in Norse mythology.

Geology: Ny Friesland consists mostly of varied pre-Caledonian metamorphic rocks and granite. On the western slopes, some remnants of Carboniferous sediments are preserved, which have some significance for the reconstruction of the original deposition of these sediments and the tectonic history of the BFZ (see section 6.11 *Wijdefjord*).

A large plutonic body intruded about 400 million years ago and cooled down to form granite, since brought to the light of day by erosion in more recent geological times, now forms Newtontoppen and surrounding mountains.

There are well-developed series of raised beaches on coastal plains near Verlegenhuken.

Landscape: Ny Friesland is an uplifted plateau, most of which is now situated at elevations between 700 and 1,000 metres. Being a gently rolling lowland until about 100 million years ago, uplift then turned those lowlands into a high plateau that was subsequently dissected by fluvial and later glacial erosion. This, in a very few words, is the story of the creation of Spitsbergen's landscape with its elevated plateaus, valleys and fjords. The parts that experienced most pronounced uplift (and have hard rocks) are still the highest areas today, including Newtontoppen. The general appearance of this area is a strongly glaciated high-mountain area, although most mountain tops are flat rather than pointed. The large, high block of Ny Friesland receives relatively high precipitation and is thus heavily glaciated over large areas: The elevated plateau is almost completely covered by the ice cap Åsgårdfonna.

Flora and fauna: Most parts of Ny Friesland are a totally inhospitable ice- and rock desert, but some steep slopes are home to seabird colonies, and it is astonishing to find a little oasis on a seemingly dead rocky ridge far inland, totally surrounded by large glaciers, but warmed up by the rays of the summer sun and covered by small but surprisingly rich patches of vegetation.

History: The first person to stand on the summit of Newtontoppen was the Swede **Helge Backlund,** a member of the Swedish-Russian Arc-de-Meridian expedition in 1900. The first crossing of Ny Friesland from north to south was made in 1913 by a Norwegian rescue expedition for the ill-fated Schröder-Stranz expedition.

6.13 Sorgfjord

"The fire of the Dutch continued heavy till 1 o'clock and was warmly replied to by the French."

Martin Conway, *No Man's Land*

General: Sorgfjord is a relatively small fjord in northeastern Spitsbergen, 15 kilometres long and without any branches. There are nice opportunities for tundra walks and mountain hikes. The eastern part of Sorgfjord belongs to the Nordaust Svalbard Nature Reserve. For map, see section 6.14 *Hinlopenstretet* (page 342).

Placenames: Crozierpynten: after a member of Parry's expedition. **Eolusneset:** after *Æolus*, a Norwegian sealing ship that was chartered by several expeditions, including Torell and Nordenskiöld in 1861. **Heclahuken:** after Parry's expedition ship *Hecla*. **Sorgfjord:** name used since the 17th century as a reminder of troubles that whalers had in this area due to ice or competitors.

Geology: The area around Sorgfjord consists of sediments that belong to the basement, mostly quartzite, dating into the upper Proterozoic (600-700 million years ago). The layers are strongly deformed and dip steeply, but are of a low metamorphic grade so that fine sedimentary details have been preserved. Small quantities of colourful minerals such as hematite bring soft, but pleasant colour shades into the landscape. The prominent flat-topped mountain on the east side of Sorgfjord called Heclahuken is the type locality of the "Hecla hoek", as the basement of Spitsbergen has been called for a long time.

Landscape: The gentle scenery around Sorgfjord is in strong contrast to the northern coast of Spitsbergen further west. Low mountains capped by wide-stretching plateaus often end at steep cliffs that fall down to wide coastal plains, many of which are covered with well-developed series of raised beaches. The tundra seems empty at first glance, but there are many interesting details for anyone who is open to the more subtle aspects of the Arctic: a beautiful flower within the barren polar desert, patches of colourful lichens or moss beds, bizarre frost-patterned ground, large amounts of driftwood along the coast, old beach ridges, …

Flora and fauna: Barren tundra of the high-arctic "Svalbard poppy type".

History: Sorgfjord was called Treurenburg Bay for a long time, and many dramas have happened in this small fjord over the centuries since the whalers' days. The oldest visible traces can be seen on a little hill near **Eolusneset** on the west side of the fjord, where whalers used to bury their dead.

If anybody had happened to stand on top of that hill in 1693, he would have been a witness to a sea battle that is said to be the northernmost one ever fought, when three French warships attacked 40 Dutch whaling ships. 13 of these ended up being caught by the French; the rest escaped.

Parry's ship *Hecla* spent some weeks in Sorgfjord during the summer of 1827, while Parry himself tried to reach the Pole – but in vain (see section 5.5 *Early expeditions and science*). In 1861, the Swedish explorers **Torell** and **Nordenskiöld** had to spend some weeks in Sorgfjord while the ice closed the entrance to the bay. Nordenskiöld complained that Sorgfjord was already one of the best-known parts of Spitsbergen and there was not much left for them to do.

Crozierpynten on the east side of the fjord was chosen in 1899 for the Swedish station of the very successful **Arc-de-Meridian expedition**. The house and a little observatory were used for a wintering in 1899-1900 and for astronomic observations to determine latitude and longitude with the best-possible precision, and it served as a summer base until 1902. Remains can still be seen at Crozierpynten.

Sorgfjord (then still called Treurenburg Bay) became pivotal once again during an arctic drama, when the ship *Herzog Ernst* of the German **Schröder-Stranz expedition**, was trapped by the ice. At this time, the expedition suffered from a total lack of leadership, as the leader, lieutenant Schröder-Stranz, was away on a sledge journey on Nordaustland, together with three other expedition members; none of them was ever to be seen again. Although sufficient provisions were present on board, several parties tried to walk along Wijdefjord in the early winter to reach the settlements in Isfjord. Several dramas happened along the way. Three Germans got lost in Wijdefjord and only Captain Ritscher managed to reach Longyearbyen after an incredible forced march. One Norwegian died from illness on board the *Herzog Ernst* in Sorgfjord. The survivors were finally rescued by a Norwegian expedition and brought across Ny Friesland to Longyearbyen, a journey that was "by the way" the first north-south crossing of this mostly unknown, completely glaciated area.

6.14 Hinlopenstretet

"The whole scene was marvellous beyond all power of words; most memorable was the gravity of the colouring, the dark-green sea, the purple rocks, the blue glacier cliff, the near grey, the remote yellowish snow, and over all the dull leaden-grey of the clouds, combined into a solemn harmony of tone over which brooded the great silence of the north."

Martin Conway, *The First Crossing of Spitsbergen*
Describing Hinlopen Strait

General: Hinlopenstretet separates the main island of Spitsbergen from Nordaustland, the second-largest island of the Svalbard archipelago. The strait is approximately 100 kilometres long and at the narrowest part, is only nine kilometres wide; there are a number of small and medium-sized islands in the middle and southern parts. The surrounding landscape is characterised by low, extensive mountain plateaux, barren polar deserts and large ice caps.
A strait has by definition two open ends, neither of which is generally the "entrance" or "exit". The northern mouth of Hinlopenstretet is, however, often referred to as the "entrance", since most tourist circumnavigations of Spitsbergen follow a clockwise direction. It is certainly less ambiguous to use the official terms **Nordporten** for the northern end and **Sørporten** for the southern one.

Strong tidal currents run through Hinlopenstretet that can, at any time during the summer, quickly move large masses of drift ice from either north or south into the strait, effectively blocking it. In historical times, Hinlopenstretet was feared amongst seafarers for its unpredictable, often dangerous ice conditions. There is still an element

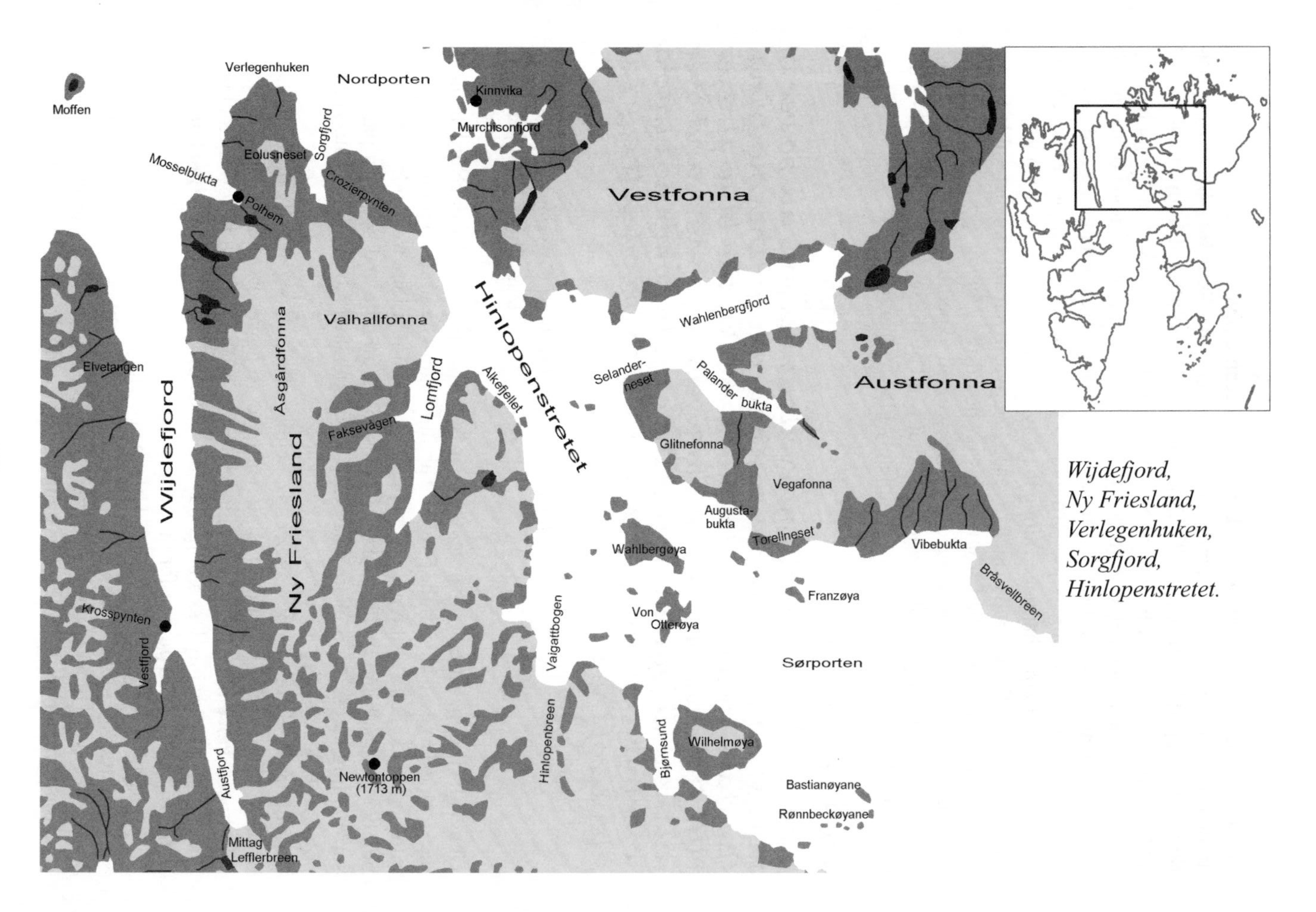

Wijdefjord,
Ny Friesland,
Verlegenhuken,
Sorgfjord,
Hinlopenstretet.

of unpredictability even today. The ice chart that is regularly updated by the Norwegian meteorological institute gives an overview of the drift ice distribution in Svalbard waters, but changes are often sudden and unexpected due to the action of winds and currents. This is generally true throughout Svalbard, but more so the further northeast you get, and Hinlopenstretet is often a challenge. The regional pattern of currents can cause the seemingly paradoxical situation where Nordporten is clear but Sørporten is blocked by ice.

In winter and spring, Hinlopenstretet does not freeze reliably because of the strong currents, but fjords and bays that cut into the surrounding coasts are normally covered by fast ice.

There are still blank patches on nautical charts of Hinlopenstretet, making access to some areas difficult. The Norwegian authorities are considering closing badly charted waters for navigation to prevent accidents, and there have already been several groundings of medium-sized cruise ships in Hinlopenstretet. The whole area is part of the Nordaust Svalbard Nature Reserve.

See the following sections for descriptions of the individual fjords and islands in and near Hinlopenstretet.

Placenames: Hinlopenstretet: "Hinlopen Strait". Name given during the 17th century, possibly after Thymen Jacobsz H., director of a Dutch whaling company, or after the town Hindelopen in the Netherlands.

Geology: The basement is exposed over large areas around northern Hinlopenstretet. Comparison with areas further west makes it clear that this is a different basement province. There are three basement provinces in Svalbard, all of them believed to be of completely different origin and only later brought together by tectonic movements. The crystalline rocks that are so characteristic of northwestern Spitsbergen and southern Ny Friesland are absent; the basement in Nordaustland consists of weakly metamorphosed upper Proterozoic sediments (ages between 600 million and one billion years). These sediments include quartzite and carbonates such as dolostone and are multicoloured due to their varying mineral content, the commonest being iron oxide (hematite). The layers have often been tilted into a steeply dipping or vertical position, but the metamorphic grade is low. Filigree sedimentary structures such as ripple marks and desiccation cracks have often been preserved, and stromatolites can be found in some of the carbonate layers, for example near Sparreneset south of Murchisonfjord. Refer to the individual sections (6.14.1-6.14.6) for further information on the geology of the individual areas.

Flora and fauna: The tundra in Hinlopenstretet and on Nordaustland is mostly extremely barren polar desert or scarcely vegetated tundra of the high-arctic "Svalbard poppy type", largely characterised by the absence of flowering plants. This gives moss patches and lichens an increased ecological importance. Mosses especially are vulnerable and should not be stepped on.

Limiting factors for plant growth often include lack of moisture and winter snow cover (that could provide protection from frost and drying up), and low nutrient availability. The smallest local changes of ecological frame conditions can produce surprising results. For example, the fine-grained sediment core of stone circles (frost patterned ground) has a better ability to store water, while old decaying whale bone or reindeer antlers slowly give their nutrients back to the tundra. In this way, seemingly insignificant landscape details can create small patches of life in a hostile environment; oases in the polar desert.

Terrestrial animal life is also very scarce. Some shy reindeer survive on Nordaustland; Arctic fox and Rock ptarmigan are occasionally seen, but life is mostly concentrated near and in the sea. The abundance of zooplankton is the basis for a number of seabird colonies in Hinlopenstretet. There are Walrus resting places, and the chance (or risk) of meeting a Polar bear is good anywhere in the area, especially if there is still drift ice or fast ice.

Even the extremely rare Bowhead whale has been seen in the Hinlopenstretet area in recent years. Chances of actually seeing one are near zero, but you never know …

History: The whalers have known Hinlopenstretet since the 17th century, but have largely refrained from frequenting these difficult and dangerous waters. No remains from whalers are known in Hinlopenstretet or on Nordaustland. A number of scientific expeditions have visited the area in the late 19th and early 20th century. The very successful Russian-Swedish **Arc-de-Meridian expedition** (main working period 1899-1902) deserves some attention. During this expedition, accurate topographic surveys were carried out to map a longitudinal section from Sjuøyane in northernmost Svalbard to the southern point of Spitsbergen. Hinlopenstretet was an important connecting link between the northernmost areas and Spitsbergen. The large number of islands provided convenient opportunities to build cairns for triangulation, many of which can still be seen. Next to these trigonometrical points, a number of placenames are reminders of the well-organised, internationally coordinated and successfully realised Arc-de-Meridian expedition. Refer to the following sections (6.14.1-6.14.6) for further details.

Miscellaneous: Stricter regulations to control traffic in the large nature reserves in eastern Svalbard have to be expected in the near future. This may include closing larger areas within the large nature reserves of eastern Svalbard.

6.14.1 Murchisonfjord

General: The westernmost fjord of Nordaustland is separated from Hinlopenstretet by a group of smaller islands. Murchisonfjord cuts 15 kilometres inland and is completely inside the Nordaust Svalbard Nature Reserve. The old research station Kinnvika on the north side of the fjord is not automatically protected because it is younger than 1945, but the Sysselmannen has announced a plan to establish a legal protection status for the station buildings, interior and surroundings. For map, see section 6.14 *Hinlopenstretet* (page 342).

Placenames: Kinnvika: after Kinneviken, a bay of lake Vänern in Sweden. **Murchisonfjord:** Sir Roderick M. (1792-1871), English geographer and geologist.

Geology: All rocks in Murchisonfjord are sediments that belong to the pre-Caledonian basement (see section 6.14 *Hinlopenstretet*). They are steeply dipping and follow a north-south trend that is evident in the landscape and on topographic maps. Nice stromatolites can be found in some carbonate banks in the Murchisonfjord area; these are amongst the oldest fossils in Spitsbergen that are visible to the naked eye.
Landscape: The most striking feature of the scenery is the vastness and the seeming emptiness, which is characteristic for large parts of Nordaustland. The scenery around Murchisonfjord is characterised by wide, rolling lowlands and coastal plains, but a closer look reveals many interesting details including bizarre frost-patterned ground, or evidence of post-glacial isostatic land uplift in the form of raised beaches with very old driftwood or whalebones far behind and above today's coastline. Light-grey dolostones give the landscape a bleak appearance. The islands in Murchisonfjord follow an interesting pattern that is determined by the north-south trend of geological structures.
Flora and fauna: Polar desert with very low vegetation cover of the high-arctic "Svalbard poppy type".
History: The Pomors took advantage of the rich marine life and placed at least one hunting station in Murchisonfjord. Two large, wooden orthodox crosses that are still standing on islands in Murchisonfjord are reminders of the Pomors, and are the only original crosses of their kind that are still standing in Svalbard.

Finland and Sweden together established a scientific station in **Kinnvika,** on the north side of Murchisonfjord, during the International Geophysical Year in 1957/58, to carry out internationally agreed observations in various fields of geophysics (meteorology, northern lights, earth magnetism etc.). The scientific programme was carried out successfully, but the station was abandoned after the completion of the original plan. The buildings are still in good condition and are currently used by scientists within the framework of the International Polar Year (IPY) 2007/08. This time, international groups of scientists will follow a wider spectrum thematically than their predecessors; investigations include the glaciology of the regional ice caps Vestfonna and Austfonna, regional pollution by environmental toxins, consequences of climate change on regional ecosystems, archaeology and more.

6.14.2 Lomfjord

General: Lomfjord is a fjord about 30 kilometres long in northeast Spitsbergen, with one side bay, Faksevågen, on its western side. Lomfjord is part of the Nordaust Svalbard Nature Reserve and mostly blank on nautical charts, which makes navigation difficult. For map, see section 6.14 *Hinlopenstretet* (page 342).
Placenames: Faksevågen: "Fakse bay", after a horse in Norse mythology. **Lomfjord:** "Guillemot bay", referring to the near-by birdcliff Alkefjellet, in Hinlopenstretet.
Geology: The fjord follows a large fault zone that has been important for the regional geological development, the so-called Lomfjorden-Aghardbukta fault zone (LAFZ). One of the results is the presence of totally different rocks on either side of Lomfjord.

Footnote one: Drift ice and circumnavigations

During any present-day ship's voyage that is scheduled to circumnavigate Spitsbergen, the question always arises sooner or later "will we make it around?". Drift ice can, at any time, be an obstacle in northern and eastern parts of Svalbard, and Hinlopenstretet is rather like the eye of a needle; many intended circumnavigations have "failed" there, on vessels ranging from sailing boats to icebreakers. The question is not simply "is it possible to enter the strait?" but also "will it be possible to get right through in a reasonable time?". This may seem quite trivial, but it can turn out to be full of excitement.

One thing to be aware of is that even Captains and experienced expedition leaders with dozens of circumnavigations under their belts cannot predict exactly what will happen, even if they have already been to the area in question earlier during the same season. Every single voyage is different and if you want to know how conditions are, then the best idea is to go there and have a look. Circumnavigations of Spitsbergen are not zoo visits where different animals get fed at a scheduled time every day; they are expedition voyages of exploration. The unpredictability of events is part of the excitement of such a voyage and passengers soon realise that a printed itinerary is at best, a general idea of what *could* happen during such a voyage.

While I am on the subject, I would like to write a few lines about terms such as "success" and "failure" with regard to these circumnavigations. Amongst the many Spitsbergen voyages that I have made were a number of ship voyages that were "supposed" to sail around the main island or even the whole archipelago, but were forced to turn back because of massive fields of drift ice. Did these voyages "fail"? In my opinion, they certainly did not. They may have "failed" to follow a specific route, but they will have been successful in their experience of Spitsbergen, its scenery, wildlife, tundra, history … in fact all those aspects of Spitsbergen which will be far more important to most travellers than a particular geographical destination. Nature and luck have presented me with some of my most precious arctic experiences during such "failed"' circumnavigations.

In the end, of course, you have to decide what is most important to you, but remember that nature rules. If you are keen on completing a voyage right around Spitsbergen, then make sure you do not come too early in the season (see section 3.1 *Spitsbergen – seasons*).

The east side is made up of horizontal layers of upper Permian and lower Carboniferous sandstones and carbonates, with a marked dark horizontal basaltic intrusion (upper Jurassic or lower Cretaceous). The west and north sides, in contrast, show steeply dipping basement sediments (see section 6.14 *Hinlopenstretet*) with some very nicely preserved ripple marks and desiccation cracks.

Landscape: The main landscape feature is a vast plateau, situated at elevations of between 300 and 400 metres, that has been dissected by erosion, forming today's valleys and fjords (Lomfjord, Faksevågen). The valleys near Lomfjord are a bit of a

Footnote two: Through Hinlopenstretet or around Nordaustland?

When approaching Hinlopenstretet, there is another question that is raised regularly and is often the subject of heated discussion. Will the route take us through Hinlopenstretet or around Nordaustland? The term "big circumnavigation" has been invented for the passage around the eastern side of Nordaustland. This raisesexpectations, but expectations of what, really?

Both routes are possible; both can be extremely interesting, beautiful and exciting and, if you are unlucky, both can be spoiled by wind and fog. There are fascinating landscapes and good chances for unforgettable wildlife encounters, both in Hinlopenstretet and on the north and east side of Nordaustland. Both areas also have interesting historical sites. The decision on which to attempt must be based on these possibilities. One must face this dilemma in a relaxed manner and make a decision based on major factors such as weather and ice conditions in order to maximise the chances of some unforgettable experiences.

Remember there is a word in the Greenlandic language, which applies to life anywhere in the Arctic (and Antarctic). It is "imaqa" and it means "maybe" ☺

regional exception due to the fact that their lower sections are not now glaciated, but filled with large moraines or river plains. The inland at some distance from the coast is almost completely covered by large ice caps. The mighty predecessors of these ice masses covered the entire region at several stages during the ice age and have left obvious traces of their former presence almost everywhere in the landscape, for example in the form of erratic boulders. A splendid specimen of an erratic boulder is seen lying on top of the highest ridge north of Faksevågen at about 355 metres above sea level; this rock certainly enjoys one of the finest panoramas in the area, with clear views of Lomfjord and Faksevågen and the mountains further inland. The area has nice opportunities for energetic hikers.

Flora and fauna: Sheltered terrain in Lomfjord has surprisingly rich tundra, with almost complete vegetation cover in favourable places and an abundance of species such as Mountain avens and Arctic bell-heather, that are considered characteristic species for "middle-arctic" tundra types of central Spitsbergen. They remind visitors more of the dense tundra in Isfjord than the barren polar desert of Hinlopenstretet. The local reindeer population benefits from the rich vegetation.

Steep cliffs, especially on the intrusion on the east side of Lomfjord, have seabird colonies with Brünich's guillemot as the dominant species.

6.14.3 Alkefjellet

General: A visit to Alkefjellet is an experience that you will not forget. You need the weather gods on your side, as these steep cliffs are exposed to winds from northerly or easterly directions. Strong tidal currents make navigation for small boat pilots a challenge at times. In some places it is possible to get very close to breeding birds, who seem not much bothered about human presence, but respectful behaviour is certainly due. There may be dense congregations of birds on the water, especially in the late season when the chicks have left the cliffs and sit on the water, just about to start the long voyage towards their wintering areas. Small boats should stay clear of such concentrations of birds. The risk of rockfalls and snow avalanches must not be ignored, especially early in the season. Alkefjellet is inside the Nordaust Svalbard Nature Reserve. For map, see section 6.14 *Hinlopenstretet* (page 342).

Placenames: Alkefjellet: "Mount Guillemot", name given for obvious reasons. **Kapp Fanshawe:** after a mate on the *Hecla*, one of Parry's ships in 1827.

Geology: Alkefjellet would not exist without a thick, lens-shaped intrusion of dolerite which stretches from the thickest part somewhere in the centre of the island, thinning outwards from a good hundred metres to zero in a distance of a few kilometres. This lens has been cut by ice-age glacial erosion to create the near-vertical cliff: what you see at Alkefjellet is a cross-section through central parts of the doleritic intrusion; thinner, marginal parts are exposed at Kapp Fanshawe, the point north of Alkefjellet at the entrance of Lomfjord, and on the east side of Lomfjord. The doleritic ("basaltic") rocks show a large-scale columnar structure, but no perfect basalt columns; the reasons for this have to do with the exact chemical composition of the rock and the rate of cooling.

The dolerite was intruded into the pre-existing rocks between 150 and 100 million years ago (Jurassic or upper Cretaceous). The older, surrounding rocks are horizontal layers of Permocarboniferous sediments that are still exposed in places at the top and bottom of the cliff. Being heated up by the large body of molten rock, layers of limestone directly neighbouring the intrusion have re-crystallised to form marble (contact metamorphism). The contact zone between white marble/limestone and dark dolerite creates a nice colour contrast.

Landscape: The sheer cliffs, more than 100 metres high, would certainly be worth a visit even without any birds. Individual columns have been dissected out of the cliff by erosion that followed the columnar structure, and Alkefjellet might well be the scene for a fairy tale or fantasy film, especially in fog and quickly changing light.

The inland area behind Alkefjellet, the peninsula between Hinlopenstretet and Lomfjord, is mostly covered by the ice cap Odinjøkulen. Several smaller outlet glaciers drain this ice cap and reach the shore of Hinlopenstretet, and there are some nice waterfalls with glacial meltwater flowing out of channels in the ice and falling down the cliffs in some places. The milky colour of the meltwater contrasts nicely with clear, green seawater.

The steep terrain of Alkefjellet does not allow any landings.

Flora and fauna: A large breeding colony of Brünich's guillemots is the obvious main attraction at Alkefjellet. During the summer, several tens of thousands of breeding pairs occupy almost every square inch, and there is constant frantic activity. Birds fly out to the open sea to secure food for their chicks and return in large numbers, always making an incredible noise. Exact counts of the birds have not yet been made, but estimates are in the order of 60,000 breeding pairs. It is hard to believe that this makes Alkefjellet "only" a medium-sized Brünich's guillemot colony, but there are indeed larger ones in other places in Svalbard. The great advantage of Alkefjellet from a tourist perspective is the terrain that allows a close approach to the birds with boats, as opposed to most other colonies where the actual breeding sites are far above sea level.

Common neighbours of breeding Brünich's guillemots, including large, predating Glaucous gulls, and some Kittiwakes are also present at Alkefjellet.
Miscellaneous: Guano-proof clothing is strongly recommended.

6.14.4 Wahlenbergfjord, Palanderbukta

General: Wahlenbergfjord has a relatively constant width of about ten kilometres and cuts about 50 kilometres or so from Hinlopenstretet into Nordaustland. It has one side branch, Palanderbukta, on the south side. The waters of Wahlenbergfjord are partly blank on nautical charts and thus difficult for navigation. There are two small islands in the entrance of the fjord, called Gyldénøyane, which are very similar to the smaller islands in southern Hinlopenstretet (see secton 6.14.5 *The islands in Hinlopenstretet*). Wahlenbergfjord is inside the Nordaust Svalbard Nature Reserve. For map, see section 6.14 *Hinlopenstretet* (page 342).
Placenames: Wahlenbergfjord: Göran W., (1780-1851), Swedish botanist and geologist. **Palanderbukta:** Baron Adolf Arnold Louis P. (1842-1920), Swedish polar explorer, member of several expeditions of Adolf Erik Nordenskiöld. **Selanderneset:** Nils Haquin S. (1804-70), Swedish astronomer. **Vegafonna:** After the *Vega*, Nordenskiöld's ship during his famous expedition through the Northeast Passage (1878-79). Captain during this expedition was the above-mentioned Palander.
Geology: Weakly metamorphosed basement sediments (dolostone, limestone, quartzite) north of Wahlenbergfjord (see section 6.14 *Hinlopenstretet*). Horizontal layers of Permocarboniferous sediments on the south side, mostly carbonates, often rich in shallow-water marine fossils including Brachiopods. The youngest sediments date into the Triassic and can be seen in the upper slopes of Selanderneset at the fjord entrance. These fine-grained Triassic sediments can roughly be distinguished from the underlying Permian carbonates by their darker colour. The youngest solid rocks are doleritic intrusions from the Jurassic or lower Cretaceous, that have been uncovered by erosion and form a small steep cliff with columnar structures in the uppermost slope section of Selanderneset. The islands in Wahlenbergfjord and some points on the northern side also consist of doleritic intrusions.
Landscape: The meagreness of this vast, open polar desert is impressive. Wahlenbergfjord is surrounded on all sides by large ice caps that provide an appropriate background for the high-arctic scenery. There are small strips of more or less level ground near the coast in some places, interrupted by steeper cliffs. The most impressive cliffs are those of Selanderneset south of the entrance to Wahlenbergfjord. Being a good 200 metres high, the steep slopes have been dissected by meltwater streams to leave

individual, regular protrusions that resemble towers. This characteristic appearance is reminiscent of some mountains in Isfjord (Ekmanfjord, Dickson Land, Tempelfjellet), which have a similar geology – rocks make landscapes. There are other, less impressive coastal cliffs further into Wahlenbergfjord, but the coast gets less and less steep there. It is typical for the rock types in this area that walking is mostly quite dry and easy, although lagoons and small streams are as wet as anywhere else and rubber boots are the appropriate footwear for most activities in summertime.

Palanderdalen is a passage from the west side of Palanderbukta, leading across the peninsula Scaniahalvøya between the ice caps Glitnefonna and Vegafonna, to Augustabukta in Hinlopenstretet.

Most flat areas near the coast have well-developed series of raised beaches. These young sediments include shells of bivalves that were living in Spitsbergen waters a few thousand years ago when the average water temperature was slightly warmer than today. These shells are mostly covered with carbonate crusts that originated in micro-organisms. The overall appearance of such encrusted shells is that of very old fossils, but the truth is that they are geologically very recent (which does not make them any less interesting).

Flora and fauna: It is difficult to imagine a landscape more barren. Flowering plants are mostly restricted to singular occurrences of hardy plants such as Svalbard poppy and Purple saxifrage, next to colourful moss beds that mostly follow little streams and wet spots. The innermost part of Wahlenbergfjord, however, has been described as "perhaps the most fertile part of North East Land". It is hard to believe but true that some reindeer can survive in this environment. Chances for encounters with high-arctic wildlife including seals, Walrus and Polar bears are definitely good and even better if there is some drift ice or fast ice in Wahlenbergfjord.

History: Wahlenbergfjord has rarely been visited due to its relative remoteness and difficult ice conditions. The only known activity of trappers was in the season 1933-34 when two Norwegians, who wintered in Augustabukta, had a "bistasjon" (secondary station, small hut) in Palanderbukta, the ruin of which is still there. The two trappers died in their main hut in Augustabukta in January 1934.

6.14.5 The islands in Hinlopenstretet

General: There are several larger and a great many smaller islands in central and southern parts of Hinlopenstretet. The largest are Wilhelmøya with a surface area of about 100 sq km and Wahlbergøya with 28 sq km. The other islands are much smaller (mostly less than two sq km); most of them are concentrated in two groups: Vaigattøyane west and south of Wahlbergøya, and Bastianøyane/Rønnbeckøyane southeast of Wilhelmøya. Some isolated examples are found between Alkefjellet and Wahlenbergfjord and near Torellneset. The whole area is inside the Nordaust Svalbard Nature Reserve. For map, see section 6.14 *Hinlopenstretet* (page 342).

Most **placenames** have been given during a limited number of expeditions, see *history* further down in this section.

Geology: Most of the islands are composed entirely of dioritic intrusions that have been uncovered by erosion in the more recent geological past. These intrusions date into the Jurassic or lower Cretaceous. Rocks of other ages and types are seen only as erratic boulders.

There are two exceptions to this rule; Wahlbergøya and Wilhelmøya. Wahlbergøya has remnants of Permian limestones on its western side, but the island is otherwise made up of the ubiquitous dolerites. The larger exception is Wilhelmøya where dolerite intrusions play only a subordinate rule, but a larger volume of the sediments that once covered the whole area is present. Geologically speaking, Wilhelmøya is part of neighbouring Spitsbergen; it is one of the northernmost major outposts of the Mesozoic province of eastern Svalbard (Olav V Land in easternmost Spitsbergen, Barentsøya, Edgeøya, Hopen). The geology of these areas including Wilhelmøya is mostly characterised by horizontal layers of Mesozoic sediments, dominated by siltstones and shales, that are quite uniform, dark in appearance and not well solidified.

Landscape: All the islands are very barren, rocky, unglaciated and more or less flat or gently undulating with elevations below 100 metres. Steep terrain is largely restricted to low coastal cliffs. Only Wilhelmøya has a different appearance (see further down), but shares the large amounts of driftwood and plastic rubbish that litters many beaches.

The dolerites are quite interesting because they show a different weathering behaviour that depends on the details of their mineralogical composition. Some blocks still show freshly polished surfaces as if they had been exposed to the destructive effects of the atmosphere only a few days ago, although the glaciers that once created those surfaces disappeared more than 10,000 years ago. Other dolerite blocks are slowly disintegrating into black sand, leaving bizarre shapes behind for a while, created and destroyed at the same time by wind and frost.

Wilhelmøya has a totally different landscape due to its different geological background. The scenery reminds one of Barentsøya and Edgeøya in southeastern Svalbard, rather than of Hinlopenstretet. Central parts of the island show a plateau at an elevation of 300 to 500 metres that is covered by a smaller ice cap. This ice cap has several outlet glaciers, but none of these reaches the coast which is mostly wide bays with dark beaches and lots of driftwood, separated by four capes of harder doleritic rocks. The softer sediments are responsible for mostly rounded, gentle slopes and the very dark appearance of Wilhelmøya; sharp ridges and pointed peaks are missing and replaced by rounded hills or plateau-topped mountains.

It is as well to know that these soft sediments weather quickly under the influence of repeated freezing and thawing, disintegrating into fine-grained mud that is prone to solifluction over much of the lower slopes and even on almost level ground near the shore. This solifluction sediment is a viscous and **extremely sticky mud**, which hikers should definitely avoid. If you happen to get stuck in mud, then the most important thing is to stay calm and avoid panic: frantic movements will only make the situation worse. If you are a witness to such an event, make sure that people don't rush to the mudhole in order to help – a whole group stuck in the mud is not a very pleasant situation (all you need to complete a worst case scenario is a Polar bear showing up at this time). Pieces of driftwood can be useful, but unless requested to do otherwise, stay where you are and take some pictures. The victim may have to sacrifice his boots to get out, but will appreciate photos at a later time.

To be safe from such unpleasant surprises, stay on ridges of dolerite rocks that are obvious due to their large boulders, although the huge rocks themselves make walking difficult.

Flora and fauna: The doleritic islands are very rocky and barren and vegetation is scarce or absent over large areas. When walking around you will, however, find patches with colourful mosses and lichens – count the number of species of lichens on suitable rocks and you will quickly have more than ten or even 20. Life as a flowering plant is not a great pleasure in this area, but hardy plants such as Svalbard poppy and Purple saxifrage occur here and there.

Wilhelmøya is again the exception to the rule. There, tundra vegetation on more or less protected areas is surprisingly rich, with a vegetation cover of almost 100 % of the surface on favourable terrain that is reminiscent of the green plains on parts of Barentsøya, Edgeøya or even Nordenskiöld Land in central Spitsbergen, with Polar willow as one of the most common species.

History: The "Erste Deutsche Nordpolarfahrt" from 1868, the Swedish section of the Arc-de-Meridian expedition, and Adolf Erik Nordenskiöld's voyage of 1873 are amongst those expeditions that have surveyed parts of Hinlopenstretet and deserve to be mentioned.

The "**Erste Deutsche Nordpolarfahrt**" ("First German North Polar Voyage") of 1868, initiated by the armchair geographer August Petermann and led by Captain **Karl Koldewey**, was bound for the east coast of Greenland and from there to the North Pole; all this on board the *Grönland* which was a yacht rather than a ship. Due to the ice conditions, that were quite normal but totally different from what Petermann had expected, the *Grönland* finally ended up in Hinlopenstretet where Koldewey and his men took the opportunity to survey some areas around Kapp Torell and Wilhelmøya; previously been believed to be part of Spitsbergen, but circumnnavigated on this occasion for the first time.

Placenames given during the **Erste Deutschen Nordpolarfahrt** include **Kapp Koldewey**, after the leader of the expedition, and **Wilhelmøya,** after emperor Wilhelm I. The small archipelago Bastianøyane and its individual islands were named after German scientists, mostly geographers, geologists and ethnologists. **Roonbreen, -øya, Moltkebreen, -neset**: after leading Prussian politicians. **Bismarckstrasse** has later been re-named as **Bjørnsund** ("Bear sound"). Geographical features on the coast of Nordaustland named during this expedition were **Augustabukta** after Marie Louise A. Catharine, married to emperor Wilhelm I. and **Kapp Oetker** after Friedrich O., lawyer and sponsor. Islands in that area: **Perthesøya**, after Petermann's publisher in Gotha. **Franzøya**, after Friedrich Franz II., grand duke of Mecklenburg. **Karl Alexanderøya**: Carl Alexander August Johann, grand duke of Sachsen-Weimar-Eisenach.

The individual islands of **Vaigattøyane** have also been named by Koldewey, mostly to commemorate Swedish scientists that were members of Nordenskiöld's 1868 expedition (Nyström, Palander, Von Otter, Wijkander). The name **Vaigatt** itself is older and its origin not exactly known, but it is assumed that it means something like "hole (gatt), through which the wind blows". This name can be found on maps from different parts of the Arctic including west Greenland and the Russian Arctic.

The southernmost islands of Hinlopenstretet have been named after the Norwegian sealing Captain **Nils Rønnbeck**, who may have been the first one to circumnavigate the whole Svalbard archipelago in 1850. He reached Franz Josef Land in 1865 – eight years before the "official" discovery of these islands – and sailed through Hinlopenstretet and around Spitsbergen in 1867. On the latter voyage, he discovered the islands that still bear this brave man's name.

Miscellaneous: The information that you have just read in the sections on landscape and flora and fauna of these islands may not seem too encouraging for a visit to this area. The opposite is really the case and all of these islands are exciting. There are many fascinating little details to be seen, including colourful mosses and lichens, weathered rocks with bizarre shapes, a lot of old driftwood, occasional old whalebones, and the feeling of being on a small island at the end of the world that only a very few people have touched before. You never know what sort of unexpected wildlife may happen to be on the island at the same time ... **Caution** is certainly needed at all times. In 1995, a man was killed and another one badly injured by a Polar bear on Kiepertøya (Bastianøyane). The men belonged to a small group that was not sufficiently armed and met the Polar bear by surprise on the shore; the bear was later shot.

6.14.6 Augustabukta, Vibebukta

General: There is a relatively large area of ice-free land in the southweast of Nordaustland, allowing long hikes in this impressive, high-arctic landscape. The whole region belongs to the Nordaust Svalbard Nature Reserve. For map, see section 6.14 *Hinlopenstretet* (page 342).

Placenames: Augustabukta, Franzøya, Kapp Oetker, Perthesøya: see 6.14.5 *The islands in Hinlopenstretet*, section on *history*. **Vibebukta:** Andreas V. (1801-60), Norwegian topographer.

Geology: Horizontal layers of Permocarboniferous sediments; mostly fossil-rich, yellowish carbonates, covering almost the whole area. Younger sediments (Triassic) occur in elevated positions, and remnants of doleritic intrusions form dark hills in places. The wide coastal plains are completely covered by young deposits, mostly raised beaches.

Landscape: Vibebukta especially is characterised by vast, open polar desert that is very impressive due to the sheer emptiness of this huge, wide landscape. Augustabukta is slightly more varied: the glacier Mariebreen has a low calving front, and a hill rises towards the elevated, glaciated inland not far from the coast. Coastal plains are everywhere covered by well preserved series of raised beaches that have been created by post-glacial land uplift during the past 10,000 years. Some of the depressions between the shallow ridges hold narrow but elongated ponds, or at least wet spots, with mosses and bacteria. Decaying whalebones mark places where large whales were stranded thousands of years ago when the relevant spot was part of the shoreline.

The inland is completely glaciated. The ice cap Vegafonna covers the inland behind Augustabukta. Vegafonna is an ice cap on its own, but connected to the larger ice cap Austfonna that includes Bråsvellbreen east of Vibebukta (see section 6.15.5 *Isispynten, Austfonna, Bråsvellbreen*).

Flora and fauna: The most obvious quality of the regional flora is its absence; the wide coastal plain of Vibebukta in particular has hardly any vegetation. Only singular occurrences of Svalbard poppy and Purple saxifrage survive on favourable spots, often where an old whalebone has provided the stone desert with some nutrients, or the fine-grained core of some frost patterned ground has retained some moisture. Colourful moss beds grow in little streams; the dark-red colour of the mosses is usually due to malnutrition. Some denser vegetation grows near the glacier in Augustabukta, where the meltwater stream provides water and where local conditions are a little less hostile. It is hard to believe that reindeer can survive in this extreme environment, but a few are constantly roaming the polar desert in search of anything digestable.

History: Remains of a hut can be seen near the beach in Augustabukta, that was built in 1933 by two Norwegian trappers who wanted to hunt Polar bears during the following winter. The wintering resulted in a drama, because both died in January 1934 under unknown circumstances, possibly an explosion. Further details remain unknown, but at least nobody has so far suggested terrorism.

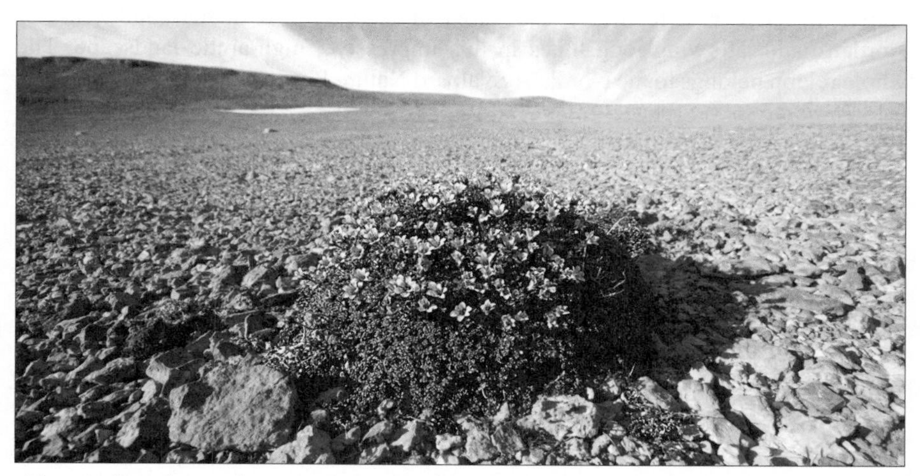

A lonely Purple saxifrage in the polar desert. Palanderbukta, Nordaustland.

6.15 Nordaustland

"The barrenness of the country and the severe weather conditions had attached to North East Land a peculiarly evil reputation, increased by the disappearance of Schroeder Stranz and three other members of the German Arctic Expedition in 1913, and by the Nobile disaster of 1928."

R.A. Glen, *Under The Pole Star*

See section 6.14 *Hinlopenstretet* for western and southwestern parts of Nordaustland (Murchisonfjord, Wahlenbergfjord/Palanderbukta, Augustabukta, Vibebukta).

General: Nordaustland is the second largest island in the Svalbard archipelago, with a surface area of 14,443 sq km, which makes it similar in size to Wales. This barren, remote and still quite inaccessible island exerts a strong fascination on everyone who has studied its landscapes, wildlife and history. The north coast is weakly influenced by the West-Spitsbergen current ("Gulf stream") and thus is ice-free much earlier in the summer than the east and south coast of Nordaustland. The climate is nevertheless colder and rougher than on the west coast of Spitsbergen because Nordaustland is on Svalbard's cold side, shielded from the mild influence of the Atlantic by Spitsbergen, but exposed to the ice and cold waters of the Arctic Ocean. The average summer temperatures (July-August) on Phippsøya (Sjuøyane), recorded by an automatic weather station, are 0.6°C compared to 3.8°C in Ny Ålesund.

Nordaustland and all surrounding islands belong to the Nordaust Svalbard Nature Reserve. Stricter regulations on traffic, including total traffic bans in certain areas, may be introduced in the future.

Geology: Almost all bedrock exposed in northern Nordaustland belongs to the basement, which can be subdivided broadly into two main groups:

- **Weakly metamorphic sediments** (quartzite, dolostone, limestone, slate) dating into the upper Proterozoic with ages around 600 to 700 million years. Younger tectonic movements have deformed these rocks, and the strata are accordingly often steeply dipping or vertical, bent and cut by folds and faults. Metamorphism is only weak, and filigree sedimentary structures such as ripple marks, desiccation cracks, fine cross-bedding and some fossils (stromatolites) are preserved. Trace minerals including iron oxides often give nice colours to the rocks, that can be found in northwestern Nordaustland (Murchisonfjord-Lågøya), on the west side of Rijpfjord, and also in northern Prins Oscars Land east of Rijpfjord.
- **Strongly metamorphic gneisses,** and **granites** and other magmatic rocks, mostly very old (around one billion years and older), partly re-activated during the Caledonian orogeny 400 million years ago. These crystalline rocks are exposed in Sjuøyane, the large peninsulas southwest of Sjuøyane (Laponiahalvøya and

Botniahalvøya) and in the far northeast, and to the east of Rijpfjord and Duvefjord. The oldest radiometric ages found in Svalbard, well beyond one billion years, have been obtained from single mineral grains in these rocks.

To summarise, the northern part of Nordaustland has some of the oldest rocks within Svalbard. The only non-basement (post-Caledonian) rocks are a few outcrops of dioritic intrusions on Lågøya and Botniahalvøya. These are the same rocks that are more common further south, for example in Hinlopenstretet. Their Jurassic and lower Cretaceous ages (150-100 million years) make these intrusives the youngest rocks in Nordaustland.

Landscape: Nordaustland is large and extremely barren and contrasts dramatically with landscapes elsewhere in Spitsbergen that are generally more mountainous. Typical landscape features of northern parts are relatively low mountains and hills topped by wide plateaux; isolated mountains are the exception. Elevations are mostly under 400 metres and often less than 300 metres; the highest single "mountain" on Nordaustland is Snøtoppen (620 metres), a glaciated elevation on Laponiahalvøya. Large central areas of the ice cap Austfonna are a good 700 metres high, though, and northern parts of Vestfonna are still 630 metres above sea level at Snøhatten, an ice dome in the northernmost part. The rocky elevated plateaux are often cut abruptly by steep slopes that drop down to coastal plains or directly into the sea. Coastal plains are often covered by raised beach ridges of coarse gravel and stones.

The north and west coast is strongly dissected by fjords, indicating former drainage systems of earlier Pleistocene ice caps. An area of 11,500 sq km out of a total land area of 14,443 sq km is covered by ice caps and glaciers; a proportion of 80 % as opposed to an average of 60 %, for the whole archipelago. The most important ice caps are Vestfonna (2,450 sq km) and the complex of Austfonna and Vegafonna (together 8,450 sq km). The northeastern, eastern and southern coasts are almost entirely made up of ice cliffs from Austfonna and Bråsvellbreen; this glacier front stretches from Kapp Laura in the northeast to Vibebukta in the south with a total length of about 190 kilometres, making it the longest glacier front in the northern hemisphere.

The glaciers of Nordaustland have a complex and not yet fully known history. There is evidence that at least some of them, for example Franklinbreane, were smaller several thousand years ago than they are today (see also section 6.15.5 *Isispynten, Austfonna, Bråsvellbreen*).

Amazing amounts of driftwood and plastic rubbish are lying on many beaches of northern Nordaustland, but substantial volumes of the latter have been removed by passengers of cruise ships who participated in the "Clean Up Svalbard" project in recent years.

Flora and fauna: The tundra is extremely barren and flowering plants are scarce, although there is a local abundance at favourable spots. The most common species are Svalbard poppy and various saxifrages, but 83 flowering plants have been found on Nordaustland up to 1999 (173 in Svalbard) and more may be found in the future. The inner fjord areas are more favourable to plant life than the outer coasts.

Lichens in particular are far better adapted to this extreme environment and cover large areas on the surface of many rocks, while algae can be found almost anywhere on wet tundra areas, forming a thin, inconspicuous blueish-black cover. The ability of algae to fix atmospheric nitrogen makes them an important factor for the terrestrial ecosystem.

This vegetation is enough to support a regional reindeer population, and occasional animals can be found in almost all ice-free areas. The fauna of the tundra in Nordaustland is not exactly rich in species: next to the Arctic fox, there are a few birds including Purple sandpiper, Snow bunting, Arctic skua, Rock ptarmigan and geese, but none of them is really abundant compared to other parts of Spitsbergen; some of these species are associated with the shoreline or the sea, but they are also seen on land.

There is a surprisingly large number of insect species on Nordaustland. At least five different spiders and 34 Collembola (Springtails. 49 in Svalbard) are creeping around under the rocks, but they are very small and only occur in small numbers of individuals.

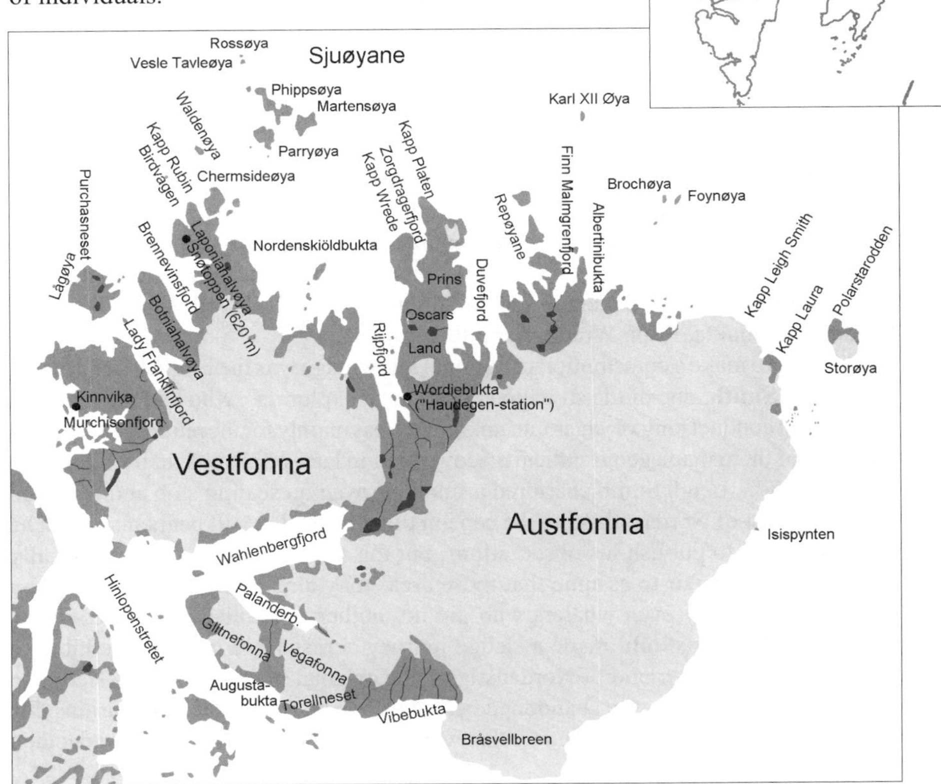

The sea is, as usual, by far the most productive part of the regional ecosystem, and many more species and individuals are found by the sea or near the coast than on shore, ranging from bird cliffs to seals, whales and Polar bears. There are many small bird cliffs in northern Nordaustland inhabited by Brünich's guillemots, Kittiwakes, Fulmars and Black guillemots, and locally also by Puffins and Ivory gulls; the latter only in small numbers and often far inland. Arctic terns and Arctic skuas breed on lowland areas, and there are at least two breeding sites of the very rare Sabine's gull.

Walrus regularly occupy several haulout sites during the summer, and Polar bears are constantly roaming along the rocky coast and over the drift ice.

History: The northeastern and eastern parts of Nordaustland were hardly visited and accordingly not well known until the early 20th century because of the difficult ice conditions, and even today these waters are inadequately charted, which makes navigation difficult. On the other hand, the early whalers soon got a general idea of the northwestern coasts and islands (Lågøya, Sjuøyane) that are more easily accessible due to the influence of the mild West-Spitsbergen current. The coastal waters have never been a classical whaling area, in contrast to the ice edge further north. This ice edge was often east and north of Sjuøyane, stretching from there to the southwest; the open water between the coast and the ice was commonly referred to as "Whalers' bay".

Some early expeditions including **Phipps** (1773) and **Parry** (1827) came through the area on the quest for highest latitudes, but the islands and land were only of secondary interest to them and the north coast of Nordaustland remained largely unknown.

One of the first scientific expeditions to produce some basic knowledge of the nature and geography of northern Nordaustland was the one led by the Swedish geologist **Otto Torell** in 1861; with him was, amongst others, **Adolf Erik Nordenskiöld**. The coast was roughly surveyed using a small, open boat, while the expedition ship remained in Spitsbergen. This brave voyage produced a first overview of the geology and topography of the areas visited (Brennevinsfjord, Beverlysund, Sjuøyane, Nordenskiöldbukta, Kapp Wrede, Kapp Platen).

The next to make a contribution to regional knowledge was the Englishman **Benjamin Leigh Smith**, one of the so-called "gentleman explorers", who had the financial resources to conduct long voyages into unknown areas mainly for the purpose of hunting, but some of them made geographical discoveries and later published their findings. In 1871 and 1873, Leigh Smith chartered a small Norwegian sealing ship and followed the north coast of Nordaustland to the cape in the far east that still bears his name; he left it to others to publish his observations, but this new knowledge was eventually made public. It is fair to assume that those areas may already have been visited by sealers and possibly even whalers who did not bother to publish their discoveries.

In 1873, **Nordenskiöld** made a sledge journey across large parts of the hitherto totally unknown hinterland of Nordaustland; the original plan had been to sledge to the North Pole, but this was abandoned before it even started because of various difficulties; amongst others, all reindeer that were to pull the sledges had wisely decided to escape well in advance.

The Swedish section of the **Arc-de-Meridian expedition** (1899-1902) made triangulations from Sjuøyane to Hinlopenstretet. Many cairns still remind one of the extensive and precise surveys of this successful expedition.

In 1928, this remote corner of the world attracted worldwide media and public attention when **Umberto Nobile** and the crew of his airship *Italia* crash-landed on the ice north of Nordaustland. A large number of expeditions with aircraft, ships and dog sledges were sent out from various countries to find Nobile and his men; some new details of geographical knowledge resulted, but there was of course no time for detailed surveys and the production of new charts.

During the spring of 1929, the Norwegian trapper **Karl Bengtssen** and two companions made a remarkable sledge journey from Lågøya to Kapp Leigh Smith and back, hoping to find some remains of the *Italia*. Apart from this, the region was much less used by trappers than Spitsbergen or Edgeøya, and several of the few winterings in northern Nordaustland resulted in catastrophes due to scurvy or shipwreck.

The first real scientific work in Nordaustland was carried out by **scientists from Oxford** who made several expeditions between 1921 and 1936, covering different scientific fields with a focus on glaciology; topographical surveys were also made in most parts of Nordaustland. The 1935-36 expedition even included a wintering with field stations in Brennevinsfjord ("Brandy Bay") and on the nearby ice cap Vestfonna, following the example that Alfred Wegener had set in 1929-30 with a wintering in central parts of the Greenland ice cap. Several remarkable sledge journeys were made over the whole island during this expedition.

Systematic aerial photography, the basis for modern topographic mapping, followed for the first time in 1938 as part of Norway's efforts to make topographic surveys of the whole archipelago.

Miscellaneous: Northern and eastern Nordaustland is an area where the effects of current climate change ("global warming") can be experienced directly. Well into the 1980s and early 1990s it was still relatively unusual to be able to sail around Nordaustland, but since the late 1990s, even Kvitøya east of Nordaustland has been reached in summer. This is an island that was always closed off by dense drift ice year-round in earlier years and if landings were possible at all, only in the late summer when the ice edge is usually at its furthest north. In 2006, the first landings on Kvitøya were being made as early as late June, and ice-strengthened ships (not icebreakers) were reaching 82°N at the same time – far north of the northernmost islands of Svalbard. One must not be tempted to derive a general trend from single situations in exceptional years; climate has always had pronounced short-term fluctuations and the ever-shifting ice conditions are certainly no exception. Dramatic variations from year to year have been known since men started to navigate these waters. It is to be hoped that the exceptionally ice-free summer of 2006 will remain an exception but, sadly, the opposite seems more likely.

6.15.1 Lady Franklinfjord, Brennevinsfjord, Lågøya

General: The northwestern fjords of Nordaustland, Lady Franklinfjord and Brennevinsfjord, are amongst the least visited areas in Svalbard because the few depth indications on nautical charts indicate dangerous shallows. The same is the case for the offshore island of Lågøya (53 sq km). Ships have to keep a distance of several nautical miles from Purchasneset, the northernmost tip of Lågøya, which means that the price to be paid for an excursion to this island is a long ride in a small boat through open waters. A very barren but individual landscape is the reward for those few who make it ashore on Lågøya. The region is part of the Nordaust Svalbard Nature Reserve and access may be restricted in the future. For map, see section 6.15 *Nordaustland* (page 357).

Placenames: Beverlysund/Birdvågen: After members of Parry's expedition in 1827. **Botniahalvøya:** After the northernmost part of the Baltic sea between Sweden and Finland ("Bottenhavet"). **Brennevinsfjord:** "Brandy bay", name in use since the 17th century, origin unknown, possibly to commemorate a booze-up amongst whalers or hunters. **Chermsideøya:** After a member of Leigh Smith's expedition. **Lady Franklinfjord**: Lady Jane F., second wife of the English polar explorer Sir John F., organised a number of relief expeditions after her husband had disappeared in the Northwest Passage in 1845 together with 129 men. **Franklinsund**: After Lady Jane Franklin's husband Sir John F. **Laponiahalvøya:** After a region in Sweden ("Lappland"). **Lågøya:** "Low island", descriptive name of this mostly flat island. **Purchasneset:** Samuel P. (1577-1626), English author of geographical literature. East of Brennevinsfjord, there are a number of placenames to commemorate Amundsen's expedition in 1925 that had to make an emergency landing after a failed attempt to fly to the North Pole (see section 5.6 *Attempts to fly to the pole: Virgohamna and Ny Ålesund*).

Geology: Weakly metamorphic sediments that are part of the basement (see section 6.15 *Nordaustland*) west of Lady Franklinfjord and Lågøya. Doleritic intrusions (Jurassic or lower Cretaceous) in northern and eastern parts of Lågøya; the northermost of their kind in Svalbard.

Botniahalvøya between Lady Franklinfjord and Brennevinsfjord consists of very old crystalline rocks, mostly granites (around one billion years old, "Grenville event") and some Mesozoic intrusions at the northern tip. There are also weakly metamorphosed lavas that date back to volcanic eruptions long ago (Mesoproterozoic, almost two billion years ago). These rocks are the only surviving evidence of this early volcanism, the volcanoes themselves having been eroded long ago.

Laponiahalvøya east of Brennevinsfjord consists largely of old granites and granitoid rocks (one billion years old, "Grenville event"). The youngest rocks of Laponiahalvøya are in northeastern parts of this peninsula and on Chermsideøya; these are Caledonian granites. Their age of "only" 400 million years has been obtained from complicated laboratory analysis and is not obvious in the field, of course.

Landscape: The landscape is mostly typical for the region, with low plateau-topped mountains. The northern slopes especially, which are exposed to the open sea, often fall steeply down to sea level. There are some extensive lowlands west of Lady Franklinfjord, and on Lågøya that owes its name to this landscape characteristic. This former coastal plain continues underwater: it is no deeper than 15 metres three miles north of Lågøya. The island is largely covered by raised beaches. In other places, solid rocks are exposed: coarse blocks in areas with dolerites (northeastern coast). Fascinating details can be found where the ground consists of basement quartzitic sediments, like rosette-shaped frost-patterned ground.

Lågøya has a large number of shallow lakes and lagoons, but no significant elevations and no glaciers. The nearby peninsulas of Nordaustland are unglaciated except for one outlet glacier of Vestfonna that reaches the shore in Lady Franklinfjord, and a local ice cap on Snøtoppen.

Flora and fauna: Barren polar desert, where mosses, lichens and algae are more prominent than flowering plants.

History: See section 6.15. *Nordaustland* for expeditions that visited the general area. The ice conditions around Lågøya are relatively light, at least compared to the other islands and coasts further east. Lågøya has thus been visited relatively frequently by different expeditions, but all of them went their ways after short excursions. Norwegian **trappers** have hardly ever used the area, and only two winterings are known, one of which ended in a catastrophe. There is a decaying hut standing near the eastern tip of Lågøya that was built in 1908 by Norwegian trappers. This trio caught 30 Polar bears during the following winter. Their nearest neighbours were four Norwegian trappers who wintered at Kapp Rubin in Beverlysund, about 30 kilometres further east, and when the Lågøya party went to visit their neighbours in the spring of 1909, they were shocked to find all four dead from scurvy. Insufficient provisions and equipment and lack of experience often contributed to such tragic events. Several diaries were found, and it was written that the leader of the party at Kapp Rubin, a certain Sivertsen, had occasionally locked his companions in the hut while he was hunting. The use of meat for meals was possible only with special permission from their hard-hearted boss, despite successful hunting.

The Sivertsen-hut in Beverlysund near Kapp Rubin played an important rule during another polar adventure only a few years later, in 1913, that could also easily have taken a tragic course. The German journalist **Theodor Lerner** had organised his own relief expedition for the surviving members of the Schröder-Stranz expedition, who were marooned in Sorgfjord (see section 5.5 *Early expeditions and science*). In Sorgfjord, Lerner learned that a Norwegian relief expedition had beaten them to it and so decided to continue towards Nordaustland in a search for Schröder-Stranz who had disappeared during a sledge expedition that had been launched in Nordenskiöldbukta during the previous summer of 1912. Lerner's ship was wrecked near Kapp Rubin, and the expedition spent several weeks in the Sivertsen hut until the ice conditions allowed the voyage back to Spitsbergen in a life boat. Attempts in 2005 to find Lerner's ship have not been successful.

An English scientific **expedition from Oxford** wintered in 1935-36 in Brennevinsfjord. The main hut was at Depotodden near the fjord's entrance under the mountain Snøtoppen, and another hut was built in the inner fjord near a glacier that provided access to the ice cap. The latter hut, together with another that was used by trappers in 1908-09, was destroyed in 1944 by a German submarine that transported men and materials of the "Haudegen" war weather station to Rijpfjord (see section *Nordenskiöldbukta, Rijpfjord, Duvefjord*).
Roald Amundsen had to land near Brennevinsfjord together with five other men on board a seaplane after their emergency landing at almost 88°N during a failed attempt to fly to the North Pole. The men were soon rescued by a Norwegian sealing vessel (see section 5.6 *Attempts to fly to the pole: Virgohamna and Ny Ålesund*).

6.15.2 Sjuøyane

General: Sjuøyane is a small archipelago north of Nordaustland. Vesle Tavleøya and the little skerry Rossøya are the northernmost islands in Svalbard. Rossøya is located at 80°50'N, which is 9°10' = 550 minutes of latitude = 550 nautical miles = 550 x 1.852 km = 1,018 kilometres = 633 statute miles from the North Pole, 1,074 kilometres north of Nordkapp (north cape) of Norway (71°10'N) and 1,650 kilometres north of the arctic circle (66°34'N).

Sjuøyane translates as "Seven islands", but the exact number of islands depends on how you count. There are nine islands including Waldenøya that lies some miles away from the main islands of Sjuøyane to the west, not counting smaller rocks and skerries. The largest islands are Phippsøya (26 sq km), Martensøya (19 sq km) and Parryøya (18 sq km). The northernmost islands, Vesle Tavleøya and Rossøya, hardly allow any landings due to the steep terrain. Landings are possible on beaches in most bays of the larger islands, but it takes some luck to set foot (or even two) on one of the northernmost islands of Svalbard. The weather is often bad or the shore is blocked by ice or the beach is occupied by a Polar bear or ... it is amazing how many things can go "wrong" in these difficult latitudes. Another difficulty lies in the badly charted waters, and long, cold small boat rides are always necessary. Sjuøyane are part of the Nordaust Svalbard Nature Reserve; access may be restricted in the future. For map, see section 6.15 *Nordaustland* (page 357).
Most **placenames** were given in 1861 by Otto Torell and Adolf Erik Nordenskiöld, after persons who had been in the area during previous expeditions. The following islands were named after members of **Phipps**' expedition (1773): **Nelsonøya**: Horatio N. (1758-1805), midshipman destined to become more than a little famous. **Phippsøya**: John P. (1744-92), commander. **Waldenøya**: John W., midshipman, surveyed the island that was then named after him.

The following islands were named after members of **Parry**'s expedition (1827): **Parryøya**: William Edward P. (1780-1855), commander. **Rossøya**: James Clark R. (1800-1862), who was later to become a famous polar explorer himself.

Other names: **Martensøya**: Friedrich M., ship's doctor from Hamburg who visited Spitsbergen on a whaling ship in 1671 and subsequently published the first accurate description of Spitsbergen's nature. **Tavleøya** ("Table island") and **Vesle Tavleøya** ("Little Table island") are descriptive names and refer to the flat-topped mountains.

Geology: Caledonian and older granites, migmatites and strongly metamorphic rocks with, in addition, many crystalline erratic boulders from Nordaustland; altogether a nice, colourful open-air museum of the regional geology.

Landscape: See also section 6.15 *Nordaustland*. The typical Nordaustland landscape is also widely represented on Sjuøyane with plateaux at elevations between 300 and 400 metres, the highest being 465 metres on Phippsøya. The plateau is frequently cut by steep slopes that fall down to the sea or end in coastal plains which are covered by old raised beaches, usually coarse gravel and stones. It is easy to imagine that Sjuøyane consisted of a much larger number of smaller islands about 12,000 years ago, when post-glacial isostatic land uplift was just about to begin and the land surface was more than 100 metres lower relative to sea level. Only today's mountains were above water, and the coastal flats were at depths of around 100 metres. Subsequent isostatic land uplift has left wide series of raised beaches on all of today's coastal plains, which now are often cut by well-developed ice wedges.

The little island of Nelsonøya has a column-shaped, flat-topped mountain about 140 metres high that looks like a top hat from a certain perspective.

The larger islands are quite similar to each other, landscape-wise. There are no glaciers on Sjuøyane.

Flora and fauna: High arctic. The tundra is very barren, and flowering plants have mostly given way to mosses and lichens. Occasional patches with a favourable microclimate can have a surprisingly rich vegetation of Svalbard poppy, saxifraga species and other plants.

Seabirds are breeding on some of the steeper cliffs. A faunal highlight is a small colony of Ivory gulls on top of a mountain on Sjuøyane. Vesle Tavleøya has the northernmost breeding colony of Puffins in the Atlantic; it is a bit of a surprise to see these colourful Alkets flying around in this high-arctic environment, often with drift ice in the background. If there is ice around, it is always worth keeping a look-out and having binoculars ready; high arctic wildlife, including large mammals, is never far away in this area, and rare gulls such as Pomarine skua, Ivory gull or even Sabine's gull are sometimes seen. First prize would undoubtedly be a sighting of the extremely rare Ross' gull, but don't expect it …

History: Expeditions commemorated in the placenames have been to the area, but were mostly not particularly interested in these islands, which were surveyed by **Torell** and **Nordenskiöld** in 1861 and more accurately by the **Arc-de-Meridian expedition** (1899-1902).

At the first sight of the small jagged island of Waldenøya, it is hard to believe that several expeditions have spent time there, including Walter Wellman whose ship sank in 1894 not too far away. This did not keep Wellman from hoping that he could reach the North Pole during the same summer, but he had to return to Waldenøya until he was rescued.

6.15.3 Nordenskiöldbukta, Rijpfjord, Duvefjord

General: This is the central part of the north coast of Nordaustland with several long fjords. The waters are badly charted and have shallows, so navigation is accordingly difficult. This applies especially to the western half of Nordenskiöldbukta and the whole coast east of Duvefjord. The area is part of the Nordaust Svalbard Nature Reserve; access may be restricted in the future. For map, see section 6.15 *Nordaustland* (page 357).

Placenames: Albertinibukta: Gianni A. (born 1902), member of a relief expedition during the *Italia* catastrophe in 1928. **Duvefjord**: "Dove bay", name given in the early 18th century, origin unknown. **Finn Malmgrenfjord**: F. M. (1895-1928), lost member of Nobile's expedition. **Kapp Wrede:** Fabian Jacob W. (1802-93), Swedish officer and scientist. **Repøyane**: Outger R. (17th/18th centuries), Dutch whaling Captain. **Rijpfjord**: Jan Cornelisz R., member of all of Willem Barents' expeditions. **Wordiebukta**: James Mann W. (1889-1962), English geologist and polar explorer. **Zorgdragerfjord:** Cornelis Gisberts Z., Dutch whaling Captain and chronist.

Geology: See also section 6.15 *Nordaustland.* Granitic rocks on Laponiahalvøya west of Nordenskiöldbukta, around one billion years old ("Grenville event"). Weakly metamorphic, upper Proterozoic sediments west of Rijpfjord and east of Nordenskiöldbukta. Reddish Caledonian granites on the east side and around the head of Rijpfjord.

Landscape: Rocky and barren (see section 6.15 *Nordaustland*). There are no glaciers near the coast except for an outlet glacier of the ice cap, Austfonna, that drains into Duvefjord.

Flora and fauna: See section 6.15 *Nordaustland.*

History: There are two "historical highlights" in addition to those expeditions that have visited the general area (see section 6.15 *Nordaustland*): The ill-fated German Schröder-Stranz expedition and the German weather station "Haudegen" from the Second World War (see also relevant sections in chapter 5. *History*).

The **Schröder-Stranz expedition** in 1912/13 was officially called "Die Deutsche Arktische Expedition" ("The German Arctic Expedition"). In August 1912, its leader Herbert Schröder-Stranz ventured, together with three other men, dogs, sledges and boats, on a journey that was hazardous rather than brave, with the purpose of crossing Nordaustland and then meeting the expedition ship *Herzog Ernst* in Spitsbergen (!). The sledge party with Schröder-Stranz left the *Herzog Ernst* at 80°25'N/21°15'E, in the middle of Nordenskiöldbukta, in dense drift ice. Nothing has ever been seen of the four men since; some bits and pieces of equipment are all that was found scattered on the coast of Nordaustland in the following decades. Several attempts have been made in recent years to reveal the secrets; the details of the last weeks and days. The most significant discovery may be remains of a camp in inner Duvefjord where one person died; the camp could be identified as part of the Schröder-Stranz expedition.

In September 1944, a German submarine and a Norwegian boat brought a naval meteorological detachment, led by **Wilhelm Dege,** to Wordiebukta in innermost Rijpfjord. This remote site had been chosen to protect the weather station, code name "**Haudegen**" (something like "warhorse") as usual derived from the name of the station commander. Additional depots were established in inner Wahlenbergfjord, Albertinibukta and in inner Duvefjord, and coded meteorological reports were sent four times every day to Norway. After the end of the war, "Haudegen" continued to send its weather data uncoded, and mine belts and hand grenades were destroyed. Geographer Dege used the remaining time for excursions and scientific work, until the party was picked up by a Norwegian boat that reached Rijpfjord on 03 September 1945. The "Haudegen" detachment was the last German military unit officially to surrender (on 04 September 1945) after the end of the war; an event the men had been looking forward to, given the uncertainty about their future.

The main building of the "Haudegen" station, a "Hartpapier-Hütte" ("hard paper hut"), is still in relatively good condition, the only war weather station in Svalbard that is still standing. It is subject to general strict regulation to protect the cultural heritage in Svalbard and it is highly important to exercise great care when moving around in the former station area in order to prevent further damage. Make sure you do not step on any objects; it cannot be excluded that there is still ammunition or unexploded ordnance somewhere around. Stricter rules, including a complete ban on traffic, may be imposed in the future, although the remoteness of the site and the badly charted waters provide a good degree of protection; the frequency of visits does not compare with other important historical sites such as Virgohamna or Smeerenburg.

6.15.4 Karl XII Øya, Brochøya, Foynøya

General: The end of the world! It is hard to imagine anything more remote than these small islands. The surrounding waters are not well charted, as usual in this region. The islands are part of the Nordaust Svalbard Nature Reserve; there are plans to introduce access restrictions in the future. For map, see section 6.15 *Nordaustland* (page 357).

Placenames: Brochøya: Ole Jacob B. (1818-1889), Norwegian mathematician and politician. **Foynøya**: Svend F. (1809-1894), Norwegian entrepeneur, invented the explosive harpoon that made industrial whaling of large whales possible. **Karl XII Øya**: King of Sweden (1682-1718).

Geology: Metamorphic basement rocks, partly Caledonian, partly older (which does not make a visible difference).

Landscape: Foynøya is the largest of these islands, with a mere ten sq km. Brochøya and Foynøya are massive, rounded rock ridges that rise steeply and inhospitably from the sea. There are no beaches or bays on these islands.

The northern part of Karl XII Øya is a steep rock tower, connected to a low gravel ridge that stretches to the south. Karl XII Øya was a little archipelago of two separate islands in the late 19th century, between which a gravel ridge has since grown; a so-called "tombolo". The mass of driftwood found on these islands is quite surprising.

Flora and fauna: There is hardly any vegetation; Brochøya and Foynøya especially are completely barren and there is hardly any "stationary" wildlife apart from a little Arctic tern colony and a few breeding black Guillemots, Little auks and Fulmars on Foynøya. A small Kittiwake colony is breeding on the rock tower at the northern end of Karl XII Øya.

History: Karl XII Øya was seen in 1861 by **Torell** and **Nordenskiöld**. The first known sightings of Foyn- and Brochøya were made ten years later by the Englishman **Benjamin Leigh Smith**. It can be assumed that all islands had previously been seen by sealers, but these observations have not been published.

These three islands would be totally unknown remote rocks in the sea, if **Umberto Nobile**'s airship ***Italia*** had not crashed north of Karl XII Øya, at approximately 81°14'N/25°25'E, on the way back from the North Pole to Ny Ålesund on 25 May 1928 (see section 5.6 *Attempts to fly to the pole: Virgohamna and Ny Ålesund*). Six men disappeared, together with part of the airship, and another was found dead on the ice after the crash. Two men, including Nobile, had suffered fractures. The nine remaining (including the two injured) collected all useful bits and pieces of equipment they could find on the ice near the crash site and made themselves comfortable as much as they could. The story of their camp was to become famous as the "Red Tent", due to the colour of their airy accommodation that was far too small for the whole group. Land was seen on 30 May, most likely Foynøya. A group of three men decided to walk over the ice to reach land, but it is doubtful what the three, the two Italians Zappi and Mariano and the Swede **Finn Malmgreen** who had been meteorologist and second in command of the expedition, were hoping to find on this uninhabited coast. Zappi and Mariano were later rescued by the Soviet icebreaker *Krassin*, but Malmgren had disappeared under highly disputed circumstances. A Swedish airplane managed to land near the "Red Tent" on 23 June and evacuated the injured Nobile and his little doggy Titina, but the airplane crashed during the second landing attempt and the pilot was then also stuck with the remaining Italians on the ice. During all these weeks, the ice had been drifting, first towards Foynøya and then further to the east, until the remaining men were finally picked up by the Soviet icebreaker *Krassin* at 80°38'N/29°13'E on 12 July, after 49 days on the ice. Amongst many relief expeditions was a dog sledge party with the Dutch Josef van Dongen and the Italian Gennaro Sora, who finally became stuck on Foynøya on 04 July; they were rescued on 13 July by a Swedish seaplane.

6.15.5 Isispynten, Austfonna, Bråsvellbreen

General: The east and south of Nordaustland is mostly covered by the ice cap Austfonna that, together with the adjacent ice cap Vegafonna, occupies approximately 8,450 sq km; combined, they are thus amongst the largest glacial systems outside Greenland and Antarctica. The coastline is mostly dominated by the calving ice cliff of Austfonna, interrupted only by a few rock outcrops in the northeast. The total length of the ice cliff is nearly 190 kilometres, which makes it the longest glacier front in the northern hemisphere. Few crevasses are visible on the surface of Austfonna, but torrential summer rivers of meltwater flow in deeply incised channels towards the ice cliff, from which they fall in some places, for example Bråsvellbreen, as grand waterfalls.
Bråsvellbreen is the southern part of Austfonna, forming a separate drainage system to transport ice from central parts towards the coast from the ice cap, with ice velocities above average. Bråsvellbreen looks just like any other part of Austfonna, but it is the part that is most often approached by ships, as the shallow waters south and east of Nordaustland are better charted here and the waterfalls that fall down the 10 to 25 metres high ice cliff provide extra excitement. The coastal waters in the east and northeast of Nordaustland are almost uncharted. The area is part of the Nordaust Svalbard Nature Reserve. For map, see section 6.15 *Nordaustland* (page 357).
Placenames: Austfonna: "East ice cap". **Bråsvellbreen:** "brå" (Norwegian) = sudden, "svell" = swell. Bråsvellbreen made a very sudden and pronounced advance in 1937-38, a so-called surge. **Isispynten:** after a river that runs through Oxford, name given by an expedition from Oxford in 1935/36.
Geology: Metamorphic and magmatic basement rocks, mostly granite and different gneisses, with relatively little bedrock exposed.
Landscape: Only those few square kilometres of ice-free land that have recently been exposed from the slowly retreating glacial coastline have some "landscape" in a stricter sense. Isispynten was a peninsula that was connected to the ice cap well into the 1990s, but it is now a separate island that can be circumnavigated in small boats because the ice cliff has retreated; Isispynten's surface area may be in the order of one square kilometre. It consists largely of fresh moraines, muddy if wet, and generally rocky with a colourful selection of erratic boulders – a nice open-air display of the regional geology that is otherwise not accessible. The geomorphology of Isispynten is typical for fresh moraines, with little ponds and mudholes, and this young landscape is not yet stable, as is evident from frequent small landslips on steep slopes, which often expose dead ice – old, inactive glacier ice, that still makes up most of the volume of Isispynten. It follows that there are several options for the future development of Isispynten: it is possible that only a flat island of sand, gravel and some boulders will be left after a few centuries, when the remaining dead ice has disappeared. Alternatively, nothing will be left because global sea level will have risen so much that Isispynten becomes a part of the shallow sea floor. Thirdly, nothing may be left because Austfonna could advance again and bury Isispynten once more under the ice cap, where it has been for millenia in the past.

Miscellaneous: The current state and future development of the ice cap is not exactly known and is the subject of current research. Scientific activities have increased during the IPY (International Polar Year) 2007/08 and international scientists are working with different methods to reveal the secrets of Austfonna's past, present and future. It is known that the margins have retreated slightly during recent decades, but the retreat has so far been much less pronounced compared to many other glaciers in Svalbard. There is an indication of increasing surface elevations in the central parts of Austfonna, indicating a balanced or slightly positive mass budget. The reasons for, and significance of this observation are not yet fully understood; it could be due to long-term growth or a sign of very rapid advance ("surge") in the future.

The moraine island of Isispynten with Austfonna in the background.

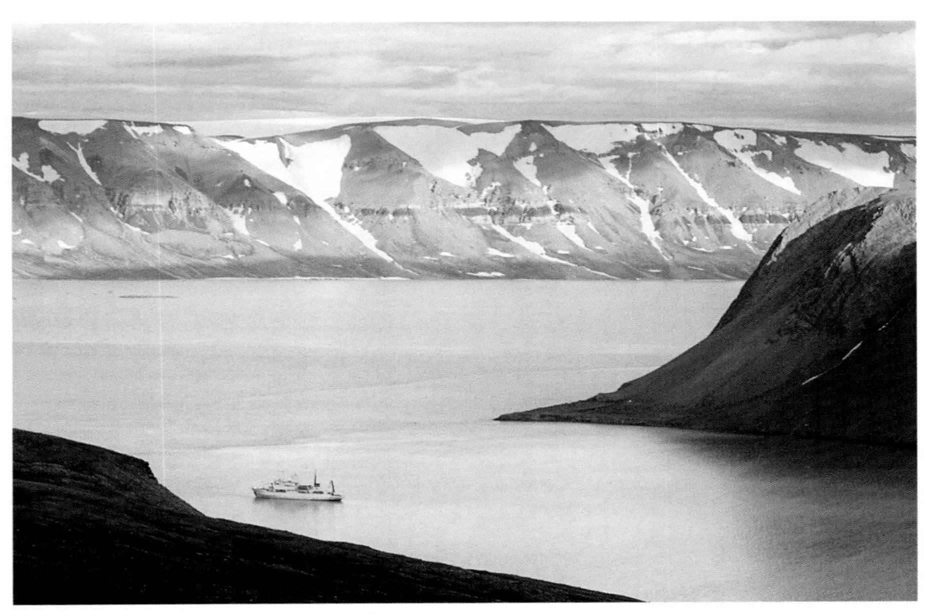

6.14.2-1: Lomfjord, with Faksevågen in the foreground.

6.14.2-2: Faksevågen, a side branch of Lomfjord.

6.14.3-1: Alkefjellet, a colony of Brünich's guillemots in Hinlopenstretet.

6.14.3-2: Brünich's guillemots at Alkefjellet.

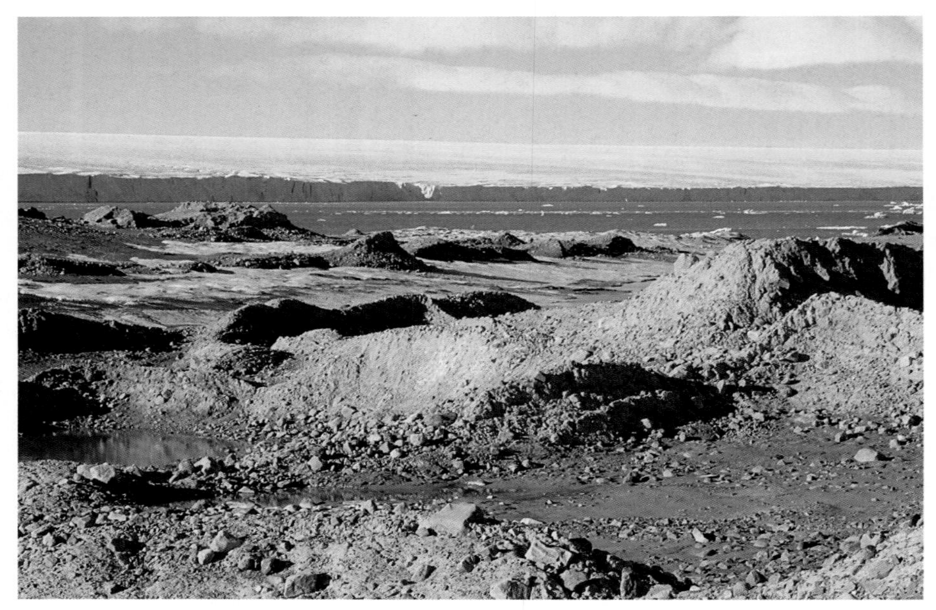

6.15.5-3: The moraine island Isispynten.

6.16-1: Storøya.

6.16-2: Andrée-memorial on Kvitøya.

6.17: Svenskøya, Kong Karls Land.

6.18.1: Agardhdalen at the east coast of Spitsbergen.

6.18.2-1: Freemansund with Barentsøya in the background.

6.18.2-2: Freemanbreen in 1960, shortly after a surge.
Photo: Horst-Günter Wagner.

6.18.2-3: Freemanbreen in 2005.

6.18.2-4: Sundneset, Barentsøya.

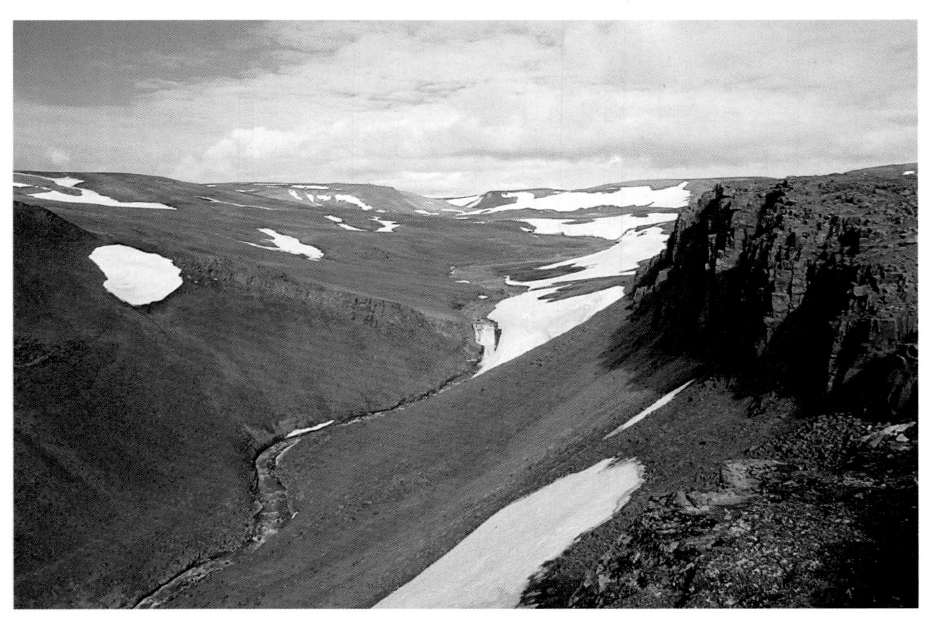

6.18.2-5: Inland of Barentsøya near Sundneset.

6.16 Storøya, Kvitøya

"Giles Land was glittering white from its highest summit down to the very edge of the sea. It was covered throughout with its soft mantle of snow; not a rock projected through it to break its spotless purity. The island rose in regular curves to an altitude of 600 or 700 feet, and was one continuous mass of ice and snow. ... With the sun shining upon it White Island (Giles Island) must be a fascinating object."

Alfred G. Nathorst, *Geographical Journal* August 1899

General: These two islands are east of Nordaustland, in the remotest part of Svalbard. The name "Storøya" means "Great island", which was either a joke or a mistake, considering the size of 40 sq km and its position next to the much larger Nordaustland. The name Kvitøya which means "White island" is well justified in view of the ice cap that covers 99 % of the approximately 700 sq km island. "Officially", there are three small patches of ice-free land on Kvitøya: Andréeneset in the west, Hornodden in the southeast and Kræmerpynten in the east. The latter one is the easternmost part of Svalbard. Storøya and Kvitøya have been closed off by dense drift ice throughout the whole summer in most years until the late 20th century. This has changed dramatically and further changes have to be expected (see *Miscellaneous* in section 6.15 *Nordaustland*), but you still need luck to be able to make a landing on one of these islands. Drift ice is always around and can block the shore; neither Kvitøya nor Storøya have protected bays, which means good weather and calm seas are necessary for landings. The waters are partly shallow and not well charted.

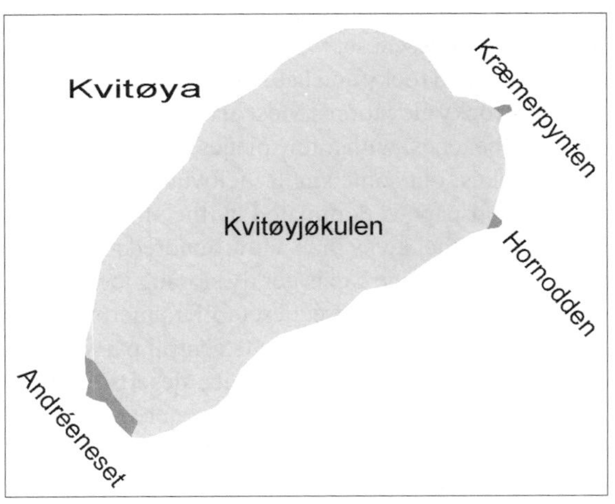

Great care is needed ashore. Polar bears may be present even if you cannot see any; there may be one behind a rock and it has happened many times on these islands that landings have had to be aborted and everybody evacuated in a rush, because a bear has suddenly appeared uncomfortably close by. In 2006, a Polar bear unfortunately had to be shot in self defence by the armed guides of a tourist group on Storøya; the bear was hungry and about to attack and it was shot from a distance of about ten metres.

Next to the high-arctic scenery and chances for wildlife, it is the dramatic history of Kvitøya that fascinates visitors. Both islands are part of the Nordaust Svalbard Nature Reserve; access may be restricted in the future. For map of Storøya, see 6.15 *Nordaustland* (page 357).

Placenames: Andréeneset: after Salomon August A., see *history* further down in this section. **Hornodden:** after Gunnar H., a Norwegian polar explorer, early 20th century. **Kræmerpynten:** Waldemar Kræmer, Norwegian trapper (see section 6.7.4 *Fair Haven, Fuglefjord, Sallyhamna*). **Kvitøya:** "White island", descriptive name referring to the ice cap that covers most of the island. **Storøya:** "Great island".

Geology: Basement rocks. Gabbro on Storøya and on the east side of Kvitøya. Andréeneset consists of a varied mixture of reddish migmatite and dark gneiss with many light-coloured intrusions. The rocks on Andréeneset are probably very old and date into the Mesoproterozoic (more than one billion years); future research is intended to throw some more light on the complex history of these rocks.

Landscape: Both Storøya and Kvitøya are mostly ice covered. **Storøya** has approximately five sq km of ice-free land at the north tip of the island. The appearance is rather dark due to the colour of the rocks. The ice free land is mostly flat with very low rocky elevations and an extensive series of ancient raised beaches – a topography that provides many little depressions where wildlife may be hidden, hence great care is generally needed when landing on Storøya and Kvitøya. The coastal plain has many small ponds and is gently rising towards the shallow dome-shaped ice cap. The coast has some open bays that are separated by small rocky points.

The largest ice free land on **Kvitøya** is Andréeneset with about five sq km at the western point of the island. The coast is low and rocky and has several rocky shallows. The terrain is almost level with only small rocky elevations. Most of the plain is covered by marine gravel and stones from raised beaches, with a few pieces of old driftwood or whalebones in places. There are no lakes, but some small meltwater streams run across the land towards the coast. The landscape is dominated by the almost 700 sq km ice cap Kvitøyjøkulen, which is never further away than a few hundred meters, no matter where you are on shore. The margin of the ice cap is gently sloping ice without the slightest trace of a moraine. The distance from Andréeneset to Kræmerpynten is 40 kilometres across the ice cap, which is 410 metres high in its central parts.

Flora and fauna: Both Storøya and Kvitøya are mostly dead ice deserts, and the ice free areas hardly deserve to be called tundra. Vegetation is extremely scarce and consists mostly of lichens and mosses, the latter being quite lush by small streams. The red colour of some mosses is due to a lack of certain nutrients. Mosses are generally very vulnerable to footsteps, so please avoid stepping on them. Both islands have breeding Arctic terns and the next Polar bear is never far away, even if it is not in sight at the moment.

History: Legend has it that a mysterious "Giles Land" was sighted for the first time in 1707, somewhere northeast of Nordaustland, by the Dutchman **Cornelis Giles**. "Giles Land" (several spellings exist) has since then appeared on various maps with different shapes and sizes and in different positions. In the late 19th century, when the ice conditions slowly became a bit easier, Norwegian sealing ships ventured to sail to northeastern Svalbard and Franz Josef Land and brought back some first-hand information of the geography, even though most of the newly acquired knowledge was never published or was inaccurate. "Giles Land" must be Kvitøya, as there is no other land near the position where the elusive island was marked on old maps, although it could be a mirage mistaken for an island – a rather common phenomenon in the ice. Even today, many maps wrongly show Kvitøya with a very long and narrow shape; the real shape is half as wide as it is long.

Kvitøya became famous in 1930 when the remains of Salomon August Andrées last camp were found. Andrée had left from Virgohamna, together with two companions in the balloon *Örnen* ("Eagle"), in an attempt to reach the North Pole. The balloon crash-landed on the ice after a difficult flight, somewhere near 82°56'N, almost due north of Andréeneset but at a distance of more 300 kilometres. The three men tried to walk over the ice to Franz Josef Land, but the currents took the ice further west, and they finally landed on the west side of Kvitøya on 05 October 1897 after an extremely strenuous forced march. They died there after a few weeks.

A number of relief expeditions were sent in subsequent years to many parts of the Arctic to look for the Andrée expedition, but their last camp was only discovered in 1930 by chance, when a Norwegian expedition led by **Gunnar Horn** on the way to Franz Josef Land to build a weather station, made a landing on Kvitøya. Faced with the sensational discovery, Horn decided to cancel the voyage to Franz Josef Land, and the bodies and most items were soon brought back to Sweden, where the brave deceased received a state funeral in Stockholm; the news quickly went through the press and around the globe. Some of the photographic plates could still be developed after 33 years on Kvitøya. The site was visited again by another Swedish expedition on board the *Quest* to secure further items; the *Quest* men did not miss the opportunity to erect a simple, small concrete memorial to themselves which can still be seen next to the larger concrete block that was erected in memory of Salomon August Andrée, Knut Frænkel and Nils Strindberg, who had died just a few metres away. The site has been investigated again in recent years, and it is believed that there are now no artefacts remaining, related to Andrée.

It is hard to imagine a more desolate place for a desperate attempt to survive an arctic winter than the barren plain of Andréeneset on the almost completely glaciated island of Kvitøya. A little museum in Gränna, Andrée's birth place in Sweden, is dedicated to the memory of the expedition.

6.17 Kong Karls Land

"*Some fifty-five miles east of Barendsz Land and twenty-five miles south of North-East Land is a group of rather large islands properly called Wiches Land, but now generally known as King Carl's Land. These we had the rare good fortune to approach very closely, a thing seldom possible.*"

Martin Conway, *The First Crossing of Spitsbergen*

General: Kong Karls Land is a small archipelago in easternmost Svalbard, separated from Nordaustland by the 75 kilometres wide Erik Eriksenstretet (-strait) and from Spitsbergen, Barentsøya and Edgeøya by the 100 kilometres wide Olgastretet. The main islands are (from west to east) Svenskøya (136 sq km), Kongsøya (191 sq km) and Abeløya (13 sq km). Kong Karls Land is part of the Nordaust Svalbard Nature Reserve. Beyond this, they enjoy special protection because of their importance for the regional Polar bear population: there is a year-round ban on all traffic within 500 metres of the nearest part of the shoreline (this includes even the smallest rock above water). Kong Karls Land has, as a consequence, no tourist interest as landings are not possible and there is not a lot to see from a distance. Tourist ships normally only happen to come near these forbidden islands if there is "good" ice (not too open, not too close) in the area.

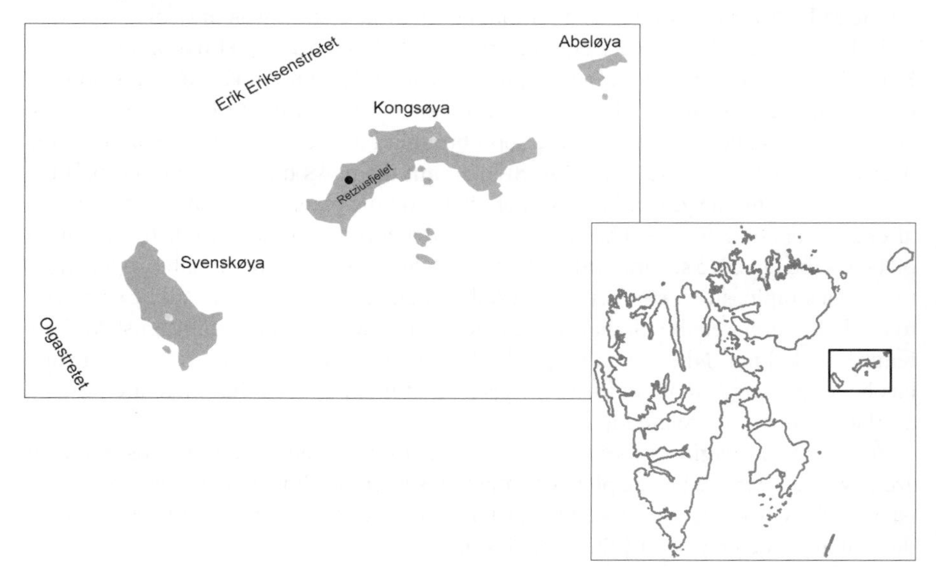

Placenames: Abeløya: Niels Henrik A. (1802-29), Norwegian mathematician. **Erik Eriksenstretet**: E. E., see *history* further down this section. **Kong Karls Land** (earlier also called Wiches Land), after Karl I. (1823-91) of Württemberg, name given by the German geographer August Petermann in 1871. Only some years later, the name has been changed in Norway to commemorate Karl XV (1826-72), king of Norway and Sweden – in other words, the name was changed from Kong Karls Land to Kong Karls Land. Really! **Kongsøya**: "King's island". **Olgastretet**: Olga (1822-92), Queen of Württemberg, wife of Karl I. of Württemberg. **Svenskøya**: "Swedish island".

Geology: Horizontal layers of sediments (sandstone, siltstone, shale) from the upper Triassic to the lower Cretaceous with dioritic intrusions. Unusually for Svalbard, the Mesozoic volcanic activity not only produced intrusions, but also surface volcanism that created tuff and lava with flow structures, indicating subaerial cooling of lava flows.

Landscape: There are wide coastal plains on all islands in Kong Karls Land, and the small island of Abeløya is completely flat. The coastal plains are mostly covered with coarse gravel from raised beach ridges. Svenskøya and Kongsøya have plateau-topped mountains that reach elevations between 200 and 300 metres. The highest elevation is Retziusfjellet on Kongsøya at 320 metres.

The Mesozoic sediments are poorly solidified and weather quickly into fine-grained soft sediment that is prone to solifluction. There are no glaciers in Kong Karls Land, but some permanent firn snow fields.

Flora and fauna: The cold waters of the East-Spitsbergen current wash the coasts of Kong Karls Land year-round and bring masses of heavy drift ice for most of the year. The ecosystem is accordingly high arctic, and the tundra is barren polar desert where mosses and lichens thrive better than flowering plants. The steeper slopes are home to several Kittiwake colonies, and Kong Karls Land has the largest breeding population of Ivory gulls in Svalbard, a species that clearly indicates (and depends on) high arctic conditions.

It is the very high density of Polar bear dens that give Kong Karls Land biological importance beyond Svalbard. It is one of the favourite areas for female bears to give birth to their offspring, and one den neighbours the next on the slopes on Svenskøya and Kongsøya. The highest density has been observed on Kongsøya with up to 10 dens per square kilometre. This means that a large proportion of the Polar bears in the northeast Atlantic is born in Kong Karls Land.

History: Kong Karls Land was probably seen for the first time in the early 17th century and was called Wiches Land. The discovery was of no importance to whalers and other arctic seafarers and was soon forgotten again. The islands were seen on several occasions, from areas further west, in the middle of the 19th century. This created some confusion, as this newly sighted land was, by some geographers, believed to be the elusive "Giles Land" (see section 6.16 *Storøya, Kvitøya*) and appeared on various maps in fantastic sizes and shapes. The Norwegian sealing Captain Erik Eriksen made the first known landing on the westernmost island (Svenskøya) in 1859, and more and more sealing ships came into the area in the following years. The first scientific expedition that visited Kong Karls Land was Nathorst's in 1898; the main purpose of which was to find the missing Andrée expedition (see section 6.16 *Storøya, Kvitøya*).

News about the high Polar bear density in Kong Karls Land spread quickly amongst Norwegian sealers, but difficult ice conditions prevented hunters from reaching these inaccessible islands, and fears about the risk of ice preventing a group from being picked up, probably kept trappers away from Kong Karls Land. It was not until 1908 that six trappers from Tromsø built a hut at Kapp Hammerfest at the southern end of Svenskøya. Their bag was no less than 90 Polar bears during the following winter and spring, including 21 living young bears. In 1909, the group could not be picked up because dense ice closed the islands off for the whole summer and, in early September when a second wintering seemed almost unavoidable, necessaties were packed into a small boat and pulled over the floes. After a forced march of one week, the six reached the octagonal hut at Kapp Lee on Edgeøya, rested for three days and then rowed 24 hours across Storfjord, finally making another forced march from Agardhbukta at the east coast of Spitsbergen to Longyearbyen – not without some detours due to lack of geographical knowledge (it is hard enough if you know the route and have all the equipment you need). After 18 days, the group finally arrived at Longyearbyen.

Miscellaneous: For centuries, Kong Karls Land has been largely unknown because of the large masses of heavy drift ice that surrounded the islands for twelve months of the year. These heavy ice conditions are also the main reason, as well as the presence of suitable terrain, for Kong Karls Land's exceptional importance for the regional Polar bear population. As elsewhere in northeastern Svalbard, ice conditions have been changing dramatically in recent years (see also *Miscellaneous* in section 6.15 *Nordaustland*). Consequences for the regional ecosystem including the bears have been subject to scientific work and many educated guesses, but it must be assumed that the environment, as we know it, will deteriorate. While we are waiting to see what the future brings, we may as well do something to keep the man-made component of climate change as small as possible (see also chapter 7 7. *Arctic environmental problems and tourism*).

6.18 Southeastern Svalbard

"I saw Foul bay and Wybe Jans Water, the quantities of ice upon the sea, all glittering in sunshine; and then, on the remote horizon, the snow-decked mountain front of Edges land, ... We ran down the moraines, and were at once on the swampy flat that fills the head of Foul (Agardhs) bay. A stream was waded, and we walked far out on to the flat to an amorphous region that was half land, half water. Stranded icebergs in the bay looked upon us over the mud-flat. We had crossed to the east coast for the first time on record. I leave you to imagine our satisfaction."

Martin Conway, *The First Crossing of Spitsbergen*

General: The landscape of southeastern Svalbard is very different in character from most parts of the west and north coasts of Spitsbergen, apart from those areas in central Spitsbergen with similar geology. The waters east of Spitsbergen have the heaviest **ice conditions** in Svalbard, due to the cold East-Spitsbergen current that brings cold water and ice from the Polar ocean.

Spitsbergen is separated from Edgeøya and Barentsøya by the 200 km long **Storfjord** ("Great fjord"), which is 150 kilometres wide at its mouth. Strictly speaking, Storfjord is a sound rather than a fjord, as it communicates with the open sea further east via a very small channel (Heleysund/Ormholet) in the north and a larger one in the east (Freemansund).

Storfjord is very important for **regional ice formation**, which starts as soon as the surface water layer has cooled sufficiently in the winter to allow freezing. The young ice will be repeatedly blown out of Storfjord to the south by northerly winds, leaving a large area of open water which then freezes again. A lot of ice is generated during the freezing season as this process is repeated over and over. A "lot of ice" is a bit theoretical, since new ice is only formed once older ice has disappeared; this gives a cumulative thickness with a theoretical value that is much higher than the maximum thickness actually reached. The cumulated, "theoretical" thickness is nevertheless very important for the seasonal formation of high salinity watermasses: during freezing, the water layer under the young ice is enriched with salt. This water has then a slightly higher density due to the increased salt content and can thus sink to greater depths. Sea ice formation is therefore an important factor for deep water currents in the world's oceans and for the so-called "global conveyor belt", a system of surface and bottom currents that is a major force in the Earth's climate system, distributing large watermasses and energy over the globe. Important areas for ice formation in the Arctic are to the north of Siberia and near northeast Greenland, but Storfjord also makes a significant contribution. This process works as long as sufficient volums of sea water freeze. If this is not the case anymore, for example due to regional warming in areas of important sea ice formation, then the production of high salinity bottom waters will decrease to a degree that is supposed to have global climatic significance, implying a weakening of important parts of the global conveyor belt. Many scientists think that the Gulf stream could be seriously affected in such a scenario. Regional cooling in areas currently heated by the Gulf stream and its branches, especially the UK and Norway, could thus be the consequence of warming in certain key areas in the Arctic. There is evidence of repeated breakdown of the Gulf stream during the geologically recent past (Holocene). Storfjord is one brick in the wall of this complex system; not the biggest one, but certainly not without significance.

Parts of the east coast of Spitsbergen (Agardh-, Duner- and Mohnbukta) are within reach for well trained hikers in the summer. There are some small glaciers on the route, but the numerous rivers, some quite large, are the main obstacle during the crossing from Longyearbyen to the east coast; a demanding trip that should not be underestimated and that requires several days. It can much more comfortably be done in the winter by snow mobile, when the east coast is suddenly only a day trip away; a popular excursion for guided groups during the spring season. The islands in the southeast – mainly Barentsøya and Edgeøya – are mostly accessible to ship-based travellers, as it is not allowed to use snow mobiles in the Nature Reserves; hardly anybody ventures on such a long trip on skis or with a dog sledge, although this is generally possible. The northern part of Storfjord is normally frozen during the spring, which makes non-motorised traffic (ski, dog sledge) at least theoretically possible, for example to Barentsøya; this would be a demanding journey with expedition character that would require solid experience, thorough planning and careful judgement of risks, including possible break-up of fjord ice during storms.

As in many other areas in eastern Svalbard, some of the waters are not charted and are thus difficult for navigation; for example the northernmost Storfjord and the east coasts of Barentsøya and Edgeøya. It is not unlikely that waters that are deemed hazardous for navigation will, in the future, be closed by the Norwegian authorities.

All islands east of Spitsbergen are Nature Reserves now, the latest one having been established in 2003 (Hopen). In the future, there may be access restrictions for tourists in the Nature Reserves.

Geology: Large areas in southeastern Svalbard are characterised by horizontal layers of Mesozoic sediments (mostly Triassic) with some Jurassic/lower Cretaceous doleritic intrusions.

Landscape: Extensive flat-topped hills and plateau-shaped mountains are prominent in most parts of southeastern Svalbard, from central Spitsbergen to Kong Karls Land and Hopen. Wide coastal plains are common, especially on Barentsøya and Edgeøya. Glaciation differs regionally and is strongest north of Storfjord (Olav V Land) and at the southern east coast of Spitsbergen. Most of these glaciers are currently retreating, many of them dramatically, and with few exceptions. The wide, open and sometimes

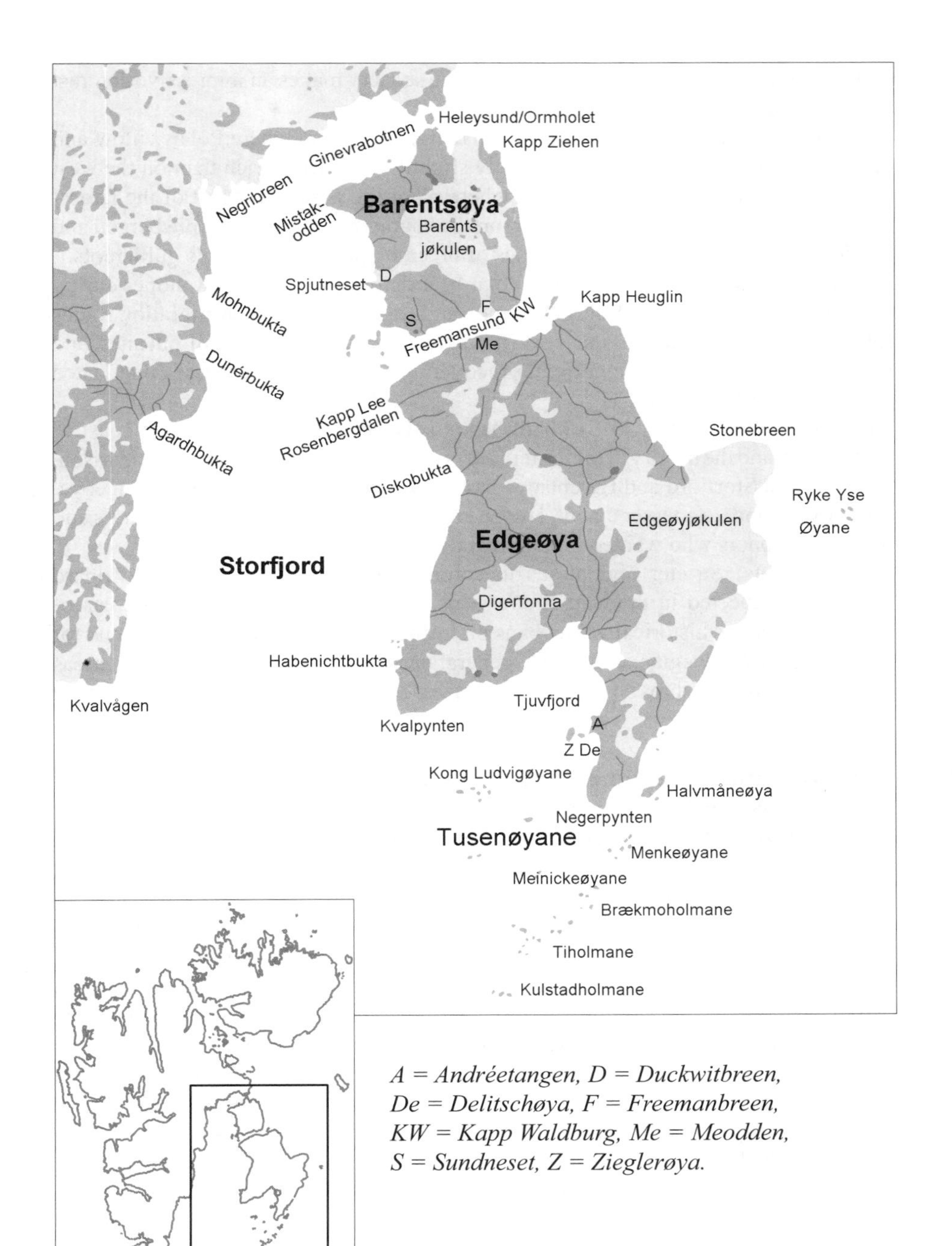

A = Andréetangen, D = Duckwitbreen, De = Delitschøya, F = Freemanbreen, KW = Kapp Waldburg, Me = Meodden, S = Sundneset, Z = Zieglerøya.

dark or even slightly gloomy appearance of the scenery makes an impressive contrast to the west and north coast of Spitsbergen.
Flora and fauna: The tundra varies from dense vegetation where Polar willow and other plants are abundant (though usually slightly less species rich than on the west coast of Spitsbergen) to polar deserts where plant life is scarce. Most of the largest seabird cliffs in Svalbard can be found on the southern east coast of Spitsbergen and on Hopen, with many tens of thousands of breeding pairs of Brünich's guillemots.

There is a much higher density of Polar bear dens on suitable snow slopes during the winter than further west in Spitsbergen and traditional summer migration routes follow the general pattern of the ice drift. There are several Walrus haul-out sites, and these majestic creatures are currently recovering from hunting excesses that lasted well into the 20th century.
History: Human activity in Svalbard has mostly taken place on the west coast of Spitsbergen and the history of the eastern areas is shorter and less varied by comparison. The northern Storfjord and Barentsøya have never been used for whaling. Edgeøya, Tusenøyane and, to a lesser extent, Hopen have been favourite places for Pomors and for those trappers who wanted to hunt mainly Polar bears.
Miscellaneous: Stricter regulations to control tourist traffic in eastern Svalbard have to be expected in the near future. This may include closing certain areas of high biological or historical value, bans on traffic in areas considered hazardous for navigation by Norwegian authorities, general bans on tourist landings in large areas and a general ban on ships beyond a certain size/passenger capacity or carrying certain fuel types (crude oil).

6.18.1 Agardhbukta, Dunérbukta, Mohnbukta

General: Agardhbukta is the coastal end of Agardhdalen, the only ice-free valley on the east coast of Spitsbergen in Storfjord. There is a "corridor" of several ice free valleys that leads from Nordenskiöld Land to this part of the east coast. Only two glaciers need to be crossed on this classic "Conway-route" (see below, *history*) from Adventdalen to Agardhdalen; none if you come from Sveagruva. It is a demanding, several-day-long hike, with all the features that make hiking in Spitsbergen exciting: torrential rivers, wet tundra, small, but deeply incised streams and moraines. The eastern half of Agardhdalen, in particular, is very wet and walking is accordingly tiring. Most routes require crossing of one or several glaciers, which can have (hidden) crevasses and, in the melting season, deeply incised meltwater channels. Sleeping in a tent in Polar bear country (all of Spitsbergen, but more seriously on the east coast) is not everybody's cup of tea. If you are happy to take this problem on board, then you can experience the huge arctic landscapes of the east coast and the feeling of being alone at the end of the world; this is not really true, of course, but it comes quite close. Ship-based travelling is certainly more comfortable, although navigation is hampered by uncharted waters in some areas. Not too many ships make landings on the east coast of Spitsbergen. The same landscape, but with a totally different appearance, can be seen during the spring by snow mobile excursion from Longyearbyen; often a day trip where the whole distance from Longyearbyen to Storfjord and back is covered during one rather long day.

The east coast of Spitsbergen, in Storfjord north of Kvalvågen, is not part of any protected area, but you need to notify the Sysselmannen about your plans in advance (see section 3.6.3 *Registration of tours with the administration*). For map, see section 6.18 *Southeastern Svalbard* (page 393).

Placenames: **Agardhbukta**: Jacob Georg A. (1813-1901), Swedish botanist. **Dunérbukta**: Nils Christopher D. (1839-1914), Swedish astronomer, member of expeditions to Spitsbergen with Otto Torell (1861) and Nordenskiöld (1864). **Elfenbeinbreen**: originally called the "Ivory gate" in 1896 by Martin Conway due to its shining appearance. "Elfenbein" is Norwegian for ivory. **Ginevrabotnen**: after the yacht of the Englishman James Lamont, who visited Spitsbergen in 1858 and 1859. **Hayesbreen**: Isaac Israel H. (1832-81), American Polar explorer. **Mohnbukta**: Henrik M. (1835-1916), Norwegian meteorologist. **Negribreen**: Christoforo N. (1809-96), founder and first president of an Italian geographical society. **Ulvebreen**: Erik Andreas U. (1833-96), Norwegian Captain, member of Leigh Smith's expeditions (see section 6.15 *Nordaustland*). **Usherbreen**: Thomas Leslie U., supported the Scottish polar explorer William S. Bruce.

Geology: Horizontal layers of fine-grained Mesozoic sediments: sandstone, siltstone and shale, often dark due to a relatively high content of organic matter. In Agardhbukta, the rocks represent most of the Mesozoic from Triassic near sea level to lower Cretaceous at elevations of more than 500 metres. Some layers, especially from the Jurassic, are very fossil-rich and contain, for example, Belemnites, Ammonites and bivalves. Parts of dinosaur skeletons, and even related footprints, have been found near the east coast. The sediments have been intruded by dioritic dykes and sills during the Jurassic and lower Cretaceous; these intrusions are often quite prominent geomorphologically, as they are much harder than the sediments.

An important tectonic structure runs across central Agardhdalen, for a distance of about seven kilometres from the shore (on the north side of the valley): the "Lomfjorden-Agardhbukta fault zone" (LAFZ, see also section 6.14.2 *Lomfjord*). The LAFZ was active mainly in upper Palaeozoic times, but some activity continued into the Mesozoic and visibly influenced the Triassic sediments in Agardhdalen. It seems as if the LAFZ also has some influence on today's groundwater system, as there is a pingo in Agardhdalen situated directly on top of the fault, marking the line to the east of which the tundra is much wetter in summer, compared with areas further inland.

Landscape: Olav V Land, north of Storfjord and forming the easternmost part of Spitsbergen, is almost completely ice covered. The largest of many glaciers that reach the coast is Negribreen. Almost resembling an ice shelf in appearance, though on a smaller scale, it used to have a glacier front 30 kilometres wide, but the term "ice shelf" does not strictly apply to Negribreen, as the whole glacier is resting on the ground (which is below sea level near the front), rather than actually floating. Nevertheless, large icebergs do break off the front of Negribreen, including some with a tabular shape, but these have to slide some distance over the muddy sea bottom before they really float, allowing them to drift further south into Storfjord. The degree of glaciation decreases southwards from Negribreen: there are two smaller glaciers in Mohnbukta, one in Dunérbukta and none in Agardhbukta. Usherbreen in Mohnbukta has created an impressive series of push end moraines during a rapid advance ("surge") in 1978.

The scenery generally is reminiscent of the geologically similar islands of Barentsøya and Edgeøya. The Mesozoic sediments weather quickly to produce a fine-grained mud that can be very sticky and should be avoided (see also 6.14.5 *The islands in Hinlopenstretet*, remarks on Wilhelmøya in the *landscape* section). Smaller cliffs and headlands often consist of hard, local dioritic intrusions, while the sedimentary slopes tend to create more rounded slopes that are generally unsuitable for climbing because of the softness of the rocks. The appearance of the landscape is altogether dark, verging on gloomy, especially in grey weather and fog.

If you have hiked from Longyearbyen to the east coast, then you have seen text-book glacial and periglacial geomorphology along the way, including several nice pingos, moraines and glaciers. The current trend of glacial retreat is quite pronounced in the area, and moraines are growing wherever glacier ice melts. Elfenbeinbreen, so proudly called "The Ivory Gate" ("gate" to the east coast) by Martin Conway during his crossing of Spitsbergen in 1896, is a mere shadow of its past appearance: large areas of then shining glacier ice have changed into a muddy, chaotic moraine, and the lower tongue of the remaining ice body has recently been cut off from the main glacier by a meltwater river, it can thus be expected to melt completely during years to come. Should you ever get into the area Jøkulvatnet-Elfenbreinbreen, then do not trust the topographic map, but be prepared for a dramatically changed landscape and choose your route once you can see the terrain. The meltwater rivers are torrential and hazardous at times of high water.

Flora and fauna: In protected valleys, the tundra is dense and rich, covering 100 % of the surface over large areas. Polar willow is very abundant, but also species such as Mountain avens, and the tundra at the central Storfjord coast of Spitsbergen is regarded as "middle-arctic tundra" of the "Mountain avens type" on vegetation maps of the Norwegian Polar Institute. Arctic cottongrass is growing on wet ground that covers wide areas for example in Agardhdalen. In contrast, exposed areas on slopes and geomorphologically active surfaces such as young moraines and solifluction slopes, are completely barren and have an almost lunar appearance in places.

The Storfjord coast is the highest risk area that is within reach of summer hiking tours starting from Longyearbyen, so far as meeting Polar bears is concerned.

History: The first known crossing of Spitsbergen, from Adventfjord to Agardhdalen, was made by the Englishman **Martin Conway** with companions in 1896 (see *history* in section 6.1.8 *Adventfjord*). Some Norwegian trappers repeated this challenging adventure unintentionally in 1909 on their way from Kong Karls Land to Longyearbyen (see section 6.17 *Kong Karls Land*). In mid-20th century, Agardhbukta and the adjacent

Storfjord were the "backyard" of the legendary trapper **Hilmar Nøis** who had, together with his wife Helfried, a comfortable home in Sassendalen and went by dog sledge to Storfjord to hunt Polar bears. The west side of Storfjord has not been used a lot for hunting apart from this, and only eight winterings are known in the 20th century before WWII, while popular areas such as southern Edgeøya were almost overcrowded with Polar bear hunters at times.

Quite remarkable is the adventure of a Swede who wanted to winter on his own and went in 1920 to Agardhbukta where he had expected to find a hut. There was none, and the man had to spend the winter under an old boat that he found on the beach (probably the one from the trappers who came from Kong Karls Land in 1909, see above). Today, there are two huts standing on the north side of Agardhbukta, one belonging to the Sysselmannen and the other to a club in Longyearbyen.

6.18.2 Barentsøya

General: Barentsøya has a surface area of 1,330 sq km and is thus the fourth largest island in Svalbard. It is very similar to its larger neighbour Edgeøya, in terms of geology, landscape and biology, but has a very short history due to the extremely difficult ice conditions in historical times. Well into the early 19th century, it was widely believed that Barentsøya was part of the main island, Spitsbergen, although Heleysund had already been seen. Spitsbergen and Barentsøya are actually separated by two narrow straits, Heleysund and Ormholet, either side of a small island. Heleysund is well charted and deep but difficult to navigate because of very strong tidal currents of up to 10 knots (18 km/h), and Ginevrabotnen, the adjacent part of Storfjord, is shallow and mostly uncharted. Northern Barentsøya is accordingly hardly ever visited by larger ships. Freemansund, between Barentsøya and Edgeøya, has strong tidal currents and quickly moving drift ice which has often caused surprises there, usually not of the pleasant sort. The wide tundra and characteristic landscape of Barentsøya are inviting for walks and long hikes, but drift ice, weather or a Polar bear on the coast, often make changes of plans necessary, adding to the excitement of travelling in southeastern Svalbard. Barentsøya is part of the Søraust Svalbard Naturreservat. There may be access restrictions in the Nature Reserves for tourists in the future. For map, see section 6.18 *Southeastern Svalbard* (page 393).

Placenames: Barentsøya: Willem B. (ca. 1550-1597), Dutch seafarer who discovered Spitsbergen in 1596. **Duckwitzbreen**: Arnold D. (1802-81), mayor of Bremen. **Frankenhalvøya:** after Franken, a province in southern Germany. **Freemanbreen, -sund**: Alderman Ralph F. (early 17th century), a director of the English Muscovy Company. **Heleysund**: William H. of the Muscovy Company, saw the strait in 1617 and called it after himself (indecent!). **Kapp Waldburg**: Carl Marie Eberhard count of Waldburg-Zeil-Wurzach (1825-1907), sponsor and leader of an expedition to Spitsbergen in 1870 together with the German naturalist Theodor von Heuglin. **Mistakodden**: "Mistake point", old name of unknown origin. **Ormholet:** "Worm hole", descriptive name of the very narrow sound. **Spjutnes**: "Spear tip", descriptive name referring to the long and narrow shape of the peninsula. **Sundneset**: "Sound point", headland reaching into Freemansund.

Geology: The geology of the larger islands in southeastern Svalbard (Barentsøya, Edgeøya, Hopen) is almost identical. The basement is buried under thick layers of younger Palaeozoic and Mesozoic sediments and is thus nowhere exposed. The oldest exposed rocks are Permian carbonates, although outcrops are restricted to a few limited areas in the inland of Barentsøya and Edgeøya. The only exposure near the coast is at Kapp Ziehen, the northeastern corner of Barentsøya. Most of Barentsøya, Edgeøya and Hopen consist of rather poorly solidified horizontal sediments, sandstone, siltstone and shale, that have been deposited in near-coastal parts of shallow shelf seas during the Triassic. The composition of some layers points to a coastal origin: deltaic sands that even have some thin coal seams of inferior quality. Some of the marine layers are rich in fossils such as Ammonites and bivalves.

One particular layer within this Triassic sequence, that is relatively homogenous in appearance, deserves to be mentioned: it is a black shale that is quite prominent on both sides of Freemansund and in other places of Barentsøya and northern Edgeøya. These sediments were deposited on the sea bottom at some greater distance from the coast, as is indicated by the absence of grain sizes larger than clay. The dark colour is caused by a high content of organic matter that was not mineralised because of a lack of oxygen in bottom waters (similar to large parts of the Baltic sea today). This shale weathers quickly, but has nevertheless relatively high stability and is accordingly the only sedimentary layer on Barentsøya and Edgeøya that tends to form small, steep cliffs that extend across slopes that are otherwise rather rounded. In many places, meltwater erosion has created small canyons in these layers. The only other cliff-forming rocks

Sampling solifluction mud with rubber boots is not one of the greatest pleasures in life.

are hard dioritic intrusions that are more localised than the shale. These intrusions date to the Jurassic and lower Cretaceous and are the same as the abundant dolerites for example from Hinlopenstretet. Being exposed by more or less recent erosion, the dolerites tend to form islands, headlands or steep cliffs. They are quite common on Barentsøya and Edgeøya, but are missing on Hopen.

Again, a warning is due regarding the weathering products of the Triassic bedrock. They are prone to create very sticky mud and solifluction-influenced soil. The mud can be sticky to a degree that can even be dangerous and should definitely be avoided (see also 6.14.5 *The islands in Hinlopenstretet*, remarks on Wilhelmøya in the *landscape* section). Thorough boot cleaning is certainly required after every landing on Barentsøya or Edgeøya.

Landscape: The landscape is strongly influenced by the geology and consists of a vast plateau that has been uplifted to its present position at elevations between 300 and 600 metres, and subsequently dissected by erosion, first by rivers and then, during the ice-age, by glaciers. This has created today's fjords and straits. The interior is covered by several medium-sized ice caps (Barentsøya: Barentsjøkulen 570 sq km. Edgeøya: Edgeøyjøkulen 1,365 sq km and Digerfonna 270 sq km). Several outlet glaciers have calving fronts at the coast. The best known is **Freemanbreen** on the north side of Freemansund. Freemanbreen made a rapid advance ("surge") in the 1950s, blocking Freemansund for some years until its tongue started to disintegrate. Freemanbreen is now again in line with the coastline or even slightly behind it. Duckwitzbreen on the west side of Barentsøya also made a surge, in 1918. Since then, it has retreated back to its original size but has left an impressive moraine landscape that now forms most of the peninsula Spjutneset. The contrast between the young moraine hills with their lunar appearance and the adjacent lush tundra is remarkable.

There are several coastal plains on Barentsøya, for example Sundneset at the southwestern corner. There are some rolling lowlands of dioritic bedrock that was polished by ice age glaciers, and some smaller lakes at Sundneset. A little river cascades down over dioritic cliffs in several small waterfalls and rapids that are very small but pleasant in appearance, just north and east of Sundneset.

Flora and fauna: There is a striking contrast between the east and west coasts of Barentsøya and Edgeøya, despite the geographical separation of less than 50 kilometres. The eastern sides are quite barren, with polar deserts where large areas are mostly free of vegetation. The western sides, in contrast, have lush tundra that covers almost 100 % of the ground on suitable terrain. The regional tundra belongs to the high arctic "Polar willow zone", but is still surprisingly diverse: a number of different saxifraga species, together with buttercups, cottongrass, both lousewort species, and others, add colourful spots of colour and varying shades of green. Plants with yellow flowers (Snow buttercup, Bog saxifrage and others) confuse and delight amateurs. Relatively large numbers of fungi grow in the late summer. The rich tundra provides food for a large local population of reindeer that certainly enjoy a better life than their comrades on barren Nordaustland.

Seabirds commonly breed on steep cliffs, for example in the above-mentioned small canyons that are cut into some stable layers of shales. The colonies are of small to medium size and dominated by Kittiwakes as by far the most important breeding species. An exceptionally lush local vegetation benefits from fertilisation provided by seabirds, and Arctic foxes make sure that eggs or chicks that fall down from the narrow ledges are not wasted.

The tundra in southeastern Svalbard is an important area for birds. Geese are common in the late summer near the shoreline or on small lakes where Red-throated divers and Long-tailed ducks also breed; Common eiders are often seen. Most of these birds are easily disturbed, and care is needed when moving around in their breeding or resting areas.

History: No remains from whalers' or Pomors' times are known from Barentsøya, although whalers have at least visited the general area. Pomors must have known Barentsøya, even though they did not use it a lot, if at all. Only one wintering by Norwegian trappers is known. A hut was built in 1894 on a small group of islands near Duckwitzbreen called Anderssonøyane, where four men wintered. One of them disappeared in the pack ice during the winter and was not seen again. The others returned home in 1895 after a winter that was hampered by various difficulties, including disagreements between the men and their leader. Anderssonøyane were partly covered when Duckwitzbreen advanced in 1918; the island with the hut was nearly buried under the advancing ice masses, but has since then become a part of the peninsula Spjutneset.

Between 1959 and 1967, a series of geo-scientific expeditions led by the geographer, **Julius Büdel** from south Germany, investigated the regional geomorphology in eastern Svalbard, focussing on southwestern Barentsøya where a hut was built at Sundneset. The hut, called "**Würzburger Hütte**" after the home of the builders, is still there. Landscape phenomena, including post-glacial isostatic land uplift, frost-patterned ground and periglacial erosion were investigated in detail.

6.18.3 Edgeøya

General: Edgeøya is the third-largest island in Svalbard with an area of 5,030 sq km and in many respects is the larger sister of Barentsøya, as both islands are very similar in terms of geology, landscape and ecology. Edgeøya has always been more easily accessible due to the slightly lighter ice conditions, which is the reason for a more intense and varied history compared to Barentsøya.

Coastal waters, especially those east and south of Edgeøya, are badly charted, making navigation difficult. Edgeøya is part of the Søraust Svalbard Nature Reserve. There are plans with the Norwegian authorities to close sites of special historical or biological importance as well as larger areas in general and to close waters that are considered hazardous for navigation. For map, see section 6.18 *Southeastern Svalbard* (page 393).

Placenames: **Andréetangen**: Karl A. (1808-75), German geographer. **Diskobukta**: Possibly derived from Duckes Cove, after ducks or after the garbled surname of the English whaler Thomas Marmaduke. **Dolerittneset**: after the rock-type dolerite. **Freemansund**: see section 6.18.2 *Barentsøya*. **Grunnlinesletta:** "Base line plain", where the Russian division of the Arc-de-Meridian expedition measured a base in 1899. **Habenichtbukta**: Hermann H. (1844-1917), German cartographer. **Hassensteinbukta:** Bruno H. (1839-1902), German cartographer. **Kapp Heuglin**: Theodor von H. (1824-76), German naturalist, visited Spitsbergen in 1870. **Kapp Lee:** Origin unknown. Strictly speaking, the name Kapp Lee is applied to the cliffs at the northwestern corner of Edgeøya, but it is commonly used to refer to Dolerittneset, approximately five kilometres south of Kapp Lee proper. **Kvalpynten**: "Whale point". **Meodden**: refers to the position in the middle of Freemansund. **Negerpynten**: Norwegian translation of the original English name from the 17th century, referring to the appearance of the mountain that consists of dark Triassic sediments. **Rosenbergdalen**: Karl Benjamin Herman von R. (1817-88), German zoologist and discoverer. **Stonebreen**: possibly after someone who worked for the Muscovy Company. **Tjuvfjord**: Tjuv (Norw.) = thief, origin unknown, possibly after a person or of "dy" (Norw.) = mud.
Geology: See *geology* section in 6.18.2 *Barentsøya*.
Landscape: In addition to the landscape section in 6.18.2 *Barentsøya*, the following paragraphs contain some information concerning different parts of Edgeøya, starting in the northeast and following the coast counter-clockwise.

There is a vast coastal plain in the northeastern part of Edgeøya, at **Kapp Heuglin**; it is so low that it is hard to see from a distance. The coastal waters are shallow.

In **Freemansund**, the terrain gradually steepens towards the impressive massif of **Kapp Lee** (355 metres high) at the northwestern corner of Edgeøya; level ground is restricted to some valleys.

Dolerittneset is five kilometres south of Kapp Lee, although the latter name is commonly, but inaccurately used when referring to Dolerittneset. Dolerittneset itself is a small dolerite peninsula and, on its northern side, it has something that is quite rare on Edgeøya: a small bay that has some limited protection against swell from the south. However, the bay is so small that ships have to stay outside. Dolerittneset is like a little open-air exhibit of everything that is typical for the region: the landscape with wide, elevated plateaux, steep cliffs to the north and more gentle slopes to the south, all broken by nicely curved doleritic intrusions, sticky solifluction sediment, nice tundra and the ice-free valley Rosenbergdalen within reach. **Rosenbergdalen** has beautiful tundra with well-developed ice wedges and raised beaches with large whalebones, some of them quite far inland, and slopes with smaller basalt cliffs that are so typical for the area. Sitting on top of one of those cliffs and enjoying the scenery on a fine day is certainly an excellent way to spend a little while, before you continue with a walk or a long hike that could take you as far inland as time allows. But this all needs luck, because the beach near Rosenbergdalen is prone to high surf unless the weather is really good.

The west coast of Edgeøya is very shallow, and again good luck with the weather is needed for landings in **Diskobukta**. It can be difficult to get ashore during low tide because of shallow water and rocks. An interesting landing site is not far from an old hut on the north side of the very wide and open Diskobukta. The coast is separated from the slopes by a plain that is still relatively narrow here, but widens further south towards the very large plain, Raddesletta. The dark slopes behind the above-mentioned old hut are dissected by several small canyons that have steep walls where they cut into stable layers of uniform black shales.

In **southwestern Edgeøya**, about ten kilometres north of Kvalpynten (the southwestern point), there is a level lowland formed of dioritic rock that has been polished by ice-age glaciers. A number of names are attached to different small points and bays of this lowland, so different names are often used for what is basically one and the same area. Near the southern end of an even more extensive lowland, an outwash plain of several smaller rivers is called **Grunnlinesletta**, and the largest of several small bays that cut into the low-lying dioritic headland is **Hassensteinbukta**. Even smaller is **Habenichtbukta,** near the southern end of the dioritic part of the plain; it is so shallow that more than one Zodiac outboard engine propeller has had to be sacrificed for landings. Wherever you choose to land, compensation for an approach that is likely to have been difficult due to shallow and rocky waters, is that walking is mostly dry and easy apart from some rocks, and the tundra on dioritic bedrock does not have that treacherous sticky mud that is so typical for other parts of Edgeøya with sedimentary subsoil. Whalers and Pomors have taken advantage of the relatively well sheltered natural harbour of Habenichtbukta.

Both capes in the south of Edgeøya, **Kvalpynten** in the west and **Negerpynten** in the east, are impressive massifs of table-shaped mountains that are a good 400 metres high. Between them, the wide-open fjord **Tjuvfjord** cuts into Edgeøya's south coast. Tjuvfjord, the only fjord in southeastern Svalbard, is quite shallow and badly charted. In Tjuvfjord and southwards, countless small, rocky islands form the archipelago that is so aptly named **Tusenøyane** ("Thousand islands"), see next section 6.18.4 *Tusenøyane, Halvmåneøya, Ryke Yseøyane*. On the east side of Tjuvfjord, there is another dioritic lowland called **Andréetangen** that is not too different in general appearance from that mentioned above, at Hassensteinbukta/Habenichtbukta. Andréetangen is a vast peninsula with only a few very low hills of dolerite outcrops especially near the southern end. Otherwise, it is mostly table-flat and covered by the inconspicuous remnants of an extensive series of old raised beaches with whalebones in unexpected places far inland. The near-by massif of Negerpynten provides a nice background.

Glaciation is mostly restricted to the inland area. The largest ice cap is Edgeøyjøkulen, which is 1,365 square kilometres in area and covers most of southeastern Edgeøya, including the southeast coast where it forms a large calving glacier called **Stonebreen**. The glaciers and ice caps follow the worldwide trend of general retreat, and Stonebreen is thus not as large anymore as it looks on the map. According to old reports, it must have been very impressive in past centuries.

Finally, a warning needs repeating here concerning the weathering products of the Mesozoic bedrock – a very sticky mud and many solifluction-influenced surfaces. The mud can be sticky to a degree that can even be dangerous and should definitely be avoided. The differences are difficult to see and even experienced travellers are not entirely safe from unpleasant surprises (see also 6.14.5 *The islands in Hinlopens-tretet*, remarks on Wilhelmøya in the *landscape* section). A common ritual after every landing on Edgeøya is intense boot cleaning.

Flora and fauna: Very similar to Barentsøya, see section 6.18.2 *Barentsøya*.

History: Edgeøya has, at least in comparision to Barentsøya, a longer and more varied human history, mostly relating to the exploitation of its biological resources. There are a number of historically interesting sites, some of which have been used during subsequent chapters of the regional history. The importance of respectful behaviour in order to protect the remains, which are often inconspicuous to the unexperienced eye and always fragile, cannot be overstressed.

Dolerittneset/"Kapp Lee": The most obvious artefacts are the huts on the north side of a little rocky ridge that cuts through the tundra at Dolerittneset. The oldest remains, however, are those of a Pomor hunting station on the south side of the ridge, probably from the 18th century. What can be seen are foundations of a hut, and brick fragments that are typical for Pomors as opposed to later trappers from Scandinavia. The Pomors used to bring bricks to build a stove, whereas Scandinavian trappers brought ovens ready-made of metal. Bones of different animals, mostly Walrus, are still bleaching on the tundra around the Pomor site.

A bit further north, not far from the huts, is a real "Walrus graveyard" near the beach – sad, silent witnesses to the slaughter that continued for centuries, but probably started by whalers in the 17th century although they have not left any archaeological traces. The Pomors were followed by Norwegian trappers who came for the first time in 1904 and built the conspicuous octagonal hut from parts ready-made in Tromsø; a house type that was used by several expeditions in those years, for example in Franz Josef Land (Alger Island, Cape Flora, Cape Tegethoff). The hunting territory around Kapp Lee remained in use for several decades, often together with southern Edgeøya. Polar bears were the main target species of Norwegian trappers, although foxes provided a welcome extra income.

In 1968/69, Dolerittneset was finally dedicated to more peaceful activities when it was chosen by a Dutch expedition that spent one year there on biological research. After 1969, Dutch scientists continued to work at Dolerittneset for some years on summer expeditions. One of the Dutch was badly injured during a Polar bear attack; the man did not carry any weapons. The bear was later shot by the police. The building raised for the wintering in 1968 was later completely removed. With its semi-circular cross-section, it did not follow the regional style of traditional huts, but looked rather like a modern-day polar station.

Habenichtbukta: A relatively large number of foundations can be seen on the northern side of this shallow, narrow bay. Some foundations have been made of local stones and carried log-cabin style walls. It is not readily apparent, but this "settlement" was actually used twice during subsequent periods, for the first time in the 17th century by whalers who came probably from England, and later by Pomors. In the 20th century, Norwegian trappers occasionally wintered south of Habenichtbukta, where remains of a hut can still be seen.

6.18.4 Tusenøyane, Halvmåneøya, Ryke Yseøyane

General: There are many small islands and rocks on the south side of Edgeøya, in Tjuvfjord and adjacent open waters, that together are aptly named Tusenøyane ("Thousand islands"). All of them have in common that they are small and very rocky, without significant elevations. The surrounding waters are shallow and biologically productive and have accordingly a rich marine fauna that has attracted hunters from differing origins for centuries. There is accordingly a high density of cultural remains at Tusenøyane. All of the islands consist of dioritic intrusive rocks similar to the islands in Hinlopenstretet (see section 6.14.5 *The islands in Hinlopenstretet*).

The islands on the east side of Edgeøya, Halvmåneøya and Ryke Yseøyane, are very similar to Tusenøyane in terms of geology and landscape. The islands of Tusenøyane are geographically subdivided into several mini-archipelagos that are indicated by place names that end with -øyane or -holmane.

The waters between the islands are shallow and little charted. The whole area is part of the Søraust Svalbard Nature Reserve. Norwegian authorities are currently considering closing areas of special historic or biological importance and waters that they consider hazardous for navigation; this could include parts or even all of Tusenøyane. For map, see section 6.18 *Southeastern Svalbard* (page 393).

Placenames: Bölscheøya: Wilhelm B. (1843-93), German geologist. **Brækmoholmane:** Sivert Johansen B. (1853-1931), legendary Norwegian sealing Captain. **Delitschøya**: Otto D. (1821-81), German geographer. **Halvmåneøya**: "Half moon island", after the shape. **Kong Ludvigholmane**: Ludwig II., king of Baviaria (1845-86). **Meinickeøyane**: Carl Eduard M. (1803-76), German geographer. **Menkeøyane**: Heinrich Theodor M. (1819-92), German cartographer. **Tiholmane**: "Ten little islands". **Zieglerøya**: Possibly after Alexander Z. (1822-87), patron of August Petermann, a German armchair geographer who organised several arctic expeditions around 1870. **Ækongen**: Origin unknown, possibly after an old Norwegian word for King eider.

The large number of German placenames in Tusenøyane originates from the expedition of Count Waldburg-Zeil and the naturalist Theodor von Heuglin, who visited the area in late August of 1870.

Geology: Exclusively dioritic intrusions from the Jurassic and lower Cretaceous, that were brought to the light of day by erosion during more recent times in earth history. Other rock types occur only as erratic boulders.

Landscape: All islands are more or less flat and there are no elevations higher than a few metres above sea level. The largest have a surface area of one or two square kilometres, only Halvmåneøya being significantly larger (twelve sq km). The coasts consist either of large boulders or of very low cliffs and are thus quite inaccessible, but there are small beaches and even some protected bays in places.

Fossil coastal cliffs, that resemble today's coasts but are now situated further inland, can be found on some islands, giving evidence of the emergence of these islands from the sea in post-glacial times due to isostatic land uplift. The same process formed raised beaches which are restricted to relatively small areas, but are nevertheless prominent because they form the only surfaces that are comfortable to walk on: everything else is very rocky and uneven. The larger islands have small lakes.

Flora and fauna: Most of the smaller islands are almost free of vegetation, apart from some moss beds. Others have tundra-covered areas, with mosses which cover a large part of the ground. Try to walk around them or step on stones, rather than on mosses which are quite vulnerable.

The birdlife of Tusenøyane is rich, although cliff-breeding seabirds are absent due to a lack of suitable terrain apart from some Black guillemots that are happy with the small coastal cliffs, either active or fossil (see *landscape* section above). Many birds that breed on flat tundra have found good breeding sites in Tusenøyane: Arctic terns, Common eider and Long-tailed ducks are abundant, benefiting from the absence of Arctic foxes. Red-throated divers breed on those islands that have small lakes. All of these species are easily disturbed at their breeding sites, and landings during the breeding season should only be made with greatest care, if at all.

History: Whalers, most likely from England, had several shore stations on Tusenøyane to process whale blubber (fat). This is a bit surprising due to the dangerous waters. The large number of rocks and rocky reefs and currents, combined with rapid weather changes and drift ice, must have taken a considerable toll. But whaling must nevertheless have been profitable, as remains of several stations can still be seen. The best preserved blubber ovens in Svalbard, including a double oven and the only clearly preserved foundations of a triple oven, are in Tusenøyane, together with the foundations of houses.

Pomors too seem to have appreciated the rich wildlife in Tusenøyane: foundations of houses, and graves are evidence of widespread activity over a long time. Life in the arctic was dangerous in those days, and scurvy and accidents followed the brave hunters wherever they went. It was not unusual for ice conditions to prevent a group's safe return home after a year of hunting in the north. Legend has it that in 1743, four Pomors left their small ship in an open boat for a hunting excursion in Tusenøyane and got lost in fog and ice with not much more than the clothes and very basic equipment for a trip of an intended duration of only a few hours. Those few hours were to become no less than six years, until they were found by coincidence. Only one had died from scurvy in the meantime, the others having managed life under those extreme conditions quite well, mostly by applying stone-age hunting techniques.

The Pomors finally left "Grumant", as they called Svalbard, by the middle of the 19th century, and were followed by Norwegian trappers who made southeastern Edgeøya and the surrounding islands one of their most extensively used Polar bear hunting districts. At least ten huts were built within this relatively small area, from Zieglerøya and Delitschøya (near Andréetangen) in the west, to southeastern Edgeøya (Andréetangen, Negerdalen) and adjacent Halvmåneøya with its tiny satellite islands of Tennholmane. This area is one of the most important Polar bear migration routes in Svalbard, as the bears come with drift ice from the northeast and follow the prevailing currents east of Edgeøya southwards and around Negerpynten. The most famous site is Halvmåneøya, where the well-known Norwegian hunter Henry Rudi brought in a record-breaking 115 bears during the season of 1935-36; a number that earned him the title of uncrowned "Polar bear king". In 1946-47, even Rudi's record was beaten, also on Halvmåneøya, but the busiest days of Polar bear hunting were without any doubt in the early 20th century. Several groups, totalling no fewer than 20 men, crowded southeastern Edgeøya in 1906-07, competing for anything white and furry, and using self-shots, rifles and poisoned bait. The last wintering of Polar bear hunters in Svalbard was in 1969-70 on Halvmåneøya, shortly before the bears were protected by Norway.

It happened several times that hunters who had lost their ship in fog and ice had to risk the return journey to Norway in a small, open boat. Even in modern times, the business of wintering in the arctic is not entirely without risk and in 1967, two adventurous young Norwegians built a hut on the southernmost island of Ryke Yseøyane, a group of three small islands east of Edgeøya – the easternmost, remotest outlier that might be considered part of the Tusenøyane. Dense ice remained around the lonely and rocky shores throughout the whole of the following summer, and it was not until 1969 that a boat could finally reach those desolate islands. Only one man was found; the other had disappeared in the ice during the previous winter.

The number of gloomy stories from Edgeøya and Tusenøyane is endless, and to some extent history becomes confused with storytelling.

6.18.5 Hopen

General: Hopen (46 sq km) is an amazing little island on the edge of Svalbard. Biologically, it is important in several ways and it has a long, sometimes dramatic history. Hopen is rarely visited by tourists. The reason for this lies in the remoteness of the island and in landing conditions that are anything but convenient; there are no protected bays and the near-shore waters are badly charted, so ships have to stay at some distance. Access to some beaches is made difficult by rocky reefs, but the shores are nevertheless exposed and surf is frequent, especially on the east side of the island, which is where there are some interesting sites (Koefoedodden, weather station, Nordhytte/Hermansenskaret). It is possible to walk across the island near the weather station.

The waters around Hopen are strongly influenced by the East Spitsbergen current that brings cold water waters from the northeast. Drift ice is often around the island well into the summer, and later, when the boundary between cold and milder Atlantic watermasses is near Hopen, fog is a frequent guest that leaves only reluctantly.

Hopen was declared a Nature Reserve in 2003, except for the immediate station area.

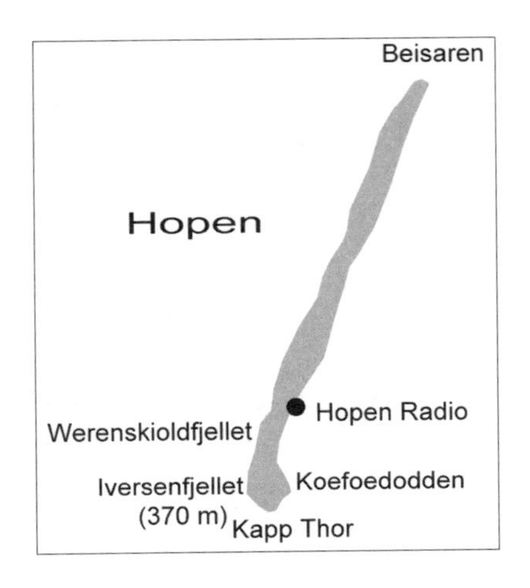

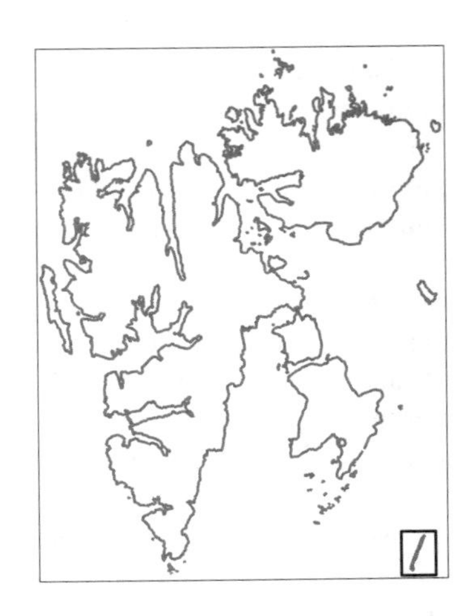

Placenames: Beisaren: after Berner Jørgensen (1861-?), Norwegian trapper who was commonly called "Beisaren". **Hopen**: probably after the "Hopewell", the ship of the English whaler Thomas Marmaduke (1613). **Iversenfjellet**: Thor I. (born in 1873), Norwegian Captain on Einar Koefoed's expeditions to Hopen in 1923 and 1924. **Koefoedodden**: Einar Laurentius K. (born in 1875), see Iversenfjellet. **Kapp Thor**: T. Iversen, see Iversenfjellet. **Werenskiöldfjellet**: Werner W. (born in 1883), Norwegian geographer, geologist and Spitsbergen-explorer.

Geology: Exclusively horizontal layers of Triassic sediments (sandstone, siltstone, shale), very similar to Barentsøya and Edgeøya, but without any intrusive rocks. See also section 6.18.2 *Barentsøya*.

Landscape: The most striking landscape feature on Hopen is the shape of the island itself: 37 kilometres long and almost straight, but only two kilometres wide at maximum. Hopen is a chain of narrow plateau-topped hills that are between 250 and 350 metres high and separated by lower saddles, some of which offer passes from one side of the island to the other. The plateau is a remnant of the same uplifted plateau that is also the oldest, most important geomorphological element on Barentsøya and Edgeøya (and other parts of Svalbard). The highest part is Iversenfjellet at the southern end with a summit plateau at an elevation of 370 metres above sea level. Iversenfjellet drops down to the sea at Kapp Thor, a massive, steep slope. Many other parts of the coastline consist of steep cliffs, and beaches are narrow and few. The longest continuous beach is the one on the southeast coast from Egsetstranda to Koefoedodden. Starting not far south from the station, it can be followed easily all the way through until Koefoedodden is reached, the only level area on Hopen of some size. Unfortunately, the eastern side of Koefoedodden, that could offer at least some protection against western swell, is not easily accessible due to some rocky reefs.

There are no rivers on Hopen, only a few short meltwater streams some of which have cut deeply into the slopes. The sedimentary bedrock gives the whole island a relatively dark appearance that can be quite gloomy in grey and foggy weather. Due to their softness, these rocks are prone to frost shatter and often produce quite sticky mud that makes walking difficult in places, especially on very gently sloping surfaces like the lower passages between both coasts.

Flora and fauna: There is not much tundra due to a lack of suitable terrain, with some exceptions (mainly Koefoedodden), but examples of high-arctic flora such as Svalbard poppy and Purple saxifrage grow here and there. Hopen's steep coastal cliffs are of great importance for the regional seabird populations. Brünich's guillemots are especially abundant, with more than 100,000 breeding pairs. A large part of Svalbard's population of these birds lives at the northern end of Hopen, together with tens of thousands of Kittiwakes and Fulmars. Snow buntings, Arctic skuas and Common eiders are also breeding in good numbers.

Hopen used to have substantial Walrus haulout sites, but these have fallen victim to centuries of excessive hunting. Whales were also frequent, but have become scarce for the very same reason. Finally, Hopen is an important denning area for Polar bears. The large and so-far reliable ice masses that surround the island for most of the year, together with suitable slopes with snow drifts that female bears use to build their dens, make Hopen a convenient place for Polar bear cubs to be born. Decades of hunting, not least by the crews of the weather station since WWII, have luckily had little effect so Hopen is still important for the northeast Atlantic Polar bear population, almost like Kong Karls Land. The decrease of surrounding drift ice has brought the numbers of denning bears dramatically down in recent years (17 dens in 2003), including seasons without a single den at all (2007).

History: Hopen was discovered by **whalers** during the early 17th century, possibly as early as 1613 by the Englishman **Thomas Marmaduke**. The strategic position of the island far away from any other land, was the reason why a land station was soon established, despite the difficult nautical and landing conditions. Some inconspicuous remains of blubber oven foundations at Koefoedodden date back to those years. Not only whales, but also the abundant Walrus were targeted by whalers, possibly even as the most important prey. Despite relative quiet during the 19th century, there was not a single Walrus anywhere on Hopen when the island once more became busy during the early 20th century.

The first Norwegian **trappers** came to Hopen in 1908, attracted by Polar bears that were said to be numerous on this island especially during seasons with drift ice. There are still the remains of huts at Koefoedodden ("Rudihytta"), near the weather station ("Nilsebu") and at Hermansenskaret ("Nordhytta"). **Henry Rudi** who was later to become famous as "Isbjørnkongen" ("Polar bear king") wintered during that first season at Koefoedodden and shot his very first bears, up to six within 24 hours! Rudi took the little cub "Maja" with him back to Tromsø and walked through the town with the little Polar bear on the lead; Maja was then sold to Italy. The result of that first wintering on Hopen was 89 bears. Further hunting expeditions followed. From 1923, and after the Second World War, hunting was a popular leisure time activity for the station crew. 90 bears were caught by station members as recently as 1969-70. Total catches made during the 20th century on Hopen are estimated to be around 1,500 Polar bears.

The first landing of a "scientific" expedition on Hopen was made in 1871, when **Julius Payer** and **Karl Weyprecht** visited the island on board the *Isbjørn* on a reconnoissance expedition to investigate the ice conditions in the eastern Barents sea. Systematic investigations were not made until 1924, 1929 and 1930, during expeditions on behalf of the Norwegian fishing authority in Bergen. During these expeditions, led by **Thor Iversen** together with Captain **Einar Koefoed**, Hopen was for the first time mapped systematically.

The Dutch tourist **Hogendorp** survived an astonishing adventure on Hopen in August 1928, when he was left behind by accident during a rare cruise ship visit. It must have been four very long, cold and unpleasant weeks until he was found by chance by a Norwegian sealing ship.

During the Second World War, Hopen was to become the scene for dramatic and even tragic events. In October 1942, the Sovjet cargoship ***Dekabrist*** left Iceland together with a convoy, bound for Murmansk, with about 80 men and one woman on board. On 04 November, *Dekabrist* was attacked by several German aircraft and so badly damaged that the crew abandoned her in four lifeboats; *Dekabrist* was sunk during a second attack on the following day. Many details of the dramatic events that followed remain unclear. It is likely that more than one lifeboat managed to land on Hopen some days later but, apart from one short and obscure sighting, three boats disappeared and were never seen again. The 18 men and one woman from the fourth boat landed on Hopen, but most died soon in the cold, dark and stormy polar night. The others finally found a small hut where they survived the most difficult winter months. Only four were left in July 1943 when a German submarine turned up and took the survivors on board as prisoners of war, only to put three of them ashore again after a short time – "aus Sicherheitsgründen", "for security reasons". The same submarine returned to Hopen more than two months later, on 05 October, and took the remaining three on board again, where one died tragically a few hours later from cold and exhaustion. Out of about 80 souls, only the Captain, the female doctor and one sailor survived the *Dekabrist* tragedy and returned to Russia after the end of the war. The original landing site of the lifeboat is 3.5 kilometres north of the weather station and is aptly called "Livbåtstranda" ("Lifeboat beach"); the hut, that provided scanty shelter, was the old trapper cabin at Hermansenskaret. In 1975, Russians from Barentsburg erected a small memorial stone on the area of the Norwegian station, and a piece of the lifeboat is on exhibition in the "museum" that is in the old trapper hut from 1908.

It did not take more than a few weeks after the last survivor of the *Dekabrist* had left Hopen, before the island received its next inhabitants, also for non-peaceful reasons. In October 1943, the German air force established a weather station called "Svartisen" in Husdalen, the same place where the modern Norwegian station still stands. "Svartisen" was crewed by four men and operated until late July 1944 without any incidents. A trapper hut that was built in 1934 served as base station (it was destroyed during a fire in 1948). This successful operation led the German air force to re-occupy the site with a new weather station in October 1944, called "Helhus", again with a crew of four. The station leader Dr. Neunteufl had a scientific education and used the time after the end of the war for excursions and investigations over the whole island, but could not add anything to the results of Iversen and Koefoed. "Helhus" was evacuated in early August 1945 by the Norwegian garrison in Spitsbergen.

In the meantime, when "Helhus" was sending its weather data uncoded to Norway, the meteorological importance of the station was realised and the Norwegian navy continued operating the station after an interruption of only a few weeks. In 1946, a new house was built that was soon called "Villa gjennomtrekk", which means "Villa draught" and refers to unwanted permanent ventilation due to a lack of insulation. Responsibility for the operation was handed over to the civilian Norwegian meteorological institute from the summer of 1947, and the station was staffed with four men, later increased to six. Life on Hopen was mostly peaceful, and interruptions from the daily routine work were few. In the summer of 1962, the station was noticeably shaken by some "earthquakes" caused by the Soviet Union testing nuclear weapons on Novaya Zemlya.

In the early 1970s, the oil industry became interested in the remote island, and explorative drillings were made in 1971 on Koefoedodden and in 1973 on Lyngefjellet. The investigations did not yield any commercially interesting results and all installations disappeared from Hopen without leaving any trace, thanks to the careful procedures not leaving tracks or anything else behind (wheel tracks visible on Koefoedodden are from a trial landing of a German weather reconnoissance aircraft during WWII).

Some more calm years were unexpectedly followed by tense weeks when a Sovjet combat aircraft, armed with live ammunition, crashed into the steep slopes of Werenskioldfjellet on 28 August 1978.

On 13 June 1986, the station on Hopen was declared an official postal station and received a postal stamp that showed a Walrus and the designation "9174 Hopen 76°30°N", but this status was withdrawn again in 2003. The operation of the weather station on Hopen is certain to be continued for a long time into the future.

Miscellaneous: Hopen is visited relatively rarely and visitors to **"Hopen Radio"**, the weather station, are usually welcome unless they come at a busy time (crew change, supply ship, ...). Surprise visits are not convenient and early notification to the station is a necessary courtesy. Next to a little insight into life and work on an outpost in the arctic, the station has a small selection of the usual souvenirs (postcards, mugs) for sale. If you are interested in the station stamp, then you should bring your diary or some postcards or whatever you may want to stamp.

There is no infrastructure whatsoever (accommodation, supplies) for public use.

6.19 Bjørnøya

"The 12th of June in the morning, wee saw a white beare, which wee rowed after with our boate, thinking to cast a rope about her necke ; but when wee were neare her, shee was so great that wee durst not doe it, … being well furnished of men and weapons, wee rowed with both our boates unto the beare, and fought with her while foure glasses were runne out (two hours), for our weapons could doe her little hurt ; and amongst the rest of the blowes that we gave her, one of our men stroke her into the backe with an axe, which stucke fast in her backe, and yet she swomme away with it ; but wee rowed after her and at last wee cut her head in sunder with an axe, wherewith shee dyed ; … This island wee called the Beare Island."

Journal from Barents' voyage in 1596,
from Martin Conway *No Man's Land*

General: Bjørnøya is quite different from the rest of Svalbard. The 178 sq km small island (20 km long; maximum width 15 km) is distinguished by its remoteness – at least in a Spitsbergen-centred world view. It is half-way between the north cape of Norway and Spitsbergen and thus actually much closer to civilisation than the rest of the archipelago. Most visitors to Spitsbergen have at least flown over Bjørnøya at an altitude of some 30,000 feet, with the island usually being hidden under a persistent cloud cover. Ships from Norway to Spitsbergen pass Bjørnøya, although only a few approach close.

In "normal" years, because a branch of the cold East-Spitsbergen current reaches the area and brings ice from the far north, Bjørnøya is surrounded by drift ice during the spring and early summer. This cold current follows an underwater plateau on the Barents shelf, on which Hopen is also located, with relatively shallow depths of around 100 metres. Next to this steady current, there are the ever-changing tidal currents that can be surprisingly strong around Bjørnøya; the difference between the tides is 2.2 metres maximum.

The strong influence of the Barents sea produces a markedly maritime climate on Bjørnøya. The coldest month, January, has an average temperature of a relatively mild –7.9°C, and July is only 12° warmer with an average of 4.4°C. Precipitation falls mostly during the winter and amounts to 366 mm at the weather station on the north coast, but is much higher in the more mountainous south of the island. The result is pronounced differences in the spacial distribution of environmental toxins that reach the island by air currents and precipitation. Bjørnøya has a bad reputation

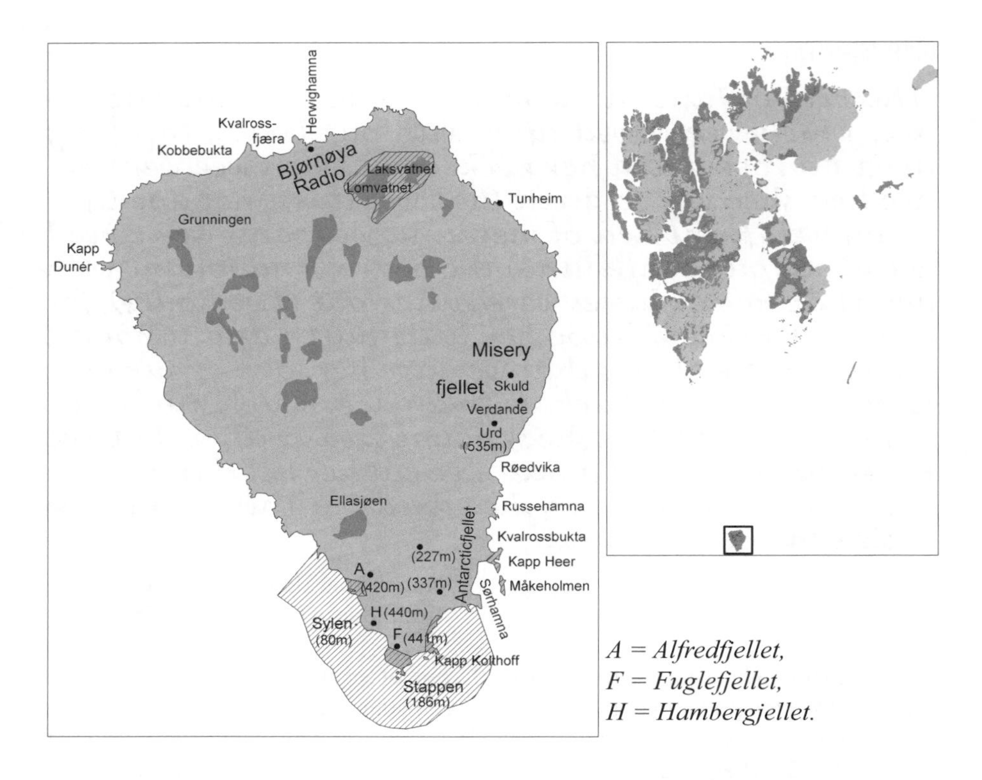

A = Alfredfjellet,
F = Fuglefjellet,
H = Hambergjellet.

for its poor weather. Fog is frequent, especially in July and August, with up to 25 days per month with a visibility below one kilometre. Calm days are about as rare as clear ones. The wind is often strong, the highest storm frequency being between October and January.

Tourist visits to Bjørnøya are few, and not many have the chance to set foot on this remote but very interesting island. This is largely due to its position far away from the "usual" cruise ship routes, but also to the fact that the sight of Bjørnøya is rarely hospitable: the weather often makes life difficult, and the steep topography, together with the lack of protected bays, does not make life any easier.

The main attractions characteristic of the arctic, that many visitors are keen to see, are absent: no calving glaciers, no Walrus, and only rare Polar bear sightings during the summer when the ice edge is far away (but they do occur and the same safety measures need to be applied here as elsewhere in Svalbard). In other respects, Bjørnøya has a lot to offer in terms of scenery, wildlife and history, all of which is unique not only within Svalbard, but also within a wider context. This was a good reason for giving the island, apart from the immediate station area, protection status as a Nature Reserve in 2002. Two areas enjoy special protection. The lakes Lomvatnet and Laksvatnet and their surroundings, southeast of the station and between the station and Tunheim, are now a bird sanctuary because of breeding occurrences of the Great northern diver – a bird that is more common on the west side of the north Atlantic and is not seen elsewhere in Svalbard. All traffic is banned in the area around those lakes between 15 June and 31 August. The second specially protected site is the southern tip of the island with large seabird colonies. All vessels must keep a distance of one nautical mile during the breeding period which is defined as 01 April to 31 August, except for boats that are shorter than 40 feet (ca 12.2 metres), which are allowed to approach the cliffs.

All traffic within the twelve mile zone around Bjørnøya must be notified to the Sysselmannen in advance and is subject to permission (see section 3.6.3 *Registration of tours with the administration*).

Placenames: Bjørnøya: see *history* further down this section. See the following sections (6.19.1-6.19.4) for further placenames.

Geology: Sediments ranging in age from the basement (upper Proterozoic to Silurian) to the Triassic. See the following sections (6.19.1-6.19.4) for further details.

Landscape: The two main geomorphological elements on Bjørnøya are the inland plateau and the steep coast. The plateau is mostly lower than 100 metres, rising from about 35 metres above sea level steadily towards the south. Only the mountainous southern tip rises above the plateau, the highest "peak" is Urd, the southern top of Miseryfjellet, at 535 metres. There are no remains of ancient raised beaches on this plateau, not even on the lowermost parts. Characteristic of the plateau is the large number of lakes, 740 of them in total, most of them very small and shallow. The plateau was created near sea level during very long periods of erosion well before the ice age, and was uplifted when the north Atlantic was formed during Cretaceous times, a history that is similar to the other islands of Svalbard, further north.

The second important, much younger, landscape element is the coast which is mostly steep cliffs. There are no fjords and hardly any protected bays. The most spectacular section is the southern tip with its near-vertical cliffs that rise more than 400 metres from the sea, with several large offshore rock stacks. These are witnesses to the size of Bjørnøya in earlier times and to the constant retreat of the coastline due to wave action. The coastal cliffs allow landings only in a few places.

There are no glaciers on Bjørnøya, although traces of local glaciation during the ice age are evident in the south. Bjørnøya must have been completely covered by large ice caps at earlier stages, but probably not at the last glacial maximum about 18,000 years ago. It is still in the area of continuous permafrost with a frozen layer approximately 50 to 70 metres thick.

Another interesting type of landscape seen are karst features, caused by solution of water-soluble limestone bedrock in southwestern Bjørnøya, where several rivers run partly in caves under the surface.

Flora and fauna: Bjørnøya is much more barren than Spitsbergen despite its position further south. Large parts of its inland are almost vegetation free and plant life is mostly restricted to coastal areas, especially near the bird cliffs, where vegetation is lush and appears with a strong green colour, although poor in species. Scurvy grass is the only plant that really thrives at locations that are strongly fertilised with guano. Further inland, Ymerdalen, a relatively protected valley in the south, is the site which has most vegetation, but the plateau is otherwise dominated by lichens and mosses. 54 species of flowering plants have been found on Bjørnøya up to 2004, including at least seven species that have not been found anywhere else in Svalbard. There is one native plant, the Bjørnøya dandelion (*Taraxacum cymbifolium*), that does not occur anywhere else.

By far the dominant faunal element is the rich bird life on the steep cliffs at the southern end of Bjørnøya (see also section 6.19.1 *Southern Bjørnøya: the bird cliffs*). Its position as the only land in a large, biologically productive sea, makes Bjørnøya extremely important for north-Atlantic seabird populations. The most abundant species are Brünich's and Common guillemot, but there are also large breeding populations of Kittiwakes (estimated at 100,000 breeding pairs) and Fulmars (50,000-60,000 pairs), Glaucous gulls and several smaller Little auk colonies. Approximately 30 pairs of Skuas breed on Bjørnøya. Unique within Svalbard are two or three breeding pairs of Great northern divers in northeastern Bjørnøya, near the lakes Laksvatnet and Lomvatnet. The island is an important stepping stone during the annual migrations of geese to and from Spitsbergen. Rock ptarmigans were last seen in 1965. Arctic char are common in some of the larger lakes.

The mammalian fauna is rather poor and mostly restricted to Arctic foxes. Polar bears are not uncommon when there is drift ice around the island, although there are exceptions to this rule, and "summer bears" are quite rare, but even more dangerous. Walrus were once abundant, but are locally extinct due to excessive hunting. Whales must have been equally abundant in times long gone by, but are still commonly seen in good weather (which is even rarer in that area).

History: Bjørnøya was the very first island that **Willem Barents** saw on 10 June 1596, during his third voyage. His men met a Polar bear and killed it after a long fight (see quotation at the beginning of this chapter). The island owes its name to this encounter, as it was subsequently called "Beeren Eyland". Other names including Cherry (or Cherrie) island have been attached to the same island during following decades, but "Beeren Eyland" finally survived, until it was Norwegianised and turned into Bjørnøya. It did not take more than a few years for **whalers to** follow in Barents' wake. The first came in 1603 from England and concentrated on the abundant Walrus rather than on whales, but lost interest in the island after a while when the Walrus tended to stay away from such dangerous beaches.

The whalers were soon followed by **Pomors** who built hunting stations at several places around Bjørnøya. It is astonishing that the Walrus kept returning to Bjørnøya despite regular hunting by Pomors, and it was only when western Europeans started to come again in the early 19th century that the Walrus population was driven to local extinction.

Bjørnøya was not only the first island to be discovered, but also the first one that was visited by scientists. In 1827, it was the first stop on the voyage of **Barto von Löwenigh** from Germany, who had invited the Norwegian geologist **Balthazar**

Matthias Keilhau to join him on his trip that was otherwise mostly for the adventure. They spent a few days on Bjørnøya before they continued to south Spitsbergen and southwestern Edgeøya. Löwenigh and Keilhau were followed by a large number of scientific expeditions and it became a common habit to make a stop at Bjørnøya on the way to Spitsbergen.

A remarkable chapter in the history of Bjørnøya was the occupation of large parts of the island in 1898 and 1899 by the German journalist **Theodor Lerner**, but Lerner did not have the resources or political support to maintain his property, although at one point he drove away the Russian cruiser *Svetlana*. The Russians did not want to risk diplomatic trouble and were thus content with setting up annexation signs in other parts of the island, while Lerner left Bjørnøya for good in 1899.

During the 20th century, Bjørnøya was not saved from any of the varied human activities in Spitsbergen: a whaling station, mining, hunting, a Norwegian weather station and, during the War, a German weather station, were chapters in the history of the island. Most of these chapters were episodes and closed not long after they had started, with the exception of the Norwegian weather station, which is still operating today. See the following chapters 6.19.1-6.19.4 for further details.

Environmental situation: Bjørnøya plays an exceptionally important role in Svalbard with respect to the environmental situation. The main reason is its position in the area of influence of the marine and atmospheric conveyor belts (Gulf stream and air masses) that transport **environmental toxins** from industrialised countries in northwestern Europe to the Arctic, where they are deposited together with snow, rain and fog. There are no local sources for such toxins (see also section 4.5 *Driftwood, rubbish and environmental toxins*). Some species on Bjørnøya such as Glaucous gulls and Arctic char are amongst those animals that are the most strongly contaminated in the entire Arctic, with concentrations well beyond thresholds that are believed to be significant for health. Scientists fear consequences for the immune system and reproduction. It is believed that environmental toxins are the main reason, direct or indirect, for the decline of the local Glaucous gull population by 60 % since the 1980s up to 2004. Concentrations of substances that have been banned since the 1980s have dropped noticeably, but are still high. They have been replaced by substitute compounds that are very similar to the banned chemicals. Legislation is slow and takes time to react. Another problem is the long life of many of these pollutants: it takes a long time for them to be fully broken down and removed from the ecosystem. Finally, there is the illegal use of banned substances, also in the EU. Concentrations vary strongly on Bjørnøya due to the different precipitation levels which are much higher in the mountainous southern part.

Another problem is the extensive fishery in the Barents sea, that threatens to reduce vital biological resources to near-collapse levels. After years of excessive fishing, the regional population of capelin (*Mallotus villosus*) collapsed, followed in consequence by the Common guillemots that were breeding on Bjørnøya, which collapsed by 85 % within one year: 245,000 breeding pairs in 1986 were reduced to only 36,000 by the following summer. Some may have survived that difficult year at sea, but the breeding season was certainly lost, probably together with a larger part of the population. The Common guillemots have still not recovered. In 2004, the numbers were only 50 % of the 1986 level. The Brünich's guillemot population, similar in size, was not affected because it has a more varied diet and can thus more easily divert to other food resources.

6.19.1 Southern Bjørnøya: The bird cliffs (Hambergfjellet-Sørhamna)

General: The south end of Bjørnøya is the most spectacular part of the island in terms of scenery and wildlife. Landings are not possible due to legal restrictions and the steep topography, but the cliffs and rock stacks, together with the massive bird colonies, can be a fantastic experience from small boats. Guano-proof clothing is recommended and be aware of potential rockfalls! Boats may find protection from westerly winds in Sørhamna, but the steep cliffs prevent access further inland. See section 6.19 *Bjørnøya* for regulations and restrictions in protected areas. The east side of Sørhamna (Kapp Heer, Måkeholmen is also part of the protected area of southern Bjørnøya. For map, see section 6.19 *Bjørnøya* (page 412).
Placenames: Antarcticfjellet: after the *Antarctic*, a Norwegian ship that was used during Nathorst's expedition in 1898, which visited Bjørnøya. **Ellasjøen:** after Nathorst's wife Ella. **Hambergfjellet:** Axel H. (1863-1933), Swedish geographer. **Kapp Kolthoff:** Gustaf Isak K. (1845-1913), Swedish zoologist, member of Nathorst's expedition in 1898. **Perleporten:** "Perl portal", a coastal cave. **Stappen:** "High rock", 186 metre high offshore rock stack. **Sylen:** "The awl", 80 metre high rock stack.
Geology: The steep cliffs at the southern tip of Bjørnøya consist of basement sediments, dark to black dolostone and quartzite, upper Proterozoic to Ordovician. The layers are near horizontal. The highest sections of the southwestern mountains (Hambergfjellet, Fuglefjellet) include fossil-rich, horizontal layers of Permian sandstone and limestone.
Landscape: The interior is hilly rather than mountainous; steep slopes are found only at the coast. The mountains are topped by plateaux rather than peaks, at elevations around 400 metres; the highest area in the south is Hambergfjellet at 440 metres. The southernmost lake on Bjørnøya, Ellasjøen, is also the deepest, with a depth of 43 metres; additionally it is the one that is most strongly contaminated with environmental toxins brought in with precipitation and guano.

The dominant landscape feature is the impressive coast with near-vertical cliffs that are up to 400 metres high. The coastline is slowly moving inland under the constant influence of the powerful sea, but some single rock stacks remain for a while until they also disappear. These include Sylen (80 metres) near Hambergfjellet and Stappen (186 metres), the southernmost part of Bjørnøya. A little northeast of Stappen is Kapp Kolthoff, another impressive headland, with the 170 metres-long coastal cave, Perleporten.

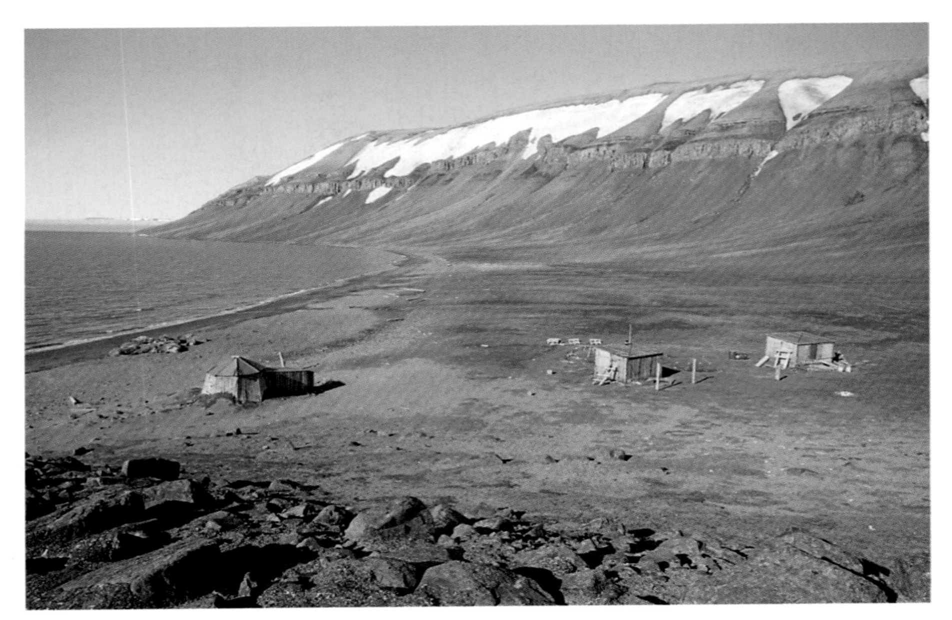

6.18.3-1: Dolerittneset ("Kapp Lee"), Edgeøya.

6.18.3-2: Rosenbergdalen, Edgeøya.

6.18.3-3: Canyon with Kittiwake colony. Diskobukta, Edgeøya.

6.18.3-4: Remains of a whaling station and Pomor settlement. Habenichtbukta, Edgeøya.

6.18.4-1: Double oven of English whalers. Delitschøya, Tusenøyane.

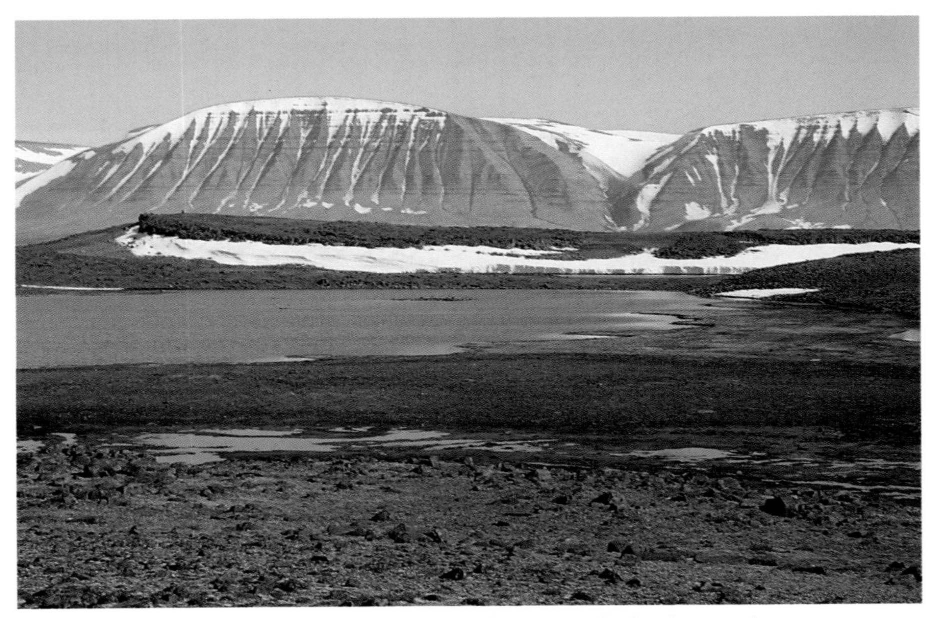

6.18.4-2: Landscape of Tusenøyane, with Edgeøya in the background.

6.18.4-3: "Bjørneborg", an old trappers' hut on Halvmåneøya. Edgeøya in the background.

6.18.5: The weather station on Hopen.

6.19.1: The 80 metre high coastal stack Sylen near the south coast of Bjørnøya.

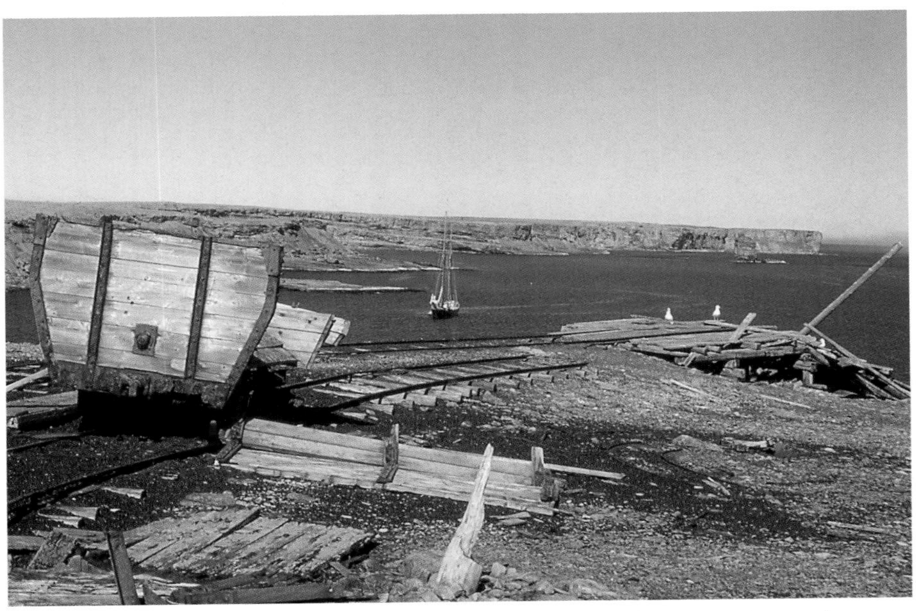

6.19.3-1: Tunheim. Remains of coal mining and coastal scenery in northeastern Bjørnøya. Photo: Jens Götz.

6.19.3-2: Tunheim, Bjørnøya. Photo: Jens Götz.

6.19.4: The weather station at Herwighamna, Bjørnøya.

6.20: Trollosen, the largest spring in Spitsbergen. Stormbukta, Sørkapp Land.

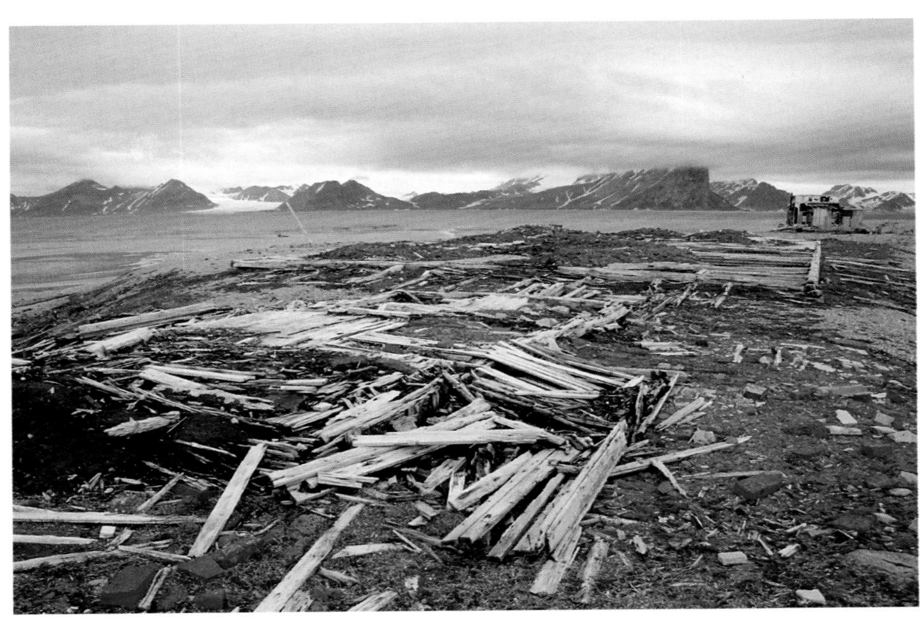

6.21.1: Remains of the Russian main station of the Arc-de-Meridian expedition ("Konstantinovka") at Gåshamna, Hornsund.

6.21.2-1: Hornsundtind, 1,431 metres.

6.21.2-2: Samarinvågen, Hornsund.

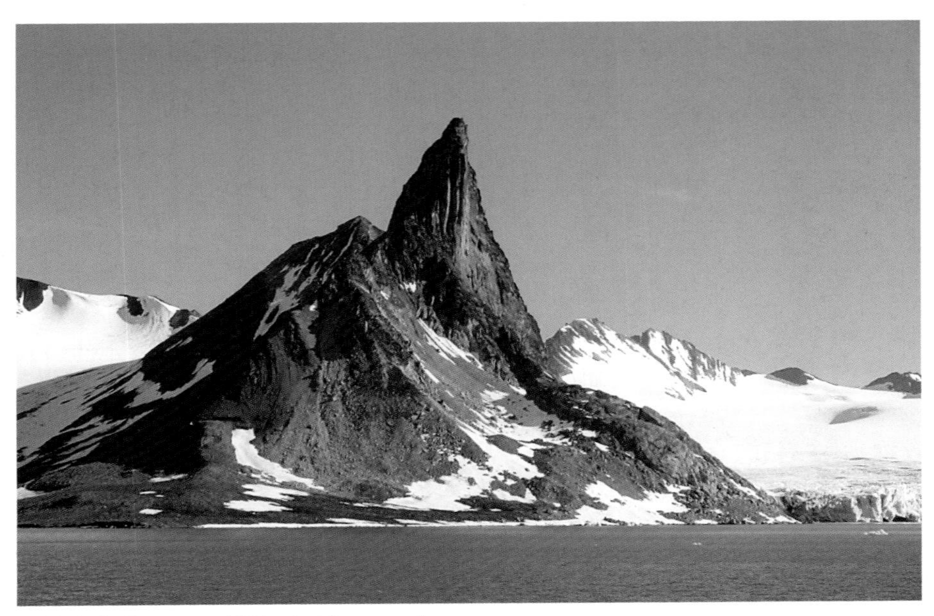

6.21.3-1: Bautaen (475 m), Hornsund.

6.21.3-2: Brepollen seen from Ostrogradskijfjellet, Hornsund.

6.21.4-1: Hyrnefjellet, Hornsund.

6.21.4-2: Austre Burgerbukta, Hornsund.

6.21.4-3: Sofiekammen in Vestre Burgerbukta, Hornsund.

6.21.4-4: Gnålodden at the southern tip of Sofiekammen, Burgerbukta.

6.21.4-5: Gnålodden, Hornsund.

6.21.5: The Polish research station in Isbjørnhamna, Hornsund, with national flags of guest scientists.

6.22: Wreck of German aircraft from the Second World War at Kapp Borthen.

6.23.1: Asbestodden, Recherchefjord.

6.23.2-1: Ahlstrandodden with boats used during White whale hunting in the early 20th century. Berzeliustind (1,205 metres) in the background. Mid-June, Van Keulenfjord, Bellsund.

6.23.2-2: View from Ahlstrandodden over Van Keulenfjord to Bravaisberget.

6.23.2-3: Trapper cabin from 1898. Midterhukhamna, Bellsund.

6.23.3-1: View from Akseløya towards Ingeborgfjellet, Bellsund.

6.23.3-2: View from Midterhuken over Van Mijenfjord to Fridtjovbreen in late April.

6.23.3-3: Old mine carts at Camp Millar, Vårsolbukta, with view over Bellsund to Midterhuken and Recherchefjord.

Flora and fauna: Small patches of suitable terrain within the bird cliffs have bright green, lush vegetation, mostly Scurvy grass. Vegetation further inland is scarce but richer than elsewhere on Bjørnøya. Fertilisation from seabirds on hills near the bird cliffs has led to moors coming into being: mosses that have kept growing on top of older mosses, thus creating thick piles of peat. The greatest thickness found so far is around five metres, and the lowermost peat layers have been shown to be 8,700 years old. Such peat deposits are unique in the Atlantic Arctic and important also for science, as a climatic archive.

The seabird colonies on the cliffs of southern Bjørnøya are amongst the largest in the north Atlantic. Brünich's guillemots have been estimated at 245,000 breeding pairs in 1986 and Common guillemots at 123,000 in 1991, four years after the population collapse in 1987 (see section *Environmental problems* in 6.19 *Bjørnøya*). Their numbers had not yet reached pre-1987 levels by 2004.

History: Hardly anything has happened at the south coast of Bjørnøya, due to the inhospitable terrain, apart from some occasional egg collecting.

6.19.2 Western Bjørnøya

General: The west coast of Bjørnøya has comparatively little to offer for tourist interests, but there are several possible landing sites that can be used in case weather conditions make landings on the north or east coasts impossible. These include Kapp Dunér on the northern west coast, where the interior can easily be reached. See section 6.19 *Bjørnøya* for regulations and restrictions and for map (page 412).

Placenames: Kapp Dunér: Nils Christopher D. (1839-1914), Swedish astronomer and polar scientist, member of Otto Torell's expedition to Spitsbergen in 1861 and Nordenskiöld's in 1864.

Geology: Carboniferous sediments (limestone, sandstone).

Landscape: Low coastal cliffs with, in places, narrow rocky beaches. The interior is a barren, mostly very rocky plain with a large number of small lakes.

Flora and fauna: Not much beyond mosses, lichens, single flowering plants and some small seabird colonies on the coastal cliffs.

History: Grunningen, one of the largest lakes on Bjørnøya, is about two kilometres east of Kapp Dunér. A German special aircraft landed in 1943 a few hundred metres northwest of Grunningen, to install an automatical weather station. East of Grunningen, there are some remains of a postal plane that crashed there in 1954 on a return flight from Spitsbergen. All eight crew members perished in the crash.

6.19.3 Northern Bjørnøya: Bjørnøya Radio

General: There are no protected bays on the north coast of Bjørnøya and landings are only possible at a few places during good weather and in good sea conditions. The relatively shallow coastal waters prevent ships from anchoring close in. There is a small pier near the station, but the beach close to the houses is better for Zodiac landings. See section 6.19 *Bjørnøya* for regulations and restrictions and for map (page 412).

Placenames: Herwighamna: Walter H. (1838-1912), president of the "German Sea Fishing Association". **Kobbebukta:** "Seal bay". **Kvalrossfjæra:** "Walrus coast" **Nordhamna:** "Northern harbour".
Geology: The northern part of Bjørnøya is made up of Carboniferous sandstones and limestones west of the station, and similar rocks of Permian age further east.
Landscape: The interior is a rolling, rocky plain with a large number of small lakes. The coast consists mostly of low cliffs, but there are several wide bays with sandy beaches (Kobbebukta, Kvalrossfjæra in Nordhamna).
Flora and fauna: Barren, rocky tundra. Unique in Svalbard is a breeding occurrence of Great northern divers at Lomvatnet, with two or three pairs.
History: Other than the east coast, it is the north of Bjørnøya that has the longest and most interesting history. The large Walrus herds attracted **whalers** to the island, which thus has the longest history of exploitation of its natural resources, mainly at former Walrus haulout sites such as Kvalrossbukta in the southeast and Kvalrossfjæra on the north coast. According to historical records, an almost unbelievable 3,000 animals were killed between 1603 and 1612, to supply European markets with ivory. After those years of slaughter, Walrus gave Bjørnøya a wide berth for a long time, and the whalers lost interest in the island.

After the whalers, Pomors came to hunt whatever they could find. There are still some inconspicuous graves at Gravodden, west of the weather station.

In **1818**, a large **English expedition** with two ships that were supposed to find a passage across the North Pole to China, made a stop at Bjørnøya and killed no less than 900 Walrus during a few hours; the population had obviously recovered since the early 17th century. One of the commanders was **John Franklin**, who was lost in the Northwest Passage in 1845.

The news of these rich catches met receptive ears in north Norway, and it did not take long before the first hunting expeditions were sent north. The first Norwegian hunters wintered in 1823-24 on Bjørnøya in a house that was already built in 1822. It was named **"Hammerfesthuset"** after the origin of its builders and is still standing on the station area; now the oldest intact building in Svalbard. In was enlarged in 1865 by Sivert Tobiesen. The extension is still known as **"Tobiesenhuset"** and serves now as a venue for social occasions for the crew of the weather station. A **"Walrus graveyard"** on the beach at Kvalrossfjæra, some hundred metres to the west of the station at the mouth of the little stream Lakselva, is still a reminder of the Walrus slaughter of the past.

In 1899, the **"German Sea Fishing Association"** occupied the northern part of Bjørnøya and built a house ("Tyskehytte") at Gravodden west of the station; some remains can still be seen. This occupation was independent of Theodor Lerner's activities at the same time further south on Bjørnøya (see *history* section in 6.19 *Bjørnøya*); both parties actually regarded each other as competitors.
Bjørnøya Radio: The Norwegian weather and radio station was originally founded at Tunheim on the east coast, but moved in 1947 to Herwighamna. It is now one of

three Norwegian stations in the north Atlantic that are still operating, together with Jan Mayen and Hopen. Nine persons make sure that weather data are recorded and sent to Norway, and they also take care of maintainance responsibilities and some limited research facilities, but Bjørnøya Radio should not be regarded as a scientific station. The most important part of the operation, from a meteorological point of view, is the regular ascent of a weather balloon that records data not only on the ground, but also at higher elevations of up to 30,000 metres. This data is crucial for weather forecasting and requires a manned ground station. There is a clear political decision in Norway for the operation of a permanently manned station on Bjørnøya. Supplies are brought in by ship or helicopter. The position half-way between Norway and Spitsbergen enables the large coast guard helicopters to reach Spitsbergen and Hopen from Norway.

Life on a polar station is mainly determined by routine work and everybody has regular tasks. Occasional visitors are, nevertheless, usually welcome unless they come at an inconvenient time (crew change, supply ship or helicopter, ...). Surprise visits are accordingly not advisable and early notification to the station is self-evident. Next to a little insight into life and work on an outpost in the arctic, the station has a small selection of the usual souvenirs (postcards, mugs, T-shirts) for sale. If you are interested in the station stamp, then you should bring your diary or some postcards or whatever you may want to stamp. There is no infrastructure whatsoever (accommodation, supplies) for public use.

6.19.4 Eastern Bjørnøya: Kvalrossbukta, Russehamna, Miseryfjellet, Tunheim

General: The east coast of Bjørnøya has some relatively well protected bays, with the best landing sites on the island and several places with amazing scenery and some historical interest. For map, see section 6.19 *Bjørnøya* (page 412).

Placenames: Kvalrossbukta: "Walrus bay". **Miseryfjellet:** originally "Mount misery", name in use since the 17th century, exact origin unknown. The three tops of Miseryfjellet are, from north to south, **Skuld** (454 m), **Verdande** (462 m) and **Urd** (535 m), after the Norns (goddesses of destiny) in Norse mythology, possibly named in connection with a Swedish expedition to Spitsbergen in 1882 that used vessels named *Urd* and *Verdande*. **Måkeholmen:** "Gull islet". **Russehamna:** "Russian bay", after an old Pomor station. **Røedvika:** Ole R. (1879-1937), Norwegian lawyer and businessman, engaged in Bjørnøen A/S, the company that founded Tunheim. **Tunheim:** Karl T., temporary foreman of the mine.

Geology: The southern east coast (Måkeholmen-Røedvika) consists of basement dolostone that dates into the upper Proterozoic. North of Røedvika, Devonian sediments make up the bedrock: siltstone, sandstone and conglomerate, including several coal seams which are amongst the oldest examples of coal formation on Earth. The only younger rocks are Permian limestones and sandstones at Miseryfjellet, overlain by Triassic sediments (darker sandstone and siltstone) at elevations above 300 metres.

Landscape: The steep coastal landscape has the most varied scenery on Bjørnøya, second only to the cliffs at the southern tip. There are several smaller, more or less protected bays **south of Miseryfjellet**. **Sørhamna** is the best natural harbour, but steep cliffs prevent access to the interior. Landing sites that have access to the inland are at Kvalrossbukta and Russehamna. The coastline is very rocky, with many small offshore rocks and tiny islets, but the coastal cliffs are much lower than further south. Inland of the southern east coast is a landscape that was clearly formed by glaciers during the ice age, which have left obvious traces including smaller U-shaped valleys such as Ymerdalen between Antarcticfjellet and Alfredfjellet, and other landforms typical of glacial erosion. Sharp ridges and peaks are missing; instead there are rounded hills and plateau-topped mountains.

The **central east coast** is dominated by **Miseryfjellet** with its three rounded peaks, the southernmost being the highest elevation on Bjørnøya at 535 metres. The coast is steep, but not vertical as around the south point. A large landslipped mass is still lying on the slope under Urd.

The coast **north of Miseryfjellet** is a cliff about 20 to 30 metres high, with the typical rocky plain and a lot of small lakes further inland. The near-coastal waters have numerous rocks and reefs. Landings with access to the interior are possible at several points on the easternmost coast of Bjørnøya (Kapp Levin, Rifleodden, Kapp Nordenskiöld) and near the old mining settlement Tunheim or, more precisely, at the mouth of the little stream Engelskelva in the bay Austervåg, and a little further east, at Siloodden.

Flora and fauna: The inland is rocky and mostly free of vegetation except for small spots within and near bird cliffs. These have lush vegetation that is poor in species, with Scurvy grass being the most common flowering plant that thrives on this extremely well-fertilised soil; peat layers have even developed in some places. Smaller seabird colonies exist in many places on the cliffs. The species are the same as further south, mainly Brünich's and Common guillemot, Kittiwakes, Glaucous gulls and Fulmars, but the numbers are nowhere near the magnitude found on the cliffs at the south point.

History: Walrus herds in **Kvalrossbukta** were exploited by 17th century whalers and, occasionally, by later hunting and other expeditions, together with Walrus on the north coast.

Pomors had a hunting station in **Russehamna**, but there is hardly anything left of it. In 1976, a hut was built on the historic site for leisure time use for the crew of the weather station. Other remains had already been destroyed in the early 20th century when the Norwegian **Ingebrigtsen** built a little quay as part of a **modern whaling station**. This Norwegian station, consisting of three houses, operated in Russehamna from 1905 to 1908, while a second, similar one was sited in Grønfjord in Spitsbergen. A few remains can still be seen at Russehamna. A small, by now largely overgrown track leads up to the cliffs between Russehamna and Sørhamna, where the German journalist and "fog prince" **Theodor Lerner** built a hut in 1899 as a base for his intended occupation of Bjørnøya.

After the closing down of Tunheim in 1925, Bjørnøen A/S tried for some years to exploit lead ore at **Blyhatten** southwest of Russehamna, on the northern side of Antarcticfjellet, but without commercial success.

Tunheim, further north on the east coast, was the place where Bjørnøen A/S from Stavanger tried to extract Devonian coal in the years from 1915 to 1925. A settlement of altogether 25 houses was built, where 60 to 80 persons lived and worked. In 1918, a weather station was added and a wireless telegraph station followed in 1919. The whole enterprise did not yield the economical success that Bjørnøen A/S had been hoping for, and after 1925, Tunheim started to decay. Today, there is not too much left of most of the buildings, but four are still standing, all in a state of disrepair (cow house, two residential buildings, smithy). There is still a lot of old "rubbish" lying around, providing interesting photographic opportunities: old mine carts, two old, rusty railway engines, and mining equipment. The terrain does not provide a convenient natural harbour and a shipping station had to be built at Siloodden, connected with Tunheim by a railway track.

During the Second World War, the **German weather station "Taaget"** operated near **Kvalrossbukta** from late autumn 1944 to April 1945, staffed by a Russian and a Norwegian. The Norwegian disappeared under mysterious circumstances, and the Russian was subsequently evacuated. Hardly anything is left of "Taaget".

6.20 Sørkapp Land

"Sørkapp har vært en av de beste fangstplasser for bjørn."

"South cape was one of the best hunting territories for Polar bears."

Gustav Rossnes,
Norsk Overvintringsfangst på Svalbard 1895-1940

General: Sørkapp Land, the southernmost part of Spitsbergen south of Hornsund, is rarely visited except from the south side of Hornsund (see section 6.21 *Hornsund*). On ship voyages, the south point of Spitsbergen is normally passed in the middle of the night on the passage from Edgeøya to Hornsund or vice versa. The southern tip of Spitsbergen is flat lowland that is scarcely visible from a distance – in other words, no reason to get up in the middle of the night, unless the midnight sun casts its beautiful light on a mirror-like sea when it is a good opportunity to watch out for whales. Such weather conditions are unfortunately quite rare. Landings are seldom made because there are no protected bays with convenient landing sites in Sørkapp Land. Stormbukta is an interesting place, but difficult to reach because the shore is exposed to the open ocean and partly blocked by reefs. Sommerfeldbukta is too shallow even for small boats. The actual south cape (Sørkapp) is on a low island with many lagoons, Sørkappøya.

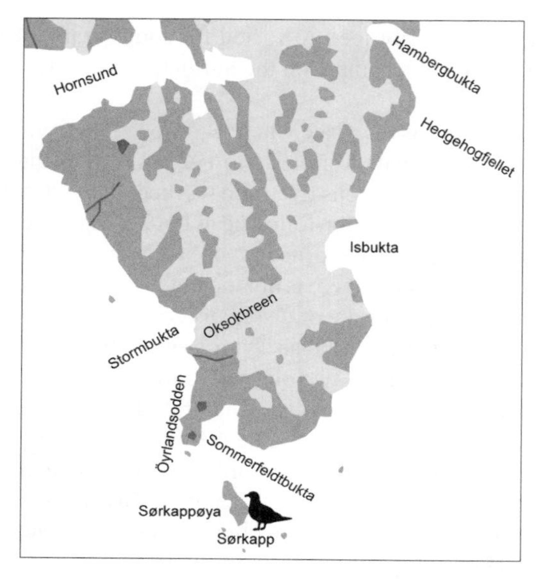

= *Bird sanctuary*

Drift ice is often encountered around Sørkapp and can stay well into the summer by which time the west coast further north is already ice free. This is because the cold waters of the East-Spitsbergen current that come from the northeast, drift around Sørkapp and influence the southern west coast, before giving way to the milder waters of the West-Spitsbergen current, at least on the surface.

Sørkapp Land is part of the South Spitsbergen National Park. Sørkappøya including all adjacent islets and rocks is a bird sanctuary (all traffic banned within 300 metres from the shore from 15 May to 15 August).

Placenames: Hambergbukta: Axel H. (1863-1933), Swedish geographer. **Isbukta:** "Ice bay". **Olsokbreen:** After Saint Olav. Norwegian scientists including Adolf Hoel visited the glacier on 29 July 1920, Saint Olav's name day. **Sommerfeldtbukta:** Søren Christian S. (1794-1838), Norwegian botanist. **Stormbukta:** Erik S. (1904-36), Norwegian pilot. The translation "Storm bay" was not the reason for this placename, although it would be appropriate. **Trollosen:** "Troll spring".

Geology: The west coast is made up of a complicated tectonic mosaic of various sediments: Permian to Tertiary south of Olsokbreen. Further north (Stormbukta) weakly metamorphosed basement carbonate rocks (Ordovician to Silurian in age). The east coast of Sørkapp Land consists of younger, near-horizontal sediments (lower Tertiary and lower Cretaceous): siltstone, sandstone, conglomerates and some coal seams.

Landscape: Wide coastal plains near the west and south coasts, that continue into the sea as extensive shallows or islands. The plain is covered by a beautiful series of raised beaches, especially south of Olsokbreen; with a lot of luck, you may have good views of these fantastic geometric patterns from the scheduled flight from or to Spitsbergen.

The interior is strongly glaciated. There is one calving glacier, Olsokbreen, on the west coast that has a four kilometres wide front.

The east coast is steeper and has hardly any lowlands, but there are several glaciers that reach the shore, especially in Isbukta which is surrounded by glaciers on all sides, although the general trend of retreat is certainly also affecting this area.

There are some interesting geomorphological phenomena in **Stormbukta**, mostly because of the presence of carbonate rocks that are very slightly water soluble. The largest spring in Svalbard is Trollosen north of Olsokbreen, a karst spring where a river flows out of a cave near the coast. There are some much smaller springs further south, closer to the glacier. None of these springs is related to volcanic activity, although there is a sulphurous smell, but this is derived from sulphur-bearing compounds in some of the sediments.

Flora and fauna: The cold East-Spitsbergen current makes itself felt climatically and the tundra is classified as part of the high-arctic "Svalbard-poppy zone", in contrast to the middle-arctic fjords further north. As well as some reindeer and Arctic fox, there are small or medium-sized Kittiwake colonies on steep rockwalls.

When Sørkapp Land is surrounded with drift ice that comes around the south cape on the cold current from the northeast, during the spring or early summer, then it is one of the areas in Spitsbergen with the highest densities of Polar bears …

History: … which made the area including Sørkappøya a favourite area for hunters of various generations. **Pomors** had no less than three stations on the small island of Sørkappøya, which are amongst those six in Spitsbergen that are believed to date into the middle of the 16th century. This is interesting because it would mean that the Pomors had reached Spitsbergen before Barents voyage in 1596, but this is still a matter of scientific dispute.

Norwegian **trappers** came to Sørkapp Land for the first time in 1908 and there were many winterings during following years until 1933. The first of these winterings resulted in a catastrophe, when two men out of a group of four were caught in drift ice with their small rowing boat and never seen again.

The English **NEC (Northern Exploration Company)** was out for different natural treasures and, in 1920, investigated **coal** occurrences at Hedgehogfjellet on the east coast. This was simplified by the presence of a very convenient small natural harbour, but the occurrence turned out to be economically uninteresting and, as if by a strange whim of nature, the entrance to the natural harbour soon became silted up by marine sediments.

The madness of the **Second World War** left some traces in Sørkapp Land. The British cargoship *Chumleigh*, part of a convoy to Murmansk, ran into some rocky reefs near Sørkappøya and was soon afterwards bombed by German aircraft (see section 6.1.11 *Festningen, Russekeila, Kapp Linné/Isfjord Radio*). In 1944-45, the German air force operated a weather station called "Landvik" in Stormbukta, which was manned by two Norwegians. The foundations of the building, made of local stones, can still be seen hidden behind a low hill north of Olsokbreen.

6.21 Hornsund

"The most remarkable mountains I have seen, are situated near Horn Sound, ... Horn Mount, or Hedge-hog Mount, so called from an appearance of spines on the top when seen in some positions, takes its rise from a small tract of alpine land, on the southern side of Horn Sound."

William Scoresby,
An Account Of The Arctic Regions

General: Hornsund, almost 30 kilometres long and ten kilometres wide at the entrance, is not only the southernmost fjord in Spitsbergen, but also, as many say, the most beautiful (just as Kongsfjord, Magdalenefjord, Smeerenburgfjord, Liefdefjord and others). Eight large glaciers have calving fronts along its shores, near which several impressive mountains rise, including Hornsundtind the third-highest mountain of the Svalbard archipelago at 1,431 metres. This impressive peak and the glacier scenery are the main attractions of Hornsund, but the weather gods have to be friendly for good views of their full splendor. Quite often, the higher parts of the mountains are hidden by clouds, and complete views of Hornsundtind are rare. Hornsund can also be quite rough with strong winds in an east-west direction.

Hornsund is influenced by the cold watermasses that come around Sørkapp as a branch of the East-Spitsbergen current. As a consequence, drift ice blocks the fjord in some years well into the early summer, even when the fjords further north along the west coast are clear. Hornsund is subdivided into several basins by submarine ridges. Colder and consequently denser watermasses tend to stay in the deeper basins, separated from the surface by slightly warmer and/or less saline surface waters. The result is a side-by-side arrangement of high-arctic and sub-arctic watermasses with their individual physical characteristics and plankton communities, of interest to marine biologists and others. There is a permanently staffed Polish research station in Isbjørnhamna (see section 6.21.5 *Isbjørnhamna*). Hornsund is part of the South Spitsbergen National Park.

Placenames: Hornsund: "They brought a piece of a Deeres horne aboard, therefore I called this sound Horne Sound." Jonas Poole, English whaler (1610). See the following sections for further placenames.

Geology: Varied: most of the geological spectrum of Spitsbergen is represented within a relatively small area in and around Hornsund, from the basement in central and outer parts (400 million years and older) to the lower Tertiary (40-50 million years old) in the inner reaches (see also the following sections 6.21.1-6.21.5).

A closer look at the rough picture of the geological structure in Hornsund is interesting, even without paying too much attention to the individual rock types. As a general rule, the rocks are older and more strongly deformed the closer to the west

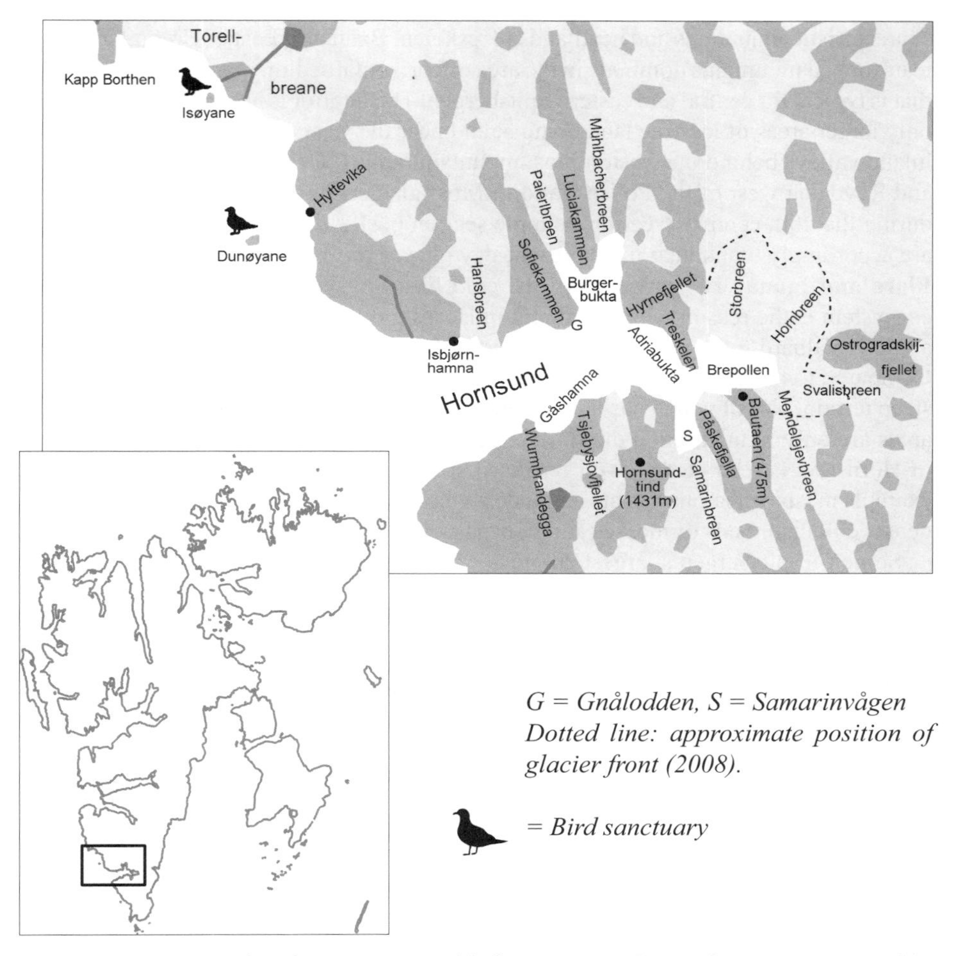

G = Gnålodden, S = Samarinvågen
Dotted line: approximate position of glacier front (2008).

= Bird sanctuary

coast you are, ranging from metamorphic basement rocks on the outer coast and in central Hornsund, to steeply dipping Palaeozoic sediment layers further east and finally to horizontal layers of Mesozoic and Tertiary sediments in the innermost reaches of the fjord. This structure visibly influences the overall appearance of the landscape.

Landscape: The striking mountain and glacier scenery, with some outstanding mountains such as Hornsundtind, Bautaen, Sofie- and Luciakammen (see sections 6.21.2-6.21.4.), is well worth seeing.

The geomorphology is strongly influenced by the geological structure, which has created a cross section from west to east as follows: Wide coastal plains in basement rocks on the west coast, then ranges of mountains in the area of strongly uplifted basement rocks (western and central Hornsund, including Hornsundtind). Further east follows a north-south trending belt of steeply dipping sedimentary rocks with

characteristic mountains and headlands (Treskelen, Bautaen). East of Brepollen, plateau-topped mountains dominate in the area of horizontal sedimentary layers in a way that is typical for central and eastern Spitsbergen. The interior is heavily glaciated, the only larger areas of ice-free land being at and near the west coast, including the first inland valleys behind the westernmost mountain range (Gåshamna on the south side and Revdalen west of the Polish station). Most glaciers have retreated significantly during the 20th century (see for example section 6.21.3 *Brepollen*). Nautical charts are accordingly blank near most present-day glacier fronts.
Flora and fauna: The influence of the cold East-Spitsbergen current on the local ecosystem is the reason why the tundra in Hornsund is considered part of the high-arctic "Svalbard poppy zone", in contrast to the middle-arctic fjords further north. Compared to the latter, there is not much vegetation in Hornsund anyway due to the steep terrain, part of which has only recently been exposed by glaciers. Larger tundra areas are only found around the fjord entrance, while lush plant life in central parts of Hornsund is restricted to well fertilised surfaces and slopes near bird cliffs, for example in Isbjørnhamna and at Gnålodden, where a rich nutrient supply has produced dense, colourful beds of mosses and lichens.

Some of Spitsbergen's largest colonies of Little auks occur in Hornsund, but the breeding sites are on steep scree slopes and thus rather inaccessible. The colony north of the Polish station is the one that is most easily reached so far as the terrain is concerned, but visits have to be coordinated with the station in advance, not only because it is in the immediate neighbourhood, but also because it is an important research site, and tourist visits are not always convenient.

Hornsund is part of a classical migration route for Polar bears when drift ice comes from the east coast and around the south point of Spitsbergen into the fjord. The bears seem to know the route over the glaciers back to the east coast. It is always worthwhile to keep a lookout and have binoculars ready to hand when in Hornsund, watching the coastline, slopes, water and ice: there could always be a bear or a pod of White whales.
History: Hornsund has been visited throughout all the chapters of Spitsbergen's history, from the 17th century whalers to Pomors, trappers and finally scientific expeditions. See the following sections (6.21.1-6.21.5) for further details. One expedition that deserves to be mentioned here is the one made in 1872 by count **Hans Wilczek** from Austria. The main purpose of this expedition was to lay a depot on Novaya Zemlya for the Austrian-Hungarian North Pole expedition led by Julius Payer and Karl Weyprecht, that was to become famous because it discovered Franz Josef Land in the Russian arctic. Wilczek, being the main sponsor of the expedition and himself very interested in the Arctic, led the support expedition on board the Norwegian sealing ship *Isbjørn*. On the way to Novaya Zemlya, some days were spent in Hornsund to construct topographic maps and to climb some mountains; Wilczek made good use of the opportunity to spread the names of expedition members, along with those of his family and friends, all over the freshly-drawn map of Hornsund.

6.21.1 Gåshamna

General: Open bay on the south side of Hornsund, part of the South Spitsbergen National Park. For map, see section 6.21 *Hornsund* (page 441).

Placenames: Gåshamna: "Goose bay", origin unclear. Possibly after a person. **Konstantinovka:** Grand duke Konstantin Konstantinovitsch (1858-1915), Russian scientist. **Nigerbreen:** after the dark (moraine covered) surface. **Tsjebysjovfjellet:** Pafnutij Ljvovitsch T. (1821-94), Russian mathematician. **Wurmbrandegga:** Gundaker W. (1838-1901), Austrian politician.

Geology: Basement. Weakly metamorphosed carbonates on the west side of Gåshamna, and quartzite and slate on the east side. The Quaternary geology is interesting. The little glacier Nigerbreen flows down the western slope of Tsjebysjovfjellet and ends in a moraine that gradually developes further downslope into a very nice rock glacier. The braided (multi-channelled) meltwater river and the moraine of Gåsbreen are prominent. Nice frost-patterned ground can be seen in some places on the gently rising slopes under Tsjebysjovfjellet, including both stone rings and similar phenomena that have been deformed by solifluction, producing half-moon shaped and linear structures.

Landscape: The mountain ridges Wurmbrandegga (west of Gåshamna, 392 metres) and Tsjebysjovfjellet (east side, 920 metres) picturesquely surround the three kilometre wide bay. The glacier Gåsbreen terminates on land at a distance of about two kilometres from the shore in a typical moraine landscape. The wide, flat valley bottom is completely covered with young deposits left by the meltwater river.

Flora and fauna: The wide river plain is free of vegetation, but there is tundra on both sides under the slopes, where Yellow mountain saxifrage, otherwise not a very common plant in Spitsbergen, flowers in August. Several pairs of Arctic skuas nest on the flat tundra areas and attack potential aggressors who come too close to their nests; a strategy that is well known also from Arctic terns that breed near the shore and on the river plain not far from Konstantinovka (see *history* further down this section). Try to keep a distance from both terns and skuas and leave the area quickly once you are under attack.

History: Whalers, probably from England, operated shore stations in Gåshamna. Blubber oven foundations that look like small mounds, and large whalebones can still be seen on both sides of the bay. There are some remains of Pomor house foundations near the point west of Gåshamna. The Russian division of the Arc-de-Meridian expedition had their wintering station and astronomical observatory called "Konstantinovka" on the east side of the bay the foundations are still clearly seen (see also section 5.5 *Early expeditions and science*). The hut that is standing directly next to the remains of Konstantinovka was built in 1906 by trappers and used for winterings over many years. One Norwegian hunter liked it so much that he spent no less than eight years there between 1927 and 1939, four of them on his own. Today, the hut is used and maintained by scientists from the Polish station on the other side of Hornsund.

6.21.2 Hornsundtind, Samarinvågen

General: The central part of Hornsund has spectacular landscapes on both sides. The whole area is part of the South Spitsbergen National Park. For map, see section 6.21 *Hornsund* (page 441).

Placenames: Hornsundtind: see 6.21 *Hornsund.* **Meranfjellet:** Franz M. (1839-91), friend of count Wilczek. **Påskefjella:** "Easter mountains". The massif delayed the prompt return journey of a Russian sledge expedition, who wanted to celebrate Easter at Konstantinovka. **Samarinvågen, -breen:** After a member of the Russian section of the Arc-de-Meridian expedition. **Traunkammen:** Otto T. (1818-54), Austrian count.

Geology: Hornsundtind consists of a complicated tectonic mosaic of more or less metamorphic basement rocks dating to the Ordovician, mostly crystalline carbonates ("marble"). A narrow, north-south trending belt on the west side of inner Samarinvågen, that continues to the south, consists of near-vertical, Devonian Old Red sandstone with a marked purple colour. The Meranfjellet-Påskefjella-massif, east of Samarinvågen, is made up of Carboniferous sediments (sandstones, siltstones, conglomerates) that are the youngest rocks in this area.

Landscape: Very steep, mountainous landscape dominated by Hornsundtind, 1,431 metres high and thus the third-highest mountain in Spitsbergen and adjacent islands. The top of Hornsundtind is a conspicuous twin peak, that is unfortunately often covered in cloud. Both the Hornsundtind-massif and the inland are extensively glaciated : two smaller side glaciers creep down the steep slopes of Hornsundtind to Samarinvågen, and the larger Samarinbreen has a wide glacier front at the head of the bay. Samarinbreen is often very active and can fill the bay with smaller icebergs and brash ice at times. In recent years in particular, the result has been a pronounced retreat of several kilometres, exposing a small rocky islet in 2006. See also section 6.21.3 *Brepollen* for the younger glacial history.

Flora and fauna: Hardly any on shore due to the steep topography.

History: The first successful ascent of Hornsundtind was made during the German mountaineering expedition of **Dr. Rieche** in 1938. Earlier attempts had been made by, amongst others, Garwood in 1896, who was a member of Martin Conway's expedition (see 6.1.8 *Adventfjord*), but Garwood had to turn back only shortly before the summit was reached due to lack of time and thick fog.

6.21.3 Brepollen

General: Wide bay with an almost completely glacial coastline in innermost Hornsund. The whole of Hornsund is part of the South Spitsbergen National Park. For map, see section 6.21 *Hornsund* (page 441).

Placenames: Bautaen: "The monolith". **Brepollen:** "Glacier bay". **Chomjakovbreen:** After a member of the Russian section of the Arc-de-Meridian expedition. **Hornbreen:** see section 6.21 *Hornsund.* **Mendeléjevbreen:** Dmitri Ivanovitsch M. (1834-1907), Russian chemist. **Storbreen:** "Great glacier". **Svalisen:** "Cold ice", telegraphic address of a predecessor of the Norwegian Polar Institute. **Treskelen:** "The threshold".

Geology: The entrance to Brepollen has steeply dipping sediments from the Permian, Triassic and Jurassic, the layers being successively younger towards the east. On the north side, Permian carbonates form a relatively small strip on the west side of the peninsula Treskelen, most of which, together with the peninsula and islands on its eastern side, consists of Jurassic and Triassic rocks (dark sandstone and siltstone). The steeply dipping attitude of the layers, that follow almost exactly a north-south trend, has created an interesting geometric pattern of parallel peninsulas and islands at Treskelen and on its east side.

On the south side of the entrance to Brepollen there is a similar succession, but it has been moved further to the east by tectonics: Meranfjellet opposite Treskelen consists of metamorphic basement rocks, and sedimentary cover rocks are exposed east of Meranfjellet. Hard, steeply dipping sediments from the Permian are responsible for the striking shape of **Bautaen** (475 metres), which is the northernmost end of a long ridge but appears as an isolated, almost needle-sharp rock from a particular position near the entrance to Brepollen.

East of Bautaen, the mountains comprise Mesozoic rocks (Triassic and Jurassic) where tectonic deformation is much less pronounced. The dark colour of these siltstones, sandstones and shales is obvious in the mountain slopes that rise above the large glaciers around Brepollen, and the horizontal position of the layers has favoured the development of plateau-topped mountains that are typical for central and eastern parts of Spitsbergen and that contrast strongly with the more alpine scenery in central Hornsund.

Landscape: See *geology* for the unglaciated part of the landscape. The most striking features in Brepollen are the many, large glacier fronts that surround this wide bay on all sides. Why is this the only part of Hornsund where count Wilczek did not leave any placenames in 1872? Because the bay, Brepollen, did not exist until the early 20th century! In 1900, all the glaciers were combined in one large glacier front west of Treskelen, even including Samarinbreen. Since then, these glaciers have retreated and thus created the bays of Samarinvågen and Brepollen. The glaciers around Brepollen have retreated by five kilometres just from 1983 to 1999. Partly responsible for this dramatic development is the geometry of their circular arrangement around the bay: the further they retreat, the wider the calving glacier fronts that contribute to ice loss: several glacier fronts around Brepollen are now (summer 2007) a good seven kilometres wide (Hornbreen, Storbreen). At the same time, the accumulation area, that catches snowfall and thus produces ice, is shrinking.

This process started in the late 19th century at the end of a global cold phase that is known as the Little Ice Age and before the onset of what we usually call, slightly imprecisely, "global warming" which is, at least in part, man made. It is evident that recent climate change has markedly increased the rate of retreat of the glaciers in Brepollen, which have now retreated so far that they do not have a combine glacier front anymore, and are separated from one another by moraine peninsulas or mountains. The only glacier that has not retreated (by 2007), but has even advanced slightly, is

Mendeléevbreen on the south side of Brepollen. This shows the complexity of the relationship climate-glacier: each glacier has its individual response mechanisms to changes of frame parameters and may thus show different reactions to the same changes compared to its direct neighbours. The advance of Mendeléevbreen is due to a rapid advance (surge) in 2000. In the long term, however, Mendeléevbreen will follow the same trend of retreat that is so obvious in this area.
Flora and fauna: Ice-free land at sea level is very limited and has until recently been glacier-covered. The short time span has not yet allowed much tundra to grow. There are some small seabird colonies on steep slopes (Meranfjellet, Bautaen).

6.21.4 Burgerbukta, Gnålodden

General: The north side of central Hornsund is something like "Spitsbergen in a nutshell", because a lot of those features that attract visitors to the arctic are there: wild scenery with impressive mountains and glaciers, a bird cliff, a lonely trapper's hut in picturesque surroundings and a bay that is often filled with icebergs and bergy bits (small pieces of glacier ice). Gnålodden is an interesting place, but landings are difficult at low tide because of offshore rocks. The whole of Hornsund is part of the South Spitsbergen National Park. For map, see section 6.21 *Hornsund* (page 441).
Placenames: Adriabukta: After the Adriatic sea. **Burgerbukta:** Wilhelm B. (1844-1920), member of count Wilczek's expedition in 1872. **Gnålodden:** gnåle (Norw.) = making a constantly humming sound, referring to the bird cliff. **Hyrnefjellet:** "The mountain at the corner". **Luciakammen** and **Mariekammen:** L. Pálffy (1862-1958) and M. Kinsky, (1858-1938), daughters of count Wilczek. **Mühlbacherbreen** and **Paierlbreen**: Ferdinand M. (1840-1913) and Georg P. (actually Bäuerle), members of count Wilczek's expedition. **Sofiekammen:** S. Öttingen-Öttingen (maiden name Metternich), daughter of a friend of count Wilczek.
Geology: Complex and colourful. Sofiekammen/Gnålodden, Luciakammen: weakly metamorphic, but strongly deformed basement carbonates (Ordocivian-Silurian).

East side of Burgerbukta/Adriabukta: reddish Devonian sandstones and conglomerates (Old Red) in lower slope sections, overlain by yellowish-brown Carboniferous and Permian carbonates and finally dark Triassic sandstones and shales in the highest slopes. Altogether, the slopes show a beautifully coloured succession that comprises (from bottom to top) Devonian, Carboniferous, Permian and Triassic strata, that are quite easily distinguished in good light conditions. The best exposure is at Hyrnefjellet where the layers show a nice upward bend.
Landscape: Burgerbukta has two branches, Vestre (western) and Austre (eastern) Burgerbukta, that are separated by Luciakammen. Both end at medium-sized glaciers that have two-kilometre-wide glacier fronts (Mühlbacher- and Paierlbreen) which have retreated several kilometres during the 20th century. These glaciers are often very active, and at times the whole of Burgerbukta can be filled with pieces of glacier ice of all shapes, sizes and colours.

The surrounding mountains have near-vertical slopes close to the shore and reach 925 metres (Sofiekammen), 695 metres (Luciakammen) and 815 metres (Urnetoppen). The only level ground is a small area, with a pond that is often dry in the late summer at Gnålodden, the southern point of Sofiekammen.
Flora and fauna: The only tundra area is at Gnålodden where a large seabird colony provides rich fertilisation for the rich moss beds. The breeding sites are high above the beach.
History: Being one of only a few sites in this part of Hornsund where the terrain allows some activity on shore, Gnålodden has received attention through several centuries. There was a Pomor hut during the 18th and early 19th centuries, although hardly any traces are left. A grave from those times can still be seen on the little point at the corner of Burgerbukta. The trapper hut, that has been there more or less in its present shape at least since 1919, is an eye-catcher in these picturesque surroundings. It was used by Norwegian trappers for decades during the early 20th century, because Hornsund had a reputation as a good hunting area for Polar bear and also for Arctic fox. The hut at Gnålodden was a "bistasjon", a secondary hut that was used during travelling. "Hovedstasjonen", the main house, was usually a hut in Hyttevika on the west coast north of Hornsund. **Wanny Woldstad**, a woman from north Norway, spent the years from 1932 to 1937 in Hornsund, together with her partner Anders Sætersdal. For two years, she also brought her two sons who were at an age where today's boys still face several years at school. There were not too many women wintering in lonely huts in Spitsbergen in those years, and most of them would rather take care of the housework while their husbands or partners went out hunting, but Woldstad shot bears and took part in all kinds of work, no matter how hard or dangerous it was. Woldstad died in a traffic accident in north Norway not too long after her final return; she is still a legendary figure from those adventurous years in Spitsbergen. The huts in Hyttevika and at Gnålodden were used by trappers until 1971.

6.21.5 Isbjørnhamna

General: Isbjørnhamna is the site of the permanently staffed Polish research station and thus the southernmost permanently inhabited place in Spitsbergen. Visits to the station and its surroundings need to be coordinated with the station leader in advance. The shoreline is rocky and the landing site, which is on the eastern beach, requires a careful approach because of underwater rocks. Isbjørnhamna is, together with the rest of Hornsund, part of the South Spitsbergen National Park.For map, see section 6.21 *Hornsund* (page 441).
Placenames: Hansbreen: H. Rafael Wilczek (1861-1929), son of count Wilczek. **Isbjørnhamna:** Norwegian sealing ship, chartered by count Wilczek in 1872. **Wilczekodden:** Count Johann (Hans) Nepomuk W. (1837-1922).
Geology: Metamorphic basement (marble, schist).

Landscape: The area is a typical geomorphological cross-section through the west coast of Spitsbergen and near-coastal ranges. The outer coast is a wide plain, behind which mountains rise up to between 400 and 700 metres. There is a regional rarity between this westernmost mountain range and the Polish station: an unglaciated valley with a small lake. The mountains directly north of the station are Ariekammen (510 metres) and Fugleberget (569 metres high). The westernmost calving glacier in Hornsund is Hansbreen with a 2.5 kilometre wide glacier front, situated about two kilometres east of the station. As with most other glaciers, Hansbreen has retreated during the 20th century, but to a less dramatic extent: between 1936 and 1990, the position of the glacier front has moved about one kilometre landwards.

Flora and fauna: The lower slopes of the mountains near the station (Fugleberget) are covered with coarse scree which is home to large colonies of Little auks. Exact numbers are unknown, but several tens of thousands of breeding pairs are likely to be there. The colony is an important research field for the scientists, and visits need to be arranged with the station in advance. A very dense, colourful carpet, mostly of mosses and lichens but including some colourful plants such as Moss campion and Purple saxifrage, has developed on the well-fertilised tundra near the bird colonies.

History: The topography that provides a more or less sheltered bay and some level ground has attracted visitors through the centuries. Older traces of whalers, Pomors and trappers have largely given way to the station buildings, that now dominate the scene.

Polish station: Poland established the research station in Isbjørnhamna during the International Polar Year (IPY) in 1957/58. The station was kept serviceable beyond the end of the IPY, at first for more or less regular summer expeditions, but as a year-round research facility since the early 1970s. One advantage of the station was that it was one of a very few opportunities for Polish scientists to meet western colleagues during the Cold War. The tradition of international cooperation has been retained since then, and scientists from a large number of countries benefit from the infrastructure during the busy summer season. The most important work, though, is the long-term programme with measurements in classical fields of geophysics such as meteorology, earth magnetism, seismic studies, northern lights and so on. Another important, almost traditional field of research concerns the adjacent glaciers, including long-term mass-balance studies of Hansbreen. Throughout recent years, the focus has changed from geology and geomorphology to biology and ecology, following a common trend within (non-commercial) polar science. The nearby Little auk colony plays an important role, and so does the marine-biological cross section of Hornsund with its sub-arctic and high-arctic watermasses.

The buildings and facilities have been modernised in recent years. Next to a larger building for accommodation and main laboratories, there are several smaller warehouses.

Visits need to be arranged with the station leader in advance; surprise visits to a busy station are not a good idea. Guests should respect some obvious rules including:

- Do not enter any buildings without explicit invitation.
- Dirty boots and Polar bears are not permitted inside any buildings.
- Do not touch any scientific installations.
- Do not leave the station area without a weapon.

Often the station staff have some souvenirs for sale (postcards, buttons). If you are interested in the station stamp, then you should bring your diary or some postcards or whatever you may want to stamp.

6.22 Dunøyane, Isøyane, Kapp Borthen

"A little to the northward of Horn Sound, is the largest iceberg I have seen. It occupies eleven miles in length, of the sea-coast. The highest part of the precipituous front adjoining the sea is, by measurement, 402 feet, and it extends backwards toward the summit of the mountain, to about four times that elevation. Its surface forms a beautiful inclined plane of smooth snow; the edge is uneven and perpendicular."

William Scoresby, *An Account Of The Arctic Regions*
(referring to Torellbreane)

General: This rather exposed coast is normally passed during the night on the passage between Hornsund and Bellsund or Isfjord. The whole area is inside the South Spitsbergen National Park. The islands of Isøyane, Dunøyane and Olsholmen north of Kapp Borthen are bird sanctuaries, where all traffic is banned within 300 metres from the coast from 15 May to 15 August. For map, see section 6.21 *Hornsund* (page 441).
Placenames: Dunøyane: "Down islands". **Kapp Borthen:** Harry B. (born in 1884), Norwegian businessman and sponsor of expeditions to Spitsbergen. **Torellbreane:** Otto T. (1828-1900), Swedish geologist and arctic explorer. **Isøyane:** "Ice islands".
Geology: Complex mosaic of basement rocks, mostly schist. Large areas are covered with Quaternary deposits.
Landscape: The very gently rising glaciers Torellbreane dominate almost 20 kilometres of the coast between Hornsund and Bellsund. The coast near Torellbreane, as well as the small offshore islands (island groups, strictly speaking) Dunøyane and Isøyane, consist of young moraines. In contrast, the terrain is table-flat wherever meltwater rivers have deposited their freight, for example the plain between Kapp Borthen and the moraine ridges near the glacier.
Flora and fauna: There is not much vegetation in the Kapp Borthen area and the young moraine landscapes appear almost lunar. The small islands Isøyane and Dunøyane are important breeding sites for Common eiders.

History: One of the last Pomor groups to winter in Spitsbergen in the middle of the 19th century is said to have been murdered on Dunøyane by the Danish-Norwegian sealing Captain Andersen, who did not recoil from multiple manslaughter to misappropriate the results of hard work during the winter. Legend has it that nature soon did justice to Andersen, who drowned when an iceberg that he had climbed as a lookout, turned over.

Trappers regularly went to Dunøyane and Isøyane during the later spring to collect the down of Common eiders from their nests; a habit that was kept into the second half of the 20th century. If done carefully, this is not harmful to the ducks or their offspring, but inconsiderate collecting pressed hard on the birds until the bird sanctuaries were established in the 1970s. An important wintering station for the hunting and trapping area in and near Hornsund was at Hyttevika east of Dunøyane (see section 6.21.4 *Burgerbukta, Gnålodden*).

There is a historical curiosity near Kapp Borthen in the form of a German aircraft that had to make a forced landing after it had been damaged during an attack on a convoy on 14 September 1942. The crew survived without injuries and were soon picked up by another plane that landed a bit further north on the tundra. The wreck is still lying in the plain near Kapp Borthen, not far from the moraine ridges of Vestre Torellbreen.

6.23 Bellsund

"On 25th (1838) July La Recherche cast anchor in Bell-Sound. Here a grand and terrible panorama opened to our view; I wish I could describe its gigantic proportions and wonderful beauties."

Xavier Marmier, in *Spitsbergen Gazette*, 20 July 1897

General: Bellsund is the entrance to a fjord system with several branches that cut up to 80 kilometres inland. Bellsund itself is about 20 kilometres wide. The branches are the small Recherchefjord on the south side, Van Keulenfjord and Van Mijenfjord.

The local climate in Bellsund is relatively mild because the cold waters of the East-Spitsbergen current that come from the south give way to the warmer West-Spitsbergen current at the surface. The ice conditions are accordingly easier and Bellsund is usually accessible in the early summer when Hornsund further south is still blocked with dense drift ice. This, and other resources including the presence of protected bays with unglaciated shorelines, mineral occurrences and the wildlife, are the reasons why almost everybody who wanted to become rich in Spitsbergen has tried his luck in Bellsund since the days of the early whalers. There is still large-scale commercial activity in the innermost reaches of Van Mijenfjord where Sveagruva is situated; the centre of Norwegian coal mining and currently the largest mine in Spitsbergen. The noise and dust are far away, however, unless you visit the settlement itself which is

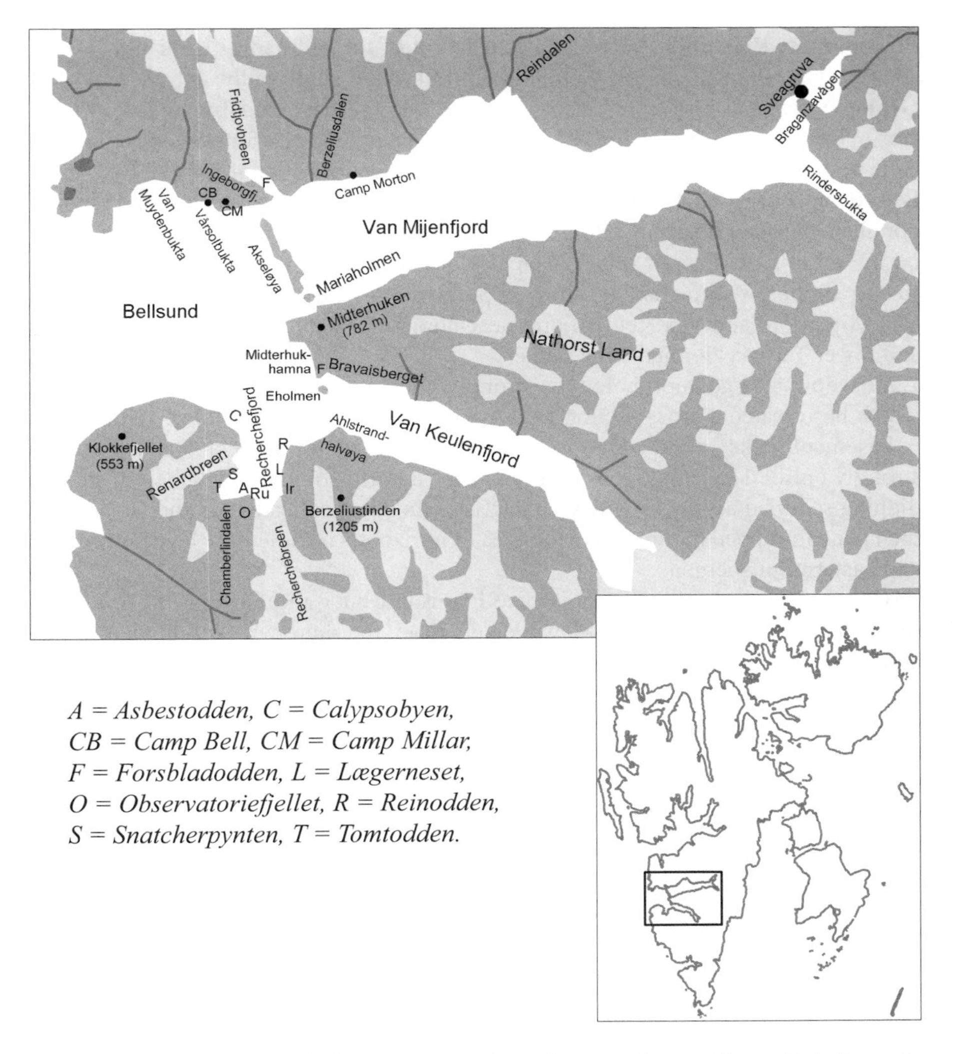

A = Asbestodden, C = Calypsobyen,
CB = Camp Bell, CM = Camp Millar,
F = Forsbladodden, L = Lægerneset,
O = Observatoriefjellet, R = Reinodden,
S = Snatcherpynten, T = Tomtodden.

not a tourist place. Instead, there are a number of interesting and beautiful places in Bellsund with attractive scenery and typical wildlife. Remains from earlier days, when people tried to make their fortune here, are still rusting away, but as soon as you have left those behind, the tundra can be enjoyed for walks or long hikes.

The north side of Bellsund is within reach for energetic hikers from Longyearbyen or Barentsburg. Together with the north side of Van Mijenfjord (except Sveagruva), it is part of the Nordenskiöld Land National Park. The south side of Bellsund and Van Keulenfjord are in the South Spitsbergen National Park. Refer to the sections 6.23.1 to 6.23.3 for the individual branches of Bellsund.

Placenames: Bellsund: Norwegian translation of the old name "Klok bay", "Bell sound". After the bell-shaped mountain **Klokkefjellet** south of the entrance.
Geology: Bellsund has a representative cross section with rocks and structures from most eras of Spitsbergen's geological history; worth seeing, not just for trained geologists. Both age and degree of deformation of the rocks decrease from west to east, as in Isfjord and Hornsund. Strongly deformed basement rocks such as schist and phyllite dominate the outer reaches of Bellsund including Recherchefjord and the coastal plain on the north side. East of this basement block, there is a belt of deformed, mostly steeply dipping sediments, that show impressively in the landscape. Further east, in Van Mijenfjord and Van Keulenfjord, near-horizontal sediments from the Mesozoic and lower Tertiary dominate the scenery.
Landscape: The geomorphology is strongly influenced by the geological structure, which has created a cross section from west to east as follows: Wide coastal plains in basement rocks on the west coast, then the first range of mountains in the area of strongly uplifted basement rocks. Further east, a north-south trending belt of steeply dipping sedimentary rocks with characteristic mountains, headlands and islands and then plateau-topped mountains in the area of horizontal sedimentary layers in central and eastern Spitsbergen.

Bellsund is not as strongly glaciated as Hornsund, but is more so than the south side of Isfjord, further north. Only a few glaciers reach the shore with calving ice-fronts, and all glaciers follow the current trend of retreat.

Many coastal plains show excellent series of raised beaches.
Flora and fauna: Bellsund has a varied ecological pattern. The relatively mild local climate makes itself felt, and the tundra on the lowlands is regarded as middle-arctic "Mountain avens zone" or "Arctic bell-heather zone". Local factors such as bedrock and fertilisation from birdcliffs have created a varied mosaic.

There are a number of seabird colonies on steeper slopes in Bellsund, where representatives of a rather sub-arctic avifauna breed next to common species such as Brünich's guillemots, Kittiwakes and Little auks: Puffins and even a few Common guillemots, indicate the mild influence of the West-Spitsbergen current. The breeding colonies are inaccessible on high slopes. Some of the smaller islands are important breeding sites for Common eiders, and there may always be the odd King eider within a group of Common eiders.
Reindeer and Arctic fox roam the tundra, especially in the vicinity of bird colonies, and Polar bears are not uncommon. In the early summer, bears plunder the nests of tundra breeders (Common eiders, Arctic terns) and may then migrate through the fjords and over the glaciers back to the east coast.
History: Bellsund was for a while believed to have the longest history in Spitsbergen, until rumours of a stone-age population were disproved during systematic investigations of potential sites in 1997. Akseløya in particular had previously been believed to be a place where stone-age people might possibly have lived. There is no doubt, though, that Willem Barents saw Bellsund in 1596, when he called it "Inwyck". During the

following centuries, whalers, Pomors, scientific expeditions, hopeful mining enthusiasts and trappers have all been to Bellsund and left traces of their presence in different places (see the following sections 6.23.1-6.23.3).

6.23.1 Recherchefjord

General: Recherchefjord is a relatively small fjord, eight kilometres long, on the south side of Bellsund, and you can discover a number of decaying witnesses to Spitsbergen's adventurous past, while strolling over the beautiful tundra. Recherchefjord is inside the South Spitsbergen National Park. There are plans to restrict access to the historical site at Lægerneset in the future. For map, see section 6.23 *Bellsund* (page 451).

Placenames: Asbestodden: after the mineral asbestos. **Calypsobyen:** after a ship used by an English expedition in 1895. **Chamberlindalen:** Thomas Chrowder C. (1843-1928), US-american geologist. **Jarnfjellet:** "Iron mountain", after ore occurrences. **Lægerneset:** "Lair point". **Recherchefjord:** after the French expedition ship *Recherche*. **Renardbreen:** (French/Norwegian) "Fox glacier". **Observatoriefjellet**: referring to an astronomical observatory that was operated on top of the mountain during the *Recherche* expedition. **Rubypynten** and **Snatcherpynten:** after ships used by an English expedition in 1895. **Tomtodden:** Tomt (Norwegian) = dwelling site.

Geology: Mostly basement rocks: deformed, metamorphic schists, phyllites, quartzites and carbonates. "Staining" with minerals, mostly iron oxides, causes nice discolouration of these rocks in places. Younger rocks are restricted to the coast on both sides of the entrance: Carboniferous and Permian sandstones, conglomerates and carbonates on the east side; lower Tertiary sandstones, shale, conglomerates and some coal seams on the west side.

Landscape: Pointed mountains and ridges with heights of between 500 and 800 metres rise on both sides of Recherchefjord. Both major glaciers, Renardbreen on the west side and Recherchebreen at the head, are retreating; Recherchebreen does not have a calving front anymore, but is separated from the fjord by a lagoon and a beach. There are more or less level tundra areas everywhere around the fjord and one major, ice free valley, Chamberlindalen, leads nine kilometres inland from the southwest corner of Recherchefjord, with several pingos on the valley floor.

Flora and fauna: Rich tundra vegetation on suitable terrain in inner Recherchefjord and Chamberlindalen, especially at Asbestodden.

History: The very **first wintering of Europeans** in Spitsbergen was probably in Recherchefjord, when eight whalers were accidentally left behind in 1630. The eight men managed to survive the winter, probably near **Renardbreen** on the west side of the fjord. The site was later destroyed during an advance of the glacier. Bellsund was, at this time, an important area for whalers and there was a shore station with buildings and several blubber ovens at **Lægerneset**. Some foundations and graves can still be seen. Another station was located a little to the south of **Snatcherpynten** on the west side, although there is not much left to be seen today.

The first major non-commercial expedition that went to Recherchefjord was the Russian one in 1764 led by Vasilij Vakovlevitsj **Tsjitsjagov**. The main purpose of this expedition was to reach the North Pole, and a base with no less than 16 huts was built at **Tomtodden** where a party was left for the winter. All eight survived the first winter, but a second winter during the following year (1765-66) proved fatal and all eight died. The rest of the expedition was not much more successful. Neither was the North Pole reached, nor was the chance used to do some research elsewhere. Only some foundations remain at Tomtodden. They look pretty much like those of Pomor houses, and it can be assumed that the buildings were indeed used by Pomors once Tsjitsjavog's expedition had left.

The Russians were followed by a French expedition in 1838, that sailed to different places in the north Atlantic on board the ***Recherche***. They spent two weeks in the fjord that received its name on this occasion, and did much better than their predecessors in terms of research work. Amongst other projects, they operated a small observatory on top of the 565 metre high mountain **Observatoriefjellet** south of Asbestodden.

The next to visit was an English squadron, that charted Recherchefjord in 1895 during a training cruise.

The early 20th century was the time of hectic mining attempts in Spitsbergen, and Bellsund, especially Recherchefjord, was a focus for those who hoped to find treasures in the frozen rocks. The English **NEC** (**Northern Exploration Company**) tried its luck at no less than four sites within this relatively small fjord. The NEC claimed to have found "a mountain of iron" (Jarnfjellet) on the east side. It can be assumed that the mountain was mostly of rocks rather than pure metal, just as it had been during earlier investigations and just as is now, and activities during the year 1918-19 did not go beyond the stage of investigation. Four quite large buildings, proudly named "Iron mountain Camp", were erected; today, there is still one collapsing ruin left.

The NEC left a pile of mine carts at **Snatcherpynten** on the southwest side of the fjord. It is a bit unclear why the place was chosen, because there are no occurrences of potentially economical minerals there. It is assumed that Snatcherpynten was only used for temporary storage, although it is hard to believe that the effort was taken to offload the mine carts at a place where they would obviously never be used. The house at Snatcherpynten does not have anything to do with the NEC (or other mining companies); it was built in 1904 by the Norwegian consul **Johannes Gjæver** for reasons that are not entirely clear. It is assumed that Gjæver, a clever businessman, had plans to bring tourists to this scenic fjord with its good reindeer-hunting opportunities. The house, still known as **Gjævervilla,** was too large to be used as a private hut for hunting purposes alone. Later, Gjæver sold his property to the NEC. The one thing that Gjæver had in common with the NEC was that neither went beyond the preparatory stages in Recherchefjord, but the area was used for hunting by Norwegian trappers. Not all of them were lucky enough to return home alive: there are some early 20th century graves not far from Gjævervilla.

At **Asbestodden**, there is a small occurrence of – guess what – yes: asbestos. Both a Norwegian company and the almost ubiquitous NEC have left a hut each, but neither took operations to the stage of actual mining, although the leader of the NEC-group in 1919 was none other than **Frank Wild**, Ernest Shackleton's courageous and firm second-in-command on his famous *Endurance* expedition to Antarctica. Shackleton himself was supposed to lead the NEC expedition in 1918, but the British government decided to send him to military service in northern Russia.

There is a fourth place in Recherchefjord where NEC tried to extract potentially valuable minerals; a seam of lower Tertiary coal at Calypsostranda, on the west side of the fjord entrance. During its heyday in 1918-20, **Calypsobyen** was almost a little village and one of NEC's largest operations in Spitsbergen, next to Camp Mansfield on Blomstrandhalvøya – in other words, it was one of those places where most money was "burnt". In 1919, a radio station was established there, and 133 tons of coal were broken during the following winter. Four buildings are still in good condition, and not only maintained as a cultural heritage site by the Sysselmannen, but regularly used by Polish scientists from the university of Lublin, who do field work during the summer.

The oldest hut at Calypsostranda is a single building a few hundred metres east of Calypsobyen. "Camp Jacobsen" was built already in 1901 as accommodation during investigations of the coal seam, by order of Christian Michelsen, then shipowner and later to become Norway's first prime minister. Camp Jacobsen is one of the oldest houses in Svalbard that is still standing.

All NEC houses were used by trappers who were occasionally even paid by the NEC for "guarding functions", in addition to trapping foxes.

6.23.2 Van Keulenfjord

General: Van Keulenfjord cuts 35 kilometres into Spitsbergen. Its inner reaches are rarely visited by tourists, but the entrance area near Bellsund has very attractive scenery and tundra that is inviting for walks of various durations. The south side of Van Keulenfjord is part of the South Spitsbergen National Park. Norwegian authorities are considering to restrict access to the historical site at Midterhukhamna in the future. For map, see section 6.23 *Bellsund* (page 451).

Placenames: Ahlstrandodden: Johan August A. (1822-96), "Swedish librarian, interested in polar research". Back then it was obviously easier to get a place named after oneself than it is today. **Berzeliustind:** Jöns Jakob B. (1779-1848), Swedish chemist. **Bourbonhamna:** Henry prince of B. (1851-1905). **Bravaisberget:** August B. (1811-63), member of the *Recherche* expedition. **Eholmen:** "Common eider islet". **Forsbladodden:** Nils Jacob F. (born in 1874), Swedish Captain and member of polar expeditions. **Kapp Toscana:** after an Austrian aristocratic family that was related to the family of Parma-Bourbon. **Midterhuken, Midterhukfjellet:** after the position in the middle of the surrounding fjords. **Nathorstbreen:** Gabriel N. (1850-1921), Swedish geologist and polar explorer. **Van Keulenfjord:** after a family of Dutch cartographers in the early 17th century.

Geology: The only outcrop of basement rocks (metamorphic carbonates) is the western point of Midterhuken; the rest of the area is made up of sediments from the Carboniferous and Permian into the lower Tertiary. Age and degree of deformation decrease from west to east. There is a north-south trending belt where the strata are strongly deformed, folded and tilted to an inclined or vertical attitude. Midterhukfjellet, Forsbladodden, Eholmen, Ahlstrandodden and Berzeliustind are part of this belt. Especially hard layers of fossil-rich Permian carbonates and flint, the so-called Kapp Starostin formation, are prominent as they create conspicuous islands, headlands and free-standing walls on the tundra. Berzeliustind (1,205 metres), the highest mountain of Van Keulenfjord, has a dramatic, jagged slope that is made up of these hard strata in a near-vertical attitude. These rocks continue under water across the entrance to Van Keulenfjord, but depths are large enough for medium-sized ships to sail through. East of this belt, the steep attitude of the strata decreases from near-vertical to sloping and finally to near-horizontal. The dip of the layers gives a markedly tilted-over appearance to the mountains east of Berzeliustind (south side) and Midterhukfjellet (north side). The age of the sediments in this area is Mesozoic and they are markedly darker and more uniform in appearance than the Permian strata further west. The youngest rocks are horizontal layers of lower Tertiary sandstones and several coal seams in the inner reaches of Van Keulenfjord, where the mountains are topped by vast plateaux.
Landscape: The general geomorphology is clearly influenced by the geological structure. Flat tundra is mostly restricted to the south side of the fjord around Ahlstrandhalvøya near the entrance to Bellsund. The only flat area on the north side is Forsbladodden, opposite Ahlstrandhalvøya. The only calving glacier of Van Keulenfjord is Nathorstbreen at the head of the fjord, which is hidden round a bend.

There are beautiful geometric patterns of raised beaches on the plains near the entrance (Ahlstrandhalvøya, Forsbladodden) that have some well-developed ice wedge polygons. Relatively well protected bays include Van Keulenhamna on the east side of Forsbladodden and Bourbonhamna east of Ahlstrandodden.
Flora and fauna: Depending on local factors such as microclimate and subsoil, the tundra on the coastal lowlands is rather scarce, but mostly quite rich. There are bird colonies on the high, steep slopes of Berzeliustinden and Midterhukfjellet. The small islands in the entrance to Van Keulenfjord are important breeding sites for Common eiders, and geese feed on the tundra after the spring migration. Arctic terns and Arctic skuas are breeding on level ground, both of them ready at any time to attack anything that comes too close. Small birds such as Snow bunting and Purple sandpiper are common, and Grey phalarope often search for food at the shore of Ahlstrandodden.

Pods of White whales used to be common up to the early 20th century, but the population was then decimated by excessive hunting and has not returned to original levels again.
History: Whalers ran one of several shore stations in Bellsund, in **Midterhukhamna** under the slopes of the magnificent Midterhukfjellet, with the usual facilities: several blubber ovens, buildings and a grave field.

Bellsund was one of the first trapping fields that were taken into use by Norwegian trappers in the late 19th century, and in 1898, a smaller cabin was built in **Midterhukhamna** that was primarily used during travelling; the main hut was on Akseløya. The small building is still standing and being maintained by the Sysselmannen, as it is one of the oldest of its kind in Spitsbergen. The main target species of the trappers was the Arctic fox, but they took basically anything they could get hold of, including White whales, of which some bones are still bleaching in the sun. Midterhukhamna is a sensitive site because of remains spanning more than 350 years of Spitsbergen history, and some lush, but vulnerable moss beds. Visitors should move around with care. Special regulations for visits to Midterhukhamna may be imposed by Norwegian authorities in the future.

In 1891 and 1892, Bellsund had noble visitors when Prince **Henry of Bourbon** sailed to the arctic with his yacht *Fleur de Lys* and spent some time charting Van Keulenfjord.

A number of huts were built in Van Keulenfjord by the **NEC** (see section 6.23.1 *Recherchefjord*) to underpin claims, but activities never went beyond claiming territory and building huts. These were later used by trappers, but none of the buildings still exist.

The latest period of whaling in Spitsbergen, on a level that was more or less industrial, was an intense White whale fishery that was carried out with nets in the entrance area of Van Keulenfjord. The two kilometre long beach east of Ahlstrandodden is still called "Kvitfiskstranda" ("White whale beach"). There is a large and robust hut at the eastern end of this beach called **Bamsebu** and, near that hut, several large piles of Beluga bones are bleaching in the midnight sun. Further west at Ahlstrandodden, several old rowing boats that were used in those times in the 1930s are lying upside down on the beach.

Miscellaneous: A Norwegian has harvested down from Common eider nests from some colonies in Bellsund, especially Eholmen where almost 3,000 pairs breed within a small area. The down is cleaned in a hut at the south end of Akseløya and then sold. Collecting down from Common eider nests in a careful, considerate way does not harm the adult birds or their offspring and is still done commercially in Iceland, for example. The down collecting activity in Bellsund is one more good reason to stay clear of the ducks' nesting sites. This should be done anyway, and the most important breeding colonies are now bird reserves and are thus inaccessible during the sensitive season, regardless of whether one wants to collect memories and photographs or down.

6.23.3 Van Mijenfjord, Akseløya, northern Bellsund

General: Van Mijenfjord is separated from Bellsund by the long and narrow island of Akseløya and cuts 50 kilometres into Spitsbergen. It has two inner branches, Braganzavågen and Rindersbukta. Akseløya, which is eight kilometres long but less than one kilometre wide, protects Van Mijenfjord from the swell of the open ocean which can be troublesome in Bellsund. On the other hand, it keeps the fjord ice stable longer into the summer than elsewhere in fjords along the central west coast, much to the disgust of the Norwegian coal mining company *Store Norske Spitsbergen Kullkompani* (SNSK), because icebreakers are needed to start the coal shipping season at the mining settlement of **Sveagruva**. This is expensive and it does not meet with sympathy from environmentalists. The nautically challenging passage of the large coal ships through the narrow passage north of Akseløya, with its strong tidal currents, is another matter that has attracted attention. While some probably have secret dreams of blowing up Akseløya (or at least one half of it), for others it is a pearl of arctic scenery, nature and history.

During spring, the ice conditions in Van Mijenfjord east of Akseløya are quite reliable, to the advantage of sledgers, be they driven by engines or dogs, and of brave ski travellers, but the narrow sounds north and south of Akseløya stay ice-free due to the strong tidal currents. Attention also needs to be paid to the date of the first icebreaker that cuts a passage to Sveagruva, making a sledge journey across the fjord impossible. The date is published in the local press (Svalbardposten) or can be obtained from the Sysselmannen or tourist information in Longyearbyen.

Van Mijenfjord is within reach for several-day-long hiking or skiing trips from Longyearbyen. In the summer especially, the outer reaches are attractive due to their varied scenery and ecology. Energetic hikers can reach outer Van Mijenfjord or Bellsund within a few days from Longyearbyen, and Barentsburg is even closer. Some crossings of torrential rivers are part of the adventure, but it is not advisable to attempt to cross Reindalselva, certainly not near the mouth. It is one of the largest rivers in Spitsbergen and definitely dangerous or even impossible at times during the melting season.

The northern side of Van Mijenfjord, except for the inner part east of Reindalen, is part of the Nordenskiöld Land National Park. The establishment of this protected area in 2003 has hopefully put an end to any discussion about a road between Longyearbyen and Sveagruva that would cut through some of the largest and richest tundra areas of Svalbard, namely in Reindalen. For map, see section 6.23 *Bellsund* (page 451).

Placenames: Akseløya: after the Norwegian sealing ship *Axel Thordsen*, that was used in the late 19th century. **Berzeliusdalen:** Jöns Jakob B. (1779-1848), Swedish chemist. **Braganzavågen:** Aldegonda princess of B. (born in 1858), married to prince Henry of Bourbon (see section 6.23.2 *Van Keulenfjord*). **Camp Millar:** Herbert M., shareholder of the Northern Exploration Company. **Fridtjovbreen**: after a Norwegian sealing ship. **Ingeborgfjellet:** after a legendary figure of Norse mythology. **Mariaholmen:** small island near Akseløya, probably following the Swedish poem "Axel and Maria". **Paulabreen:** P., born as baroness Hagen (born in 1871), related to prince Henry of Bourbon (see section 6.23.2 *Van Keulenfjord*). **Reindalen:** "Reindeer valley". **Rindersbukta:** Michiel R., Dutch whaler (17th century). **Sveagruva:** "Swedish mine". **Van Mijenfjord:** wrong spelling of Van Muyden, a Dutch whaler. **Van Muydenbukta:** Willem van M., commander of the Dutch whaling fleet in 1612-13. **Vårsolbukta:** after a Norwegian sealing ship.

Geology: The geology of Van Mijenfjord is very similar to that of its southern neighbour Van Keulenfjord. The rocks and structures influence the scenery in a very striking way that inspires not only trained geologists. The local history is also strongly related to mineral occurrences.

Basement is exposed east of Ingeborgfjellet with quartzites and phyllites. The structural boundary between basement and younger sedimentary cover rocks runs exactly under the old huts of Camp Millar, but there are no good outcrops.

Steeply dipping strata, including hard Permian sediments, form a north-south trending belt that includes Akseløya. These strongly deformed sediments from the upper Palaeozoic (Carboniferous and Permian) and lower Mesozoic (Triassic and Jurassic) continue northwards in Ingeborgfjellet and southwards in Midterhukfjellet: an especially beautiful pattern of folds is exposed on the northern slope of Midterhukfjellet. The intricate combination of larger and smaller folds makes a nice contrast to the larger, elegant curves of Ingeborgfjellet. The deformation must be younger than the youngest involved rocks, which date into the lower Cretaceous and even include lower Tertiary sediments in other places, meaning that it is related to the opening of the north Atlantic that started about 100 million years ago.

East of this deformed belt, tectonic structures and accordingly also the landscape features, are gentler and more widely spaced, with relatively uniform, horizontal sedimentary strata (sandstone, siltstone, shale, conglomerates) from the lower Tertiary that contain those up to four-meter-thick coal seams which are mined in the coal field of Sveagruva.

Landscape: The centre-piece of the exciting scenery is Akseløya, which is the prominent boundary between Bellsund and Van Mijenfjord with their marked differences in geology, scenery and ice conditions. The direct influence that geology has on geomorphology, ecology and history can hardly be more evident than in Van Mijenfjord. The beautiful patterns of folded layers are evident on Akseløya and to the north and south of it. A more local contrast is seen on the east side of Akseløya where Triassic rocks are exposed, creating low-lying level ground with much more vegetation than on the adjacent ridges of harder Permian rocks that are up to 60 metres high.
The scenery around inner Van Mijenfjord is dominated by plateau-topped mountains that are in strong contrast to Ingeborgfjellet and Midterhuken.

West of Ingeborgfjellet is a very wide coastal plain covered with ancient raised beaches. These provide mostly excellent footpaths with their dry and solid surface, only the outlet rivers of some lakes providing obstacles in places. A lot of interesting details, like frost-patterned ground, can be seen on this seemingly empty plain.

The hinterland to both sides of Van Mijenfjord is not strongly glaciated. Nordenskiöld Land on the north side is well-known for its ice-free valleys, the largest in Svalbard. The largest is Reindalen that has a twelve kilometres wide mouth and debouches into Van Mijenfjord. Berzeliusdalen west of Reindalen and Kjellströmdalen near Sveagruva, are not much smaller. Soft tundra can make walking difficult. The large rivers may be difficult or even impossible to cross during the melting season, and when you have followed one huge valley for two days, seeing the same landscape the whole time, you may prefer smaller side valleys next time.

Only two glaciers reach the shores of Van Mijenfjord. Paulabreen in Rindersbukta in the innermost reaches of the fjord has a strongly incised calving front. The dramatic retreat during recent centuries has left huge moraine ridges on both sides of the fjord, reaching beyond Sveagruva, a distance of more than 20 kilometres from today's glacier front. The second calving glacier in Van Mijenfjord has an interesting history. Fridtjovbreen had a calving front in inner Fridtjovhamna in the early 1990s, until it made a very rapid and pronounced advance in 1996, filling almost the whole bay and threatening to destroy a trapper's hut. This was first moved a short distance during hurried rescue operations and was later replaced by another hut at the south end of Akseløya, more than far enough from the dangerous glacier. Fridtjovbreen has, since then, retreated again and its surface, that was very crevassed and broken after 1996, has become much more even again.

Flora and fauna: The large valleys north of Van Mijenfjord have extensive rich tundra areas with strong reindeer populations. Plains near mountains with bird cliffs also have lush vegetation, which is the case under Ingeborgfjellet and Midterhukfjellet. Arctic foxes thrive in these places. Another area with relatively rich plant life is the smaller area of level ground on the east side of Akseløya, that contrasts with the relatively barren ridges that form the backbone of the island. The west coast plain north of Bellsund becomes relatively barren, as soon as you are away from the area influenced by the bird cliffs at Ingeborgfjellet.

The largest seabird cliffs of the area are at Midterhukfjellet and Ingeborgfjellet. Brünich's guillemots, Kittiwakes and Fulmars breed in large numbers on the higher, steep slopes, always in the company of Glaucous gulls, and even some sub-arctic Common guillemots which are said to be breeding in Bellsund. Little auks have breeding sites in the lower slopes that are covered with scree. The noise level is quite impressive in the early summer, when the colonies are busy and air traffic is accordingly intense.

Flat tundra areas with rich vegetation, for example near Ingeborgfjellet, are important feeding grounds for geese after the spring and before the autumn migrations. Eider ducks breed in large numbers on small offshore islands and gather in large groups near the coast, and there is always the chance for the odd King eider to be amongst them. Reindeer are common on all tundra areas.

History: The history of outer Van Mijenfjord, including Akseløya and Bellsund, is long and varied, corresponding with the richness that nature provides. There are a number **Pomor sites** with relics of hunting stations from the 17th and 18th centuries. Three of them, all on the outer coast north of Bellsund, have been dated to the middle of the 16th century by Russian archaeologists. This would be before Barents' discovery of Spitsbergen in 1596 but is, however, debatable.

The south end of **Akseløya** was the place chosen by an early pioneer of modern (mostly Norwegian) trapping in Spitsbergen. **Johan Hagerup** built a hut there in

1898 and, together with four companions, a number of smaller cabins for use during travelling. One of these huts is still standing, at Midterhukhamna. Trappers in Bellsund would mostly target Arctic foxes. Hagerup used the area for a number of years, with relatively large parties of up to nine men. Next to the reduction of local wildlife populations, Hagerup was also interested in science. For several years, he made complete records of meteorological data at a time when there were no weather stations in Spitsbergen and, in 1902-03, he provided accomodation to a scientist of the "Norwegian Northern Light Expedition" which observed the aurora simultaneously from Iceland, north Norway Novaya Zemlya and Akseløya. Hagerup's house on Akseløya is a bit unusual compared to other trappers' huts, as it is largely made of local stone and not of wood. Located in the immediate neighbourhood of the modern house, it is still in good condition thanks to maintenance work done by the Norwegian administration. Small concrete blocks not far from the house were foundations for astronomical instruments used in 1902-03. The oldest traces at the site are foundations of Pomor houses.

The English **NEC (Northern Exploration Company)** had a number of huts in northern Bellsund and Van Mijenfjord, that were supposed to be used during prospecting and mining operations. Some were not really used and probably only built to underline claims to the territory while the NEC had hopes for prosperous mining at other locations. The following places were the most important NEC sites (from west to east).

A minor occurrence of zinc ore, originally found by the Norwegian geologist Adolf Hoel in 1913, was investigated on **Sinkholmen**, a small island belonging to a small group of islets called Reiniusøyane, between Van Muydenbukta and Vårsolbukta. A hut was built and 20 tons of zinc ore were extracted in 1924 followed by 240 tons in 1925. In 1926, a vertical mine shaft was dug 34 feet down and 30 tons of ore were broken out.
Camp Bell (Vårsolbukta): The NEC was hoping to find coal in Carboniferous strata in Vårsolbukta with its attractive scenery, not far from the mighty Ingeborgfjellet with its large bird cliffs, but met with no success. The hut belongs now to the Sysselmannen and was moved inland in 1999 to protect it from encroaching marine erosion.

Only a few hundred meters further east, the NEC expected gold occurrences in the boundary zone between metamorphic basement and sedimentary cover rocks. Instead of using Camp Bell, two new huts were built and called **Camp Millar**. The gold vein, as it turned out, did not exist. A little pile of mine carts and a small mine shaft are evidence of busy digging at Camp Millar. Both huts are still in good condition and the original appearance has been preserved. One is owned by the Sysselmannen, the other by a club in Longyearbyen.
Camp Morton: approximately 50 persons wintered in 1918-19 under the leadership of **Frank Wild**, who had been second-in-command during Ernest Shackleton's famous *Endurance* expedition, to prepare for mining of coal seams. The quality and quantity of the occurrence did not meet expectations, and activities were not continued beyond this first season when four houses were standing at Camp Morton. One had already

been built in 1901 by Christian Michelsen, who was later to become Norway's first prime minister, for leisure time purposes and possibly to promote (hunting) tourism, but it was apparently not used a lot. One of the old NEC huts is still maintained by a club in Longyearbyen and is accordingly in good condition, and some mining equipment is still lying around.

Norwegian trappers were happy to use the solid and comfortable NEC huts and, instead of paying some rent to the NEC, they themselves were paid for their presence so that the NEC could make a pretence of maintaining them. Some of the old huts at Camp Morton, Camp Millar and Camp Bell are still standing and some other remains can still be seen. Anyone who is attracted to the area by the scenery and nature should not miss the spectacle of visible reminders of bad investments in the early 20th century. The huts, as usual, have their respective owners and must not be used without permission; they are normally locked.

While the NEC built one hut after the other without ever scratching anything of value out of the ground, a Swedish mining company started a coal mining operation in the innermost Van Mijenfjord in 1917. The mine was aptly called **Sveagruva**. The Swedes did not have much more luck than their competitors and finally sold their property in 1934 to the Norwegan SNSK (Store Norske Spitsbergen Kullkompani). The small evacuated settlement was largely destroyed in 1944 by a German submarine, but mining was re-started in 1946 to supply Norway's urgent domestic needs. In 2000, Sveagruva was modernised and extended and by then, it had replaced Longyearbyen as the centre of Norwegian coal mining activity in Spitsbergen. A new coal field, "Sentralfeltet" has been opened some kilometres north of Sveagruva, where coal seams up to five metres thick are mined. Sentralfeltet is situated under a local ice cap with an ice thickness of up to 250 metres, which causes difficulties due to meltwater. 4,000,000 tons of coal were exported in 2007, of which 70% was bought by German companies (steel and energy production), and production is planned to increase gradually. A new mine at Lunckefjellet north of Sveagruva is planned to be opened in 2013. Despite technical difficulties and an accident in which one man died, the SNSK has even made some profit in Sveagruva in favourable years, a rarity in the company's history. Most miners actually live in Longyearbyen and commute to Sveagruva by air for their tour of duty; some of their families even live in Norway.

Sveagruva is a mining settlement and other economic activities, including tourism, are not provided for. It is not an attractive place for individual (and most other) tourists, although the hotel is used during organised snow mobile excursions on the way from or to the east coast. Sveagruva is conveniently located about half-way between the east and the west coast. Kapp Linné and Barentsburg are possible destinations that have overnighting facilities. Individual tourists should not expect any services (opportunities to stock up foodstuffs, accommodation) to be available in Sveagruva.

Miscellaneous: The house at the south end of Akseløya is owned by a Norwegian who collects Eider down in Bellsund during the early summer. It is private property and the immediate vicinity should be considered private and not be invaded without the house owner's permission, especially if he is around (although he is not the land owner).

Trapper huts at the south end of Akseløya. The small one to the far left is the oldest one, built in 1898, called "Hagerup-hytta". The large one to the right is still in use. Midterhukfjellet is in the background.

Chapter 7 – Arctic environmental problems and tourism

There continues to be widespread and, in some cases, dramatic evidence of an overall warming of the Arctic system.

Arctic Report Card 2008, NOAA
(National Oceanic And Atmospheric Administration,
United States Department Of Commerce)

„Civilization exists by geological consent ... subject to change without notice“,

Will Durant, American historian, 1885-1981

Currently, the fragile arctic environment has to cope with a whole number of man-made burdens. Most of these originate in countries far to the south of the north Atlantic; others are more local. Norway has announced that Svalbard will be developed to become one of the best preserved wilderness areas in the world, and there cannot be any doubt that many regulations are getting stricter and stricter. More steps still need to be taken before Svalbard, including the surrounding marine environment, is fully protected from the harmful influences of fishery, mining and the oil industry; the attention of the oil and gas industry from Norway and Russia is focussing increasingly on the Barents shelf.

I do not want to go deeper into details of problems related to fishery, mining and hydrocarbons, although they will need a lot of attention in the future. I prefer to write some paragraphs on simple measures that everyone can take to improve the environmental situation. A welcome side effect is the fact that many of these measures also affect Antarctica and the whole globe. We all have the opportunity to decrease our own environmental impact greatly. Our influence on other problems is limited and rather indirect, but no less important. One important step is to develop an awareness of individual responsibility for the (arctic) environment. This can start during a voyage in polar regions, but it is vital to keep the awareness beyond the end of the trip and let small but important steps follow at home.

Means of transportation

Environmentally friendly ways of travelling are hiking, cross-country skiing and dog sledging.

Ship-based voyages create CO_2 and other emissions, but usually on a reasonable level, although the situation can be different for individual vessels depending on age and technical outfit.

Nautical safety is of decisive importance. Next to danger to life and limb of all people on board, it is the environment that is seriously threatened in the case of oil spills. Compared to heavy fuels such as crude oil that can pollute for many years, light marine diesel disappears relatively quickly from the environment. In Svalbard, the Norwegian government has recently banned ships that use heavy fuels from most areas; waters that are poorly charted may be closed for navigation in the near future, at least until good charts are available. Ships used in polar waters should be ice-strengthened; this does not mean that they necessarily have to be ice-breakers. Bilge waters must be discharged to special facilities in larger ports.

Other forms of propulsion, used on some cruise ships in polar areas, are sails and nuclear energy. The respective environmental advantages and disadvantages of both are well-known and should be considered when you decide for or against a certain voyage.

Getting to Spitsbergen

This is getting tricky. One return flight from London Heathrow via Oslo to Longyearbyen and back creates almost two tons of carbon dioxide (in the higher atmosphere, where the greenhouse gas effect is stronger), whereas three tons per person (at sea level) for a whole year is considered to be a sustainable level for the control of climate change. The additional influence of vapour induced by aircraft is not yet fully understood, but there can be little doubt that it is significant and needs to be addressed. The general problem of global climate change, at least partly induced by man, with its dramatic social, economic and ecological consequences, is now well-known and does not require further discussion here; see the reports of the IPCC (*Intergovernmental Panel on Climate Change*, provides the United Nations and governments with scientific advice, www.ipcc.ch). The consequences for polar areas, especially the Arctic, will be dramatic and are already starting to show. The decrease of sea ice in many parts of the Arctic in recent years, including Svalbard, is an evident fact and only one of many examples. It is a dilemma that all who travel to the Arctic to enjoy its seemingly untouched nature increase the environmental pressure on it at the same time. Currently, changes for example in sea ice cover that are already observed exceed predictions in velocity and magnitude.

What can we do?

The first and most important thing is to consider whether the flight in question is really necessary. Isn't there a train, a bus or a ferry? Is it really true that all attractive destinations are on the other side of the globe?

If you want to travel in Spitsbergen, then a flight is usually unavoidable. If we cannot avoid CO_2-emissions, then we can do something to support carbon storage or support some means of saving CO_2 emissions elsewhere – this can be anywhere on the globe. A number of organisations offer to estimate the amount of CO_2 that a certain flight creates and the amount of money needed to save this amount elsewhere. The amount can then be donated to an appropriate project to save the relevant amount of CO_2. This procedure should follow the CDM (Clean Development mechanism) rules that were established during the Kyoto conference. Various standards have been introduced to ensure maximum quality, for example the "gold standard", which has been developed under WWF leadership and requires even higher ecological and social standards than the CTM criteria. See the author's website (www.spitzbergen.de) for links to relevant organisations.

It has to be clear that terms like "neutralizing emissions", "climate-neutral flying" or even "climate-friendly flying" are misleading. Emissions are a fact and cannot be neutralized, and flying is never climate-friendly. Again, the best thing to do is to avoid flights, but once you have decided to fly, helping to reduce emissions is certainly a good way to take responsibility in a way that follows the "polluter pays" principle.

At home

Many tend to think green during their holidays, but it is all very far away again once back home. Pay attention 365 days a year, business and private. Save energy at home. Buy green energy. Leave the car at home unless you can't avoid it. Use biodegradable chemicals.

Environmental toxins

The arctic environment is suffering from slow toxification. This concerns animals that are high in the food web such as Glaucous gulls and Polar bears, but also indigenous people not in Spitsbergen but in other parts of the Arctic, who use local food resources. These toxins come from industries and agriculture in industrialised countries; local sources are largely irrelevant. Most of us cannot directly influence the production methods of our economies, but we can all choose products that have been produced with minimal environmental damage, that come from local producers.

Fishing

There would hardly be any life in polar areas if the sea was not so incredibly productive. The biological productivity of the marine ecosystem is seriously threatened by overfishing, and the consequences start to show now in many of the world's seas including the Barents sea (see 6.19 *Bjørnøya*, section on *environmental situation*). Currently, neither fishing industries nor politics seem to be able to control the problem. Consequently, the consumer needs to take action. The WWF recommends looking for seafood products with the *Marine Stewardship Council* (MSC) label in restaurants and supermarkets.

Support environmental organisations

Environmental organisations help to introduce and promote green products and give threatened ecosystems a voice in politics on all levels. The more members they have, the bigger the voice and the more likely it is that they will be heard when decisions are made. The WWF website (www.panda.org) can be recommended for further information.

Association of Arctic Expedition Cruise Operators (AECO)

AECO was founded in 2003 and is an international organization for expedition cruise operators. The organization is dedicated to managing respectable, environmentally-friendly and safe expeditions in the Arctic. AECO-members are obliged to operate in accordance with national and international laws and regulations as well as agreed AECO rules and guidelines.

The main objective for AECO is to ensure that expedition cruises and tourism in the Arctic are carried out with the utmost consideration for the vulnerable, natural environment, local cultures and cultural remains, as well as for the challenging safety hazards at sea and on land.

The strategies are:

- To be recognized as one of the primary organizations representing the concerns and views of the expedition cruise tourism companies operating in the Arctic.
- To agree upon and encourage the incorporation of specific standards and guidelines for operating expedition cruises in the Arctic.
- To encourage the use of the best qualified guides and staff, knowledgeable and experienced in the arctic environment and its natural and human history.
- To stimulate and encourage coordination among expedition cruise operators offering voyages to the Arctic.
- To serve as a contact and advisory group to government ministries and agencies responsible for managing and regulating the lands, surrounding marine waters, and human activities in the Arctic
- To interact with and maintain an open dialogue with non-governmental organizations interested in the Arctic.
- To educate all interested groups and people about the Arctic and its unique environment, culture and natural history.

AECO has a set of guidelines, "The AECO guidelines for expedition cruise operations in the Arctic", that have been developed to support members in their efforts to give their visitors memorable experiences of the arctic's unique nature, local cultures, wildlife and cultural remains, while at the same time striving to support the protection of the environment for the future.

For more information, please visit www.aeco.no

Other books written by the same author

Next to a growing number of German books, I have written and published in English:

- Rocks and Ice. Landscapes of the North. A geographical traveling accompaniment for Spitsbergen and East Greenland (68-74°N).
- East Greenland in Winter. On skis through Liverpool Land.

Please visit my website at

www.spitzbergen.de

for books or further information about Spitsbergen and Arctic!

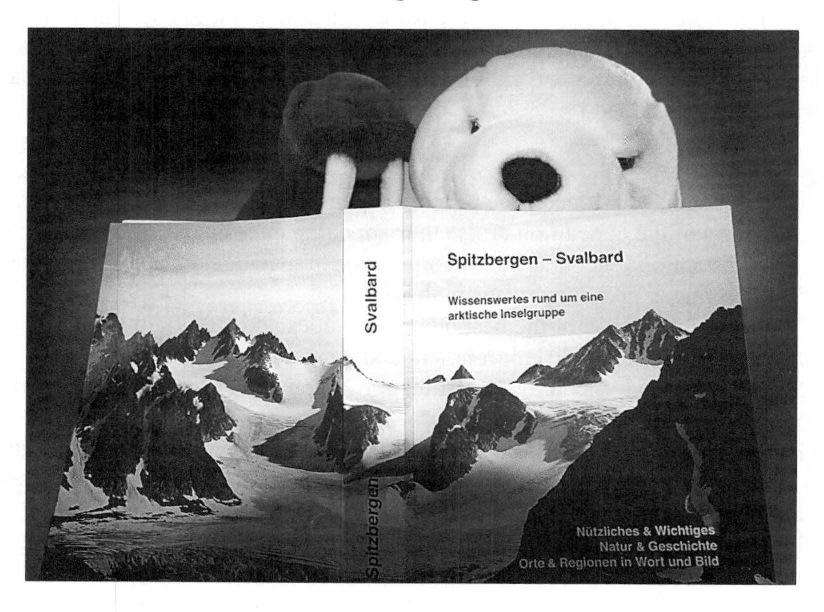

I have also contributed several chapters to "Polar Essays of the Arctic", edited by Monika Schillat and Ian Stone; a very readable book with chapters on subjects ranging from acoustic communication of large whales to the biology of the Svalbard reindeer, the little-known island of Jan Mayen, 17th century whaling in the Arctic, recent environmental threats to Polar bears, Arctic birds and other geological and historical topics. Published in 2007 by Editorial Fuegia, Teuk 882, 9410 Ushuaia, Republica Argentina. ISBN 978-987-05-3490-7.

The author: Rolf Stange

Since I can remember, my parents always went north with me during our summer holidays, often as far as Denmark ☺ I found it exciting if our holiday home was a beach further north than the previous year. I have never lost the desire go north again. In 1993, I went to Norway and Sweden for the first time, followed by Spitsbergen in 1997. While at home, I studied geography in Münster and Bonn.

Three long summers of hiking and trekking in Spitsbergen as well as a three-month winter season at Kapp Linné on the west coast, were followed by my first arctic season on small, ice-strengthened expedition cruise ships to experience the far north together with nature-enthusiasts from many countries of the world. More than 100 expedition cruises in the Arctic and the Antarctic have followed – and I am sure that some more are still to come …

Somehow, I still find some time for private travelling to the north. Next to a larger number of hiking and cross-country skiing trips in Spitsbergen, Norway and Sweden, several-week long cross-country skiing trips in Spitsbergen and East Greenland were highlights of my passion for the north. During the spring of 2006, I spent three months in Ittoqqortoormiit (=Scoresbysund, East Greenland), taking care of and using my own sledge dog team.

I enjoy photography as well as writing books about the Arctic, which I publish myself. Additionally, I am running my own Spitsbergen website (www.spitzbergen.de).

When I am not in the far north or deep south, I am at my home near Rostock in northeast Germany on the Baltic Sea coast.

Thank you!

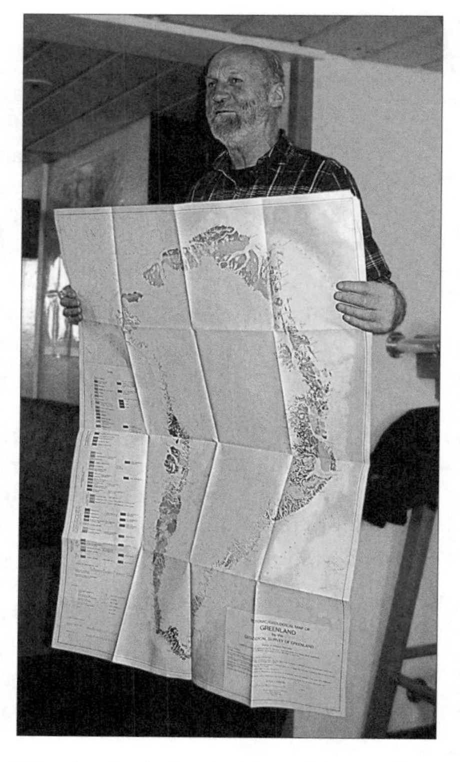

A number of kind people have enabled me in different ways to write this book. But at first, I need to say that I have always insisted on having the last word, and all mistakes and shortcomings of this book are my sole responsibility.

It was **David Matthews** from Scotland who has corrected my first English draft and made sure it would be readable for native English speakers.

Dave publishes unusual writings and translations, mainly polar books, working on a small scale from his workshop in the Scottish Highlands.
Visit him at
http://www.tswpublishing.co.uk/

A lot of what I know about Swiss chocolate and humour, about polar areas and travelling there, and first of all, about the respect that these beautiful areas deserve, I owe to **Peter Balwin**, an experienced expedition leader in the Arctic and Antarctica. Peter has read large parts of the German manuscript and made valuable comments and suggestions.

Paolo Bernat, Piero Bosco and **Stefano Poli** have helped me with Italian names of animals and plants.

My mother **Helke Stange** has filtered the text for remaining misprints, spelling and punctuation mistakes (but I have made sure some mistakes have survived).

Michelle van Dijk, Spitsbergen-friend and fellow countryman of Willem Barents has made her vast knowledge of Spitsbergen's vegetation and the confusing world of the internet available to me.

Claus Wöckener was not only the one, who gave me a first introduction into Spitsbergen's plants and animals in 1997, but he has helped me again with important advice.

For photos and illustrations, I want to thank **Peter Balwin, Arjen Drost, Sabine Formella, Jens Götz ("Wenzel"), Jan Leiendecker, Roman Ruettiman, Horst-Günter Wagner, Michelle van Dijk, Rinie van Meurs**.

Norwegian glossary

The definite article, that is at the end of a Norwegian noun, is in parentheses. Pl. = plural.

Boge(n) = open bay
Bre(en), Pl. Breane = glacier
Bukt(a) = bay
By(en) = town
Dal(en) = valley
Egg(ane) = sharp mountain ridge
Elv(a) = river
Fjell(et), Pl. Fjella = mountain
Fjord(en) = fjord
Fly(a) = plain
Fonn(a) = snow field, glacier, ice cap
Gruve(gruva) = mine
Halvøy(a) = peninsula
Hamn(a) = natural harbour
Holme(n), Pl. Holmane = small islet
Huk(en) = headland
Hytte (hytta) = hut
Jøkul(en) = glacier, ice cap
Kam(men) = ridge
Kapp(et) = cape, headland
Sjø(en) = lake
Slette(sletta) = plain
Sund(et) = sound, strait
Tind(en) = mountain peak
Vatn(et), Pl. Vatna = lake

Geological glossary

Ammonite: Extinct group of marine cephalopods (molluscs) with shells that often resemble rams' horns. Ammon was an ancient Egyptian god with a ram's head. Silurian to Cretaceous.

Anhydrite: see EVAPORITE.

Basalt: dark-coloured volcanic rock derived from molten magma with a low silica content. When cooled at depth below the surface of the earth's crust, forming larger crystals, it is called **gabbro**. **Dolerite** is a sub-volcanic variation of basaltic rocks, which means that it cooled below the surface, but not at great depth, resulting in medium-sized crystals. **Hyperite** is occasionally used synonymously with dolerite.

Basement: In Svalbard, the geological basement comprises all rocks that are older than or contemporary with the Caledonian orogeny during the Silurian. The basement is very inhomogenous in terms of rock types and ages. There are at least three different basement provinces in Svalbard: a belt of metamorphic rocks along the west coast of Spitsbergen, typically phyllite and schist; a zone of metamorphic and magmatic rocks in northern Spitsbergen and northeastern Svalbard; and thirdly, weakly metamorphosed sediments around the northern Hinlopenstretet. All basement rocks have generally been deformed by tectonic movements to a higher degree than the SEDIMENTARY COVER ROCKS that were deposited after the Caledonian orogeny.

Beach ridge: Ridge of sand and gravel above the high tide line, thrown up by waves during heavy storms. In the case of land uplift or a fall in sea level, a beach ridge is left further from the sea and becomes inactive or "fossil". Also called raised beach.

Belemnite: Extinct group of marine cephalopods (molluscs) that were very similar to today's squid. Mostly, only a part of the skeleton that resembles a bullet is preserved. Devonian to Cretaceous.

Brachiopod: Marine invertebrate that resembles bivalves, although they are biologically markedly distinct. Cambrian to recent. Brachiopods are common in Carboniferous and Permian sediments in Spitsbergen.

Breccia: Coarse-grained sediment with large, sharp-edged clasts (rock fragments) that indicate shorter transportation distances (longer movement in flowing water produces rounded edges). The pores are filled with sand and mud.

Carbonate: Carbonate-bearing rock, for example limestone, dolostone.

Cleavage: Parallel orientation of planar minerals, often resulting in the tendency of a rock to split into very thin slices. Typical characteristic of metamorphic rocks such as SCHIST and, PHYLLITE.

Conglomerate: sediment deposited in fast-flowing water, consisting of rounded pebbles and a fine-grained matrix.

Deformation: Combined FOLDing and FAULTing.

Diabas: See BASALT.

Doline: Funnel-shaped holes in the ground after the collapse of caves in water-soluble rocks (CARBONATES, EVAPORITES).

Dolostone: A CARBONATE rock, also called dolomite, but dolostone is more convenient to prevent confusion with the mineral dolomite. Dolostone is chemically similar to limestone. Dolostones comes into being either directly as a sediment or through later chemical changes of LIMESTONE.

Dyke: INTRUSION of magma in a steep or vertical attitude.

Evaporite: Chemical sediment left after the evaporation of large volumes of water, for example GYPSUM, ANHYDRITE and halite (salt).

Fault: Large fracture cutting through rocks, caused by tectonic activity.

Fault zone: Area with a series of more or less parallel faults.

Fjord: Glacial valley submerged by the sea. A classical fjord is surounded by steep slopes and is quite deep, but often has a shallower ridge near the entrance area. Strictly speaking, a fjord should have only one entrance.

Gabbro: See BASALT.

Geomorphology: A branch of earth sciences that describes and explains surface landforms.
Graben: Tectonic structure where a crustal block subsides along two bounding faults, causing deposition of large volumes of sediments. An important example in Spitsbergen is the Devonian Andrée Land Graben; a recent example is the Upper Rhine Valley in southeastern Germany.
Granite: See MAGMATITE.
Grenville-event: Important tectonic phase (OROGENY), approximately 950 to 1,300 million years ago. Evidence for this event is found mostly in the form of radiometric ages of crystalline BASEMENT rocks in northern Spitsbergen and elsewhere. During the Grenville-event, landmasses collided to form a "supercontinent" called Rodinia. About 800 million years ago Rodinia broke into several pieces, long before the creation of the next (and so far youngest) supercontinent Pangea (300-150 million years ago) and Gondwana (the southern part of Pangea).
Gypsum: EVAPORITIC sediment of commercial value.
Hecla Hoek: Local name for the BASEMENT in Svalbard, now regarded as old-fashioned and not commonly used in modern scientific literature.
Hematite: Reddish iron oxide, developes as a weathering product in warm, not too dry climate. Hematite is responsible for the intense red colouration of much of the Devonian OLD RED in Spitsbergen.
Hiatus: A hiatus indicates that rocks of a certain age were never deposited at a particular place or that they have been removed by erosion at a later time. There is a series of hiatuses in Svalbard, the most important being in the uppermost Devonian, upper Permian, several smaller ones in the Mesozoic, upper Cretaceous and upper Tertiary. Rocks of these ages do not exist in Svalbard (anymore). See also UNCONFORMITY.
Holocene: most recent part of earth history, including the present time. See also QUATERNARY.
Hyperite: See BASALT.
Ice age: Period that is characterised by cold climate and glaciation on a continental scale. Ice ages are known from all eras of earth history, the most recent one being the QUATERNARY.
Intrusion: Molten rock mass that has penetrated other rocks under pressure and crystallised.
Kar: Small glacial valley with the shape of an amphitheatre on a steep slope. Many kars have a small lake.
Limestone: Typical and widely spread CARBONATE rock; origin mostly as a BIOLOGICAL SEDIMENT (reefs, deposition of calcarous skeletons of marine organisms).
Magmatite: Crystalline rock derived from completely molten rock mass. If this forms slowly at great depths in the earth's crust, then the process is slow enough to allow large crystals to grow that are visible to the naked eye. In this case, the result

is called **plutonite**, of which **granite** is an example. If the molten rock mass cools quickly at the surface, then the resulting volcanite has crystals that are too small to be seen without a magnifying glass ("lava"). If cooling is abrupt, under water or under glacier ice, then no crystals can grow at all and the result is a volcanic glass. If the rock mass was not completely molten, then remains of the original rock structure are visible in the magmatite after cooling. Such a rock is called **migmatite**.

Marble: Metamorphic, crystallised LIMESTONE.

Metamorphism: Change of mineralogical composition and crystal structure of a rock without changing its chemistry, caused by heat and/or pressure.

Migmatite: See MAGMATITE.

Moraine: Young sediment deposited by a glacier, usually not solidified.

Old Red: Sediments, mostly sandstones and conglomerates, from the Devonian period, deposited as the result of weathering of the Caledonian mountains (see CALEDONIAN OROGENY), often with an intense reddish colouring due to a high HEMATITE content. In Svalbard, the Old Red is not metamorphic, but is somewhat deformed and thus occupies an intermediate position between BASEMENT and SEDIMENTARY COVER. The Old Red is also known, for example, in England, Scotland, Wales, Northern Ireland and East Greenland.

Orogeny: Tectonic phase of mountain formation as a result of continental collision.

Orogeny, Alpine: Tectonic phase from the Cretaceous into the upper Tertiary, during which several ancient oceans were closed, leading to the formation of a chain of mountain areas from the Himalayan ranges, Iran, Turkey to south Europe. At the same time, the north Atlantic ocean opened, separating Norway and Spitsbergen from Greenland. In the early stages (starting in upper Jurassic times), wide-spread intrusive activity took place in Svalbard (mainly eastern parts), followed by pronounced DEFORMATION, but without METAMORPHISM.

Orogeny, Caledonian: Tectonic phase, mainly during the Silurian, that led to the closure of an ancient ocean called Iapetus and thus to the formation of a large continent called Laurasia, that comprised present-day North America (including Greenland) and Europe (including Spitsbergen). Intense DEFORMATION, METAMORPHISM and magmatism occurred over large areas.

Palaeontology: A branch of science concerned with fossils.

Permocarboniferous: Combined term for Permian and Carboniferous, when the geological development is continuous and similar in certain respects during both periods.

Phyllite: Low grade metamorphic rock that shows a strong CLEAVAGE, usually silver-grey.

Pingo: Permafrost-phenomenon; a 20 to 30 metres high hill of ice with a thin cover of sand and gravel.

Pleistocene: Largest part of the most recent ice age, see QUATERNARY.

Plutonite: See MAGMATITE.

Quartz vein: See VEIN.
Quaternary: The most recent ICE AGE, starting approximately 2.7 million years ago. The Q. is subdivided into the PLEISTOCENE (2.7 million to 10,000 years ago) and the HOLOCENE, which includes present time.
Quaternary geology: A branch of geology that is concerned with young, mostly unsolidified, deposits of the Quaternary; in Svalbard a mosaic of moraines, fluvial deposits, raised and active beaches, solifluction soil and so on.
Schist: METAMORPHIC rock that shows strong fissility due to parallel arrangement of mineral crystals, usually micas.
Sediment, biogenic: Sediment such as coal or most LIMESTONES formed by biological processes.
Sandstone: CLASTIC SEDIMENT composed of sandgrains.
Sediment, clastic: Mechanically deposited sediment, created by water, ice or wind.
Sedimentary cover rocks: Sediments younger than the BASEMENT, and usually showing only weak or absent deformation and metamorphism unless involved in a younger OROGENY. In Svalbard, the sedimentary cover comprises rocks from the Carboniferous to the lower Tertiary (the Devonian OLD RED has an in-between position between basement and cover rocks).
Shale: Silty SEDIMENTary rock composed of particles that are too small to be seen with the naked eye.
Sill: INTRUSION that runs parallel to the main structure of the host rocks, for example the bedding of sediments.
Siltstone: Silty SEDIMENTary rock composed of particles that are smaller than sand.
Sound: Strait with at least two connections to adjacent waters.
Stromatolite: Colony of calcarous algae or bacteria, often with a concentric structure resembling an onion or cabbage.
Surge: Sudden, pronounced advance of a glacier.
Svalbardian phase: Late phase of the CALEDONIAN OROGENY in the uppermost Devonian, that resulted in deformation of the OLD RED and in the creation of a pronounced angular UNCONFORMITY.
Unconformity: Break in a sedimentary succession. An unconformity is caused by a period of time during which no rocks were deposited and existing ones possibly eroded. An **angular unconformity** is a special case where the rocks on either side of the break are not parallel. An unconformity represents a HIATUS during which some tilting of the older rocks occurred.
Vein: Filling of cracks or fissures by minerals that precipitate from circulating water.
Volcanite: See MAGMATITE.

Table earth history of Svalbard

Period [Ma = million years)	Tectonic activity	Depositional environments: sediments	Magmatism
Quaternary	Calm. The Atlantic ocean is growing steadily.	Ice age: moraines, beach ridges, permafrost, ...	Local volcanism (Bockfjord).
2.5 Ma **Tertiary**	**Alpine orogeny** Opening of the north Atlantic. Deformation of some older rocks, pronounced uplift.	Uplift, no sedimentation. Alternating shelf sea and coastal/ fluvial conditions: deposition of marine shales and siltstones, fluvial conglomerates and sandstones, coal.	Lava flows (Andrèe Land).
65 Ma **Cretaceous**		Uplift, no sedimentation. Sedimentation in shallow sea and coastal environments: sandstones, siltstones, shales, coal.	Dioritic intrusions, announcing start of spreading of the Atlantic ocean.
163 Ma **Jurassic**	Tectonically rather calm.		
213 Ma **Triassic**			
248 Ma **Permian**	Phases of subsidence. Activity of distinct fault zones, Graben formation. Increasingly calm.	Uplift, no sedimentation. Shelf sea in sub-tropical climate, sandstone, limestones.	
286 Ma **Carboniferous**		Lakes, lagoons, swamps, shelf seas, reefs, ... in tropical climate: gypsym, anhydrite, carbonates, coal, sandstone, ...	Local intrusions (Vestfjord).
360 Ma **Devonian**	Late phase of the Caledonian orogeny (Svalbardian phase). Graben formation.	Erosion of the Caledonian mountains, terrestrial sedimentation: mainly fluvial sandstones and conglomerates (Old Red).	
408 Ma **Silurian** 438 Ma	**Caledonian orogeny** Metamorphism and deformation of older rocks.		Granites (Hornemanntoppen, Newtontoppen, Nordaustland).
Ordovician, Cambrian 570 Ma		Non- or weakly metamorphic basement rocks. Limestone, dolostone, quartzite, ... (Northern Hinlopenstretet).	
Proterozoic 2,500 Ma **Archaean**	Grenville-event (1,000 million years ago). Various older tectonic phases.	Metamorphic basement: gneisses, marble.	Various granites and volcanic rocks, later metamorphosed.

Note: The terms **Tertiary** and **Quaternary** do not officially exist anymore and have, since 2004, been replaced by **Palaeogene** (65 to 23 million years ago) and **Neogene** (23 million years ago to recent). I have decided to use the old terminology, as it is still commonly used both in general language and geological literature.

Literature

The following list contains most printed sources that have been used during the writing of this book. Some titles that are easily available and which offer useful introductions to certain fields of interest, are marked with **bold letters and underlined**; the others are out of print, very specialised or in Norwegian.
NPI = Norwegian Polar Institute.

- Aga, Ole J. (Editor, 1986): *The Geological History of Svalbard. Evolution of an arctic archipelago.* Published by Statoil in Stavanger, 121 pp, ISBN 82-991255-0-2. Very nice introduction to the geology of Svalbard, unfortunately difficult to find.
- Amundsen, Birger (Editor, series of books): *Svalbardboka.* Collection of very interesting articles on different subjects. Norwegian.
- Anker-Nilssen, T., Bakken, V., Strøm, H., Golovkin, A.N., Bianki, V.V., Tatarinkova, I.P. (scientific editors, 2000): *The Status of marine birds breeding in the Barents Sea region.* Rapport Nr 113, NPI. 213 pp, ISBN 82-7666-176-9. Overview of seabirds populations in the Barents sea.
- Arlov, Thor (1996): *Svalbards Historie 1596-1996.* Aschehoug, Oslo. ISBN 82-03-22171-8. Currently the only modern introduction to the history of Svalbard, rather focussed on a Norwegian perspective. Norwegian.
- Arlov, Thor Bjørn and Reymert, Per Kyrre (2001): *Svalbard – en ferd i fortidens farvann.* Tapir Akademisk Forlag, Trondheim. 275 pp, ISBN 82-519-1715-8. Narration of a boat trip to Bellsund and Krossfjord with some historical background, Norwegian.
- Bengtssen, Karl J. (1996): *Tretti år rundt Svalbard.* Published by Vågemot forlag. Adventures of trappers in Spitsbergen. Norwegian.
- Born, E.W., Gjertz, I., Reeves, R.R. (1995): *Population Assessment of Atlantic Walrus.* Meddelelser Nr. 138, NPI. Overview of Walrus populations in the north Atlantic.
- Bruce, William S. (1908): *The exploration of Prince Charles Foreland, 1906-1907.* The geographical journal.
- Brusewitz, Gunnar (1981): *Arktisk Sommar. Med Ymer genom Ishavet.* ISBN 91-46-13905-2. Narration of an artist on board the Swedish research icebreaker *Ymer* in 1980, nicely illustrated. Swedish.
- Conway, Martin (1897a): *The First Crossing of Spitsbergen.* The geographical Journey, April 1897, Vol IX.
- Conway, Martin (1897b): *The First Crossing of Spitsbergen.* 371 pp, London.
- Conway, Martin (1906): *No Man's Land. A History of Spitsbergen from its discovery in 1596 to the beginning of the scientific exploration of the country.* Faksimile edition, 1995, Damms Antikvariat A/S, Oslo. Nice reading.
- Dallmann, W. (Editor, 1999): *Lithostratigraphic Lexicon of Svalbard. Review and recommendations for nomenclature use. Upper Palaeozoic to Quaternary*

Bedrock. NPI, Tromsø. 318 pp, ISBN 82-7666-166-1. Quite technical, but a treasury for everybody with some interest in the regional geology, richly illustrated with photographs, diagrams and distribution maps.

- Dowdeswell, J.A. and Hambrey, J.J. (2002): *Islands of the arctic.* Cambridge University Press, Cambridge. 280 pp, ISBN 0521 81333 6. Very readable and nicely illustrated, up-to-date general introduction to the Arctic, with a focus on geology and glaciology.
- Dufferin, Frederick Hamilton (first edition 1856): *Letters from high latitudes. Being some account of a voyage in 1856 in the schooner yacht 'Foam' to Iceland, Jan Mayen and Spitzbergen*. London. Classic about a hunting voyage to Iceland, Jan Mayen, Spitsbergen and Lappland. Nice reading.
- Edwards, Bernard (1990): *The Merchant Navy goes to War*. Hale, 208pp.
- Ellingsve, Eli Johanne (2005): *Stedsnavn på Svalbard/Names on Svalbard.* Tapir Forlag, Trondheim. 186 pp, ISBN 82-519-2011-6. Short explanations of the most important placenames in Svalbard, for the historically interested. Not comprehensive, but definitely more handy than the voluminous standard book "Placenames of Svalbard". English and Norwegian.
- Elvebakk & Prestrud (Editors, 1996): *A catalogue of Svalbard plants, fungi, algae and cyanobacteria.* Skrifter 198, NPI, Oslo. "Official" catalogue of Svalbard's vegetation.
- **Gjærevoll, Olaf, Rønning, Olaf I.: *Flowers of Svalbard.*** Tapir Forlag, Trondheim 1999. 121 pp. ISBN 8251915295. Nice little book, useful for beginners. 55 "important" plant species are described and illustrated with photographs, unfortunately not all of excellent quality.
- Goldberg, Fred (2003): *Drama in the Arctic. S.O.S Italia. The Search for Nobile and Amundsen. A diary and postal history*. 144 pp, ISBN 91-631-3971-5. Detailed overview of Nobiles *Italia* expedition in 1926 from Ny Ålesund and related relief expeditions.
- Hadaè, Emil (1944): *Die Gefässpflanzen des "Sassengebietes", Vestspitsbergen.* Edited by Norges Svalbard- og Ishavs- Undersøkelser (today: NPI) as Skrifter No 87. 72 pp. Scientific report of botanical investigations in Nordenskiöld Land, with distribution maps. German.
- Harland, Brian (1977): *The Geology of Svalbard.* 521 pp, ISBN 1897799934. London, The Geological Society. Standard book at its time.
- **Hjelle, Audun (1993): *Geology of Svalbard.*** NPI, No 7 in the series "Polar Handbooks". 162 pp, ISBN 82-7666-057-6. For amateurs, but some basic knowledge is useful.
- Holm, Kari (latest edition 2006): *Longyearbyen – Svalbard. Historisk veiviser.* ISBN 82-992142-0-3. Interesting facts about Longyearbyen and Spitsbergen. Norwegian.

- Houghton, John (third edition 2004): *Global warming. The complete briefing.* Background about climate change, presented by a former IPCC chairman. ISBN-13 978-0-521-52870-0. Cambridge University Press, Cambridge.
- *King's Mirror (Speculum Regale Konungs Skuggsja).* Translated from the old Norwegian by Laurence Marcellus Larson. The American-Scandinavian Foundation. Oxfjord University Press, 1917.
- Linder, Elke and Meister, Kay (2006): *Die kleine Spitzbergenflora. Portraits interessanter Pflanzen des Archipels.* Nice introduction into Spitsbergen's flora, mail-order polarflora@kaboina.de, ISBN: 3-8334-5132-7. German.
- Isaksen, Kjell and Bakken, Vidar (Editors., 1995): *Seabird populations in the northern Barents Sea. Source data for the impact assessment of the effects of oil drilling activity.* NPI, Meddelelser No 135, Oslo. ISBN 82-7666-087-8.
- Kovacs, K., Gjertz, J. and Lydersen, C. (2004): *Marine Mammals of Svalbard.* NPI, Oslo. ISBN 82-7666-208-0. 64 pp. Nice little book about Spitsbergen's marine mammals.
- **Kovacs, Kit (Hrsg., 2005): *Birds And Mammals Of Svalbard*.** NPI, No 13 of the series "Polar Handbooks". 203 pp. ISBN (13) 978-82-7666-221-4. Highly recommended book about Spitsbergen's wildlife.
- Lamont, James (1861): *Seasons with the Sea-horses; or Sporting Adventures in the Northern Seas.* New York.
- Meurs, Rinie van (2005): *Polar Bears of Spitsbergen/Svalbard.* Published by Oceanwide Expeditions (www.oceanwide-expeditions.com), ISBN 83-9195777-7-2. Nice read, background and stories about Polar bears and Spitsbergen, with many beautiful photographs.
- Nathorst, A. G., Hulth, J. M., De Geer, G. (1909): *Swedish Explorations in Spitzbergen 1758-1908.* Ymer 1909, volume 1.
- NPI (1990): *Den Norske Los / Arctic Pilot. Sailing directions, Travellers' guide. Svalbard and Jan Mayen.* Stavanger. Sailing directions, volume 7, 2nd edition, 433 pp, Norwegian and English.
- NPI (1991): *The Placenames of Svalbard.* Rapportserie Nr. 122 (reprint). A real treasure regarding the explanations of placenames, with a lot of interesting historical details.
- Phipps, Constantine John (1774): *Voyage towards the North Pole undertaken by His Majesty's command 1773.* London.
- Ritter, Christiane (1955): *A woman in the Polar Night.* Narrative of a wintering in Woodfjord. Nice reading to get into the mood for Spitsbergen.
- Roberts, Davids (2003): *Shipwrecked on the top of the world. Four Against the Arctic.* ISBN 0-7515-3689-x, 304 pages. The true and exciting story of four Pomors who survived several years on Edgeøya after the loss of their ship.
- Rossnes, Gustav (1993): *Norsk Overvintringsfangst på Svalbard 1895-1940.* NPI, Meddelelser No 127, Oslo. Details about trappers in Svalbard. Norwegian.

- **Rønning, Olaf I. (1996): *The Flora of Svalbard.*** NPI, No 10 in the series "Polar Handbooks". 184 pp. ISBN 82-7666-100-9. Standard book about Svalbard's flora, not the easiest book for beginners, but currently the most comprehensive book on the market.
- Sakshaug, Egil (main editor, 1994): *Økosystem Barentshavet.* Universitetsforlaget, Oslo, ISBN 82-00-03963-3. Oceanography and biology of the Barents sea. Norwegian.
- **Schillat, Monika and Stone, Ian (editors, 2007): *Polar Essays of the Arctic.*** Very readable book with chapters written by different authors (including the author of the present books) on various fields of interest, including biology, history and geology of Spitsbergen, Greenland, Jan Mayen. ISBN 978-987-05-3490-7.
- Scoresby, William (1820): *An Account Of The Arctic Regions. With A History And Description Of The Northern Whale-Fishery.* Reprint, 1969.
- Selinger, Franz (2001): *Von "Nanok" bis "Eismitte". Meteorologische Unternehmungen in der Arktis 1940-1945.* –Schriften des Deutschen Schiffahrtmuseums, Band 53, Bremerhaven. ISBN 3-934613-12-8. Very detailed book about the Second World War in the Arctic. German.
- Seton, Gordon (1922): *Amid Snowy Wastes. Wild Life on the Spitsbergen Archipelago.* London.
- Soper, Tony (2001): *The Arctic. A Guide To Coastal Wildlife.* Bradt Travel Guides (UK)/The Globe Pequot Press Inc (USA). 143 pp. ISBN 1 84162 020 3. Overview of arctic wildlife.
- Sysselmannen på Svalbard (2000): *Kulturminneplan for Svalbard 2000-2010.* Longyearbyen. Norwegian.
- Søreide, Oddmund (1994): *Hopen. Ishavsøy og meteorologisk stasjon.* Friske Tankar A/S, Øystese. 158 pp, ISBN 82-91386-05-6. Comprehensive book about the island of Hopen. Norwegian.
- Theisen, Fredrik (Red., 1997): *Dokumentasjon og vurdering av verneverdier på Bjørnøya.* NPI Meddelelser No 143, Oslo. Overview of natural and cultural resources of Bjørnøya. Norwegian.
- Thorén, Ragnar (1978): *Svenska arktiska expeditioner under 1800-tallet.* Publication No 66 of the Marinlitteraturföreningen, 365 pp, ISBN 91-85944-00-9. Overview of Swedish arctic expeditions of the 19th century. Swedish.
- Tromsø Universitet Museum (editor, 2004): *Bjørnøya – Historie, natur og forskning.* Ottar populærvitenskapelig tidskrift fra Tromsø Museum – Universitetsmuseet, nr. 253, 2004. General introduction to the island of Bjørnøya, focussing on environmental aspects. Norwegian.

Index

Entry with **bold** page number: main entry.
Entry with underlined page number: refers to illustration.

A

Administration area 10 46
Advent City 208, 239
Adventdalen 87, 209, 264
Adventelva 87
Adventfjord **233**, 264
AECO **467**
Agardhbukta 390, **394**
Agardhdalen 382
Ahlstrandhalvøya 456
Ahlstrandodden 430
Airport 53, 264
Akseløya 431, 452, **457**, 459, 460, 463
Ålandvatnet 227
Albertinibukta 365
Alkefjellet **347**, 370
Alkhornet 92, **217**, 257
Amsterdamøya **303**, 323
Amundsen, Roald 200, 201, **360**, 362
Andøyane 172, **313**
Andrée Land 311, 312, 319
Andrée, Salomon August 198, **200**, 226, 302, 386, **387**
Andréeneset 93
Andréetangen 402
Arc-de-Meridian expedition 198, 333, 339, 340, 344, 359, 363, 401, 423, 443
Arctic char 251, 320, 414, 415
Arctic cottongrass 396
Arctic tern 138, **148**
Augustabukta 350, 352, **353**, 373
Aurora borealis 17, 18
Austfjord 319, 320
Austfonna 354, 356, **367**, 379

B

Baby, first one born in Spitsbergen 245
Bansö 209, 240
Barents, Willem 13, 187, 189, **191**, 273, 298, 414, 452

Barentsburg 22, 208, 209, 211, 221, 230, 233, **243**, **246**, 266, 451, 458, 462
Barentsøya 166, 171, 351, 382, 384, 388, 392, 394, 396, **397**, 407
Basement 79
Bautaen 425, 441, 445
Beach, raised 75, 91, 237, 249, 250, 313, **318**, 338, 340, 345, 353, **361**, 363, 386, 438, 452, 459
Bell-heather, Arctic 172, **183**
Bellsund 81, 191, 233, 244, 431, **450**, 455, 456, **457**, 460
Beluga **117**
Bengtssen, Karl 359
Bicycling 26
Billefjord 22, 175, **226**, 260, 261, 319
Billefjorden Fault Zone 227, 231, 320
Birch, Dwarf 161, **178**
Bird sanctuaries 40, 41
Birdvågen 96, 374
Bjørndalen 235, 240, 265
Bjørneborg 420
Bjørnfjord **300**, 322
Bjørnøya 40, 191, 205, 210, 212, **411**, 421, 422
Bjørnøya Radio **434**
Blomstrandhalvøya 207, **289**, 321
Blomstrandhamna 41
Bockfjord 97, 98, 310, **316**, 330
Bohemanflya 41, 165, **219**, 245, 258
Borebukta **219**
Bråsvellbreen 354, 356, **367**, 379
Brennevinsfjord 201, 359, **360**
Brepollen 442, **444**
Brochøya **365**
Bruce, William Spiers 230, 274
Brucebyen 228, 230, 261
Büdel, Julius 401
Bünsow Land 226
Burgerbukta 427, **446**
Byrd, Richard 201

C

Calypsobyen 455
Camp Bell 461
Camp Jacobsen 455

Camp Millar 432, 459, 461
Camp Morton 461
Camp Zoe 293
Camping site 238, 264
Chickweed, Tundra 163, **179**
Chumleigh 251, 439
Clavering, Charles 308
Clean up Svalbard 102
Colesbukta 208, 211, **240**
Colesdalen 208, 242, 243
Common eider **124**, 135
Conway, Martin 239, 396, 444
Conwaybreen 272, 288
Copper Camp 255
Coraholmen **221**
Cottongrass 174, **184**
Cress, Polar 173, **184**
Crozierpynten 198, 333, 340

D

Dandelion, Arctic 175, **185**
Dandelion, Polar 175, **185**
Danskøya 200, **301**, 323
De Geerdalen 232, 263
Dei Sju Isfjella **295**
Dekabrist 409
Delitschøya 419
Diabasodden 85, 231, 232
Dickson Land 23, 84, 86, **223**, **226**, 259, 260, 288, 319
Dicksonfjord 168, **223**
Dinosaurs, foot imprints of 249, 395
Diskobukta 402, 418
Diver, Great northern 413, 414, 434
Diver, Red-throated **122**, 134
Diving 30
Dolerittneset 50, 401, 403, 417
Dolines 228, 249, 250
Driftwood 38, **101**
Duck, Long-tailed **126**, 135
Duckwitzbreen 400
Dunérbukta **394**
Dunøyane 41, **449**

Duvefjord **364**
Dwarf birch 238

E

Ebeltofthamna 293, 294
Edgeøya 50, 94, 174, 351, 388, 390, 392, 394, 396ff, **401**, 407, 417ff
Eider, Common **124**, 135
Eider, King **125**, 135
Ekmanfjord **221**, 259
Elfenbeinbreen 396
Emergency telephone numbers **54**
Engelskbukta **255**, 268, 285
Eolusneset 340
Esmarkbreen 219, 258

F

Fair Haven **305**
Faksevågen 176, 345, 369
Festningen **248**, 249, 267
Filchner, Wilhelm 232
Finneset 205, 245
Fire 38
Fjortende Julibukta 90, 291ff, 321
Flintholmen 171, **221**, 259
Fog 99, 104
Forlandsund **253**, 256
Forsbladodden 456
Fossils 38, 69, 223, 227, 236, 395
Fox, Arctic **108**, 129
Foyn, Svend 204, 365
Foynøya **365**, 378
Fredheim 233
Freemanbreen 383, 399
Freemansund 382, 391, 398, 399, 401
Fridtjovbreen 233, 432, 460
Fringed sandwort 164, **179**
Frost patterned ground 77
Fuglefjellet 237, 240
Fuglefjord **305**, 325
Fuglehuken 191, 256, 273
Fuglesangen **306**, 326
Fugløya **306**

Fulmar **123**, 134
Fungi 176, **185**

G

Gåshamna 198, 423, 442, **443**
Gåsøyane 41, 227, 231
Giles Land 387, 389
Gipsdalen 228, 232
Glaciers **74**, 75
Global warming 359
Gnålodden 427, 428, 442, **446**
Gneiss 93
Goose, Barnacle **128**, 136
Goose, Pink-footed **127**, 136
Gråhuken 311, 312
Gravneset 297, 298
Grey phalarope 138, **147**
Grønfjord 205, 209, **243**, 436
Grumant 13, 189, 405
Grumantbyen 146, 208, **240**, 265
Grunnlinesletta 402
Guillemot, Black 144, **158**
Guillemot, Brünich's 143, **156**, 335, 370
Guillemot, Common 143, **155**
Gull, Glaucous 141, **153**, 415, 466
Gull, Ivory 140, **152**, 239, 279, 286, 363, 389
Gull, Ross' 141, **153**
Gull, Sabine's 140, **151**, 319, 358, 363
Gullybreen 297

H

Habenichtbukta 174, 402, 403, 418
Hagerup, Johan 460
Halvmåneøya **404**, 420
Hamburgbukta **295**
Hamiltonbukta 309, 327
Hares 121
Hassensteinbukta 402
Haudegen 210, 362, 365, 377
Hecla Hoek 79, 340
Heleysund 391, 397
Helhus 410

Herwighamna 422
Hinlopenstretet 163, 333ff, **341**, 346, 347, 370
Hiorthamn 235, 239, 240
Hoel, Adolf 199
Hopen 210, 212, 392, 398, **406**, 420
Hopen Radio **410**
Hørbyebreen 84, 227
Hornsund 198, 204, 211, 423ff, **440**
Hornsundtind 239, 424, 440, 441, **444**
Hotellneset 239
Hyttevika 447, 450

I

Ice formation 391
Ice wedges 76, 92, 217, 237, 401, 456
Ichthyosaurs 232
Ingeborgfjellet 459
IPCC 465
Isachsen, Gunnar 293
Isbjørn 209, 246
Isbjørnhamna 211, 428, 440, 442, **447**
Isfjord 191, **216**
Isfjord Radio 212, **248**, 251, 267
Isispynten **367**, 379, 380
Isøyane 41, **449**
Italia 201, 280, 359, 364, **366**

J

Jacob's ladder, Boreal 173, **184**
Jakobsenbukta 310, 312
Johansen, Hjalmar 220
Jotunkildene 316

K

Kaffiøyra **255**
Kapp Borthen 429, **449**
Kapp Fanshawe 348
Kapp Guissez 41, 291
Kapp Lee 50, 390, 401, 403, 417
Kapp Linné 22, 41, **62**, 153, 212, **248**, 251, 267, 462
Kapp Mineral 251
Kapp Rubin 361

Kapp Schoultz 232
Kapp Smith 225
Kapp Starostin 190, 249
Kapp Starostin formation 80, 456
Kapp Thordsen 198, **226**, 260
Kapp Torell 352
Kapp Toscana 455
Kapp Wijk 225, 226
Kapp Wrede 378
Karl XII Øya **365**
Keilhau, Balthazar Matthias 196, 415
Kiepertøya 353
King eider **125**, 135, 314
Kingodden 87
Kinnvika 211, 336, 344
Kittiwake 142, **154**
Klovningen **306**
Knospe 209, 293
Knotweed 162, **178**
Kobbefjord 302, 303
Kokerineset 245
Koldewey, Karl 352
Kong Karls Land 40, 381, **388**, 392, 396, 397, 408
Kongsbreen 288
Kongsfjord 41, 271, 272, **275**, **286**, 321
Kongsøya 388
Kongsvegen 271, 272, 288
Konstantinovka 443
Kreuzritter 314, 316
Kronebreen 288
Krossfjord 90, 209, **291**, 321
Krossøya 336
Kvadehuken 277
Kvalpynten 402
Kvalrossbukta **435**
Kvitøya 93, 200, 381, **385**

L

Lady Franklinfjord **360**
Lægerneset 453
Lågøya **360**, 374
Landvik 439

Leigh Smith, Benjamin 358, 366
Lerner, Theodor 220, 361, 415, 436
Lernerøyane 315, 329
Lichens 176
Liefdefjord 91, 133, 172, 174, 210, 310, 313, **314**, 328ff
Likneset 300, 301
Lilliehöökbreen 292
Little auk 144, **157**, 238, 297, 305, 307, 326, 442, **448**, 452, 460
Lloyds Hotel 293
Lomfjord 90, 176, **345**, 369
Lomonossov, Mikhail 195
Longyear, John Munro 208
Longyearben 233
Longyearbyen 22, **53**, 83, 88, 89, 208, 210, 211, 240, 451, 458, 462
Lousewort, Wooly 174, **184**
Lovén, Sven 197
Lunckefjellet 462
Lundstrømdalen 82, 84
Lyckholmdalen 86, 225, 259

M

Magdalenefjord 40, 197, **296**, 322
Mansfield, Ernest 207
Martens, Friedrich 195, 295, 363
Martensøya 91, 375
Mathiesondalen 228
Midnight sun 104
Midterhuken 81, 431, 432, 456, 459, 460
Midterhukhamna 456, 461
Miseryfjellet 413, 435
Mittag-Lefflerbreen 89, 320, 331
Mobile phone 43, **54**, 244
Moffen 40, 41, **318**, 331
Mohnbukta **394**
Monaco, Duke Albert of 199, 274, 292, 293
Monacobreen 314ff, 330
Moskushamn 235, 240
Mosquitos 48
Moss campion 165, **180**
Mosselbukta 197, 226, 337
Mountain avens 172, **183**
Mountain sorrel 162, **178**

Mouse 146
Mouse-ear, Arctic 163, **179**
Murchisonfjord 336, **344**
Muscovy Company 192
Mushamna 93, 310, 312
Muskoxen 121

N

Nathorst, Alfred 197, 390
National parks **39**
Nature reserves **40**
Negerpynten 402
Negribreen 395
Nelson, Horatio 196
Nelsonøya 363
Newtontoppen 24, 338, 339
Ninavarden 233
Nobile, Umberto 201, 359, 364, 366
Nodding lychnis 164, **179**
Nøis, Hilmar 204, 233, 312, 314, 316, 396
Nordaustland 96, **355**, 374
Nordenskiöld, Adolf Erik 197, 226, 337, 340, 358, 362, 363, 366
Nordenskiöld Land 82, 84, 92, 263
Nordenskiöldbreen 22, 261
Nordenskiöldbukta **364**
Nordenskiöldfjellet 236, 237, 239
Nordporten 341
Nordvestøyane **306**
Norge (Airship) 280
Norskøya, Ytre 307, 326
Norskøya, Ytre/Indre **306**
Northern Exploration Company 207, 255, 288, 293, 439, 454, 461
Nunatak 152
Nussbaum 209, 293
Ny Ålesund 201, 208, 211, 270, 271, **275**, **277**
Ny Friesland 319, 332, **338**
Ny London 321

O

Old Red 79, 221, 223, 225, 249, 272, 286, 288, 309, 311, 313, 315, 317, 320, 328, 444, 446
Olsholmen 41

Operafjellet (plane crash) 246
Oxaas, Arthur 204, 225, 306
Oxford 359, 362, 367

P

Palanderbukta 167, **349**, 371
Parry, William Edward 196, 340, 358, 363
Payer, Julius 409, 442
PCB 102, 152
Permafrost 76
Phipps, Constantine John 196, 358, 362
Phippsøya 355, 362, 363, 375
Pike, Lord Arnold 302
Pingo 76, 92, 238, 245, 292, 395, 396, 453
Plain, coastal **313**
Plant protection 38
Platåberget 88, 233, 238
PLB 45
Plesiosaurs 223, 231
Polar bear 42, **105**, 129, 233, 246, 389, 394, 396, 403, 408, 414, 439, 442, 452, 466
Polar night 104
Polhem 337
Polish research station (Hornsund) 212, 428, 440, 442, **447**
Pomors 87, 187, **189**, 252, 298, 337, 345, 402, 403, 405, 414, 439, 460
Poolepynten 102
Poppy, Svalbard 166, **180**
Precipitation 104
Prins Karls Forland 87, 115, 132, **256**, 269
Ptarmigan 137, **145**
Puffin 142, **154**, 363
Purple sandpiper 138, **146**
Pyramiden 22, 208, 210, 211, **226**, **229**, 260

R

Rabies 50, 108
Raudfjord 166, **308**, 327
Razorbill 293
Recherche expedition 196, 298, 454
Recherchefjord 195, 196, 429, 450, 452, **453**
Red-throated diver 134
Reindalen 458, 459

Reindeer **109**, 130
Reindeer antlers 38
Reinsdyrflya 125, 312, **313**
Richardvatnet 166
Rijpfjord 210, **364**, 377
Rijpsburg 220, 258
Ritter, Christiane 312
River crossing 87
Rock glacier 76, 238, 443
Rønnbeck, Nils 353
Rosenbergdalen 401, 417
Ross' gull 363
Rossøya 362, 376
Rudi, Henry 204, 293, 406, 408
Russehamna **435**
Russekeila 190, **248**, 252
Ryke Yseøyane **404**

S

Sabine, Edward 308
Sallyhamna **305**, 325
Samarinvågen 424, **444**
Sarkofagen 235
Sassendalen 82, 231ff, 263, 397
Sassenfjord 85, **230**
Satellite phones 44
Saxifrag, Tufted 171
Saxifrage, Alpine 169, **182**
Saxifrage, Bog 170, **182**
Saxifrage, Drooping 170, **182**
Saxifrage, Hawkweed-leaved 169, **182**
Saxifrage, Purple 168, **181**
Saxifrage, Tufted **183**
Saxifrage, Yellow mountain 168, **181**
Scharnhorst 210
Schröder-Stranz expedition 199, 288, 337, 339, 341, 361, 364
Scoresby, William jr 195, 277
Scurvy grass 167, **181**
Sea battle, northernmost one 195, 340
Seal, Bearded **110**, 130
Seal, Harbour **115**, 132, 273, **304**
Seal, Ringed **111**, 131

Seasons 16
Seed Vault **67**
Selis 209, 246
Sentralfeltet 462
Signehamna 209, 293
Sjuøyane 91, 355, **362**, 375, 376
Sjursethfossen 228
Skansbukta 22, 173, **226**, 230, 262
Skansdalen 95, 225
Skottehytte 230
Skua, Arctic 139, **150**
Skua, Great 139, **149**
Skua, Long-tailed 140, **151**
Skua, Pomarine 139, **149**, 363
Smeerenburg 193, 300, **303**, 323, 324
Smeerenburgfjord **300**
Snatcherpynten 453, 454
Snow bunting 137, **145**
Snow Buttercup 165
Snow-buttercup 165, **180**
Solifluction 77, 250, **351**, 389, 399, 401, 403, 443
Sørdalsbukta 314
Sørgattet **300**
Sorgfjord 195, 196, 198, 199, 333, **339**
Sørkapp **437**, 440
Sørkapp Land 423
Sørkappøya 41
Sørporten 341
Sparreneset 343
Spider plant 171, **183**
Spiders 357
Spitsbergen **13**, 188, 191
Spitsbergen Treaty 188, **205**, 206
Spitzbergen **13**
Spjutneset 166
Spring, largest 423, 439
St. Jonsfjord **254**, 268
Starostin, Ivan 190, 252
Stasjonsøyane **313**, 328
Stone circles / Stone rings 77, 93, 250, 344
Stone stripes 250
Store Norske Spitsbergen Kullkompani 208, 211, 458, 462

Storfjord 390, **391**, 392, 394, 396, 397
Stormbukta 210, 423, 437ff
Storøya 380, **385**
Strandflate **313**
Stromatolite 355
Sundneset 384, 401
Svalbard **13**, 15, 188, 206
Svalbard poppy 166, **180**
Svalbard Treaty 206
Svartisen 409
Sveagruva 208, 211, 450, **458**, 459, **462**
Svenskehuset 260
Svenskøya 381, 388
Sverdrupbyen 238
Sverrefjellet 97, 317
Sysselmannen 37, 45, **54**, **56**

T

Taaget 437
Tarantellen 89, 229, 331
Tavleøya 376
Tempelfjellet 230, 232
Tempelfjord 22, **230**
Texas Bar 313, 316, 329
Tides 99, 411
Tinayrebukta 291
Tirpitz 210
Tjuvfjord 402
Topographic maps 48, 51
Torell, Otto 197, 340, 358, 362, 363, 366
Torellbreane 449
Torellneset 163
Torun Polar Station 255
Toxins, environmental **101**, 107, 114, 152, 154, 411, 415, 416, 466
Tre Kroner 288
Treskelen 445
Treurenburg Bay 340
Trinityhamna 297
Trollkildene 317
Trollosen 423
Trygghamna 22, 81, **217**, 257
Tsjitsjagov, Vasilij Vakovlevitsj 195, 454

Tundra 160
Tunheim 421, 422, **435**
Tusenøyane 394, 402, **404**, 419

U
UNIS **56**, 73, 88

V
Van Keulenfjord 430, 450, 452, **455**
Van Mijenfjord 81, 86, 99, 211, 432, 450, 452, **457**
Vårsolbukta 432, 458, 461
Vegafonna 354
Vegetation zones 159
Verlegenhuken 320, 332, **338**
Vesle Raudfjord 102
Vesle Tavleøya 362, 376
Vest-Spitsbergen **13**
Vestfjord 319
Vestfonna 356, 359
Vibebukta **353**, 373
Vikings 187, **188**
Virgohamna 40, 52, 200, 277, 300, **301**, 323, 387
von Löwenigh, Barto 196, 414
Von Otterøya 371

W
Waggonwaybreen 297
Wahlbergøya **350**
Wahlenbergfjord 334, **349**, 365, 371
Waldburg-Zeil, Count 397, 404
Waldenøya 362, 364
Walrus **113**, 131, 273, 335
Walrus colonies 215
War weather stations 209, 240, 293, 314, 316, 365, 409, 437, 439
Wellman, Walter 200, 302, 364
Weyprecht, Karl 197, 409, 442
Whale, Bowhead **120**, 192
Whale, Fin **119**, 133
Whale, Humpback **118**, 133
Whale, Minke **117**, 132
Whale, Right 192
Whale, White **117**, 133

Whitlow-grass 167, **181**
Wijdefjord 217, **319**, 331, 341
Wilczek, Johann ("Hans") 442, 445
Wild, Frank 455, 461
Wilhelmøya **350**, 351, 372
Willow, net-leaved 177
Willow, Polar 161, **177**
Wintering, first 194, 453
Woldstad, Wanny 204, 447
Woodfjord 93, 132, **310**, 328
Worsleyneset 313

Y

Ymerbukta 22, 217, **219**, 258
Ytre Norskøya **306**

Z

Zachariassen, Søren 207, 220, 245
Zeeussche Uytkyk 308
Zeppelin, Ferdinand Graf 276, 298
Zorgdragerfjord 378